30.00
4.95

WARNING
from the
FBI

The war against spies and saboteurs demands the aid of every American.

When you see evidence of sabotage, notify the Federal Bureau of Investigation at once.

When you suspect the presence of enemy agents, tell it to the FBI.

Beware of those who spread enemy propaganda! <u>**Don't repeat vicious rumors or vicious whispers.**</u>

Tell it to the FBI!

J. Edgar Hoover, Director
Federal Bureau of Investigation

The nearest Federal Bureau of Investigation office is listed on page one of your telephone directory.

TIM WEINER

ENEMIES

A HISTORY OF THE FBI

RANDOM HOUSE | NEW YORK

Published in the United States by Random House, an imprint of
The Random House Publishing Group, a division of
Random House, Inc., New York.

RANDOM HOUSE and colophon are registered trademarks of
Random House, Inc.

ISBN 978-1-4000-6748-0
eBook ISBN 978-0-679-64389-0

Printed in the United States of America on acid-free paper

www.atrandom.com

9 8 7 6 5 4 3

Book design by Simon M. Sullivan

For Robert D. Loomis, who taught me to write;
for Professor Dora B. Weiner, who taught me to read;
for Kate, Ruby, and Emma Doyle, who teach me to live

Safety from external danger is the most powerful director of national conduct. Even the ardent love of liberty will, after a time, give way to its dictates. The violent destruction of life and property incident to war, the continual effort and alarm attendant on a state of continual danger, will compel nations the most attached to liberty to resort for repose and security to institutions which have a tendency to destroy their civil and political rights. To be more safe, they at length become willing to run the risk of being less free.

ALEXANDER HAMILTON, 1787

CONTENTS

AUTHOR'S NOTE

ENEMIES IS THE HISTORY of the Federal Bureau of Investigation as a secret intelligence service. We think of the FBI as a police force, arresting criminals and upholding the rule of law. But secret intelligence against terrorists and spies is the Bureau's first and foremost mission today, and that has been true for most of the past hundred years.

This mission creates a conflict that the authors of the Constitution foresaw ten generations ago. A free people must have both security and liberty. They are warring forces, yet we cannot have one without the other. Secret agents can be scofflaws; their traditions include wiretapping, bugging, and burglary. Over the decades, the Bureau has best served the cause of national security by bending and breaking the law. A secret police is anathema in a democracy. But the FBI's powers make it America's closest counterpart.

Enemies is the chronicle of a century of constant conflict over the conduct of secret intelligence in an open democracy, the tug-of-war between national security and civil liberties, the saga of our struggle to be both safe and free. It is written on the record, without anonymous sources or blind quotations. It is based on a foundation of more than seventy thousand pages of recently declassified documents, including an extraordinary collection of the intelligence files of J. Edgar Hoover, and more than two hundred oral histories recorded by agents who served during and after his forty-eight-year tenure as the leader of the FBI.

Hoover stands at the center of the American century like a statue encrusted in grime. His loyalists saw him as a visionary genius. His opponents saw him as "a goddamned sewer," in the words of President Kennedy's national security adviser. Today millions of Americans know him only as a caricature: a tyrant in a tutu, a cross-dressing crank. None of that is true. The files opened over the past few years strip away layers of myth and legend. They show him in a new light. He carried out secret missions that were almost inconceivable in their time, spying directly on the leaders of the

Soviet Union and China in the darkest days of the Cold War, sending detailed intelligence warnings of suicidal airborne attacks against New York and Washington, controlling a coup against a democratically elected foreign leader, and subtly undermining presidents of the United States.

Hoover was not a monster. He was an American Machiavelli. He was astute, he was cunning, and he never stopped watching his enemies. He was a founding father of American intelligence and the architect of the modern surveillance state. Every fingerprint on file, every byte of biographic and biometric data in the computer banks of the government, owes its origins to him.

He was a masterful manipulator of public opinion. He practiced political warfare and secret statecraft in pursuit of national security, often at the expense of morality. He fought communism and terrorism with a consuming passion for fifty-five years. From the 1940s onward, until the day he died, he foresaw the apocalyptic threats we face today. Yet he left behind an institution that almost died along with him, and has only revived its national-security mission under law in the past three years.

The FBI has never had a legal charter beyond the president's oath to take care that the laws are faithfully executed, and presidents have strained against the strictures of that oath since World War I. They ordered Hoover to persecute pacifists as well as terrorists; they targeted the heroes of the civil rights movement along with the knights of the Ku Klux Klan. At their command, the Bureau has violated the freedoms of the Bill of Rights to enforce the president's powers as commander in chief. "The Constitution has never greatly bothered any wartime president," Franklin D. Roosevelt's attorney general once wrote—and every president since has seen himself at war.

Enemies is a record of illegal arrests and detentions, break-ins, burglaries, wiretapping, and bugging on behalf of the president. By design, it touches only briefly on famous criminal-justice cases—like the war on gangsters in the Great Depression and the bloody confrontation with the Branch Davidians cult—to focus on the FBI's secret intelligence operations. But that is the heart of the story of America's hundred-year war against terrorists, spies, anarchists, and assassins. The commanders in this battle—presidents, attorneys general, and FBI directors alike—have used and abused their powers in the name of national security. Yet even their powers have limits in our democracy. Late in his life, Hoover refused to execute illegal orders from President Nixon. And Robert Mueller, the

Bureau's director since September 4, 2001, resisted President Bush's commands to carry out unlawful secret surveillance; he offered his resignation in protest. He has said we will not win the war on terrorism if we lose our freedoms in the battle.

The FBI's leaders live each day in that state of continual conflict. Americans need to know the history of that struggle. If not, when the next crisis comes, they will surrender guarantees of liberty for promises of security. They may be more safe, but they will be less free.

PART I

SPIES AND SABOTEURS

The September 1920 bombing of Wall Street:
a terrorist attack that went unsolved.

ANARCHY

J. EDGAR HOOVER WENT TO WAR at the age of twenty-two, on Thursday
morning, July 26, 1917. He walked out of his boyhood home in Washington, D.C., and set off for his new life at the Justice Department, to serve as
a foot soldier in the army of lawmen fighting spies, saboteurs, Communists, and anarchists in the United States.

America had entered World War I in April. The first waves of her troops
were landing in France, unprepared for the horrors that faced them. On the
home front, Americans were gripped by the fear of sabotage by German
secret agents. The country had been on high alert for a year, ever since an
enemy attack on a huge warehouse of American munitions bound for the
battlefront. The blast at Black Tom Island, on the western edge of New York
Harbor, had set off two thousand tons of explosives in the dark of a mid-
summer night. Seven people died at the site. In Manhattan, thousands of
windows were shattered by the shock waves. The Statue of Liberty was
scarred by shrapnel.

Hoover worked for the War Emergency Division at the Justice Department, charged with preventing the next surprise attack. He displayed a
martial spirit and a knack for shaping the thinking of his superiors. He won
praise from the division's chief, John Lord O'Brian. "He worked Sundays
and nights, as I did," O'Brian recounted. "I promoted him several times,
simply on merits."

Hoover rose quickly to the top of the division's Alien Enemy Bureau,
which was responsible for identifying and imprisoning politically suspect
foreigners living in the United States. At the age of twenty-three, Hoover
oversaw 6,200 Germans who were interned in camps and 450,000 more
who were under government surveillance. At twenty-four, he was placed in
charge of the newly created Radical Division of the Justice Department,

and he ran the biggest counterterrorism operations in the history of the United States, rounding up thousands of radical suspects across the country. He had no guns or ammunition. Secret intelligence was his weapon.

Hoover lived all his life in Washington, D.C., where he was born on New Year's Day 1895, the youngest of four children. He was the son and the grandson of government servants. His father, Dickerson, was afflicted with depression; deep melancholy cost him his job as a government cartographer and likely hastened his death. His mother, Annie, was doting but dour. Hoover lived at home with her for the first forty-three years of his life, until the day she died. He told several of his closest aides that he remained a single man because he feared the wrong woman would be his downfall; a bad marriage would destroy him. Hoover's niece, Margaret Fennell, grew up alongside him; she stayed in touch with him for six decades. She knew him as well as anyone could. "I sometimes have thought that he really—I don't know how to put it—had a fear of becoming too personally involved with people," she reflected. If he ever expressed love beyond his devotion to God and country, there were no witnesses. He was sentimental about dogs, but unemotional about people. His inner life was a mystery, even to his immediate family and his few close friends.

Hoover learned how to march in military formation and how to make a formal argument. The drill team and the debate team at Central High School were the highlights of his youth. Central High's debate squad was the best in the city, and Hoover became one of its stars; his school newspaper praised his competitive spirit and his "cool relentless logic." He told the paper, after a stirring victory over a college team, that debating had given him "a practical and beneficial example of life, which is nothing more or less than the matching of one man's wit against another."

Hoover went to work for the government of the United States as soon as he had his high school diploma. Its monuments were all around him. His two-story home sat six blocks southeast of Capitol Hill. At the crest of the hill stood the chandeliered chambers of the Senate and the House, the colossal temple of the Supreme Court, and the Library of Congress, with its vaulted ceilings and stained glass. Hoover dutifully recited the devotions of the Presbyterian Church on Sundays, but the Library of Congress was the secular cathedral of his youth. The library possessed every book published in the United States. The reverent hush of its central reading room imparted a sense that all knowledge was at hand, if you knew where to look. The library had its own system of classification, and Hoover learned its complexities as a cataloguer, earning money for school by filing and retrieving information. He worked days at the library while he studied in the early evenings and on summer mornings at George Washington University, where he earned his master's degree in law in June 1917. He registered for military service but joined the Justice Department to fight the war at home.

"The gravest threats"

On April 6, 1917, the day America entered World War I, President Woodrow W. Wilson signed executive orders giving the Justice Department the power to command the arrest and imprisonment, without trial, of any foreigner deemed disloyal. He told the American people that Germany had "filled our unsuspecting communities and even our offices of government with spies, and set criminal intrigues everywhere afoot." The president's words stoked fear across the country, and the fear placed a great weight on the Justice Department. "When we declared war," O'Brian said, "there were persons who expected to see a veritable reign of terror in America."

O'Brian watched over Hoover and his colleagues as they labored day and night in cramped and smoky rooms at the War Emergency Division and the Alien Enemy Bureau, poring over fragmentary reports of plots against America. They were like firemen hearing the ceaseless ringing of false alarms. "Immense pressure" fell upon them, O'Brian recalled; they faced demands from politicians and the public for the "indiscriminate prosecution" and "wholesale repression" of suspect Americans and aliens alike, often "based on nothing more than irresponsible rumor." Before Black Tom, "the people of this nation had no experience with subversive activities," he said. "The government was likewise unprepared." After Black Tom, thousands of potential threats were reported to the government. American leaders feared the enemy could strike anywhere, at any time.

The German masterminds of Black Tom had been at work from the moment World War I began in Europe, in the summer of 1914. They had planned to infiltrate Washington and undermine Wall Street; they had enlisted Irish and Hindu nationalists to strike American targets; they had used Mexico and Canada as safe havens for covert operations against the United States. While Hoover was still studying law at night school, at the start of 1915, Germany's military attaché in the United States, Captain Franz von Papen, had received secret orders from Berlin: undermine America's will to fight. Von Papen began to build a propaganda machine in the United States; the Germans secretly gained control of a major New York newspaper, the *Evening Mail*; their front men negotiated to buy *The Washington Post* and the New York *Sun*. Political fixers, corrupt journalists, and crooked detectives served the German cause.

But after a German U-boat torpedoed the British passenger ship *Lusitania* on May 7, 1915, killing 1,119 people, including 274 Americans, the German ambassador glumly cabled Berlin: "We might as well admit openly that our propaganda here has collapsed completely." Americans were enraged at the attack on civilians; Germany's political and diplomatic status in the United States was grievously damaged. President Wilson ordered that all German embassy personnel in the United States be placed under surveillance. Secretary of State Robert Lansing sent secret agents to wiretap German diplomats. By year's end, von Papen and his fellow attachés were expelled from the United States.

When Hoover arrived at the Justice Department, O'Brian had just tried and convicted a German spy, Captain Franz von Rintelen. The case was front-page news. Von Rintelen had arrived in New York a few weeks before the sinking of the *Lusitania*, carrying a forged Swiss passport. On orders from the German high command, he had recruited idle sailors on New York's docks, radical Irish nationalists, a Wall Street con artist, and a drunken Chicago congressman in plans to sabotage American war industries with a combination of business frauds and firebombs. But Captain von Rintelen had fled the United States, rightly fearing the exposure of his secret plans. British intelligence officers, who had been reading German cables, arrested him as he landed in England, roughly interrogated him in the Tower of London, and handed him over to the Justice Department for indictment and trial.

"America never witnessed anything like this before," President Wilson told Congress after the captain's arrest. "A little while ago, such a thing would have seemed incredible. Because it was incredible we made no preparation for it."

Terrorists and anarchists represented "the gravest threats against our national peace and safety," the president said. "Such creatures of passion, disloyalty, and anarchy must be crushed out. . . . The hand of our power should close over them at once."

J. Edgar Hoover and the FBI would become the instruments of that power.

2

REVOLUTION

"I BELIEVE IN POWER," President Theodore Roosevelt wrote in June 1908, at the hour he decided to create the force that became the FBI. His presidency possessed "more power than in any other office in any great republic or constitutional monarchy of modern times," he recorded with pride. "I have used every ounce of power there was." Catapulted into the presidency by an anarchist assassin at the turn of the twentieth century, Roosevelt fought to enforce democracy, to impose political order, to build a nation under law.

Born in revolution and dedicated to liberty, America had been ripped asunder by civil war, reunited, and reshaped by great migrations of foreigners seeking freedom. At the turn of the twentieth century, the last wild and ungoverned western territories were on the verge of becoming states. The frontiers of exploration in the mountains and deserts were closing. Roughly 76 million people lived in the United States, more than half of them in small towns and villages. As America fought to civilize its frontiers, great swaths of the land remained lawless. U.S. marshals acted as sheriffs and formed posses; they faced death at the hands of desperadoes.

In American cities, the dynamos of money and power, invention and information, the poorer quarters teemed with immigrants seeking the promise of freedom and fortune in the New World. By 1900, American industry and its laborers had become the biggest creators of capital on earth, producing nearly one-quarter of the globe's manufacturing output. As America became a giant, the influence of corporate wealth grew immense; captains of industry sought to command and control the millions of workers whose labor had made them rich. As America became a global force, each new wave of immigration from the Old World fueled the fear of foreign subversion. Revolutionaries were importing dangerous ideas from

Germany and Italy and Russia. Their pamphlets and protests raged against the American political and economic order. The mines and factories and sweatshops of America were filled with people who had once lived under kings and czars. They dreamed of a better world. The most radical imagined the death of the old order and the rise of a political utopia where the wretched of the earth would rule.

"The time of the great social revolutions has arrived," Roosevelt had written in 1895, the year he became the police commissioner of New York City, and the year J. Edgar Hoover was born. "We are all peering into the future to try to forecast the action of the great dumb forces set in operation by the stupendous industrial revolution which has taken place during the present century. We do not know what to make of the vast displacement of population, the expansion of the towns, the unrest and discontent of the masses."

Anarchy was among the great dumb forces loosed upon the world. The anarchists aimed to destroy power itself; to pull down the pillars of western civilization. They had assassinated the president of France in 1894, the prime minister of Spain in 1897, the empress of Austria in 1898, the king of Italy in 1900—and the president of the United States, William McKinley, in 1901. McKinley's murder made Theodore Roosevelt president at the age of forty-two, the youngest in American history.

In his first major address to Congress, in December 1901, Roosevelt declared that "anarchy is a crime against the whole human race." He called for new laws to bar revolutionaries and subversives from living in the United States.

"THESE PEOPLE SHOULD ALL BE MARKED"

President Roosevelt had tasted imperial power and liked it. He acted alone when he carved a great canal out of the Panama jungle; he alone chose to send the American navy on a global show of force. He knew that foreigners might fight back when America projected its power across the world. But in the first years of his presidency Roosevelt had no real power to fight crimes against the United States. His Justice Department was only beginning to learn to uphold the rule of law.

Created in 1870, five years after the end of the Civil War, the Justice Department and its chief, the attorney general, were charged with imposing order on a nation torn apart. The attorney general and his lawyers had set up shop a block from the White House, on three upper floors of the Freedman's Savings Bank—a foul place, stinking from the sewers running beneath it—and there they remained for the rest of the nineteenth century. Congress gave them the authority to detect and prosecute crimes against the United States, along with the grand sum of $50,000 a year for that high purpose, but it failed to create a federal code of law regulating how justice was to be served.

Four nineteenth-century presidents had turned to the nation's most powerful private police force, the Pinkerton National Detective Agency, as an instrument of law enforcement, a source of secret intelligence, and a tool for political combat. "I have always been averse to appointing and paying detectives," Attorney General Benjamin Brewster wrote in 1884. But he did it nonetheless. The agency's founder, Allan Pinkerton, had run espionage missions during the Civil War and helped created the Secret Service for President Abraham Lincoln. Its detectives served railroad and steel barons by spying, breaking strikes, and cracking skulls to defeat labor organizers; they paid secret informants whose identities were protected with code names. They did not shrink from breaking the law to uphold the law, or using violence in the name of order. In 1892, Congress banned the government from hiring the firm after a confrontation at the Carnegie Steel Company in Homestead, Pennsylvania, left three Pinkerton men and five workers dead. The White House was now bereft of the skills, cunning, and force of the private eyes.

After the McKinley assassination, a Pinkerton man proposed creating a new government agency dedicated to eradicating America's radicals. "These people should all be marked and kept under constant surveillance," Robert A. Pinkerton wrote. In 1903, under new laws banning anarchists from living in the United States, the Justice and Labor departments began keeping secret files on foreign radicals.

The Republican Roosevelt wanted to fight plutocrats as well as anarchists. Their plunder of oil, coal, minerals, and timber on federal lands appalled him, in his role as the founder of America's national parks. Corporate criminals, carving up public property for their private profit, paid bribes to politicians to protect their land rackets. Using thousand-dollar bills as weapons, they ransacked millions of acres of the last American frontiers.

In 1905, a federal investigation, led in part by a scurrilous Secret Service agent named William J. Burns, had led to the indictment and conviction of

Senator John H. Mitchell and Representative John H. Williamson of Oregon, both Republicans, for their roles in the pillage of the great forests of the Cascade Range. An Oregon newspaper editorial correctly asserted that Burns and his government investigators had used "the methods of Russian spies and detectives." The senator died while his case was on appeal; the congressman's conviction was overturned by the U.S. Supreme Court on grounds of "outrageous conduct," including Burns's brazen tampering with jurors and witnesses. Burns left the government and became a famous private eye; his skills at tapping telephones and bugging hotel rooms eventually won him a job as J. Edgar Hoover's boss at the FBI.

The rape of virgin land by swindlers and speculators continued unabated. The president was enraged.

"ROOSEVELT, in his characteristic dynamic fashion, asserted that the plunderers of the public domain would be prosecuted and brought to justice," according to a 1943 memo to Hoover from FBI special agent Louis Findlay, who had joined the Bureau in 1911. The memo is a unique record of the birth of the FBI, whose origins, with reason, were obscured by its founders.

"ROOSEVELT called Attorney General CHARLES J. BONAPARTE to the White House and told him that he desired that the land frauds be prosecuted vigorously, and directed that he obtain the necessary investigative personnel." Bonaparte was a rare American blueblood—the grandnephew of Emperor Napoleon I of France and the grandson of the king of Westphalia. He had been a close friend and adviser to Roosevelt for years. Both men were aristocrats as well as progressives, reformers, and moralists; both supported the judicious use of force in the name of the law. Roosevelt favored giving strikers a taste of the nightstick and the blackjack; Bonaparte believed that violence by vigilantes could serve to vindicate the social order.

"BONAPARTE applied to the United States Secret Service for trained personnel to make the proper and necessary investigation, and was assigned quite a force of men" to root out the rampant land frauds, Findlay recounted. The president was unsatisfied. "He told Mr. BONAPARTE in most emphatic language characteristic of President ROOSEVELT that the report was a whitewash. He wanted the facts, all the facts, and the true facts, and if there was any whitewashing done he would do it himself," the record states.

"President ROOSEVELT directed BONAPARTE to create an investigative service within the Department of Justice subject to no other department or bureau, which would report to no one except the Attorney General." The president's order "resulted in the formation of the Bureau of Investigation."

By law, Bonaparte had to ask the House and the Senate to create this new bureau. "The Department of Justice has no executive force, and, more particularly, no permanent detective force under its immediate control," Bonaparte wrote to Congress; it was thus "assuredly not fully equipped for its work." He formally sought the money and authority to create "a small, carefully selected, and experienced force."

On May 27, 1908, the House emphatically said no. It feared the president intended to create an American secret police. The fear was well-founded. Presidents had used private detectives as political spies in the past.

"American ideas of government" prohibited "spying on men and prying into what would ordinarily be considered their private affairs," said Representative Joseph Swagar Sherley, a Kentucky Democrat. Representative Walter I. Smith, an Iowa Republican and later a federal appeals court judge, objected strongly to the creation of a "system of espionage" in America. Representative John J. Fitzgerald, a New York Democrat, warned against "a central police or spy system in the federal government." Representative George E. Waldo, a New York Republican, said it would be "a great blow to freedom and to free institutions if there should arise in this country any such great central secret-service bureau as there is in Russia."

Congress banned the Justice Department from spending a penny on Bonaparte's proposal. The attorney general evaded the order. The maneuver might have broken the letter of the law. But it was true to the spirit of the president.

Theodore Roosevelt was "ready to kick the Constitution into the back yard whenever it gets in the way," as Mark Twain observed. The beginnings of the FBI rose from that bold defiance.

"THE ATTORNEY GENERAL KNOWS OR OUGHT TO KNOW"

Bonaparte waited until after Congress adjourned at the end of June. Then he dipped into the Justice Department's expense fund to hire eight veteran Secret Service agents as permanent full-time investigators. On July 26, 1908, Bonaparte signed a formal order establishing a new investigative division with a thirty-four-man force of "special agents." He would have to beg, borrow, or steal the money and the men the president wanted. He appointed one Stanley W. Finch—a clerk unqualified to practice law in Washington, D.C.—as the first chief of the Bureau of Investigation.

"The difficulties encountered in recruiting a trustworthy and efficient detective force are serious," Bonaparte privately warned the president. The force had to have "some acquaintance with the haunts and habits of criminals, and its members are obliged to frequently associate with and use in their work persons of extremely low moral standards." Detectives were "often tempted to manufacture the evidence desired," Bonaparte said. The attorney general had to be the man "justly to be called to account" for their work.

Congress was notified about the creation of the Bureau of Investigation after the fact, in December 1908, in a few lines of Bonaparte's annual report on the work of the Justice Department. "It became necessary for the department to organize a small force of special agents of its own," he wrote. "Such action was involuntary on the part of this department." This shaded the truth, since the president had ordered the Bureau's creation.

Bonaparte personally swore to Congress that the Bureau would not be a secret police. It would be above politics. The attorney general, as the nation's chief law enforcement officer, would command and control its agents. "The Attorney General knows or ought to know at all times what they are doing," he promised.

The precipice between "knows" and "ought to know" would become a dangerous abyss when J. Edgar Hoover came to power.

3

TRAITORS

O N AUGUST 1, 1919, Hoover became the chief of the Justice Department's newly created Radical Division. He held a combination of powers unique in the government of the United States.

He oversaw hundreds of agents and informants working for the Bureau of Investigation. He could call for the arrest of almost anyone he chose. He began organizing a nationwide campaign against the enemies of the state. He was still only twenty-four years old.

The United States had fought and won its military battles abroad in the two years since Hoover had joined the government. Now it was engaged in political warfare against enemies on the home front.

The Justice Department and the Bureau of Investigation had used their powers against Americans and aliens alike from the start of World War I. President Wilson had warned that "vicious spies and conspirators" had "spread sedition among us." He had asserted that "many of our own people were corrupted" by foreign agents. He told citizens who opposed the war that they were in effect enemy combatants. "Woe to the man or group of men that seeks to stand in our way," Wilson said.

Hoover had learned the mechanics of mass arrests and detentions during his first year at Justice. The department had a list of 1,400 politically suspect Germans living in the United States on the day war was declared. Ninety-eight were jailed immediately; 1,172 were deemed potential threats to national security and subject to arrest at any time. They were the first political suspects over whom Hoover kept watch.

The Bureau launched its first nationwide domestic surveillance programs under the Espionage Act of 1917, rounding up radicals, wiretapping conversations, and opening mail. The Espionage Act made possession of information that could harm America punishable by death; imprisonment awaited anyone who would "utter, print, write, or publish" disloyal ideas. One thousand fifty-five people were convicted under the Espionage Act. Not one was a spy. Most were political dissidents who spoke against the war. Their crimes were words, not deeds.

Rose Pastor Stokes, a Russian immigrant married to a millionaire American socialist, was sentenced to ten years in prison under the Espionage Act for saying that "no government which is for the profiteers can also be for the people." Eugene V. Debs, the leader of the American Socialist Party, was indicted for speaking out against her conviction. He had won close to one million votes running against President Wilson, but he would conduct his next campaign from prison. "I believe in the right of free speech, in war as well as in peace," Debs said at his trial. "If the Espionage Law finally stands, then the Constitution of the United States is dead." His prosecutor, Edwin Wertz of the Justice Department, responded that Debs was a threat to society because his words inflamed American minds: if he went free, then "a man could go into a crowded theater . . . and yell 'fire' when there was no fire." A unanimous Supreme Court upheld the ten-year sentence. Justice Oliver Wendell Holmes, the most famous jurist in America, wrote that the Socialists had used "words that may have all the effect of force." They created "a clear and present danger" to the nation.

As the war went on, Senator Lee Overman, Republican of North Carolina—a prominent member of the Judiciary Committee, which oversaw the Justice Department—demanded stronger action by the Bureau against "traitors, scoundrels, and spies." The senator warned that 100,000 foreign espionage agents stalked the United States. Citing the Bureau as his authority, he would double and redouble the number when he pleased—200,000 one day, 400,000 the next.

Attorney General Thomas Gregory wrote to a Justice Department prosecutor: "There is quite a deal of hysteria in the country about German spies. If you will kindly box up and send me from one to a dozen I will pay you very handsomely for your trouble. We are looking for them constantly, but it is a little difficult to shoot them until they have been found."

The hunt for foreign spies became a wild-goose chase. The army and the navy, the State Department, the Secret Service, U.S. marshals, and big-city police forces competed with one another and the Bureau of Investigation in the fruitless pursuit. The Bureau faced "an enormous overlapping of investigative activities among the various agencies charged with winning the war," remembered one agent, Francis X. Donnell. "It was not an uncommon experience for an agent of this Bureau to call upon an individual in the course of his investigation, to find out that six or seven other government agencies had been around to interview the party about the same matter."

The search became a free-for-all. Attorney General Gregory and the Bureau of Investigation's wartime director, A. Bruce Bielaski, backed business executives across the country who financed the ultrapatriotic American Protective League—gangs of citizens who spied on suspected subversives. They worked in posses, wearing badges proclaiming them members of a "secret service." At its height the league claimed more than 300,000 loyalists. Its more zealous members reveled in burglarizing and beating their fellow Americans in the name of justice and the flag. The rumors, gossip, and innuendo gathered by the league filled the files of the Bureau of Investigation.

President Wilson's son-in-law, Treasury Secretary William G. McAdoo, told the president that the Bureau's alliance with the league posed "the gravest danger of misunderstanding, confusion, and even fraud." That gave the president pause; Wilson asked Attorney General Gregory if these vigilantes were the best force America could muster. He said it was "very dangerous to have such an organization operating in the United States, and I wonder if there is any way in which we could stop it?" The president said he knew he had been "derelict in not having sought a remedy" to the disorder in the government's ranks—but he was "still in doubt as to what the best remedy is."

Attorney General Gregory had an answer. As the searchlights played across America and the sirens of warning wailed louder, he put the Bureau of Investigation to work as a political strike force.

The Bureau conducted two major political raids during the war. The first was a nationwide attack on the Industrial Workers of the World (IWW), a left-wing labor movement with 100,000 members in the United States. The IWW had passed a resolution against the war; the rhetoric alone was a political crime under the Espionage Act. The attorney general intended to put the IWW out of business. President Wilson heartily approved. *The New York Times* opined that the union's leaders were "in effect, and perhaps in fact, agents of Germany," under the theory that the Germans paid the IWW to subvert American industries. The newspaper suggested that "Federal authorities should make short work of these treasonable conspirators." Bureau agents and American Protective League members did so. They kicked in the doors at IWW offices, homes, and union halls in twenty-four cities across America, seizing tons of documents and arresting hundreds of suspects. Three mass trials led to the Espionage Act convictions of 165 union leaders. Their prison sentences ran as long as twenty years.

Politicians and the public applauded the arrests. Calls for the jailing of traitors, scoundrels, and spies rang from the pulpits of churches and the chambers of state legislatures. The attorney general found an easy target. He authorized the Bureau of Investigation to round up the "slackers"—men who had failed to register for the military draft—in the spring and summer of 1918.

The biggest slacker raid by far was a three-day roundup set for September 3, the most ambitious operation in the decade-long history of the Bureau of Investigation. Thirty-five agents gathered under the direction of Charles de Woody, the head of the Bureau's New York office. The Bureau's men were backed by roughly 2,000 American Protective League members, 2,350 army and navy men, and at least 200 police officers. They hit the streets of Manhattan and Brooklyn at dawn, crossed the Hudson River in ferries, and fanned out across Newark and Jersey City. They arrested somewhere between 50,000 and 65,000 suspects, seizing them off sidewalks, hauling them out of restaurants and bars and hotels, marching them into local jails and national armories. Some 1,500 draft dodgers and deserters were among the accused. But tens of thousands of innocent men had been arrested and imprisoned without cause.

Attorney General Gregory tried to disavow the raids, but the Bureau would not let him. "No one can make a goat of me," de Woody said defiantly. "Everything I have done in connection with this roundup has been done under the direction of the Attorney General and the chief of the Bureau of Investigation."

The political storm over the false arrest and imprisonment of the multitudes was brief. But both Attorney General Gregory and the Bureau's Bielaski soon resigned. Their names and reputations have faded into thin air. Their legacy remains only because it was Hoover's inheritance.

"The gravest menace to this country"

The Red threat began to capture the imagination of the American government in the last weeks of World War I.

President Wilson sent some 14,000 American troops into combat against Bolshevik revolutionaries on the frozen frontiers of Russia. They were still fighting when the guns fell silent in Europe on November 11, 1918. The first battle of America's war on communism was fought with live ammunition.

The president also launched a political attack on Russia's radicals. To the shock of his top aides, Wilson personally authorized the publication of secret dossiers purporting to show that the leaders of the Russian Revolution were paid agents of the German government. These documents had been delivered to the White House by one of Wilson's experts on propaganda, who thought he had produced "the greatest scoop in history." The president consulted no one about their authenticity. They were fakes—crude forgeries sold to a credulous American by a czarist swindler—but they changed the political conversation in America.

Congress now joined the war on communism. In January 1919, the U.S. Senate began hearings on the threat, led by Senator Lee Overman of the Judiciary Committee. The Justice Department gave Senator Overman open-ended access to Bureau of Investigation records. In turn, his committee gave the Bureau copies of all its reports from every other branch of government. These files formed a cornerstone for the foundation of J. Edgar Hoover's career.

The tone of the hearings was set by the testimony of a New York lawyer named Archibald Stevenson, a largely self-taught expert on the subject of the Soviets.

"The idea, then, is to form a government within this Government?" asked Senator Overman. "And to overthrow this Government?"

"Precisely," Stevenson said.

"You think this movement is growing constantly in this country?"

It was, Stevenson said, and it constituted "the gravest menace to this country today."

"Can you give us any remedy?" asked the senator.

"The foreign agitators should be deported," he said. "American citizens who advocate revolution should be punished."

Senator Overman concluded by saying it was high time to start "getting this testimony out to the American people and letting them know what is going on in this country."

As the Senate's alarm at the Red threat increased, the fighting spirit mustered for the world war festered. Nine million American workers in war industries were being demobilized. They found new jobs scarce. The cost of living had nearly doubled since the start of the war. As four million American soldiers started coming home, four million American workers went out on strike. The United States never had seen such confrontations between workers and bosses. The forces of law and order felt the Reds were behind it all.

On January 21, 1919—the day that the Senate took its first testimony on the Red threat—thirty-five thousand shipyard workers in Seattle walked off their jobs. Federal troops put down their uprising, but the spirit of the strike spread to coal mines and steel mills, to textile workers and telephone operators, and to the police force in Boston. Hundreds upon hundreds of strikes threw sand in the gears of the American engine. Political and economic fear ran across the country.

The White House was vacant. President Wilson had set sail across the Atlantic aboard the USS *George Washington*, seeking to bring an end to all wars. He and his most trusted aides went to France in pursuit of his dream of a League of Nations, a global alliance to keep the peace. Wilson called his proposal a covenant; a messianic element tinged his mission. His wartime allies, the leaders of England and France, found Wilson unbearably sanctimonious. They were far more interested in punishing Germany than in building a new world founded on Wilson's visions.

Without a peace treaty, the United States was still in a state of war abroad. Without a president in the White House, the nation had no one to lead the war at home.

Wilson was out of the United States from December 4, 1918, to February 24, 1919. Nine days later, he left again for France, and he stayed away for four months. On the day he set sail for the second time, Wilson named an old political ally as the new attorney general.

A. Mitchell Palmer was a handsome man of forty-seven, a three-term congressman from Pennsylvania, a pacifist Quaker and a smooth talker with flexible principles and soaring ambitions. A ranking member of the Democratic National Committee, he had served as Wilson's political manager at the 1912 Democratic convention. During 1918, he had run the Justice Department's Alien Property Office as a fief, giving friends and cronies custody of seized German property and patents worth millions. Now he leaped at the chance to run the Justice Department.

Palmer had one great goal in mind. He fancied himself the next president of the United States.

"We will dynamite you!"

Thirty-six brown paper packages of dynamite made their way through the U.S. mails in late April 1919. They constituted the biggest conspiracy to commit political murder in the history of the United States.

On April 29, the first bomb arrived at the Atlanta home of Thomas W. Hardwick, who had just left his seat as a U.S. senator from Georgia. Hardwick had helped pass the new Anarchist Exclusion Act, aimed at deporting radical foreigners. The bomb blew off the hands of his housekeeper.

Not one of the mail bombs reached its intended victim. A postal clerk in New York found sixteen of them on the postage-due shelf; the bombers hadn't used enough stamps. The would-be assassins were evidently semiliterate; they had garbled some of the addressees' names. But their hit list was sophisticated.

Attorney General Palmer led it. Supreme Court Justice Oliver Wendell Holmes was on it. So was Judge Kenesaw Mountain Landis, who had overseen more than one hundred Espionage Act convictions. Five members of Congress were marked for death, including Senator Overman. The secretary of labor and the federal immigration commissioner, both responsible for deportation proceedings under the Anarchist Exclusion Act, were on the list. So were the mayor and the police commissioner of New York. The most famous targets were the nation's foremost bankers, John D. Rockefeller and J. P. Morgan. The least famous was a plump, balding twenty-nine-year-old Bureau of Investigation agent named Rayme Finch.

Finch had spent months chasing members of a gang of Italian anarchists led by Luigi Galleani, the founder of an underground journal called *Cronaca Sovversiva*—the Subversive Chronicle. Galleani had perhaps fifty followers who took to heart his calls for violent revolution, political assassination, and the use of dynamite to sow terror among the ruling class. Literate revolutionaries drew a bright line between propaganda of the word and propaganda of the deed. Galleani believed in deeds. Finch and a handful of his fellow Bureau of Investigation agents had followed a broken trail from the Ohio River Valley to the Atlantic Ocean, ending in a February 1918 raid on *Cronaca Sovversiva*'s offices in Lynn, Massachusetts. The raid led to Galleani's arrest and, a year later, to a judicial order for his deportation, along with eight of his closest adherents, under the new Anarchist Exclusion Act. Late in January 1919, Galleani had filed his final appeal when a flier appeared in the mill towns of Massachusetts and Connecticut, signed by "The American Anarchists." It promised a coming storm of "blood and fire."

"Deportation will not stop the storm from reaching these shores," it said. "Deport us! *We will dynamite you!*"

On the night of June 2, 1919, nine more bombs went off in seven cities. Again, each target escaped alive. In New York, it was a municipal judge, though a night watchman on the street was killed. In Cleveland, it was the mayor; in Pittsburgh, a federal judge and an immigration inspector; in Boston, a local judge and a state representative. In Philadelphia, the bombers hit a church; in Paterson, New Jersey, a businessman's home.

In Washington, D.C., a young man blew himself up on Attorney General Palmer's doorstep. The blast rocked a row of elegant town houses. Franklin Delano Roosevelt, the thirty-seven-year-old assistant secretary of the United States Navy, was coming home from a late supper with his wife, Eleanor, when the explosion shook the spring night. The front windows of their home at 2131 R Street in Washington were blown out. Across the street, Palmer was standing in the ruins of his front parlor. The façade of his house was shattered.

The sidewalks were filled with shards of glass and broken branches and bits of flesh and bone. It took a very long time to determine that the fragments of the disintegrated body were in all likelihood the mortal remains of a twenty-three-year-old immigrant named Carlo Valdinoci, the publisher of the *Cronaca Sovversiva.*

Copies of a fresh diatribe against the government, printed on pink paper, fluttered in the wreckage. "It is war, class war, and you were the first to wage it under cover of the powerful institutions you call order, in the darkness of your laws," it read. "There will be bloodshed; we will not dodge; there will have to be murder: we will kill, because it is necessary; there will have to be destruction; we will destroy to rid the world of your tyrannical institutions." It was signed "The Anarchist Fighters."

"THE BLAZE OF REVOLUTION"

The Boston and Pittsburgh field offices of the Bureau of Investigation were the first to report that Moscow was behind the bombings.

Palmer presumed that the Reds were responsible. He had become the attorney general in the same week that the Soviets had proclaimed the Comintern—the international Communist movement. Announcing that the movement aimed to overthrow the existing world order, Lenin had openly invited Americans to join them.

On the morning of June 3, sitting in the ruins of his library, Palmer received a small delegation of Senate and House members. "They called upon me in strong terms to exercise all the power that was possible," he recounted. " 'Palmer, ask for what you want and you will get it.' "

On the front page of every newspaper in America, he vowed to hunt down the bombers. Now he needed hunters.

First he chose a new leader for the Bureau of Investigation: William J. Flynn, the former chief of the U.S. Secret Service. Palmer proudly introduced him to the press as America's finest detective. An old-time New York cop with a high school education, Flynn had worked as a plumber before finding his calling. He cut a fine rotogravure figure with his derby, his cigar, and a big belly rounded by beer and beefsteaks. He had a number of newspaper reporters in New York and Washington wrapped around his finger, and he had cultivated a reputation as a master sleuth who never gave up on a case.

Flynn had warned the nation that hundreds of thousands of foreign agents were within the United States. The government, he believed, was well within its rights to jail any number of suspects to catch a spy or a saboteur. His first move was to raid the Reds.

On June 12, 1919, Bureau of Investigation agents and New York state police sacked the newly opened Soviet diplomatic offices at 110 East 40th Street in Manhattan. They seized reams of files—but nothing to link the Reds to the bombings.

The next day, Attorney General Palmer went to Congress and asked for money and new laws to stop the Reds and radicals. He warned that the next attacks could come within days or weeks, perhaps on the Fourth of July. He had started to see a growing global conspiracy of Communists and common crooks, parlor pinks and sexual perverts—"a mass formation of the criminals of the world to overthrow the decencies of private life." He took the bombing of his house as the clearest sign that "the blaze of revolution was sweeping over every institution of law and order" in America, "licking into the altars of churches, leaping into the belfry of the school bell, crawling into the sacred corners of American homes."

On June 17, Palmer and Flynn met at the Justice Department with a handful of aides. They emerged to announce that the Bureau of Investigation would round up the bombers in short order. Flynn was convinced the attacks were the work of the Russian Bolsheviks.

Six days later, the Bureau's agents interviewed Luigi Galleani, who was sitting in a holding cell on Deer Island in Boston Harbor, awaiting deportation. They got nothing from him. The next morning, he was on a ship to Italy, never to set foot in America again. Galleani and his anarchist gang were never charged; the investigation went on for twenty-five years without resolution. His followers would soon strike again, carrying out the biggest terrorist attack America ever had witnessed.

"Secret agencies planted everywhere"

Two ships crossed in the Atlantic. One took Galleani away from America. The other brought the president home.

On July 8, Woodrow Wilson returned to the United States after five futile months fighting for his League of Nations. His vision of world peace was slipping away, evanescent as the ocean waves. He had scant support from America's wartime allies. The U.S. Senate was increasingly scornful. Wilson soon was off on a cross-country campaign, taking his argument to the citizenry. No national radio stations existed in 1919; the president had to deliver his message in person. He traveled over eight thousand miles by railroad, making forty speeches in fifteen states.

The president appeared as a prophet of doom. Wheezing, coughing, seeing double, blinded by headaches, Wilson delivered an apocalyptic vision to the American people. He foresaw the nation and the world under the never-ending threat of war. He spoke of the Russian Revolution as if it were a gigantic cloud of deadly gas, floating west across the Atlantic, bringing "the poison of disorder, the poison of revolt, the poison of chaos" to America.

"Do you honestly think, my fellow-citizens, that none of that poison has got in the veins of this free people?" the president asked. "Men look you calmly in the face in America and say they are for that sort of revolution, when that sort of revolution means government by terror." Without peace, "that poison will steadily spread, more and more rapidly until it may be that even this beloved land of ours will be distracted and distorted by it."

He warned that the United States would have to be ready to fight "in any part of the world where the threat of war is a menace." The enemies of the United States would not rest: "You have got to watch them with secret agencies planted everywhere." The nation would have to keep a great standing army and navy in a constant state of high alert.

"And you can't do that under free debate," the president said. "You can't do that under public counsel. Plans must be kept secret. Knowledge must be accumulated under a system which we have condemned, because we have called it a spying system. The more polite call it a system of intelligence."

As the president whistle-stopped westward across the Great Plains, a new American intelligence system was taking shape in Washington.

"When the time came for a Revolution"

On August 1, 1919, the attorney general assigned J. Edgar Hoover to crush the Communist conspiracy against the United States. He had taken an instant liking to Hoover, whose tireless work won strong commendations from his chiefs at Justice.

Hoover, as the new chief of the Radical Division, had sixty-one Bureau of Investigation agents and thirty-five undercover informers at his command. He began to fill the Bureau's files with information from military intelligence, the State Department, and the Secret Service. He enlisted the aid of the immigration and passport services, postmasters, police commissioners, private detectives, and political vigilantes. Teams of lock pickers and safecrackers from the Bureau and the Office of Naval Intelligence broke into foreign embassies and consulates to steal codes and ciphers.

He used the authority granted him as a magnetic force, pulling together fragments of secret information scattered throughout the government, creating classified cases against tens of thousands of political suspects. Americans and aliens alike could land on Hoover's enemies list by attending a political rally alongside an informant or by subscribing to any of the 222 radical foreign-language newspapers published in the United States.

Hoover's cache of secrets formed the foundation of a primitive system of central intelligence. Within three months after taking office, he controlled files on more than sixty thousand people; the Bureau compiled at least as many dossiers on the places where these people gathered, the publications they read, and the political groups they joined. Every one of these people had to be weighed as a potential threat to national security. Each might have a role in a secret underground, each might be a camouflaged soldier in what Hoover came to call "the mad march of Red fascism," dedicated to creating a Soviet America.

Lenin and Stalin were rising to power out of the political chaos in Russia. The fear that their revolution would spread was immense.

On August 12, his second week on the job, Hoover began "a vigorous and comprehensive investigation" of American citizens and aliens "advocating change in the present form of government by force or violence." The Justice Department wanted evidence "of every nature, whether hearsay or otherwise," against American Communists. The hearsay evidence could be used in prosecutions under new laws that Palmer was urging upon Congress. Palmer had scoured the statutes searching for new ways to arrest and jail outspoken Americans for sedition in peacetime. In 1919, seventy such bills were introduced in Congress. None passed.

On August 23, Hoover began a series of meetings with the immigration commissioner, Anthony Caminetti, a sixty-five-year-old California politician with a big white handlebar mustache. Hoover had worked closely with Caminetti's enforcers during the war. Caminetti controlled records on roughly 13 million immigrants—one of every eight people in America, including 1.7 million born in Germany, 1.6 million in Italy, and 1.4 million in Russia. Hoover suspected that the shock troops of Red fascism were among them. Together they began to work out a plan to rid the nation of its enemies. The Anarchist Exclusion Act gave them the power to exile foreigners advocating revolution with only a summary hearing, without indictments or convictions. Hoover proposed winning public acclaim by making two of the most famous rabble-rousers in America their first deportees: Emma Goldman and Alexander Berkman. Happily for Hoover, both of them were already in jail for agitating against the war, both were due to be released within the month, and both could be charged swiftly and shipped back to their native Russia.

Goldman preached atheism, free love, birth control, and other outlaw doctrines. Hoover called her "the Red Queen of Anarchy." Berkman, her former lover, had spent half his life in prison for trying to murder the steel magnate Henry Frick. He never claimed to be an American citizen; the case against him was open-and-shut. But Goldman asserted she was an American by marriage, a bar to her deportation. Hoover personally took charge of the challenge.

That same week, late in August 1919, Hoover sent his agents to infiltrate two of America's leading left-wing organizations. Both were convening in Chicago over the Labor Day weekend.

One was the Socialist Party. The Socialists had tried to work openly within the American political system for years; their candidates had run in state and local elections across the country, sometimes winning. But with their leader, Eugene Debs, in prison, their hierarchy was fractured. Their most radical members revolted, led by the flamboyant John Reed, a secret Soviet agent and the author of a romantic account of the Bolshevik uprising, *Ten Days That Shook the World*. Reed was joined by his friend Benjamin Gitlow, a radical New York state assemblyman, in a raucous faction calling itself the Communist Labor Party.

The second group under surveillance was the little-known Union of Russian Workers. Hoover's eye had fallen on a report about the union filed by an enterprising Bureau of Investigation agent named Edgar B. Speer. Once a newspaper reporter in and around Pittsburgh, Speer had good sources among the coal and steel bosses of the Midwest; his son grew up to be the chairman of the U.S. Steel Corporation. The bosses had alerted Speer to the presence of the Union of Russian Workers among the miners of Pennsylvania, Ohio, and West Virginia. He had studied a cache of documents seized from the union's headquarters in Manhattan. He concluded that the Russian Workers constituted a conspiracy of thousands of immigrants—atheists, Communists, anarchists—preparing to rise up against America. They were "terrorists," he reported, "ready for any sort of work when the time came for a Revolution."

Hoover began to prepare for an American counterrevolution.

4

COMMUNISTS

T HE COMMUNIST PARTY of the United States of America was born at the Russian Federation hall in Chicago on September 7, 1919. At least five government agents attended its birth. Their reports went directly to J. Edgar Hoover. They are among the first dispatches of the Cold War in America.

The hall was festooned with red ribbons, red streamers, and red flags, reported Bureau special agent August H. Loula. The Chicago police tore the decorations down before the delegates were called to order, though they left hanging a seventy-five-foot red muslin banner that read, LONG LIVE THE DICTATORSHIP OF THE PROLETARIAT.

The 137 official delegates at the convention were zealots with a talent for machine politics. Over the summer, they had siphoned off thousands of card-carrying, dues-paying Socialists, many of them members of the Union of Russian Workers.

The delegates included the Bureau of Investigation's Confidential Informant No. 121, a Russian native from the steel town of Gary, Indiana, listed on the roster as N. Nagorowe. He was assigned to spy on "secret sessions of the heads of the Communist movement or any other secret procedure that may be contemplated by the radicals" outside of the convention hall, as Agent Loula reported.

The meeting was open to the public; mimeographed minutes were distributed in the hall. But Confidential Informant No. 121 reported that "the whole game has been played behind closed doors," run by "the Russian Steam Roller, as the American delegates later referred to it."

While the police were tearing down the red ribbons on the first floor, the Russians and their Slavic allies were meeting secretly on the second floor.

They vowed that "this party must be made an exact copy of the Russian original." They would incite rebellion among American workers and "train them in the tactics of the Bolsheviks for the overthrow of the government and the seizure of the state by the Communist Party."

On September 7, Confidential Informant No. 121 sent the Bureau's Russian-speaking special agent Jacob Spolansky a draft version of the new group's constitution.

"The name of this organization shall be THE COMMUNIST PARTY of America," it read. "Its purpose shall be the education and organization of the working class for the establishment of the Dictatorship of the Proletariat, the abolition of the capitalist system, and the establishment of the Communist Society."

"To overthrow the Government"

By September 8, 1919, Hoover had studied dozens of reports from Chicago—the speeches and tracts denouncing lawmen as "cutthroats and pimps," calling for nationwide strikes, a workers' revolution, and the creation of a Soviet America.

Hoover thought the nation faced an insurrection unlike any since the Civil War. He concluded that the Reds in Chicago were controlled by the Communist International in Moscow. He wrote in a report to Congress that their aims were one: "to overthrow the Government of the United States by force and violence."

Hoover correctly intuited a Moscow connection. Soviet archives exhumed after the Cold War ended show that the Comintern was trying to underwrite its American allies with smuggled gold and diamonds—and that John Reed was one of the smugglers. How much money actually arrived in the coffers of the American Communists from revolutionary Russia is another question. It could have been tens of thousands of dollars, hundreds of thousands, or more; many middlemen were involved, not all of them honest brokers. The Comintern also sent a secret communiqué to its American allies that summer, calling on them to incite strikes and strife across the country. Though its effect cannot be measured, the facts were clear. American workers rose up against their bosses in a new wave of protest after Labor Day 1919.

On September 9, three-quarters of the Boston police department walked out when their commissioner rejected their call for a union. The cops were no more Communist than Woodrow Wilson, but the president called them criminals, and Massachusetts governor Calvin Coolidge called out the National Guard and fired every one of the 1,117 protesting policemen.

September 10 brought a call for a national strike by iron and steel workers. Immigrant Russians and Slavs worked many of the hardest steel mill shifts, laboring seventy hours a week under killing conditions for less than a living wage. At least 275,000 steelworkers walked out, seeking an eight-hour day, a six-day week, and the right to bargain collectively. Attorney General Palmer and the Justice Department worked to blame the steelworkers' strike on Communists, in particular a labor organizer named William Z. Foster, later a secret leader of the American Communist movement. Hoover would be hunting Foster for the next forty years. The nation's steel executives called on soldiers, police, private detectives, and local militias to crush the workers. The War Department granted requests from states and cities to put down the steel strikes; the army imposed martial law where it was warranted.

No one sought President Wilson's approval. The president had fallen silent.

On September 25, while campaigning for his League of Nations, on a train outside Pueblo, Colorado, the president had turned to his doctor and said he could not breathe. He took to his berth, but he could not rise at the next stop, in Wichita, Kansas. "I seem to have gone to pieces," he muttered. The train sped back to Washington. Wilson collapsed at the White House a week later. On October 2, a catastrophic stroke took him to the edge of death.

The president lay on the Lincoln bed, his left side paralyzed, his speech gone. The press and the public were told he was exhausted, nothing more. His stroke was kept a secret from all but his inner circle. In this hour of crisis, the country had no leader. The president remained invisible, locked away in the White House, as his power slipped away.

"Doomed to Siberia"

Attorney General Palmer saw himself as the president-in-waiting. He needed a swift political success to seize national attention.

The pressure on Palmer was growing. Congress was demanding action.

On October 17, the Senate passed a resolution pointedly asking Palmer if he had done anything to fight the forces trying to overthrow the government—"and if not, why not." His Justice Department had convicted no revolutionaries, the nationwide bomb plots remained unsolved, and the Communist Party chiefs in Chicago openly taunted Bureau agents who confronted them, saying they could say and write what they pleased under the Constitution.

Palmer turned to J. Edgar Hoover for results.

On October 27, Hoover was in New York, eyeball to eyeball with Emma Goldman in a small room off the great main hall of the immigrant center on Ellis Island; the Statue of Liberty stood a half mile away in the harbor, lifting her lamp. Hoover had spent days in the city preparing the deportation case; in a spare moment, he had watched mounted police clubbing Russian demonstrators during a pro-Soviet march on Fifth Avenue.

Hoover, at the government's table, sat before stacks of Goldman's speeches and writings, anarchist diatribes dating back a decade. He used her own words against her. The ruling by the immigration inspector was never in doubt: he asked Goldman if she was an anarchist; she declined to answer. The inspector determined that she was; she thus could be deported to Russia. The only remaining question was how. Hoover solved that problem. Working with the War Department and the State Department, he requisitioned an army troop transport ship, the *Buford*, decommissioned only days before. The ship was just shy of thirty years old, she leaked and rolled, but she was still seaworthy enough to have brought 4,700 American soldiers home from France that year.

The *Buford* would carry hundreds of America's most despised radicals back where they came from.

On October 30, Hoover ordered his agents to prepare for their first pitched battle: a mass arrest of members of the Union of Russian Workers. "It is the desire of the Bureau of Investigation to shortly have taken into custody the leaders of each of the locals of the Union of Russian Workers," Hoover wrote to the immigration chief Caminetti on November 3. He requested "the cooperation of the immigration inspectors at the time when the round-up of these persons will be made." Caminetti gave the go-ahead. The raids were set for Friday evening, November 7, 1919—the second anniversary of the Russian Revolution. It was no secret that supporters of the Soviets were planning to mark the day with speeches and rallies in cities across America.

Hoover's men struck the first blow around eight o'clock that night. The Bureau's agents, accompanied by the New York police, surrounded the Union of Russian Workers' national headquarters on East 15th Street. They took everyone out of the building, more than two hundred people in all, beating some of them with blackjacks and broken banisters and a steel crowbar, cracking skulls and bones, sacking the building so thoroughly that the rooms looked like they had been dynamited. The New York police executed seventy-one search warrants across the city and arrested every card-carrying Communist they could find. The Bureau's men worked long and hard all across the country. They meted out rough justice in Chicago, Detroit, Cleveland, Pittsburgh, and a dozen more cities and towns. Hoover worked furiously to pump the newspapers full of the incendiary Communist propaganda his agents seized that night.

The publicity was tremendous. Palmer was hailed as a conquering hero. The acclaim from politicians and the press grew. The Palmer for President bandwagon began rolling. Filled with pride and the intoxicating spirit of self-promotion, Palmer proclaimed that the arrests had destroyed a Communist plot against America.

But the aftermath was hidden from public view. The Bureau's men had seized many more people than they had planned to arrest; Hoover had obtained far fewer warrants than were needed. The Bureau's files would show that 1,182 suspects had been arrested in eighteen cities and towns across eight states—nearly one thousand more people than Palmer publicly acknowledged. In the days to come, 199 among them were found worthy of deportation under the law. That left nearly one thousand detainees in limbo. Some disappeared into city and county jails for months; the unluckiest suffered beatings and torture by Bureau agents and local police.

The raids on the Union of Russian Workers were only the beginning. Hoover planned a far bigger crackdown in a few weeks.

He was preparing legal briefs holding that every member of a Communist group was a criminal engaged in a conspiracy against the United States. "They would destroy the peace of the country and thrust it into a condition of anarchy and lawlessness and immorality that passes imagination," he wrote. He held this belief all his life.

On November 18, Hoover sent fresh orders to all the Bureau's field agents, marked "personal and confidential" and bearing his initials, JEH.

He wanted legal affidavits naming anyone and everyone in America who was "prominent in Communist activities." The affidavit would serve as proof that a person was a card-carrying Communist; party membership alone justified deportation under the Anarchist Exclusion Act. The scope of the assignment was breathtaking: New York City alone had seventy-nine local branches of the Communist Party and the Communist Labor Party, each with its own set of leaders. "To gather a correct, up-to-date list of these would entail quite some investigation by both undercover and open investigators," a daunted Bureau special agent, M. J. Davis, warned headquarters on December 4. But Hoover wanted immediate results. He alerted Caminetti on December 16 that he was ready to send over "a considerable number of affidavits." He did not say how many.

On the night of December 20, Hoover took a cutter across New York Harbor, accompanied by five congressmen and a contingent of reporters. Ice drifted down the Hudson and a cold wind swept snowdrifts against the barracks at Ellis Island. Inside the walls, 249 alien anarchists awaited—the rabble of the Russian Workers and the renowned rebels Emma Goldman and Alexander Berkman among them. Midnight passed. The deportees filed out toward a docked barge.

"The crowd was very cocky," Hoover recounted, "full of sarcasm." Hoover sparred with them. He came face-to-face again with Emma Goldman, the emblem of radical America. "Haven't I given you a square deal, Miss Goldman?" Hoover asked. "Oh," she replied, "I suppose you've given me as square a deal as you could. We shouldn't expect from any person something beyond his capacity."

The barge took the Reds to the edge of the harbor at Fort Wadsworth on Staten Island, the oldest military site in the United States, where the *Buford* was docked. Emma Goldman was among the last to board.

"It was 4:20 A.M. on the day of our Lord, December 21, 1919," she wrote years later. "I felt dizzy, visioning a transport of politicals doomed to Siberia. . . . Russia of the past rose before me. . . . But no, it was New York, it was America, the land of liberty! Through the port-hole I could see the great city receding into the distance, its sky-line of buildings traceable by their rearing heads. It was my beloved city, the metropolis of the New World. It was America, indeed America repeating the terrible scenes of tsarist Russia! I glanced up—the Statue of Liberty!"

The *Buford* slipped out of New York Harbor, its prisoners bound for

Soviet Russia. Hoover boarded the first train back to Washington. Over the next ten days he perfected his plans for the war on communism.

Hoover marked his twenty-fifth birthday at home—his mother's home, where he still lived—on New Year's Day. Then he went back to work. He made sure that the war began on time.

5

"WHO IS MR. HOOVER?"

O N THE AFTERNOON of December 30, 1919, the chief of the Communist Party of America, Charles E. Ruthenberg, went to lunch in New York with seven of his closest comrades. One of them was an undercover spy whose reports went to the Justice Department marked "Attention— Mr. Hoover."

Ruthenberg was rail-thin and balding; he looked much older than his thirty-seven years. He had run for high office on the Socialist ticket in Ohio, winning a fair number of votes. He had gone to prison in 1918, convicted under the Espionage Act for opposing the war, and he had come out a hard-core Communist. He had just been arraigned on a charge of criminal anarchy for publishing the Party platform in New York. Now he was afraid a new wave of arrests was coming. "The Communist Party is practically busted," he said, according to the secret agent's report to Hoover. "Most of the leaders are either in jail, in hiding, or afraid." If the federal government struck anew, he feared, the Party would have to go underground or die.

At that moment, Hoover was counting down the hours until the crackdown.

Hoover had the names of 2,280 Communists at hand, and he was adding hundreds more to the list on the morning of December 31. His men had worked nonstop for six weeks gathering the names. The Bureau had identified at least 700 Communists in New York alone. Hoover had enlisted help from undercover informers inside the Communist ranks, military intelligence officers, state and local police, business executives, private detectives, vigilantes from the American Protective League and veterans from the newly founded American Legion. By nightfall on New Year's Eve, Hoover had won the approval for roughly 3,000 arrest warrants from the acting secretary of labor, who oversaw the immigration department, and he had convinced the immigration authorities to change their rules of procedure, in order to deny the arrested suspects the right to see a lawyer.

"Arrange with your undercover informants to have meetings of the Communist Party and the Communist Labor Party held on the night set," read the orders to the Bureau's agents in charge of the crackdown across twenty-three states. The agents were told not to bother with search warrants unless they were absolutely needed. They were instructed to break into homes and offices, probe ceilings and walls for hiding places, ransack records, and take "literature, books, papers, and anything hanging on the walls."

"Communicate by long distance to Mr. Hoover any matters of vital importance or interest which may arise during the course of the arrests," said the orders, signed by Frank Burke, Hoover's immediate superior. "Forward to this office by special delivery marked for the 'Attention of Mr. Hoover' a complete list of the names of the persons arrested." Agents were reminded that secrecy was paramount: "in order that no 'leak' may occur," they were to tell no state or local police about the planned attack until a few hours beforehand.

A final set of orders went out under Hoover's initials. "All instructions previously issued to you for carrying out arrests of Communists should be executed in detail," they read. "Bureau and Department expect excellent results from you in your territory." The orders authorized the thirty-three special agents in charge to tell reporters that "arrests are nationwide in scope and being directed by Attorney General."

The biggest mass arrests in American history began at 9:00 P.M. on Friday, January 2, 1920. They went down in history as the Palmer raids. But Palmer neither organized nor directed them. Hoover did.

"A HUMAN NET NO OUTLAW CAN ESCAPE"

The Bureau broke into political meetings, private homes, social clubs, dance halls, restaurants, and saloons across America. Agents hauled people out of bookstores and bedrooms. Hoover worked around the clock, answering the ringing telephones and reading the urgent telegrams as his squads checked in from across the country.

Not all the raids went off smoothly. "About 25 aliens were apprehended in the course of the night on suspicion and while in a number of cases we were satisfied that they were members of the Communist Party, we were in possession of no evidence to prove it," the special agent in charge in Buffalo, New York, reported to Hoover. "As they denied it, they were released."

The Bureau took 2,585 prisoners on Friday night and Saturday morning, but their job was only half done. The raids went on into the next week. Agents sought at least 2,705 new warrants. In addition, hundreds of people, perhaps thousands, were arrested without warrants. All told, somewhere between 6,000 and 10,000 people were swept up in the raids. No one will ever know precisely how many were arrested and imprisoned, how many questioned and released. No official accounting ever took place.

The raids sent the Communist Party reeling. Charles Ruthenberg and his inner circle survived by going underground, taking false names, communicating in code, living clandestine lives. A few of Ruthenberg's handwritten reports turned up in the Comintern archives at the end of the century. "The attack upon our organization," he wrote, had made it "impossible for the party to function on a national scale." He spent the next and last seven years of his life on the run, under indictment, on trial, in prison, or fleetingly free on bail.

By Wednesday, January 7, roughly five thousand captives crowded county jails and federal detention centers across the country. Ellis Island was overflowing. Chicago's prisons were jammed. In Detroit, eight hundred suspects filled a corridor on the top floor of the post office; the mayor protested the lockup, and a prominent citizen compared it to the Black Hole of Calcutta. In Boston Harbor, more than six hundred huddled in the unheated prison on Deer Island.

"The Department of Justice of the United States is today a human net that no outlaw can escape," Attorney General Palmer wrote. His aides sent every major newspaper and magazine in America sheaves of press releases and political cartoons and photographs of disheveled detainees. Palmer declared that he was "sweeping the nation clean of such alien filth," inspired by "the hope that American citizens will themselves become voluntary agents for us in a vast organization."

"What will become of the United States Government if these alien radicals are permitted to carry out the principles of the Communist Party?" Palmer asked. "There wouldn't be any such thing left. In place of the United States Government we should have the horror and terrorism of Bolshevik tyranny. . . . The Department of Justice will pursue the attack of these 'Reds' upon the Government of the United States with vigilance, and no alien advocating the overthrow of existing law and order in this country shall escape."

Congress now seriously debated the sedition statutes Palmer had proposed, new laws that would imprison Americans for politically charged speech in peacetime. The House of Representatives voted to bar its lone Socialist member from holding his seat. The New York legislature expelled its five elected Socialist assemblymen. Public acclaim for Palmer poured in. Politicians pronounced him a clear choice for the next president of the United States.

Hoover bathed in the reflected glory. He was now a public figure, quoted across the country as the Justice Department's top authority on communism.

The first pictures of Hoover in office show an element of his pride. He is fit and trim, snappily dressed. His suit is stylish and his necktie slightly rakish. The tie is tightly knotted beneath a slightly jutting chin. He has the barest hint of a smile, but his eyes are dead serious. He signs an order with a fountain pen. He looks astonishingly young.

He began to cultivate reporters as his superiors did. He kept a bulging scrapbook of his newspaper clippings. (He was sometimes misidentified as J. A. Hoover or J. D. Hoover. Not for long.)

He worked to promote his reputation inside and outside the government with regular bulletins on Reds and radicals in America. The first went out a few days after the January 1920 raids. He contended that all the threats of the past year—the terrorist bombings, the nationwide strikes—arose from a master plot hatched in the Kremlin.

"The revolutionary conspiracy is international, it is being fiercely pushed, and most cunningly led," read one of his first reports to Congress, a warning of a threat to America's existence. "Civilization faces its most terrible menace of danger since the barbarian hordes overran West Europe and opened the dark ages." He theorized that the Communists might organize secret cells in Mexico, stockpile arms from Germany and Japan, cross the border, and plant the seeds of revolution among black men in the American South. He believed that he was in a battle with the world in the balance.

Hoover went on his first counterterrorism raid on February 14, 1920. The Bureau and the local police swept into the tenements and industrial warehouses of Paterson, New Jersey, and found seventeen members of an Italian anarchist gang called L'Era Nuova. The Bureau had placed an undercover informant inside the group four weeks before. TERRORISTS CAUGHT IN PATERSON RAIDS, read the headline in *The New York Times.* The Bureau announced that reams of blank pink paper seized in the raid resembled those used in the broadside "Plain Words," which had been found near Attorney General Palmer's shattered home in June 1919—"the first clue to the origin of the bomb outrages which stirred the nation," the newspaper said.

But it was not a clue that Hoover had time to pursue. He was called to a federal courthouse in Boston to defend the Bureau's conduct in the war on communism.

"DEMOCRACY NOW SEEMS UNSAFE"

Political revulsion had been rising against the raids, a public reaction Hoover had not imagined possible.

The chief federal prosecutor in Philadelphia, U.S. Attorney Francis Fisher Kane, had resigned in an open letter to the president. "I am strongly opposed to the wholesale raiding of aliens that is being carried on throughout the country," he wrote. "The policy of raids against large numbers of individuals is generally unwise and very apt to result in injustice." The chief federal immigration officer in Seattle reported to his superiors in Washington, D.C., that the Bureau had swept up uncounted innocents to find a handful of suspects. And in Boston, a federal judge named George W. Anderson, addressing two hundred people gathered at a banquet convened by the fledging Harvard Liberal Club, issued an open invitation for a legal challenge to the raids.

Judge Anderson contended that the government was concocting conspiracies. "As an aftermath of our 'war to make the world safe for democracy,' real democracy now seems unsafe in America," he said. "The same persons and newspapers that for two years were faking pro-German plots are now promoting 'The Red Terror' . . .

"I cannot say there will not be some bomb thrower. There are Reds—probably there are dangerous Reds. But they are not half as dangerous as the prating pseudo-patriots. . . .

"Real Americans, men who believe in law, order, liberty, toleration of others' views on political and religious subjects, are not given to advertising themselves and their patriotism. They have too much respect for Americanism and for patriotism to disgrace these fine words as they are being daily disgraced by those using them for personal or political notoriety."

The next day, a petition for a writ of habeas corpus arrived at the federal courthouse in Boston, filed on behalf of prisoners held at Deer Island. Judge Anderson had engineered the petition, secretly arranging to hear the case himself, after consulting a young Harvard law professor and Liberal Club stalwart named Felix Frankfurter. Boston's federal immigration commissioner, Henry J. Skeffington, who was named as the lead defendant, was outraged. "I'll take great pleasure in getting some of these Harvard Liberal Clubs myself," he exclaimed. "If I have a warrant in my pocket I'll take pleasure in getting them."

Attorney General Palmer, preparing to announce himself as a candidate for president, did not wish to be burdened with the details of the case. He told Hoover to handle it.

The Justice Department would have to defend the Bureau's arrests and the Deer Island deportations before a hostile judge in an open court. Hoover knew this posed a problem. The Bureau had overstepped its authority. Its conduct could not withstand close scrutiny.

At dawn on Wednesday, April 7, 1920, Hoover arrived in Boston on the sleeper train from Washington to face his first legal challenge. In Judge Anderson's court, Felix Frankfurter, representing the prisoners, quickly offered into evidence the telegram that had gone out to the Bureau's agents: eschew search warrants, seize anything they laid their hands on, and report directly to Hoover. Seated at the government table, whispering to the U.S. attorney, Hoover had good reason to wonder how his secret orders from headquarters—marked "strictly confidential" and carrying his name—had wound up in the hands of radical suspects. He listened as Frankfurter questioned George Kelleher, Hoover's ranking agent in New England:

Q: It is a fact, is it not, Mr. Kelleher, that men and women were picked up that night without any warrant in your possession for their custody? *Objection. Overruled.*

A: That is so.

Q: Did your men search the bodies and the homes and the halls at which the various men and women were arrested? *Objection. Overruled.*

A: Yes.

Q: And they made seizure, did they not, of papers, documents, books and what not? *Objection. Overruled.*

A: Pursuant to the Department's instruction . . .

Q: Searches were made by the arresting officers irrespective of the production of a search warrant? *Objection. Overruled.*

A: . . . That was left to the discretion of the various officers.

Q: What did you do with those whom the warrant did not fit, or who did not fit the warrant? *Objection. Overruled.*

A: They were detained at the station or brought to Boston and taken down to Deer Island.

The testimony turned to the government's use of undercover informers. "Somebody who is employed to go around under an alias or pseudonym, or some kind of disguise, to pretend to be a Communist or Socialist or Anarchist. . . . [T]hat is an exceedingly dangerous thing, isn't it?" said the judge. "I wonder that there have been no witches hung in the past six months."

The judge himself then questioned Henry J. Skeffington, the Boston immigration commissioner:

Q: Were these arrests for what you call the "raids" made by your forces, or by the Department of Justice?

A: Department of Justice, your Honor. . . .

Q: Can you point out any rule or any statute under which the Department of Justice agents have power to arrest?

A: No, I don't know anything about that, Judge. . . .

Q: Did you have instructions as to this procedure?

A: We had an understanding.

Q: Written instructions?

A: No. We had a conference in Washington . . . with Mr. Hoover. . . .

Q: Who is Mr. Hoover?

A: Mr. Hoover is an officer in the Department of Justice.

Hoover was not eager to testify about the raids under oath. After sitting through a day and a half of damning testimony, he left the courthouse and packed his bags.

"This case seems to have been conducted under the modern theory of statesmanship: Hang first and try later," Judge Anderson wrote in a ruling freeing thirteen Deer Island prisoners on $500 bail. In a final judgment, he called the Bureau's conduct lawless and unconstitutional. The government had created a "spy system" that "destroys trust and confidence and propagates hate," he concluded. "A mob is a mob whether made up of government officials acting under instructions from the Department of Justice, or of criminals, loafers and the vicious classes."

The Justice Department never challenged Judge Anderson's ruling.

"Seeing red"

Hoover returned to Washington to confront a new nemesis: Louis F. Post, the seventy-one-year-old assistant secretary of labor. On April 10, three days after Hoover's disastrous trip to Boston, Post threw out more than a thousand of the remaining deportation cases.

Post was a lifelong liberal who had known and admired Emma Goldman. As the Labor Department official overseeing the federal immigration system, he also had signed the order deporting her. Now he had used his administrative powers to review the files of some 1,400 people who had been arrested in the Red raids. He found that in about three out of four cases the Bureau had violated the law. Many hundreds of the detainees were not members of the Communist Party: their names had been copied off Socialist Party rolls, they had wandered into a Communist meeting hall out of curiosity, or they had simply been swept up by mistake. Post also dismissed cases where prisoners had been denied counsel or had been judged by illegally seized evidence. He was proceeding by the letter of the law, not the spirit of the times. At the rate he was going, four or five thousand of the Red raid cases would be lost.

Hoover mounted a furious counterattack. This marked the start of an

American institution: the political surveillance of his prominent opponents.

He compiled a dossier on Post's political associations with leftists and sent it to key members of Congress. His goal was to remove Post from office and reverse his rulings. His first foray into political warfare at the highest levels of the government met with an initial success. The House Rules Committee accepted the petition for a formal inquiry into Louis Post's conduct and set hearings to begin in four weeks.

Attorney General Palmer took Hoover's case directly to the White House. Palmer demanded to see the president immediately. This led directly to the first cabinet meeting convened by Woodrow Wilson in seven months. The White House had been an isolation ward ever since Wilson's cataclysmic stroke.

At 10:00 A.M. on April 14, 1920, Palmer passed through the guarded entrance alongside the locked gates of the White House, walked upstairs to the president's study, and saw a dying man. Wilson could not move unaided. His thoughts were fleeting, his speech halting. The president was only dimly aware of the war on communism being waged in the United States.

A few minutes after the cabinet meeting began, Palmer tried to take control. One reliable eyewitness account survives, from the diaries of the navy secretary, Josephus Daniels, who described the "red-hot debate" Palmer started. Palmer argued that the country faced the threat of revolution and insurrection. He steered the president's attention to the crisis being created by Louis Post. He demanded that Post be fired.

The president "told Palmer not to let the country see red"—"a much-needed admonition," as Daniels heard it, "for Palmer was seeing red behind every bush." Palmer chose to interpret the president's words in a completely different way. He heard what he wanted to hear: a go-ahead for his campaign to cleanse the country of the Communists.

On April 29, Palmer announced that the United States would face a terrorist attack on May Day. His warning came straight from Hoover and the Bureau of Investigation—a red alert of an international conspiracy to kill American leaders and destroy American landmarks.

"The plot is nationwide," the attorney general told the newspapers. He said government officials and corporate executives were targets for assassination; warnings had gone out to all those on the list of marked men. Bureau agents, state militiamen, and police officers were on guard across the country, concentrating on New York, Chicago, Philadelphia, and New Orleans; watching over railroad stations, harbors, Wall Street offices, and the homes of the most powerful men in America.

It was a false alarm. May Day came and went uneventfully. "While the night is not over, it looks as if the expected disturbances have been headed off," Hoover told reporters late that evening. A perceptible snickering began—a smattering of suspicion, as Hoover himself recorded, that the May Day plots were "creatures of the imagination of the Attorney General." In short order, the press, the public, and the political establishment began to question the judgment of the nation's chief law enforcement officer. Congress quickly cut Palmer's budget request for the Bureau of Investigation by one-third.

On May 7, Hoover sat on a back bench in a congressional hearing room and took notes as Louis Post appeared before a hostile House Rules Committee. Over the course of two days' testimony, Post made mincemeat of the charges of political misconduct that Palmer and Hoover had lodged against him. Case by case, Post argued that not one in one hundred of the men arrested in the January raids could be rightfully accused of planning to overthrow the government by force. He contended that even a despised alien was entitled to due process; warrantless arrests, forced confessions, and guilt by association were not the American way. After ten hours of testimony, the congressmen decided they would not impeach or condemn him. Instead they would summon Palmer to answer Post's accusations himself.

Hoover immediately began to prepare testimony for the attorney general. He revised his closely reasoned legal briefs arguing that membership in the Communist Party constituted a crime against the United States and a deportable offense. He told Palmer that he had the perfect opportunity to tell the world "the real story of the red menace."

But Louis Post struck back first. His lawyer had mobilized a coalition calling itself the National Popular Government League, and it was about to publish a broadside, "Report to the American People upon the Illegal Practices of the Department of Justice," signed by twelve prominent law school deans and lawyers—among them Hoover's new archenemy, Felix Frankfurter, the Harvard liberal. Hoover ordered the Bureau's chief in Boston, George Kelleher, to open a file on the future Supreme Court justice.

The "Report to the American People," published on May 28, 1920, accused Palmer and Hoover of torture and illegal imprisonment. It said they had mounted an "assault upon the most sacred principles of our Constitutional liberties."

"Wholesale arrests both of aliens and citizens have been made without warrant or any process of law; men and women have been jailed and held incommunicado without access of friends or counsel; homes have been entered without search warrants," it said. "We do not question the right of the Department of Justice to use its agents in the Bureau of Investigation to ascertain when the law is being violated. But the American people have never tolerated the use of undercover provocative agents or 'agents provocateurs' such as have been familiar in old Russia or Spain. Such agents have been introduced by the Department of Justice into radical movements . . . instigating acts which might be declared criminal."

Hoover worked feverishly for the next three days preparing Palmer's response to Congress. He put everything he had into it—his bulletins on the Red menace, the seized records of American leftists, his agents' affidavits against the deportees, paragraphs copied out of radical pamphlets, the annals of the Russian Revolution, the public decrees of the Comintern, Karl Marx's *Communist Manifesto* of 1847. The document went back and forth across decades and nations—more than thirty thousand words thrown together in seventy-two hours.

The presidency was at stake: the Democratic National Convention was in four weeks, and Palmer remained among the front-runners in a weak field. The future of America's war on communism could turn on his performance. So might the future of his chief strategist. If Palmer won, Hoover could succeed him as attorney general.

On the morning of June 1, Palmer and Hoover ascended together to the top floor of the Capitol. The small hearing chamber of the House Rules Committee overflowed with reporters and spectators. One window looked south from Capitol Hill toward Hoover's home. Congressman Philip Campbell, Republican of Kansas, called the hearing to order at 10:00 A.M.

Hoover sat silently at Palmer's side. The attorney general looked down and began to read, and he did not stop until the afternoon of the following day. He described a world on fire. Communism was attacking the nation's political institutions, its churches, its schools, its factories, its newspapers, winning converts through its insidious lies. Its "revolutionary disease" had spread from the slums of New York to the huts of Afghanistan through "the poison virus" of its ideology. Palmer invited anyone who doubted the nature of the threat to look at the photographs of the prisoners taken by the Bureau of Investigation, to see the "cruelty, insanity, and crime" staring from their "sly and crafty eyes."

"My own life is threatened daily," he said; his character assassinated by the "friends of these criminals" who represented them in court and before Congress. Palmer saved his most bitter words for Louis Post and the lawyers who signed the "Report to the American People." Such men, he said, were no better than the Communists. "They have not hesitated to give the widest publicity to their defenses of all of these communists and criminal anarchists and to their charges that these people have been outrageously treated. . . .

"I think the public is entitled to know what is going on in the country," Palmer said. "I have tried to tell them. I have told them the truth."

But it was not the whole truth. Late on the second day of his testimony, Palmer placed into the *Congressional Record* a document Hoover had prepared about the work of the Radical Division of the Bureau of Investigation. It contained "the complete story . . . of the bomb plot which broke out in a dozen cities a year ago today," Palmer said. Buried deep within this report were a few plaintive paragraphs revealing that, in retrospect, the government might have been wrong to blame the bomb plots on the Communists. But the attorney general did not read a word of it. "It would take up too much time," he said. "It is a story which might beguile an hour or so."

Palmer's public image had been scarred by his warnings of threats that never materialized. By the time he arrived at the 1920 Democratic National Convention, which opened in San Francisco at the end of June, his political reputation was plummeting and his dreams of nomination disappearing. Hoover, making his first trip to the West Coast, was one among many Justice Department aides who gathered at Palmer's suite in the St. Francis Hotel, holding out hopes that he could still win. But after forty-four ballots, Palmer withdrew. His life in politics was over.

Palmer and Hoover were called once more to the Capitol, in the last days of the Wilson administration, to testify about the Red raids of January. Palmer insisted he was unaware of the details. Not even how many search warrants had been signed? asked Senator Thomas J. Walsh, a Montana Democrat. "I cannot tell you, Senator," Palmer replied. "If you would like to ask Mr. Hoover, who was in charge of this matter, he can tell you." The senator turned to the young crusader.

Hoover said he had no idea. "You know nothing about it at all?" Senator Walsh asked. And Hoover said: "No, sir." For the rest of his life, he disavowed his role in the raids. He was learning that secrecy and deception were essential to political warfare.

"We'll get them"

Hoover prepared a report to Congress claiming that the raids had resulted in "the wrecking of the communist parties in this country"—a premature boast. A total of 591 aliens had been ordered deported. The United States held 178 Americans convicted under the espionage and sedition laws. Hoover's own records showed that at least nine out of ten people jailed in the January 1920 raids were now free. He had set out to remove thousands of radicals from the American landscape, and he had fallen short.

Hoover determined that it was time to revamp the Radical Division.

He renamed it the General Intelligence Division. This was not a cosmetic change. Hoover now intended to cover "not only the radical activities in the United States" but also those "of an international nature," and not only radical politics, but "economic and industrial disturbances" as well. His ambitions were expanding. So was his understanding of what it would take to protect America.

In a word, it was intelligence. He wrote that it was better to fight subversives in secret; the government could not handle "the radical situation from a criminal prosecution standpoint." The law was too weak a force to protect America. Only secret intelligence could detect and disrupt the threat from the left and protect America from attack.

Shortly after noon on Thursday, September 16, 1920, as Hoover was putting the final touches on his plans for the General Intelligence Division, a horse-drawn wagon exploded at the corner of Wall and Broad streets in Manhattan. It had been a pleasant day, and hundreds of people had left their desks for a lunchtime stroll, a brief respite from the great money machine. A bomb turned the center of American capitalism into a slaughterhouse. Blood ran in the streets where the first Congress of the United States had convened and the Bill of Rights had become law. Shrapnel scarred the walls and shattered the windows of J. P. Morgan and Co., America's most formidable bank. The scars are still there, graven into the cornerstones facing the sidewalk.

The bomb killed thirty-eight people and injured roughly four hundred. It was the deadliest terrorist attack in the history of the United States, and it held that distinction for the next seventy-five years.

Minutes before the explosion, three blocks away, a postman had emptied a mailbox. He found five crudely misspelled pamphlets, handmade with rubber stamps and red ink. "Free the political prisoners or it will be sure death for all of you," they said. They were signed "American Anarchist Fighters."

The Wall Street bombing was almost surely an act of revenge for the indictments of two Italian anarchists, Nicola Sacco and Bartolomeo Vanzetti, charged five days before in the murder and armed robbery of a shoe-factory paymaster and his guard outside Boston. Hoover pushed the investigation to no avail. No suspects were ever brought to justice.

"We'll get them," vowed Hoover's boss, Bill Flynn. But the Bureau never did.

6

UNDERWORLDS

"I AM NOT FIT for this office and should never have been here," President Warren G. Harding lamented in the White House. His judgment, for once, was sound.

Harding was a small-town newspaper publisher who had risen beyond his station in life as a Republican U.S. senator from Ohio. When he became president on March 4, 1921, he brought his crooked friends with him to Washington. The closest was his campaign manager, Harry M. Daugherty, who became the attorney general of the United States.

Two prominent Republican senators strongly warned Harding against the nomination. "Daugherty has been my best friend from the beginning in this whole thing," the president-elect replied. "He tells me he wants to be Attorney General *and by God he will be Attorney General!*" A skilled political fixer, Daugherty had spent years twisting arms as a lobbyist in the Ohio statehouse; his specialty was killing legislation opposed by big companies. He cut deals between businessmen and politicians with common interests in money and power. His reputation preceded him to Washington. Once he arrived, Daugherty grew in office. He became one of the nation's leading white-collar criminals.

Though the Justice Department and the Bureau of Investigation would fall into deep dishonor during the Harding years, J. Edgar Hoover would thrive.

Hoover won promotion to the number-two position at the Bureau of Investigation at the age of twenty-six. His reputation was unblemished, his aptitude for infighting undiminished, his focus on the Red threat unrelenting, his expertise unquestioned. He saw no great distinction among American radicals—Communists, Socialists, anarchists, pacificists. They were enemies of the state.

While Hoover took care of the war on communism, Harry Daugherty took care of his friends. The new attorney general placed an old pal, William J. Burns, in charge of the Bureau in August 1921. Hoover, by now an accomplished cultivator of his superiors, assured Burns that the Bureau had been infiltrating the ranks of American radicals for years. "We made an effort to have an informant in every one of the leading movements of the country," he said, and the General Intelligence Division was on guard against new threats from the Left.

Burns, at the age of sixty, was America's most famous private detective. His talent for self-promotion was impressive. After gaining notoriety as a jury-tampering federal investigator in the 1905 land-fraud cases championed by President Theodore Roosevelt, he had won acclaim by tapping telephones and bugging hotel rooms to convict two labor racketeers in the 1910 dynamite attack on the headquarters of the *Los Angeles Times*, which had killed twenty-one people. He came close to going to prison himself in 1915 for stealing documents from a New York law firm. Hours after the 1920 Wall Street bombing, Burns publicly announced that the Communists were behind the attack and vowed to bring them to justice. He offered a $50,000 reward on behalf of the W. J. Burns International Detective Agency for information leading to the arrest and conviction of the bombers. Now, as the Bureau of Investigation's director, Burns promised the public that the Bureau would find the Wall Street bombers.

Bureau agents in Chicago, looking for clues in the bombing, intercepted a letter from the Communist Party underground in New York. The government was "holding us responsible for the Wall Street disaster," it said, warning against a new crackdown. "The January raids are past history," it began. "So some of our members are beginning to think that EVERYTHING IS SAFE. WE WANT TO CALL YOUR ATTENTION TO THE FACT THAT THE DEPARTMENT OF JUSTICE IS STILL ON THE JOB. It will continue ON THE JOB as long as we exist as a *Revolutionary Organization*. Spies, stool pigeons, provocateurs, and every form of scum is bound, in some way or other, to get into the organization or learn of its activities. . . . EXERCISE GREAT CAUTION. . . . IF YOU ARE ARRESTED . . . ANSWER NOTHING."

"AN OUTLAW ORGANIZATION"

Hoover mobilized his growing network of informers. He combed through reports and tips from Bureau agents, army and navy intelligence officers, leaders of the American Protective League, commanders of the American Legion, police chiefs, corporate executives, bankers, insurance men, telephone and telegraph companies. He warned that the Reds were burrowing into labor unions, factories, churches, schools, colleges, newspapers, magazines, women's clubs, and Negro organizations. His weekly bulletins to the attorney general hammered home the threat. Daugherty needed no convincing. "Soviet Russia is the enemy of mankind," he maintained. "They have set out to conquer not only America but the world."

In the spring and summer of 1921, dozens of Bureau agents under Hoover's command spied on suspected Communists across the country, infiltrated their meetings, and broke into their headquarters. When Bureau agents and the New York bomb squad crashed into an apartment on Bleecker Street, seizing Party membership lists, internal reports, and encoded communiqués, they found a pamphlet entitled "Rules for Underground Party Work."

The rules were explicit:

1) DON'T betray Party work and Party workers under any circumstances.
2) DON'T carry or keep with you names and addresses, except in good code.
3) DON'T keep in your rooms openly any incriminating documents or literature.
4) DON'T take any unnecessary risks in Party work.
5) DON'T shirk Party work because of the risk connected with it.
6) DON'T boast of what you have to do or have done for the Party.
7) DON'T divulge your membership in the Party without necessity.
8) DON'T let any spies follow you to appointments or meetings.
9) DON'T lose your nerve in danger.
10) DON'T answer any questions if arrested.

The pamphlet concluded: "AVOID ARREST BY ALL POSSIBLE MEANS." That was a tall order for America's top Communists. Almost all the men who led the Communist Party over the next four decades did jail time for their political work between 1918 and 1923. Few went more than a few months without facing a policeman, a judge, or a jail cell—locked up or under indictment on charges of conspiracy or sedition.

"Spies are on the job every day in every city bent upon ferreting out our members, our meetings and working places," the Bleecker Street pamphlet warned. The Communists believed they were under surveillance by the government every minute of their lives, whether they worked openly or underground.

One of the Bureau's spies attended the "Unity Convention of Communist Parties" held at the Overlook Mountain Hotel in Woodstock, New York, in May 1921—a secret four-day meeting of Communist leaders from across America. FBI documents declassified in August 2011 suggest the infiltrator was Clarence Hathaway, a founding member of the Communist Party of the United States and, according to the documents, an informant for the Bureau from the start.

The Bureau's report on the Woodstock gathering noted that Moscow had sent $50,000 to the American Communists, along with orders to stop their quarrels and unite. The Soviets urged American Communists to come up from underground and into an open struggle for power. It was hard to see how that could happen. "The Communist Party is definitely an outlaw organization in the United States," founding father Charles Ruthenberg wrote from Sing Sing prison that summer, while serving time on state charges of criminal anarchy. If the party stayed underground, it would wither and die. If it tried to function openly, it would be attacked and killed. It had to have two wings, he argued—"onc out in the open, functioning publicly, the other unseen, secret, underground."

The Bureau's spy in Woodstock also reported that the American labor organizer William Z. Foster, who had tried to lead the nationwide steel strike two years before, was traveling to Moscow. The report was accurate. Foster went to meetings of the Comintern and the World Congress of Revolutionary Trade Unions in Moscow in June and July 1921. He met Lenin, and found him entrancing. He returned to Chicago as a dedicated Soviet agent, and the Comintern's chief labor union man in the United States. He started traveling the country organizing coal workers, mine workers, and autoworkers; Moscow financed his work. As he rose to the top of the Communist Party in America, the Bureau of Investigation tried to watch him every step of the way.

"THE WORD WENT OUT THROUGH THE UNDERWORLD"

President Harding outwardly pursued peace and reconciliation. He sent an American team to help the Soviets confront an immense famine in the fall of 1921, delivering a billion pounds of food, though five million Russians still died of hunger. He signed a proclamation ending America's state of war with Germany. He made a front-page decision to grant a Christmas Eve pardon to America's leading Socialist, Eugene Debs, voiding his ten-year sentence and inviting him to the White House.

But William J. Burns of the Bureau of Investigation made the biggest newspaper headlines that Christmas. It seemed America's top sleuth had cracked his biggest case: the Wall Street bombing had been the work of Lenin and the Comintern. The story was astonishing: four New York Communists had been paid $30,000 for the job, delivered through the Soviet diplomatic representative in New York. But the source turned out to be a swindler who worked as a professional stool pigeon for the Burns Detective Agency in New York. He had claimed to have chatted with Lenin at the Comintern convention in Moscow, where the Soviet ruler pronounced himself satisfied with the Wall Street bombing and ordered up a new terrorist attack on the United States. It was the purest invention.

BURNS HOODWINKED, read the headlines.

Burns was too corrupt to be embarrassed. But his old vices were starting to catch up with him. He had a bad habit of putting his private eyes on the public payroll. The worst of them was running rampant at the Bureau of Investigation. In the course of his long career, Gaston Bullock Means would stand accused of murder, larceny, perjury, forgery, and espionage against the United States, and yet Burns had hired him as an agent at the Bureau, and kept him on as a paid informant after his sordid past began to become public knowledge in February 1922. Means set up shop at the Justice Department in partnership with a political fixer from Ohio named Jess Smith, Attorney General Daugherty's oldest friend from Ohio and his roommate at the Wardman Park Hotel in Washington. Jess Smith was the man to see at Justice to fix a case.

Prohibition, the law of the land since 1920, created a corrupt political culture in America. Citizens across the country thirsted for bootleg liquor. Bootlegging financed the growth of organized crime. The bootleggers paid federal, state, and local police for protection. The crooked connections between lawbreakers and law enforcers ran all the way to the top in Washington. Jess Smith and Gaston Means had a lucrative sideline at Justice, selling government-confiscated whiskey to liquor smugglers.

"The word went out through the underworld that there was a man at the Department of Justice who could 'fix things,' " Hoover recounted in a ghostwritten memoir published in 1938, which recorded the wheeling and dealing of the Harding years. The pitch of the political fixers, as Hoover imagined it, was enticing: "I'm a great friend of the President. As a high official of the Department of Justice, I know everybody in the Cabinet. . . . So if you'll just pay me so much a barrel, I'll see that you get all the whiskey you want. To be perfectly frank with you, I've got so much power in Washington that I can take care of anything . . . except murder."

The White House itself was a speakeasy. Alice Roosevelt Longworth, the late president's daughter, whose husband was a powerful Republican congressman from Ohio, went upstairs at the White House during one of Harding's twice-weekly socials. The president's study was filled with cronies like Harry Daugherty and Jess Smith, she wrote; "trays with bottles carrying every imaginable kind of whiskey stood about, cards and poker chips ready at hand, an atmosphere of waistcoat unbuttoned, feet on the desk, and the spittoon alongside." She had tried to warn Harding, but she had wasted her breath. "Harding was not a bad man," she wrote. "He was just a slob—a slack, good-natured man with an unfortunate disposition to surround himself with intimates of questionable character."

Chief among them were the attorney general and the director of the Bureau of Investigation.

"THE RADICAL CHIEFTAINS"

Hoover kept his head down and fixed his gaze on the Red threat as it spread from New York and Chicago to the coal mines, steel mills, and rail yards of the Midwest. Organized labor unions battled America's industrial barons throughout the 1920s. The great majority of the workers were neither Reds nor radicals. They had no grand political agenda; they wanted a living wage and a decent life, not an armed revolution to overthrow the ruling class.

The Bureau backed the barons. Hoover saw the fight between capital and labor as a lifelong struggle in the war on communism. "Communists and most subversive activities are always attached to labor situations," he wrote years later. "It is a practical impossibility to divorce Communism from labor situations."

As the confrontations began boiling over in the summer of 1922, hundreds of thousands of coal miners and railroad workers began mounting strikes across the country. The Bureau struck back.

For three years, Hoover and the Bureau had been receiving reports from a shipyard worker named Francis Morrow, an informant code-named K-97, who had risen to a trusted position inside Communist conclaves. Morrow alerted the Bureau that a secret national meeting of American Communist leaders was convening on the shores of Lake Michigan. He knew about the meeting well in advance—he was the official delegate from Philadelphia. Four agents from the Bureau's Chicago office drove for two hours into the countryside, rounded up a posse of sheriff's deputies, and staked out a summer resort outside Bridgman, Michigan. The Reds saw the Red-hunters lurking. Fearing a raid, they took a hurried referendum on the main issue before them: whether to continue illegal underground work. It passed by one vote. The deciding ballot was cast by Agent K-97.

On the morning of August 22, 1922, the Bureau's men and the sheriff's deputies arrested fifteen Communists in Bridgman, among them the Party leader Charles Ruthenberg, who had been freed from prison only four months before. They seized a trove of Party records and tracked down another sixteen delegates in Chicago, including William Z. Foster, the leading Communist in the trade union movement, and Earl Browder, a rising Party ideologue—both dedicated lifelong Comintern agents.

The leaders of American communism trudged under a hot sun, hand-cuffed in pairs, from the county jail to their arraignment at the courthouse in St. Joseph, Michigan. They were charged under state law with conspiracy to overthrow the government of the United States by sabotage and violence. "The radical chieftains—financed, it is charged, by the Russian soviet to set up a soviet in this country—were herded at the county jail like a chain gang, while armed deputy sheriffs and federal agents stood guard," the local newspaper reported. "Federal authorities hoped to link the Communists with the Wall Street bomb blast that wrecked the offices of J.P. Morgan & Co. more than a year ago."

Among the twenty-seven indicted on sedition charges, only Ruthenberg was convicted. He spent the next five years fighting the case in court until he died at forty-four. His ashes were buried in the Kremlin Wall.

Foster's case led to a hung jury. He went free, to Hoover's great chagrin.

The judge had instructed the jurors that to convict him they had to find that he had "advocated crime, sabotage, violence, and terrorism." They were divided six to six. "The prosecution didn't prove that the Communist Party advocated violence," one of the jurors who voted for acquittal said. "That was the only thing we split on."

None of the other Bridgman defendants ever went to trial. But the raid drove the Party deeper and deeper underground. The dues-paying faithful were winnowed down to six thousand people or fewer—only one in ten an English-speaking native-born American citizen—and the influence of their leaders neared a vanishing point. Some kept dreaming of a rank-and-file uprising in America's rail yards and coal mines; their pamphlets still read like Soviet propaganda manufactured in Moscow. But as Foster himself reported to the Comintern, in a request for $25,000 in funds, he was trying to organize the American Communist movement with two workers on his payroll.

Hoover himself would write, later in his life, that the Communist Party's influence on American life was "virtually nonexistent" in the early 1920s. That was not what he said at the time.

Hoover and his General Intelligence Division warned constantly of a violent Communist revolution; Daugherty told the president that the nation was threatened by civil war. Ten days after the Bridgman arrests, the attorney general demanded and won a federal court injunction barring striking railroad workers, who were protesting a government-imposed pay cut, from taking any action in support of their demands. The ban was more sweeping than any in the history of American labor; in essence it ordered 400,000 workers with legitimate legal grievances to sit down and shut up. Members of Harding's own cabinet denounced the decision as unlawful and unwise.

But Daugherty and Hoover escalated the battle: they dispatched scores of special agents across the country to collect evidence that labor leaders were conspiring to violate the injunction. The agents relied on informants to infiltrate the ranks of the strikers. Daily reports poured into the General Intelligence Division from Bureau agents across the country, stoking the fear that the strike was organized warfare against the government. Federal marshals and local police, aided by legions of private detectives working for the railroads, charged laborers and organizers with seventeen thousand crimes under the injunction.

In a matter of weeks, the attorney general broke the railroad strike. But the burdens of power would soon begin to break him.

Daugherty collapsed, physically and mentally, in December 1922. He had suffered a nervous breakdown, replete with hallucinations; he thought he smelled poison gas coming from the flowerpot decorating the stage as he gave a speech. Bedridden in Washington, he began seeing Soviet spies everywhere—even in Congress.

"The most colossal conspiracy"

The Bureau of Investigation had been created as an instrument of law. It was turning into an illegal weapon of political warfare.

By the time Congress reconvened in March 1923, Daugherty and Burns were conducting political espionage against senators whom the attorney general saw as threats to America. The Bureau was breaking into their offices and homes, intercepting their mail, and tapping their telephones, just as it had done to members of the Communist Party. The only rationale was the political movement in the Senate toward American diplomatic recognition of Soviet Russia.

If recognition came, there would be Soviet embassies and diplomats in the United States. If there were diplomats, there would be spies. The Bureau spied on Senator William E. Borah of Idaho, chairman of the Foreign Relations Committee; Daugherty thought the senator had "played into the hands of the radicals" by supporting recognition. It spied on both of Montana's senators: Thomas J. Walsh, the Judiciary Committee member who had tried to question Hoover about the Red raids, and the newly elected Burton K. Wheeler, who set out on a fact-finding trip to Moscow two weeks after his swearing-in. Wheeler, a former U.S. attorney in Montana, already had a file at the Bureau; he had defended a radical newspaper editor named Bill Dunn, who was elected to the Montana legislature after the state courts threw out his conviction on sedition charges. In Washington, at least two more senators and two other members of the House of Representatives, all critics of the president and the attorney general, also became targets for political investigation by the Bureau.

Senator Wheeler's April 1923 expedition to Russia left him half convinced that capitalism and freedom of religion might emerge from the chaos and terror of the revolution. On his return to the United States, the senator said he would support diplomatic recognition. The attorney general was outraged.

"My image as a Bolshevik grew in his mind," Wheeler recounted. Daugherty denounced Wheeler, first privately, then publicly, as "the Communist leader in the Senate" and "no more a Democrat than Stalin, his comrade, in Moscow." He called him "part of an effort to capture, by deceit and design, as many members of the Senate as possible and to spread through Washington and the cloakrooms of Congress a poison gas as deadly as that which sapped and destroyed brave soldiers in the last war."

Hoover's own role in the political battle against Russian recognition was more subtle. He carefully fed documents from the Bureau's files to trusted politicians and privately financed anti-Communist crusaders. He helped a former Associated Press reporter named Richard Whitney research a series of incendiary articles, later collected in a book, *Reds in America*, in which Whitney gratefully acknowledged Hoover's personal assistance. Whitney argued that Soviet agents had an all-pervasive influence over American institutions; they had infiltrated every corner of American life. He called the Bridgman meeting a key moment in "the most colossal conspiracy against the United States in its history." He looked at the silent-movie studios of Hollywood and named Charlie Chaplin as a secret Communist. He charged his alma mater, Harvard, with harboring Communist sympathizers like Felix Frankfurter. He warned that the Comintern's political agents in America were spearheading the Senate's move to recognize Russia.

The movement toward Russian recognition halted; it would not revive for a decade. The argument against it seemed simple: why recognize a regime that wanted to overthrow the United States?

But the American government now seemed likelier to fall by the weight of its own corruption. The Justice Department and the Bureau of Investigation were at the rotten core of it.

"A SECRET POLICE"

A gunshot inside the attorney general's hotel suite marked the beginning of the end. At daybreak on May 30, 1923, Jess Smith, Daugherty's roommate and right-hand man, put a bullet through his head at the Wardman Park Hotel. Their downstairs neighbor—William J. Burns, director of the Bureau of Investigation—raced upstairs and took charge of the crime scene. But he could not keep the suicide quiet.

Three weeks later, President Harding left Washington for a long summer vacation, traveling cross-country to the Pacific Coast and embarking on a cruise to Alaska. Secretary of Commerce Herbert Hoover was aboard the ship when it set sail from Puget Sound on July 4. President Harding summoned him for a meeting in his cabin; Hoover recorded the conversation in his memoirs.

"If you knew of a great scandal in our administration," Harding asked, "would you for the good of the country and the party expose it publicly or would you bury it?" The scandal, he made clear, was at the Justice Department. "Publish it," Hoover replied. The president said that would be "politically dangerous" and he "abruptly dried up" when Hoover asked if Daugherty was the malefactor.

Harding's heart stopped four weeks later, on August 2, 1923, at the Palace Hotel in San Francisco. He was dead at fifty-seven. His successor was the upright Calvin Coolidge, the former governor of Massachusetts, whose national reputation rested on his breaking of the Boston police strike. Coolidge was a dry and dour man, but he had morals. He needed them: the American presidency had sunk to its lowest state since the end of the Civil War.

The decay that had consumed the government of the United States slowly began to reveal itself, like wreckage after a flood. Senators Walsh and Wheeler investigated the worst of the scandals, though Daugherty and Burns did their best to stop them. They sent at least three Bureau agents out to Montana to drum up cases against the senators. The agents concocted a phony bribery charge against Wheeler; the indictment and prosecution were palpable frauds, founded on perjury. The jury quickly acquitted him.

Truths eventually came out. The Harding administration, from the top down, had been led by men who worshipped money and business, disdained government and law, and misled the American people. The secretary of the interior, Albert Fall, had taken some $300,000 in bribes from oil companies; in exchange, he let them tap the navy's strategic oil reserves in Elk Hills, California, and Teapot Dome, Wyoming. The Justice Department had gotten wind of the scandal but had quashed an investigation. There was more: the head of the newly created Veterans Bureau, Charles Forbes, a poker-playing pal of Harding's, had pocketed millions in kickbacks from contractors. A Justice Department official, Thomas Miller, had banked bribes from corporations trying to free seized assets—and, years later, the evidence showed that Attorney General Daugherty had gotten at least $40,000 of the swag.

When Senator Wheeler announced that he and his colleagues had been the targets of the Bureau's spies, the political outrage was sharp, and the public shared it. On March 1, 1924, the Senate resolved to investigate the Department of Justice. John H. W. Crim, the chief of the Criminal Division, was a willing witness. He was about to retire after eighteen years at Justice, including a stint at the Bureau. His advice to the Senate was blunt: "Get rid of this Bureau of Investigation as organized."

The senators subpoenaed Daugherty, demanding the Bureau's internal records. Daugherty defied the order, and that was his undoing. It took weeks of pressure, but on March 28, President Coolidge announced that the attorney general was resigning. Daugherty eventually was indicted for fraud, but he avoided jail after two juries deadlocked. He escaped conviction by the grace of the Fifth Amendment's constitutional safeguards against self-incrimination.

President Coolidge named his new attorney general: Harlan Fiske Stone, the longtime dean of the Columbia Law School, a pillar of legal scholarship, and a friend to Coolidge since college. Stone was not a liberal, by his own standards, but he stood foursquare in favor of civil liberties. He had been a pointed critic of the 1920 Red raids. He had urged the Senate to investigate the arrests and deportations of the radicals as an assault on the law and the Constitution.

Stone was sworn in on April 8, 1924, and he spent the next month walking the corridors of the Justice Department, talking to people and taking notes. Those notes show that he found the Bureau of Investigation "in exceedingly bad odor . . . filled with men with bad records . . . many convicted of crimes . . . organization lawless . . . many activities without any authority in federal statutes . . . agents engaged in many practices which are brutal and tyrannical in the extreme."

On May 9, Stone fired William J. Burns as director of the Bureau of Investigation. He then issued a public statement whose power resounds to this day:

> A secret police system may become a menace to free government and free institutions because it carries with it the possibility of abuses of power which are not always quickly comprehended or understood.

The enormous expansion of Federal legislation, both civil and criminal, has made the Bureau of Investigation a necessary instrument of law enforcement. But it is important that its activities be strictly limited to the performance of those functions for which it was created and that its agents themselves be not above the law or beyond its reach.

The Bureau of Investigation is not concerned with political or other opinions of individuals. It is only concerned with their conduct and then only with such conduct as is forbidden by the laws of the United States. When a police system passes beyond these limits, it is dangerous to the proper administration of justice and to human liberty, which should be our first concern to cherish. Within them it should rightly be a terror to the wrongdoer.

On May 10, Harlan Fiske Stone summoned J. Edgar Hoover, second in command of the lawless Bureau. Still seven months shy of thirty, his hair slicked back, thick neck straining at his tight shirt collar, Hoover looked up at Stone, who stood a head taller at six foot four. Stone looked down, with steely eyes under thick gray brows. He told Hoover that he was on trial.

For the time being, Stone said, Hoover would serve on an interim basis as the acting director of the Bureau of Investigation. Hoover was to report directly to Stone. And the rules of the game were going to change.

The Bureau would only investigate violations of federal law. The political hacks and the blackmailers were to be fired forthwith. No more midnight break-ins at the Capitol. No more cloak-and-dagger work. No more mass arrests. The Bureau would no longer be an instrument of political warfare. It was out of the spy business.

Hoover said yes, sir.

Stone made his terms plain and he made them public. He was in no hurry, he told the press. He was putting Hoover to the test. He wanted just the right man for the job. And until he found that man, he would run the Bureau himself.

Harlan Fiske Stone stayed on for nine months before ascending to the Supreme Court. Hoover lasted forty-eight years.

7

"THEY NEVER STOPPED WATCHING US"

T HE SURVIVAL OF the Bureau—and its revival as a secret intelligence service—depended on Hoover's political cunning, his stoic patience, his iron will. In time, the man became the institution. They would withstand every political storm for the rest of his life. He never lost his faith that the fate of the nation lay with him and his work. And he never took his eyes off his enemies.

While Hoover was still on probation as acting director of the Bureau, Attorney General Stone heard a warning from a friendly acquaintance, Roger Baldwin, the head of the American Civil Liberties Union (ACLU). Baldwin was an American aristocrat who traced his roots three hundred years back to the *Mayflower*; he had been investigated by the Bureau for political subversion and imprisoned for resisting the draft in World War I. The ACLU itself was created in 1920 chiefly to defend the constitutional rights of people prosecuted under the espionage and sedition laws.

Baldwin urged Stone to study a new ACLU report, "The Nation-Wide Spy System Centering in the Department of Justice." It accused the Bureau of wiretapping, opening first-class mail, bugging, burglaries, political blacklisting, and spying on lawful organizations and individuals. The ACLU said the Bureau had become "a secret police system of a political character." It noted that Hoover's files were the fuel for the espionage machine—the General Intelligence Division, and its predecessor, the Radical Division, had driven the Bureau's spying operations since 1919.

Stone read the report with intense interest. It described precisely the kind of conduct he had forsworn. He handed it to Hoover and asked him what he thought.

Hoover's future depended on the skill of his scalding seven-page rebuttal. He insisted that the Bureau had investigated only "ultra-radical" people and groups breaking federal laws. Many if not most were "charged with activities inimical to our institutions and government." The Bureau's work since 1919 had been "perfectly proper and legal." It had never wiretapped or burglarized anyone. "The Bureau has very rigid rules on matters of this kind," he wrote. The ACLU, for its part, was "consistently and continually advocating . . . on the part of the communistic element," taking civil liberty as criminal license. One week later, on August 7, 1924, Hoover, Baldwin, and Stone sat down for a conversation at the Justice Department. Hoover did most of the talking, as was his custom when confronted with a conversation that posed the potential for trouble. He maintained, as he did all his life, that he was not a willing participant in the Red raids. He assured Baldwin that the days of political espionage were over. He said the General Intelligence Division would be shut down—though he would keep its files unless Congress ordered him to burn them—and the Bureau would stick to the investigation of violations of federal law. He renounced his own past. He was utterly convincing. "I think we were wrong," Baldwin wrote to Stone a few days later. He told reporters that Hoover was the right man for the job. Hoover responded with a gracious thank-you note. It was his goal, he wrote, "to leave my desk each day with the knowledge that I have in no way violated the rights of the citizens of this country."

The FBI kept right on infiltrating the ACLU throughout these exchanges of pleasantries, and in the months and years thereafter. In the fall of 1924, the Bureau maintained a spy on the ACLU's executive board, purloined the minutes of its meetings in Los Angeles, and kept tabs on its donor lists. Seven weeks after his cordial meeting with Baldwin, Hoover was receiving new and detailed reports on the ACLU board's legal strategies. His files grew to include dossiers on the group's leaders and prominent supporters, among them one of the world's most famous women, the deaf and blind Helen Keller. Hers became one file among thousands in the FBI's unique history of the American civil-liberties movement.

"We never knew about the way that Hoover's FBI kept track of us," Baldwin said half a century later. "They never stopped watching us."

Nor did Hoover abolish the General Intelligence Division. On paper, the division disappeared. But its lifeblood, the files, remained. To preserve their secrecy, Hoover created an entirely new record-keeping system called "Official and Confidential." These documents were kept under his control. In theory, the Bureau's centralized records belonged to the Justice Department. They were vulnerable to discovery in the courts or subpoena by Congress. The "Official and Confidential" files maintained by Hoover were his and his alone. For fifty years they remained his inviolate cache of secrets. His power to spy on subversives depended on secrecy, not publicity. Confidential files were far better than blaring headlines. Despite the dangers of discovery, Hoover and the Bureau maintained surveillance over America's Communists.

"See that every secrecy is maintained"

Attorney General Stone had told Hoover to stick to law enforcement. He had asked Hoover more than once what federal laws made communism illegal. There were none. "The activities of the Communists and other ultra-radicals have not up to the present time constituted a violation of the federal statutes," Hoover wrote on October 18, 1924. "Consequently, the Department of Justice, theoretically, has no right to investigate such activities."

The Bureau of Investigation had no authority to conduct political warfare. The Espionage Act of World War I was null and void now that the war was over. The remaining federal sedition law, dating from the Civil War, required proof of a plan to use violence to overthrow the government. The Bureau never had been able to prove to the satisfaction of any court that American Communists conspired to that end. An even older law, the Logan Act of 1790, outlawed the communication of hostile conspiracies between Americans and a foreign country. Communists in the United States clearly communicated with Moscow. But Congress never had voted to grant the Soviet Union diplomatic recognition—it was not a country, in the eyes of American law—so the Logan Act was out. Hoover had no law to enforce. He had bent his authority to the limits and beyond in the realm of anticommunism.

Yet he had met the attorney general's standards. On December 10, 1924, Stone said he had passed the test. Hoover would become the director of the Bureau of Investigation.

Remarkably, that same week, Hoover found a legal basis for secret intelligence investigations of the American Left. It lay buried in an eight-year-old Justice Department budget authorization bill. In 1916, the Wilson administration, newly vigilant against foreign diplomats engaged in espionage, had started using the Bureau's agents to eavesdrop on the German embassy. The administration had slipped a line into the Justice Department budget giving the Bureau the power to investigate "official matters under the control of the Department of Justice *and the Department of State*" [emphasis added]. The bill became law and its provisions remained. When the Senate held hearings on the question of Soviet recognition in 1924, Secretary of State Charles Evans Hughes asked Hoover to prepare a report on Moscow's influence over American Communists. Hoover responded with nearly five hundred pages detailing his belief that Soviet communism sought to infiltrate every aspect of American life.

He maintained that the continuing diplomatic and political controversy gave him license to investigate communism in the United States. Hoover made that fragment of a sentence the foundation of his secret intelligence service.

Harlan Fiske Stone now ascended to the Supreme Court, where he served for the rest of his life, ending his days as chief justice. He watched over Hoover, and the new director knew it. To that end, Hoover hewed to Stone's edicts. He had to avoid the barest hint of lawbreaking if he wanted to rebuild the Bureau from the rubble bequeathed to him. "This Bureau cannot afford to have a public scandal visited upon it," Hoover wrote in a "personal and confidential" message sent to all special agents in May 1925. "What I am trying to do is to protect the force of the Bureau of Investigation from outside criticism and from bringing the Bureau of Investigation into disrepute."

He fired crooks and incompetents, cutting his forces until he had fewer than three hundred trustworthy special agents. He banned drinking on and off the job in light of the Prohibition laws. In time, he instituted uniform crime reports, constructed a modern criminal laboratory, built a training academy, and assembled a national fingerprint file. And for the next decade, he kept his spying operations small and tightly focused.

The risks of being caught spying on Americans were great. Hoover ran them; the risks of not spying seemed greater. Throughout the rest of the 1920s, Hoover and the Bureau tracked the work of American Communists with the help of paid informers, Party defectors, police detectives, and State Department officials.

Hoover investigated the national movement to stop the 1927 execution of the Italian anarchists Sacco and Vanzetti. Their murder conviction was seen as a frame-up by liberals across the country, chief among them Hoover's old nemesis Felix Frankfurter, who had fought Hoover face-to-face during the Deer Island deportations. He instructed his agents to "keep fully informed" on the local Sacco and Vanzetti defense committees and to "keep me advised"—but to "see that every secrecy is maintained." Hoover had always suspected that Italian anarchists had carried out the 1920 terrorist bombings that targeted American leaders and left Wall Street running in blood. But he was never able to prove it; the cases remained forever open.

Hoover spied on William Z. Foster, the Communist Party's perennial presidential candidate, the Comintern's favorite American labor organizer, and the head of the Party's Trade Union Educational League. FBI files from 1927, detailing secret meetings of Communist Party leaders in Chicago and New York, reported on the Reds' resolve to redouble recruitments and burrow into the ranks of the American Federation of Labor. Hoover told his most trusted confidant at the State Department that Communists controlled "the entire membership of all New York unions" and conspired "to take over the executive power of the unions in this country." He went on high alert when Foster and his followers traveled to Moscow in May 1929. He took note when Stalin directly addressed the American delegation, and he kept the file on hand for the rest of his days.

"The moment is not far off when a revolutionary crisis will develop in America," Stalin said. "Every effort and every means must be employed in preparing for that, comrades."

The crisis came quickly. It began with the Wall Street crash in November 1929, it grew mightily with the Great Depression, and it lasted until World War II.

8

RED FLAGS

"THE WORKERS OF this country look upon the Soviet Union as their country, is that right?" Congressman Hamilton Fish of New York asked the American Communist leader William Z. Foster. "They look upon the Soviet flag as their flag?"

"The workers of this country," Foster said, "have only one flag and that is the red flag."

The ruins created by the Great Depression provided cornerstones for the Communist movement. Roughly eight million people lost their jobs in 1930. Thousands of banks failed. One-quarter of the nation's factory lines stopped. President Herbert Hoover seemed unwilling or unable to act. Congress did little or nothing to help. The Communist Party of the United States, despite vicious internal battles, began to build significant support among labor unions and unemployed workers.

Congress responded with its first formal investigation of American communism in 1930. The House Committee to Investigate Communist Activities was a long-running spectacle, but not a success. The congressional investigators were befouled from the start by forged documents, fake evidence, and grandstanding witnesses.

J. Edgar Hoover tried to keep his distance from the public crusade led by Congressman Fish, a cantankerous Republican who represented Franklin D. Roosevelt's home district in New York State. But he did agree to testify before the investigative committee, and he shared some of his voluminous files on American radicals. Hoover issued a pointed warning about the power of Communist propaganda, which he called a new instrument of warfare for an armed conflict between workers and bosses, a class struggle that could threaten the shaky foundations of American capitalism.

But he said the Bureau could not attack American Communists unless

Congress once again outlawed revolutionary words. He wanted federal laws to make communism itself a crime.

In 1931, as the misery of the Great Depression spread and protests against the government grew, Congressman Fish ended his hearings in a state of rage. He had concluded that "no department of our government had any authority or funds from Congress to investigate Communism, and no department of the government, particularly the Department of Justice, knew anything about the revolutionary activities of the Communists in the United States. We have about 100,000 Communists in New York, and if they were so minded, they could raid the White House and kidnap the President, and no department of the government would know anything about it until they read it in the newspapers the next day."

But Congress gave Hoover no fresh ammunition for the war on communism; nor did the Supreme Court. The new chief justice, Charles Evans Hughes, the former secretary of state, was from the progressive wing of the Republican Party. He held that even Communists had constitutional civil liberties. The chief justice wrote a majority opinion overturning the California conviction of Yetta Stromberg, a nineteen-year-old counselor in a Communist Party summer camp who was sentenced to five years in prison for raising a red flag each morning. The Court said her conviction violated the Constitution and the Bill of Rights. The red flag could be waved freely in America.

Congressman Fish wanted to strike that flag. He wanted to outlaw Communist words and deeds. He wanted the Bureau back on the case. So he called on Hoover.

The director explained his precarious position to the congressman. The Bureau's power to spy on Americans had "never been established by legislation," Hoover said to Fish on January 19, 1931. It operated "solely on an appropriation bill"—the slender reed of the 1916 budget language saying the Bureau could work for the secretary of state. This was not a technicality: legislative language cloaked in a spending bill was only language, not law. If Congress and the Supreme Court wanted to outlaw communism, they should do so. But until then, the Bureau had no power to openly investigate political conduct. Hoover was walking a very fine line.

Hoover also told Attorney General William D. Mitchell that secret undercover work was crucial "to secure a foothold in Communistic inner circles" and to stay abreast of their "changing policies and secret propaganda." But "the Bureau of Investigation may be given the closest scrutiny at all times"—and it "would undoubtedly be subject to charges in the matter of alleged secret and undesirable methods," Hoover warned. Under law, he could not investigate political acts "which, from a federal standpoint, have not been declared illegal and in connection with which no prosecution might be instituted."

Hoover nevertheless kept spying on the Communists, hewing to his reading of the law by reporting in secret to the State Department.

On January 20, 1931—one day after his conversation with Congressman Fish—Hoover sent a letter to the State Department's most respected Russia hand, Robert F. Kelley, the chief of the Eastern European division. He summarized a series of reports from the Bureau of Investigation's New York office, based on the work of confidential informants within the Communist Party.

Hoover reported on an organization called the Workers' Ex-Servicemen's League—which he called an "active Communist unit" of American military veterans of World War I. The veterans wanted the government to pay a promised "bonus" for their military service—a payment that was not due until 1945. The group was "trying to organize an impressive number of ex-servicemen for the purpose of a 'Hunger March' to Washington," Hoover wrote. "The campaign is conducted by the league under the direction of the Central Committee of the Communist Party." The veterans and the Communists had joined forces, Hoover said, and they were planning to mount a protest march the likes of which no one had ever seen.

Hoover's intelligence report on the evolving plans for the Bonus March was prophetic. In the summer of 1932, thousands of ragged and unemployed World War I veterans from across the country gathered for a demonstration against the government. One Bonus Army banner read: IN THE LAST WAR WE FOUGHT FOR THE BOSSES/IN THE NEXT WAR WE'LL FIGHT FOR THE WORKERS. Marching on Washington, many accompanied by their families, they set up ragged encampments. They built a hobo jungle on Capitol Hill, pitched tents by the Anacostia River, and squatted in abandoned federal buildings.

On July 28, the president called out the troops—led by General Douglas MacArthur and his aide-de-camp, Major Dwight D. Eisenhower. They met the Bonus Army marchers with tanks, mounted cavalry, machine guns, and infantry with fixed bayonets and tear gas. General MacArthur's soldiers burned down the camps by the river; one of the Bonus Marchers was killed in the melee. The spectacle of the United States Army chasing the unarmed veterans, their wives, and their children out of the shadow of the Capitol was a scene of American urban combat without parallel since the Civil War. The newspaper pictures and the newsreels of the rout were a political disaster for President Hoover, who had just won the Republican Party's nomination for a second term.

Attorney General Mitchell announced that the Communists were to blame. He turned to J. Edgar Hoover to back the charges. Bureau agents in New York, Chicago, and St. Louis worked for months trying to prove that the Communist Party had planned and financed the march. Infiltrating meetings and rallies, searching bank records and shadowing leaders of the march, they investigated in vain. A grand jury convened to gather proof that the Bonus Army was a Communist conspiracy. It found none.

The Bureau of Investigation had only a few hundred agents with professional expertise and a devotion to the principles of the rule of law, among whom were a few dozen experienced in the techniques of espionage and counterespionage. Neither the Bureau nor Hoover had much of a claim to fame. If Americans knew the director's name, it was probably because the president had named Hoover "coordinator of federal assistance" in the 1932 kidnapping of the infant son of Charles and Anne Lindbergh. The case was "the crime of the century" and the search for the perpetrator would go on for two years.

"THE CRIMINAL STANDING ARMY"

Despite the political and social torments of the Great Depression—a national disaster in which the American people might have followed any politician promising a way out—the Communist Party was still a weak force when Americans went to elect a new president in November 1932. The Party had a few thousand members who devoted their lives to Stalin and the Soviets. They had made some small inroads with American workers and American unions, and their ideas held a growing attraction for intellectuals and radicals who despaired over the American political system.

The war on crime and the war on communism were not the battles in which Americans were engaged. They were struggling to survive. They were starved for a strong leader. They were ready for a president who would create "an American dictatorship based on the consent of the governed," in the startling words of Congressman Fish. The election of Franklin D. Roosevelt was foreordained from the moment he was nominated. FDR was ready to use every power the Constitution granted—and more—to save the Republic from political and economic chaos.

The FBI won its place in the firmament of American government under President Roosevelt. But it almost lost Hoover as its leader. He barely survived the transition of power.

President Roosevelt, sworn into office on March 4, 1933, had chosen Senator Thomas Walsh of Montana to be attorney general. Walsh had been a primary target of the Bureau of Investigation's political espionage a decade before, at the height of the Harding era. He had fought Hoover and his bosses, and they had hit back. The chances that Hoover would keep his job were slim. But on the eve of Roosevelt's inauguration, riding to Washington in a sleeper car with his young bride, Walsh died of a heart attack at seventy-two.

Roosevelt scrambled for a replacement. His secretary of state, Cordell Hull, recommended Homer S. Cummings, a onetime Democratic National Committee chairman. Cummings had been FDR's floor manager at the 1932 Democratic Convention, delivering delegates and a rip-roaring seconding speech. More importantly, Cummings had served for ten years as a state prosecutor in Connecticut, and he knew a great deal about law enforcement from personal experience, unlike many of his predecessors at the Justice Department.

"We are now engaged in a war," Attorney General Cummings proclaimed in a speech to the Daughters of the American Revolution in August 1933, "a war with the organized forces of crime."

Cummings created the "public enemies" list of gangsters like John Dillinger, Pretty Boy Floyd, Baby Face Nelson, Bonnie and Clyde. Cummings gave the Bureau the power to carry guns, execute warrants, and make arrests. Cummings conceived, and Congress passed, a new federal criminal code giving the Bureau the jurisdiction to enforce laws like racketeering—running an interstate criminal enterprise. If you fled a state in a stolen car, if you assaulted a federal officer, if you robbed a bank of its United States currency, you had committed a federal crime. Cummings's hope was that Hoover's men would enforce the law where corrupt city police and tinhorn county sheriffs failed.

Cummings called on Hollywood to join the battle. Hollywood made the movies; the movies helped make Hoover a star. Cummings could not be the leading man. He looked like a librarian. Hoover fit the role far better. He was happy to pose for publicity shots holding a machine gun or smiling at a starlet. He had many a cinematic model for his newly glamorous role. *G-Men,* starring Jimmy Cagney as a dashing FBI agent, featured a congressional hearing with a fictional Hoover testifying on behalf of the Cummings crime program. "These gangs will be wiped out!" he vows. "This is war!"

Within a year, Hoover became the public face of the war on crime, the star of a show that captured the imagination of the American people, the name in the headlines, an icon in the American political theater. His public performances, the speeches he made, and the statistics he produced for Congress became as dramatic as the movies. He would claim that 4.3 million Americans had joined "the criminal standing army" threatening the nation—"murderers, thieves, firebugs, assassins, robbers, and hold-up men." By that reckoning, one of every thirty men, women, and children in the United States was armed, dangerous, and at large in the land. These dire pronouncements about the war on crime went unquestioned at the time. Upon inspection, many proved to be inventions. But they won publicity and power for Hoover.

With his broad new authorities and his growing national reputation came a new name for his institution: the Federal Bureau of Investigation.

There was another war coming—the war against the enemy within. It could not be fought in public. FDR enlisted Hoover to fight it with the greatest secrecy and the utmost power a president could command.

Across the Atlantic, Adolf Hitler was establishing his dictatorship, and Roosevelt soon foresaw that one day he might have to confront the Nazi threat face-to-face. Inside the Kremlin, Joseph Stalin was demanding American recognition, if Roosevelt and the Senate would grant it, and Roosevelt came to realize that Russia might one day be a bulwark against Hitler and his storm troopers. J. Edgar Hoover was ready to do whatever his new commander-in-chief asked, against all enemies, foreign and domestic.

PART II

WORLD WAR

J. Edgar Hoover and President Roosevelt
at the start of the war against the enemy within, 1934.

9

THE BUSINESS OF SPYING

P RESIDENT ROOSEVELT DELIVERED his first battle orders to Hoover on May 8, 1934. FDR said he wanted "a very careful and searching investigation" of American fascism.

The president wanted Adolf Hitler's agents and admirers investigated on all fronts. Who were they? How strong were they? How broad a threat did they represent? Were Nazis at work in German diplomatic offices? Was Germany buying influence on Wall Street? Was Hitler controlling secret agents and secret funds inside the United States?

Hitler already represented a threat to America's allies in Europe. FDR and Hoover both knew well what Germany's secret agents had done to try to subvert and sabotage the United States during World War I. Now Hoover had orders to serve as the clearinghouse for all the evidence the United States government possessed. Prosecutions were not the point. The president wanted intelligence.

Hoover moved slowly and cautiously in the field of antifascism. He did not evince the boundless enthusiasm he had shown in fighting communism. He issued careful instructions to all his field offices, ordering "so-called intelligence investigations" into the American fascist movement. The director's choice of words was apt. Over the next two years, the Bureau's work was largely limited to collating files from state and local police, monitoring public rallies, and gathering newspaper clippings. It kept an eye on swastika-waving outfits like the German-American Bund (founded with the backing of the American automaker Henry Ford) and home-grown fascist groups like the Silver Shirts. It took note of the widely publicized right-wing rhetoric of groups like the Liberty Lobby and the increasingly popular Father Charles Coughlin, the anti-Semitic radio preacher. It even looked into an organization called the National Committee Against Communism. But the FBI's Adolf Hitler file was mostly filled with crackpot death threats against the dictator.

Hoover did his best to steer Roosevelt's attention back to the war on communism. Early in the Roosevelt administration, after a decade of debate, the United States had officially recognized the Soviet Union. That allowed Stalin to open an embassy and consulates in the United States; where there were diplomats, there were spies. Congress had passed the National Labor Relations Act, which allowed workers to organize; where there were trade unions, there were Communists. Between 1930 and 1936, Party membership had quadrupled to about thirty thousand. Now American leftists were starting to volunteer to fight fascist forces in Spain.

Hoover viewed these developments as deeply ominous. He asked to see the president in private, one-on-one.

On August 24, 1936, FDR invited Hoover to the White House. Throughout his presidency, Roosevelt routinely refused to keep written accounts of crucial meetings, especially on matters of secret intelligence. Only one record of this talk exists—Hoover's.

Roosevelt wanted to talk about "subversive activities in the United States, particularly Fascism and Communism," and he wanted "a broad picture" of their influence on the politics and economics of the nation, according to Hoover's notes. But Hoover kept the focus on the FBI's continuing investigations of communism in America. He warned the president that the Communists were taking over the longshoremen's union on the West Coast, that they had designs on the United Mine Workers union and the nation's supply of coal, and that they had great sway over the press through the Newspaper Guild.

"I told him," Hoover recorded, "that the communists planned to get control of these three groups and by doing so they would be able to paralyze the country . . . stop all shipping . . . stop the operation of industry . . . and stop publication of any newspapers." Hoover went on to say that Communists were boring into the government itself through the National Labor Relations Board.

Hoover then told the president that the FBI needed a renewed authority for secret intelligence operations. He cited the 1916 statute under which the State Department gave the FBI its secret intelligence powers.

FDR called for Secretary of State Cordell Hull, and the three men met at the White House the next day, August 25, 1936. The president said that since the threat was international and "Communism particularly was directed from Moscow," the secretary of state should give Hoover his approval to go after Soviet spies in America.

Nothing in writing came from the president or the State Department. Hoover did not record the precise language of the conversation. The legend at the FBI is that Hull turned to Hoover and said: "Go ahead and investigate the cock-suckers."

Hoover now had an open-ended order from the president to run secret intelligence operations against America's enemies. He cited the authority granted him that day for the rest of his life.

His command went out immediately to all FBI field offices: "Obtain from all possible sources information concerning subversive activities being conducted in the United States by Communists, Fascisti, and representatives or advocates of other organizations or groups advocating the overthrow or replacement of the Government of the United States by illegal methods." Hoover tried to coordinate his intelligence work with the army, the navy, and the State Department, as he had done in the heady days of the great Red raids.

The FBI set out to investigate every member of the Communist Party and its affiliates, along with the leaders of American fascist and antifascist movements. It went after left-wing labor leaders in the coal, shipping, steel, newspaper, and garment industries. It sought to find Communists and subversives at schools and universities, in the federal government, and in the armed forces. Hoover ordered his agents to recruit new informants and to write new reports on prominent subversives. He started classifying "subversive activities" under the broadest headings of American political and economic life.

"MEN OF ZEAL"

With the new authority vested in him by the president, Hoover revived one of the FBI's most valuable intelligence techniques: wiretapping.

Governments had been tapping wires ever since there were wires to tap. Army spies on both sides listened in on telegraph lines throughout the Civil War. Police departments and private detectives had been secretly recording conversations for decades. On the authority of President Wilson, the government took over the operation of public telephone lines during World War I. The Bureau had listened in on countless people during the lawless years after the war—not only Communists, but senators, congressmen, and judges.

And wiretapping now was legal—as long as it was secret.

The Supreme Court had drawn that fine line in a 1928 case, *Olmstead v. U.S.*, a 5–4 ruling in which Chief Justice William Howard Taft, a former president of the United States, cast the deciding vote. Roy Olmstead was a Seattle bootlegger; Prohibition agents from the Treasury Department had tapped his telephone. His lawyers had argued that the secret installation of wiretaps to gather criminal evidence violated the Fourth Amendment's protections against illegal trespasses and unlawful searches and seizures.

The majority in *Olmstead* had ruled that the government was within its rights: "A standard which would forbid the reception of evidence, if obtained by other than nice ethical conduct by government officials, would make society suffer and give criminals greater immunity than has been known heretofore."

The minority, led by Justice Louis Brandeis and Hoover's old boss, Justice Harlan Fiske Stone, had issued a powerful dissent. Brandeis warned: "The greatest dangers to liberty lie in insidious encroachments by men of zeal, well-meaning but without understanding."

"Crime is contagious," Brandeis wrote. "If the government becomes a law-breaker, it breeds contempt for the law; it invites every man to become a law unto himself; it invites anarchy. To declare that in the administration of the criminal law the end justifies the means—to declare that the government may commit crimes in order to secure the conviction of a private criminal—would bring terrible retribution."

Brandeis compared wiretapping and bugging to the "writs of assistance" and "general warrants" that the British had used to search the homes of American colonists before the war of independence that created the United States: "As a means of espionage, writs of assistance and general warrants are but puny instruments of tyranny and oppression when compared to wiretapping." And he shrewdly pointed out that one wiretap was in effect infinite: "Tapping of one man's telephone line involves the tapping of the telephone of every other person whom he may call, or who may call him." Hoover's men knew that well.

Six years after *Olmstead*, in 1934, Congress passed the Communications Act, a law banning the interception of telephone calls and the disclosure of their contents. The lawmakers thought they had made wiretaps a crime.

But they had left Hoover a loophole. He interpreted "disclosure" in a lawyerly way: wiretapping was not illegal if the information was not used as evidence in court. Therefore, if it was secret, it was legal. The FBI thenceforth used wiretaps whenever Hoover authorized it. Wiretapping, bugging, and break-ins became a holy trinity for FBI intelligence operations from the 1930s onward. Hoover believed that they were essential tools for protecting the United States against spies and saboteurs. President Roosevelt knew such methods were standard practice in the game of nations.

At the highest levels of power in Washington, an awareness dawned that Hoover might be listening to private conversations. This sense that the FBI was omnipresent was its own kind of power. In a 1936 investigation into the suspected leaking of Supreme Court decisions, the FBI tapped the home telephone of a court clerk. Chief Justice Charles Evans Hughes suspected that Hoover had wired the conference room where the justices met to decide cases. If you had to watch what you said in the chambers of the Supreme Court, times had changed.

"How unprepared we are"

In 1937, Hoover began to understand that his FBI was no match for an experienced foreign espionage service. He saw—too late, to his sorrow—that the Soviets, the Germans, and the Japanese had been spying for years on America's shipyards, aircraft plants, military bases, and maneuvers in the Atlantic and Pacific oceans.

His understanding came through the work of military code breakers. The army's Signal Intelligence Service was working on stealing radio communications from abroad. The navy had been trying to crack Japan's military codes and ciphers, with a weather eye on a potential attack in the Pacific; they had an under-the-table agreement with RCA, the Radio Corporation of America, to receive copies of Japanese cable traffic.

The navy's intermittently successful efforts led the FBI to arrest the first American tried and convicted for espionage since World War I. The investigation started when a navy cryptanalyst, Aggie Driscoll, stared at an odd word in a Japanese radio message: "TO-MI-MU-RA." The word *mura* means "town," but it also can mean "son." Thinking out loud, she heard the name "Thompson." Her insight led to the FBI's arrest of Harry Thompson, a former navy yeoman and a spy for Commander Toshio Miyazaki, a Japanese Imperial Navy officer studying English in California. Thompson had sold top secret weapons and naval engineering data to Japan.

Broken codes also led to the conviction of John Farnsworth, a Naval Academy graduate, a former lieutenant commander, and a desperate alcoholic who had been dismissed for misconduct. Farnsworth was hanging around navy bases up and down the Pacific Coast, flashing wads of cash, picking up bar tabs, and asking old shipmates about codes, weapons, and warship designs. The navy turned the case over to the FBI. In 1937, Farnsworth was arrested, tried, and convicted of selling secrets to Japan for $20,000.

These cases paled in comparison to the FBI's first great international espionage investigation: the Rumrich case.

"Nazi Spies in America"

On Valentine's Day, February 14, 1938, Hoover was on vacation in Miami. He was mourning the death of his mother, with whom he had lived all his life. He was forty-three years old and looking for a new home. He was also about to publish his first book, *Persons in Hiding*, a ghostwritten rehash of some of the FBI's gang-busting stories. When he first heard about the arrest of Guenther Rumrich, in a telephone call from headquarters, Hoover had deep doubts about the facts of the case. The story was far stranger than his crime-fighting yarns.

A senior British intelligence officer, Guy Liddell, had warned the U.S. Embassy in London about a Nazi spy ring in the United States. A few days later, a clerk at the State Department's passport office in New York answered the telephone. The caller said he was Cordell Hull, the secretary of state. He ordered the clerk to deliver thirty-five blank passports to the McAlpin Hotel in Manhattan.

The New York police arrested Guenther Rumrich when he picked up the package of passports. They searched his room and found a note describing a plot to steal the American military's plans to defend the Atlantic Coast.

Rumrich, the weak-chinned son of an Austrian diplomat, was twenty-six, an American citizen, AWOL from the U.S. Army—and, as he freely confessed, a spy for the German military intelligence service, the Abwehr.

Hoover assigned a star FBI agent, Leon Turrou, to the investigation. He had one of the highest profiles of any of Hoover's men; he had cultivated newspaper reporters all over New York. He saw the Rumrich case as a path to fame and fortune. In April 1938, while Turrou was supposed to be preparing for the presentation of the case to a federal grand jury in New York, he was meeting at night with a newspaper reporter, readying a series of first-person stories to be serialized in the *New York Post* and published in a heroic (and half-invented) true-crime adventure book entitled *Nazi Spies in America*.

Turrou had learned that the German espionage operation had run free in the United States for years; some of its members had been stealing American military technologies since 1927. Their leader was Dr. Ignatz Griebl, a physician in Manhattan, a public figure who ran an openly pro-Nazi political group called the Friends of New Germany. Within two months, with help from Rumrich, the FBI had identified eighteen members of the ring, both Germans and Americans, who had stolen the blueprints and specifications for a new generation of American warplanes and destroyers. The ring also distributed funds from Berlin to the ever-growing German-American Bund and members of American Nazi militias, whose numbers now ran into the tens of thousands.

It could have made a great movie. But Turrou made a mistake. He told every one of the eighteen members of the Abwehr spy ring that they would be subpoenaed to appear before a grand jury on May 5, 1938. Fourteen of them immediately fled the United States, some stowing away on German passenger ships whose captains and stewards were German intelligence agents. Rumrich, who had pleaded guilty in a bargain with the government, remained in New York along with three relatively minor co-conspirators. Dr. Griebl of the Abwehr turned up in Berlin—where, as the head of the FBI's New York office ruefully noted in a letter to Hoover, he and his fellow spies "probably have laughed time and again at our efforts in connection with the instant case." The case was all but destroyed. When Turrou took the stand at the trial of the remaining suspects, he was painted as a pathological liar.

The case made the FBI a laughingstock. That was Hoover's greatest fear.

"The utmost degree of secrecy"

The Japanese and the Germans were not the only foreign intelligence services spying on America. By the time Rumrich entered prison for a two-year sentence, a Soviet intelligence agent named Mikhail Gorin was arrested in Los Angeles. In the first case of its kind, the Soviets stood accused of re-cruiting a spy within the American military. The mole worked for the Of-fice of Naval Intelligence—Hoover's best source for the secrets of foreign espionage.

President Roosevelt expressed outrage. He reflected on "how unpre-pared we are to cope with this business of spying which goes on in our country." The president said: "Only by reinforcement of our intelligence services can we successfully combat the activities of foreign agents."

On October 14, 1938, Hoover gave the president and the attorney general a bold proposal to create an immense intelligence service under his control. His plans were an awesomely ambitious grasp for power in a nation where few were prepared for the next war.

Hoover had 587 agents in the FBI. He proposed to hire 5,000 more. He would take over the immigration and customs services. He would run the Federal Communications Commission, which controlled the national and international networks of radio, cable, and telegraph systems. He would be responsible for the security of every factory holding a government contract and every military research facility. He would oversee the issuance of pass-ports and visas by the State Department. He would have the power to inves-tigate anyone in the United States suspected as a foreign agent.

He proposed that all this should be done in secret, by presidential fiat.

"The utmost degree of secrecy" was required "for the expansion of the present structure of intelligence work," Hoover wrote in a memorandum to the president on October 20, 1938. The goal was "to avoid criticism or ob-jections which might be raised to such an expansion."

Espionage was "a word that has been repugnant to the American peo-ple," Hoover continued. "Consequently, it would seem undesirable to seek any special legislation which would draw attention to the fact that it was proposed to develop a special counter-espionage drive of any great magni-tude."

On November 2, 1938, the president called Hoover to the White House. Once again, the only record of the conversation is Hoover's secret memo-randum. It read: "He stated that he had approved the plan which I had prepared."

But Hoover found that secrecy could cut both ways in the exercise of power.

10

THE JUGGLER

As was often the case when Franklin D. Roosevelt issued secret orders in the White House, there was a catch.

"You know I am a juggler, and I never let my right hand know what my left hand does," FDR once said of his strategies in statecraft. "I may have one policy for Europe and one diametrically opposite for North and South America. I may be entirely inconsistent, and furthermore I am perfectly willing to mislead and tell untruths if it will help win the war."

The president told no one that he had "approved the plan" Hoover had proposed for a gigantic increase in the power of the FBI. Nor did the president give Hoover the money or the people he requested. FDR did reach into his secret cache of White House funds to give Hoover $600,000 under the table, a 10 percent increase over the FBI budget authorized by Congress. With this small windfall, Hoover began hiring 140 new special agents, roughly 4,860 men short of the force he sought.

But after months of struggle, Hoover won a new presidential order, giving him a measure of the authority he desired. He had to use all his powers of persuasion on the president and a new attorney general, Frank Murphy, whose tenure began in January 1939. Murphy was the eighth attorney general whom Hoover had served; the director was by now skilled at telling a new boss what he thought he wanted to hear. Murphy had a civil liberties streak; Hoover had to persuade him that the FBI's control over intelligence work was crucial to avoid the chaos and unconstitutional conduct that had characterized the Red raids of old.

On June 26, 1939, FDR issued a secret directive placing the FBI, army intelligence, and navy intelligence jointly in charge of all espionage, counterespionage, and sabotage investigations. Hoover and his military counterparts would meet weekly at the FBI to coordinate their work, with a senior State Department officer sitting in as a consultant. Their conference became known as the Interdepartmental Intelligence Committee; Hoover was its permanent chairman, since military chiefs came and went on two-year rotations. The directive made Hoover an American intelligence czar as World War II enveloped Europe.

The war exploded before summer ended. On September 1, 1939, Hitler's armies invaded Poland and began their war of conquest. Two days later, France and Great Britain declared war on Germany. Hitler and Stalin had already signed their nonaggression pact; to the shock of most of the leftists and liberals in America, the Communists in Moscow had made their peace with the Nazis in Berlin. Their concord freed Germany to attack eastward in Europe without fear of the Red Army.

The Nazis would soon drive west toward the Atlantic. Japan had rampaged through China and would seek a wider war in the Pacific. No one knew if or when the war might come for the United States.

FDR formally declared American neutrality. But from September 1939 onward he set out to support the British by delivering warships and sharing intelligence, to counter Axis spying and subversion in the United States, to try to divine what the Soviets would do next—and to keep a close eye on his enemies at home, with help from J. Edgar Hoover.

The relationship between the president and the director was by now growing into one of trust. It was founded on a mutual understanding of their respective powers. Hoover had a reverential respect for the presidency. Though not every authority he sought would be granted by the president, Roosevelt gave him plenty, and he was grateful for what he had received. FDR had a high regard for clandestine intelligence. Though not every secret he sought would be revealed by spying, he was greatly pleased when Hoover could provide them.

To Hoover's immense satisfaction, on September 6, 1939, five days after the start of the war in Europe, FDR issued a public statement to the American people. Expanding on his earlier secret order, the president said the FBI would "take charge of investigative work in matters relating to espionage." He ordered every law enforcement officer in the United States to give the FBI "any information obtained by them relating to espionage, counterespionage, sabotage, subversive activities and violations of the neutrality law." FDR said he wanted "to protect this country against . . . some of the things that happened over here in 1914 and 1915 and 1916 and the beginning of 1917, before we got into the war."

Everyone in power—the president, the justices of the Supreme Court, the attorney general and his inner circle, and Hoover himself—remembered the Black Tom explosion of 1916. They hadn't forgotten the Red raids of 1920. But this time, Attorney General Murphy reassured the nation, America's civil liberties were in good hands.

"Twenty years ago inhuman and cruel things were done in the name of justice," he told the press. "We do not want such things done today, for the work has now been localized in the FBI." Murphy said: "I do not believe that a democracy must necessarily become something other than a democracy to protect its national interests. I am convinced that if the job is done right—if the defense against internal aggression is carefully prepared—our people need not suffer the tragic things that have happened elsewhere in the world and that we have seen, even in lesser degrees, in this land of freedom. We *can* prevent and publish the abuse of liberty by sabotage, disorder and violence without destroying liberty itself."

"Disastrous catastrophes"

Hoover had no time for sentimental statements about civil liberties. He was already at war, and he required three new weapons in his arsenal.

First, Hoover wanted stronger laws against subversion. He had wanted them for twenty years. He got them. Congressional hearings had already begun on the statute that would ultimately be known as the Smith Act. It was aimed, initially, at the fingerprinting and registration of aliens. By the time it passed, it had grown to become the first peacetime law against sedition in America since the eighteenth century. The Smith Act included the toughest federal restrictions on free speech in American history: it outlawed words and thoughts aimed at overthrowing the government, and it made membership in any organization with that intent a federal crime.

Second, Hoover revived and strengthened the practice of maintaining a list of potential enemies to be arrested and detained when war came. The mechanics of making the list closely resembled the work that Hoover had done at the Alien Enemy Bureau during World War I.

On December 6, 1939, Hoover signed a "personal and confidential" order to every FBI agent under his command, headlined "Internal Security." It ordered them to prepare a list of people—Americans and aliens alike— who should be locked up in the name of national security. Hoover had in mind Communists and socialists, fascist followers of Hitler, "pro-Japanese" people, and anyone else his men thought capable of fighting political warfare. He wanted the names of the enemies of the state. The compilation of the list was called the Custodial Detention Program.

Third, Hoover wanted to wiretap at will. But a new and seemingly insurmountable obstacle lay in his way. On December 11, 1939, the Supreme Court, reversing itself, said that government wiretapping was illegal.

United States v. Nardone pitted the government against gangsters. The evidence rested heavily on the transcripts of five hundred tapped telephone calls. The defense lawyers looked to the Communications Act of 1934, which banned the disclosure of wiretapped conversations. The Supreme Court had ruled that the law was clear: its "plain words . . . forbid anyone . . . to intercept a telephone message, and direct in equally clear language that 'no person' shall divulge or publish the message or its substance to 'any person.'"

The Court made it just as plain that the law applied to federal agents.

On its face, the decision looked like a ban on wiretapping. Not to Hoover. Two days later he instructed his agents that nothing had changed: "Same rule prevails as formerly—no phone taps without my approval." So long as he and he alone approved the taps in secret, and the work was done in the name of intelligence, everything would be fine.

The prosecutors in *Nardone* took the case back to trial and convicted the defendants by sanitizing, summarizing, and paraphrasing the transcripts of the wiretapped conversations. This lawyerly tactic worked at the retrial, but it did not sit well with the Supreme Court. *Nardone II* was decided in a scathing opinion written by Hoover's old archenemy: Justice Felix Frankfurter, the Liberal Club lawyer from Harvard who had crushed Hoover in a Boston courtroom during the Deer Island deportation cases two decades before.

Wiretapping was "inconsistent with ethical standards and destructive of personal liberty," Frankfurter wrote for the Court. And the trick of summarizing a transcript would not work: "the knowledge gained by the Government's own wrong cannot be used." Case closed: The government could not use wiretaps or the intelligence that flowed from them.

On January 18, 1940, Attorney General Murphy became the newest justice of the Supreme Court. He was succeeded by Solicitor General Robert Jackson, later the lead prosecutor at the Nuremberg trials of Nazi war criminals and a Supreme Court justice of distinction. Attorney General Jackson quickly declared that the Justice Department had abandoned wiretapping. On March 15, he instituted a formal ban. It lasted nine weeks.

Hoover moved to undermine the new attorney general and find a way around the law. He was shrewd, and he was relentless when his superiors blocked his way. He sandbagged Jackson by leaking stories suggesting that the FBI was being handcuffed in the war against spies and saboteurs. He sought support from his political allies at the War Department and the State Department. He personally and pointedly warned that the fate of the nation rested on wiretaps and bugs.

Hoover was "greatly concerned over the present regulation which prohibits the use of telephone taps," he wrote to Jackson on April 13, 1940. Taps were "essential" for the FBI in its intelligence investigations and in espionage cases. Without them, "a repetition of disastrous catastrophes like the Black Tom explosion must be anticipated." The FBI "cannot cope with this problem without the use of wire taps," Hoover contended. "I feel obligated to bring this situation to your attention at the present time rather than wait until a national catastrophe focuses the spotlight of public attention upon the Department because of its failure to prevent some serious occurrence."

Hoover was telling the attorney general that he would have American blood on his hands unless he overturned the ban in the name of national security.

"A MENACE TO THE PUBLIC"

Their confrontation deepened. Attorney General Jackson was appalled to learn about Hoover's Custodial Detention Program. Keeping track of enemy aliens was one thing. Compiling files on Americans who would be rounded up in a national emergency was another.

Hoover warned Jackson to stand down. A fight over the Custodial Detention Program risked "the very definite possibility of disclosure of certain counterespionage activities." Any challenge to his power could force the FBI "to abandon its facilities for obtaining information in the subversive field." The list remained.

Hoover had commanded every FBI agent in the United States to report on "persons of German, Italian, and Communist sympathies" as candidates for detention, Americans and aliens alike. He wanted the names of editors, publishers, and subscribers to all Communist, German, and Italian newspapers in the United States. He wanted the membership rolls of every politically suspect organization in the United States, down to German singing clubs. He told his agents to set informants and infiltrators spying on "the various so-called radical and fascist organizations in the United States," identifying their "personnel, purposes and aims, and the part they are likely to play at a time of national crisis."

The FBI had started drawing up a list of thousands of people whose "liberty in this country in time of war or national emergency would constitute a menace to the public peace and safety of the United States Government." The files held intelligence compiled by FBI agents across the country from "confidential sources"—not only informants, but intelligence gathered by break-ins, wiretaps, and bugs planted on Hoover's authority. It came from public and private records, employment records, school records, and interviews.

The people on the list fell into two categories. The first were to be arrested and interned immediately upon the outbreak of hostilities between the United States and the nation to which they were loyal. The second were to be "watched carefully" when war came, based on "the possibility but not the probability that they will act in a manner adverse to the best interests of the Government of the United States." Hoover instructed his agents to keep their interviews and inquiries "entirely confidential." He told them to say, if asked, that they were conducting lawful investigations in connection with the 1938 Foreign Agents Registration Act, which required people representing foreign principals or powers to register with the State Department. This was a deception.

"WHAT IF IT IS ILLEGAL?"

Hoover now played power politics at the presidential level. At war with the attorney general over wiretapping and surveillance, he needed allies in the cabinet.

He found one in Treasury Secretary Henry Morgenthau. Hoover knew him as a lifelong friend to Roosevelt, as the grandson of a Jewish immigrant from Germany, and as a sophisticated economist intensely interested in the flow of funds between the Axis and American banks.

On May 10, 1940, Hoover told Morgenthau of a Nazi scheme to subvert the president. He said the FBI needed wiretaps to investigate it.

For years, Germany had been running an intelligence program in the United States. The program, subsidized by seized and stolen Jewish assets, was highly profitable both to the Nazis and to American bankers. It was Hitler's best tool for identifying and recruiting Germans in America.

The Third Reich sold specially denominated German marks— *Rueckwanderer* or "returnee" marks—in exchange for American dollars. To open a *Rueckwanderer* account, a German resident in the United States went to a German consulate, swore allegiance to the Third Reich, and stated his intent to return to the fatherland. He transferred American dollars to the Reich and thus invested in Germany victory.

Four banking companies in the United States handled the lucrative *Rueckwanderer* exchange. The best known was Chase National. The least known was Robert C. Mayer & Co., led by August T. Gausebeck, a resident alien and a member of the Nazi Party.

Hoover said Gausebeck was laundering money, sending tens of thousands of dollars in untraceable $5 and $10 bills to Father Charles Coughlin, the notorious right-wing radio preacher who railed against Roosevelt and the "Jew Deal," rallied an armed militia movement called the Christian Front, and prayed for the triumph of fascism over communism. Coughlin was one of FDR's strongest political foes, along with the world-famous aviator Charles Lindbergh, a potential Republican candidate for president in 1940. There was more: Hoover reported that Gausebeck planned to mail $500,000 in small bills to the Republican presidential campaign committee.

In short, said Hoover, German intelligence officers had a network of money and information that ran through the American banking system. Nazi gold was flowing to FDR's political enemies in the United States.

And the FBI had no way of wiretapping them.

"I spoke to J. Edgar Hoover and asked him whether he was able to listen in on spies by tapping the wires and he said no; that the order given him by Bob Jackson stopping him had not been revoked," Morgenthau wrote in his meticulous daily diary, preserved in the FDR presidential library, on May 20, 1940. "I said I would go to work at once. He said he needed it desperately."

Morgenthau immediately rang Edwin Watson, the president's personal secretary. "I called up General Watson and said this should be done and he said, 'I don't think it is legal.'"

"What if it is illegal?" Morgenthau replied—meaning *who cares if it is illegal?*

Watson called back in five minutes: "He said he told the President and the President said, 'Tell Bob Jackson to send for J. Edgar Hoover and order him to do it and a written memorandum will follow.'"

The president wrote a secret note to Attorney General Jackson the very next day. It said, in so many words, to hell with the Supreme Court.

The *Nardone* decision was "undoubtedly sound," FDR began. "Under ordinary and normal circumstances wire-tapping by Government agents should not be carried on for the excellent reason that it is almost bound to lead to abuse of civil rights." But these were extraordinary times. "I am convinced," Roosevelt wrote, "that the Supreme Court never intended [its decision] to apply to grave matters involving the defense of the nation."

"It is, of course, well known that certain other nations have been engaged . . . in preparation for sabotage, as well as in actual sabotage," the president said. "It is too late to do anything about it after sabotage, assassinations, and 'fifth column' activities are completed."

The president said he authorized the FBI to use "listening devices" against "persons suspected of subversive activities against the Government of the United States, including suspected spies." The order was signed and initialed "FDR." It stood for the next quarter of a century.

In those years, the FBI installed at least 6,769 warrantless wiretaps and 1,806 bugs in the name of national security. These figures are almost surely understated, since some taps, bugs, and break-ins went unreported in order to protect the secrecy of the operations, according to Justice Department records that survived the passing years and the changing politics of the era.

With Roosevelt's blessing, Hoover now wiretapped at will. Wiretapping remained illegal. Nothing in the president's order made it lawful. Roosevelt had made the FBI a presidential intelligence service. Hoover had wrested a great authority from the Justice Department.

And he had learned to juggle as well as the president did.

The attorney general fought back. "The Federal Bureau of Investigation is the subject of frequent attack as a Gestapo," Jackson wrote in a secret memo that circulated at Justice. "These attacks, if believed by a large number of people, are disastrous to its work and its standing in court when we seek convictions." He wanted the FBI to hew to the law: the straight and narrow course of investigating crimes against the United States.

But Hoover won this battle as well. He responded by schooling the attorney general on "the difference between 'investigative' activity and 'intelligence' activity." The FBI's intelligence work was not aimed at indicting criminals after they committed crimes. It was intended to stop spies and saboteurs before they struck. "It is imperative, if the internal security of this country is to be maintained, that the FBI be in a position to have in its files information concerning the activities of individuals and organizations of a subversive character," Hoover insisted. When the FBI did intelligence operations, it was not working for the attorney general and the Justice Department. It was working for the president of the United States.

The confrontation was a turning point.

Over the next two decades, Hoover told attorneys general what he was doing if and when he wanted. He made it impossible for Jackson and many of his successors at Justice to exercise their lawful authority over the FBI.

Hoover was operating outside the law, and he knew it. Wiretap evidence was useless in court; any judge would dismiss a case based on illegal government conduct.

But wiretapping worked. It was one of the most powerful tools the FBI possessed to gather intelligence. Its power was unchecked once it was unleashed. One tap could open a window into a world of secrets. And Hoover now ruled that realm.

"The President thought you might like to look them over"

The relationship between Roosevelt and Hoover had been cordial but correct. It was deepened now by the sharing of secrets.

On May 21, 1940, the same day that FDR issued his wiretap order, he also gave Hoover copies of telegrams sent to the White House in support of the anti-intervention policies of Charles Lindbergh. ("I am absolutely convinced that Lindbergh is a Nazi," FDR had told Treasury Secretary Henry Morgenthau the day before.) A note from FDR's secretary atop the sheaf of telegrams said: "The President thought you might like to look them over noting the names and addresses of the senders."

For the next five years, Hoover sent FDR a steady stream of political intelligence and innuendo about people who opposed the president's policies. The targets of the FBI's surveillance included Lindbergh; the America First coalition of conservatives, anti-Communists, and pro-Hitler reactionaries; three United States senators whom Hoover suspected of German sympathies, including his old enemy from the 1920s, Burton Wheeler of Montana; FDR's hometown congressman, the Red-baiting Hamilton Fish; and hundreds more who simply hated Roosevelt and everything for which he stood.

When the president was irritated by an America First pamphlet opposing his policy of lending ships to Britain, he ordered an aide to "find out from someone—perhaps FBI—who is paying for this?" Hoover proceeded to investigate not simply the source of the pamphlet but the entire financial structure of America First. He eventually was able to inform the president that America First received substantial and secret support from two of the nation's most powerful newspaper publishers: Joseph Medill Patterson of the New York *Daily News* and Robert R. McCormick of the *Chicago Tribune*. Hoover also implied that America First might have received secret funds from foreign fascists. All of this provoked the president to order the Justice Department to open a federal grand jury investigation of America First. A wiretap on one prominent America First leader, Lindbergh's fellow aviator Laura Ingalls, led to her indictment and conviction as a paid agent of influence for the German government.

On June 14, 1940, FDR sent Hoover a thank-you note "for the many interesting and valuable reports that you have made to me regarding the last few months." Hoover kept it all his life. Three months later he let the White House know that he was listening in on "all telephone conversations into and out of the following embassies: German, Italian, French, Russian, and Japanese," and conducting a wide range of intelligence investigations against the espionage agents of the Axis.

Hoover now was the president's intelligence chief.

11

SECRET INTELLIGENCE

AMERICA'S WAR AGAINST Germany went worldwide a year and a half before Pearl Harbor. The FBI became America's first real foreign intelligence service. Many of its battles stayed secret through the end of the century.

The FBI's attack against Nazi spies began in May 1940 with a Morse code message, sent by shortwave radio from a wood-frame bungalow on the beach in Centerport, New York, a little town on Long Island. It vaulted over the Atlantic Ocean and landed in the Hamburg office of the Abwehr, the German military intelligence service.

The Abwehr responded with a steady stream of commands for secret intelligence from German agents in America. The Abwehr wanted reports on American military readiness, troop training, aircraft production, deliveries of warplanes to Britain, the construction of aircraft carriers, chemical-warfare manuals, machine tool factories, bombsights, and the movements of ships at sea. It radioed instructions to a ring of thirty-three agents. Some worked for companies like Westinghouse Electric, Ford, and Chrysler; others served on ships that plied the Atlantic.

The Abwehr thought the radioman receiving its orders at the Long Island bungalow and reporting reams of intelligence back to Hamburg was a forty-year-old naturalized American citizen, William Sebold.

But the FBI, not Sebold, was at the controls.

Sebold was a German army veteran of World War I, a drifting merchant seaman and aircraft mechanic who had lived and worked in New York and San Diego, and then returned to Germany at the start of 1939. Armed with a new American passport, orders from the Abwehr, and $500 in cash, he had been sent back to New York. He delivered himself to the FBI on February 8, 1940, after disembarking at the end of a trip from Italy on the SS

Washington. He said that upon his return to Germany he had been coerced by German intelligence, which had shanghaied him into a spy school in Hamburg, where he had been trained in code making and secret communications.

FBI agents watched as Sebold took off his wristwatch, opened the back, and withdrew five tiny photographs. Read under a microscope, the documents contained the Abwehr's demands for information on American military secrets including antiaircraft gunnery, chemical warfare, and troop movements.

The Abwehr had ordered Sebold to contact a man named Herman Lang and construct a clandestine shortwave radio base to communicate with German intelligence in Hamburg. The identification of Lang convinced the FBI beyond all doubt: he was an inspector at the factory that made the Norden bombsight, one of the closely guarded secrets of American military technology.

Hoover sent this startling information to President Roosevelt on February 12, 1940, four days after Sebold arrived in New York.

The question for the FBI was how to use Sebold to double-cross the Germans and roll up their spy network in the United States. Hoover and his men had no experience in the use of double agents. A successful double-agent operation is a con game, based on deception. Sebold had to look like he was working for the Abwehr while he was working for the FBI.

The radio was the key. When the clandestine station at Centerport went on the air, on May 19, 1940, an FBI agent named Morris Price was at the controls, not Sebold.

Over thirteen months Price would transmit 302 messages to the Abwehr and receive 167 replies. Coordinating with army and navy intelligence, the FBI sent information, misinformation, and disinformation to Germany. The Abwehr replied with a steady list of orders for its agents and demands for information. Hoover reported regularly to the White House on what the Germans wanted from their spies in the United States—chiefly information on America's war potential and its shipments of military materiel to England.

The Abwehr's officers played into America's hands. They radioed orders to Sebold to open a bank account in New York and to serve as a paymaster for the spy ring. This gave him control over the ring's operations and ready access to its thirty-three agents.

The FBI set up a sting operation built around a dummy company, wiretaps, and hidden cameras—financed in part by the unwitting Abwehr and underwritten by President Roosevelt's close friend Vincent Astor.

Astor already was working as a spy for FDR. An heir to one of America's great fortunes, Astor had won a commission from the president to coordinate intelligence operations in New York. In his capacity as director of Western Union, he organized the interception of international cable traffic, in violation of federal law. In Bermuda, where he owned a vast estate, Astor ran an equally illegal operation with British intelligence, opening diplomatic pouches and international mail carried on ships and airplanes stopping on the island en route to and from the United States. In New York, at the West 42nd Street headquarters of *Newsweek,* the magazine Astor owned and operated, he gave a suite of three sixth-floor offices to the FBI.

The *Newsweek* building became the headquarters of the Diesel Research Corporation, run by William Sebold, financed by $5,000 checks sent to New York by Abwehr agents in Mexico, and wired with hidden microphones and cameras by the FBI. Sebold used the offices to pay the members of the ring and receive their reports. Couriers delivered messages to Sebold that showed the movements and the whereabouts of every valued member of the ring.

The FBI recorded eighty-one meetings between Sebold and the Abwehr's agents at Diesel Research, with moving pictures and still photographs shot through a trick mirror, and with hundreds of reels of audiotape recorded with hidden microphones. Within the year, the FBI had arrested them all.

Successes in counterintelligence were rarely as smashing as the Sebold case. The investigation opened Hoover's eyes to the power of deception in warfare.

"Spies, saboteurs and traitors"

The FBI's shortwave radio communiqués with the Abwehr also began providing clues that the Germans were running spies in Mexico, Brazil, and Peru. Hoover used that information to create a new global intelligence operation.

Hoover's crucial ally was Adolf A. Berle, a tough-minded assistant secretary of state. Berle ran the intelligence side of American diplomatic affairs; he served as State's liaison to the FBI, the army, and the navy; before that, he had held the Latin America portfolio. He was one of the brainiest members of FDR's brain trust. And though he was a high-minded Harvard liberal, the kind of man Hoover loved to hate, Berle won Hoover's trust as well. They shared the quality of the clandestine mind.

In May 1940—as France fell to the Nazis, the British faced attack, and the newly installed prime minister, Winston Churchill, reached out for American help—Hoover and Berle talked about setting up a worldwide American intelligence agency. The Atlantic coasts of the Americas were rife with U-boats; five months before, German and British ships had battled in the mouth of the Río de la Plata in Uruguay.

Berle proposed that the FBI investigate Nazi spies from Havana down to Rio de Janeiro. The FBI already had sent one special agent down to Mexico City, where he had started working with the chief of police and the Interior Ministry to find German spies and subversives, and another to Rio, where he was training the Brazilian secret police.

Hoover and Berle brought in Brigadier General Sherman Miles, the chief of army intelligence, and Rear Admiral Walter Anderson, head of navy intelligence. Hoover and the military men had been squabbling over their responsibilities and authorities. Their coordination was scattershot, their sharing of secrets scant. General Miles and Hoover particularly detested one another. The army and the navy fought one another on principle. But, prompted by Hoover, they all brought the question of worldwide intelligence back to the president. It was already on his mind.

On May 26, 1940, in one of his fireside chats, the radio addresses that were heard by tens of millions of Americans, FDR had let his thinking show.

"Today's threat to our national security is not a matter of military weapons alone," the president told the American people. "We know of other methods, new methods of attack.

"The Trojan Horse. The Fifth Column that betrays a nation unprepared for treachery.

"Spies, saboteurs and traitors are the actors in this new strategy. With all of these we must and will deal vigorously."

On June 3, 1940, Berle went to Hoover's office at FBI headquarters. They had "a long meeting on coordinated intelligence," and they agreed, as Berle wrote in his diary, "that the time had come when we would have to consider setting up a secret intelligence service—which I suppose every great foreign office in the world has, but we have never touched." Eight days later they approved a plan, hastily drawn up by their lieutenants, to create something without precedent in the history of the United States.

The FBI would operate a spy agency under the deepest cover. Its existence would not be acknowledged. To an outsider, it would look like a corporation based in New York with branch offices throughout the world. Its international representatives would stealthily gather information based on secret assignments sent from headquarters, without knowing who would read it back in the United States. It would be called the Special Intelligence Service.

Once again the president put nothing in writing. He told Berle on June 24, 1940, that the FBI was now responsible for foreign intelligence in the Western Hemisphere from the Texas border down to Tierra del Fuego. The army and the navy would carve up the rest of the world.

"The President said that he wished the field to be divided," Berle reported. It was a fateful phrase. The juggler had dropped the ball.

12

"TO STRANGLE THE UNITED STATES"

HOOVER ESTABLISHED THE Special Intelligence Service (SIS) on July 1, 1940, with funds from a secret account created by the president. Congress knew nothing about it. No law authorized it. Very little was written about it, outside a secret FBI history compiled after World War II and kept classified for more than sixty years.

The plan was impressive on paper, but it ran headlong into reality. This was not the FBI's kind of war.

Hoover gave the leadership of the SIS to one of his favorite lieutenants, Percy Foxworth, the smooth-talking and courtly thirty-three-year-old special agent in charge of the New York bureau. Everyone called him Sam. Born and raised in Mississippi, Foxworth looked like a purebred bull terrier; he bore more than a passing resemblance to a younger J. Edgar Hoover.

Foxworth was a social animal, comfortable chatting with a countess or the chief of the Cuban secret police. He had cultivated members of Manhattan's upper crust; his closest contacts included Vincent Astor and Nelson Rockefeller, the Chase bank heir newly appointed as an assistant secretary of state for Latin American affairs, in charge of cultural and commercial relations. Rockefeller was a perfect front man for the SIS: an incalculably wealthy man with commercial connections and diplomatic credentials throughout the Western Hemisphere. FDR wanted Rockefeller to use his name and his wealth, which included oil and industrial holdings, to counter the economic and political influence of Germany and Japan.

Hoover wanted Foxworth to find out how to spy against the Axis. Roughly one million Germans and Japanese lived in Brazil, Argentina, Chile, and Peru. They ran mines that produced gold and silver, along with rare and crucial war materiel like platinum and industrial diamonds. The Japanese had shipping routes that ran from Mexico down to Antarctica, and the Germans had considerable clout with South American leaders who favored the jackboot and the goosestep.

In August 1940, with Rockefeller acting as real estate broker, SIS set up shop as the Importers and Exporters Service Company, doing business in Room 4332 at 30 Rockefeller Plaza in New York. On the surface, Importers and Exporters offered to help clients develop international trade opportunities. In reality, the company was the clearinghouse where FBI agents from across the country picked up their cover assignments for their secret overseas missions. They would go out as reporters for *Newsweek,* with the blessing of the magazine's boss, Vincent Astor. They would pose as stockbrokers for Merrill Lynch. They would pretend to be executives for the United Fruit Company, the Armour Meat Corporation, American Telephone and Telegraph, or U.S. Steel. Under these covers, they would identify Nazi and Soviet spy rings operating from Mexico and Cuba down to Brazil and Argentina. In their spare time they would mine and refine nuggets of secret information on politics, economics, and diplomacy.

The FBI was hiring hundreds of new men, increasing its ranks by 80 percent. It grew from 898 agents in 1940 to 1,596 agents in 1941. By 1943 the Bureau had tripled in size, with 4,591 agents backed by 7,422 staffers. But the number whose training and experience qualified them to serve in the Special Intelligence Service was vanishingly small. The mismatch between the men and the mission was tremendous. Hoover said so himself.

"We certainly picked some fine lemons in our original selection for SIS" was the way he put it.

Foxworth wanted 250 agents at his command as soon as possible; eventually, the SIS would grow to nearly 600 strong. But over the course of the first year, he found only 25 men who fit the bill. Few FBI agents spoke foreign languages. Few knew their way around foreign countries. Few knew how to act like a stockbroker or a steel executive. Posing as a reporter was simpler: you carried a pen and a pad, asked questions, and wrote things down; every FBI agent could do that. But *Newsweek* could hardly staff every foreign bureau in the hemisphere with Hoover's agents. And there was no time to learn to live your cover, as a good spy must.

Two of Hoover's top intelligence aides, Stanley Tracy and W. Richard Glavin, met in a conference room outside Hoover's office at FBI headquarters. They were joined, implausibly, by the poet Archibald MacLeish, who as the wartime Librarian of Congress under FDR created a Division of Special Information to provide basic data on foreign countries to American

intelligence officers. The three men stared at a large map on an easel showing the twenty nations of Central and South America.

Dallas Johnson, Foxworth's clerk, took notes as Tracy selected "the
names of agents that he knew of that might well fit in to each of these
places," Johnson remembered. "We'd pull the personnel files down on the
people, say, with Spanish language capability," he said. "If they looked
like they were good prospects, then we'd send them in to Foxworth to
look over. And that's how the first agents then were pulled out." Johnson
recorded the names of the men with potential on the blue paper Hoover
used for his "Do Not File" files. (Hoover had created this ingenious system in the name of secrecy. The "Do Not File" documents were never
indexed, so the originals could be destroyed without a trace, and the records of the most sensitive operations—involving espionage, buggings,
break-ins, wiretaps, and political investigations—could be protected in
the event of outside inquiries from the courts or Congress. The system
survived until Hoover's death.)

"In the beginning," the FBI's own secret history of the SIS recounts,
"agents selected for these Latin American assignments were brought into
Washington from the Domestic Field and furnished with brief training."
Very brief indeed: they learned about the country of their assignment from
thin dossiers that might include old reports from military or naval attachés,
a sheaf of newspaper clippings, and a tourist handbook. As for training on
the targets of their intelligence work, there was next to none: "It was not as
a rule possible to brief the Agents with regard to subversive activities and
conditions of this kind for the reason that such information was not available in the United States."

"There had arisen in the United States considerable apprehension with
regard to the extent of Nazi penetration and Nazi activities throughout
Latin America," the secret history continues. But "the Bureau discovered
upon undertaking the program that there was a complete absence of any
accurate data or details concerning the true extent or nature of subversive
activities, current or potential, in Latin America."

On December 29, 1940, during a fireside chat, FDR underscored the urgency of protecting the Americas. "There are those who say that the Axis
powers would never have any desire to attack the Western Hemisphere," the
president told the American people. "That is the same dangerous form of
wishful thinking which has destroyed the powers of resistance of so many
conquered peoples. The plain facts are that the Nazis have proclaimed, time

and again, that all other races are their inferiors and therefore subject to their orders. And most important of all, the vast resources and wealth of this American Hemisphere constitute the most tempting loot in all of the round world."

If and when the United States joined the battle, the plan was to go after Germany first, with blockades at sea, bombing from the air, and covert operations in occupied France. That plan demanded close liaison between American and British intelligence services.

London had practiced the arts of deception in espionage, diplomacy, and military intelligence since Queen Elizabeth I reigned in the sixteenth century. British intelligence officers schooled Hoover's emissary, Hugh Clegg, in the tracking and detection of spies, the protection of manufacturing plants and shipping ports, the compiling and maintenance of lists of suspect citizens and aliens, the installation of hidden cameras for surveillance photos, the placement of undercover agents at embassies and consulates, and the undetected opening of mail. While Clegg went to spy school in London, Hoover sent two reports to the White House outlining British plans to sabotage the Axis and predicting British aims "to be in a position at the end of the war to organize the world, particularly Europe, on an economic basis for the purposes of rehabilitation, profit, and the prevention of the spread of Communism." Hoover's Special Intelligence Service chief, Percy Foxworth, flew south with a delegation led by Nelson Rockefeller for a two-month tour of the Americas. Using a false passport, he visited fourteen nations where the SIS was trying to spy on the enemy. He reported back to Hoover in February 1941. His assessment was dismal. The agents were floundering. They had no idea of where they were, or what they were supposed to do.

The FBI knew there were Nazis to be hunted. But it did not know where to hunt, or how.

"The volume of intelligence information from each Agent was in the beginning and for some time thereafter quite small and of little real value," the secret SIS history says. "The Agents were, of course, more or less completely unfamiliar with the countries in which they were trying to operate and usually very deficient with regard to the use of the language thereof. The chance of worthwhile accomplishment in the way of local orientation and the establishment of worthwhile informants and sources of information naturally required considerable time. Meanwhile, of course, the Agent, who was usually alone in the particular country to which he had been as-

signed, was possessed of a very poor pretext for clandestine operations. . . . The Bureau learned through very difficult experience that
virtually any information referred to a diplomatic officer of the State Department, the Army or the Navy . . . would invariably result in denunciation of the information as well as its source."

Hoover sensed a failure in the making. On March 15, 1941, he tried to get
rid of the Special Intelligence Service.

Hoover told Attorney General Jackson that the SIS should be handed
over to army or navy intelligence. But Hoover had no takers for the job of
policing the Americas. The army and the navy had their hands full trying to
decipher the intentions and the capabilities of the Germans in Europe and
the Atlantic and the Japanese in Asia and the Pacific. He repeated his recommendation three weeks later, saying that "the Bureau is marking time in
so far as any extension of its coverage in the Latin Americas is concerned."

The spread of Soviet communism in the United States remained
Hoover's greatest concern. Among the ever-growing list of his responsibili-
ties was the wiretapping of the Russian diplomatic posts in the United
States, including Amtorg, the Soviet economic and commercial office in
New York, which spent millions of dollars buying American technology.

In April 1941, the FBI opened an espionage investigation into Amtorg,
spurred by a British intelligence alert. A twenty-nine-year-old American, a
Princeton dropout named Tyler Kent, had served for six years as a clerk at
the American embassies in Moscow and London. The British, on the trail
of a suspected Nazi agent, had followed the suspect to Kent's London flat.
When they broke into the room and searched it, they found copies of 1,500
American diplomatic cables, codes, and ciphers. Kent had spent his career
pilfering encoded communiqués and handing them over to Soviet and Axis
agents; thanks to his work, Moscow and Berlin could read the American
diplomatic code used for secret communications between London and
Washington.

Among Kent's stolen documents was a British intelligence report on Soviet agents working for the chief of Amtorg's New York office, Gaik Balado-
vich Ovakimian, a forty-two-year-old chemical engineer. On May 5, 1941,
the FBI arrested Ovakimian on a charge of violating the Foreign Agents
Registration Act, which required people spreading foreign propaganda in
the United States to register with the Justice Department. But before the
FBI had a chance to interrogate him, he was released on $25,000 bail into
the custody of the Soviet consul general in New York. Ten weeks later, after

Hitler invaded the Soviet Union, the State Department ordered the charges dropped as a diplomatic gesture toward Moscow. Ovakimian left New York, never to return.

Back in Moscow, he became the chief of Soviet intelligence operations against the United States.

A successful interrogation and prosecution of Ovakimian would have changed history. Not until the end of the decade did the FBI understand that he had served as the Soviet spy chief in New York and a leader of Soviet intelligence in North America since 1933; that he had established American espionage networks of safe houses, recruiters, and couriers; that his rings ran throughout the United States, Mexico, and Canada. Though Stalin's purges had torn Soviet intelligence apart in the 1930s, Ovakimian had endured.

Nor was this the only lost chance to trace and trap the leaders of Soviet espionage in America. Shortly before his arrest, the FBI had trailed Ovakimian to a meeting with Jacob Golos, a middle-aged travel agent who promoted trips to Russia in the 1930s. Golos had been convicted of passport fraud and a foreign-registration act violation only fourteen months before; he had received a $500 fine and a suspended sentence. The FBI did not know, and would not know for years, that Golos was among the highest-ranking members of the Communist Party in America and a linchpin connecting Soviet intelligence to the American Communist underground.

Before he returned to Moscow, Ovakimian had been handing off control of his networks of American agents and couriers. Their names would be world-famous one day.

On May 5, 1941, the same day that the FBI arrested Ovakimian, the Japanese ambassador in Washington, Kichisaburo Nomura, an old friend of President Roosevelt's, received a bulletin from the Foreign Ministry in Tokyo: "It appears almost certain that the United States government is reading your code messages."

This startling intelligence came from the Germans. For six months, the army and the navy had been deciphering and decoding Japanese diplomatic cable traffic encrypted in a system called Purple. The intelligence derived from the decryptions was code-named Magic.

On May 20, the Japanese ambassador replied that he had discovered that the United States was indeed reading "some of our codes." But he did not know which ones. Incautiously, and inexplicably, Japan continued to use the Purple system. The Magic decryptions went on. They made bone-chilling reading—for the very few Americans authorized to read them. Among those cleared for Magic were the president, the secretaries of war and state, and the chiefs of army and navy intelligence. Those not cleared included Rear Admiral Husband J. Kimmel, the commander of the Pacific Fleet; Lieutenant General Walter J. Short, the army commander in Hawaii; and J. Edgar Hoover.

The failure to analyze Magic and turn its secret information into a plan of action would prove fatal. Collecting intelligence was one thing. Coordinating it—connecting the dots—was quite another. The army did not tell the navy what it knew. The navy did not tell the army. Neither told Hoover.

FDR had said that he wanted the field of intelligence divided. It was, and so it would remain for many years.

By May 1941, Magic had revealed that the Japanese had started to create an elaborate intelligence network in the Western Hemisphere in anticipation of a global war. Orders from Tokyo to Washington commanded a nationwide effort to gather political, economic, and military intelligence using "U.S. citizens of foreign extraction (other than Japanese), aliens (other than Japanese), communists, Negroes, labor union members, and anti-Semites" with access to American government, scientific, manufacturing, and transportation centers.

"In the event of U.S. participation in the war, our intelligence set-up will be moved to Mexico, making that country the nerve center of our intelligence net," the orders continued. "In anticipation of such an eventuality, set up facilities for a U.S.-Mexico international intelligence net . . . which will cover Brazil, Argentina, Chile, and Peru." Reports flowing back to Tokyo from Japanese spies and secret agents in America during May 1941 covered the movement of American ships and planes over the Pacific, plans to infiltrate military manufacturing plants, and attempts to make spies out of second-generation Japanese Americans who served in the United States Army. By summer's end, Tokyo was seeking intelligence on the correlation of American forces in the Pacific, including the location of American warships and aircraft carriers based at Pearl Harbor.

The FBI, the army, and the navy each possessed bits and pieces of this intelligence puzzle. No one put the pieces together. None of them foresaw an attack against American bases in the Pacific. Their eyes were fixed in the opposite direction.

On May 27, 1941, President Roosevelt declared an "unlimited national emergency," based in great part on the threat of a Nazi attack on the Americas. He spoke from the White House, surrounded by ambassadors and ministers from throughout the Western Hemisphere.

"What we face is cold, hard fact," the president said.

"The first and fundamental fact is that what started as a European war has developed, as the Nazis always intended it should develop, into a world war for world domination," FDR continued. "It is unmistakably apparent to all of us that, unless the advance of Hitlerism is forcibly checked now, the Western Hemisphere will be within range of the Nazi weapons of destruction." Nazi torpedoes were sinking merchant ships throughout the Atlantic Ocean. "Control or occupation by Nazi forces of any of the islands of the Atlantic," FDR said, threatened "the ultimate safety of the continental United States itself."

The president warned that Hitler could soon control "the island outposts of the New World—the Azores and Cape Verde Islands." The Cape Verde islands were "seven hours' distance from Brazil by bomber or troop-carrying planes," and they lay along key shipping routes across the South Atlantic. "The war is approaching the brink of the Western Hemisphere itself," he said. "It is coming very close to home. . . . The safety of American homes even in the center of this our own country has a very definite relationship to the continued safety of homes in Nova Scotia or Trinidad or Brazil."

FDR could not have been more blunt: "I merely repeat what is already in the Nazi book of world conquest. They plan to treat the Latin American nations as they are now treating the Balkans. They plan then to strangle the United States of America."

Hoover knew that a Nazi network was alive and well somewhere in Latin America, and that it could penetrate the United States unless the SIS succeeded in its mission. The need for intelligence on the Axis in the Western Hemisphere had never been more urgent. But success seemed unlikely for the men of the SIS.

Hoover's agents abroad reported little except "rumors, etc.," the secret history recounts. Those rumors came from "professional informants" who "could earn money by furnishing information of an intelligence nature. Their information was never investigated or checked for accuracy." The con artists found the SIS men easy pickings: "Ordinarily they were shrewd enough to realize quite early in the game that they could increase their earnings and the sale price of their information, the more startling its nature."

They became "so enthusiastic with regard to the money to be made from this sort of thing that they engaged in seeking out Americans and British on a somewhat wholesale basis, always striving to enlist new clients and new customers for their thriving trade." It took months, sometimes years, to sort out fact from fiction, for "the information furnished by the sources was, of course, not always fictitious," the secret history explains with the wisdom of hindsight. "As a matter of fact, the information was frequently based upon considerable truth. It was also upon occasion manufactured out of whole cloth and all kinds of forgeries, fraudulent enemy codes, etc., were being foisted off not only on Bureau representatives, but also on United States Military Attachés, United States Naval Attachés and other allied intelligence representatives in Latin America, including the British, in return for substantial payments of money."

"I'LL WIRE MY RESIGNATION TONIGHT"

A similar scam heralded the arrival of William J. "Wild Bill" Donovan as America's new intelligence majordomo.

They didn't call him Wild Bill for nothing. Donovan had a hundred ideas a day, of which ten might be brilliant. The president liked his derring-do. Like Roosevelt, he was an aficionado of foreign intelligence, enamored by espionage. He had wandered into the field of spying after a failed career in politics, and he was largely self-taught. But he thought himself an expert, and by American standards, he was.

He had been pushing the president hard to establish his own spy service. On June 10, 1941, Donovan had proposed that he take charge of a "central enemy intelligence organization" overseeing the FBI, army intelligence, and navy intelligence. He would mesh the machinery of American intelligence, get it humming, unify its work, synthesize its secrets, and report the results directly to the president.

FDR had sent him twice to London as an emissary. He had met with Prime Minister Churchill, British intelligence chief Stuart Menzies, and the British navy's intelligence director, Rear Admiral John Godfrey. The British enthralled him (and they paid for his second trip). He sent a four-page report to his close friend and fellow Republican warhorse, the new secretary of the navy, Frank Knox, describing the British intelligence system, much as Hoover had done one month before, but in far more glowing words. Hoover had his own relationships with the British intelligence service, but he kept them at arm's length. Donovan, by contrast, was being recruited by experts.

Donovan had reworked his intelligence plans at his home in New York, with strong and constant encouragement from William Stephenson, the British intelligence officer who ran American operations from an office in Rockefeller Center. Two British acquaintances looked over Donovan's shoulder, making helpful suggestions: Admiral Godfrey and his aide, Commander Ian Fleming, later the creator of the most famous fictional spy of his generation, James Bond.

Donovan's ambitions had the unusual effect of uniting the FBI, army intelligence, and navy intelligence: Hoover and his military counterparts stood foursquare against him. They signed a formal statement to the War Department calling Donovan's idea a serious detriment to national security. They said "the resultant super-Intelligence Agency would be far too cumbersome and complicated."

On July 5, 1941, Hoover's rage over Donovan's rise was recorded in a telephone conversation with Vincent Astor. Astor was still playing his role as "coordinator of intelligence" in New York and underwriting the undercover work of the SIS. He had criticized Hoover's work in Latin America, having heard the scuttlebutt from South America.

Hoover thought Astor and Donovan wanted to overthrow him. He taped the call:

HOOVER: About this idea of having a new Director come into the Bureau . . . I think as you probably know this job doesn't mean that much to me anyway.

ASTOR: Why, sure it does, Edgar. You've got as good a job as there is—

HOOVER: And it's a terrible headache and if anybody wants it . . . they can have it merely for the asking because I am not very keen about it anyway.

ASTOR: Well, Edgar, I don't think you should talk about giving up your job just at a time—the situation of—the country is in now—

HOOVER: Right. That's the only thing that has held me . . . If they want Colonel Donovan to come in or they want you to come in . . . Hell, I'll wire my resignation tonight if that's the way the President feels about it. . . . It doesn't make one damn bit of difference to me. . . . The job doesn't mean enough to me.

Hoover had been in genuine fear for his job for months. He had made enemies in high places.

The first lady, Eleanor Roosevelt, was outraged when the FBI began checking the political background of her social secretary, Edith Helm. She wrote a personal letter to Hoover: "This type of investigation seems to me to smack too much of the Gestapo methods."

Members of Roosevelt's cabinet were unnerved after the FBI ruined Undersecretary of State Sumner Welles, FDR's favorite foreign-policy man and a leading architect of his Latin America strategies. The Bureau had conducted a lengthy investigation into his homosexuality, revealed in full when Welles, intoxicated, tried to fellate a Pullman porter on a passenger train.

Hoover's reputation was founded in great part on the power of his secret surveillance. People respected him, but some simply feared him, and a fair number despised him. Hoover knew it.

Hoover told his right-hand man at the FBI, Clyde Tolson, that there was "a movement to remove me as Director." He was right: Donovan was a force behind it. Donovan and Hoover had hated one another heartily since 1924, when Donovan briefly served as Hoover's superior at the Justice Department. Hoover had fought him at Justice, successfully opposed Donovan's subsequent bid to become attorney general, and decried the idea of any secret intelligence service under Donovan's command.

Hoover believed that Donovan was a dishonest and dangerous man, and he spread rumors that Donovan was a Communist sympathizer. Donovan believed that Hoover was a failure at foreign intelligence, and he spread rumors that Hoover was a secret homosexual.

Hoover had been the subject of those rumors since at least 1937—the year that the Bureau began its long-running efforts to root out homosexuals in government. The innuendo is probably the most famous aspect of Hoover's life today.

The one thing everyone seems to know about Hoover is that he had sexual relations with his constant companion Clyde Tolson. The idea was imprinted in the public mind long ago, in a book by a British journalist that included indelible descriptions of Hoover in drag. It would be fascinating if it were true. But it is almost surely false. The allegation rests on third-hand hearsay from highly unreliable sources. Not a shred of evidence supports the notion that Hoover ever had sex with Tolson or with any other human being. They were personally and professionally inseparable, Hoover left Tolson his worldly possessions in his will, and there are photographs of the two men together that can be read as revealing human feelings deeper than fondness. One of Hoover's biographers called their relationship a sexless marriage, and perhaps that was close to the truth. But no one who knew Hoover personally or professionally believed anything beyond that.

"He abhorred homosexuality," said Cartha "Deke" DeLoach, a loyal Hoover lieutenant for many years. "That's why so many homosexuals were dismissed by the Bureau." If Hoover was himself a repressed homosexual whose secret frustrations soured into fury against his enemies, his inner rages were known to no one.

"I HAVE IN MY POSSESSION A SECRET MAP"

Hoover did not lose his job, nor did he lose his nerve to fight Donovan. But on July 11, 1941, the president named Wild Bill the national "Coordinator of Information," giving him "authority to collect and analyze" any and all intelligence bearing on national security. Having divided the field of American intelligence, FDR now fragmented it.

The British intelligence officer William Stephenson cabled London: "You can imagine how relieved I am after months of battle and jockeying in Washington that our man is in position." His choice of words bears attention. British intelligence did regard Donovan as their man, and it used him in pursuit of its highest goal in the desperate months of 1941: to get the United States into the war.

"I have in my possession a secret map made in Germany by Hitler's government—by the planners of the new world order," the president announced in a nationally broadcast speech on October 27, 1941. "It is a map of South America and a part of Central America, as Hitler proposes to reorganize it. Today in this area there are fourteen separate countries. The geographical experts of Berlin, however, have ruthlessly obliterated all existing boundary lines; and have divided South America into five vassal states, bringing the whole continent under their domination. And they have also so arranged it that the territory of one of these new puppet states includes the Republic of Panama and our great life line—the Panama Canal."

"That is his plan," FDR said. "This map makes clear the Nazi design not only against South America but against the United States itself."

The president got the secret map from Wild Bill Donovan. Donovan got it from his good friend Bill Stephenson, the British station chief in New York. And what was the source of the secret map? One of Stephenson's top lieutenants, H. Montgomery Hyde, claimed it had been purloined by British intelligence from a courier of the German embassy in Rio de Janeiro. "The President was greatly impressed," Hyde wrote. "The discovery of the map was convincing proof of Germany's intentions in Latin America and came as a considerable shock to all good citizens of the United States." But it was a fake, manufactured by British intelligence. The ploy, calculated to help draw the United States into the war in Europe, remained a secret for decades.

The President had fractured the field of intelligence. One result was a false map of the world. Another was surprise attack.

13

LAW OF WAR

WHEN JAPAN ATTACKED the United States at Pearl Harbor on Sunday, December 7, 1941, Hoover had his war plans ready. His agents had been gathering intelligence on political suspects in America for months.

The new attorney general, Francis Biddle, started signing orders for the detention of 3,846 German, Italian, and Japanese aliens. Hoover and his men already had started rounding up hundreds of people deemed most dangerous, warrants be damned. They had identified the suspects by any means necessary, including black-bag jobs. FBI agent Morton Chiles had broken into the apartment of a suspected German sympathizer, stolen his address book, and then fled in a hurry when the suspect returned home. Chiles dropped it into a mailbox; the post office turned it over to the FBI the next day.

"It was illegal. It was burglary," Chiles said. But "I put 114 people in a concentration camp" based on the names in that book.

Hoover did not endorse the president's orders for the incarceration of the 112,000 Japanese and Japanese Americans who were carted off to camps after Pearl Harbor. He did not want people imprisoned on the basis of race. He wanted them investigated and, if necessary, jailed for their allegiances.

The president expanded Hoover's powers in wartime. Hoover took the responsibility of conducting background investigations into the reputations of every applicant for a government job. He began to work with the passport and immigration authorities to control America's borders, airports, and railway stations. He had to secure hundreds of factories making war materiel. He was charged with censorship of the American press. Hoover and his men started opening first-class mail in New York and Washington, as well as the telegrams and cables sent by Western Union, the

International Telephone and Telegraph Company, and the Radio Corporation of America.

In the first months of the war, as American soldiers, sailors, and airmen began to fight and die in North Africa, Western Europe, and the South Pacific, the FBI battled at home and abroad against the threat of spies and saboteurs.

Two German submarines left their base in Lorient, France, in the last days of May 1942. The first sub, carrying four Nazi saboteurs dressed in the uniforms of the German marines, landed on the beach at Amagansett, Long Island, on the night of June 13. The second, carrying four more Nazi agents, had set its bearings for Jacksonville, Florida.

The eight infiltrators, all Germans, had lived for years in the United States. They were recruited for their ability to speak unaccented English, their knowledge of American cities, and their stated willingness to blow up bridges, tunnels, railway stations, department stores, and military plants. They were equipped with waterproof cases containing high explosives, bombs molded and shaped to resemble lumps of coal, primers, fuses, detonators, forged Social Security cards, and roughly $180,000 in cash. They were under the control of an Abwehr lieutenant named Walter Kappe, who had lived and worked in the United States from 1925 to 1937. He had been the chief of propaganda at the German-American Bund, the premier organization of American fascists and Nazi sympathizers. Returning to Germany, he served Hitler by organizing international spy rings.

George Dasch was the team leader in the sub that landed on Long Island. Dasch had fought in the German army during World War I as a fourteen-year-old child soldier. He first came to the United States as a stowaway on a ship at the age of nineteen. He had served a year as a private in the United States Army, married an American woman, and worked as a waiter in and around New York. His loyalties were divided. He had applied for American citizenship, but he did not complete his application nor swear allegiance to the United States.

Dasch and his fellow saboteurs landed on the beach around midnight, and they were instantly spotted by a United States Coast Guard patrol. Guardsman John Cullen saw four men struggling with a raft and he heard them speaking German. One of the men was carrying a gun. Cullen retreated, returning at daybreak with a Coast Guard team. They quickly dug up a buried cache including bombs, cigarettes, and brandy, and they called the police, who called the FBI. Meanwhile, the German team caught the

6:00 A.M. train into New York, where Dasch and his partner, Ernest Burger, checked into a midtown hotel. Burger was a naturalized American citizen. He had lived in Detroit and Milwaukee, where he had worked as a machinist from 1927 to 1933. Returning to Germany in 1933, he had loyally served as a Nazi propagandist until he was arrested by the Gestapo in 1940 during a political purge. He served seventeen months in a concentration camp before he was recruited by the Abwehr as a saboteur.

Dasch and Burger had a long talk in their hotel. They had grave doubts about the mission. Their loyalties to the Third Reich were wavering. The suitcase full of cash was tempting. Burger wanted to take the money and run. Dasch said he had a better idea. He called the New York field office of the FBI.

The agent who answered the phone thought Dasch was crazy. The New York office had a three-drawer file cabinet, called the nut box, filled with the records from years of conversations with drunks and cranks. The FBI man made a note of the call, and then he tossed it in the box.

On June 18, Dasch became desperate. He took a train to Washington, went to FBI headquarters, and demanded to see J. Edgar Hoover. As Dasch told his story, he had to open his suitcase and toss $82,350 in cash on the table before anyone took him seriously. Dasch talked for the next eight days. He gave the FBI all the information it needed to immediately arrest the three remaining Germans in New York, and he knew enough to help the Bureau round up the second unit, which had landed in Florida. By June 27, 1942, all eight of the German saboteurs were under arrest.

"High treason"

Hoover shaped the story of the Nazi saboteurs. The way he told it to the president and, eventually, the press, Dasch never defected, Dasch never walked into FBI headquarters, Dasch never told all. Writing to Roosevelt, Hoover claimed that Dasch had been apprehended by the FBI on June 22, which was four days after he turned himself in.

"Nothing was said about Dasch's long, minute, rambling confession," Attorney General Biddle wrote twenty years later, "and it was generally concluded that a particularly brilliant FBI agent, probably attending the school in sabotage where the eight had been trained, had been able to be on the inside, and made regular reports to America."

The president, the attorney general, and Hoover convened one of the most extraordinary military tribunals in the history of the United States. Its conduct echoes down to this day. On June 30, 1942, two days after the Dasch story hit the newspapers, Attorney General Biddle received a note from FDR, reprinted here with Biddle's comments in brackets:

I have not had an opportunity to talk with you about the prosecution of the eight saboteurs landed from two German submarines nor have I recently read all the statutes which apply [Note the Rooseveltian touch, as if to say: I know all about law, and anyway I don't have to read the statutes: this is War.]

It is my thought, however:

1. That the two American citizens are guilty of high treason. This being war-time, it is my inclination to try them by court-martial. I do not see how they can offer any adequate defense. Surely they are as guilty as it is possible to be and it seems to be the death penalty is almost obligatory.

2. In the case of the other six, who I take it are German . . . I can see no difference [i.e., don't split hairs, Mr. Attorney General].

F.D.R.

But the laws of the United States and the rulings of the Supreme Court stood in the way. In a Civil War case, the Court had held that a civilian could not be tried in a military court unless martial law had been declared and the civilian courts closed. Biddle had to find a way around that ruling. He told the president to appoint a special military commission. It would run a secret trial against the saboteurs under military law. When this decision came to the Supreme Court for a review, as it inevitably would, Biddle would argue that enemy combatants, waging a secret war against America, could be tried and punished by a military tribunal under the laws of war. The same argument would be raised in America's twenty-first-century war on terror.

FDR signed an executive order creating the military commission immediately. The secret trial began the next week, with seven army generals presiding. Armored vans flanked by soldiers with machine guns brought the prisoners from the District of Columbia jail to a closed chamber on the fifth floor of the Justice Department, a small lecture hall that served, in ordinary times, as a classroom for FBI agents.

Biddle led the prosecution. Hoover sat at his right side, passing him dossiers on each defendant, summaries of the evidence, transcripts of their statements and confessions under arrest. Dasch and Burger were the last to testify in the two-week trial. Each made full confessions; each said he had had no intent to carry out his mission of destruction.

On August 3, the seven generals reached a unanimous verdict. It was up to the president to pass sentence. He already had decided that death was "almost obligatory." And that was the sentence he pronounced. But Biddle persuaded him to commute Burger's penalty to life and Dasch's to thirty years. The attorney general thought that their confessions had value—and he knew that the FBI could never have made the case without Dasch.

Starting at seven o'clock on the morning of August 8, General Cox informed the saboteurs of their fates. One by one, the six condemned men were led to the death row of the District jail, served a breakfast of bacon and eggs, sent to the barber to have their heads shaved, and, starting at one minute after noon, seated in the electric chair, fitted with a rubber mask and a steel helmet, and electrocuted. They were buried in the potter's field at the edge of the nation's capital; six planks of wood with no names served as their headstones.

Dasch and Burger went to the federal penitentiary in Atlanta; Dasch to solitary confinement, where no one could hear his story. Barely seven weeks had passed from the day of his defection to the date of execution.

The Supreme Court had convened before the verdict to weigh whether the president had the power to create secret military tribunals in cases of sabotage and terror. But the proceedings had been so secret that no record was presented to the Court. The case deeply troubled Chief Justice Harlan Fiske Stone—the secrecy of the trial and the verdict, the rules that governed the commission, the president's having the power to put the defendants to death. But it was his opinion to write. And he wrote carefully. *Ex Parte Quirin,* named after one of the executed German saboteurs, remained the last word on the subject of military tribunals for the next sixty years.

The Court could not "define with meticulous care the ultimate boundaries of the jurisdiction of military tribunals to try persons according to the law of war," said Stone's opinion, dated October 29. Nor could it write the rules that could create a constitutional basis for a military commission. That was up to Congress. But in this case, the government did have the power to try the defendants as unlawful enemy combatants.

The Supreme Court had been painted into a corner by the president and the FBI. The six condemned men were already dead. What if the Court had found the proceedings unconstitutional? Or what if it had discovered that Hoover had promised Dasch freedom in exchange for a confession? As Chief Justice Stone wrote in a private memorandum for the record, the Supreme Court would then be placed "in the unenviable position of having stood by and allowed six men to go to their death without making it plain to all concerned—including the President—that it had left undecided a question on which counsel strongly relied to secure petitioners' liberty."

That question was whether the commission was constructed lawfully by the president. It would go unanswered until after the United States confronted a new kind of enemy combatant in 2001.

The Nazi saboteur case brought two windfalls for the FBI, one public, one secret. The publicity was great: the American people universally believed that the Bureau had broken the case by itself. They knew nothing about the defection and confession of George Dasch. The FBI's public relations machine prepared a Congressional Medal of Honor citation for Hoover. Though the medal never came, the case could not have been a better boon for the Bureau's image.

The second bonanza from the Nazi saboteur case was the FBI's deepening understanding of how the *Rueckwanderer* system worked. The Bureau, investigating the past lives of the saboteurs in the United States, found that three of them had established their allegiance to the Third Reich by buying the Nazi marks at banks in New York and Chicago. Their applications to exchange dollars for marks let German intelligence know who they were, where they lived, and how to reach them. The Abwehr had paid their passage back to Germany and trained them as sabotage agents.

Thousands of German Americans had bought the marks and gone to Germany. How many had returned to the United States as Nazi spies?

In the fall of 1942 the FBI intensified a national investigation, one of the biggest and most complex cases it had ever handled. The Bureau eventually interrogated 997 German aliens in the United States; 441 were detained or jailed on orders from the attorney general for their allegiance to Germany. The case involved hundreds of agents, tens of thousands of documents, and the biggest bank in America: Chase National.

In New York, Percy Foxworth, now Hoover's assistant director for national security affairs, took charge of the case. He obtained documents suggesting lucrative financial connections among American bankers, multinational companies doing underground business with Germany, the

German-American Bund, and the Nazi government. Precisely how Fox-worth got his hands on the documents was a sensitive matter.

The FBI had recruited an assistant cashier and a midlevel manager in the foreign department of Chase's main office in New York. At night, FBI agents sneaked in and spent hours upon hours combing through the foreign department's files. These searches were conducted without warrants; they fell somewhere in the gray area between a black-bag burglary and an intelligence investigation. Either way, they were illegal.

The FBI had a theory that Chase was acting on behalf of the German government in violation of the Foreign Agents Registration Act, the same law Justice had used to indict suspected spies. This was more than a thorny political issue. It was tantamount to a charge of collaborating with Hitler.

The charge could not be proved. The bank outmaneuvered the Bureau. Chase hired John Cahill, a very knowledgeable lawyer who had been the federal prosecutor in charge of the grand jury investigating the case. He was well aware that the FBI had gathered evidence against Chase illegally. Cahill knew enough to turn the tables. He threatened to put the FBI on trial. Its black-bag jobs would be revealed if the case proceeded, and that was a cost Hoover would not pay. The politically explosive investigation collapsed.

"WE HAD NO ONE TO GIVE US COUNSEL"

The FBI suffered another misfortune that winter. On January 15, 1943, Percy Foxworth died when his plane crashed in the jungles of Dutch Guiana, on the northeast edge of South America. Foxworth and a fellow FBI agent were en route to Morocco, where Roosevelt and Churchill were holding a war council. Foxworth had been assigned by the War and State departments to interrogate an American citizen and alleged Nazi collaborator who had been arrested in Casablanca as a potential threat to the president.

His death was a heavy blow to the Special Investigative Service, which by 1943 had grown to 583 FBI agents but was still struggling to achieve its mission.

Hoover tried repeatedly to rid himself of the SIS. "I do strongly recommend that the FBI be relieved of all responsibility for the handling of any special intelligence work in the Western Hemisphere, and that this responsibility be completely and fully placed upon Colonel Donovan's organization," he wrote to the new chief of army intelligence, Major General George

Veazey Strong: "I am most anxious and willing to withdraw entirely and completely from the Latin Americas."

There are few examples of Hoover offering to cede power, certainly not to a political enemy like Donovan. He did so only when he sensed the risk of embarrassment. And the SIS was a ceaseless source of chagrin.

"You must remember that we were starting from absolute scratch in the intelligence business," said John Walsh, an FBI agent on the national security beat who went to Medellín, Colombia, for the SIS in 1943. "We had no one to give us counsel on this thing."

The SIS assignments in Colombia were to hunt Nazi spies and shut down the clandestine radio networks that linked espionage agents and officers to their masters in Germany. But Walsh quickly discovered upon his arrival in Colombia that he was at a loss for work. "All the German aliens had been arrested by that time," he remembered. "Colombia had declared war on Germany and they had rounded up all the Germans.

"I spent a lot of time at the country club," he said. "I really didn't have much in the way of an assignment."

The FBI would claim in later years that the work of the SIS had led to the arrests of 389 Axis agents and the destruction of 24 Nazi spy-ring radio stations, mostly accomplished in 1942 and 1943. Hoover stole the credit that rightfully belonged to the Radio Intelligence Division (RID) of the Federal Communications Commission, the New Deal bureaucracy that oversaw broadcasting in the United States. Hoover had a knife out for the chairman of the FCC, James Lawrence Fly; the two fought for years over the FBI's power to plant wiretaps.

The civilians of the Radio Intelligence Division intercepted clandestine German communications with spies in Latin America. They worked with American embassy officials and local police to shut the networks down. In 1942, the RID picked up a plan to sink the *Queen Mary*, which was carrying ten thousand American and Canadian troops to war, and led the Brazilian police to arrest more than two hundred German spies. That one case alone accounted for half the Axis spy arrests claimed by the FBI and the SIS in Latin America throughout all of World War II.

The FBI's secret history recounts: "An Agent could not be expected to produce any worthwhile information until after he had served on assignment for a number of months at the very minimum in order to learn local customs, the language, etc."

But more than a few months abroad proved too much for many FBI agents. Scores if not hundreds resigned from their undercover work with the SIS or requested transfers home, "thoroughly disgusted" and "completely disillusioned when faced with something entirely different from the glamorous picture envisioned by them before undertaking the assignment." They were "subjected to all kinds of ridicule" by American soldiers and sailors throughout Latin America asking "why they were not in uniform and were trying to sell soap, magazines, or perform some other ostensibly unimportant and non-war connected job." State Department diplomats and military attachés delighted in "uncovering, exposing and embarrassing the Bureau's undercover agents," the secret history continues, calling them slackers and draft dodgers. "Unfortunately," the secret history records, "the Bureau's undercover representatives were in large measure young, healthy, intelligent, personable Americans of draft age and obvious military potentiality operating under weak and frequently illogical covers."

SIS men were called worse names, like turncoat and traitor. Trying hard "to obtain the confidence of pro-Nazi individuals and thus obtain information from within pro-Nazi ranks," they were "engaging in what appeared to local United States State Department, Military and Naval officials to be extremely questionable and suspicious activities and associations," the secret history recounts. "Many of the men also became suspected by the British, some legitimately and others apparently solely due to the fact that the British suspected them of being Bureau representatives and desired to expose them by embarrassment."

All his life, Hoover had a rule: Don't embarrass the Bureau. He had to repair the ill repute and lowly status of the FBI abroad. His confidant at the State Department, Assistant Secretary of State Adolf A. Berle, came up with an ingenious solution.

A new position began to open for the FBI in American embassies throughout the Western Hemisphere: the "legal attaché." Like the military attaché and the naval attaché, the post held diplomatic status, with the attendant rank, perquisites of office, and protections afforded by the embassy. The legal attaché was required to keep the American ambassador informed about what the FBI was doing in his country. He was ordered to work in harmony with his army and navy counterparts, if possible. He was, in theory, "the responsible American official with regard to clandestine intelligence matters, particularly in the field of subversive activities," the secret history records.

The legal attaché system salvaged the FBI's foreign intelligence service.

Hoover put the attachés to work making friends with the police chiefs and internal security ministers of Latin America. Wining, dining, and sometimes bribing the chief of police—preferably, the chief of the secret police—was a far more effective means of gathering intelligence than posing as magazine stringers and soap salesmen.

Liaison programs established by the legal attachés became the cutting edge of FDR's Good Neighbor Policy in wartime. They grew with great speed, driven by the flow of American money and power and authority from United States embassies to Latin American presidents and police forces. Legal attachés and ambassadors persuaded politically insecure Latin American presidents that it would be wise to have an FBI man as a paid security adviser for protection. The adviser, of course, served double duty as a spy.

From the summer of 1943 onward, FBI liaisons made it "feasible to obtain almost any type of investigative assistance and information from the police in practically every country in Latin America," the secret history recounts. Police chiefs and interior ministers, some of them now on the FBI's payroll, provided Hoover's men with access to intelligence from post offices, telephone and telegraph company networks, airlines and shipping companies, customs offices and a rich variety of government agencies— "including in many places the Presidential Palace."

Every police chief and every president in Latin America had one thing in common with Hoover, if only one: anticommunism. Alliances built by the legal attachés during World War II lasted as long as there were leftists to fight in Latin America.

By the summer of 1943, German espionage in the Western Hemisphere was dying out. The danger of an Axis invasion was disappearing. As the tide of the war against Hitler began turning, American leaders started to envision the world after the war.

Hoover and a handful of like-minded men in Washington looked over the horizon and saw Stalin and the Red Army marching westward. They saw their battle would not end when fascism was defeated. They saw that the war on communism would go on.

But at this moment, Hoover faced the greatest challenge to his authority to fight that war.

14

THE MACHINE OF DETECTION

E VER SINCE WORLD WAR I, Hoover had been hunting for an under-ground Communist conspiracy against the United States. After a quarter century of investigation, he finally saw the first earth-shaking evidence. In the spring and summer of 1943, the FBI secretly recorded conversations that would change the course of history.

The Bureau had been spying on Steve Nelson, the local Communist Party leader in Oakland, California, since 1940. In May 1941, the special agent in charge in San Francisco had placed Nelson on the Custodial Detention list, the secret index of Americans and aliens whom the FBI judged worthy of military detention in a time of national emergency.

Hoover convinced Attorney General Francis Biddle that a wiretap on Nelson would be "a very likely source of information concerning the policies of the Communist Party." The FBI had bugged Nelson's home and tapped his telephone since February 1942. The files on Nelson revealed that he was a tough guy with an eighth-grade education. His real last name was Mesarosh. He was a Slav who had come to the United States on a false passport in 1920, joined the Communist Party in 1925, won nineteen votes as a candidate for Congress in Pennsylvania in 1936, and shed blood in the Spanish Civil War in 1937. He served on the national committee of the Party, and he skulked around with graduate students from the University of California at Berkeley.

On the night of March 29, 1943, the FBI recorded a conversation between Nelson and a man named Joe, aka "Scientist X." Joe was a committed Communist and a physics student. He described a project at the Berkeley Radiation Laboratory dedicated to enriching uranium. He said thousands of people worked on the project in Los Alamos, New Mexico, and Oak Ridge, Tennessee.

Nelson took notes. A few days later, the FBI trailed him to a meeting on the grounds of a nearby hospital, where he passed some papers to a man who worked at the Soviet consulate in San Francisco.

On April 10, 1943, the FBI recorded Nelson talking with a Soviet diplomat named Vassili Zarubin, aka Zubilin. The FBI did not know it at the time, but he was the chief of Soviet espionage in the United States.

From the start, though, they knew he was *somebody* important. "It was obvious that Zubilin was in control of the intelligence organization," the FBI reported after it transcribed the conversation. The Soviet was counting out money, apparently paying Nelson for "placing Communist Party members and Comintern agents in industries engaged in secret war production."

On May 7, Hoover sent a report to the White House saying that the government of the Soviet Union was using the American Communist Party to create a spy network in the United States.

The FBI saw, for the first time, in real time, a link between Soviet intelligence and American Communists. It was everything Hoover had ever feared, and worse. Soviet espionage was aiming to steal a secret so highly classified that Hoover himself knew next to nothing about it—not yet. A few weeks later, Hoover was informed for the first time about the Manhattan Project, the secret nationwide program to build an atomic bomb. Then he learned about the United States Army's effort to read the encrypted cables used by Soviet spies and diplomats in their communications with Moscow.

It can take years to build a secret operation—to invent a new weapon, to create or destroy an espionage network, to crack a code. Now Hoover opened up two intelligence investigations that would consume the FBI for a decade. One was called CINRAD, short for Communist Infiltration of Radiation Laboratory. The other was called COMRAP, Comintern Apparatus. Both aimed to gain a grasp of the Soviet espionage networks in the United States. Starting in May 1943, roughly fifty FBI agents in New York and fifty more in Washington began trying to track and tap the Soviet spies who posed as diplomats and government purchasing agents at Amtorg, the Soviet trade mission. Shortly thereafter, Hoover sent 125 agents across the country, from New York to Chicago to San Francisco, to try to find the Soviet spies who worked under deep cover, without the protection of diplomatic immunity. The hunt at home would go on far longer than the war abroad.

"Like children lost in the woods"

FBI agents confronting Soviet espionage during World War II were "like children lost in the woods," the State Department's Lawrence Duggan, a Communist agent himself, told the Soviet intelligence officer who debriefed him in Washington. The FBI knew very little about the workings of Moscow's intelligence services. It had met Gaik Ovakimian, the Soviet espionage chief in New York, without understanding who he was. It had listened to Walter Krivitsky, a Soviet spy who defected, without understanding what he said.

The FBI was not incompetent or indifferent. It did not know what it did not know. Intelligence is a war in which the weapons are knowledge and foresight. Information is the most powerful force. If you have a spy in the enemy's camp, you can win a battle. If you know your enemy's mind, you can win a war.

The FBI had no reliable Soviet sources—and the government of the United States was not eager for a fight with the Soviets. Stalin was killing more Nazis than Roosevelt and Churchill combined. But if Americans who were collaborating with Soviet intelligence could be caught in the act of espionage, Hoover could use the powers of the Custodial Detention list to arrest them in secret, without a trial, and stick them in a military stockade for the duration of the war.

Then Attorney General Biddle found out about the list.

The courtly and patrician Biddle considered himself something of an expert on the subject of J. Edgar Hoover. He had studied the man from the start of the four years they worked side by side. He saw "a human side of Edgar Hoover with which he is not always credited. . . .

"Hoover's character interested me," he wrote many years later. "I sought to invite his confidence; and before long, lunching alone with me in a room adjoining my office, he began to reciprocate by sharing some of the extraordinarily broad knowledge of the intimate details of what my associates in the Cabinet did and said, of their likes and their dislikes, their weaknesses and associations . . . I confess that, within limits, I enjoyed hearing it."

Within his limits, Biddle admired many of the ways in which Hoover used his power at the FBI. The attorney general signed his share of wiretap orders, and he faced the wartime threats posed by America's enemies with all the laws at his command. But he was disturbed all his life by the secret operations of the FBI, "this great machine of detection with its ten million personal files" and "its obvious possibilities of misusing the trust it has won."

Biddle wanted no repeat of the 1920 Red raids on his watch. He had ordered the FBI to work with a new Justice Department office he created, the Special War Policies Unit. Civilian panels oversaw wartime detentions of enemy aliens—only aliens, not American citizens. Biddle kept the work under the rule of law throughout the war.

In the nineteen months since Pearl Harbor, the FBI had arrested 16,062 suspected foreign subversives. But roughly two-thirds of them, about 10,000 people, were released after the civilian panels deemed they were not a clear and present danger to the United States. As had happened a generation before, the FBI had swept up thousands of people who were innocent. The steady dismissal of these cases had made the attorney general inquire into the depth and the accuracy of the FBI's intelligence files.

On July 6, 1943, Biddle discovered that Hoover kept a list of Americans deemed deserving of military internment. He was aghast. No law allowed Hoover to have "a 'custodial detention' list of citizens," the attorney general told the director. He thought the secret files were themselves a danger to the United States.

The job of the FBI was "investigating the activities of persons who may have violated the law," the attorney general wrote in his order abolishing the program. "It is not aided in this work by classifying persons as to dangerousness. . . .

"It is now clear to me that this classification system is inherently unreliable," Biddle wrote to Hoover. "The evidence used for the purpose of making the classifications was inadequate; the standards applied to the evidence for the purpose of making the classifications were defective; and finally, the notion that it is possible to make a valid determination as to how dangerous a person is in the abstract and without reference to time, environment, and other relevant circumstances, is impractical, unwise, and dangerous."

The director tossed the order aside. He disobeyed it in secret. He did not tell the attorney general or anyone else outside the FBI what he was doing. He simply started calling the list the Security Index. Nothing else changed, except the secrecy surrounding the index. His decision stayed secret until after his death.

Hoover, of course, retained his unquestioned powers to place people under surveillance. That gave him broad authority to conduct intelligence investigations into the political beliefs of Americans. Among the thousands of people added to Hoover's Security Index during the war, the greatest number were American Communists—not merely Party members but people who wrote books or articles with Communist ideas, who spoke at Communist rallies, who went to meetings "where revolutionary preachings are given." The leaders of the German-American Bund and Italian Fascist organizations were on the list as well, along with homegrown American racists who belonged to groups like the Ku Klux Klan.

Hoover had standards: those who qualified for the list were people "opposed to the American way of life."

The attorney general wanted the FBI to focus on Axis agents. He did not think the time was ripe for a war on communism in America. "Hoover must have suspected that I would be too soft, particularly now that a war was on; too soft with Communists—so many liberals had not yet realized what the Communists were after," wrote Biddle. "Hoover . . . was clearly not reflective or philosophic. Edgar Hoover was primarily a man of immediate action."

Hoover had watched in frustration as the membership of the Communist Party, buoyed by America's alliance with Stalin, grew toward an all-time high of 80,000 card-carrying members during World War II. His orders to the field required the investigation of every last one of them.

On August 14, 1943, Hoover ordered his agents to intensify their search for suspects to be placed on the Security Index, and to ensure that the index was kept secret within the Bureau, hidden from the attorney general. The list of people "who may be dangerous or potentially dangerous to the public safety or internal security of the United States" was to be shared only with trusted military intelligence officers "on a strictly confidential basis." "Potentially dangerous" meant people who might have committed no crime beyond political disloyalty.

Generals are often accused of fighting the last war. Hoover was preparing to fight the next one.

Stalin was still America's most powerful military ally. And Wild Bill Donovan and his intelligence officers at the Office of Strategic Services wanted to work hand-in-glove with the Soviets. But Hoover now refocused the FBI's Security Index on "key figures" and "potential key figures" in the

Communist subversion of America, not just card-carrying Party members. Soon ten thousand people were listed in the index—almost all Communists and, to Hoover, potential Soviet spies.

The FBI would have to go it alone, or close to it, for the next two years. But the intelligence battles of the Cold War had begun.

15

ORGANIZING THE WORLD

S PYING ON THE SOVIETS required spying on Americans. Hoover spied hardest against his enemies within the government of the United States.

Hoover wrote to FDR's closest White House aide, Harry Hopkins, on February 10, 1944, warning him about Wild Bill Donovan's scheme to invite Soviet spies to America:

> I have just learned from a confidential but reliable source that a liaison arrangement has been perfected between the Office of Strategic Services and the Soviet Secret Police (NKVD) whereby officers will be exchanged between these services. The Office of Strategic Services is going to assign men to Moscow and in turn the NKVD will set up an office in Washington, D.C. . . .
>
> I think it is a highly dangerous and most undesirable procedure to establish in the United States a unit of the Russian Secret Service which has admittedly for its purpose the penetration into the official secrets of various government agencies . . .
>
> In view of the potential danger in this situation I wanted to bring it to your attention and I will advise you of any further information which I receive about the matter.
>
> Sincerely,
> J. Edgar Hoover

The problem was that the president himself had dispatched Donovan on his mission to Moscow. FDR had sent Donovan and the American ambassador, W. Averell Harriman, to meet with the Soviet foreign minister, Vyacheslav Molotov. They had gone to the Soviet intelligence headquarters on Dzerzhinsky Street, named after Lenin's chief of espionage and terror. They met with the chief of Soviet foreign intelligence, General Pavel Fitin, and his deputy. That deputy was Gaik Ovakimian, the same spy who had run Soviet intelligence operations in America for eight years before he was arrested by the FBI in New York and then released at the State Department's behest in the summer of 1941.

The four toasted the inauguration of the American station in Moscow and the Soviet station in Washington. Stalin swiftly gave his imprimatur.

On January 11, 1944, Donovan went to win FDR's approval. They sat in the Map Room, the intelligence center at the White House. Donovan pointed out the advantages of intelligence liaison with the Soviets in the war against Hitler, which were significant. As for the question of Soviet spying in America, he told the president: "They are already here."

The president ran Donovan's deal past the White House military chief of staff, Admiral William D. Leahy. Bad idea, Leahy said, and he bucked it up to the military chiefs. They told Hoover, and Hoover went to battle. He refused to let the Soviets set up a new intelligence station a few blocks from the White House. He suspected—correctly—that Donovan's OSS had been penetrated by the Soviets and that one of his top aides was spying for Stalin.

Hoover underscored the threat in a memo to the attorney general, entrusting Biddle with the highly confidential information that Soviet spies were inside Donovan's domain. Biddle pointed out the implications to the president. First, the Foreign Agents Registration Act would require the Soviet spies to file forms stating their identities. Second, those papers were documents that could be disclosed; public knowledge of the arrangement could have political consequences. And third, as Hoover had warned, the Soviets were trying to steal the biggest secrets of the government of the United States. Admiral Leahy formally told Donovan that the deal was off. Wild Bill had lost a major battle.

Now Hoover began to contemplate taking control of United States intelligence when the war was over. He saw himself as the commander in chief for anticommunism in America. The FBI, in partnership with the military, would protect the nation as it projected its power around the world.

Hoover now commanded 4,886 special agents backed by 8,305 support staff, a fivefold increase since 1940, with a budget three times bigger than before the war. The FBI devoted more than 80 percent of its money and people to national security. It was by far the strongest force dedicated to fighting the Communist threat.

By December 1944, Hoover had defined that threat as an international conspiracy in which the Soviet intelligence service worked with the American Communist Party to penetrate the American government and steal the secrets of its wartime military industries. The FBI already worked closely with British intelligence and security officers in London. As the Nazis retreated, FBI agents had set up shop in Moscow, Stockholm, Madrid, Lisbon, Rome, and Paris. FBI legal attachés established permanent offices at the American embassies in England, France, Spain, and Canada. Hoover's men investigated the threat of espionage inside embassy code rooms in England, Sweden, Spain, and Portugal; in Russia they looked into the sensitive question of whether the Soviet government was exploiting any part of $11 billion worth of lend-lease aid from the United States to steal American military secrets. In Ottawa, FBI men worked in liaison with the Royal Canadian Mounted Police. FBI attachés and their new friends among Latin American police and politicians were creating international networks for a war on communism.

As Hoover put it, "the system that has worked so successfully in the Western Hemisphere should be extended to a world-wide coverage." He had to deep-six the history of the struggles of the SIS as he set out his first proposals for taking the FBI global. Only its successes would be made known in Washington.

The FBI continued to find fragments of the immense puzzle of Soviet espionage. On September 29, 1944, FBI agents burglarized the New York apartment of a middle-aged man who worked at a record company selling Communist songs. He went by the name of Arthur Alexandrovich Adams, and he was a skilled mechanical engineer. He had probably come to the United States in the 1920s, and he may have been one of the first deep-cover Soviet spies in America. He was certainly the first one the FBI ever found.

The black-bag job produced a bonanza.

Adams had notebooks that made little sense to the FBI agents who saw them. "He was in possession of a document that talked about some type of water," FBI agent Donald Shannon, a member of the Bureau's Soviet espionage squad, said in an oral history interview six decades later. "We weren't sure of the information so we turned it over to the Atomic Energy Commission for evaluation." Upon expert review the notes revealed intimate knowledge of highly technical and deeply secret phases of the Manhattan Project. They included work on heavy water, a linchpin of secret research into the atomic bomb.

"We were informed that the person who had this certainly had some information on America's atomic research," Shannon said. Adams soon was indicted by a federal grand jury in New York under the foreign agents registration law—and the State Department ordered him deported.

Eighteen months had passed since the FBI's first clue that Stalin's spies were trying to steal the bomb. The second clue was now in hand.

Hoover understood in broad terms what the Manhattan Project was about. The War Department had told him about its own search for spies at Los Alamos. He began to realize that control of the bomb was not simply a matter of winning the war. It was about national survival after the war was won.

Not long before Pearl Harbor, Hoover and his aides had written about the wartime goals of British intelligence: "to be in a position at the end of the war to organize the world." Hoover thought that role rightfully belonged to the United States. The atomic bomb would be the key to its supremacy. And Hoover believed that only the FBI could protect the secrecy and the power of America's national security.

The final battles of the war still lay ahead. But Hoover had started his struggle for control of American intelligence. He set out to command the course of the Cold War for the government of the United States.

PART III

COLD WAR

*President Kennedy and his brother,
the attorney general, struggled to control
Hoover's power over secrets.*

16

NO GESTAPO

I N THE FIRST days of February 1945, President Roosevelt lived in the Livadia Palace, the summer home of the last czar of Russia, Nicholas II. The ruined villages of the Yalta Mountains lay around him, covered in snow, ravaged by war.

Roosevelt met Churchill and Stalin at Yalta to chart the course of the world after the war. They all believed, as Churchill said, that "the right to guide the course of history is the noblest prize of victory."

Back home, on February 9, the headlines in big-city daily papers owned by FDR's political archenemies read: PROJECT FOR U.S. SUPER-SPIES DISCLOSED . . . SUPER GESTAPO AGENCY . . . WOULD TAKE OVER FBI. There in black and white, word for word, was every inch of Wild Bill's blueprint for a worldwide intelligence agency. A follow-up story began: "The joint chiefs of staff have declared war on Brigadier General William J. Donovan."

Fifteen copies of Donovan's plan had circulated at the highest levels of the government; one copy went to the FBI. The likeliest source of the leak was the officer who ran the White House Map Room, FDR's intelligence center: Colonel Richard Park, Jr. The colonel had compiled a devastating report to the president on Donovan and the OSS. He had left FDR's side at Yalta and traveled throughout Europe and North Africa, interviewing army generals and intelligence officers in the field. Colonel Park owed his career to the chief of army intelligence, the imperious and devious General George Veazey Strong, who respected Hoover and despised Donovan. The leak likely came at the general's direction. Only one other person could have authorized it, and that was the president.

On April 4, 1945, FDR sent his last word on the future of American intelligence. Writing from Warm Springs, Georgia, where he had gone to rest his

weary body and soul, he ordered Donovan to convene his allies and enemies, and achieve an agreement. Eight days later, a cerebral hemorrhage
killed him at the age of sixty-six. Victory in Europe was four weeks away.

The word that the president was gone began reaching Washington at
about five o'clock on a beautiful spring afternoon. It spread quickly by telephone through the highest levels of the government.

When the phones started ringing, Attorney General Biddle was deep in
conversation with Secretary of State Edward R. Stettinius, Jr., and Navy
Secretary James V. Forrestal. They were about to weigh the merits of having
J. Edgar Hoover run a new national intelligence service.

When Hoover got the word about the president, he immediately called
for the FBI's files on Harry S. Truman.

The vice president had rushed to the White House from his traditional
five o'clock bourbon with his friends in an unmarked hideaway at the Capitol. After a long search for a Bible, Chief Justice Harlan Fiske Stone swore
him in as the new commander in chief of the most powerful nation on
earth. It was a moment of overwhelming sadness and fear. Truman said he
felt like the moon and the stars and the planets had fallen upon him. He
had served only eighty-two days as vice president; he had been a cog in the
Kansas City political machine before arriving in Washington as a senator
from Missouri. Truman came to the White House with a good deal of common sense, a fair dose of courage, and a capacity for making gut decisions,
including saying *no*. But he knew none of the secrets of the American government.

Friday the thirteenth of April 1945 was his first full day in office. He spent
the morning in the Oval Office with Secretary of War Henry L. Stimson
and Secretary of State Stettinius, his top military chiefs, and FDR's military
aide, Admiral Leahy, learning his first lessons in the command and control
of presidential power. Truman then went to the Map Room, where Colonel
Park handed over his report on the wartime performance of Wild Bill Donovan. It was a dagger, honed by Hoover and the army. It said that the officers of the OSS had done serious damage to the national security of the
United States; their incompetence made "their use as a secret intelligence
agency in the postwar world inconceivable." In a cover letter to Truman
marked TOP SECRET—a copy somehow found its way into Hoover's files—
Colonel Park advised the new president to take "drastic action" against the
OSS—"abolishing it altogether and transferring its better personnel where

they will do some good." It concluded: "General Donovan should be re-placed, above all."

The initiation of Harry Truman into the world of secret weapons, secret intelligence, and the secret operations of the United States began that day, a journey from innocence to experience.

"THIS MUST STOP"

Ten days passed before Hoover first saw Truman, in a short meeting at the White House on April 23. He made a bad impression on the president.

Hoover began to try to tell Truman about the secret world of the FBI. The president still did not know about the atomic bomb, much less the Soviet espionage plot to steal it. Nor did he yet know about the political warfare FDR had authorized with his imprimatur for Hoover's warrantless wiretapping, or about the FBI's operations overseas, or about Hoover's plans to expand them worldwide.

Truman quickly called Harry Vaughan into the meeting. Vaughan was one of his closest friends, going back to their service together in World War I. The president had picked Vaughan as his personal military aide and made him a brigadier general.

Truman said that in the future, when Hoover had something to tell the White House, he should say it to Harry Vaughan, and he left the two men alone.

Hoover got along fine with Vaughan, a back-slapping, bourbon-sipping, barnyard-joking political fixer. The director shared his intimate knowledge of the personal lives of Roosevelt's inner circle. He offered to conduct a "White House Security Survey" to see who was loyal to Truman and who was not. He gave Vaughan transcripts of conversations among the movers and shakers of Washington.

"I said, 'What the hell is this?' and they said, 'This is a wiretap on so-and-so,' " Vaughan recounted.

"Harry told me, 'What the hell is that crap?'

"I said, 'That's a wiretap.'

"He said, 'Cut all of them off. Tell the FBI we haven't got any time for that kind of shit.' "

But President Truman found the time. Hoover's reports gave him cause to wonder if the White House was a nest of vipers. Would FDR's aides be loyal to him? Could Truman trust them?

Hoover had a fresh file on a White House aide suspected of leaking to the newspapers: Edward Prichard, once a law clerk for Hoover's old nemesis, Supreme Court Justice Felix Frankfurter, a founding father of the American Civil Liberties Union. Vaughan quickly told Hoover that the president had read the report on Prichard with great interest and wanted "future communications along that line . . . whenever, in your opinion, they are necessary."

Hoover put a wiretap on Prichard. The tap quickly produced transcripts of his conversations with Justice Frankfurter—the first of twelve justices of the Supreme Court overheard or mentioned on FBI wiretaps. The investigation of Prichard's loyalties led to taps on the influential Washington newspaper columnist Drew Pearson and a politically wired Washington lawyer, Tommy Corcoran. All four men were sources of scathing scuttlebutt on the new president. A second Truman aide—another Kansas City crony, Ed McKim—reported back to the FBI that the president was duly impressed. All this happened within seven weeks after Truman took office. All of it was done in the president's name, for the purpose of plugging leaks and overhearing political gossip.

Vaughan let Hoover know that if the FBI got caught breaking the law, it was on its own. The White House would deny all knowledge of the illegal taps.

Truman may have savored this first taste of political intelligence, but he placed no faith in Hoover. On May 4, 1945, he told the White House budget director, Harold D. Smith, that he feared Hoover was "building up a Gestapo." The president returned time and again to that theme. The word had a certain resonance in the week that Adolf Hitler committed suicide in his bunker and the Third Reich collapsed. "We want no Gestapo or Secret Police," President Truman wrote in his diary on May 12. "FBI is tending in that direction. They are dabbling in sex-life scandals and plain blackmail . . . *This must stop.*"

It did not stop. Two weeks later, the president, racked by suspicion, decided that he could not trust Attorney General Francis Biddle. He summarily dismissed him. It was one of the poorer decisions of his presidency. Biddle went on to serve with great distinction prosecuting Nazi war criminals at the international military tribunal convened at Nuremberg. Truman replaced him with a political hack, Tom Clark—a professional oil lobbyist from Texas who had joined the Justice Department as an antitrust lawyer and worked his way up to chief of the Criminal Division. Truman concluded many years later that Clark was not a bad man, just "a dumb son of a bitch."

Hoover sensed this from the start. After Tom Clark took office on July 1, Hoover immediately prepared a letter for the new attorney general to send to the president. The letter said that FDR had given Hoover the power to wiretap without warrants. But Hoover omitted a key fact: Roosevelt also had ordered him to keep the taps to a minimum and to limit them, insofar as possible, to aliens. Clark rubber-stamped this letter and sent it to President Truman over his own name after the July 4 holiday. Truman gave his approval. Two months into the new administration, Hoover had renewed his power to wiretap at will. The attorney general henceforth chose a course of willful ignorance when it came to wiretaps, bugs, and break-ins by the FBI. He did not want to know what Hoover was doing beyond the boundaries of the law.

That week the president turned again to the subject of the FBI's powers. He approved six more months of secret White House funds for the FBI's Special Intelligence Service, but with evident distaste. He told his budget director, Harold Smith, that he wanted "to confine the FBI to the United States" and that "the FBI should be cut back as soon as possible." Truman trusted Smith. The president relied on him to find out what was really going on in the government. The budget director knew all about the secret White House funds with which FDR had financed the covert operations of the United States during World War II. The Congress in which Truman had served knew nothing about the money—even though, under the Constitution, the president cannot spend a penny without congressional authorization. Smith knew precisely what FDR had siphoned out of the Treasury—tens of millions of dollars a year for espionage, two billion for the Manhattan Project to build the atomic bomb.

"A NEW WEAPON OF UNUSUALLY DESTRUCTIVE FORCE"

Truman set off on the cruiser *Augusta* on July 7, 1945, his first trip to Europe since World War I. He was met eight days later in Antwerp by General

Dwight D. Eisenhower, the supreme Allied commander. They traveled overland to Brussels and flew to Berlin, once the fourth-largest city in the world. American and British warplanes had bombed most of Berlin to rubble and the Soviets had crushed what remained. On July 16, a motorcade took Truman through the city. The ruins stank of death. Corpses rotted in the rubble and wild dogs scavenged their bones. A civilization lay in a state of collapse. "I thought of Carthage, Baalbek, Jerusalem . . . ," Truman wrote in his diary. "I hope for some sort of peace—but I fear that machines are ahead of morals by some centuries and when morals catch up there'll be no reason for any of it." It was afternoon in Berlin, morning in America. Above the desert near Alamogordo, New Mexico, came a blinding flash brighter than the rising sun.

Truman met Churchill and Stalin at Potsdam, east of Berlin, in terrain held by the conquering Red Army. They convened at the Cecilienhof Palace, once the summer residence of Crown Prince Wilhelm of Prussia. Truman was unsure of how to use the immense power in his hands. Churchill seemed elderly and exhausted; he was voted out of office as prime minister that week. Stalin was stone-faced, impossible to read. Truman wrote in his diary that "Uncle Joe looked tired and drawn and the P.M. seemed lost." The next day, the president got the word from New Mexico. He arrived at Stalin's banquet that night looking supremely happy.

The seventeen-day Potsdam conference settled one big issue: the bomb would fall on Japan. Truman and Churchill met with their military chiefs at 11:30 A.M. on July 24. Truman took Stalin aside late that afternoon. "I casually mentioned to Stalin that we had a new weapon of unusually destructive force," Truman wrote in his memoirs. "The Russian Premier showed no special interest. All he said was that he was glad to hear it and hoped we would 'make good use of it against the Japanese.' "

Thanks to the efforts of Soviet intelligence, Stalin already knew about the bomb.

In two weeks, the secret weapon was no secret. Two atomic bombs had killed perhaps two hundred thousand Japanese, almost all of them civilians, at Hiroshima and Nagasaki. While the second bomb was on its way, the *Augusta* tied up in Virginia. Harry Truman returned to the White House, a million Soviet troops invaded Manchuria, and the Emperor Hirohito gathered his war council in the Imperial Library in Tokyo to decide how to bear the unbearable. The word of Japan's surrender reached Washington on August 14, 1945.

"SECRET WORLD-WIDE INTELLIGENCE"

President Truman now knew how little he knew of what was going on in the world. He did not know how to gain that knowledge. Hoover promised to deliver what the president desired. He wanted power in return.

"The future welfare of the United States necessitates and demands the operation of an efficient world-wide intelligence service," Hoover wrote to the attorney general on August 29. The FBI was "well qualified to operate such a service," Hoover maintained. "It is a fact, as you well know, that the SIS program operated by the Bureau in the Western Hemisphere has been completely successful."

On September 6, Hoover hammered harder on the president's door, in a note with two Freudian-slip misspellings that betrayed his anger. Railing at "Donovan's plans for the perpetration of his dynasty" and "Donovan's deadly died-in-the-wool secrets," he demanded a decision.

He got one. Truman fired Donovan on September 20. He broke up the Office of Strategic Services. The end of the summer of 1945 found the United States without an intelligence service.

The next day, Hoover personally pressed his blueprint into the attorney general's hands and urged him to send it to the president at once. It was entitled "FBI Plan for United States Secret World-Wide Intelligence Coverage." It made Hoover the unquestioned overseer of American national security.

Under Hoover's leadership, the FBI's agents would spy on the Soviets abroad and at home; their work would be sifted by intelligence analysts from the State Department. Hoover would synchronize his secret operations with the secretaries of state and war. He wanted the president to know that dividing American intelligence into foreign and domestic realms was an invitation to disaster. He was already sending Truman intelligence bulletins, including hundred-page reports on the subversive activities emanating from a dozen different foreign embassies in the United States.

On October 2, 1945, Hoover sent an FBI special agent to the White House to make sure President Truman had read his proposal. He cannily selected Morton Chiles, the son of an old friend of the president's; Truman had known Chiles since he was a baby. "I visited President Truman for approximately 35 minutes," Chiles reported in writing to Hoover that day. "We discussed thoroughly the Bureau's participation in World Wide Intelligence in the Western Hemisphere and the advisability of expanding the Bureau's jurisdiction to worldwide coverage."

Chiles immediately realized that the president appeared unaware of Hoover's proposition. If he had seen it, he had not read it. "I had the opportunity to fully explain to him the Bureau's plan, the Bureau's method of operation and all the reasons why the Bureau should expand to coverage of the world," Chiles reported. "He expressed concern regarding the possibility that a World Wide Intelligence organization would gain the reputation of a 'Gestapo.'"

This was not the first time Hoover had heard his men compared to Nazis. It was the first time he had heard it from a president.

Truman turned to the most experienced hands at the State and War departments to find a new bearing for American intelligence and national security. On November 20, a dozen of them gathered in the gilded chambers of the secretary of state. Led by Undersecretary Dean Acheson, the talks settled very little save for the fact that "the President had stated flatly that the FBI was not to operate outside the United States."

Sitting silently at the meeting was a man who was highly interested in the future of American intelligence: Alger Hiss of the State Department's Office of Special Political Affairs. A rising star in American diplomacy, Hiss had been at Yalta while Roosevelt, Churchill, and Stalin tried to chart the way of the world after the war. He had been a Communist agent inside the government of the United States for ten years.

That same day, the chiefs of foreign espionage in Moscow received an electrifying flash sent by their leading spy in London. "The Americans are currently investigating another Soviet intel. organization in the U.S.," reported Kim Philby, a senior British intelligence officer and a Soviet mole. Philby had picked up the secret information in a cable from William Stephenson, the British intelligence commander in Washington. Stephenson's unimpeachable source was the director of the Federal Bureau of Investigation.

Hoover laid out the case a week later, delivering a startling seventy-one-page top secret report to the president, the attorney general, and the secretary of state. His dossier, "Soviet Espionage in the United States," was dated November 27, 1945. It named many names. One was Harry Dexter White, who was hard at work drawing up blueprints for the International Monetary Fund and the World Bank on behalf of the United States Treasury. Another was Alger Hiss, who was helping to build the framework for the United Nations. Hoover was telling the president that two of the leading intellectual architects of America's plans for the postwar world were Communist spies.

The president disregarded Hoover. He rarely read the FBI's files and memoranda on national security. "President Truman was not a man who appreciated or understood intelligence," said Cartha DeLoach, Hoover's trusted aide. "He thought that Mr. Hoover was his enemy. He treated him that way."

The director and the president were now implacable foes. Their political struggle became a war over the national security of the United States. Hoover had served seven chief executives since World War I. He had never faced a president as an enemy. He had received extraordinary powers in secret from Franklin Roosevelt to conduct political warfare in America. He intended to use them whether Truman knew it or not.

Hoover was convinced that the president was a weak link in the chain of command. He believed that he himself would have to lead generals and politicians and the American people in the war on communism. He saw the FBI as America's strongest force in a life-and-death fight on the home front.

Hoover had a big map in his mind. His intelligence did not stop at the American border. The threats he had faced had come from Berlin to New York, Moscow to New Mexico, and Tokyo to Hawaii. He believed that the Soviets were planning a sneak attack on the United States, and that American Communists would serve as the shock troops. He had to radiate intelligence and power from Washington around the globe to protect the United States. The world was his battlefield.

17

SHOWDOWN

Hoover opened a secret intelligence file at the end of 1945. He took unique copies of the reports his lieutenants sent him, and he wrote his thoughts in the margins, bearing down with a fountain pen, bringing forth scrawls of royal blue ink. The imprimatur of his initial—*H.*—made his words into commands.

Reading his handwritten notes is like hearing him think out loud. His rage was personal and political, bitter and implacable, barking and biting. He had high-soaring ideas, and he had hissing fits. His sense of humor was sarcastic, sometimes petulant. His knowledge was enormous, though his mind was narrow.

These files went on for twenty-seven years. They are, in effect, Hoover's diary; they constitute his secret history of the Cold War. They reveal above all his abiding fear that America could lose the war on communism.

In 1946 and 1947 Hoover fought his battles on three fronts. He struggled for control of American intelligence. He fought to convince American leaders that the Cold War could last for the rest of their lives. And he started a campaign of political warfare against the president.

Hoover was enraged when he learned of Truman's plans to create a new director of Central Intelligence who would claim dominion over the FBI's operations against spies and traitors. "Completely unworkable," he wrote to Attorney General Tom Clark on January 15, 1946. It would "wreck any existing agencies, including the Federal Bureau of Investigation." The attorney general objected to his blunt language. Hoover fired back: "I most certainly don't share views of A.G. . . . Appeasement can eventually bring about even more difficulties. H."

To Hoover's great consternation, on January 24, 1946, the president selected a rear admiral in the navy reserve, Sidney Souers, a Democratic Party stalwart from Missouri, as the first director of Central Intelligence. In an impromptu ceremony in the Oval Office, Truman gave Souers a black cloak, a black hat, and a little wooden dagger, knighting him as the chief of the "Cloak and Dagger Group of Snoopers." The next day, Hoover summoned Souers to his office at FBI headquarters. He soon had the admiral eating out of his hand. "He wanted it understood very clearly that he intended to depend upon the FBI to a large extent for advice and counsel," Hoover wrote to his top assistants. He added the admiral to his list of useful underlings.

By himself, Hoover could not kill the blueprint for what became the Central Intelligence Agency. But he would do everything he could to protect his power. He went to the Pentagon to consult with General Dwight D. Eisenhower, the most powerful man in the American military. Hoover argued that Truman was going to ruin American espionage with the new Central Intelligence system. "General Eisenhower inquired how this would affect the Federal Bureau of Investigation," Hoover recorded. The director replied that "it appeared that the FBI would withdraw from foreign operations." Eisenhower "expressed amazement and real concern." Hoover added the general to his list of powerful allies.

"A DIRECT PENETRATION"

Having failed to stop the investiture of the director of Central Intelligence, Hoover penetrated and sabotaged the fledgling spy agency.

Hoover had received a call for help from Colonel Bill Quinn, an army man who was trying to create a new Central Intelligence corps for covert operations and espionage. The colonel faced fierce opposition from the uniformed military, who told him his outfit was riddled with Communists. The FBI had files filled with rumors that Central Intelligence was hiring Reds.

Hat in hand, Quinn went to Hoover. This is how the colonel recalled it:

"What do you want me to do?" Hoover asked.

"Mr. Hoover," Quinn said, "the simple answer to your question is to find out if I have any commies in my organization."

"Well, we can do that," Hoover said.

"While you're doing it subversively, would you please check them criminally?"

"All right."

"Before we decide on how to do it, for posterity, and for ultimate cooperation, I would like to ask that you send me a representative to be your liaison with my organization."

At this, Hoover almost fell out of his seat, the colonel recalled. "I know what was going on in his mind," Quinn recounted. "He was probably thinking, 'My God, this guy is asking for a direct penetration in his agency.'"

Quinn had just invited Hoover to spy on his spies. Liaison was penetration. You shook hands with the right hand and picked pockets with the left.

The Bureau investigated the political loyalties of dozens of Central Intelligence officers, many of whom were hired specifically for their Russian and Eastern European backgrounds, making them suspect in Hoover's eyes. The first three directors of Central Intelligence asked Hoover to provide them with seasoned FBI officers, field training, formal reports, the names and identities of trusted informants and recruited foreign agents. Hoover took pleasure in rejecting their pleas.

His resentment over his exclusion from worldwide intelligence smoldered. He aimed to regain his preeminence.

"A TIME OF SOME HYSTERIA"

At Hoover's request, Admiral Souers wrote to President Truman on April 17, 1946: "It is of the utmost urgency that the Federal Bureau of Investigation be permitted to continue its security functions . . . in the countries of the Western Hemisphere, in London, Paris, Rome, Manila, Tokyo, and the American Zone in Germany. The security mission which it performs may be illustrated by the Canadian investigation in Ottawa which reaches into the United States as well as England."

The "Canadian investigation" was about to begin to reveal the reach of Soviet espionage into America's atomic arsenal.

The case began with the carelessness of a thirty-six-year-old Red Army lieutenant, Igor Sergeyevich Guzenko, who served as one of Stalin's spies in the office of the Soviet military attaché in Ottawa, Canada. He was a code clerk who handled secret cables and ciphers. One night he tossed aside two rough drafts of encoded messages to Moscow. A cleaning woman who doubled as a Soviet security officer found the crumpled communiqués and informed the ambassador. The penalty for security violations in Stalin's secret service was Siberian exile or death. Guzenko gathered up every secret cable he could carry and fled for his life. He spent three days on the run before convincing the Royal Canadian Mounted Police to protect him.

The FBI's legal attaché in Ottawa joined in the interrogation of Guzenko. Hoover soon put seventy-five agents on the case.

The Guzenko case revealed four facts: Ottawa was a command center for Soviet espionage throughout North America. The Soviets had placed a spy somewhere inside the State Department. A British nuclear physicist named Allan Nunn May had penetrated the Manhattan Project for Moscow. The theft of the secret of the atomic bomb was the highest priority of Soviet intelligence.

Another defector from the world of Soviet espionage now was in the FBI's hands. Her name was Elizabeth Bentley; she had been a committed American Communist. She had first approached the FBI in 1942, but the Bureau did not take her at her word. She was confused, intellectually and ideologically, about why she was switching sides.

"She was a flake. A wacko, really," said FBI special agent Jack Danahy, who worked the case for years. "She had a series of crazy lovers, Fascists in Italy and Communists in the United States." When she turned to the FBI, "she made a play for every agent in the office that she talked to. . . . We worried about it. But, hey, we weren't finding informants in convents, you know."

The Bureau always had its doubts about Bentley. She was a heavy drinker, but she seemed to have a good memory when sober. Her story was strange, but this much was true: Bentley had been a courier who served a network of Soviet spies. She named names—eighty in all, though none would ever go to jail for espionage, and only two would ever be convicted of any crime.

Hoover decided to accept the confessions of this eccentric turncoat.

Her revelations let the FBI begin to trace the outlines of a Soviet intelligence system that had been aiming to penetrate the United States government for a dozen years. After the FBI accepted Bentley's bona fides, Hoover assigned 227 agents to the investigation. But he had already shared the gist of the case with his British intelligence counterpart in Washington. The word had been passed to London. And it had been relayed to Moscow, courtesy of Kim Philby, the Soviet mole inside the British service.

The Soviets had swiftly heeded Philby's alert. They ordered most of their wartime intelligence officers out of the United States, and cut off contact with many of their networks of agents. When the FBI went looking for the Soviets, they found they were trying to lasso shadows.

President Truman read Hoover's next report to the White House on May 29, 1946, with disbelief.

"There is an enormous Soviet espionage ring in Washington," Hoover wrote in a "personal and confidential" message to the president and the attorney general. "A number of high Government officials whose identities will be set out hereinafter are involved." Some of the names on the list were shocking. Hoover's suspects included the undersecretary of state, Dean Acheson, and the former assistant secretary of war, John J. McCloy, two pillars of the American establishment whose anti-Communist credentials never had been questioned.

The attorney general did not believe it either. "It *was* a time of some hysteria," Clark said. But he was learning to take the power of Hoover's secret intelligence seriously. He discovered that Hoover was keeping watch on him as well. "Whenever any derogatory information about me would come into the Department, why, they would put it in that file," Clark said. "It was outrageous."

"We ought to have a showdown"

Hoover continued trying to convince the White House that Stalin's spies were trying to steal America's atomic secrets. He was urged on by the FBI's intelligence chief, Mickey Ladd, the son of a United States senator from North Dakota. Ladd called for an all-out, no-holds-barred war on communism—including mass arrests and detentions of suspected subversives—in the name of counterespionage. Ladd wanted to put every one of the roughly eighty thousand members of the Communist Party of the United States on the FBI's secret Security Index. Once indexed, they could be arrested in a national roundup under a mass warrant "in the event of an emergency."

Hoover agreed. Without revealing the existence of the Security Index, he told Attorney General Clark that the FBI was going to "intensify its investigation of Communist Party activities" and "list all members of the Communist Party and others who would be dangerous in the event of a break in diplomatic relations with the Soviet Union." Hoover wrote in the plainest

possible language that a political crisis could make it necessary "to immediately detain a large number of American citizens."

Hoover's war with the White House intensified. He had requested the
money to hire hundreds more men to investigate Soviet espionage and
Communist subversion. Truman instead eliminated six hundred of Hoover's
agents, nearly one out of seven from the FBI's front ranks, in the first budget
he sent to Congress. The FBI had not faced such a drawdown since Hoover
became its director. Hoover reacted to the cutbacks by ordering his overseas
agents back home.

On July 8, 1946, Hoover told his agents in Latin America and the Caribbean to close down their operations immediately. He had promised the
new director of Central Intelligence, General Hoyt Vandenberg, a year for a
smooth transition. But by summer's end, the FBI had left behind nothing
but empty offices and angry ambassadors.

"Move rapidly & get out of it as quickly as possible," he commanded.
Seven weeks later, the FBI was all but gone from Central America and the
Caribbean, and it soon would be out of South America too. "All investiga-
tive files, both pending and closed, were burned," Hoover's field lieutenant,
C. H. "Kit" Carson, reported to headquarters as he shut down operations in
Mexico, Guatemala, Costa Rica, Nicaragua, El Salvador, Honduras, Venezu-
ela, Haiti, and Cuba.

Hoover went to the White House and laid down the law. If the president
wanted the FBI out of the realm of foreign intelligence, if he wanted the
director of Central Intelligence in charge, that was what he would get.

But nobody who had ever worked at the Bureau—active, retired, first-
rate, third-rate—would be allowed to work for the new Central Intelligence
Agency, Hoover told the president's chief of staff, Admiral Leahy. The admiral advised General Vandenberg "to avoid offending Mr. Hoover." But
when Vandenberg proposed to create a global registry of foreign contacts,
Hoover warned his top FBI aides: "Watch with meticulous care *any* & *all*
Directives of this outfit as I think it is *drunk* with power & will slyly grasp
for everything." When Hoover saw newly drafted legislation that would
give the director of Central Intelligence more authority, he wrote: "The
'empire builders' . . . perpetuate their present monstrosity and intrude even
more into civilian and domestic fields."

Hoover's refusal to work with the fledgling CIA approached insubordi-
nation. His defiance of the State Department neared rebellion. Hoover's
spiteful decision threatened "a major blow to the effectiveness of our secu-

rity and intelligence work," wrote Undersecretary of State Acheson. Hoover was undeterred. He had all but declared war on the White House.

"I think we ought to have a showdown," he wrote to Mickey Ladd.

His rage at the president's reluctance to fight a full-bore war on communism grew ferocious. He began to petition members of the Senate and House to give him the power to protect America against "the threat of infiltrating foreign agents, ideologies and military conquest." His views on the threat were so strong that they started to sway the liberals of Washington—and through them, the president himself.

Hoover was creating the political culture of the Cold War in the United States.

Origins of the cold war

18

"RED FASCISM"

O N SEPTEMBER 26, 1946, the White House counsel Clark Clifford and his assistant George Elsey delivered a secret report to Truman telling him to prepare for war with the Soviets. They drew from the work of Hoover and the FBI as they sketched out a battle plan for Armageddon.

They told Truman that he had to prepare to fight a third world war with atomic and biological weapons. The enemy was a Soviet dictatorship aiming for world conquest, aided by an insidious intelligence service, and assisted by an American underground. Every American Communist, they wrote, was potentially a spy and a soldier for Moscow. Truman wrote in his diary that week: "The Reds, phonies, and 'parlor pinks' seem to be banded together and are becoming a national danger. I am afraid they are a sabotage front for Uncle Joe Stalin."

In November 1946, for the first time since before the Depression, the Republicans swept the national elections and won majorities in the Senate and the House. Their campaigns had struck a strong new anti-Communist tone. Their message was that Americans had to choose between "Communism and Republicanism."

The Republicans' political rhetoric flowed directly from a forty-page pamphlet published by the United States Chamber of Commerce, which printed and distributed 400,000 copies nationwide. Its title was "Communist Infiltration in the United States." Its message was preached from political stumps and church pulpits throughout the land. Its author was Father John F. Cronin, a Baltimore priest who had many adherents among the heavily Catholic ranks of the FBI. His material came straight from the Bureau's secret and confidential files, including passages from Hoover's reports to the White House. Father Cronin befriended a freshman member of the 80th Congress who had been elected on the issue of the Communist threat and arrived in the capital from California in January 1947.

Richard Milhous Nixon was thirty-four years old, a politician of high intelligence, immense ambition, and a barely tapped but bottomless talent for intrigue. He had risen from humble roots by virtue of hard work fueled by frustrated dreams. Ten years before he came to Washington to be sworn in to the House of Representatives, while he was still in law school, Nixon had applied for a job at the FBI. He never heard back. But he would make the most of his contacts with the Bureau for the next quarter of a century. In February 1947, Father Cronin helped him make the first of those connections. He personally briefed Nixon on the FBI's investigations into American communism and Soviet espionage, introduced him to agents who specialized in Red-hunting, and became Nixon's back-channel liaison with the Bureau.

In his first days as a member of Congress, Nixon took a seat on the House Committee on Un-American Activities. Its chairman was J. Parnell Thomas, Republican of New Jersey, a petty-minded vulgarian who soon would be doing prison time for political corruption. The committee's excesses were notorious. Back in 1939, its headline-grabbing investigation of the film industry faltered when, by implication, it called the curly-headed moppet Shirley Temple a Communist. But by now the committee's professional staff included ex-FBI men and former Party members whose files constituted a secret if highly selective history of American communism. The staff's liaison with the Bureau would become one of the strongest forces in Cold War politics.

"A MALIGNANT AND EVIL WAY OF LIFE"

On March 26, 1947, the committee convened to hear public testimony from J. Edgar Hoover. It was an epic moment in Hoover's life. He was fifty-two years old; he had run the FBI for nearly a quarter of a century. He was the face of anticommunism in America.

On this day, Hoover broke with higher authority. For the next quarter of the century, until the day he died, he would obey executive orders when he saw fit. His testimony was an act of defiance against the Truman administration, a declaration that Hoover now stood in alliance with the president's strongest political enemies in Congress.

He held sway over presidential powers. Five days before, after months of pressure from Hoover, Truman had signed an executive order commanding the biggest government investigation in American history: the Federal Loyalty and Security Program. The FBI would run background checks on more than two million government employees, and launch deep investigations into the personal lives and political beliefs of more than fourteen thousand of them. The program would unearth no Soviet spies inside the government. But the hunt for the disloyal spread throughout the American political system.

Hoover now told Congress and the American people that the Communist Party, driven by Soviet Russia's dreams of world domination, was burrowing into the social and political frameworks of the United States on a mission to overthrow America—and that the Truman administration was not taking the threat seriously. "Communism, in reality, is not a political party," he testified. "It is a way of life—a malignant and evil way of life. It reveals a condition akin to disease that spreads like an epidemic, and like an epidemic, a quarantine is necessary to keep it from infecting the nation."

The Communist Party, on paper, might look like an insignificant force in American politics—Hoover said it had seventy-four thousand members —but he said its influence was infinitely greater: "For every party member there are ten others ready, willing and able to do the party's work. Herein lies the greatest menace of communism—for these are the people that infiltrate and corrupt various spheres of American life."

Hoover said that far too few Americans "possessed the zeal, the fervor, the persistence and the industry to learn about this menace of Red fascism. I do fear for the liberal and the progressive who has been hoodwinked and duped into joining hands with the Communists. I confess to a real apprehension so long as Communists are able to secure ministers of the gospel to promote their evil work . . . I do fear so long as school boards and parents tolerate conditions whereby Communists and fellow travelers, under the guise of academic freedom, can teach our youth a way of life . . . I do fear so long as labor groups are infiltrated, dominated, or saturated with the virus of Communism . . . I fear for ignorance on the part of all of our people who may take the poisonous pills of Communist propaganda."

Hoover proclaimed his political support for the Committee on Un-American Activities and its members in the war on communism. They were now a team. The FBI would gather evidence in secrecy, working toward the "unrelenting prosecution" of the subversives. The committee would make its greatest contribution through publicity—what Hoover called "the public disclosure of the forces that threaten America."

Hoover and Nixon met eye-to-eye at the hearing that day, and they hit it off famously. Nixon asked where American Communists posed the greatest dangers. Hoover pointed him to subversion on campus, on the airwaves, in the movies, and above all inside the government itself.

Nixon's performance impressed Hoover.

"Who's that young man?" Hoover asked an old friend after the hearing. "He looks like he's going to be a good man for us."

19

SURPRISE ATTACK

T HE PRESIDENT WAS increasingly convinced of the dangers of the Communist threat. But he was also deeply wary of J. Edgar Hoover. "Very strongly anti-FBI," the White House counsel Clark Clifford wrote in his notes of a May 2, 1947, conversation with Truman. "Wants to be sure to hold FBI down."

Truman felt that Hoover led "a sort of a dictatorial operation," said Treasury Secretary John Snyder, an old friend and a political confidant to the president. "That was, I think, Mr. Truman's general feeling, that Mr. Hoover had built up a Frankenstein in the FBI."

Hoover knew what the president thought. He used his knowledge skillfully as he kept up his struggle to take control of American intelligence. He artfully twisted the arms of ranking members of Congress as they weighed a new National Security Act in the spring and summer of 1947.

The bill proposed to unify the American military services under the aegis of the Pentagon; to create a secretary of defense to oversee the army, the navy, and a nuclear-armed air force; to form a new National Security Council to coordinate military, intelligence, and diplomatic powers at the White House; and to establish the first permanent peacetime American espionage service. "Espionage is as old as man," Hoover began. "We have always had it and we will continue to have it until the brotherhood of man becomes a reality as well as an ideal." Until then, the United States had to have a permanent and professional spy service established under law. He said no one was better qualified to run it than he himself.

Hoover acknowledged "the uneasiness and apprehension of responsible leaders" starved for information on the intentions and capabilities of the Soviet Union and its allies. He said he would meet their needs. He would oversee foreign intelligence collected by FBI agents, diplomats, and military officers overseas. State Department experts in Washington would analyze the work. The Bureau would continue hunting foreign spies and tapping into Communist plans in the United States.

Good intelligence could prevent another Pearl Harbor. "A future attack might be launched against American territory," Hoover said. "Its disastrous effects can be minimized through intelligence coverage which will forewarn us and thus make it possible to be prepared. The modern advances of science and its military application are a warning of what we might expect, but that is not sufficient: we must prepare ourselves by knowing when and where and how an attack will be directed at us. We can do this only by possessing adequate intelligence coverage on a worldwide basis."

Hoover said "the FBI could provide the worldwide intelligence coverage with a staff of approximately 1,200 employees at an estimated cost of $15,000,000" a year. By contrast, he pointed out, the plan for the CIA ran to estimates as high as "3,000 employees at an annual cost of $60,000,000." Hoover condemned the proposal for the CIA as nothing but the "dreams of visionary but impractical empire-builders."

Rear Admiral Roscoe Hillenkoetter had just become the third director of Central Intelligence in fourteen months. (Hoover and his aides had met the admiral and found him "very frank in his statement that he knew nothing" about his new job.) Hoover argued that intelligence should be "a career and not just another tour of duty"; hiring time-serving military men to run intelligence operations for a year or two was "unfair to the nation." Above all, Hoover asserted, America did not want a Central Intelligence Agency led by a shadowy czar who would run America's spying operations, evaluate the secrets they gathered, and pass judgment on the work of the FBI's foreign espionage agents.

Hoover capped his secret briefing by playing on the president's fears of a secret police. "Luckily for us," he said, "there is no more horrible example of what can happen through the creation of one vast central superstructure that both investigates and judges than the German Gestapo."

"IT IS A TRAGEDY"

Hoover was surpassed by a rival whose rhetoric flew higher. Allen Dulles was Wild Bill Donovan's leading protégé, a star at Donovan's Wall Street law firm, and the brother of John Foster Dulles, the Republican Party's shadow secretary of state. Puffing on his pipe, he gave suave, sophisticated, and factually slippery testimony to a closed congressional hearing on the National Security Act on June 27, 1947.

Dulles testified that the blueprint for the new CIA was sound. The United States had "the raw material for building the greatest intelligence service in the world," he said. A few dozen skilled men serving abroad should do the trick. "I do not believe in a big agency," he said. "You ought to keep it small. If this thing gets to be a great big octopus, it should not function well. . . . The operation of the service must neither be flamboyant nor over-shrouded in mystery and abracadabra which the amateur detective likes to assume. All that is required for success is hard work, discriminating judgment, and common sense."

One month later, on July 26, President Truman signed the National Security Act. The FBI was given no new powers to prosecute the Cold War. The director of Central Intelligence was given many.

Hoover began spying on the CIA from that day forward. He started wiretapping CIA officers suspected of Communist sympathies or homosexual tendencies. Reading reports on "utter confusion" at the Agency, Hoover commented: "It is a tragedy that the true phoniness of CIA isn't exposed." The Agency begged for FBI men experienced in espionage. Hoover consented, with the hope and expectation that his agents would serve as his spies inside the CIA. Few did—too few for Hoover's satisfaction—although one soon reported: "If the people of this nation are depending upon CIA in its present form to prevent another Pearl Harbor disaster, they should start digging fox holes now."

Hoover's political warfare intensified month by month. "It strikes me as a waste of time to cultivate this outfit," he wrote after offering CIA officials a tour of the FBI's training academy. He furiously rejected an aide's draft of a polite letter to the director of Central Intelligence: "*Please* cut out all of the slobbering palaver. We know they have no use for us & I don't intend to do a Munich." When the CIA asked the FBI what it knew about the Comintern, Hoover swatted down the request: "Waste no time on it. We have more pressing matters."

Hoover quickly formed an alliance with the new secretary of defense, James Forrestal, a Wall Street magnate who had been running the navy. On October 24, 1947, Hoover dominated a Pentagon meeting attended by leaders of the CIA, army and navy intelligence, and the president's national security staff. He invoked "the present widespread belief that our intelligence group is entirely inept." He inveighed against State Department leaks about a New York grand jury's investigation into the Communist Party. He explained the FBI's suspicions about the influence of left-wing scientists working for the newly formed Atomic Energy Commission, the civilians overseeing America's deadliest weapons. The commissioners told him that America knew nothing about the Soviet threat.

"The smuggling into the United States of an atomic bomb"

Hoover sent a terrifying letter to Forrestal the next week. He warned against "the smuggling into the United States of an atomic bomb, or parts thereof which could be later assembled in this country." He envisioned Moscow's spies carrying the components of a bomb in diplomatic pouches, saboteurs assembling them in secret, and suicide bombers blowing up the landmarks of the government of the United States. The fear of a surprise attack ruled the day.

Hoover's warning in November 1947 was the first of its kind. Over the next decade he issued a steady stream of alerts against the threat of terrorists and spies wielding atomic, biological, and chemical weapons against American cities, a nightmare that still haunts the nation's leaders. Forrestal convened a secret group he called the War Council, comprising the uniformed and civilian chiefs of the American military, to respond to Hoover's alarm. The council reached out to Vannevar Bush, the government's chief science adviser, and Karl Compton, the president of the Massachusetts Institute of Technology; both men had advised President Truman to drop the atomic bomb on Japan without warning. The War Council led a highly classified project to assess the threat of weapons of mass destruction as instruments of political terror. It explored "the use of biological agents" and "fissionable materials"—a dirty bomb—and set off a search for a shield against a catastrophic attack that continues to this day.

"Your original letter was the thing which first prompted us to undertake this study," the secretary of defense wrote to Hoover. "Because of the major responsibilities of the Federal Bureau of Investigation for the development of information which bears upon the whole subject," Forrestal continued, "preparedness in this particular field will require the very closest cooperation between our two organizations."

Having defined the threat as a question of national survival, Hoover pushed for a powerful series of indictments that would charge the leaders of the Communist Party of the United States with a conspiracy aimed at "destroying the Government by force and violence." The charges required a political and legal judgment that a state of emergency existed between the United States and the Soviets, and that American Communists were unlawful combatants in the Cold War.

Eleven Communist Party leaders were convicted at the first trial and faced five-year sentences. Six went to prison; five jumped bail. In the coming months, 115 more American Communists across the country faced identical charges. Ninety-three were convicted. All the indictments were brought under the 1940 Smith Act, which had outlawed membership in the Party. Each case rested on a 1,350-page document Hoover filed in court, a new version of the case he had been making since World War I. But now he had witnesses. The Bureau had been running a double agent inside the Party for five years. He was a middling and mild-mannered Communist functionary who delivered devastating testimony to the grand jury and at the trial of the eleven leaders. In time, his story became a classic black-and-white television show called *I Led Three Lives,* with an introduction instantly familiar to a generation of Americans: "This is the story, the fantastically true story, of Herbert A. Philbrick . . . Average citizen, high-level member of the Communist Party, counterspy for the Federal Bureau of Investigation."

"INSIDE THE ENEMY'S HOUSE"

Hoover's case against the Communist conspiracy was strengthened by secret evidence: a handful of files from the archives of Soviet intelligence. They came from Arlington Hall, an old girls' school across the Potomac near the Pentagon, now the center of America's efforts to read Soviet cables sent during and immediately after World War II.

The United States Army's Signal Intelligence Service had obtained copies of thousands of wartime cables sent from Moscow to its outposts in America, including Amtorg, the Soviet trade mission that had served as a front for espionage since 1920. In a 1944 black-bag job, the FBI broke into Amtorg's New York office and stole reams of Russian-language messages and their enciphered equivalents. The Soviet ciphers were five-digit numbers arranged in five separate cryptographic systems. They were supposed to have been used once and never again, giving each message a unique pattern, and making the systems unbreakable. But the Soviet intelligence service had blundered, under great pressure, during the war. After Germany invaded the Soviet Union and drove toward Moscow, duplicate sets of ciphers were sent to Soviet spies around the world. The army cryptanalysts had discovered a handful of these duplicate ciphers in October 1943. The duplication made it theoretically possible to crack the encoded communications among Soviet spies and spymasters—if a pattern could be found.

Meredith Gardner was a master of this arcane craft. Gardner worked with a pencil, a pad, and punch cards. But knowledge was growing at his fingertips. A civilian linguist, he had learned Russian and Japanese quickly after joining the army code breakers in the first months of World War II, when he was not quite thirty years old. In 1946, Gardner had begun to break fragments of Soviet intelligence communiqués, starting with a two-year-old message to Moscow from New York, within a passage in plain English spelling out a name, bracketed by two Russian code words. Gardner saw in a flash of insight that the two code words must be "spell" and "end spell." He had created a crack in the code. He broke another wartime message to Moscow that included the names of the leading scientists building the atomic bomb at the Manhattan Project. The Soviet code word for the bomb was Enormoz.

By May 1947—a few weeks after Hoover testified before the House Committee on Un-American Activities—Gardner had read two messages showing that the Soviets had had a spy inside the general staff of the War Department during the last months of World War II. Moscow had penetrated the heart of the American military. At that point, General Carter W. Clarke, the assistant chief of army intelligence, shared the secret of the code-breaking effort with Hoover.

The FBI began collaborating with the army at Arlington Hall in July 1947. Meredith Gardner worked in daily liaison with a talented thirty-year-old FBI agent, Bob Lamphere, who delivered Amtorg cables stolen by the Bureau's black-bag artists. Their work came to have its own code name: Venona.

Venona was one of America's most secret weapons in the Cold War—so secret that neither President Truman nor the CIA knew about it. On the occasions that Hoover sent intelligence derived from Venona to his superiors, it was scrubbed, sanitized, and attributed only to "a highly sensitive source." Hoover decreed: "In view of loose methods of CIA & some of its questionable personnel we must be most circumspect. H."

For nearly five years, the FBI had been trying to uncover the depths of Soviet espionage. The Bureau had not broken a single case against a Soviet spy. Soviet intelligence had started lying low after the end of World War II, alerted by their agents inside the Anglo-American alliance. But now the Soviets were starting to reactivate their networks in the United States, and the FBI was starting to pick up faint stirrings, like the fading sounds of footsteps down a dark street. Hoover was practicing the same stoic patience that the Soviets possessed.

By the summer of 1948, Venona was building a critical mass of broken Soviet ciphers, codes, and cables—clues to the twenty-year history of Soviet espionage in the United States. The investigation was on the verge of discovering evidence against the international conspiracy to steal America's atomic secrets.

"We now had dozens of entire messages in the clear," Lamphere recalled. "We were inside the enemy's house."

"Trial by fire"

At this moment, Harry Truman's political power was at its lowest ebb. "I am going through a terrible political 'trial by fire,'" Truman wrote to Winston Churchill on July 10, 1948. "We are in the midst of grave and trying times. You can look with satisfaction upon your great contribution to the overthrow of Nazism and Fascism in the world. 'Communism'—so-called—is our next great problem. I hope we can solve it without the 'blood and tears' the other two cost."

Truman put communism in quotation marks. Hoover put it in bold headlines.

Hoover knew how to work in secrecy. Now he chose publicity. As he once had used the movies to build the power and the reputation of the FBI in the war against gangsters in the 1930s, he now used politicians and newspapers and television in the war on communism. His strategy had nothing to do with law enforcement. His witnesses were unreliable; the information he gathered with warrantless wiretaps and illegal bugs was inadmissible; the broken cables were too secret to be shared.

But Hoover knew how to use intelligence as an instrument of political warfare. He furnished a powerful weapon to the Republicans and the Red-hunters in Congress, who in turn delivered a hammer blow against the president and the Democrats.

He sent assistant director Lou Nichols, who ran the FBI's public relations office and served as Hoover's liaison to Congress, to meet with members and staff of the House Un-American Activities Committee and a Senate investigations subcommittee. Nichols carried a sheaf of secret and confidential FBI files. He leaked the names of two FBI informants to congressmen and their staffs. His work was no secret in Washington: the muckraking newspaperman Drew Pearson soon reported that Nichols was flying in and out of HUAC's headquarters "like an animated shuttlecock."

On July 31, 1948, Elizabeth Bentley appeared before HUAC. She was not the ideal witness. The FBI had deemed her unreliable for years; from 1942 to 1944 her claims about Soviet espionage had been filed in the nut box. Her testimony was unusable in a court of law because of her instability and alcoholism. Any trial based on her testimony would lead to "an acquittal under very embarrassing circumstances," one Hoover aide warned.

Nonetheless Hoover sent her to Congress. She talked at length about her work as a courier for the Soviet intelligence service during World War II. She named names, thirty-two in all, including the assistant treasury secretary, Harry Dexter White; seven members of the headquarters staff of Wild Bill Donovan's Office of Strategic Services, including Donovan's personal assistant, Duncan Chaplin Lee; and Roosevelt administration figures from the military to the White House. Though much of her testimony was hearsay, it was the first public disclosure that the American government knew it had been penetrated by Soviet spies. And that knowledge flowed from Hoover.

The next day the committee subpoenaed a *Time* senior editor named Whittaker Chambers.

Chambers often spoke the truth but not the whole truth under oath. He had told his story to the FBI and to Assistant Secretary of State A. A. Berle more than six years before. Back then, the FBI had listened to Chambers in disbelief. Hoover and his men simply could not accept the word of a man who once had been a committed Communist. They did now.

He was rumpled and red-eyed and his tale was riveting. He had joined the Communist Party in 1925, and he had served as an agent of Soviet intelligence for six years in the 1930s. He said the Soviets had had highly placed spies in the Roosevelt administration. One was Laurence Duggan, a chief of the Latin American division of the State Department, who had worked on the formation of the FBI's Special Intelligence Service. Another was Alger Hiss, another State Department standout, who now ran the Carnegie Endowment for International Peace. The endowment's chairman was John Foster Dulles, who would be the next secretary of state if the Republicans won the presidency in November.

On the morning of August 3, 1948, the House Un-American Activities Committee's chief investigator, Robert Stripling, took Chambers to a closed hearing room to begin the interrogation. First question: Had Chambers been "aware at any time when you were a member of the Communist Party of a so-called espionage ring that was being set up or functioning in Washington?"

"No, I was not," Chambers replied.

That was a bald-faced lie. But when the committee convened in public that morning, before a crowd of reporters and photographers in the Ways and Means Committee hearing room, the biggest public arena on Capitol Hill, Chambers changed his story. He said he had belonged to "an underground organization of the United States Communist Party" from 1932 to 1938. He named eight members of the ring. The most recognizable name by far was Alger Hiss.

"The purpose of this group at that time was not primarily espionage," Chambers said. "Its original purpose was the Communist infiltration of the American government. But espionage was certainly one of its eventual objectives." This was a crucial point. Infiltration and invisible political influence were immoral, but arguably not illegal. Espionage was treason, traditionally punishable by death.

The distinction was not lost on the cleverest member of HUAC. Congressman Richard Nixon asked Chambers the most pointed questions that day. He knew the right questions to ask because he knew the answers in advance. He had been studying the FBI's files for five months, courtesy of J. Edgar Hoover. Nixon launched his political career in hot pursuit of Hiss and the secret Communists of the New Deal.

Truman derided Red-hunters like Nixon, and he denounced the pursuit of Hiss. But he never once criticized Hoover in public. He would not have dared.

"HE WASN'T TAKING ORDERS FROM TRUMAN"

It was a dangerous moment in American democracy. Hoover was no longer listening to the president.

"Hoover did his thing," said Stephen Spingarn, an army counterintelligence commander newly appointed as a White House security adviser. "He wasn't taking orders from Truman or anybody else, least of all the Attorney General of the United States."

Secretary of Defense Forrestal pushed the president to give Hoover sweeping national security powers over law enforcement and intelligence—to make him a secret police czar. The White House pushed back. "That was contrary to our whole tradition," Spingarn said. "You did that in Communist and Fascist countries, but you don't do that in the United States."

Hoover confronted Attorney General Clark over the FBI's power to detain thousands of politically suspect American citizens in the event of a serious crisis with the Soviet Union. Now that the broad outlines of Soviet espionage in the United States had been established, Hoover argued, the hour of crisis was at hand.

"We began to fall out," Attorney General Clark said, over the issue of "Communist infiltration."

The understanding from the first days of the FBI was that the attorney general had to know what the Bureau was doing. That way the president would know. But when Hoover distrusted the White House, he became most secretive. He hid things. In the realm of national security, he took action outside the law and beyond the boundaries of the Constitution.

Hoover now drew up plans for his biggest crackdown on American communism. They included the mass detention of political suspects in military stockades, a secret prison system for jailing American citizens, and the suspension of the writ of habeas corpus. Hoover's national security assistant, Mickey Ladd, began working out details on "the program for the detention of Communists" in October 1948, including "a draft of an agreement with the Secretary of the Army" on holding the detainees at military bases in and around New York, San Francisco, and Los Angeles, where the numbers of those arrested would overflow the federal lockups. The agreement held that the FBI, the CIA, and army intelligence officers would divide among them the duties of carrying out the thousands upon thousands of interrogations.

Almost two years passed before Hoover formally briefed the White House and the National Security Council: "For some months representatives of the FBI and of the Department of Justice have been formulating a plan of action for an emergency situation wherein it would be necessary to apprehend and detain persons who are potentially dangerous to the internal security of the country." The detentions would begin in time of war, an emergency, a national crisis, a "threatened invasion" or a "rebellion." Under the plan, the president would sign an emergency order suspending the writ of habeas corpus and instructing the FBI to begin the nationwide roundup. The attorney general would send the president a "master warrant" attached to the FBI's Security Index, whose existence Hoover finally revealed to the president. "For a long period of time the FBI has been accumulating the names, identities and activities of individuals," Hoover wrote. "The index now contains approximately twelve thousand individuals, of which approximately ninety-seven per cent are citizens of the United States." That number eventually would double. "The plan calls for a statement of charges to be served on each detainee and a hearing be afforded the individual," Hoover advised the White House. "The hearing procedure will not be bound by the rules of evidence."

Hoover made plans to fill the detention centers in a time of national emergency, and Congress secretly financed the creation of six of these camps during the 1950s. But no Cold War president seriously considered the mass incarceration of suspected subversives. It took the first president of the twenty-first century to do that.

Hoover, like his fellow Americans, assumed that the Republican governor of New York, Thomas E. Dewey, would be elected president in November 1948. Dewey, who had made his name as a crime-fighting prosecutor, would be the first conservative in the White House in a generation. Hoover was working behind the scenes to support Dewey, who shared Hoover's views on the national emergency that confronted the United States. Hoover had hoped that a new president would grant him new powers, perhaps making him the attorney general while allowing him to retain command over the FBI.

Truman looked powerless and politically spent as the election approached. Crossing through Indiana by train on a long whistle-stop campaign, with the election four weeks away, Truman caught a glimpse of a *Newsweek* magazine poll of America's fifty most prominent political reporters. Their unanimous prediction: Dewey defeats Truman. Every poll and every pundit said the same. Hoover went to sleep on election night confident in that outcome.

At 11:14 A.M. on Wednesday, November 3, 1948, the bulletin went out across the world: Truman had won the biggest upset in the history of the American presidency. A shift of only 33,000 voters in California, Illinois, and Ohio would have given Dewey victory.

When Hoover heard the news, he left his desk at FBI headquarters and did not come back for two weeks. His public relations office told the press that Hoover had pneumonia. He simply disappeared.

20

PARANOIA

THE UNITED STATES was the most powerful force on earth in the spring of 1949. "She bestrides the world like a Colossus," a British historian wrote that year. "No other power at any time in the world's history has possessed so varied or so great an influence on other nations." The British Empire had collapsed. The Soviets had lost twenty-seven million dead in the war. China was in chaos as a Communist army strode toward its capital. Germany and Japan were crushed and under occupation. The United States had half the world's wealth, half its material production, two-thirds of its machines, and its only atomic arsenal. Yet before the year was out, the United States would lose its monopoly on the atomic bomb, and with that loss came a sense of intense peril at the highest levels of government.

Hoover learned that Soviet espionage had penetrated the CIA, the Pentagon, the Justice Department, and the FBI itself.

The year began with an electrifying breakthrough by Venona. Fifteen newly decoded Soviet wartime cables described a woman who had held a job in the Economic Warfare Division of the Justice Department in New York in 1944. She had moved to Washington in 1945 to take another job at Justice—a far better posting from the Soviet point of view. She worked at the Foreign Agents Registration Division, in liaison with the FBI, tracking the political operatives of foreign powers.

Her cover name was Sima. "She gives the impression of a very serious, modest, thoughtful young woman who is ideologically close to us," reported her KGB recruiter.

The FBI quickly determined that only one woman at Justice fit Sima's profile. Her name was Judith Coplon and she had the security clearance to see classified FBI records in the Foreign Agents files, a wealth of data recording the pursuit of Soviet spies and American Communists.

Hoover had to choose a strategy to use against her. The Bureau moved fast. It was inside a Soviet espionage operation, watching it as it happened.

First came wiretaps on Coplon's home and office, the home of her parents, and the New York residence of a Soviet she had telephoned, Valentin Gubitchev, who worked at the United Nations but was clearly a Soviet spy. Fifty agents worked around the clock monitoring and recording the wiretaps. Then the FBI's Bob Lamphere set up a sting. He created a phony document showing that an attorney for Amtorg, the Soviet trading group in New York, was an FBI informant, and he slipped it like a baited hook into the stream of paper Coplon saw at work at the Justice Department. She stole it.

The FBI overheard Coplon planning a trip to New York to see Gubitchev. Agents went to Assistant Attorney General Peyton Ford for an arrest warrant. He told them they lacked sufficient evidence. He said Coplon could be arrested only if she were caught in the act of handing over classified documents to an agent of a foreign power. On March 3, 1949, Coplon took the train to New York. A team of FBI agents followed her. Coplon and the Soviet spy saw they were being shadowed. She never gave him the documents. The FBI nonetheless arrested them, without a warrant.

Coplon faced two trials: one, in April, on the charge of stealing secrets in Washington; the second, in November, on the charge of espionage in New York. They proved to be disasters for Hoover and the FBI.

Coplon was a spy, without question. But the FBI had broken the law trying to convict her. The Bureau illegally wiretapped her telephone conversations with her lawyer. At the first trial, an FBI special agent on the witness stand denied that Coplon's phone had been tapped, a lie that was later detected.

Then, to Hoover's dismay, the judge admitted into evidence FBI reports alluding to the search for information on the Soviet atomic spy ring—a threat to the secrecy of Venona.

To protect the intelligence secrets of the FBI from exposure by the court, Hoover instituted a new internal security procedure on July 29, 1949. It was known as June Mail—a new hiding place for records about wiretaps, bugs, break-ins, black-bag jobs, and potentially explosive reports from the most secret sources. June Mail was not stored or indexed in the FBI's central records but kept in a secret file room, far from the prying eyes of outsiders.

FBI headquarters issued a written order to destroy "all administrative records in the New York field office"—referring to the Coplon wiretaps—"in view of the immediacy of her trial." The written order contained a note in blue ink: "O.K.—H."

Despite Hoover's efforts, the existence of the wiretaps was disclosed at the second trial—another layer of the FBI's secrecy penetrated. Then the same FBI special agent who had lied at the first trial admitted that he had burned the wiretap records.

Coplon was found guilty, but the verdict would not stand. Judge Learned Hand, who heard Coplon's appeal, overturned her twenty-five-year sentence. He publicly rebuked Hoover—a rare event in American jurisprudence. In the words of the FBI's Bob Lamphere, who led the investigation, Hoover was furious about "the entire Coplon affair—especially in the reversal of the conviction." The judge reminded the FBI that the Supreme Court's ban on wiretapping was still the law of the land. The ban was based on "broad considerations of morality and public well-being." The warrantless arrest was illegal. The evidence seized from an illegal arrest was inadmissible—"a fruit of the poisonous tree." Judge Hand also wrote that the defense should have had the right to identify the FBI's original "confidential informant" in the case. That source, of course, was Venona, the deepest secret of American intelligence.

The FBI had been caught breaking the law again. For the first time since the raids of 1920, lawyers, scholars, and journalists openly questioned the powers that Hoover exercised. Almost everyone agreed that the FBI should have the ability to wiretap while investigating treason, espionage, and sabotage. Of course taps would help to catch spies. But so did opening the mails, searching homes and offices, stealing documents, and planting bugs without judicial warrants—all standard conduct for the FBI, and all of it illegal. Even at the height of the Cold War, a free society still looked askance on a secret police.

"THEREFORE RUSSIA KNOWS"

Hoover increased the pressure on his agents to break the secrets of Soviet espionage. The KGB saw the manhunt coming, thanks to its well-placed spies inside the American and British intelligence services.

The American spy-hunters consulted regularly with Peter Dwyer, the chief representative in Washington of the British foreign intelligence service, MI6. In August 1949, Dwyer relayed some recent Venona decryptions from the FBI to the chiefs of British intelligence in London.

They included a five-year-old Soviet cable that contained a verbatim quote from a naturalized British subject, a leading atomic scientist named Klaus Fuchs, who had worked on the Manhattan Project. It showed that Fuchs had served as a Soviet agent at Los Alamos while America was perfecting the bomb. A first-rate theoretical physicist and a hard-core Communist who had fled Hitler's Germany, he proved the best source of secret intelligence for the Soviets on the atomic bomb and its far more powerful successor, the hydrogen bomb. By September 7, 1949, informed of the evidence against Dr. Fuchs, the British were trying to decide how to arrest and convict him without revealing Venona as the source of their knowledge.

On September 20, the CIA issued a report saying the Soviets probably would not produce an atomic weapon for four more years. Three days later, President Truman announced to the world that Stalin had the bomb. American planes had picked up the radioactive fallout from the secret Soviet test. The balance of terror shifted.

Hoover sent his agents across the country to interrogate the scientists who had worked with Fuchs. The Americans pressed the British to prosecute him. He finally broke on January 31, 1950, after weeks of intense interrogation in London. Harry Truman decided publicly, at almost precisely the same hour, to build the hydrogen bomb. The president's decision coincided with Hoover's warning that Fuchs had enjoyed almost unlimited access to the secrets of Los Alamos, including long-term research on the H-bomb.

"Fuchs knew as much about the hydrogen bomb as any American scientist; therefore Russia knows," the FBI reported days after he confessed.

The FBI was desperate to find the rest of the ring that had stolen the secrets of the bomb. But British diplomats barred the Bureau from questioning Fuchs until after a formal sentencing. Hoover called the delay an outrage—especially since it was the British who had recommended Fuchs for the Manhattan Project. Precious weeks passed before the FBI questioned the spy. Fuchs withheld a good deal in his answers, much of it concerning the technological leap from atomic to nuclear bombs. But the Bureau got what it wanted: an airtight identification of the courier who had connected Fuchs to the Soviet espionage underground in America.

His name was Harry Gold, and he had been a Soviet intelligence agent in the United States for fifteen years. His name had been in the FBI's files since 1947. Agents from the Bureau's New York office had interviewed Gold, and he had freely admitted being part of the network of wartime Russian agents served by Elizabeth Bentley. "But after that connection with Gold, three years went by," said FBI special agent Donald Shannon. The interview had been sent to FBI headquarters, filed, and forgotten.

Hoover discovered, to his intense chagrin, that the FBI had overlooked its own records on Klaus Fuchs for four years. They were English translations of captured German army documents, and they had been in the FBI's possession since shortly after the end of World War II, when Fuchs was still spying for the Soviets in the United States. They revealed that Fuchs was well-known as a "communist of relatively important character."

The fault lay with a brilliant but erratic FBI counterintelligence supervisor named William K. Harvey. Hoover had fired him for alcoholism in 1947; he had then joined the CIA. The evidence went unseen until after Fuchs confessed.

"Take note," Hoover wrote to his national security chief on February 16, 1950. "We can't tolerate such slip-shod methods."

"WHAT THE COMPETITORS HAVE"

The KGB knew with uncanny precision how the case would unfold after Fuchs confessed. It predicted that Fuchs would give up Gold, and that Gold would betray the rings of Soviet spies and couriers who had worked to obtain America's atomic secrets. The KGB lamented: "What the competitors have on them is not only their clear and incontrovertible involvement in our work, but also evidence that they passed secret materials on the atomic bomb to us." The "competitors" were the FBI.

The KGB's knowledge came from a Soviet spy named William Weisband. He had been inside Venona headquarters at Arlington Hall for five years.

Much about Weisband remains mysterious today, including his birthplace —Alexandria, Egypt? Odessa, Russia?—and the year he first came to the United States. He likely trained at the Comintern's Lenin School in Moscow during the early 1930s. He spoke fluent Russian, unaccented English, and fair Arabic. By 1936 he was working as a courier for Soviet intelligence in

New York. He became an American citizen in 1938. He joined the United States Army and he served with Signals Intelligence in England, Italy, and North Africa.

Weisband came to Arlington Hall as a Russian translator in 1944. He was a social animal, affable in the extreme. "At the Hall he had a reputation as a stroller. He wandered around, chatting and picking up pieces of gossip," reads a secret history of the case prepared by the National Security Agency. "He was also adept at getting himself on distribution for documents that did not directly concern the work of his section. Highly gregarious, Weisband had a wide circle of friends . . . His postwar wedding party was talked about as a who's who of Army cryptology." His new wife also worked at Arlington Hall.

From February 1948 onward he sent Moscow reams of intelligence describing Venona. In short order, Moscow changed its codes. The Soviets "implemented a set of defensive measures, which resulted in a significant decrease in the effectiveness of the Amer. decryption service," Weisband's KGB file shows. Six weeks before the Soviets tested their first atomic bomb, he reported that American intelligence "was all of a sudden no longer able to read our cipher telegrams."

The secret National Security Agency history picks up the story. "The FBI began piecing together information" on why Venona had gone dark. The Bureau "was aghast to learn in 1950 that Weisband was employed at Arlington Hall" as a section chief working on the Soviet cables. He was arrested, but he never talked. He served a year in prison for contempt of court after he refused to testify before a federal grand jury. He worked in and around Washington selling cars and tending apartments for sixteen years before he died.

The penetration paralyzed the progress of Venona. For the next three decades, the United States could not read the Soviets' most secret messages. It could only look backwards, trying to decipher old cables from the 1940s.

The FBI never found out what Weisband told the Soviets. The National Security Agency history concludes: "His case instilled a certain paranoia within the profession."

That paranoia afflicted the FBI. Hoover insisted that the FBI would create and control its own system for secret communications. "Mr. Hoover was not one who trusted anyone," said the FBI's Ronald M. Furgerson, a leading cryptanalyst at the Bureau. "He was afraid that the National Security Agency, which manufactured everybody else's cryptographic equipment, might have been infiltrated."

Weisband had burrowed into American intelligence from the bottom up. Now another Soviet spy penetrated it from the top down.

Hoover had been convinced from the first that the CIA would be an easy target for Soviet spies. In October 1949, a suave and smooth-talking new MI6 man arrived in Washington, and in time he would personify Hoover's fears.

Kim Philby introduced himself to the leading lights at the CIA and the Pentagon. They read him into their most secret operations. Philby learned of the CIA's plans to parachute Russian and Eastern European émigrés and refugees behind the Iron Curtain to serve as spies, saboteurs, and shock troops against the Soviet Union and its satellites. His foreknowledge doomed those operations and ensured the death or capture of the CIA's recruited foreign agents. He learned all about the counterintelligence work of the FBI and the British in Venona. His reporting kept the KGB informed on the American assault on the Soviet cipher system, the fate of Klaus Fuchs, and the threat to the American members of the atom spy ring.

Philby moved freely through the corridors of the Pentagon, an institution still in a state of upheaval six months after the suicide of Secretary of Defense James Forrestal, who had suffered a psychotic breakdown and jumped from his high window at the Bethesda Naval Hospital. Forrestal had been Hoover's strongest ally in the government of the United States. His death contributed to Hoover's deepening despair over American intelligence and its ability to meet the growing Soviet threat.

While Philby started ransacking American secrets, Hoover was fighting a rearguard action against the future director of Central Intelligence, Allen Dulles. Still a lawyer in private practice, Dulles had been commissioned by the Pentagon to conduct a top-secret study of the shoddy state of American spying. He intended to use his report to the president as a fulcrum to elevate himself to the command of the CIA. Dulles had not consulted Hoover or the FBI during his yearlong investigation, a deliberate snub. When Hoover wrangled a draft copy of the report from the Pentagon, he saw that Dulles did not recognize Hoover's presidentially mandated authority in matters of national security.

"It is outrageous that FBI should be excluded," Hoover wrote.

Dulles did not respond. After a long effort, an FBI special agent back-handed the CIA's new budget out of a staff member of the House Appropriations Committee: it was buried in seven or eight different Pentagon bills. No more than four members of Congress knew about it. "This is the most shocking picture of irregular accounting I have ever seen," Hoover wrote on the memo. More shocking still: the CIA was spending five and a half times more than the FBI.

Hoover saw he had to renew his battle for the power to command the war on communism.

21

"IT LOOKS LIKE WORLD WAR III IS HERE"

I N THE SUMMER OF 1950, Americans realized that the Cold War was a real war and the survival of the world was at stake. Hoover's FBI fought hard on the home front: his force was felt in every branch of the government, every court, and every college in America.

On July 24, 1950, just a month after the Korean War began, Hoover won a formal statement from President Truman expanding the FBI's authority to investigate "espionage, sabotage, subversive activities and related matters" affecting American national security, a mandate even broader than FDR's wartime directives to the FBI. Hoover sought to justify his enhanced powers with a truly frightening top secret report to the president on August 24. He warned that an invisible army—tens of thousands of hard-core members of the American Communist underground—stood ready to do battle against the United States.

He laid out a detailed vision of the death of American cities at the hands of suicide bombers. Hoover attributed his warnings of a terrorist holocaust to "ten substantial and highly reliable informants of the FBI." Some of his secret witnesses were former members of the Communist Party who had testified before federal grand juries or in court; others had been Soviet intelligence agents for twenty years or more. So Hoover said in his report to the White House.

"Soviet leaders will utilize any method which will further their goal of complete world domination," Hoover's report said. "In the event of conflict between the United States and the Soviet Union, every Communist will do everything possible to injure this country." They would infiltrate the military, incite mutiny, start race riots, toss monkey wrenches into the weapons industry, wreck the economy with strikes and sabotage, seize radio and television stations to pump propaganda into people's eyes and ears. The

American Communists had surveyed "the major industrial centers in the United States," one informant averred, "including the strategic points to be captured or destroyed in the event of war."

Hoover saved the worst for last: "the Soviet Union would not hesitate to deliver atom bombs on any target even though such an attack involved suicide missions." Hoover foresaw "suicide planes with atom bombs" and "a large-scale attack of suicide paratroopers carrying small bombs or other destructive devices." The paratroopers would be aided by American Communists when they landed—and the scale of the attack Hoover envisioned was suggested by his assertion that millions of Russian children were training as parachutists.

Atom bombs and hydrogen bomb components could be smuggled into the United States, readied for an attack, and "detonated by remote control or by individuals ready to sacrifice themselves"—the American Communist underground. The report said that "20,000 devoted members of the Communist Party, comprising the core of the Party"—the very same people whom Hoover had placed on his Security Index, the suspects whom he wanted locked up in the name of national survival—were "willing to follow implicitly the instructions of the Soviet Government" in a time of war or crisis.

Hoover's visions of nuclear kamikazes and teenaged suicide bombers falling from the skies were intended to bludgeon the mind of the American government. His apocalyptic scenarios sounded like science fiction, but they truly represented his worst fears.

They also depicted a threat that the FBI could meet: the political mobilization of American Communists in wartime.

Hoover timed his report to the White House with precision. One week before, a federal grand jury in New York indicted the atomic spies who had helped to deliver the secrets of the Manhattan Project to Moscow. The August 17, 1950, indictment against Julius Rosenberg was ironclad. The trial jury would see the evidence as incontrovertible. So would the judge. So would the American people.

On September 23, Congress passed the Internal Security Act of 1950. It contained provisions Hoover had been demanding for a decade. The laws defining espionage and sabotage were expanded and strengthened. Subversive citizens now were subject to political imprisonment. Communist and Communist-front organizations were required to register with a new Subversive Activities Control Board. The new attorney general, J. Howard McGrath, decided that the Internal Security Act gave legal sanction to Hoover's Security Index, with its provisions for preventive detention, its proposals for the suspension of constitutional protections, and its ever-growing roster of more than twenty thousand Americans. Hoover's index was now legal—an accepted part of the American national security establishment. It remained in effect for the next twenty-one years.

The year 1950 brought many bleak days for President Truman. None was darker than November 1.

In the morning, the new director of Central Intelligence, General Walter Bedell Smith, delivered a bulletin: Communist Chinese soldiers had entered the Korean War. The CIA's reporting gravely underestimated the size of the attack. Three hundred thousand Chinese soldiers struck in a human avalanche that killed thousands upon thousands of American soldiers. They came close to driving the Americans from the mountains into the sea. Behind them stood the new dictator of China, Chairman Mao Tse-Tung. American generals assumed Stalin backed Mao, brandishing his new atomic bomb.

In the afternoon, a freakish heat wave engulfed Washington; the mercury hit eighty-five degrees. Truman lay down for a nap at Blair House, across the street from the White House; the executive mansion was in a state of collapse and undergoing renovation. On the sidewalk, at the Blair House door, stood two Puerto Rican nationalists, one armed with a German Luger, the other with a German Walther, carrying sixty-nine rounds of ammunition between them. They tried to shoot their way into Blair House and kill the president in the name of Puerto Rican independence. One of them died, as did a Secret Service agent. The second assassin was arrested, convicted, and sentenced to death. Truman commuted the sentence to life. The FBI's investigation into the leaders and followers of the independence cause lasted more than fifty years.

On November 28, 1950, after the scale of the Chinese attack in Korea was clear, Truman convened a rare full-dress meeting of the National Security Council. The threat of a third world war with weapons of mass destruction was now upon the world. Truman declared a national emergency, tripled the Pentagon's budget, appointed General Eisenhower the supreme commander of NATO, and rejected top secret calls by General Douglas MacArthur and the Joint Chiefs of Staff to drop the entire American arsenal of atomic bombs on China and Manchuria. But Truman said he was prepared to use the bomb if he had to.

"It looks like World War III is here," Truman wrote in his diary on December 9. "I hope not—but we must meet whatever comes—and we will."

"Twenty years of treason"

The FBI, tracing old leads from Venona, suspected the continuing presence of a KGB agent in the British Embassy in Washington. The Bureau knew only that he was a diplomat who held high rank and the code name of Homer.

The British and the Americans had been entwined in intelligence for a decade now, but Hoover had never been comfortable with the partnership. He scorned American Anglophiles. He looked askance at British intelligence boffins. He was appalled by their reticence on the Homer investigation.

Top British and American intelligence officers gathered on a warm Saturday night in April 1951 at the Washington home of Kim Philby. Among the guests were James Angleton and Bill Harvey of the CIA; Bob Lamphere and Mickey Ladd from the FBI; Robert Mackenzie and Jeff Patterson of British intelligence; and Philby's disheveled houseguest, a British diplomat named Guy Burgess. Dinner was unpalatable, drinks plentiful. The veterans of World War II had floated into the 1950s on a sea of alcohol. Angleton, a reigning intellectual at the CIA, liked to drink lunch with Philby, sharing details of American and British plans for commando raids behind the Iron Curtain. He predicted Philby would be the next chief of British foreign intelligence.

The party ended badly. Burgess was drunk and disorderly, inciting snarling catfights with the Americans and their wives. Mickey Ladd of the FBI wondered aloud why Philby, the leading British intelligence officer in Washington, had a character like Burgess living under his roof.

A few weeks later, on May 25, 1951, newspapers on both sides of the Atlantic reported that Burgess and Donald Maclean, chief of the American desk at the British Foreign Office in London, had disappeared together behind the Iron Curtain. Maclean had been the first secretary at the British Embassy in Washington in 1944 and 1945.

He was Homer.

His flight to Moscow brought the chief of British foreign intelligence, Sir Percy Sillitoe, to Washington. Sir Percy carried an attaché case bulging with dossiers on Philby, Maclean, and Burgess, and he shared the contents with Hoover and the FBI. The three Britons were friends of twenty years' standing, going back to their days at Trinity College, Cambridge. In the 1930s, all three had been Communists or socialists. The dossiers held more open secrets: Burgess was famous for his promiscuous homosexuality, Maclean was a closet case, and Philby had married an Austrian Communist and Soviet agent. All three were alcoholics. All this was known by their superiors, yet they were protected and promoted. Maclean and Burgess were in Moscow now; Philby had been recalled to London. Hoover argued that Philby clearly was a Soviet agent, and that he had enabled Moscow to penetrate the CIA and the Pentagon at the highest levels. Sir Percy politely disagreed, unwilling to accept that a man of Philby's rank and breeding could be a traitor.

Reflecting on the past lives of the British spies at Cambridge in the 1930s, Hoover conflated their communism with their homosexuality.

The connection seemed self-evident to him. Homosexuality and communism were causes for instant dismissal from American government service—and most other categories of employment. Communists and homosexuals both had clandestine and compartmented lives. They inhabited secret underground communities. They used coded language. Hoover believed, as did his peers, that both were uniquely susceptible to sexual entrapment and blackmail by foreign intelligence services.

The FBI's agents became newly vigilant to this threat. "The Soviets knew, in those days, a government worker, if he was a homosexual, he'd lose his job," said John T. Conway, who worked on the Soviet espionage squad in the FBI's Washington field office. Conway investigated a State Department official suspected of meeting a young, blond, handsome KGB officer in a gay bar. "It was a hell of an assignment," he said. "One night we had him under surveillance and he picked up a young kid, took him up to his apartment, kept him all night. Next day we were able to get the kid and get a statement from him and this guy in the State Department lost his job."

On June 20, 1951, less than four weeks after the Homer case broke, Hoover escalated the FBI's Sex Deviates Program. The FBI alerted universities and state and local police to the subversive threat, seeking to drive homosexuals from every institution of government, higher learning, and law enforcement in the nation. The FBI's files on American homosexuals grew to 300,000 pages over the next twenty-five years before they were destroyed. It took six decades, until 2011, before homosexuals could openly serve in the United States military.

Hoover then ratcheted up the Responsibilities Program, a new nationwide campaign launched in secret in the spring and summer of 1951. The FBI, under law, was supposed to share its investigative files only within the executive branch of government. Hoover already had breached that wall by leaking files to his favorite members of Congress. The Responsibilities Program began feeding governors, mayors, and other state and local leaders ammunition to attack subversives at home. The local special agent in charge of FBI regional offices served as the go-between for Hoover and the nation's political officials. For the next four years, the Responsibilities Program served as a tool for purging the faculties of state universities, colleges, and public schools of hundreds of suspect leftists, until its secrecy was breached by a publicity-hunting state education commissioner. Together, the Responsibilities and Sex Deviates programs resulted in the dismissals of uncounted teachers across the country.

Hoover took up the homosexual issue in his first meeting with Truman's director of Central Intelligence, Walter Bedell Smith, a four-star army general who had been Eisenhower's chief of staff throughout World War II. General Smith had earned a reputation as Ike's hatchet man, the sharp teeth behind Ike's warm grin. He had served as Truman's ambassador to the Soviet Union; he had gone eyeball-to-eyeball with Stalin. He was a man of great force and short temper, intolerant of imperfection. He and Edgar Hoover hit it off. They had a lot in common.

They sat down for an informal luncheon in a private suite at the Mayflower Hotel. After pleasantries, Hoover raised the issue of homosexuality at the CIA. "General Smith seemed to be considerably amazed at the wide prevalence of this condition," Hoover wrote. "He inquired as to the percentage of persons in the population who had tendencies along this line." Hoover said he would send over an FBI synopsis of Alfred S. Kinsey's *Sexual Behavior in the Human Male,* which reported that one man out of ten was a practicing homosexual, a far greater number than most Americans supposed.

Hoover and General Smith had greater concerns. They thought that the Soviets had infiltrated the CIA. Each and every one of the guerrilla operations the Agency had launched in the past two years had gone wrong. Hundreds of the CIA's recruited foreign agents had been parachuted behind enemy lines, inside the Iron Curtain, and almost all of them had been captured or killed. The CIA was making no headway in its war on communism overseas. The FBI was not breaking any new cases against Communist spies, either.

Some of these failures could be laid to Philby's betrayals—but not all of them. If the Soviets still had a man in the high councils of American intelligence, then the secret operations of the United States could still be sabotaged, at home and abroad.

Hoover decided that he had to change the way the FBI and the CIA worked with each other against the Soviets. Hoover assigned the FBI's Sam Papich to serve at CIA headquarters, and General Smith assigned Jim Angleton to get along with the FBI. Papich, born in Montana, with roots in Yugoslavia, had served undercover for the FBI in Rio de Janeiro during and after World War II, posing as a representative of Dun and Bradstreet. Angleton, born in Idaho, educated at Yale, was an American spy in Italy during the war. These two men kept liaison between the FBI and the CIA alive for the next two decades.

Angleton soon thereafter became the chief of the counterintelligence staff at the CIA, the man in charge of identifying Soviet spies. He made a professional practice of studying the espionage cases of years gone by, trying to decode decades of Soviet deception. He found patterns in the carpet of the past few others could see, some of them invisible to the naked eye and the rational mind.

His elevation to chief of counterintelligence was a coup for J. Edgar Hoover. The depth of Angleton's discussions with the FBI was astonishing; he was by far Hoover's best source on what was going on inside the CIA. "He has been very cooperative and, as you know, has volunteered considerable information which has been of assistance to us," Papich reported. "The fact that he has dealt with the Bureau in a very frank manner, free of the cloak-and-dagger atmosphere usually found in CIA, has made him a person who could work with the Bureau."

On July 2, 1952, Angleton told the FBI that the CIA's political front groups and propaganda organizations throughout Europe were "widely exposed to penetration by Soviet agents." He said that the KGB must have planted spies among the thousands of Eastern European and White Russian refugees the CIA recruited in Germany and England in its efforts to roll back the Soviets. The CIA's operations in Europe were filled with political exiles and "émigrés who were using the organization to feather their nests," Angleton said. He let drop that the CIA's covert operations commander, Frank Wisner, who already had spent hundreds of millions of dollars in secret, had just requested $28 million more to expand his overseas empire. Hoover wrote in his royal blue hand: "It is shocking that such waste and looseness can prevail and nothing can be done about it."

There was something to be done. The national security of the United States hung in the balance of the 1952 presidential election. Hoover worked to ensure that General Eisenhower would be president of the United States and Richard Nixon the vice president. The Republican ticket was set on July 11. The Democrats chose Governor Adlai Stevenson of Illinois on July 24. Hoover already had a report on Stevenson in hand. Assistant FBI director Mickey Ladd had dredged it up from the Sex Deviates files: "Pursuant to your request, there is attached hereto a blind memorandum concerning Governor Stevenson, who, it has been alleged, is a known homosexual."

At the hour of Adlai Stevenson's presidential nomination, a nineteen-page memo about the Democratic candidate went to the FBI's Lou Nichols, who handled relations with Congress and the press. It featured a compendium of vicious gossip, including a report from a New York police detective who said the governor not only was one of the best-known homosexuals in the state of Illinois but used the drag name "Adeline." Hoover made sure that this scuttlebutt reached Richard Nixon, the Republican campaign committee, and a large number of journalists.

The election of Eisenhower and Nixon in November 1952, along with a Republican sweep of the House and the Senate, ended two decades of Democratic dominance in Washington—the era that Senator Joseph McCarthy called "twenty years of treason." At the start of those twenty years, Hoover had led a small, weak organization with 353 special agents and a budget well under $3 million. He now led an anti-Communist army of 6,451 men with 8,206 support staff and $90 million to spend.

A few days after his victory, Ike assured Hoover that he wanted him to run the FBI for as long as he was president, and that he would have the complete support of the White House in the years to come. Some men were more respected in Washington, but not many. Some may have been more feared, but very few.

22

NO SENSE OF DECENCY

A DIRECT TELEPHONE LINE now ran from the White House to Hoover's home. Eisenhower called only on occasion, but Nixon called twice a day, early in the morning and late at night.

Hoover extended his influence into every corner of the ever-expanding national security establishment. As Hoover reported to the newly inaugurated president on January 26, 1953, FBI agents now worked "day-to-day and person-to-person" at the White House, the Pentagon, the Office of the Secretary of Defense, the Joint Chiefs of Staff, the National Security Agency, the CIA, the State Department, Congress, six American embassies, army intelligence bases in Germany and Austria, and a dozen more centers of America's global power.

Hoover took a seat at the National Security Council, alongside the secretary of defense and the secretary of state. The new attorney general, Herbert Brownell, Jr., took Hoover's word as law. Brownell's deputy and successor, William Rogers, became a close personal friend to Hoover, and he sat down twice a week for working lunches with the director. Hoover helped to shape the policies and strategies of the government on everything from national security to civil rights.

American anticommunism came to full power under Eisenhower. Hoover's men investigated nominees for posts ranging from foreign ambassador to congressional aide. They oversaw internal security purges throughout the government, destroying lives and careers over suspicions of disloyalty or homosexuality.

Hoover's impact at the State Department was immense. With the full backing of Secretary of State John Foster Dulles, an FBI agent named R. W. "Scott" McLeod took a job as the internal security chief at State. His political purges of Washington and embassies and consulates overseas used FBI methods, including wiretaps, to force liberals and suspected leftists out of the Foreign Service. An uncounted number of diplomats resigned in despair.

FBI men were ever present in the new organizations Eisenhower created to project American influence and power, such as the United States Information Agency, which broadcast American ideas throughout the world. FBI special agents Charles Noone and Joe Walsh ran the USIA's internal security operations in Washington and New York. The FBI conducted full field investigations of every USIA employee, checking every detail of their lives from childhood onward.

"Our bible was Executive Order 10450, issued by President Eisenhower," Walsh recounted. "This order related to Federal employees as affecting the country's national security. Denial of such employment was spelled out to include anyone associated with communism, homosexuals, drunks, and other social aberrants who might be considered threats to the security of the USA. It was a nasty business—seeking out and identifying people suspected of homosexuality," he said. "There were several awfully decent and intelligent people who worked within the Agency whom I got to know well and enjoyed working within the Agency programs who, suddenly and peremptorily, dropped out of the picture—disappeared! Under investigation, they had admitted their homosexuality and had resigned."

No one in government was exempt, even those who already held top secret security clearances. Stanley Grand was a State Department officer working with the CIA on the coup that overthrew the government of Guatemala in 1954. "It was not a good time for the State Department," he recalled. "We all had to be reinvestigated by the FBI and get new clearances, which most of us did. Some people were terribly damaged. . . . One officer I know, who was an excellent officer, got so fed up because he knew the kind of false charges that might be brought against him, that he committed suicide. It was a tragedy."

But Ike's new internal security regime was a triumph for Hoover. It affirmed the president's faith in the FBI as the front line of American national security.

The White House read Hoover's reports on the Soviets as the most authoritative in the government. Attorney General Brownell said: "The FBI reported to me one of the results of their counterintelligence work against the communist conspiracy. They had learned that Stalin was ill and Malenkov was acting for him and would succeed him if Stalin died. Stalin did die on March 3, 1953, and it is now history that Malenkov succeeded him."

By contrast, the United States had no ambassador in Moscow when Stalin died, and the CIA had no spies inside the Soviet Union. The first CIA officer dispatched to Moscow was seduced by his Russian housekeeper—she was a KGB colonel—photographed in the physical act of love, blackmailed, and fired by the Agency for his indiscretions in 1953. His replacement was caught in the act of espionage, arrested, and deported shortly after he arrived.

The FBI now had Communist informants across America. Through witnesses, wiretaps, bugs, break-ins, and relentless surveillance, the FBI had penetrated and infiltrated the Communist Party of the United States. Many Communists indicted and convicted under the Smith Act went to jail in silence, some went underground, but others became cooperating witnesses. Hoover took some satisfaction when top Communists went to prison, but he saw his intelligence operations as more crucial than any law enforcement work. The two missions demanded different techniques.

A cop confronting an evildoer wants to string him up. A spy wants to string him along. Waiting and watching required a terrible patience. Hoover had it. After twenty years of attack and a decade of counterattack, the FBI was starting to understand the scope of the KGB's operations in America.

The Bureau had a handful of double agents working against the KGB. The first productive break was the case of Boris Morros. Born in Russia in 1895, the same year as Hoover, Morros came to the United States in the wake of the Bolshevik revolution, making his way to Los Angeles and the world of make-believe. He worked at Paramount Pictures, arranging musical soundtracks for B movies, and he ran the Boris Morros Music Company on the side.

He had gone to the Soviet consulate in New York seeking a visa for his father, who wanted to return to Mother Russia in 1934. The visa officer, who served Soviet intelligence, asked: Will you do your country a favor in return? Morros agreed to create a legend—a ghost job with false credentials—in Paramount's Berlin office. The legend served as a deep cover for Vassili Zarubin, later the chief of Soviet espionage in the United States during World War II. Zarubin returned the favor. He paid Morros for the use of his Hollywood music company as a front for undercover Soviet spies.

The FBI had recorded Zarubin in the spring of 1943 talking to the American Communist Steve Nelson about placing Soviet agents inside the Berkeley Radiation Laboratory. That summer Hoover received an anonymous letter from a disgruntled Soviet intelligence officer in Washington. The letter identified Zarubin as the Soviet foreign intelligence chief responsible for espionage in America. It said Soviet spies were recruiting and running large networks of underground agents who were "robbing the whole of the war industry in America." It named five Soviet intelligence officers operating under diplomatic and commercial cover in the United States—including Boris Morros.

But the FBI had waited four years before sending an agent to talk to Morros in Los Angeles in June 1947. The inexplicable delay prompted Hoover to write a poignant note: "How many other like situations exist in our own files is what concerns me. H."

Happily for Hoover, Morros agreed to work for the FBI. His decision to double-cross Moscow was rare indeed. Rarer still was the fact that a flash of his old Soviet case file had become legible to the army code breakers and the FBI, confirming that Morros had deep KGB connections. The Soviet code makers were careless every once in a great while. Moscow's cover name for Boris Morros, born Boris Moroz, was Frost. The Russian word for frost is *moroz*. Any small chink in the armor of Soviet intelligence was a gift from the gods of war.

Morros had become the FBI's man after a decade of work for Moscow. The Bureau called his work the Mocase. His music company still served as a front for KGB operations in New York and Los Angeles. He had produced a breakthrough for the FBI in 1948, securing an invitation to travel to Geneva to meet Aleksandr Korotkov, the man who ran the KGB's worldwide ring of illegals. He met with Korotkov again in Moscow in 1950. For the Kremlin's benefit, Morros spun tall tales of his invitations to the White House and the Vatican. The KGB bit, despite its doubts.

The case was unique in the early 1950s: neither the CIA nor the Pentagon ran an agent inside the KGB. A few select outsiders in the White House and Congress knew that Hoover had achieved this breakthrough—very few.

"THE FBI IS J. EDGAR HOOVER"

In Congress, three investigative committees now worked with the FBI against the Communist threat. The House Un-American Activities Committee hounded Hollywood leftists and denounced fellow travelers in the clergy. The Senate Internal Security Subcommittee pursued Soviet intrigues at the United Nations and Communist sympathizers on college faculties. The Senate Permanent Investigations Subcommittee was now under the command of a new chairman, Senator Joe McCarthy, Republican of Wisconsin.

McCarthy had been in full cry for three years. A garbled version of an outdated and inaccurate FBI report had been a key source for the first false charge that brought him fame in 1950: that the State Department was infested with hundreds of Communists. He did not have a list of names, as he claimed, only a number that changed over time. But the senator nevertheless owed a measure of his fame and power to his use and abuse of FBI reports provided by Hoover's congressional liaison agents. McCarthy and his chief investigator, an ex-FBI man named Don Surine, read sheaves of Bureau reports on the Communist threat. In turn, Surine kept Hoover posted on McCarthy's work.

Like his colleagues in Congress, the senator regularly paid fealty to Hoover in public and in private. "No one need erect a monument to you," McCarthy wrote to the director in one typical tribute. "You have built your own monument in the form of the FBI—for the FBI is J. Edgar Hoover and I think we can rest assured that it always will be."

In the spring of 1953, American politics seemed ready for Senator McCarthy's pitiless brand of anticommunism, as the execution day of Julius and Ethel Rosenberg loomed. The judge who had pronounced the death sentence against the atom spies said their crimes were "worse than murder." His rhetoric matched the tenor of the times. The judge said that Julius Rosenberg had put the atomic bomb in Stalin's hands, which "caused, in my opinion, the Communist aggression in Korea, with the resultant casualties exceeding 50,000, and who knows but that millions more of innocent people may pay the price of your treason." On June 19, 1953, came the execution day. Even Hoover had doubts about the political wisdom of putting Ethel Rosenberg to death. But the FBI had made the case.

"THE VICTIM OF THE MOST EXTREMELY VICIOUS CRITICISM"

Senator McCarthy's attacks were scattershot, but on occasion, when the Bureau's reports steadied his hand, his aim was true. Sometimes he hit a bull's eye, as when he threatened to expose the fact that the CIA had a well-paid employee who had been arrested for homosexual activities, or when he tried to wring testimony from an International Monetary Fund official who the FBI suspected was a Soviet agent.

J. Edgar on McCarthy

Hoover understood McCarthy. He told a newspaper reporter: "McCarthy is a former Marine. He was an amateur boxer. He's Irish. Combine these, and you're going to have a vigorous individual who's not going to be pushed around. . . . I never knew Senator McCarthy before he came to the Senate. I've come to know him well, officially and personally. I view him as a friend, and I believe he so views me. Certainly, he is a controversial man. He is earnest and honest. He has enemies. Whenever you attack subversives of any kind, Communists, Fascists, even the Ku Klux Klan, you are going to be the victim of the most extremely vicious criticism that can be made. I know."

But when McCarthy started tearing at the pillars of national security, Hoover had to fight to control the damage that the senator was inflicting on anticommunism and the American government.

In the summer of 1953, the senator began to plan an inquisition against the CIA. McCarthy leveled accusations of Communist Party membership or Communist-front activity against CIA employees in executive sessions of his investigative committee. Allen Dulles, the director of Central Intelligence, was badly shaken; McCarthy had warned him that the CIA was "neither sacrosanct nor immune from investigation," as Dulles told his brother, the secretary of state.

Hoover's agents told him that "Senator McCarthy had found the CIA to be a very 'juicy' target." The FBI's congressional liaison, Lou Nichols, reported that the senator and his staff had lined up "thirty-one potentially friendly witnesses" prepared to testify against fifty-nine CIA employees and officials.

McCarthy's targets included James Kronthal, a homosexual CIA station chief suspected of succumbing to Soviet blackmail, who committed suicide while under investigation; a second CIA officer who had "an intimate relationship" with Owen Lattimore, a State Department officer falsely accused by McCarthy as the top Soviet spy in the United States; and sundry CIA employees suspected of "alcoholism, perversion, extramarital sex relations, narcotics violations and misapplication of CIA funds."

Many of McCarthy's charges were drawn directly from the FBI's raw and uncorroborated reporting, including third-hand hearsay. Wary about the wholesale disclosure of the FBI files, Hoover sent word to the senator to slow down. Instead, McCarthy reloaded and took fresh aim.

On October 12, 1953, the senator began a week of closed-door hearings into suspicions of Soviet espionage at the Army Signal Corps center at Fort Monmouth, New Jersey, where Julius Rosenberg had worked. Rosenberg had been an electrical engineer at the Signal Corps when the FBI first learned that he was a secret Communist. Seven engineers who worked on Signal Corps radars and radios were suspected members of the atomic spy ring—and four of them were still at large the day the Rosenbergs died.

The senator had obtained a three-page summary of a 1951 letter from Hoover to General Alexander R. Bolling, the army intelligence chief, naming thirty-five Fort Monmouth workers as suspected subversives. A radar specialist and an electronics engineer soon were fired because they once had known Julius Rosenberg. Thirty-three others were suspended pending security investigations. But the army found no spies among them.

McCarthy's fury boiled over. The stage now was set for the Army-McCarthy hearings, the first great live television news event in history. The show reached a high point on May 4, 1954.

McCarthy pulled out his copy of Hoover's letter on the thirty-five suspected subversives at Fort Monmouth, and he shoved it at the dapper secretary of the army. Hoover was mortified at McCarthy's public brandishing of the letter. Not many people knew that the senator had enjoyed access to Hoover's secret files.

Hoover and President Eisenhower now concluded that McCarthy's assault on the army and the CIA was subverting the cause of anticommunism. At their behest, Attorney General Brownell issued a ruling that McCarthy's possession of Hoover's letter was an unauthorized use of classified information—a federal crime. McCarthy responded by calling on every one of America's two million government workers to send him all the secrets they had about corruption, communism, and treason. Ike, enraged, issued a decree that no one in the executive branch of government would answer to a call to testify to Congress about anything at any time, the most sweeping claim of executive privilege in the history of the American presidency.

The strains on McCarthy grew. He was drinking bourbon in the morning and vodka at night, sleeping two or three hours before going on national television to rail against the secret Communists in the American government. The drama on TV was strong stuff. So was the shadow play behind the scenes.

On June 2, 1954, Senator McCarthy publicly renewed his vow to go after the CIA, making the announcement on television at the Army-McCarthy hearings.

The president struck back. At the White House, on June 8, Ike told his aides, including his press secretary, Jim Hagerty: "My boys, I am convinced of one thing. The more we can get McCarthy threatening to investigate our intelligence, the more public support we are going to get. If there is any way I could trick him into renewing his threat, I would be very happy to do so and then let him have it."

Hoover told his men to shut off all collaboration with the senator. Without the FBI's files to guide him, McCarthy ran aground. The CIA ran an operation to confound him. One of McCarthy's men had tried blackmailing a CIA officer, telling him that either the officer would furnish classified CIA documents to McCarthy in secret—or McCarthy would destroy him in public. Allen Dulles and his counterintelligence expert, Jim Angleton, advised the CIA officer in question to feed disinformation to McCarthy about communism in the American military, hoping to mystify and mislead him at the moment his confrontation with the army approached its crashing climax.

On June 9, 1954, McCarthy fell. The subject of the day was his futile search for spies at Fort Monmouth. McCarthy's counsel, Roy Cohn, confronted the army's lawyer at the hearing, Joe Welch. Welch was making mincemeat of him. Cohn looked like a toad in the talons of an eagle. McCarthy, burned out and hungover, came to Cohn's defense. He had cut a deal with Welch: if the army did not ask how Cohn had avoided military service in World War II and Korea, a question without a good answer, McCarthy would not bring up the issue of Fred Fisher. Welch had kept his word. McCarthy now broke it. Few in the enormous television audience could have heard of Fisher, a Republican lawyer in Welch's firm. McCarthy, his voice dripping with venom, now named him as a member of the National Lawyers Guild, "the legal bulwark of the Communist Party." Fisher had joined the guild at Harvard Law School and left it shortly after graduation.

McCarthy then turned on Welch.

"I don't think you yourself would ever knowingly aid the Communist cause," the senator said. "I think you are unknowingly aiding it when you try to burlesque this hearing." Welch was stunned but not speechless. His rebuke resounded: "Let us not assassinate this lad further, senator. Have you no sense of decency, sir, at long last? Have you left no sense of decency?"

With the fall of Joe McCarthy, Hoover regained his role as the nation's leading crusader in the war on communism. President Eisenhower relied on him more than ever to shape and sharpen American responses to the threats of espionage and subversion.

McCarthy, censured by the Senate, descended into self-destruction. He drank himself to death three years later. Hoover went to his funeral. So did the young Democrat who had served as the committee's minority counsel, Robert F. Kennedy. It was a fitting moment for the two to meet.

23

GAME WITHOUT RULES

A FTER THIRTY YEARS as director of the FBI, Hoover's political antennae were so finely tuned that news of the most sensitive presidential decisions arrived almost immediately on his desk.

On July 16, 1954, President Eisenhower summoned a retired three-star general named Jimmy Doolittle. Ten years before, Doolittle had led the first American bombing of Tokyo. Now the president wanted Doolittle to help him overhaul the CIA. Ike wanted the report done by October.

Hoover found out about this top secret investigation within days. "The President stated that he wanted General Doolittle to conduct a thorough and objective study of CIA's covert operations," Hoover learned from Pat Coyne, an FBI veteran who served as the National Security Council's most trusted intelligence staffer. Ike wanted "to unearth any evidence that the CIA was not operating efficiently and to make any recommendations which would improve the organization in any way whatever. He summarized his position by stating that he wanted Doolittle to make the survey as thorough and exhaustive as would be done if the President himself were handling the assignment."

Hoover also got word that Doolittle had told the president: "There was one individual in Government who could be of extremely valuable assistance to him regarding correct and proper administration of intelligence operations. Doolittle stated that this person was J. Edgar Hoover."

Hoover strongly doubted that the problems of the CIA could be fixed. He wrote to his national security aides: "I have a completely defeatist attitude as to any effective corrective measures which might improve CIA. H."

Hoover had made plainly evident his personal and professional contempt for the CIA's chief, Allen Dulles. He deigned to meet with Dulles no more than half a dozen times during the eight years of Eisenhower's presidency. He made sure that his aides reflected his thinking.

"How in the world can I do business with the Bureau?" Dulles had shouted at his FBI liaison in an unguarded moment. "I try and you keep striking back."

The Doolittle investigation presented Hoover one more opportunity to stake his claim to preeminence in American intelligence.

"Wipe out CIA entirely"

The FBI's intelligence division chief, Al Belmont, indoctrinated General Doolittle and his investigators for three hours on August 25, 1954.

"Doolittle viewed the Bureau as a model in guiding him," Belmont reported with satisfaction. "I placed unusually great stress on the fact that the Bureau, in addition to being a law enforcement body, was also very much in the intelligence field. I made it clear that we were expending every effort to keep apprised of all activities of the Communist Party. We had Soviet and satellite diplomats under constant observation; and that as far as the Bureau was concerned, we could never relax."

By contrast, Belmont told the Doolittle group, the CIA was shot through with "waste, inefficiency, and plain boondogglery."

Hoover granted Doolittle an audience on October 6, 1954. The CIA's right hand did not know what the left hand was doing, he told the general. Its spies had little if any idea of what was going on behind the Iron Curtain, and its analysts knew even less. No doubt, Hoover allowed, "some of its weaknesses and defects were due to the newness of its operations." But the Agency lacked trained officers. It had no internal inspection service; those overseers were a crucial part of the way in which Hoover punished and promoted the FBI's agents. The Agency needed a strong shot of the Bureau's kind of discipline.

On October 19, 1954, Doolittle delivered his grim assessment of American intelligence to the president. "We are facing an implacable enemy whose avowed objective is world domination," it began.

"There are no rules in such a game," it continued. "Hitherto acceptable norms of human conduct do not apply. If the United States is to survive, long-standing American concepts of 'fair play' must be reconsidered. We must develop effective espionage and counterespionage services and must learn to subvert, sabotage, and destroy our enemies by more clever, more sophisticated and more effective methods than those used against us."

Hoover's critique shaped Doolittle's confidential conclusion: "The ideal solution would be to wipe out CIA entirely and start all over again."

President Eisenhower could not bring himself to do that. Instead, he leaned harder on Hoover's reporting on the Soviet threat.

Hoover deepened the president's fears of a devastating attack on the United States. He heavily influenced a top secret National Security Council alert to the president on potential Soviet actions that could trigger World War III. His February 28, 1955, report warned of spies and saboteurs assassinating American civilian and military leaders; smuggling nuclear weapons components and "biological, chemical or radiological warfare agents" into the United States; exploding "weapons of mass destruction" at American military bases; using underground American Communists to direct bombing attacks against government targets; and organizing "armed insurrection in the U.S. by communist party members or persons under Soviet direction" who would be armed with "cached weapons, ammunition, explosives and military communications gear."

Hoover followed up by informing the White House that the FBI was intensifying its intelligence work along every front of the Cold War, stepping up its surveillance of Soviet diplomats and embassy personnel, looking for spies and secret agents. "Plans for the detention of enemy diplomatic personnel have been readied," Hoover assured the president. The Bureau now listed 26,500 "potentially or actually dangerous" people on the Security Index, all of whom would be arrested and detained at the president's command. Among them were American prisoners of war returned from North Korea, some of whom, the FBI suspected, had been brainwashed by Chinese Communist interrogators to serve as underground agents who would burrow into the American military and betray the nation if war came again.

Hoover told the White House and the Pentagon that the FBI's "most important goal" was "the development of good double agents" to penetrate the Soviet leadership at the highest levels and gain knowledge of the Kremlin's intentions and capabilities. He was already working on a plan to meet that theretofore unattainable goal.

24

THE LONG SHADOW

O N THE MORNING of March 8, 1956, Hoover addressed the president and the National Security Council at the White House. He said he was "using every available means"—tapping telephones, opening mail, installing bugs, and breaking into the offices and safes of suspected Communist spies and saboteurs throughout the United States—to prevent a surprise Soviet attack on the United States.

His briefing, "The Present Menace of Communist Espionage and Subversion," raised the new specter of a dirty bomb unleashed by Soviet spies. Using cobalt-60, a radioactive isotope developed for the war on cancer, the Soviets, he warned, could deliver a lethal cache in an attaché case. If unleashed in Manhattan, it could kill hundreds of thousands of people and render the city of New York uninhabitable for years. It would be a doomsday weapon.

The threat of a nuclear attack haunted Eisenhower every day. He asked Hoover what the FBI was doing to guard against the danger.

"Sometimes it is necessary to make a surreptitious entry where on occasion we have photographed secret communist records," Hoover told the president. Everyone in the room understood that "surreptitious entry" was against the law.

Hoover explained that the FBI's reports based on illegally gathered intelligence would be sanitized to guard their secrecy, and to protect the president and the attorney general. The reports would be scrubbed of any references to break-ins and bugs; the intelligence would be attributed to "confidential sources."

The president commended Hoover. The minutes of the meeting record no more questions about the FBI's methods.

Hoover went back to headquarters convinced that he had strengthened the powers of the hunting license granted him by President Roosevelt. He was certain that it would be good for at least four more years; Ike's re-election was assured—if he lived; he had suffered a serious heart attack six months before—and if Nixon became president, he would back Hoover to the hilt. Attorney General Brownell would be steadfast, too, so long as Hoover did not tell him precisely what he was doing in the name of national security.

These men tacitly understood the code of silence Hoover required. Eisenhower had run the D-day invasion, the biggest secret operation of World War II. Nixon had been steeped in raw FBI reports from his first days in Washington. Brownell knew more about secret intelligence than any of his predecessors: he had chaired the committee that created the electronic-eavesdropping, code-making, and code-breaking behemoth of the National Security Agency in 1952.

At Hoover's request, Brownell had asked congressional committee chairmen for new laws allowing wiretapping without a warrant. They had said no, time and again. Hoover had asked for the legal authorization for microphone surveillances—bugging, or "technicals," in Bureauspeak—but the lawmakers spurned the request. The director would have to depend on invoking the authorities granted him explicitly by President Roosevelt and tacitly by President Eisenhower. That was good enough for the attorney general. He just didn't want to know the details.

Hoover's intelligence operations already ranged to the edge of the law and beyond. Each one was a potential disaster if anything went wrong. Hoover deemed the risks worth the rewards. The Cold War would not be won simply by shadowing the enemy.

"We all did it, because it was the Bureau"

The FBI's budget had doubled since the end of World War II. The Intelligence Division was now the most powerful force within the Bureau, commanding the most money, the most manpower, and the most attention from the director. The division conducted uncounted break-ins and buggings in the Eisenhower years; the routine destruction of FBI files ensured that no accurate count existed.

"Surveillances weren't the answer," said the FBI's Jack Danahy, who had run more than his share, going back to the days of the atom spy rings. "We had to change our tactics. . . . We had to make every effort to develop live informants, utilize both mike and technical wiretaps, and become more sophisticated in our actual techniques."

The FBI's James R. Healy, who worked in San Francisco and northern California, recalled: "We had a group sort of like the Dirty Dozen, a very talented group of agents who effected the thorough penetration of the Communist Party underground." His squad was "hot on the trails of the COMFUGS, communist fugitives," who were running from federal and state charges of subversion. Healy and his men broke the FBI's dress codes, along with many other rules, as they went deep undercover.

"The clothing that we wore fit the scene," he said. "We were dressed in old clothes. Some of the guys let their hair grow a little bit. Didn't shave all the time. We fit in with the neighborhoods that we were following these people through . . . We knew what they were doing before some of them knew what they were doing. The placing of informants and the related techniques gave us an inside view of the whole Communist Party underground apparatus."

The "related techniques" included burglaries aimed both at stealing documents and installing hidden microphones. At the FBI's New York office, "we were using every means necessary, at that time, which was extensive use of bag jobs, surreptitious entries, mail pilferage," recalled Graham J. Desvernine, who started working with a special unit called the Underground Squad in 1956. "We were regularly going into Communist Party headquarters and into their main vault," Desvernine said. "Go in there and bag the place. We had keys to everything and all. I was pickin' locks. You know, it was kind of fun, the whole thing."

Only one FBI operation was more sensitive than the Underground Squad: a special espionage team, created in 1954, which set up "a program of intelligence collection that later became known as Program C," said Edward S. Miller, who cut his teeth on the program's San Francisco squad, and eventually became the number-three man in the FBI. This international effort included attempts to break into Soviet and Soviet-bloc embassies and consulates in New York, Washington, San Francisco, and other cities. One goal was to support the National Security Agency in its efforts to steal the secret codes and ciphers of America's enemies.

Hoover's men conducted bag jobs across the country, not just in the Communist hotbeds of the East and West coasts. In 1955, John F. McCormack, a young agent with the Cleveland office of the FBI, went on his first black-bag operation. The target was the home of a suspected Communist—a steel-mill worker with a Ph.D. from New York University. "We broke into the house, picked the lock . . . and photographed everything in the house," McCormack recounted. "We later determined that he had connections with a foreign country. Basically he was there, we assumed, to do something in case of a national emergency at the steel mill." McCormack was well aware that "you would get fired or arrested at the very least" if a break-in went wrong. "You couldn't carry your credentials or any identification" on a black-bag job, he said. "We knew that perhaps we would be on our own if something happened. I think that all the agents that were involved did it for a sense of accomplishment. They took that risk. It was no less a risk than arresting a fugitive and getting shot. And so we all did it, because it was the Bureau."

In Cleveland, the eighth-largest city in America in the mid-1950s, the FBI found six leading Communist figures to arrest and prosecute under the Smith Act, which had effectively outlawed membership in the Communist Party. All were found guilty.

But each of those convictions was overturned. The courts were starting to question the legal basis for the FBI's national security investigations.

The Supreme Court, in a series of decisions starting in 1955 and 1956, voided dozens of Smith Act convictions, undercut the FBI's use of paid informers as witnesses against the Communist Party, and upheld the right of defense lawyers to see evidence gathered through FBI surveillance. Each decision was a blow to Hoover.

The Court rejected cases built on hearsay and perjury by the Bureau's professional witnesses, culled from the ranks of ex-Communists. The worst among them was Harvey Matusow, a high school dropout and army veteran who had joined the Communist Party in 1947, volunteered his services as an informant to the FBI in 1950, and testified in court and before Congress that Communists had infiltrated every corner of American society, from the State Department to the Boy Scouts. Matusow had recanted in a 1955 book, *False Witness,* and in 1956 started serving forty-four months in federal prison for perjury.

The Court was also becoming alert to the continuing use of wiretaps and bugs. In a five-to-four decision, it upheld a state court conviction based on evidence obtained by concealed microphones planted by police during warrantless break-ins. But five justices also expressed outrage that the bug had been placed in a bedroom. That decision worried Attorney General Brownell, who privately warned Hoover about where to put his microphones.

One Supreme Court ruling especially infuriated Hoover. It allowed Communist Party members to invoke the Fifth Amendment in refusing to identify their comrades. A majority opinion was written by Hoover's oldest living nemesis, Justice Felix Frankfurter.

The justices finally ruled that the government had enforced the Smith Act too broadly by targeting words, not deeds—free speech, instead of forcible blows against the political system. That made the act almost useless for prosecuting American Communists. A decade of legal attack against the Communist Party was coming to an end. The law no longer was an effective weapon in the war on communism.

These reversals enraged Hoover. And out of that rage came the boldest attacks that Hoover ever mounted against his enemies, the most ambitious and destructive operations in the history of the FBI.

"Will it get us what we want?"

On May 18, 1956, the new plan of attack began taking shape, the brainchild of the FBI Intelligence Division chief Al Belmont and his trusted aide, William C. Sullivan.

They called the plan COINTELPRO, short for counterintelligence program. Counterintelligence, formally defined, is the work of preventing spies from stealing your secrets. COINTELPRO was more than that. Hoover and his men aimed to subvert America's subversives. Their stratagems were sharpened at the suggestion of agents in the field, toughened by Sullivan, and ultimately approved by Hoover.

The first operations began on August 28, 1956. Armed with the intelligence gathered through break-ins, bugs, and taps, COINTELPRO began to attack hundreds, then thousands, of suspected Communists and socialists with anonymous hate mail, tax audits by the Internal Revenue Service, and forged documents designed to sow and fertilize seeds of distrust among left-wing factions.

The idea was to instill hate, fear, doubt, and self-destruction within the American Left. The FBI used Communist techniques of propaganda and subversion. The goal was to destroy the public lives and private reputations of the members of the Communist Party and everyone connected with them.

In time there would be twelve major COINTELPRO campaigns, aimed at targets across the political spectrum, and a total of 2,340 separate operations. Most operations, in cases where the records were not burned or shredded, bore Hoover's personal approval in his scribble of blue ink.

"OK. H."

"I concur. H."

"Yes, and promptly. H."

The cleverest mind behind the birth and growth of COINTELPRO belonged to Bill Sullivan, the newly appointed chief of research and analysis at the Intelligence Division. Born in 1912 on a farm thirty-five miles west of Boston, Massachusetts, Sullivan remembered the spectacle of burning crosses in the fields near his hometown, ignited by the Ku Klux Klan, the racist secret society that arose after the Civil War and flared up mightily after World War I. He taught school, worked for the Internal Revenue Service, and then joined the FBI four months before Pearl Harbor.

Sullivan recalled his FBI training and indoctrination vividly—especially "the terrific propaganda that the instructors gave out: 'This is the greatest organization ever devised by a human mind.' They kept quoting Emerson: 'An institution is the lengthened shadow of one man.' They hit us with that almost every day. They drilled that into us."

He rose rapidly at the Intelligence Division by virtue of his drive and ambition. Despite his appearance—he looked like a rumpled and shifty-eyed B-movie detective—Sullivan would become Hoover's field marshal in matters of national security, chief of FBI intelligence, and commandant of COINTELPRO. In that top secret and tightly compartmentalized world, an FBI inside the FBI, Sullivan served as the executor of Hoover's most clandestine and recondite demands.

"He was a brilliant chameleon," Sullivan said of Hoover. "He was one of the greatest con men the country ever produced, and that takes intelligence of a certain kind, an astuteness, a shrewdness."

Hoover's talented political hatchet man and trusted deputy, Cartha "Deke" DeLoach, painted a matching portrait of Sullivan: "Brash, brilliant, brimming over with self-esteem, something of a bantam rooster, Sullivan had more ambition than was good for a man, combined with a slight deficiency in principle. For years COINTELPRO was his special domain. He ruled it with skill and daring most of the time, but occasionally with reck-less abandon." Some of the FBI's chieftains thought the Communist Party was so demoralized "it was no longer worth worrying about," DeLoach re-flected. "But increasingly, the architect of COINTELPRO—Sullivan—was worth worrying about."

Sullivan's quicksilver talents for palace intrigue and his political cunning were primal forces that shaped the Bureau, the national security of the United States, and the American presidency for two decades. He came within a hair's breadth of succeeding Hoover after the director's death—a very close call made by President Nixon, whose downfall Sullivan then secretly helped ensure. At the end of his era, Sullivan talked in a closed Senate cham-ber about the thinking that drove the FBI and COINTELPRO onward.

Sullivan was capable of bearing false witness, but this testimony reso-nated with the ring of truth.

"This is a rough, tough, dirty business, and dangerous. It was dangerous at times. No holds were barred," Sullivan said. And the law was not at issue: "Never once did I hear anybody, including myself, raise the question: 'Is this course of action which we have agreed upon lawful? Is it legal? Is it ethical or moral?' We never gave any thought to this realm of reasoning, because we were just naturally pragmatists. The one thing we were concerned about was this: will this course of action work, will it get us what we want?"

Sullivan said he and his cohorts at the FBI "could not free ourselves from that psychology with which we had been imbued as young men." They were soldiers in the Cold War. "We never freed ourselves from that psychology that we were indoctrinated with, right after Pearl Harbor, you see. . . . It was just like a soldier in the battlefield. When he shot down an enemy, he did not ask himself is this legal or lawful, is it ethical? It is what he was expected to do as a soldier. We did what we were expected to do."

"The things he hated, he hated all his life"

The FBI had spied on every prominent black political figure in America since World War I. The scope of its surveillance of black leaders was im-pressive, considering the Bureau's finite manpower, the burden of its re-sponsibilities, and the limited number of hours in a day. Hoover spent his career convinced that communism was behind the civil rights movement in the United States from the start.

Civilrights

Hoover gave special attention to William Edward Burghardt Du Bois. Born in 1868, the venerable Du Bois had become the head of the National Association for the Advancement of Colored People in 1910. The NAACP, the most august civil rights group in America, had been the focus of intense FBI interest since World War II.

The FBI's intelligence investigation of Communist influence at the NAACP began in the spring of 1941 and lasted for twenty-five years. The FBI's Washington field office opened the case after the navy asked it to look into "fifteen colored mess attendants" protesting rampant racist conduct (American armed forces remained segregated throughout World War II). The FBI hired an informant and sought the NAACP's "connections with the Communist party." Four months before Pearl Harbor, FBI headquarters ordered Oklahoma City agents to investigate "Communist Party domination" at the NAACP. They reported "a strong movement on the part of the Communists to attempt to dominate this group . . . Consequently, the activities of the NAACP will be closely observed and scrutinized in the future."

They were. Hoover took the investigation nationwide. FBI informants infiltrated civil rights conferences in at least ten states and filed reports on hundreds of NAACP members, including the group's counsel, the future Supreme Court justice Thurgood Marshall.

On October 2, 1956, Hoover stepped up the FBI's long-standing surveillance of black civil rights activists. He sent a COINTELPRO memo to the field, warning that the Communist Party was seeking to infiltrate the movement.

"The Negro situation is a paramount issue" for the Communists, the director wrote.

Hoover told President Eisenhower that the Communists were concentrating their efforts in Alabama, Georgia, and Mississippi; they intended to inject civil rights into every political issue in America; they would demand federal intervention to enforce the law of the land; they would seek the impeachment of Senator James Eastland of Mississippi, the Democratic chairman of the Judiciary Committee, a plantation master, and an ardent segregationist.

Hoover started watching the new leaders of the civil rights movement very closely. By 1957, COINTELPRO was primed as a weapon in the long struggle between black Americans and their government.

Three years before, in *Brown v. Board of Education,* the Supreme Court had cracked the façade of the American way of life by ordering the integration of public schools. Hoover advised Eisenhower that Communists at home and abroad saw the *Brown* decision as a victory, and that they aimed to "exploit the enforcement of desegregation in every way."

The ruling threw gasoline on the smoldering embers of the Ku Klux Klan. Days after the decision, the Klan began to burn again.

"The Klan was dead until *Brown*," said the FBI's John F. McCormack, who moved from chasing Communists in Cleveland to a series of assignments in the South in 1957. "They lived down here in their own little world. There was no problem. The blacks had their own area, the blacks had their own schools." Now the Supreme Court had told the southern whites that they had to integrate. As McCormack saw it, working-class whites feared "blacks coming into their area now. Blacks would go to school with their children, blacks gonna marry their daughters, blacks gonna take over their jobs. So that was a motivating force. . . . And the Klan grew."

The Klan began dynamiting black churches, burning synagogues, shooting people in the back with hunting rifles, and infiltrating state and local law enforcement. It became the most violent American terrorist group of the twentieth century. As the Klan revived, the high sheriffs of the old South pledged to resist the new law of the land. Senator James Eastland of Mississippi spoke for them when he proclaimed that Anglo-Saxon Americans saw resistance to integration as obedience to God.

Despite the violence, Hoover took a hands-off stance toward the KKK. He would not direct the FBI to investigate or penetrate the Klan unless the president so ordered. "Headquarters came out with instructions that we were not to develop any high-level Klan informants because it might appear that we were guiding and directing the operations of the Klan," said the FBI's Fletcher D. Thompson, based in Georgia. This was a rationalization for racism.

Hoover had been born in nineteenth-century Washington, D.C., a southern city that stayed segregated throughout most of the twentieth century. In his world, blacks knew their place: they were servants, valets, and shoeshine boys. He feared the rise of a black "messiah," to quote a COINTELPRO mission statement. He presided over an Anglo-Saxon America, and he aimed to preserve and defend it.

"He was very consistent throughout the years. The things he hated, he hated all his life," Bill Sullivan said. "He hated liberalism, he hated blacks, he hated Jews—he had this great long list of hates."

More precisely, Hoover hated ideologies more than individuals, pressure groups more than people; above all, Hoover hated threats to the stability of the American political system, and anyone who might personify that danger was an enemy for life.

Hoover's antipathy to the idea of racial equality can explain some of his hostility to the civil rights movement, but not all of it.

His alarm at a nexus between communism and civil rights intensified in early 1957. To the FBI, the newly organized Southern Christian Leadership Conference, and its theretofore obscure director, the twenty-seven-year-old Martin Luther King, Jr., represented such a threat.

Hoover first began to focus on Bayard Rustin, the principal strategist of civil disobedience and nonviolent resistance—boycotts, sit-ins, and protest marches—at the Southern Christian Leadership Conference. The Bureau already had a substantial file on Rustin, a man seemingly made by his creator to get under Hoover's skin—a socialist, a pacifist, and openly gay, with a prison record for draft resistance and sodomy. He remained the subject of FBI investigation for the next twenty years.

So did a white New Yorker with thick glasses, a businessman and legal counselor whom Rustin introduced to King in late 1956. His name was Stanley David Levison, and he helped draw up the founding documents for the Southern Christian Leadership Conference. He became King's closest confidant—writing his speeches, polishing the manuscript of King's first book, preparing his tax returns, and serving as a sounding board as King drafted his first major address to white America, delivered from the steps of the Lincoln Memorial on May 17, 1957.

By that time Levison had been in the FBI's files for five years. The Bureau suspected that he had been a key financier for the Communist Party underground since 1952. Though the evidence was circumstantial, Hoover believed it.

But only seven weeks before the Lincoln Memorial speech, the FBI took Levison off its list of top American Communists. That decision was based on information from its best informants inside the Party. Six weeks after the speech, on June 25, 1957, the FBI noted that Levison was "a CP member with no official title, who performs his CP work through mass organization activity." He appeared to have left his leading role in the Communist underground to devote himself to civil rights.

But Hoover's belief that communism stood behind Martin Luther King and the civil rights movement never wavered.

Hoover's agents in Chicago and New York had been working for years on an operation to recruit and run a man who was trusted and respected in the highest ranks of the Communist Party of the United States. The operation, code-named Solo, had no precedent in the annals of the Cold War.

Solo had one terrible consequence. It would convince Hoover that the American civil rights movement was backed by Moscow and infiltrated at the top by secret Communists. It would lead him into open political warfare against King.

25

"DON'T TRUST ANYBODY"

A T A FORMAL state luncheon for the king of Morocco on November 26, 1957, J. Edgar Hoover and Richard Nixon talked face-to-face about the fact that President Eisenhower might die at any moment. The afternoon before, Ike had suffered a stroke. Nixon had rushed to the White House, where the president's chief of staff, Sherman Adams, told him: "You may be President in twenty-four hours."

Eisenhower recovered by the spring of 1958, though sometimes his speech and his thoughts seemed slightly askew. Hoover himself appeared to suffer a mild heart attack not long after Ike's stroke, an undocumented cardiovascular event he kept hidden from everyone he could. His behavior began to change, as did the president's. Both men grew more short-tempered, impatient, and demanding. But while Ike began soul-searching, seeking a thaw in the Cold War, Hoover hardened. The few men who were close to him at the FBI saw him becoming imperious, vainglorious, and grandiose.

That summer, *Masters of Deceit,* a meandering tract on communism, made Hoover wealthy. Written by his aides, Bill Sullivan chief among them, and published in Hoover's name, with his face on the cover, the book sold hundreds of thousands of copies, many of them bought in bulk by patriotic groups like the American Legion. A desultory congressional investigation, mounted after his death, showed that Hoover laundered 20 percent of the book's net profits through a tax-exempt foundation for retired FBI officers. He banked at least $71,000, equal to more than half a million today.

Masters of Deceit was published by a fabulously rich Texas oil man named Clint Murchison, who had conceived the book as a business deal. Hoover enjoyed a separate silent partnership with Murchison: he could invest in an oil well, and if it gushed, he would profit; if it was dry, he would not lose a dime. Hoover (and his number-two man, Clyde Tolson) spent summer vacations at Murchison's elegant resort in La Jolla, California, staying in the best suite, Bungalow A, playing the ponies, dining and drinking, all on the house. "They lived in sheer opulence," Hoover's aide Deke DeLoach reflected years later. The La Jolla junkets were "the nearest thing to a genuine scandal in Hoover's life."

He liked his luxuries. A coterie of servants, all FBI employees, tended him at home on 30th Place, a leafy street of landscaped and spacious houses in northwest Washington, where he had lived for the two decades since his mother's death. The Bureau provided him with chauffeurs, handymen, gardeners, valets, and the tax accountants who sorted out the honoraria he received, totaling tens of thousands of dollars, from corporate grandees. The gifts, given for ghostwritten speeches and articles, and as private awards for public service, supplemented the freely spent tax dollars that financed Hoover's four-star style.

He had five bulletproof Cadillacs garaged and gleaming in Washington, New York, Chicago, Miami, and Los Angeles. His drivers took him wherever he wanted to go. When in Washington, as he was eleven months a year, he lunched at the Mayflower Hotel after leaving the Bureau at 11:45 A.M., usually ordering a slab of roast beef or, on doctor's orders, a bowl of chicken soup and a plate of cottage cheese. By 6:15 P.M., most evenings, he was sipping a Jack Daniel's and ordering a steak at Harvey's Restaurant, one of the few culinary palaces near the Capitol. His drooping jowls and his pouched eyes reflected his tastes in food and drink.

Hoover was now conscious that he might not live forever. By law, he could serve as director for only six and a half more years, until he turned seventy. He sought a sinecure from the Senate majority leader, Lyndon B. Johnson of Texas. Johnson had been Hoover's across-the-street neighbor on 30th Place since 1945. He would invite Hoover over for a glass of sour-mash whiskey or a Sunday breakfast from time to time. They had a friendship, or what passed for friendship in Washington. More precisely, they were political allies. Together they conceived a special bill of legislation. LBJ won a quick and uncontested vote from Congress granting Hoover his salary in perpetuity, from July 1958 onward, until the day he died. Johnson would see to it that Hoover never had to retire from the FBI.

Congress fawned over him during his annual appearances before the leaders of the judiciary and appropriations committees. In his public testimonies, the con man within took over; his ritual performances were stage pieces. He would receive the praises of the chairmen. He would respond by reciting statistics concocted by the FBI's Crime Records Division, his public relations office. He would hurl purple prose against the Red threat. "Communism," to quote the director, "represents a massive effort to transform not only the world but human nature itself."

But the Communist Party was no longer a significant force in American political life. It had been staggered by the Justice Department's indictments at the start of the 1950s, subverted by the FBI's underground squads for the next five years, split by the Soviet leader Nikita Khrushchev's 1956 denunciation of Stalin's dictatorship, knocked headlong by the first blows of COINTELPRO. The Party had lost at least three-quarters of its members since the end of World War II. Perhaps twenty-two thousand card-carrying Communists remained on the rolls. A good number among them were undercover FBI agents and informants; a greater number were superannuated survivors of the Red raids of the 1920s.

Hoover had to continue to represent the Party as a mortal threat. The power of the FBI depended on having a great enemy. So did the unwavering support he enjoyed from the American people and their president.

The only thing he feared was leaks. He worried about them constantly. He was afraid that his intelligence operations would be uncovered, to his embarrassment. He did not trust the FBI's own internal security. He kept a close eye on cases that could tarnish his reputation. What he wanted was secret intelligence that resulted in public success—national security cases that would make front-page news. They required the terrible patience he had possessed for so long.

"AMERICAN INTELLIGENCE WALKS IN BABY SHOES"

An intoxicated Soviet spy named Reino Hayhanen walked into the American Embassy in Paris in April 1957. He said he was a KGB officer, and that he had been operating in the United States for five years. Hayhanen had been ordered to return from New York to Moscow, and he rightly feared for his life, for he had fouled up. He had been given $5,000 to pass on to the American Communist underground in New York. He went on a bender instead, and bought a one-way ticket to Paris. The CIA station chief in Paris decided to fly him back to New York and turn him over to the FBI. The Bureau put him in a Public Health Service hospital on Staten Island.

"The word was that this guy's crazy," recalled FBI agent Philip Mogen.

Born near Leningrad, Hayhanen had been recruited into the Soviet intelligence service in the first months of World War II, at the age of twenty. After the war, the KGB began to build a legend for him—a false identity that became his life. After five years of training, his legend was ready, along with a forged American passport. Hayhanen had come to New York on the *Queen Mary* in 1952. He served as a courier carrying coded microfilm messages in hollowed-out coins, batteries, pens, pencils, and screws. He picked up and delivered secret intelligence at dead drops—hiding places in the parks and on the sidewalks of New York.

Once in the FBI's hands, he identified his superior as Mikhail Svirin, who had served as first secretary of the Soviet delegation to the United Nations. The Bureau knew plenty about Soviet diplomats who were KGB spies—the FBI identified sixteen such poseurs in the late 1950s, all immune from arrest by virtue of their diplomatic passports, all expelled by the State Department under the protocols of espionage. Svirin had been in and out of the United States since before World War II, but by 1957 he had left New York, never to return.

"The FBI kept a keen eye and ear on what happened within the Soviet embassy and when embassy personnel traveled," said a State Department consul, William D. Morgan. "Never could they say that the information came from eavesdropping, because they would never admit it. . . . If the man had been caught servicing a suspected mail box or lamp post—in other words, activity which involved really serious indications that the man was 'performing duties not in accordance with his diplomatic status'—that, of course, was the basis for declaring him *persona non grata*."

Hayhanen knew his second KGB contact as Colonel Rudolph Abel. He had gone on assignments for the colonel through the northeastern United States, carrying messages and money. "One thing about Reino, he loved life, but he had enough intelligence to warrant us getting onto the case," said the FBI's Edmund J. Birch, who led an espionage squad in pursuit of the KGB's Colonel Abel, following the leads Hayhanen gave him when the spy's pickled memory permitted.

The colonel used the alias Emil Goldfus and lived a cover life as an artist with a studio in Brooklyn. Birch, carrying a concealed camera in a briefcase, trailed him as he left a restaurant, clicking away as the suspect walked down the street. Birch took one final photo, hopped in a taxi, and sped to the FBI's New York headquarters on Third Avenue and 69th Street. A technician dipped the film into a vat of developer. "Beautiful pictures of trees, a fire station, and, all of a sudden, one beautiful picture of his face," Birch remembered. Hayhanen immediately identified the man in the photo as Colonel Abel.

The FBI had never fully grasped the workings of the spies who had given up their lives and their identities to serve the Soviet state outside the comfortable confines of embassies and consulates. Birch and his fellow agents kept Abel under constant surveillance, four three-man squads working around the clock. He never did anything remotely illegal. The FBI was "trying to find out what kind of apparatus he had going for him in New York," Birch said. "I don't think we ever found any . . . and after awhile, the Bureau finally said, as the Bureau always said, 'Enough is enough.'"

The arrest of Colonel Abel on June 21, 1957, was the spy story of the decade. But it was a source of endless frustration for Hoover. The colonel could not be charged with espionage; the FBI's evidence was hearsay. The arrest was executed by immigration agents under the Foreign Agents Registration Act, the statute that Justice used when a spy case could not be made in open court.

The Bureau needed to break Abel. Agents "interviewed him like crazy, every day," for months on end, Birch said. "He was telling them nothing." The first series of interrogations took place in a makeshift prison for illegal immigrants outside McAllen, Texas, on the Mexican border. Abel was being held in "a wetback camp, in a wire cage, which was hot and uncomfortable," said the FBI's Ed Gamber, who questioned Abel eight hours a day for six weeks. "He was a real stand-up guy for the Soviets. He was a gentleman; he was polite; he was a nice guy—except when you asked him about the KGB."

Teams of FBI agents, one after another, spent more than two years questioning Abel in a cell at the Atlanta federal penitentiary, one of the toughest prisons in the United States. "I'll talk with you about art, mathematics, photography, anything you want to talk about, but don't ask me about my intelligence background," Abel said to the FBI's Alden F. Miller. "I made the resolution when I was arrested in New York and I have not said anything, and I'm not going to now." The best the FBI could do was to photograph Abel's artwork and search it for signs of steganography—a message hidden in an image. They found none.

The FBI's understanding of the case took years to sink in. The Bureau eventually learned that Abel was not Abel; nor was he a Soviet. His true name was Willie Fisher, and he had been born in 1903 in Newcastle-on-Tyne,

England. He was living proof of the fact that the Soviets had a spy network in America served by men who could come from anywhere, under any name, commanded by spymasters in Moscow whose patience was hard for Americans to fathom. Fisher had been living under deep cover in the United States for nine years; his training and his legend traced back to the early 1930s.

One thing he told the FBI stuck in Birch's memory almost fifty years later: "American intelligence walks in baby shoes," the spy said.

The Abel case infuriated Eisenhower. At a National Security Council meeting, with the vice president and the attorney general at the table, he spoke in anger and frustration. "If we discovered a Soviet spy, we would have to expose all our intelligence sources and methods in order to obtain a conviction," the president said. "About all the FBI can do is keep spies under surveillance." Eisenhower muttered that he would not forget about the Abel case. He never did. And the colonel never talked. Five years later, the United States swapped him for Francis Gary Powers, the imprisoned American pilot of a downed U-2 spy plane.

The case had one consequence of lasting value for the FBI. It helped convince Hoover to go forward with the operation code-named Solo, the Bureau's boldest plan to penetrate the Soviet Union.

SOLO

The FBI's most valued secret agents of the Cold War were two brothers, Morris and Jack Childs. The operation the Bureau built on their work posed great risks and the promise of even greater rewards.

Morris Childs was a Russian Jew, born Moishe Chilovsky outside Kiev in 1902. He came to America in 1911 and became an important figure in the Communist Party in the 1930s and 1940s, serving as the editor of its newspaper, the *Daily Worker*. He had fallen out with the Party in 1948. Three years later, the FBI approached him and his younger brother Jack as part of a new program called TOPLEV, in which FBI agents tried to talk top-level Communist Party members and officials into becoming informants. Jack Childs, a born hustler and a bag man for the Party's underground financial operations, readily took the offer. He eventually convinced Morris to join him as an undercover Communist for the FBI.

Morris rose higher and higher in the secret hierarchy. He won the trust of the Party's leaders. In the summer of 1957, they proposed that he serve as their international emissary in an effort to reestablish direct personal, political, and financial ties with the Kremlin. If Moscow approved, the FBI had a chance to place a spy inside the highest councils of the Soviet Union. Morris Childs would be reporting to Hoover as the foreign secretary of the Communist Party of the United States of America.

Hoover's intelligence chief, Al Belmont, could barely contain his excitement. "We have been trying for some time to produce direct evidence of the fact that the CPUSA follows orders and takes direction from the Communist Party, Soviet Union," Belmont wrote on August 30, 1957. "If we are able to develop such evidence it would not only strengthen our case against the CPUSA but it would enhance tremendously the Bureau's prestige as an intelligence agency."

The FBI's first debriefings of Morris Childs, running 166 single-spaced pages, were declassified in August 2011. They reveal how powerfully his work affected President Eisenhower and Vice President Nixon. They help explain several mysteries of the Cold War, including Hoover's ferocious opposition to Martin Luther King, Jr., and the civil rights movement, Eisenhower's failure to go forward with the CIA's plans to invade Fidel Castro's Cuba, and Nixon's first thoughts about a détente with the Soviets.

On April 24, 1958, Morris Childs boarded TWA Flight 824 to Paris, on the first leg of his long trip to Moscow, at the invitation of the Kremlin, where he met the Party's leaders over the course of eight weeks. He learned that his next stop would be Beijing. On July 6, he had an audience with Chairman Mao Tse-tung. Was the United States planning to go to war in Southeast Asia? Mao asked. If so, China intended to fight, as it had during the Korean War. "There may be many Koreas in Asia," Mao predicted.

Returning to Moscow that summer, conferring with leaders of the Party and the KGB, Morris received a formal invitation to attend the 21st Congress of the Communist Party of the Soviet Union, and he accepted promises of cash payments for the CPUSA that would come to $348,385 over the next few months; the money would be delivered personally to Morris by a Soviet delegate to the United Nations at a restaurant in Queens, New York.

In January and February 1959, at the Party's Moscow convention, Morris Childs met Communist leaders from around the world and intelligence officers who oversaw espionage against the United States. Though the trips exhausted him, leaving him a physically broken man, he went abroad two or three times a year over the course of the next two decades. He undertook fifty-two international missions, befriending the world's most powerful Communists. He controlled the income of the American Communist Party's treasury and contributed the insights for its foreign policy. His work was undetected by the KGB and kept secret from all but the most powerful American leaders.

Solo's reporting gave Hoover an unquestioned authority in the White House. The United States never had had a spy inside the high councils of the Soviet Union or the People's Republic of China. Morris Childs would penetrate them at the highest levels and provide the FBI with insights no president had ever possessed.

Hoover briefed the cabinet about the Solo mission on November 6, 1958. For the next two years, he sent summaries of his reporting directly to the president, the vice president, the secretary of state, and the director of Central Intelligence. He took pleasure in concealing the source of his intelligence from Allen Dulles and the CIA: "I flatly *refuse* to disclose the disclosure of the informant irrespective of any 'fits' Allen Dulles or anyone else throws. H."

Hoover reported that the world's most powerful Communists—Mao Tse-tung and Nikita Khrushchev—were at each other's throats. The breach between Moscow and Beijing was a revelation to President Eisenhower. It had been the consensus of American intelligence that the Communist leaders were of one mind. For years, Eisenhower had been relying on flawed intelligence from the CIA and the Pentagon about the military and political strengths of his enemies. Solo's reporting provided Ike with insights that no eavesdropping satellite or spy plane ever could deliver, portraying Communist leaders as confused and quarreling.

Hoover said Moscow had decided that "the main task of the Communist Party, USA, is to fight for Negro equality and integration." The FBI noted that the Kremlin had asked Solo to send a copy of Martin Luther King, Jr.'s first book, the newly published *Stride Toward Freedom,* written with the help of Stanley Levison, King's close adviser and a former member of the Communist underground. This evidence of ties between international communism and the American civil rights movement was electrifying to Hoover. The idea that they were connected through covert operations was an elemental part of his thinking and his conduct for the rest of his life.

Hoover told the White House that Solo had met with Anibal Escalante, a political leader of the newly victorious revolution in Cuba, a confidant to Fidel Castro, and the most highly regarded Cuban Communist in Moscow.

Escalante said that the Cubans knew the United States was planning a paramilitary attack to overthrow Castro. This reporting gave Eisenhower pause as he weighed the CIA's proposal to invade the island with a force of anti-Castro Cubans undergoing training in Guatemala. He never approved the plan.

Hoover reported directly to Nixon as the vice president prepared to go to Moscow in July 1959, where he would engage Khrushchev in a public discussion on the political and cultural merits of communism and capitalism. Solo had met with the top Communist Party officials responsible for American affairs. Hoover distilled their thinking about the leaders of the United States and the qualifications of the leading candidates in the 1960 presidential election. Moscow liked Ike: he understood the meaning of war and he was willing to risk the chances of peace. The Democrats were less appealing: Senator John F. Kennedy was judged as "inexperienced" and Senator Lyndon B. Johnson was "a reactionary." As for Nixon himself, the Communists thought he would be a capable president, though he was "cunning" and "ambitious."

Nixon learned from the Solo debriefings that Moscow could conduct rational political discourse; a decade later, the lesson served him well as president when he sought a rapport with the Soviets.

Nixon personally introduced Khrushchev to Hoover at a state dinner in the Eisenhower White House on September 15, 1959. The jet-lagged Soviet leader wore a medal in his lapel. Nixon, already preparing to run for president, was formal and unctuous; Hoover was all ears as a translator leaned in to join their conversation with Khrushchev.

"When I introduced him to Hoover, he immediately perked up, and he says, '*I think we know some of the same people,*' " Nixon remembered. "I think it was a very astute comment on Khrushchev's part: '*We know some of the same people, so don't trust anybody.*' "

They did know one man in common. Morris Childs returned to Moscow with Khrushchev the week after the state dinner at the White House.

The counsel of the world's top Communist—"Don't trust anybody"—sounded like wisdom to Hoover as he prepared for the end of the Eisenhower years and the election of the next president of the United States.

26

IMMORAL CONDUCT

Hoover called for a full check of the FBI's files on John F. Kennedy as soon as it was clear that the senator would win the Democratic nomination, a victory gained after a freewheeling, free-spending primary campaign run by his brother Robert and financed by his father, Joseph.

Hoover knew Joe Kennedy well: a buccaneering businessman worth hundreds of millions of dollars, a famous philanderer, and a fierce anti-Communist crusader. Their friendship had survived Hoover's refusal to accept a $100,000-a-year offer to run the Kennedy family's security interests.

Hoover was getting to know Robert Kennedy; the two men had met at least three times in connection with Kennedy's work as the chief interrogator for the Senate Rackets Committee from 1957 to 1959. The committee's hearings on organized crime featured a dramatic confrontation between Kennedy and the boss of the Chicago Mafia, Momo Salvatore "Sam" Giancana. The mobster took the Fifth Amendment, snickering at Kennedy. Bobby shot back: "I thought only little girls giggled, Mr. Giancana."

Hoover felt a rivalry with the Rackets hearings; he relished moments when Robert Kennedy stumbled due to his inexperience and zeal. In March 1959, the young crusader raised a charge he could not prove: that a key witness had offered money to Senator Kennedy's presidential campaign if the committee eased up on him. "This is what happens when the prodigal son gets too far away from home and papa," Hoover wrote in a sneering aside to an internal FBI report on Robert Kennedy and the Rackets Committee.

Hoover had wanted nothing to do with the Mafia, whose existence as a force in American economic and political life was by now an open secret. In 1959, more than four hundred FBI agents based in New York covered the

Communist threat; only four covered the mob. Hoover had argued that crimes like racketeering and extortion were matters for state and local law enforcement. He thought that investigating the Mob would create the risk that agents would be bribed and bought off, recalled the FBI's Graham Desvernine: "The ensuing problems and publicity—that would overcome any of the benefits." Hoover had shied from infiltrating the Ku Klux Klan for fear his agents would be seen as aiding and abetting cross-burning racists. He balked at undercover work against the Mafia on the chance his men would be corrupted. Different reasons, same rationale: Don't embarrass the Bureau.

But the work of the Rackets Committee, and the competition he felt from the publicity attending them, compelled Hoover to change his tune. He took the tactics he had used against Communists and started to turn them on mobsters. "The decision was made that we would take the same methods and investigative techniques that we used on the Underground Squad and apply it to organized crime," Desvernine said. Bag jobs, hidden microphones, bugs, and wiretaps were "very effective in finding out what they were doing and what they were up to." It couldn't be used in court, of course—"it was strictly intelligence gathering . . . you gotta get intelligence first and then you find witnesses." The FBI tapped and bugged Giancana and his compatriots in Chicago and Las Vegas, starting in the summer of 1959.

Hoover knew Senator John F. Kennedy, too, but he did not know him well at all. He did not like what he read in the FBI's files. Dated July 7, 1960, a nine-page summary on JFK's past made Hoover uneasy about America's political future. It included charges of "immoral conduct"—sex stories, some of them accurate, including an allegation that the senator was sleeping with his wife's social secretary. Hoover dimly remembered the oldest such case: back in 1942, when JFK was a twenty-four-year-old navy man, he had conducted a notorious affair with a married woman named Inga Arvad, a Washington newspaper columnist and a onetime Nazi sympathizer. The FBI, under the impression that she was also a German spy, had placed her under surveillance, tapped her calls with Kennedy, and bugged the hotel rooms where the two made love.

The FBI's files on Kennedy also included unspecified and unverified charges of "hoodlum connections."

On July 13, 1960, the day that JFK won the presidential nomination at the Democratic National Convention, the FBI produced a biographical sketch on the candidate for Hoover. It reported that the senator and Frank Sinatra had socialized in New York, Las Vegas, and Palm Springs during the campaign. The FBI had a long-standing file on Sinatra. The Bureau surmised that the singer was trying to use his influence with the Kennedy clan on behalf of mobsters. Sinatra's FBI file included his association with Sam Giancana, who was later overheard on an FBI bug boasting that he had influence with the Kennedys. The FBI would soon learn that Sinatra had introduced JFK *and* Giancana to a woman of easy virtue named Judith Campbell, who had sexually serviced the senator during the Democratic convention and maintained intimate relations with both men.

"The President expressed amazement"

President Eisenhower called on Hoover at an urgent meeting of the National Security Council on October 13, 1960. Crushing national security concerns faced the White House that fall. The rise of Soviet-style communism in Fidel Castro's Cuba was chief among them. But the president spent much of the National Security Council meeting talking about sex.

The political tension was high in Washington. The election was now twenty-five days away, the race was neck-and-neck, and the third of the presidential debates between Nixon and Kennedy was hours away. (They argued on television that night about American intelligence and Soviet spies. "Communist espionage goes on all the time," Nixon said, in the nervous voice that cost him innumerable votes. "The United States can't afford to have a es— an es— a espionage lack or should we s— uh—lag—or should I say, uh, an intelligence lag any more than we can afford to have a missile lag.")

The president, however, spent the better part of an hour at the October 13 meeting telling Hoover to rid America of homosexuals in high places.

Two young math geniuses who worked at the National Security Agency as code breakers had defected to the Soviet Union. Bernon Mitchell, thirty-one, and William Martin, twenty-nine, had been missing from work for eight days before anyone noticed. The universal assumption— unsupported by NSA records declassified five decades later—was that Martin and Mitchell were lovers. They had flown from Washington to Havana via Mexico City, and then on to Moscow. They surfaced at a press conference in Moscow on September 6, informing the world that the NSA had been cracking the diplomatic and intelligence codes of American allies including France, Italy, Indonesia, Egypt, and Syria.

The president turned to Hoover for a full report on the case. "Mitchell had been found to have homosexual tendencies," Hoover told the president, and "Martin was noticeably unstable." But the Pentagon had granted them top secret security clearances nonetheless. The president found this outrageous. He connected communism and homosexuality, as did Hoover; they both believed without question that homosexuals were especially susceptible to foreign intelligence services.

"The President expressed amazement that these two men had been retained after such information had been developed," Hoover recorded in his dictated memorandum of the conversation. "He instructed the Chairman of the Joint Chiefs of Staff, General Lyman L. Lemnitzer, to call in the officials who were responsible for clearing these two individuals and in the words of the President, 'Give them hell.'"

The president asked Hoover how to cleanse the government of this threat once and for all. Hoover recounted:

> There was some discussion then upon the part of the President and the Attorney General as well as myself about the setting up of a list of homosexuals in order that there be some central place to which inquiries might be directed concerning individuals who may apply for Government employment or be in Government employment. . . .
>
> The President was of the opinion that this information should be in the FBI and suggested that steps be taken to see that we gathered together in the FBI any information concerning such tendencies upon the part of individuals who are either in Government or may apply for positions in Government so such information would promptly be available to all Government agencies.
>
> The President seemed to be greatly concerned about this entire problem and left no doubt . . . that he was thoroughly opposed to the employment or retention in employment of individuals who might have such tendencies.

The FBI's Sex Deviates Program had been in effect since 1951; the files filled hundreds of thousands of pages. President Eisenhower's 1953 executive order banning homosexuals from government service equated "sexual perversion" with espionage, sabotage, mental illness, drug addiction, and membership in the Communist Party as behavior that constituted a danger to national security. But there had never been a central file at the FBI comprising a who's who of homosexuals in America. Now there would be.

Hoover may not have had a sex life of his own. But he had a deep interest in other people's secret lives—notably, the life of the next president of the United States.

27

"MURDER WAS IN STYLE"

A T THE END OF 1960, Hoover and the FBI became enmeshed in President Eisenhower's plans to assassinate both Fidel Castro and Rafael Trujillo, the dictators of Cuba and the Dominican Republic respectively.

Hoover started to see the outlines of these dark conspiracies just before John Kennedy very narrowly defeated Richard Nixon in the November 1960 election. His gimlet eyes were opening to an underworld of power. He grasped connections between the American government and organized crime.

On October 18, 1960, Hoover wrote a terse memorandum to Richard Bissell, the CIA's covert operations chief, with copies to the top men at Justice, State, the Pentagon, and the FBI's chain of command. It concerned Sam Giancana and Fidel Castro.

Hoover had read FBI reports that Giancana, while enjoying a meal at La Scala, the best Italian restaurant in New York, had boasted that "Castro was to be done away with very shortly"—by November. The mobster said he had met with the hired assassin three times in Miami. The instrument of death was to be a poison pill. And, as Hoover soon discovered, the CIA was behind the plot. Hoover started an all-pervasive electronic surveillance of Giancana—not only wiretaps and bugs, but parabolic microphones that could pick up conversations at a distance of hundreds of feet, a new technology used only in the most sensitive spy cases. "You are advised that its use has been confined to top Internal Security and Espionage cases in the past," Hoover wrote to the FBI special agent in charge in Chicago. The Giancana investigation now was an intelligence case.

The FBI learned that Giancana was one among ten members of "the commission," which oversaw the work of Mafia families in the United States and the Caribbean. Mafia dons aimed to revive Mob-owned casinos in Havana from which they had been expelled by Castro, who had come to power in Cuba on January 1, 1959, by overthrowing the dictator Fulgencio Batista. Failing that, they would move their gambling and graft operations to the Dominican Republic.

The Mob liked Generalissimo Rafael Trujillo, an American ally who had held power in the Dominican Republic since 1930. He ruled by fear and fraud. His wealth, wrung from the soil of the island and the sweat of his subjects, was measured in hundreds of millions of dollars. His crimes included murder and kidnapping on American soil, the bribery and corruption of members of the United States Senate and House, and the subversion of rival Latin American leaders.

"The President was entitled to know"

Hoover had gathered a trove of political intelligence on the murderous politics of the Caribbean during the late 1950s. His best sources included an FBI veteran turned American ambassador in the Dominican Republic, his agents and legal attachés in Miami and Havana, and the CIA counterintelligence chief, James Angleton.

A common denominator of their reporting was political corruption in Washington. Ten members of Congress had been convicted of crimes during Hoover's years at the FBI; almost all of the cases involved relatively minor-league cases of graft. But Hoover learned through secret intelligence that some of his strongest allies in the Senate had been pocketing bribes from Batista and Trujillo. Hoover had received a report from Angleton, based on a tip from the Cuban consul general in New York, that "Senator Homer E. Capehart has received the sum of $20,000 as a 'fee' to effect the entrance and asylum in the United States of Batista." Capehart, an Indiana Republican, had been one of Hoover's most vocal supporters in the war on communism in the Senate since 1945. Hoover also received intelligence from the American ambassador in the Dominican Republic that his most powerful supporter in Congress, Senator James Eastland of Mississippi, received money and other favors from Trujillo, one plantation master bestowing largesse on another.

Hoover shunned criminal investigations of congressmen. He very rarely handled matters involving money, sex, and politics as law enforcement cases. He classified them as intelligence matters, fit for his files and the president's eyes only. He brought salacious political secrets about members of Congress to the White House, and presidents from Franklin Roosevelt onward usually savored them.

"If it was highly politically explosive ... the President was entitled to know," said Nicholas deB. Katzenbach, later the attorney general of the United States. "The Bureau didn't give you a lot of other stuff. They did if there was homosexuality or something of that kind involved. . . . You know, little girls or something like that."

Hoover never pursued Eastland on charges of corruption; it would have been awkward in the extreme to investigate his favorite senator, the Democratic chairman of the Judiciary Committee and its Internal Security Subcommittee. But Hoover had told President Eisenhower that other members of Congress were in Trujillo's pocket. Eisenhower himself had named two of them in a White House meeting: Senator Allen Ellender, Democrat of Louisiana, the chairman of the Senate Agriculture Committee, and Representative Harold Cooley, Democrat of North Carolina, the chairman of the House Agriculture Committee. The committees set the sugar import quotas allocated to the Dominican Republic; their decisions generated millions for the dictatorship; their chairmen received considerable largesse in return. Trujillo personally controlled roughly two-thirds of the crop and took the lion's share of the profits.

Trujillo had distinguished himself to his American allies as a bulwark against communism. He had asserted in interviews with American newspapers that he had given the United States priceless intelligence on a "Caribbean Comintern" with headquarters at the Soviet Embassy in Mexico City and bases in New York, Miami, and Puerto Rico. Vice President Nixon had toured the Dominican Republic and hailed Trujillo in public and private. Franklin D. Roosevelt, Jr., was one among many of Trujillo's well-paid Washington lobbyists. Trujillo bought favorable publicity by siphoning money into the hands of newspaper owners, broadcast magnates, advertising agencies, and syndicated columnists through his political and intelligence operatives, who worked out of fifty-four consulates in the United States. His going rate for endorsements from powerful and prominent gringos was $25,000 in cash.

The problems Trujillo presented were without real precedent in American political history. The United States had installed pro-American rulers through coups and plots. But it never had removed one.

"Get into the underground"

The president, the Dulles brothers, and J. Edgar Hoover hit upon an unusual solution to the problem of Trujillo. They sent a veteran FBI agent down to the Dominican Republic as the new American ambassador.

Joseph S. Farland was not a typical diplomat. His skill was in secret operations. Farland had become an FBI agent in 1943. His assignments included wiretapping, black-bag jobs, and undercover surveillance. As he explained, Hoover had chosen him to be "one of the very select group of individuals," part of "a secret organization within a secret organization" working against the Soviet atom spies. "Our work was to get the information as to who was who and who was doing what to whom and how they were doing it." His new assignment in the Dominican Republic was not all that different. He recalled his orders: "Get into the underground and find out what is going on and what is going to happen at this time and in the future. It's a delicate operation, but your background and training make you the best possible selection we have in the Department. We do not want to eliminate Trujillo. In other words, assassinate him. But we want him to take his loot and go off."

American military, economic, and diplomatic relationships hung in the balance if Trujillo's power was challenged. But Farland kept reporting, and he reported it all—the torture chambers, the political assassinations, and the fawning tributes Trujillo received from members of the American Senate and House in exchange for money and sex.

"Trujillo was in complete control," he said. "He was eliminating his opponents. Murder was in style. It was completely amoral."

Farland encountered his fellow Americans under unusual protocols. The list of politicos who enjoyed Trujillo's money, rum, and girls was long. The once and future Dominican ambassador to the United States, Manuel de Moya, one of Trujillo's chief intelligence officers, maintained a mansion on the edge of Santo Domingo where American congressmen were entertained—"a love nest just outside of the city that you entered by a maze of hedges so no car could be observed," as Farland described it. "It was totally wired. There were two-way mirrors. There was a supply of whatever one wanted in the way of your desire. A number of our Congressmen made use of that and were photographed and taped. I had one Senator come down and I said, 'Senator, I and my country team are prepared to brief you.' He said, 'I know all I want to know about this damn country. All I want from you is to make diddly-darn sure that I'm well-supplied with liquor in my hotel room for a week.' "

Farland started cleaning house at the American Embassy. He had a feckless CIA station chief as a counterpart in the Dominican Republic. "One day, he came to me and said, 'Mr. Ambassador, I hate to bother you, but I've locked myself out of my office.' " Farland "picked the lock and opened it up," he recounted. "This was my old FBI training." The station chief was soon replaced.

Farland also found that his second in command at the American Embassy, the deputy chief of mission, was "definitely in the pocket of Trujillo. . . . The stupid character, he even told me he had spent some time in Manuel de Moya's love house." The ambassador replaced him with a trusted number-two man, Henry Dearborn. He too was appalled at the representatives of American democracy who were Trujillo's honored guests. "Senator Eastland was one," Dearborn said. "He wasn't the only one."

Farland made friends with Trujillo, after a fashion, and gathered through him a ream of intelligence about the rise of Fidel Castro in Cuba. "Castro has among his chief lieutenants known Communists and is receiving financial support from Soviet Union," Farland wrote in a top secret cable to Washington on December 15, 1958, seventeen days before the revolutionaries took Havana. The CIA did not see that threat for many months.

On January 29, 1959, Hoover held the floor at a formal meeting at the State Department on the crisis in the Caribbean. Addressing the CIA's Allen Dulles, eight leaders of the State Department, and the immigration service chief, Hoover had boasted that he had "a considerable amount of information" about Cuban exiles working for and against Castro in Miami, New York, New Orleans, and across the country. Hoover ordered every agent in the FBI to stay on top of the Cubans. Was Castro himself a hard-core Communist? Who was working for him, and against him, in the United States?

On March 31, 1959, on orders from Hoover, FBI agents interviewed a gun-running American soldier of fortune, an ex-marine and army intelligence officer named Frank Sturgis, aka Frank Fiorini. He gave them a detailed look inside Castro's revolution. He had fought with Fidel in the mountains, and supplied him with weapons and aircraft. After the revolution, Castro had assigned him to expel American mobsters from Havana's casinos. Sturgis had looked at the house odds and bet on America. He told the FBI he had decided to change sides: he "offered his services as an 'agent' for the United States Government," reporting directly to Hoover. (Sturgis went on to work for the CIA and, years later, for the White House: he was one of the burglars arrested in the break-in at the Watergate Hotel.)

The FBI's reporting on Cuba was mostly on the mark. It opened up a world of secrets, including the connections among American casino operators in Havana, the Mafia, anti-Castro Cubans, and the CIA. The FBI named the hard-core Communists in the Castro camp and precisely placed Castro's leftward movement on the political spectrum. The Bureau confirmed Farland's reports that Castro and Trujillo were plotting coups against each other.

President Eisenhower decided to do away with both of the dictators.

First he canceled every dollar of military aid to the Dominican Republic. It fell to Farland to inform the generalissimo. "I went all by myself," Farland recounted in a tape-recorded oral history. "He had his ambassador to the United States, the head of the army, the head of the navy, and the head of the air force standing there at attention. He blew up. He turned red. He proceeded then to do the unmentionable. He began a tirade against Eisenhower, my president. He called him stupid, said that he didn't understand politics, didn't understand what was going on in the Caribbean, and he called him—I hate to say this on tape—a 'son of a bitch.' When he did that, my diplomacy took a flight out. . . . I decided the time had come when I would have to say a few words in support of my country, which I did, ending up by saying, 'As far as you are concerned, in my estimation, you're nothing but a two-bit dictator and your country compared to mine is nothing but a fly speck on a map.'"

Trujillo was wearing a revolver. Farland thought to himself: "If you blink, you're dead. . . . But I didn't blink. He blinked. He came walking around the corner of the desk and said, 'Mr. Ambassador, my friend, in moments of stress, we oftentimes make comments that we really don't mean. Let's forgive and forget.' I couldn't help myself. I said, 'Trujillo, I am a Christian. I will forgive, but I won't forget.' I turned on my heel and walked what looked like 24 miles across that office, all the time wondering if I was going to get a .38 in my back."

Farland plotted in secret with Trujillo's opponents in the Dominican Republic. Their plans involved the death of the dictator. "I was pretty close to the underground," he said—close enough that he sent the State Department a list of dissidents who were prepared "to take over the government once Trujillo was assassinated." It was crucial to the United States that these men were certifiable anti-Communists. Farland assured Washington that they were: "These were lawyers, doctors, engineers, top-flight merchants, people generally who had been trained in the United States."

Farland reported that they wanted the United States to provide them with a clandestine shipment of weapons to kill Trujillo. The conspirators' wish list, conveyed by Farland to the CIA, also included a hit squad of "ex-FBI agents who would plan and execute the death of Trujillo," in the words of Richard Bissell, the CIA's covert-operations chief.

By April 1960, Eisenhower had resolved that the United States should prepare "to remove Trujillo from the Dominican Republic." It would be done "as soon as a suitable successor regime can be induced to take over with the assurance of U.S. political, economic, and—if necessary—military support."

On May 13, 1960, the president summoned Farland and two of his State Department superiors to the White House. The president, according to notes taken by his military aide, told Farland that "he was being bombarded by people who are opposed to Castro and Trujillo"—and that "he would like to see them both sawed off."

President Eisenhower did not get the job done. The Kennedy administration inherited the conspiracies to commit murder in the Caribbean.

28

DANGEROUS MAN

THE WAR BETWEEN J. Edgar Hoover and Attorney General Robert F. Kennedy was a scorched-earth campaign that burned throughout the 1960s. It threatened to consume the FBI, the Justice Department, and the White House.

Robert Kennedy said he found Hoover "rather frightening"—a "dangerous" man who ran "a very dangerous organization." But he believed "it was a danger that we could control." RFK thought he could impose his authority over Hoover: "For the first time since he had been Director of the FBI, he had to take instructions or orders from the Attorney General of the United States—and couldn't go over his head."

But Hoover did not care to be instructed by an insolent young man who had never commanded anything but his brother's presidential campaign.

Hoover believed that "Bobby was trying to take over the FBI, and run the FBI, water down the FBI," the director's close aide Deke DeLoach said. "He was trying to re-do the whole machine to his own liking, and he didn't have the experience or respect to command things like that."

Robert F. Kennedy was thirty-five years old, born in 1925, just weeks after Hoover had taken charge of the FBI. He had not asked to be the attorney general, nor was he his brother's first choice. But there was logic to it. JFK was the third president in a row to appoint his campaign manager as attorney general; the office had become a political post, requiring loyalty above all. Robert Kennedy was first and foremost loyal to his brother. And their father, whose millions had helped win the election, demanded it. Hoover had told his old friend Joe Kennedy that he approved of the appointment. He regretted that.

The president and the attorney general tried to be deferential to Hoover at first. But deference did not come naturally to them. The president had thought an occasional private White House luncheon would satisfy Hoover. "We did it for the reason of keeping him happy," RFK said. "It was important, as far as we were concerned, that he remain happy and that he remain in his position, because he was a symbol—and the President had won by such a narrow margin."

But breaking bread at the White House a few times a year did not suffice. Nothing did. Almost everything about Robert Kennedy angered the director. The attorney general's crime was grave. "He offended the FBI," said RFK's deputy at Justice, Nicholas deB. Katzenbach.

"We don't know what to do"

The lingering problem of Rafael Trujillo shaped the start of the struggle between Hoover and Robert Kennedy.

On February 16, 1961, the fourth week of the new administration, Attorney General Kennedy signed orders aimed at uncovering the political corruption that the regime had used to maintain its power. The first of some 582 FBI wiretaps and nearly 800 FBI bugs authorized during the Kennedy administration were installed.

The FBI wiretapped the congressional office of House Agriculture Committee chairman Harold Cooley, the home of the committee's clerk, the Dominican Republic's embassy and consulates, and the law offices of Trujillo's lobbyists. As far as can be determined by existing records, it was the first time since the Harding administration that an attorney general had ordered a member of Congress wiretapped.

But RFK soon balked. The investigation hit too close to home. If it were pursued, it could ensnare congressmen, senators, and politically connected lobbyists, most of them conservative Democrats—power brokers that the Kennedys needed to hold Congress in line. The only person ever charged was the gossip columnist Igor Cassini, a Kennedy family friend, the brother of Jackie Kennedy's favorite fashion designer, a social butterfly, and a paid shill for Trujillo. And the facts in that case came from an investigative reporter, not the FBI. Robert Kennedy later called the Trujillo investigation the "most unpleasant" case he ever confronted—a high standard—and "the only investigation I've called off since I've been Attorney General."

Kennedy called off the case after the generalissimo was ambushed and assassinated by his opponents on the outskirts of his capital on the night of May 30, 1961. The moral support of the United States did not save twelve of the fourteen conspirators from brutal revenge killings at the hands of Trujillo's son, brothers, and political heirs, who quickly regained power.

"The great problem now," RFK wrote shortly after Trujillo's assassination, "is that we don't know what to do."

It took years for the White House to find an answer. The final solution lay with J. Edgar Hoover. In the end, Hoover himself would choose a new leader for the Dominican Republic.

"Firing J. Edgar Hoover? Jesus Christ!"

By Robert Kennedy's own admission, he did not lie awake at night worrying about communism or civil rights when he became attorney general. He thought about organized crime. He wanted the FBI to go after the Mob, as he had done when he served on the Senate Rackets Committee.

He tried to take control of the FBI—by law his right—and the struggle would consume him for the rest of his days at Justice.

Hoover was outraged that the attorney general wanted to go after Mafia dons instead of Moscow's agents. He was furious that Kennedy poormouthed the pursuit of Soviet espionage. He was contemptuous of his big ideas for a federal crime commission and organized-crime strike forces. He was appalled at his penchant for off-the-shelf operations, his back-channel deals, his one-on-one meetings with a Soviet embassy officer who was known as a KGB spy, and his role as the president's all-purpose political fixer for problems foreign and domestic.

Hoover was genuinely infuriated that his titular superior summoned him, rather than the other way around. It was a short walk down the corridors of the Justice Department from Hoover's suite to Kennedy's soaring chambers. But Hoover refused to take it. "Bobby was just about never in Mr. Hoover's office or Hoover in his," Katzenbach said. Unable to bear the sight or sound of one another, Hoover and RFK worked out the appointment of a go-between. An FBI agent both men knew and liked, Courtney Evans, served as their official liaison for three years. "Courtney would explain something to Bobby one way and explain something to Hoover another way," Katzenbach said. "When he was trying to sell something Hoover wanted to Bobby, it was explained in a way that would make it palatable to Bobby, and vice versa." Trying to serve these two masters was a task few men could fulfill.

Later in life, Evans claimed: "I kept the Kennedys from firing Hoover. They were incensed at him from time to time. They felt he was wasting his manpower investigating national-security cases." But the idea of dismissing the director was close to inconceivable. "Firing J. Edgar Hoover? Jesus Christ!" Katzenbach said. "I seriously question whether President Kennedy could have made a firing stick."

But the president vowed to fire Allen Dulles after the disaster that befell the United States at the Bay of Pigs in April 1961. Dulles had sold his plans to invade Cuba and overthrow Castro as a sure thing. The Bay of Pigs invasion left 114 of the Agency's Cubans dead, 1,189 captured, Castro triumphant—and the president vowing, in his words, to break the CIA into a thousand pieces and scatter it to the winds.

JFK ordered his brother to conduct a postmortem of the invasion and to fix the apparatus of American intelligence. Among the many open questions was whether the president would appoint RFK as the director of Central Intelligence. On April 20, the day after the invasion collapsed, Bobby Kennedy called Hoover for his thoughts on how to harness the CIA.

Hoover's never-ending disdain for the CIA was recorded in his handwritten memos of the day: "For years CIA has not played clean with us. . . . CIA hasn't changed its stripes anymore than a zebra. H." But he found the rumor that the president might place his brother in charge of the Agency intriguing and appealing. At one blow, it would remove RFK as Hoover's superior and condemn the cocksure Kennedy to the impossible task of washing the stain of the Bay of Pigs from the family coat of arms.

Hoover assembled a sophisticated three-part report on American intelligence and hand-delivered it to the attorney general. It covered the history of the CIA and the key personalities at the Agency. Hoover outlined the story of American espionage since 1941, stressing that Kennedy could not "analyze the weaknesses of US intelligence today without going back to past history"; Communist infiltration during World War II had "created situations and problems which even to this day affect US intelligence operations." He also warned against a long roster of top CIA officers, singling out the former FBI agent William K. Harvey, who was responsible for the clandestine collection of communications intelligence at the CIA, but was also a notorious alcoholic who had fouled up the investigation of the atomic spy Klaus Fuchs.

It is unlikely that Robert Kennedy read a word of the report. Harvey became a principal participant in the CIA's revived plots against Fidel Castro, closely overseen by the attorney general.

"Agents did not drive buses"

Hoover defied the attorney general at will. In those same days of May 1961 came the first clear case of his contempt.

The Freedom Riders, a contingent of black and white civil rights demonstrators, aimed to challenge segregation in the South by traveling together on a Greyhound bus through Alabama. The FBI, through open and secret sources, including informers, knew their plans days in advance. The Bureau tipped off state and local law enforcement officers in Alabama. The police and the Ku Klux Klan, working in concert, planned to waylay the demonstrators and beat them half to death. The FBI knew that too.

Hoover had made a conscious decision not to tell the Justice Department what he knew about the Freedom Riders and the Klan. His written reports to Kennedy about the Freedom Riders primarily concerned the Communist Party's capabilities in Alabama.

Hoover defied direct orders from the attorney general to protect the integrationists, as he called them. Joseph G. Kelly, a thirty-seven-year-old FBI agent in the small civil rights division of the FBI, watched the story unfold at headquarters.

"The driver of the bus refused to continue driving the Freedom Riders," he recounted. "We had a call from the Attorney General's Office, from Nick Katzenbach. He said that the Attorney General, Mr. Kennedy, wanted an agent to drive the Freedom bus. Of course, in those days, we didn't always do what the Department requested if we thought it was not in the best interest of the case or the Bureau.

"So we told Katzenbach that agents did not drive buses, it wasn't included in their resume, and that he had a number of Civil Rights Division attorneys down there who might be able to drive it. And Katzenbach said— 'Well, this is a request from the Attorney General.' And I said, 'I know, but that's our answer.' So I hung up the phone and called the Director's office and alerted them to the fact that Kennedy would be calling, and he did. The Director told him the same thing."

"No one was safe from the inquisition"

RFK began to grasp the ubiquity of Hoover's power. He saw that Hoover had wired the national security establishment of the United States. The director had more information and power than the attorney general.

Hoover picked up secrets across the spectrum of American politics and foreign policy. His liaison agents and his loyalists told him what was going on at the CIA, on Capitol Hill, and at the State Department. The attorney general tried to identify and neutralize Hoover's spies inside the Kennedy administration. The battle started at the State Department—a classic armed standoff, Kennedy and Hoover, guns drawn, daring the other to fire.

"We had a leak," said William J. Crockett, the State Department's top administrator under JFK. "Day after day, I would be called by the Senate Internal Security Committee to be grilled about why certain people had been given security clearances" and how the State Department set foreign policy.

Hoover's staunch supporter, Senator James Eastland of Mississippi, led the Internal Security Committee. When Eastland went "witch-hunting," Crockett said, "no one was safe from the inquisition." Crockett suspected a mole in the State Department was serving as Eastland's spy, and if the senator had a spy in the State Department, so did Hoover. Under a formal liaison agreement forged in 1951, the Internal Security staff had sent the FBI every shred of confidential information in their files. Since 1955, Hoover and Eastland had had an informal and highly secret agreement to share intelligence with each other.

Crockett sought help from the secretary of state, Dean Rusk, who went to the president, who went to his brother. RFK sent for his special assistant, Walter Sheridan—his favorite investigator from the Senate Rackets Committee, a former FBI agent, and a veteran of the National Security Agency's eavesdropping teams. "Sheridan was the principal so-called nigger in the woodpile" at the Kennedy Justice Department, Hoover later told Lyndon Baines Johnson. Sheridan suggested that a friend and colleague from the NSA take charge of the State Department's security. Sheridan's man was caught red-handed running bugs and black-bag jobs against the leaks. Crockett had to fire him on the spot.

But he had identified the mole. "The leaker was one Otto Otepka, a high-ranking official in the Security Office and a holdover from the McCarthy period," Crockett said. "He justified his actions by saying: 'I feel it is my higher duty to my country to reveal the security risks that this new Administration is bringing into government. I am willing to break the law and sacrifice my career to bring this practice to a halt.'" The leak investigation proved too sensitive to pursue. The bugging could not be revealed. Otepka landed a national security post seven years later in the Nixon administration.

Robert Kennedy's use of Walter Sheridan as an undercover investigator "grossly offended the FBI," said Katzenbach. Hoover thought that they were usurping the FBI's powers. The director would not let Robert Kennedy subvert his command of the government's internal security systems. He controlled the power of secret information.

29

RULE BY FEAR

HOOVER CONVINCED THE Kennedys that Martin Luther King, Jr., was part of Moscow's grand design to subvert the United States of America.

He had identified King's counselor and speechwriter Stanley Levison as a secret member of the Communist Party. His greatest and most secret source, Solo, reported that Levison had been a linchpin in the Party underground from 1952 to 1957. Levison had evidently cut his ties to the Party that year, when he began to work for King. But Hoover became convinced that Levison was still taking orders from Moscow, whispering in King's ear, indoctrinating him in Marxist thought and subversive strategies.

On January 8, 1962, Hoover advised the attorney general in writing that Levison was a secret agent of international communism. RFK remembered the moment he learned about Levison: "When I heard that he was tied up, perhaps, with some Communists, I asked the FBI to make an intensive investigation of him."

Kennedy and Hoover had a telephone conversation the next day about the techniques of wiretapping and bugging. The substance of their conversation remains classified fifty years later.

RFK took off on an around-the-world trip shortly thereafter, leaving his deputy, Byron "Whizzer" White, soon to be appointed a Supreme Court justice, in charge as acting attorney general. White asked for the FBI's files on Levison. Hoover refused to hand them over. He thought that guarding the secrecy surrounding Solo, the FBI's source for the charge of Communist influence over the civil rights movement, was more important than keeping the Kennedys informed.

Hoover was convinced that the KGB was trying to renew financial, political, and espionage links in America—to the Old Left, to the budding movement that called itself the New Left, and especially to the civil rights campaign. He was encouraged by the Bureau's breakthroughs against Soviet espionage at the United Nations, one of which gave the FBI a fresh look at Stanley Levison.

The FBI had two hundred agents keeping an eye on the United Nations. Telephone taps on UN offices were easy; planting bugs in Soviet and Soviet-bloc offices was hard; black-bag jobs inside the UN were risky and rare. But the Bureau did all three, while keeping a weather eye out for disaffected diplomats who might defect to the United States. The FBI had the UN wired: When the Soviet deputy premier Anastas Mikoyan met with the Soviet delegation at the UN in the wake of the Cuban missile crisis later that year, Hoover sent President Kennedy real-time reports on the closed-door conversations.

The FBI's Edmund J. Birch—the agent who had nailed the KGB spy known as Colonel Abel—worked the United Nations beat. Birch had his eye on a Soviet named Viktor Lesiovsky, who had just taken a top post in the United Nations secretariat, as one of three chief assistants to the new UN secretary-general, the Burmese diplomat U Thant. Lesiovsky, who lived in a beautiful apartment on Sutton Place, the most elegant address on Manhattan's East Side, had served as the KGB chief in India. Birch suspected that he was doing more than infiltrating the UN. He thought he was running political operations to reinvigorate Moscow's ties with the American Left.

The thought gained power when the FBI's United Nations surveillance team reported that Lesiovsky had met in secret with Stanley Levison.

Days later, Robert Kennedy, newly returned to Justice from his globe-trotting, personally authorized a wiretap on Levison's New York business telephone, on 39th Street off Fifth Avenue. For good measure, Hoover's men also bugged Levison's office.

On March 16, 1962, the Levison tapes started rolling, and they kept rolling for six years. For Hoover, it was the next best thing to a tap on King, since Levison was a guiding light for the movement, and King consulted him constantly by telephone.

Armed with the gleanings of the twenty-four-hour surveillance, Hoover began to bombard the president, Vice President Lyndon B. Johnson, Attorney General Kennedy, and Senator Eastland, among many others, with raw intelligence reports about King, Levison, the civil rights movement, and Communist subversion. Senator Eastland's Internal Security Committee subpoenaed Levison to an executive session, behind closed doors. Under oath, he denied that he had been a member of the Communist Party. After that, he took the Fifth Amendment on every crucial question.

Hoover never fully explained to the Kennedys why he maintained that Levison was a Communist agent. Protecting Solo was more important, the director wrote to his aides: "Under no circumstances should our informant be endangered."

"Gutter gossip"

The power of secret information was a gun that Hoover always kept loaded. He took it from his holster when he felt his power threatened—or when it gave him pleasure.

On March 22, 1962, the director had one of his rare luncheons at the White House. The conversation gave the president reason to fear that Hoover knew his deepest secrets. No record of the meeting survives, but the circumstantial evidence of what took place is strong.

The evidence suggests that Hoover let the president know what he knew about the interplay among the CIA, the attorney general, the continuing plots to kill Castro, the participation of the Mafia boss Sam Giancana, and the president's dalliance with Giancana's mistress, Judith Campbell.

Immediately before dining with Hoover, the president had a crash meeting with the attorney general. Immediately thereafter, JFK had his last telephone conversation with Campbell. By one hearsay account, after the luncheon, the president told an aide that he had to fire "that bastard" J. Edgar Hoover.

On May 9, Hoover recorded, with evident satisfaction, his face-to-face meeting on the Castro assassination plots with Robert Kennedy. They discussed "the 'gutter gossip' " surrounding the CIA and Giancana. "I expressed astonishment at . . . the horrible judgment in using a man of Giancana's background," Hoover wrote. RFK scribbled a note to his FBI liaison: "Courtney I hope this will be followed up vigorously."

Hoover followed up. It was evident to him that the mobster's girlfriend had been having sex with the president (as were, by the FBI's count, five other women not his wife). Hoover also knew that Robert Kennedy was overseeing new plots to eliminate Castro.

Hoover's knowledge of JFK's private conduct and RFK's political conspiracies were potentially lethal political weapons. He brandished them now. He let the president and the attorney general know that he knew they had committed mortal sins.

On June 11, 1962, the FBI's bugs picked up the baritone voice of Martin Luther King, Jr. He was visiting Stanley Levison at his office on 39th Street in Manhattan. Their conversation got the attorney general's attention. RFK knew much more about this surveillance than he ever admitted. He personally renewed his authorization for the taps on Levison's office, and he approved Hoover's request to tap Levison's home telephone, where King called late at night several times a week. The FBI began gaining insights, shared freely with the White House and the Justice Department, into the hopes, fears, and dreams of Dr. King. The Bureau had identified an aide to Levison named Jack O'Dell as a suspected source of Communist influence inside the Southern Christian Leadership Conference. Hoover cited the twin specters of Levison and O'Dell as the justification for an open-ended investigation of King's headquarters and aides in Atlanta.

Robert Kennedy now agreed with Hoover's surmise that Levison was a Red Svengali swaying the Reverend Dr. King. "Levison influenced him. Their goals were identical, really, I suppose," he said.

Hoover commanded the FBI in Atlanta and New York to open a new case. It was captioned: COMMUNIST INFILTRATION OF THE SOUTHERN CHRISTIAN LEADERSHIP CONFERENCE, shorthanded inside the FBI as COMINFIL/SCLC—a full-scale, full-field investigation of communism at the center of the civil rights movement.

"WE MUST MARK HIM NOW"

The confrontation over the civil rights movement grew increasingly tense. Hoover had adopted an attitude akin to civil disobedience against the attorney general.

In September 1962, when a black man named James Meredith attempted to enroll at the segregated University of Mississippi, a white riot ensued. The Kennedy administration wound up sending thousands of troops to Mississippi and arresting a retired right-wing army general on a charge of insurrection. The duty officer at FBI headquarters on the Saturday that Mississippi boiled over was a supervisory special agent named Fred Woodcock. "The Klan got involved and they were threatening violence," he remembered. "Some of these bonehead pro-Nazi organizations in this country were involved, and life was hell for me."

The phones were ringing off the hook when a Justice Department lawyer got Woodcock on the line and demanded information from the FBI's agents in Mississippi and their informants in the Klan. "I said, 'You know we can't disclose that information; we have a confidential relationship with all our informants and, if we disclose their identity we could wrap up the informant program,' " Woodcock recounted. "A few minutes later he calls me back and he says, 'Bobby Kennedy wants to see you in his office right away.' "

"I was dumbfounded," Woodcock said. "I gather up my files and stuff on the University of Mississippi and I go over to Kennedy's office. . . . Bobby's in his shirtsleeves and they're actually tossing a football around. You know, this was rumored that these things happened, but I never really believed that they would sit in their office and do this."

"I want you to go down and arrest these Klan members," Kennedy said.

"Well, what would be the basis of the arrest?" Woodcock replied. "What would we arrest them for?"

"It doesn't matter," Kennedy said. "We'll worry about that later. Just go down there and arrest them, get them off the street."

Woodcock thought to himself: "I'm in really big trouble here. This shit is getting to be pretty deep."

The FBI agent defied the attorney general: "I think I can speak for Director Hoover and say that we would not do that without a basis for an arrest. We would not make these arrests." Woodcock went back to his office and wrote a long memo to Hoover, not forgetting to mention the football and the shirtsleeves. It came back from the director "without a whole lot of blue ink"—just Hoover's "H."—"so I figured I must have done something right."

That summer, badgered by the attorney general, Hoover thought it wise to hire a handful of black FBI agents. One of the first was Wayne G. Davis, posted to Detroit. Soon he got a telephone call: Hoover wanted to meet him. "I go in to see Hoover," Davis recalled. "He talked—the whole half an hour I was with him—he talked about Martin Luther King." Hoover railed about "how awful King was, what a hypocrite he was and how his concern was that the movement that King was leading, the Southern Christian Leadership Conference, was infiltrated by Communists," Davis said. "And then he said, 'Well, nice talking to you, Wayne, you're doing a fine job, keep up the good work.' "

"Listen, Hoover was a bastard," Davis said. "He ruled by fear."

The FBI relentlessly recorded Martin Luther King planning the August 1963 March on Washington, which brought 250,000 demonstrators to the capital in the largest public protest in American history. And in the months before the march, RFK and his aides personally warned King against his associations with Communists. So did the president of the United States. King became more circumspect about his relationship with Levison, but he kept him close.

Hoover kept bombarding the Kennedys with memoranda accusing King of a leading role in the Communist conspiracy against America. He commissioned FBI reports on the deep history of the Communist Party's connections with the civil rights movement. What he wanted was a document so convincing that it would destroy Martin Luther King.

"The 19 million Negroes in the United States today constitute the largest and most important racial target of the Communist Party USA," read an August 23, 1963, report from FBI intelligence chief Bill Sullivan to the director. "Since 1919 communist leaders have devised countless tactics and programs designed to penetrate and control the Negro population."

But the report failed to provide direct evidence of Communist control. Hoover reached for his pen: "I for one can't ignore the memos re King. . . ." Sullivan kowtowed, the day after the "I Have a Dream" oration: "In the light of King's powerful demagogic speech. . . . We must mark him now, if we have not done so before, as the most dangerous Negro of the future in this Nation from the standpoint of communism, the Negro and national security."

The result was "a really politically explosive document," said Nick Katzenbach. Signed by Hoover, it went all over Washington—"to the White House—all around the damn place—about all of King's Communist contacts." It was political dynamite. Robert Kennedy ordered it withdrawn, but too late. It shocked senators and generals. The memo gave Hoover the leverage he needed for an all-encompassing surveillance of King and the civil rights movement.

"Bobby thought it was absolute blackmail," Katzenbach said. "But he felt he could not, with all of the flood of memos about his Communist associations, then turn the Bureau down on a tap."

On October 10, 1963, and again on October 21, Robert F. Kennedy approved Hoover's requests for an unlimited electronic surveillance of King and the SCLC headquarters in Atlanta. The case file was entitled MARTIN

LUTHER KING JR./SECURITY MATTER—COMMUNIST. The bugs got quick results. When King traveled, as he did constantly in the ensuing weeks, to Washington, Milwaukee, Los Angeles, and Honolulu, the Bureau planted hidden microphones in his hotel rooms. The FBI placed a total of eight wiretaps and sixteen bugs on King. The transcripts are sealed under judicial order until 2027. But their essence is an open secret. The telephone taps largely recorded King thinking out loud, planning the civil rights movement, weighing tactics and strategies. The hotel bugs sometimes picked up the sounds of late-night parties that ended in the unmistakable sounds of sex. Thomas F. McGorray, an FBI agent on his first tour of duty in 1963, drew the assignment of monitoring the surveillance on King's private apartment in Atlanta. No one questioned the wisdom of bugging King's bedrooms.

"It's a moral issue," McGorray reflected. It certainly was for Hoover.

"Hoover was telling me, '*It's a terrible thing,*'" said Jack Danahy, the FBI agent who ran investigations of Communists for decades, recalling a conversation in the director's office. "'*That Martin Luther King, a minister, a religious minister... it makes me so damn mad.*' And he banged the glass-topped desk with his fist. '*Oh, damn,*' he says. He actually shattered it." The director displayed his pique on paper, too. "King is a 'tom cat' with obsessive degenerate sexual urges," Hoover wrote in a rage on January 27, 1964.

But in private he had reasons to be happy as the end of his fourth decade in office approached, and not only because he had the dirt on his nemesis.

The FBI's technical surveillances on foreign embassies and consulates constituted something close to complete coverage. The FBI's tracking of Soviet spies and diplomats in the United States was thorough. COINTELPRO, after seven years of sabotage, had delivered results: the Bureau's own figures showed that the Communist Party of the United States of America had now been reduced to 4,453 members—about 5 percent of its strength in the years after World War II. The Bureau had the Communist menace in check.

And when an assassin's bullet brought Lyndon Johnson to power in the White House, Hoover once again had a commander in chief who delighted in sharing his secrets.

On November 22, 1963, Hoover had his last significant conversation with Robert Kennedy. It was short and brutish. Hoover had telephoned Kennedy to deliver the word that his brother had been shot. "I have some news for you," Hoover had said—not bad news, just news. Forty-five minutes later, Hoover told RFK that his brother was dead.

The FBI's investigation of the Kennedy assassination was equally brusque: Lee Harvey Oswald did it. Case closed. Hoover would not countenance talk of a conspiracy.

The Warren Commission's official investigation was a wearisome sideshow for Hoover. He distrusted its leader, Chief Justice Earl Warren, and he kept close tabs on its work through a confidential informant who served as a member of the commission: Congressman Gerald R. Ford, the future president of the United States.

Hoover still had to swat down swarms of rumors about the assassination. Senator James Eastland, the Judiciary Committee chairman, sent warning that CIA and State Department officers were charging that "Oswald was a confidential informant of the FBI's" and that "Secret Service representatives were attempting to place the blame on the FBI." That was bad enough. But Lyndon B. Johnson and Robert F. Kennedy both feared that there might have been a Communist conspiracy to kill the president. To pursue that question in public was unthinkable. It would require them to challenge the authority of J. Edgar Hoover, and neither man was prepared to do that. Both Hoover and Allen Dulles, the CIA's director from 1953 to 1961 and a member of the Warren Commission, made sure that no one breathed a word about American plans to kill Fidel Castro. If there had been a Communist plot to assassinate the president in revenge, if the Soviets or the Cubans had ordered President Kennedy killed, and if the United States had a shred of evidence to prove the case, it would have been the opening shot of a new world war.

Hoover knew full well that the FBI was guilty—in his own words—of "gross incompetency" for its failure to keep an eye on Oswald in the weeks before the assassination. The angry and unstable marine had defected to the Soviet Union and returned as a Marxist malefactor. He was known to the Dallas office of the FBI—known as a Communist demagogue, possibly deranged, who had passed out leaflets supporting Fidel Castro and held a job at the Texas School Book Depository building, overlooking the route of JFK's motorcade. Hoover learned four days after the assassination that Oswald never had appeared on the FBI's Security Index, the list of people who posed a danger due to "their training, violent tendencies, and prominence in subversive activities," to quote the Bureau's own standards.

"We failed in carrying through some of the salient aspects of the Oswald investigation," Hoover concluded. "It ought to be a lesson to us all." He disciplined agents for dereliction of duty, overruling DeLoach's warnings that official reprimands or letters of censure could be construed as "a direct admission that we are responsible for negligence which might have resulted in the assassination of the President."

But Hoover would be damned if he would let the American public think so.

30

"YOU GOT THIS PHONE TAPPED?"

"EDGAR, I don't hear you well. What's the matter? You got this phone tapped?" asked the president of the United States.

"No, I should say not," said Hoover, with a chuckle. "I can hear you perfectly, sir," he said to Lyndon B. Johnson, who himself was taping the call.

On that evening, February 27, 1964, Johnson had been president for ninety-seven days. Every sunrise brought a fresh series of crises, landing like the morning paper on the front porch. Tonight's hot spot was the fountain-of-youth tourist town of St. Augustine, Florida, racked by racist murders and the dynamiting of the Florida East Coast Railroad. LBJ ordered Hoover to get on the railroad case. "I'm not going to tolerate blowing up people with bombs," he said.

Johnson leaned on Hoover harder than any president ever had. He relied on him in matters of national security, foreign policy, and political intrigue. He praised Hoover to the skies and to his face. Some of his flattery was silver-tongued sweet talk, but some was plain truth. He wanted to believe in Hoover as a matter of faith.

The new president pledged his allegiance to Hoover. "You're my brother," Johnson told Hoover a week after John Kennedy was killed. "You have been for twenty-five, thirty years. . . . I've got more confidence in you than in anybody in town."

Their political relationship was cultivated as carefully as the White House Rose Garden, where the two stood side by side on Friday, May 8, 1964, at a ceremony in the director's honor. The coming Sunday would mark Hoover's fortieth year in power. The new year would bring his seventieth birthday and his mandatory retirement under federal law. Johnson signed an executive order that day waiving the law. Hoover would be the director till he died.

"J. Edgar Hoover is a household word," the president said that sunny afternoon. "He is a hero to millions of decent citizens and an anathema to evil . . . that would subvert our way of life and men who would harm and destroy our persons. Edgar Hoover has been my close personal friend for thirty years, and he was my close personal neighbor for nineteen years. I know he loved my dog, and I think he thought a little bit of me as a neighbor, and I am proud and happy to join the rest of the nation this afternoon in honoring this quiet and humble and magnificent public servant."

"That goddamned sewer J. Edgar Hoover"

Hoover stoked the president's fear that Robert F. Kennedy and his loyalists wanted to retake the White House. Johnson could not bear the thought. He collaborated with Hoover to excommunicate the attorney general from power, shunning him with silences and lies.

"One of the troubles with dealing with the President was that he had that goddamned sewer J. Edgar Hoover flowing across his desk," said the national security adviser McGeorge Bundy, a Kennedy man who served and suffered under LBJ. "Like many extremely skillful politicians, he had a weakness for under-the-rug information."

LBJ recorded several anguished conversations with RFK shortly before Kennedy resigned to run for the U.S. Senate in New York.

"Mr. Hoover's going down to Jackson, Mississippi. I understand they have a press conference scheduled there," RFK told LBJ. "If he's asked some of the questions about this communist situation in connection with the civil-rights movement, and answers some of them in the way that some of the memos have indicated he might, it could cause a good number of difficulties around the country."

LBJ answered: "All right. You want me to talk to him?"

RFK hesitated and stumbled. His chagrin was audible: "As I've said before, it's quite difficult for me. . . ."

A few days later: "Martin Luther King is going down to Greenwood, Mississippi, tonight and he's going to address a mass rally there," RFK told the president. "If he gets killed, it creates all kinds of problems—just being dead, but a lot of other kinds of problems."

LBJ suggested that Kennedy order Hoover to shadow King.

The attorney general said he had no power to tell Hoover to do anything. "I have no dealings with the FBI anymore," Kennedy said. "It's a very difficult situation."

"He sends all kinds of reports over to you . . . about me planning and plotting things," Kennedy told LBJ, "plotting the overthrow of the government by force and violence . . . leading a coup."

Johnson professed shock and ignorance about these reports. It was not the last lie he would tell Kennedy about his relationship with Hoover.

"Mr. Johnson at all times recognized strength and knew how to use strength," said Deke DeLoach, Hoover's newly appointed liaison to LBJ's White House. "Hoover was riding the crest of the wave at the time and Mr. Johnson knew how to use him. They were not deep personal friends by any stretch of the imagination. There was political distrust between the two of them, but they both needed each other."

"WE'RE FIXIN' TO DECLARE WAR"

Lyndon Johnson concentrated information and power in the Oval Office better than any president since Franklin Roosevelt. He admired the way Hoover used secret intelligence. He used the FBI as a political weapon in ways no president ever had done.

He needed Hoover's help to use every ounce of his presidential power—to wield his political clout as freely and as secretly as possible; to contain the Communist menace, foreign and domestic; to snoop on his friends and enemies in Congress and on the Supreme Court, to keep the lickspittles of the liberal left in check, and to slay the dragons of the far right.

LBJ never used power more effectively than when he ordered Hoover to destroy the Ku Klux Klan in Mississippi, a red-white-and-blue war against the Klan's church-burning terrorists.

Burke Marshall, the chief of the civil rights division at the Justice Department, remembered LBJ saying that "three sovereignties" were involved in the battle: "There's the United States and there's the State of Mississippi and there's J. Edgar Hoover." To handle all three required a combination of brute force and great finesse. LBJ made it work.

On Sunday, June 21, 1964, three civil rights workers disappeared after fleeing a jailhouse in Philadelphia, Mississippi, in their station wagon, with

Klansmen hot on their trail. Once they went missing they were presumed dead. Mississippi saw, on average, twenty-five civil-rights-connected shootings, beatings, bombings, and arsons every month during 1964. But a triple murder—and one that involved two white men from the North—was out of the ordinary.

Hoover called LBJ at the White House two days later. "We have found the car," Hoover told the president. It had been set ablaze eight miles outside Philadelphia.

"Apparently, these men have been killed," Hoover continued.

"Or maybe kidnapped and not killed," said LBJ, with little hope.

"Well, I would doubt whether those people down there would give them even that much of a break," Hoover said. "The car is so burned and charred with heat . . ."

"The car is still burning?" LBJ asked.

"The car is still burning," Hoover said.

"We're going to have more cases like this down south," Hoover told the president. "What's going to complicate matters is the agitators of the Negro movement."

The search began in the hot and hostile terrain of Neshoba County, Mississippi. The Klan had sworn members working for the Mississippi Highway Patrol (MHP) and the county sheriff. The FBI had a paltry presence in Mississippi; some old-time agents, who had to work and live with state and local law enforcement officers, were unenthusiastic about making a federal case out of the murder of three agitators.

On June 24, LBJ shocked Hoover by sending the retired CIA director Allen Dulles to talk with the governor of Mississippi and the chief of the Mississippi Highway Patrol. The president stroked and reassured Hoover: "I haven't got a better friend in this government than you. . . . Ain't nobody going to take over anything from you as long as I'm living. . . . Ain't nobody going to take our thirty-year friendship and mess it up."

On June 26, Dulles reported back to LBJ at the White House. The president put him on the phone with Hoover. "You ought to review the number of agents that you have in that state," Dulles told the director. The Mississippi Highway Patrol and the county sheriffs were "not really going to enforce this business, I'm afraid, unless they have somebody looking over their shoulders. . . . There are a half a dozen other situations down there that are full of difficulty and there might be terroristic activities of any kind."

Hoover was deeply skeptical. "That's going to be an almost superhuman task, don't you think, Allen?"

While LBJ listened on a speakerphone, Hoover focused on keeping the integrationists in line. "These people have been trained . . . and are going to live in the homes of the colored population," Hoover said. "They will hold meetings in each community to give them the education they're supposed to have" in order to be registered to vote under Mississippi law. "You've got to almost keep a man, keep an agent, with these individuals as they come into the state," Hoover said. "Because this Klan crowd—members of the MHP are Klansmen, many of the chiefs of police are, the sheriffs are." Hoover wanted a contingent of U.S. marshals, not the FBI, to deal with the Mississippi Highway Patrol and the National Council of Churches and the black activists alike.

LBJ got back on the line, telling Hoover to beef up the FBI's manpower in Mississippi: "Maybe we can prevent some of these acts of terror by the very presence of your people."

The president called Hoover again on the evening of June 29. LBJ had invited the mother of one of the missing men, Andy Schwerner, to the White House. Hoover was unhappy. "She's a communist, you know," he told the president. "She and her husband both have been active members of the Communist Party in New York for a number of years."

LBJ, coughing heavily, straining his voice: "Is she an actual member?"

Hoover, wearily: "Oh, yes, she's an actual member."

Hoover, nevertheless, had started to comply with the president's command. "I'm opening a main office," he said, "a full-time office at Jackson, Mississippi, with an agent in charge and a full staff as we would have in New York or San Francisco."

On July 2, 1964, LBJ asked Hoover to go to Mississippi and proclaim the omnipresence of the FBI. The director was dubious. "Whatever you do, you're going to be damned," Hoover said. "Can't satisfy both sides."

Then he got a direct order from the president of the United States.

"Ain't *nobody* going to damn *you*," LBJ said. "Nobody but a few communists and a few crackpots and a few wild people are against you in this country. They're unanimous. Ain't anybody in this country has the respect you have."

"See how many people you can bring in there," said the president. "You oughta put fifty, a hundred people, after this Klan, and studyin' this from one county to another. I think their very presence may save us a division of soldiers. . . . I think you oughta have the *best* intelligence system, *better* than you got on the communists. I read a dozen of your reports last night here 'til one o'clock on the communists. And they can't open their mouth without your knowin' what they're sayin'."

"Very true," Hoover said.

LBJ knew how to twist Hoover's arm: "Now I don't want these *Klans*men to open their mouths without *your knowing what they're sayin'*. Now nobody needs to know it but you, maybe, but *we ought to have intelligence* on that state. . . .

"If I have to send in troops . . . it could be *awfully* dangerous," LBJ said. "I'm having these demands for 5,000 soldiers. . . . To send in a bunch of Army people, divisions, is just a mistake. But I've got *ample* FBI people. . . . You figure out where you can borrow them . . . See how many we can put in next week."

"I want you to have *the same kind* of intelligence that you have on the *communists*," the president said

LBJ was telling Hoover to go after the Klan in language he understood. Hoover obeyed. The FBI would pursue the Klansmen, penetrate their ranks, subvert them, and sabotage them, so long as Lyndon Johnson commanded that it be done.

"Mr. Hoover never would have changed by himself"—not without LBJ's forceful command, Burke Marshall said. "The FBI was grudging about doing anything" against the Klan. "Mr. Hoover viewed the civil-rights activists as lawbreakers. The FBI was worse than useless, given his mind-set"—until the president ordered him to change his mind.

Hoover assigned a hard-headed but highly intelligent favorite of his, Joe Sullivan, to run Mississippi. Sullivan chose Roy K. Moore as his special agent in charge. Moore was an old marine. An unusual number of the best young FBI men he sent to Mississippi were combat veterans culled from FBI outposts across America.

"I want you to gather intelligence by trying to infiltrate the Klan," Moore told his men. "We're fixin' to declare war."

Moore tutored many first-tour agents in "techniques to gather intelligence . . . that have been used since the days of the Egyptians," said an FBI rookie named Billy Bob Williams, an ex-marine who rooted out Klan torture chambers and killing fields in desolate Mississippi Delta hamlets.

"Martin Luther King yelled and screamed that there weren't enough

Yankee agents down in Mississippi—so, lo and behold, I find myself down in Mississippi," the FBI's Donald J. Cesare said. In Philadelphia, the hotbed of the White Knights of the Ku Klux Klan, a town of about 40,000, "there must have been forty to fifty agents searching all over that place," out looking for corpses.

Cesare was an unusually experienced man for an FBI rookie. He came to Mississippi from his first tour, in Dallas, where he had investigated the Kennedy assassination. A decade before, he had been a tobacco-chewing captain in the United States Marine Corps, recruited by the CIA as a paramilitary officer during the Korean War. Among other assignments, he had trained Tibetan guerrillas loyal to the Dalai Lama. He wanted to go to East Africa in 1963, but the CIA wanted to send him back to Asia. Cesare quit—and wound up in charge of Neshoba County, Mississippi, instead of Nairobi, Kenya. Why? Because his father, chief of police in Old Forge, Pennsylvania, had always wanted his son to join the Bureau.

Cesare's chief, Inspector Joe Sullivan, found out where the three civil rights workers' bodies were buried. Sullivan was "very friendly with Maynard King, who was a Mississippi State Highway Patrol Captain," Cesare said. Sullivan never told his underlings how he got the information. But Hoover knew.

On the evening of August 4, 1964, Deke DeLoach called the White House, interrupting a war council. The president had received a startling report of a Communist attack that day on American ships in the Gulf of Tonkin—a false report, but one taken as truth. The intelligence fiasco was the opening shot of America's war in Vietnam. That night, on live television, the president told the American people that the United States had begun bombing Vietnam.

He was far happier to talk to DeLoach.

"Mr. Hoover wanted me to call you, sir, immediately and tell you the FBI has found three bodies six miles southwest of Philadelphia," DeLoach said. "A search party of agents turned up the bodies just about 15 minutes ago."

"You pretty much have in mind who did this job?" LBJ asked.

"Mr. President, we have some very excellent suspects," DeLoach said. "We have some excellent circumstantial evidence."

"How'd you find the spot? Somebody give you a lead?"

"Yes, sir, someone we have to protect with a great deal of caution, of course."

"You don't have much doubt but what these are the bodies, do you?"

"Mr. President, we feel very definitely these are the bodies," DeLoach said. "It took a hell of a lot of shoveling and digging to get at them."

Through Maynard King, who had led the FBI to the bodies, the Bureau recruited another Klansman, Delmar Dennis, a handsome twenty-seven-year-old preacher with a photographic memory. Sullivan assigned Don Cesare to handle Dennis. The preacher had a good head under his hood. He remembered license plates. He remembered phone numbers. He remembered names, dates, and places. Cesare was authorized to pay Dennis whatever it took to keep him serving as the FBI's secret agent inside the Klan.

"I paid him close to a quarter of a million dollars," Cesare said—a sum worth about $1.75 million today, far greater than any FBI informant ever before had received.

Delmar Dennis earned it. "He identified all the law enforcement in Neshoba County as Klansmen," Cesare said. He named the officers who cornered, shot, killed, and buried the outside agitators; "in particular he spelled out the order which called for the murder of the three civil rights workers which originated from Sam Bowers, who was the Imperial Wizard of the Klan in Mississippi, to the Neshoba Klavern—at that time, headed by Edgar Ray Killen," Cesare said. "Delmar was so trusted in the Klan that he served not only the Bureau, but he also served the Klan—not only as a courier of Klan information, but he was a distributor of Klan funds too."

It took a very long time before men like Killen and Bowers were brought to justice; in Killen's case it took forty years. Delmar Dennis wound up a broken and disillusioned man, torn by his role as an informer. But with his recruitment, the FBI was inside the Mississippi Klan.

WHITE HATE

The day after the corpses of the three civil rights workers were found, LBJ called Hoover. "I knew you'd do it," the president said. "If you just think that you gonna get off the payroll 'cause you're getting a little older, you crazy as hell. I don't retire the FBI."

"That's very nice of you, Mr. President," Hoover said with evident pride. "I just finished up my physical and I passed it 100 percent."

Then he got down to the Mississippi murder cases: "Each of these men had been *shot*," he said. "And we have the names of the people who did it.

Now, to *prove* it is gonna be a little tougher job. The sheriff was in on it. The deputy sheriff was in on it. The justice of the peace was in on it. And there were seven other men. So we have all those names and as I say we're concentrating now on developing the evidence."

The deep penetration of the KKK in Mississippi led Hoover to authorize a full-blown counterintelligence program against the Klan.

COINTELPRO—WHITE HATE was inaugurated on September 2, 1964, two months after the president had told Hoover to pursue the Klan just as he had chased the Communists. WHITE HATE went on for seven years, inflicting serious and lasting damage on the Klan. White-shirted agents would fight white-sheeted Klansmen like snake-killing jungle warriors, but their job called for something more subtle than kicking down doors. It required recruiting and running informants. The FBI men had to act more like spies than soldiers. Two hundred FBI agents had worked on the Mississippi killings; they had interrogated 480 Klansmen. After the Klan murdered Lemuel Penn, a black army reserve lieutenant, outside Atlanta, the FBI expanded its work to cover every major Klan group in Mississippi, Alabama, and Georgia.

These were internal security cases, not criminal investigations. They depended on the infiltration, surveillance, and sabotage of the members of the Klan and their murderous leaders.

WHITE HATE intensified rapidly in the fall of 1964. It involved all the techniques developed in the FBI's long-running attack on the Left. Once a week during the fall of 1964, FBI agents interrogated all known members of the White Knights of the KKK, blaming other Klansmen for being snitches and naming names, sowing deep suspicion among Klan members. Few knew who was an informer and who was not. The FBI dangled small fortunes before potential KKK informers, offered outright bribes to Klansmen who could serve as double agents inside state and local police forces, planted bugs and wiretaps in Klaverns, carried out black-bag jobs to steal membership lists and (on at least one occasion) dynamite caches. The FBI's infiltration of the Klan proved better than the Klan's infiltration of state and local law enforcement agencies.

"There would be a Klan meeting with ten people there, and six of them would be reporting back the next day," said the FBI's Joseph J. Rucci, Jr. "We had a pretty effective counter-Klan going. We would also communicate with them in the mail. I remember we would send them post cards; big post cards went through the mail. I remember one in particular showed a Klansman and someone peeking up a sheet and it would say, the catch would be, 'I wonder who is peeking under your sheet tonight.' "

The gung-ho mood of the FBI agents who ran WHITE HATE was remarkable, given the fact that their colleagues were fighting Communist infiltration of the civil rights movement with equal intensity.

The Communist Party COINTELPRO was focused on the movement and its white supporters among liberals and young leftists. "The Bureau was doing what it was supposed to do, keeping up with foreign influences" inside the civil rights movement, Billy Bob Williams said; the FBI had identified a significant number of civil rights activists as "trained in the Soviet Union or trained in Cuba, and all they were interested in was civil *unrest*."

"It makes me scared by God to even talk back to my wife!"

LBJ's newly declassified diaries and telephone logs show he was in constant contact with Hoover during 1964 and 1965, sometimes two and three times a day, seeking political intelligence on many matters, most of them far from the field of law enforcement.

Hoover lived for such moments.

When simmering racial tensions flared up in the streets of New York in September 1964, LBJ sent Hoover to investigate. Hoover made a quick trip to the city and reported to the president that "the race riots . . . have not been initiated by communists" but that "communists have appeared immediately" to reap political hay from them. As an aside, Hoover gave the president a report on the fortunes of his Republican rival in the upcoming election, Senator Barry Goldwater of Arizona, among New York Jews. "A lot of these Jews that were going to vote for Goldwater—thinking that he was a Jew, you know—have now decided that they're going to vote for you," Hoover told LBJ. The two men chuckled together.

With the 1964 election three weeks away, LBJ's chief of staff, Walter Jenkins, had been caught by a Washington, D.C., vice detail having oral sex with a man in a YMCA bathroom a block from the White House. Sexual entrapment for the purpose of political blackmail was widely assumed to be a time-honored technique of Communist intelligence services. In a matter of days, Hoover was able to assure Johnson that the case had no national security implications.

"I'm very grateful to you for your thoroughness and your patriotism and the way you have handled it, as I am everything else you have done," LBJ told him.

"Of course, I realize the spot that you have been in and the terrible other burdens you have had, and it's awful bad this thing happened. But I think we handled it with compassion," Hoover said.

"You just remember, my friend, you have done your duty as you have been doing all your life, and I'm proud of it. And I'm prouder of you now than I have ever been before," LBJ told him. "And as long as your Commander-in-Chief feels that way about you—"

"That's all I care about," Hoover replied.

The homosexuality of his top aide mystified the president, though. "I guess you are going to have to teach me something about this stuff," LBJ said to Hoover. "I swear I can't recognize 'em. I don't know anything about 'em."

"It's a thing that you just can't tell sometimes—just like in the case of this poor fellow Jenkins," Hoover replied. "There are some people who walk kinda funny and so forth, that you might kinda think might be a little bit off or maybe queer."

A week later, a deeply uncomfortable Robert Kennedy sat next to President Johnson in a limousine winding through the streets of New York.

LBJ had joined RFK on the campaign trail five days before the election as Kennedy campaigned for the U.S. Senate. The president began a guarded conversation about the political bombshells that had been kept in Jenkins's office safe. He told Kennedy that the safe held FBI reports detailing the sexual debauchery of members of the Senate and House who consorted with prostitutes. The president wondered aloud whether they should be leaked selectively, against Republicans, before election day.

"He told me he had spent all night sitting up and reading the files of the FBI on all these people," Kennedy recounted. "And Lyndon talks about that information and material so freely. Lyndon talks about everybody, you see, with everybody. And of course that's dangerous." Kennedy had seen some of those files as attorney general. He felt their disclosure could "destroy the confidence that people in the United States had in their government and really make us a laughingstock around the world."

Nor were these the only sex files the FBI shared with the president.

On November 18, 1964, Hoover, enraged that Martin Luther King was set to receive the Nobel Peace Prize, doubly incensed by King's criticism of the FBI's performance in the civil rights field, held a highly unusual press conference, calling a group of women reporters into his offices and proclaiming that King was "the most notorious liar in the country." LBJ, conferring with Deke DeLoach two days later, expressed a degree of sympathy for Hoover's position.

"He *knows* Martin Luther King," LBJ said with a low chuckle. "I mean, he knows him better than anybody in the country."

The FBI intelligence chief, Bill Sullivan, had run his own COINTELPRO against Martin Luther King. He had a package of the King sex tapes prepared by the FBI's lab technicians, wrote an accompanying poison-pen letter, and sent both to King's home. His wife opened the package.

"King, look into your heart," the letter read. "The American people soon would "know you for what you are—an evil, abnormal beast. . . . There is only one way out for you. You better take it before your filthy, abnormal fraudulent self is bared to the nation."

The president knew Hoover had taped King's sexual assignations. Hoover was using the information in an attempt to disgrace King at the White House, in Congress, and in his own home. DeLoach himself had offered newspaper reporters and editors a chance to hear the sex tapes. When Nicholas Katzenbach, now the acting attorney general of the United States, got wind of these offers to the press, he called DeLoach into his office and confronted him.

"He flatly denied any such activity and wanted to know who had been circulating such lies," Katzenbach recalled. "I was totally convinced who in fact was lying, but I was without the means to prove it." Convinced that the civil rights movement faced disaster, Katzenbach flew to see the president at the LBJ Ranch in Texas, where Johnson was enjoying a break after his landslide victory in the November 1964 presidential election. The president listened, asked a few questions, and moved on.

LBJ could not help but admire the Machiavellian force of Hoover's attack. "I'll tell you," he told Katzenbach on March 4, 1965, "when Martin Luther King questioned his integrity, he goddamned sure responded pretty effectively!"

LBJ's estimation of Hoover hit an all-time high on March 25, 1965, after the murder of Viola Liuzzo, a white civil rights activist driving from Selma, Alabama, with a black passenger. A car pulled alongside her on a dark highway and a gunman shot her to death. The FBI broke the case immediately. An undercover informer named Gary Thomas Rowe was riding in the car with three fellow Klansmen.

On March 26, at 8:10 A.M., LBJ and Hoover talked about the arrests.

"We had one of our men *in the car*," Hoover told an incredulous president. "Fortunately he had no gun and did no shooting. But he has identified the two men who had guns and fired guns. . . . We know who they are, and then we'll bring 'em in and shake 'em down in interrogation. . . . We've got the informant in the office and we're talking to him. He's scared to death, naturally, because he fears for his life."

"What is an infiltrator and an informant?" LBJ asked. "You hire someone and they join the Klan?"

Hoover's pride practically pulsed through the telephone line. "They go to someone who is in the Klan and persuade him to work for the government," he explained. "We pay 'em for it. Sometimes they demand a pretty high price, other times they don't. For instance, those three bodies we found in Mississippi, we had to pay $30,000 for that . . . and after we found the bodies, we ascertained the identity of one man, and from him—we broke him down, and he gave us the identities of the other nineteen, two of whom confessed."

Johnson was agog. "That's wonderful, Edgar," he said.

The case was a mixed blessing for Neil Shanahan, the FBI agent who handled the covert Klansman in the car, Gary Rowe. "We had this case wrapped up two hours after it happened," Shanahan remembered. But how was the FBI to handle the fact that Rowe was a party to a murder? "We didn't have any witness protection at that time," Shanahan said. "*I* was his witness protection plan. . . . It was a problem for which there was no solution."

LBJ and J. Edgar Hoover stood side by side in the East Room of the White House at noon on March 26, in a live address to the nation. The president announced the arrests of the four Klansmen, including the undercover FBI informant. Praising Hoover and the FBI for the swift arrests, without mentioning the FBI's man inside the car, Johnson denounced the Klan as "enemies of justice who for decades have used the rope and the gun and the tar and the feathers to terrorize their neighbors."

"We will not be intimidated by the terrorists of the Ku Klux Klan any more than we will be intimidated by the terrorists in North Vietnam," Johnson said, surely the first time a president had denounced the cross burners and the Vietcong in the same breath. Hoover stood at LBJ's right, silent and stony.

They spoke again by telephone, in a brief moment of mutual pleasure, on April 13, 1965. "I sure am proud of what you've done on this civil rights thing, and I think history will so show it," the president said. "Anybody could have a man in that car, that's the most unthinkable thing I ever heard of! And it makes me scared by God to even talk back to my wife! 'Fraid you'll have somebody there arresting *me*!"

Hoover and Johnson laughed heartily together, a rare sound in the annals of American history. That moment of mirth ended one of the last free-and-easy conversations the two men ever had. In eleven days Lyndon Johnson would face a crisis that he could not handle. He would have to turn to Hoover to save him.

31

"THE MAN I'M DEPENDING ON"

THE DOMINICAN REPUBLIC blew up on Saturday, April 24, 1965. President Kennedy had dreamed of making the country a showcase for democracy. Now it was a cauldron of fear and hate.

A right-wing junta had overthrown President Juan Bosch, the nation's first freely elected leader. Then Bosch's loyalists counterattacked. Bosch, a dreamy liberal, had fled to San Juan. His predecessor, Joaquín Balaguer, the last puppet president of the past dictatorship, had fled to New York. Blood ran in the streets of the capital, Santo Domingo.

At 9:35 A.M. on April 24, LBJ called the American diplomat he trusted most, Thomas Mann, a tough Texas conservative who served as an undersecretary of state.

"We're really going to have to set up that government down there and run it and stabilize it one way or another," LBJ told Mann. "This Bosch is no good."

The president had put himself in the position of picking the next leader of the Dominican Republic. The problem was that almost no one in the United States government knew what was happening in Santo Domingo. The CIA station chief was out of commission with a bad back. The American ambassador was visiting his mother in Georgia. The ranking American officers in the capital were dodging bullets.

But J. Edgar Hoover and his man in San Juan had a handle on the case.

The position of special agent in charge was the highest a man could hold in the FBI without working at headquarters—"the Seat of Government," as Hoover called it. The special agent in charge was the prince of his city, whether it be New York, New York, or Butte, Montana. Within those ranks, Wallace F. Estill was unique. He was the special agent in charge of Puerto Rico.

Not many men in Hoover's FBI were as worldly. Born in 1917, Estill had joined the Bureau in 1941. He had investigated Nazi platinum smugglers in Uruguay, gathered intelligence on Russia from Eskimos in Alaska, served as Hoover's official liaison with the Royal Canadian Mounted Police, and somehow managed through it all to keep his cool, a rare quality after twenty-four years under Hoover.

Wally Estill had been keeping a very close eye on Juan Bosch. Estill and the Bureau were listening to his telephone calls from San Juan as he plotted his way back to power in the Dominican Republic. The legal basis for the technical surveillance was dubious at best. "We have no evidence that Bosch has violated or conspired to violate any U.S. laws," Tom Mann had written two months earlier. "What he has done is exercise the right of free speech."

But Hoover and the Bureau had fingered Bosch as a Communist as early as 1961, and the charge, once made, was indelible.

Hoover himself authorized the "tech"—an unlimited electronic surveillance—on Bosch in San Juan; Hoover's writ extended to the island because Puerto Rico was a U.S. commonwealth, under U.S. law. "With Bureau approval a tech was placed on Bosch's phone," Estill remembered. "It was successful beyond our wildest expectations."

The FBI listened as Bosch and his aides in San Juan talked to their allies in Santo Domingo. The wiretapping showed that "Bosch was not only the nominal head of the revolt, he was the de facto leader," Estill said. "We relayed this to the Bureau which, in turn, furnished it to the White House."

Bosch became suspicious that his phone might be tapped. "He resorted to the use of pay phones throughout the city, and even the phones of friends and supporters" in Puerto Rico, Estill said. "With oral authorization"—from Hoover—"we expanded our coverage until we had the capacity, limited by available manpower, to monitor virtually every call between Puerto Rico and elsewhere."

On Tuesday morning, April 27, Undersecretary Mann advised President Johnson "to try to get a junta set up" in the Dominican Republic. In the afternoon, as the confrontation between Bosch's supporters and the regime's soldiers deepened, President Johnson sent the United States Navy to evacuate roughly one thousand Americans from the island. That night, a sleepless president, talking to the duty officer in the White House Situation Room at 3:30 A.M., monitored United States Air Force bombing runs over Vietnam.

The following day, April 28, the president swore in a new CIA director, Admiral William F. "Red" Raborn, another fellow Texan, in the Cabinet Room at the White House. Every ranking member of the CIA was present. But when the six-minute ceremony was over, the first thing LBJ did was to retreat to the Oval Office for an eight-minute one-on-one conversation with Hoover. "Mr. Hoover expressed his deep concern for the communistic activities in this hemisphere as well as affecting the Vietnamese war," according to the president's daily diary records.

As night fell, Johnson ordered four hundred United States Marines to the Dominican Republic, the first landing of American troops in the Western Hemisphere since 1928.

At dawn on April 29, the marine guards at the U.S. Embassy in Santo Domingo came under fire from snipers. LBJ ordered one thousand more marines to hit the shores. That afternoon, Hoover came to the White House for a twenty-minute briefing, alone with the president. Hoover saw a global threat: as the Communists were moving in the Caribbean, and the Kremlin was driving the Vietcong, American Marxists and their masters in Moscow were mobilizing the antiwar movement in the United States. What was happening in the Dominican Republic was part of a worldwide pattern, he said.

"THE ENEMY HAS THE ROADS"

LBJ received a good deal of unreliable intelligence on the Dominican Republic from the CIA and Red Raborn. "In my opinion this is a real struggle mounted by Mr. Castro," the admiral told the president, with little evidence.

LBJ wanted to believe in him. On April 30, the president told his lawyer, Abe Fortas, that the CIA had "men right in these operations—just like Hoover had one in that car in Alabama—that know what's happening."

"And there ain't no doubt about this being Castro now," the president told Fortas. "They are moving other places in the hemisphere. It may be part of a whole Communistic pattern tied to Vietnam. . . . Our choice is whether we're going to have Castro or intervention. . . . I think the worst domestic political disaster we could suffer would be for Castro to take over."

That same day, the president decided to intervene with the full force of the American military. He sent a three-star army general, Bruce Palmer, Jr., and the 18th Airborne Corps, including the 82nd Airborne Division, into the Dominican Republic. More than twenty thousand American soldiers and special operations forces and psychological warfare officers joined the marines. The week before, LBJ had sent forty-nine thousand more American troops to Vietnam.

On May 1, General Earle Wheeler, the chairman of the Joint Chiefs of Staff, gave General Palmer his marching orders: "Your announced mission is to save U.S. lives. Your unannounced mission is to prevent the Dominican Republic from going Communist. The President has stated that he will not allow another Cuba. You are to take all necessary measures to accomplish this mission."

American forces interposed themselves between the soldiers of the junta and the soldiers loyal to President Bosch (the "rebels," to the Americans). A tense standoff set in, marked by skirmishing, sniper fire, shelling, and savage nighttime raids against civilians.

Intelligence was the most precious commodity—but only the FBI's Wally Estill had it, by virtue of his electronic surveillance of Bosch in San Juan and his allies in the Dominican Republic.

"A rebel artillery battalion lobbed a number of rounds into the U.S. lines" in Santo Domingo, Estill recounted. "My phone rang and our receptionist announced that the Bureau was on the line." It was Al Belmont, Hoover's ranking assistant director. "Immediately I heard Mr. Belmont demanding to know whether those shots were fired with the approval of the rebel leadership. I responded that I would have to run upstairs and poll those on the tech to see what might have been intercepted and I would call him back. He responded with an emphatic NO! and said that President Johnson was holding on Belmont's other line and prepared to order our troops to respond with a devastating barrage that would demolish the rebels unless assured that the rebel barrage was an unauthorized event.

"I ran upstairs and loudly queried those on duty. We had just intercepted a call from the rebel headquarters to Bosch explaining that a young artillery officer had ordered the shots fired—for whatever reason. It had been without approval and contrary to orders. The officer had been relieved of his assignment and would be disciplined. As I relayed the information to Belmont, and he to Johnson I could feel, even over the phone, the tension ease. Our retaliatory barrage did not occur."

On May 5, LBJ talked to George Mahon, a thirty-year Democratic congressman from Texas. "With all these terroristic techniques that are developing in the world, I'm afraid that the time is coming, just like this thing in Santo Domingo, that they are refining the instruments of terror," the congressman said. "They could even blow up the Capitol someday."

"No question about it," LBJ replied. "And we've got to meet it head on."

The president met the threat by ordering Hoover to set up an FBI intelligence network at the American Embassy in Santo Domingo. The order was arguably illegal; the FBI had no jurisdiction. Hoover titled the operation DOMSIT, for Dominican Situation. He started rounding up two dozen agents who spoke Spanish, named each one a LEGAT, or legal attaché, wrangled diplomatic passports for them, and began dispatching them to the Caribbean that night.

The FBI's Paul Brana was in the first wave of ten agents. "They fly us down in this C-130," a military transport with master bedrooms in the main compartment, Brana said. "We land the C-130 in the Dominican Republic, and they have helicopters to fly us over. I said, 'How come they're flying us over in helicopters? How come we don't drive over?'"

A military officer responded: "Well, the enemy has the roads."

"I said, '*The enemy has the roads?*' Nobody had told us that there was a combat operation going on. So we're going up in this goddamned helicopter and I see this machine gun fire. I say, 'Christ, nobody told us we were coming into combat.'"

Brana's bosses had told him that the president "was very unhappy because of the fact that he knew nothing" about the political situation in the Dominican Republic. LBJ ordered the FBI to run a background check on everyone vying for power.

"HE WAS THE MAN OF THE FUTURE"

The president and Hoover called each other three times on May 14, as the FBI was setting up operations in Santo Domingo. The final call came from LBJ, at 7:05 P.M., in the middle of a two-and-a-half-hour Cabinet Room meeting with Defense Secretary Robert McNamara; national security adviser McGeorge Bundy; undersecretaries of state Tom Mann and George Ball; the CIA director, Red Raborn; and his deputy, Richard Helms.

The president told Hoover to put an FBI detail on Joaquín Balaguer, the exiled president who had served as Trujillo's figurehead. "Get right after him in New York," LBJ commanded. "I sure want your operation stepped up wherever it is for the next forty-eight, seventy-two hours unless you want to have another Castro."

Hoover promised to deliver. The results would surprise even LBJ. Within seventy-two hours, the FBI had recruited the Dominican exile as a trusted confidential source.

On the afternoon of May 17, the top State Department officer for the Dominican Republic, Kennedy Crockett, flew to New York for a hastily scheduled meeting with Balaguer. The White House wanted Balaguer on a 5:00 P.M. flight to Puerto Rico for a meeting with his rival Bosch; the plan was being improvised by LBJ's lawyer, Abe Fortas. LBJ and Hoover spoke about the anticipated meeting with Balaguer at 3:02 P.M.

"I arrived at the Regency Hotel at 3:40 P.M.," Crockett wrote in a secret memo to the White House. "Balaguer was not there. At 3:50 P.M. he had still not appeared on the scene."

Fortas and Crockett cooled their heels in the plush hotel lobby. "Balaguer turned up at about 3:55 P.M.," Crockett wrote. "I told him time was short—I had a cab standing by—I would brief him on developments since our last meeting as we drove to Kennedy Airport. Balaguer said we would have to wait until 4:00 P.M., as his suitcase was in the car which had dropped him off at the hotel and it would not be back until 4:00 P.M. He suggested we ride out to Kennedy Airport in 'his car.' I objected, pointing out that I did not want to have anyone else listening in on our conversation. He said this would not be a problem as 'his car' had been provided by the FBI."

" 'Balaguer's car' turned up at 4:00 P.M. sharp," Crockett wrote. "The senior Special Agent accompanying him was Heinrich Von Eckardt." Balaguer was now a recruited source for the FBI; Von Eckardt was his handler.

"After examining each other's credentials, we all climbed aboard and started for Kennedy Airport," Crockett reported. In the backseat, Fortas and Crockett assured Balaguer that the United States would back him to the hilt—"that he was the man of the future in the DR and we would do nothing that did not take into account both his short- and his long-range value for both the USG [U.S. government] and the Dominican people." Then Fortas bought Balaguer a ticket to San Juan; Von Eckardt caught the same flight.

In San Juan, the FBI's Wally Estill sent a driver to meet the former president and bring him to his meeting with Bosch. "We arranged for a particular cab to pick him up at the airport and take him to a particular hotel," Estill remembered. "And we had set up mikes in the hotel room and actually covered that damn conversation, so we could wire it back to D.C. It was a kind of double-check on whether Balaguer was leveling. And it was after that Von Eckardt puts Balaguer on the plane to be flown to Santo Domingo."

The president hardly could have asked for more. But he did.

"J. Edgar Hoover's man"

That same night, a minute after midnight, LBJ convened a White House meeting on the Dominican Republic. McGeorge Bundy, Tom Mann, Abe Fortas, and other top LBJ aides had been meeting with Dominican leaders in San Juan and Santo Domingo. The Americans proposed that Balaguer and Bosch could run for president after tempers cooled and soldiers left the streets. Meanwhile, a rich pro-American businessman named Antonio Guzmán could run a provisional government.

In the middle of the night, LBJ was trying to pick a cabinet for the provisional government.

"Are they going to let you bring in J. Edgar Hoover's man to come in as legal adviser to the Embassy, to advise Mr. G. on the bad characters, and have him watch them?" the president asked Mann. The answer was yes: an American Red squad in Santo Domingo, led by the FBI, would serve the provisional government. But LBJ quickly torpedoed the deal, fearing it could not guarantee a government free of Communists. His diary notes that he was up until 4:30 A.M., slept for perhaps three hours, and called the Situation Room at 8:06 A.M.

On May 19, shortly before noon, Abe Fortas telephoned LBJ. The president angrily asked him if American military officers were backing the firepower of right-wing attacks in the Dominican Republic.

LBJ: Have we done that, in your judgment?

FORTAS: Yes, sir.

LBJ: Do we *admit* that we've done it?

FORTAS: No, sir.

Fortas anxiously assured the president he almost had finished the master list of potential Dominican leaders, military and political, making sure they were free of the faintest taint of the left. Then the president cut Fortas off: "I've got Hoover waiting on the other line." Not knowing whom to trust, he wanted Hoover's help.

"Now, Edgar, here's the play," he said. "Our State Department, far as I can tell, and I wouldn't say this to anybody but you, is not worth a damn, they're a bunch of sissy fellows and they never come up with a solution . . .

"*Now,* Fortas, I called him in," said LBJ, ever more intense. "He's as close to me as you are. He wants to do what I want done if it can be honorably done . . .

"*Now!*" the president barked. "We want a democracy. We want the will of the people. We want to help *influence* that will, and help direct it. . . . But let's get an *anti*-communist government. . . . Most people are anti-*American,* 'cause we've acted such damn fools, throwing our weight around."

"Yes, we have, we have . . . ," said Hoover.

"*Now! I've got to decide today,* I've got to *decide,*" LBJ said. "But I'm not going to decide on *anybody* that either you or Raborn or somebody responsible doesn't tell me they're not a communist."

"Yes, I understand," said Hoover.

"I don't know, I'm not infallible," said the president. "Hell, I've made mistakes in my life."

"We all do," said Hoover.

"So you get the best men you got to check these names," LBJ said.

"We're getting on it and checking it now," Hoover said. "We'll have that information for you if possible by this evening."

"Check out everybody you can . . . ," LBJ said. "I don't want to work a month and make a deal and send in 30,000 soldiers and then *piss it off to the communists!*"

"That's right," Hoover said.

"And *you the man I'm depending on* to keep me from pissing it off! Now that's ugly language, but it's expressive, and you know what I want."

"We won't let you down," Hoover said.

"Playing for keeps"

Joaquín Balaguer was now the chosen one in the Dominican Republic. The blessings of J. Edgar Hoover had paved his way to power.

Balaguer had reconfirmed his bona fides to the Bureau on May 27, 1965. He reported in full to the FBI on his conversations in New York with Kennedy Crockett, the State Department's director of Caribbean affairs. The American diplomat asked the exiled leader for additional names to serve in the Dominican government and discussed Balaguer's strategies. The Dominican played back the conversation for his FBI handlers before Crockett's report reached Washington. That won Hoover's trust.

His dominion in the Dominican Republic was a glory for Hoover. It was reflected in the orders the CIA's new leader, Richard Helms, gave to his new station chief in Santo Domingo, David Atlee Phillips. Helms was famous for sending officers out to foreign assignments with laconic one-liners. Phillips, in a memoir, captured the moment:

> What would my instruction be from Helms? Certainly this time the marching orders would be detailed, the demands clearly enumerated. People were still killing each other in Santo Domingo, and the President was observing developments there with keen interest. . . . But my instruction was a one-liner too.
>
> Helms said, "Get along with the FBI."
>
> Was Helms joking? He was not. "Get along with the FBI. It is very important!"

The command reflected the degree to which LBJ depended on Hoover.

Hoover dominated a White House meeting with the CIA's leaders on September 1. Hoover strongly suggested that a two-man race would be best for the Dominican Republic; a wide-open contest with four or five candidates could "provide excellent fodder for the Communists." Hoover warned that perhaps two or three hundred "hard-core, skilled, trained Communists" remained at large on the island, and the provisional government "must identify these Communists and take them out of circulation right away; they have no guts if you pick them up and lock them up." Hoover noted that the military were "too heavy-handed and ill-trained" for this type of work; a strong national police would better serve the cause. So the

FBI would provide training and facilities to help create a new Dominican national intelligence force, a Department of Special Operations, a secret police to combat subversives.

The president asked Hoover to help pick a new United States ambassador —a man tough enough to handle the American-engineered regime change in the Dominican Republic. Hoover had in mind "a good tough individual who will stand up and be able to dominate the government." He gave his blessings to John Hugh Crimmins, an experienced Caribbean and Cuba hand, who had been spending long days and nights watching over the crisis in the Dominican Republic at the State Department's emergency center. When the new ambassador arrived in the Dominican Republic, he found twenty-six FBI legal attachés ensconced in the American embassy.

"That whole operation was really weird," said Crimmins. "The policymaking and policy execution apparatus of the U.S. Government was stretched to the absolute maximum. It was just madness. It was just chaos. . . . Oh, it was crazy."

As Ambassador Crimmins took over, LBJ called Hoover again. The tape is heavily redacted on national security grounds.

"It is an awful mess," Hoover said. "I think the situation down there is very critical. . . ."

"I'd kinda hate to see your people pull out of there until we form a government," LBJ said.

"Well, we won't pull out of there until you say so," Hoover assured him.

"This is playing for keeps. We just can't have a communist government there," the president said. "We can't lose that one, Edgar. If we do I'm gonna put it right in your lap, I'm gonna say J. Edgar Hoover did this, and I'm gonna resign." Hoover laughed heartily.

"HE WANTS TO WIN"

On September 25, Juan Bosch returned home from San Juan, where he had been under an all-pervasive FBI surveillance net for five months. American soldiers still patrolled the streets of Santo Domingo, and the FBI's legal attachés kept close watch over Bosch and his allies. President Johnson received a warning that "FBI sources in Santo Domingo are picking up an increasing number of reports that Bosch would like to see the elections postponed for several months because of what he describes as the existing state of political insecurity."

The United States proclaimed that a free election between Balaguer and Bosch would take place. But Richard Helms explained the facts of life to Desmond FitzGerald, his covert operations chief at the CIA: "The President," Helms said, "expected the Agency to devote the necessary personnel and material resources in the Dominican Republic required to win the presidential election for the candidate favored by the United States Government. The President's statements were unequivocal. He wants to win the election, and he expects the Agency to arrange for this to happen."

The United States provided as much cash as could be safely smuggled into Balaguer's hands. President Johnson had ordered that the candidate would receive all the campaign money he needed, along with information and propaganda, courtesy of the CIA and the State Department.

Balaguer won the vote by a margin of 57 percent to Bosch's 39 percent— a landslide built on American money, intelligence, and power. The American press universally reported that the vote was free and fair.

Ten days after the election, President Johnson received satisfying news from his national security adviser. "Hoover has furnished security reports on 35 of Balaguer's first appointments," the June 11, 1966, report said. "These cover the Cabinet and sub-Cabinet, the Supreme Court and some of the key independent agencies such as State Properties, Industrial Development, Immigration, Communications and Airport Administration.... Security-wise the Cabinet looks good.... Balaguer made a clean sweep of the Supreme Court.... The Attorney General is also given a clean bill. We can expect the new Supreme Court to clean house further down the ranks of the judiciary."

Hoover had helped install a government led by an FBI informant and run by three dozen FBI-approved ministers, military chiefs, and judges. Joaquín Balaguer, the FBI's man in Santo Domingo, was one of the last of the old-time Latin American strongmen. He ruled with a heavy hand for twenty-two years.

32

CLEARLY ILLEGAL

B Y THE SPRING OF 1966, LBJ had sent almost a quarter of a million American soldiers to Vietnam. Thousands of American citizens protested. Hoover watched the marches with growing alarm. He saw long shadows hovering behind the antiwar movement, reaching from Hanoi to Harvard, Beijing to Berkeley.

"The Chinese and North Vietnamese believe that by intensifying the agitation in this country, particularly on the college campus levels, it would so confuse and divide the Americans that our troops in Vietnam would have to be withdrawn in order to preserve order here," Hoover told LBJ days after he began pouring soldiers into combat. It was an agony for the president to hear his prophecy that Vietnam would become a political war on the home front.

The peace movement affected nearly every outpost of the FBI. "We were engaged almost every weekend with various antiwar demonstrations at the Alamo and at President Johnson's ranch in Johnson City," said FBI agent Cyril P. Gamber, on his first tour at the Bureau's San Antonio, Texas, office. "Most holidays and weekends were taken up with the New Left demonstrating on one side of the road and the Klan and the Nazi Party on the other side of the road." Like the road to the LBJ Ranch, America was cleft in two. The FBI had its right flank covered, but it knew less and less about what was happening on the left.

Hoover and his inner circle saw the protests through the old prism of the international Communist conspiracy. "The demonstrations have been marked by a growing militancy," Hoover wrote in a letter to all FBI special agents. "With summer approaching, the potentialities for violent outbreaks will increase immeasurably, whether demonstrations are directed at opposition toward United States foreign policy in Vietnam or protests involving racial issues. We must not only intensify and expand our coverage ... but also insure that advance signs of such outbreaks are detected."

Hoover told his men: *"We are an intelligence agency and as such are expected to know what is going to or is likely to happen."*

The FBI's agents had a hard time gaining that insight as the battles of the sixties intensified. They were ill-suited to infiltrate the New Left. And Hoover was becoming cautious about the Bureau's time-honored techniques of black-bag jobs, break-ins, bugging, wiretapping, and mail openings. He had not lost his will for political warfare. Nor had the president lost his appetite for political intelligence. But the Supreme Court and members of Congress were becoming increasingly suspicious of the power and ubiquity of secret government surveillance. And neither LBJ nor Hoover wanted to be caught spying on Americans.

"I HAD NO ILLUSIONS"

The patrician but politically astute Nicholas deB. Katzenbach, Bobby Kennedy's protégé and his successor as attorney general, battled Hoover over taps and bugs. He came to understand that there were no controls over them. The Justice Department had not kept records of their installations. Once a wiretap was approved, Hoover considered it approved forever. Hoover had asserted that the FBI was free to install bugs at will, without informing a higher authority. He told Katzenbach that this power had been granted him in perpetuity by Franklin Delano Roosevelt a quarter of a century ago.

"I was, frankly, astounded to hear this," Katzenbach recounted. "I had no illusions that I was going to bring the FBI under my control. But I did think it was possible to institute a more orderly procedure."

He began to demand facts and figures from the FBI; the Bureau slowly disclosed them. Hoover had installed 738 bugs on his own authority since 1960; the Justice Department's attorneys had been informed about only 158 of them, roughly one in five. Installing bugs in homes, offices, apartments, and hotel rooms generally required breaking and entering, which was illegal. The Bureau had conducted uncounted break-ins and black-bag jobs on Hoover's say-so.

The attorney general proposed that henceforth taps and bugs would have to have his written approval. He was even more astonished when

Hoover appeared to agree. LBJ had made it clear to both men that he wanted wiretaps kept to a minimum—except when it came to his opponents on the left. Katzenbach readily approved surveillances on the antiwar activists of the Students for a Democratic Society.

SDS had led the first big antiwar marches on Washington. The FBI had been watching the group for three years, from the moment it was conceived. The first SDS manifesto read: "Communism as a system rests on the suppression of organized opposition. The Communist movement has failed in every sense." But Hoover still saw the student movement through a Soviet prism. A purely American protest against authority was inconceivable to him. After that first march, Hoover had reported to the White House that "Students for a Democratic Society, which is largely infiltrated by communists," had made plans for antiwar protests in eighty-five more cities. He promised LBJ a full report on the Communist influence over the anti–Vietnam War demonstrations.

Hoover ordered his intelligence and internal security chiefs "to penetrate the Students for a Democratic Society so that we will have proper informant coverage similar to what we have in the Ku Klux Klan and the Communist Party itself. . . . Give this matter immediate attention and top priority as the President is quite concerned about the situation and wants prompt and quick action." But the Bureau had very few sources in the New Left. No underground squads infiltrated coffeehouses and colleges—not yet. Electronic surveillance was of the essence if Hoover wanted intelligence.

"Wire taps and microphones," Hoover reminded the attorney general, had "made it possible for the FBI to produce highly significant intelligence information to assist our makers of international policy, as well as to hold in check subversive elements within the country." Yet Katzenbach declined to authorize new hidden-microphone bugs on the student left. He was painfully aware of the pervasive surveillance that had been placed on Martin Luther King; he feared the political consequences of its exposure.

Hoover said he was "extremely concerned" at the decision. But he reported that he had "discontinued completely the use of microphones" and that he had "severely restricted" new wiretaps against the antiwar and civil rights movements.

Bewildered FBI agents wondered whether the old man was losing his nerve. What was Hoover doing? Why was he doing it? Very few understood the answer. Hoover had reason to fear that the FBI's lawbreaking would be exposed.

Senator William Fulbright, Democrat of Arkansas and chairman of the Foreign Relations Committee, was threatening to create a new committee to oversee the FBI's intelligence work; President Johnson warned Hoover to keep a very close eye on Fulbright, whom he suspected was holding secret meetings with Soviet diplomats. A far less prominent Democratic senator, Edward Long of Missouri, had started a scattershot series of hearings on government wiretapping. "He cannot be trusted," an FBI intelligence supervisor warned.

Hoover strongly suspected that Senator Robert F. Kennedy was leaking information about the FBI's bugging practices. He confronted Katzenbach. The attorney general denied it. "Just how gullible can he be!" Hoover wrote.

"HOOVER PUT US OUT OF BUSINESS"

Hoover knew a politically explosive case involving the FBI's illegal bugging of a shady Washington lobbyist was working its way up to the Supreme Court.

The defendant was Fred Black, a powerful influence peddler appealing a tax-evasion conviction. The FBI had bugged Black's suite at the Sheraton-Carlton Hotel in Washington in 1963, and it had recorded his conversations with his lawyer. The secret recordings were illegal on their face, as was the breaking and entering required to install the bugs. Hoover fought bitterly with the Justice Department over the legal necessity of disclosing these facts to the Supreme Court as it considered the case of *Black v. United States*.

Hoover used Justice Abe Fortas, newly appointed to the Court by LBJ, as a confidential informant in the case. Deke DeLoach, the FBI's liaison to the White House, served as the go-between. Over breakfast at his home, Justice Fortas laid out a political strategy to blame the bug on Bobby Kennedy. "He was always willing to help the FBI," DeLoach wrote, while noting that the justice's conduct in discussing a case before the Court was "blatantly unethical."

Despite Hoover's best efforts, the solicitor general of the United States,

Thurgood Marshall, revealed the FBI's conduct to the Court. (Marshall had been a target of FBI surveillance for many years, as the leading lawyer for the NAACP.) The Court overturned the conviction. In months to come, the justices would rule that the FBI's electronic surveillance of a public telephone booth was unconstitutional, and it would compare government eavesdropping to the "general warrants" used by the British colonialists to suppress the American Revolution.

The public disclosures of the FBI's procedures were front-page news, as Hoover had feared. Hoover had always controlled the force of secret information. Now that secrecy was starting to erode, and with it went a measure of his power.

On July 19, 1966—six days after the *Black* bug was revealed in court—Hoover banned the FBI from using black-bag jobs and break-ins. "No more such techniques must be used," Hoover instructed his lieutenants.

 The practice of breaking and entering was "clearly illegal," the FBI's intelligence chief, William Sullivan, had reminded the director in a formal memo. "Despite this, 'black bag' jobs have been used because they *represent an invaluable technique* in combating subversive activities of a clandestine nature aimed at undermining and destroying our nation."

Hoover's old guard believed the FBI would be handcuffed. The paladins of the FBI's intelligence and internal security divisions were dumbstruck by the director's order.

Edward S. Miller, rising through the intelligence ranks to the number-three post at headquarters, said: "In our time in the Bureau—and that is Hoover's time, and subsequent to that—the only thing we had was our reliance on investigative techniques that had made us very successful against the Communist Party and Soviet Communism." The Bureau would rise or fall by "conducting business the only way we felt that we were authorized to do," said Miller, who faced a federal indictment a decade later for his use of black-bag jobs.

Along with breaking and entering, Hoover also suspended the Bureau's long-standing practice of opening first-class mail.

The FBI's mail-opening program dated back to World War I. It violated the Fourth Amendment's ban on unwarranted searches and seizures. It had gone on without an interruption since 1940, when the British had taught the Bureau the ancient art of chamfering, cutting envelopes with scalpels and resealing them undetected.

The search for secret communications among spies and subversives in the satchels of the U.S. mails had expanded mightily in the seven years since 1959. The FBI ran covert mail-opening operations out of post offices in eight American cities—New York, Washington, Boston, Los Angeles, San Francisco, Detroit, Seattle, and Miami—inspecting hundreds of thousands of letters and parcels, looking for evidence of espionage. Since the start of World War II, the mail-opening program had led to the identification of four Communist spies and two Americans who had offered to sell military secrets to the Soviets. Opening mail was so patently illegal that Hoover had never thought to ask any attorney general or any president for that power. Was it worth the risk to the FBI? Hoover thought not.

Hoover's edicts created a furor inside the American intelligence community. The National Security Agency and the CIA had worked with the FBI since 1952 on a worldwide effort to steal the communications codes of foreign nations, friends and foes alike. A crucial element in that program was a gang of FBI and CIA safecrackers and burglars who could steal codebooks from foreign embassies and consulates. The ban on bag jobs threatened to bring breakthroughs in code cracking to a standstill.

The military and civilian chiefs of the National Security Agency, General Marshall Carter and Louis Tordella, went to see Hoover. They had been given fifteen minutes to make their case for reinstating the FBI's old methods. The one-sided conversation ran for two and a half hours as Hoover rambled on about his greatest cases of the 1930s and 1940s. Carter and Tordella finally got a word in, sometime during the second hour, to plead for covert intelligence collection. Hoover turned them down.

"Someone got to the old man," Bill Sullivan told Tordella. But no evidence exists that anyone twisted Hoover's arm. He knew that if his methods came to light, the Bureau would be tarnished forever. The danger of exposure was growing by the day. The political tide of civil liberties was rising. Hoover stood increasingly isolated against old-line liberals in Congress and New Left lawyers in the courts. A concerted attack on the FBI's extralegal intelligence techniques could destroy Hoover's image as the avatar of law and order in America.

The cost of his cautiousness was high for the FBI chieftains pursuing spies and saboteurs.

"Hoover put us out of business in 1966 and 1967 when he placed sharp restrictions on intelligence collection" using bugs and black-bag jobs, said Bill Cregar, a former professional football player who had become one of the Bureau's leading Soviet intelligence specialists. "We need technical coverage on every Soviet in the country. I didn't give a damn about the Black Panthers myself, but I did about the Russians."

Hoover's restrictions on illegal intelligence-gathering methods hobbled the FBI's spy hunters. The Bureau's increasingly relentless focus on American political protests drained time and energy away from foreign counterintelligence. The results were evident.

For the next decade, from 1966 to 1976, the FBI did not make a single major case of espionage against a Soviet spy.

"One big job before you go out"

The president's hunger for intelligence on the American Left grew more and more ravenous. Hoover tried to satisfy it by burrowing into the growing antiwar and black power movements with infiltrators and informants.

The Bureau instituted a nationwide program called VIDEM, for Vietnam demonstrations. It sent the White House a steady stream of intelligence on the leaders of the movement, the identities of people who sent telegrams to the president protesting the war, and the organizers of church and campus meetings on Vietnam. One peace conference in Philadelphia generated a forty-one-page FBI report, based on thirteen informants and sources, including verbatim transcripts of each speech and background checks on the chaplains, ministers, and professors in attendance.

Some FBI agents made extraordinary efforts to confirm the suspicions of the president and the director that the Soviets were behind the antiwar movement. The FBI's Ed Birch—the man who had nailed Colonel Abel of the KGB in 1957—had trailed the Soviet spy Viktor Lesiovsky across the country as he traveled from his diplomatic post at the United Nations secretariat earlier in the 1960s. He suspected that Lesiovsky, who had met in 1962 with Stanley Levison, Martin Luther King's counselor, was secretly financing the American Left with Soviet funds. "That guy traveled," Birch said. "But what got me was the places that he went to," including the University of Michigan, the seedbed of SDS. "It was always my impression—but I couldn't convince anybody in the Bureau of this—that this guy helped with the funding of the SDS." The evidence of Soviet financial support for the American antiwar and civil rights movements always proved elusive.

The nation's cities became war zones in the long hot summer of 1967. Black Americans fought the army and the National Guard as well as the police across the country; the forces of law and order suppressed seventy-five separate riots, sometimes with live ammunition and orders to shoot to kill. Forty-three people died in Detroit, where the army was deployed for eight days of combat and patrols; twenty-six in Newark, where the army was alerted for riot duty. In all, the nation suffered eighty-eight deaths and 1,397 injuries; the police arrested 16,389 people; economic damage was estimated at $664.5 million.

As Detroit smoldered on the morning of July 25, 1967, Hoover called the president with some real-time intelligence: the transcript of a wiretapped conversation between Martin Luther King and Stanley Levison, who remained under FBI surveillance.

"King was told by Levison, who is his principal advisor, and who is a secret communist, that he has more to gain nationally by agreeing with the violence," Hoover reported, confiding that this fresh intelligence was the result of an FBI tap. Hoover said that King thought "the President is afraid at this time and is willing to make concessions." The president did not fear Martin Luther King. But he *was* afraid that there was an unseen hand behind the upheavals. He thought foreign agents—maybe the Cubans, perhaps the Soviets—might be instigating the urban riots. He told Hoover to "keep your men busy to find the central connection" between the Communists and the black power movement. "We'll find some central theme," the president said.

Hoover said he would get right on it. One month later, on August 25, the FBI inaugurated COINTELPRO—BLACK HATE.

Orders went out to twenty-three FBI field offices to "disrupt, misdirect, discredit, or otherwise neutralize the activities of black nationalist hate type organizations." The Bureau singled out Martin Luther King's Southern Christian Leadership Conference along with Stokely Carmichael and H. Rap Brown's Student Nonviolent Coordinating Committee (SNCC). Hoover publicly labeled King along with his more radical counterparts as the leading "rabble-rousers" and "firebrands" inciting black riots. BLACK HATE went hand in hand with the newly created "Ghetto Informant Program." Within the year three thousand people had been enlisted as FBI sources—many of them respectable businessmen, military veterans, and senior citizens—to keep watch over the black communities of urban America. BLACK HATE and the Ghetto Informant ranks soon doubled in size and scope.

In the fall of 1967, the urban riots ebbed but the peace marches grew. The protesters in Washington chanted: "Hey, hey, LBJ, how many kids did you kill today?" The president ordered the FBI, the CIA, and the army to root out the conspiracy to overthrow his government.

"I'm *not* going to let the Communists take this government and *they're doing it right now*," LBJ shouted at Secretary of Defense Robert McNamara, Secretary of State Dean Rusk, and Director of Central Intelligence Richard Helms during a ninety-five-minute Saturday morning meeting on November 4, 1967.

On his orders, liberal-minded men—like the new attorney general, Ramsey Clark, and his deputy Warren Christopher, later President Bill Clinton's secretary of state—commanded the FBI to spy on Americans in concert with the United States Army and the National Security Agency. Some 1,500 army intelligence officers in civilian clothing undertook the surveillance of some 100,000 American citizens. Army intelligence shared all their reports with the FBI over the next three years. The CIA tracked antiwar leaders and black militants who traveled overseas, and it reported back to the FBI.

The FBI, in turn, shared thousands of selected files on Americans with army intelligence and the CIA. All three intelligence services sent the names of Americans to the National Security Agency for inclusion on a global watch list; the NSA relayed back to the FBI hundreds of transcripts of intercepted telephone calls to and from suspect Americans.

The president had created a concerted effort to organize a secret police. He was trying to synchronize the gears of the FBI, the CIA, and the army to create an all-pervasive intelligence machine that would watch citizens as if they were foreign spies.

But the political forces at work in the world in 1968 were too powerful to control. None of the intelligence the president received calmed his troubled mind. By the time of the Tet offensive at the end of January 1968—with 400,000 Communist troops striking almost every major city and military garrison in South Vietnam—LBJ believed that his enemies had encircled him in Washington.

He was a haunted man when he spoke to Hoover on February 14, 1968.

"I don't want anybody to know I called you," LBJ said in a hoarse whisper, breathing heavily, sounding exhausted.

"I want you personally to do one big job before you go out," the president said. What he wanted was an intensified search for spies in Washington. He suspected that American politicians and political aides were serving the Communist cause.

The FBI's electronic surveillance of foreign embassies and consulates now included closed-circuit television monitoring as well as wiretap coverage of the Soviets in Washington and New York. LBJ told Hoover to step up the surveillance in a search for Americans leaking information to the nation's enemies. He wanted reports on senators, congressmen, their staffs on Capitol Hill, and any other prominent American citizens who might be in secret contact with Communists in foreign embassies. He feared that congressional staff members were secretly working for the Soviets, perhaps delivering government documents to the KGB, on behalf of their bosses.

"If you don't do anything else—and that is while you and I are here—I want you to watch, with all the care and caution and judgment that you ever have built up over forty or fifty years, these embassies and what those who're dedicated to overthrowing us are doing," the president said.

"I would watch it like nobody's business and I'd make it the highest priority," LBJ told Hoover. "See who they're talking to, what they're saying . . . I just want you to personally take charge of this and watch it yourself."

He wanted Hoover to scrutinize politically suspect members of Congress with special attention. "I'm going to insist that everybody who has secret documents be carefully cleared," he said. "Say to those committee chairmen, 'The President has ordered us to check everybody.'

"Because when McNamara goes up and testifies before Fulbright that we are breaking the North Vietnamese code and a goddamn Commie sympathizer goes and tells it, they just change their codes. . . . Chase down every damn lead and see who they saw and who they talked to and when and how . . . You the only guy in the government that's watching it. I just want to order you now to be more diligent than you've ever been in your life."

"I'll give it my personal attention, Mr. President," Hoover said.

The FBI sent squads of agents to spy on the diplomatic compounds of allies and enemies alike. They gave special attention to the embassy of South Vietnam, America's faltering partner in the war on communism, trying to see if Americans were working with foreign diplomats and spies to subvert the president.

"A PILLAR OF STRENGTH IN A CITY OF WEAK MEN"

Lyndon Johnson renounced his power on March 31, 1968. He said he would not seek reelection. He spoke to the nation on television, his face a crumpled mask of exhaustion, his voice tinged with bitterness and despair.

To LBJ's anguish, and to Hoover's anger, Senator Robert F. Kennedy immediately became the front-runner for the Democratic nomination. Both men had good reason to believe that their most bitter political enemy would be the next president. Hoover feared a concomitant surge from the left wing of America, and most of all a rise among the radicals in the black power movement. RFK's campaign was catalyzing black voters across America; the candidate had a newfound fervor for the politics of liberation.

Four days after LBJ stood down from the presidential election, Hoover wrote to his field agents to be on guard against the forces he had labeled BLACK HATE: "The Negro youth and moderates must be made to understand that if they succumb to revolutionary teaching, they will be dead revolutionaries."

The next evening, Martin Luther King was assassinated in Memphis.

The killing unleashed unfettered rage across the country; the flames burned close to the White House. Returning from King's funeral in Memphis, Attorney General Ramsey Clark looked down upon Washington, D.C., from his airplane. The burning city, aglow as night fell, was in the grip of the most dangerous insurrection since the war of 1812. King's killer, James Earl Ray, eluded the biggest manhunt in FBI history by taking a bus to Toronto and an airplane to London. A Scotland Yard detective arrested him sixty-six days later as he tried to board a flight for Brussels.

On April 23, the Students for a Democratic Society seized Columbia University; six days later police stormed the campus and arrested seven hundred students. It took the FBI ten more days to respond. The response was COINTELPRO—NEW LEFT.

The first wave of the FBI's national attack on the antiwar movement included explicit instructions from Hoover and Sullivan to all field offices: Instigate conflicts among New Left leaders. Exploit the rifts between SDS and its rival factions. Create the false impression that an FBI agent stood behind every mailbox, that informants riddled their ranks. Use disinformation to disrupt them. Drive them mad. But COINTELPRO was behind the curve. More than one hundred campuses across the country had already been hit by student protests. The marches were breaking barricades, and at their fringes were militants willing to toss Molotov cocktails and more. Hoover sent out a fierce call to arms for his special agents in charge across America. "I have been appalled by the reaction of some of our field offices to some of the acts of violence and terrorism which have occurred . . . on college campuses," he wrote. "I expect an immediate and aggressive response."

Hoover saw a gathering storm unlike anything since the great police, coal, and steel strikes that swept the nation as the American Left rose up after World War I. But the FBI had no answer to the violence and rage that shook America that spring.

Robert Kennedy was assassinated in Los Angeles on June 6. Millions of Americans had put their hopes in him. Hoover was more cold-eyed. "He became a kind of Messiah for the generation gap and individuals who were pro-King and still are," Hoover wrote in a memo to his top aides after RFK's death. Kennedy's election would have been the end of Hoover's power.

The murder left the path to the White House open for a man who vowed to restore the rule of law and order. Hoover now had reason to hope for a restoration, a return to Republican verities, and a renaissance for the FBI. His old friend Richard Nixon might be elected president in November.

It was a very close call. The contest between Nixon and LBJ's vice president, Hubert Humphrey, swung on public opinion about the war in Vietnam. Half a million American soldiers now fought; they died by the hundreds each week. Ten days before the election, after an all-night meeting with his closest military and intelligence aides, Johnson was set to announce a halt to the American bombing of Vietnam and a plan for a negotiated peace. But at the last minute, President Thieu of South Vietnam balked.

"We've lost Thieu," LBJ told an aide on the eve of the election. "He thinks that we will sell him out."

The FBI had detected evidence of a plot to sabotage LBJ's plans for a cease-fire in Vietnam. The plot appeared to the president to be the work of the Nixon campaign.

Three days before the election, LBJ said he was "personally watching the traffic"—telephone calls and telegrams being intercepted at the embassy of South Vietnam by the FBI and the National Security Agency—and that he had detected Nixon's scheme to torpedo the peace talks. He ordered the FBI to place Anna Chennault, the most famous representative of Chinese anti-communism, under surveillance.

LBJ suspected that she was Nixon's go-between. FBI headquarters sent a top secret message to the president on Monday, November 4, the day before the election: "Anna Chennault traveled in her Lincoln Continental from her residence to the Vietnamese Embassy where she remained for approximately thirty minutes." After that, the FBI reported, she went to 1701 Pennsylvania Avenue and entered room 205—an unmarked Nixon campaign office.

LBJ summarized what he had learned about the Chennault affair on the eve of the election. "She says to the South Vietnamese Embassy—she was a carrier, that's what she was—she said, 'I have just heard from my boss . . . And you tell your boss to hold on a while longer.' And that's the nut of it."

Nixon won the presidency by a very narrow margin: fewer than half a million votes, roughly one-seventh of one percent of the electorate. A peace accord would surely have worked to Humphrey's advantage.

LBJ was convinced that Nixon had cut a secret bargain with the government of South Vietnam to win his victory. The essence was this: Don't make a peace agreement with Johnson and Humphrey. Wait until I'm elected. I will get you a better deal.

"Now, that is the story, Dick," LBJ said in a heated telephone call to Nixon after the election, all but accusing him of an act tantamount to treason. "And it is a sordid story."

Nixon denied it to his dying day. But the conversation left him with the indelible impression that the president of the United States had used the FBI to spy on him.

The president did not dream of going public with the accusation. The mere fact that he had ordered the FBI to put the Nixon campaign under surveillance would have been explosive enough. But a public accusation that Nixon had torpedoed the peace talks would have been the political equivalent of nuclear warfare.

LBJ had to make peace with him. On December 12, he invited Nixon to the White House for a two-hour meeting. They found common ground in their admiration for the work of J. Edgar Hoover.

In the Oval Office, Johnson picked up the telephone, and he had a three-way chat with Hoover and Nixon. The call went unrecorded. But Nixon remembered the president saying: "If it hadn't been for Edgar Hoover, I couldn't carry out my responsibilities as Commander in Chief—period. Dick, you will come to depend on Edgar. He is a pillar of strength in a city of weak men."

33

THE ULTIMATE WEAPON

Richard Nixon came to power with a soaring vision of world peace. If he succeeded, he thought he could reunite a nation at war with itself. If he failed, he feared the United States itself might fall.

He wanted to find a way out of Vietnam. He thought he could end the Cold War with Russia and China. His political calculus of the price of compromise with the leaders of world communism was brutal: "The risk of war goes down, but the risk of conquest without a war through subversion and covert means goes up geometrically."

His hopes for the world hinged on secret government in America. His policies and plans, from carpet bombings to the diplomacy of détente, were clandestine, hidden from all but a few trusted aides. But he knew the chances for the absolute secrecy he sought were slim.

"I will warn you now," LBJ had told him at the White House in December 1968, "the leaks can kill you." He advised Nixon to depend on Hoover, and Hoover alone, to keep his secrets and protect his power: "You will rely on him time and time again to maintain security. He's the only one you can put your complete trust in."

But Nixon put his complete trust in no one—not even Hoover, a man whom he called "my closest personal friend of all in public life."

They had been cronies, as Nixon put it, for more than twenty years. Hoover had schooled the callow newcomer to Congress in 1947. His tutelage in the political tactics of the war on communism had been Nixon's primal experience of power. They had shared their thoughts in confidence a hundred times throughout the 1950s. Hoover had never lost touch; he had been a source of political counsel throughout Nixon's long exile from Washington. Hoover had been more than a source of secret information;

he was a trusted political adviser. He had never ceased to feed Nixon's fears of political subversion.

The two men spoke at least thirty-eight times, face-to-face or on the phone, over the first two years of the new administration—before Nixon plugged in his hidden microphones at the White House. Every few weeks, as Nixon remembered, "he'd come in alone" and talk at length about the threats that faced America. "Much of it was extremely valuable," Nixon said. "And it never leaked."

They talked for hours over dinners at the White House, at Hoover's home, on Nixon's presidential yacht. The supper for four on the *Sequoia* included Nixon's chief of staff, H. R. Haldeman. "Almost unbelievable conversation," Haldeman wrote in his private diary. "J. Edgar went on and on," recounting "detailed reports of great FBI operations." Hoover was "a real character out of days of yore"—and Nixon was "fascinated by him."

Hoover came to see Nixon at the headquarters of the presidential transition team at the elegant Pierre Hotel in New York at the end of 1968. He was "florid and fat-faced," and "he looked unwell," recalled John Ehrlichman, who would serve as Nixon's White House counsel and Hoover's White House liaison. But his powers of speech were undiminished.

Hoover told Nixon that he should be cautious about what he said on the telephone to LBJ during the days of the transition, and careful what he said on the telephone once he took office. He could be taped. Hoover explained that the Army Signal Corps controlled the presidential communications system and monitored all calls patched through the White House switchboard; the way Nixon understood it, a corporal could listen in on the president.

The director then pointedly reminded Nixon about the powers of surveillance that were at a president's command. Years later, Nixon was compelled by an order from Congress to give a formal statement about what Hoover had told him that day.

Hoover emphasized that the FBI had "conducted, without a search warrant," black-bag jobs, break-ins, and bugging for every president since FDR, Nixon said. Its skills included "surreptitious entries and intercepts of voice and non-voice communications." The Bureau was especially adept at hunting down leakers, Hoover confided. Wiretapping was "the most effective means" it had.

Nixon also learned from Hoover how to lie to Congress about wiretapping without being caught.

"That was Mr. Hoover's common practice," Nixon said in a secret sworn deposition to Watergate prosecutors, unsealed in November 2011. "He told me about it. He said, 'You know, about a month or so before I ever go up to testify before the Appropriations Committee I discontinue all taps . . . so that when they ask me the question as to whether we are tapping anybody, I can say no.'" Once Hoover was done with his annual appearances in Congress, the FBI would turn the taps back on.

"Hoover, over a period of fifty years, always stonewalled the question," Nixon said, "and he was always technically truthful."

Nixon revived the FBI's traditions of wiretaps, bugs, and black-bag jobs. They quickly became a part of the political culture of the Nixon White House. He ordered Hoover back into the field of political warfare.

"THERE WAS ONLY ONE WAY TO DEAL WITH THIS"

Nixon had apocalyptic visions of a revolution in America, his dark thoughts driven deeper by the political assassinations, ghetto riots, and antiwar marches of the sixties. His inaugural parade on January 20, 1969, ran into a brief but furious hail of rocks, bottles, and beer cans tossed by hundreds of antiwar protesters. On the campaign trail, Nixon's mantra had been "Bring Us Together." The people he thought were ripping America apart were screaming curses at his black limousine as it rolled to the White House.

The early days of his presidency were marked by alarming bombings and shoot-outs: radicals attacked army recruiting offices and Reserve Officer Training Corps (ROTC) centers on campus; Puerto Rican nationalists blew up the draft board in San Juan; black militants aimed sniper attacks at police. Hoover had proclaimed the Black Panther Party and its photogenic leaders the greatest threat to the internal security of the United States. His intelligence chief, Bill Sullivan, had succeeded through COINTELPRO at placing informers at high levels inside the party, which by 1969 was already starting to fragment. But the FBI did not have a clue about the student movement, and the students were the ones who worried Nixon the most.

Nixon feared that they were a subversive threat as powerful as the Soviets, the Chinese, and the Vietcong. He spoke of the campus uprisings at American universities in one of his first major addresses.

"This is the way civilizations begin to die," he said. He quoted Yeats: "*Things fall apart. The center cannot hold.* None of us has the right to suppose it cannot happen here."

The correlation of forces was changing in America. Nixon would remake the Supreme Court by appointing right-wing justices. He vowed repeatedly to reestablish respect for the law and the power of the presidency. He had named the deeply conservative John N. Mitchell as attorney general to re-store order to the United States, continuing the political tradition of hiring his campaign manager to run the Justice Department. Mitchell had a placid, pipe-puffing demeanor and a passionate devotion to the president. He would do anything Nixon asked of him, and he treated Hoover with the deference the director demanded. "Attorneys General seldom directed Mr. Hoover," Nixon said. "It was difficult even for Presidents."

From his first week in office, Nixon demanded secret intelligence on the radicals. "He wanted to know who was doing it, and what was being done to catch the saboteurs," Ehrlichman wrote. The president told his White House counsel to go see Hoover, to establish himself as "his friend and White House confidant," and to set up a direct channel for secret commu-nications between the FBI and the White House.

Ehrlichman approached the director with caution. His staff had warned him "that every meeting in Hoover's office was secretly filmed or video-taped. But they did not prepare me for the Wizard of Oz approach that his visitors were required to make." From the corridors of Justice, Ehrlichman was ushered through double doors guarded by Hoover's personal atten-dants. He walked into a room crammed with tributes to Hoover—plaques and citations emblazoned with emblems of American eagles and eternally flaming torches. The anteroom led to a second, more formal room, with hundreds more awards. That led to a third trophy room with a highly pol-ished desk. The desk was empty.

"J. Edgar Hoover was nowhere to be seen," he wrote. "My guide opened a door behind the desk, at the back of the room, and I was ushered into an office about twelve or thirteen feet square, dominated by Hoover himself; he was seated in a large leather desk chair behind a wooden desk in the center of the room. When he stood, it became obvious that he and his desk were on a dais about six inches high. I was invited to sit on a low, purplish leather couch to his right. J. Edgar Hoover looked down on me and began to talk." He talked nonstop, for an hour, touching on the Black Panthers, the Communist Party of the United States, Soviet espionage, Congress, the Kennedys, and much more. But he had little to say about what the presi-dent wanted: intelligence on the radical factions of the New Left.

Ehrlichman would learn—as would Nixon—that "the Bureau dealt excessively in rumor, gossip, and conjecture" when it came to sensitive political intelligence. Even when a report was based on wiretapping or bugging, "the information was often hearsay, two or three times removed."

Such was the case with the first hot tip Hoover delivered at the end of January 1969. Nixon had invited Hoover to a dinner for twelve at the White House. The invitation crossed with a startling memo to the president. Hoover asserted that a long-standing member of the White House press corps, Henry Brandon, who covered Washington for the *Sunday Times* of London, was a threat to national security.

"I called Mr. Hoover and said, 'What is this all about?' " Nixon remembered. He knew Brandon as the most prominent foreign correspondent in Washington, an accomplished social climber, and a friend to the national security adviser, Henry Kissinger, who liked to spend Sundays in Brandon's swimming pool.

Hoover said that the reporter was suspected of spying for the British and Czech intelligence services—and that the FBI had been wiretapping Brandon for years in search of the proof. This planted the seed of an idea in Nixon's mind: wiretapping reporters was the way to find the leakers and their sources within the White House.

A few days later, on February 1, 1969, Henry Kissinger convened the National Security Council staff for a top secret meeting on the Middle East with Nixon. "Within days," Nixon remembered, "details of the discussion that had taken place were leaked to the press. Eisenhower, whom I had personally briefed on this meeting, considered any leak of classified foreign policy information, whether in war or peace, treasonable."

So did Nixon and Kissinger. Front-page stories on their strategies for dealing with the Soviet Union and Southeast Asia, seemingly taken directly from the minutes of the National Security Council, appeared almost every week. By Kissinger's account, twenty-one newspaper articles based on leaks about the president's secret foreign policies were published in the first hundred days of the administration. Nixon would explode in anger at the headlines: "What is this cock-sucking story? Find out who leaked it, and fire him!" Kissinger learned to imitate his boss; sometimes he could outdo him: "We must crush these people! We must destroy them!"

On April 23, Nixon spent twenty minutes on the telephone with Hoover, thinking out loud about a plan to plug the leaks. Two days later, the president sat down with Hoover and Attorney General John Mitchell at the White House.

Nixon's sworn account of the Oval Office meeting on the leaks was suc-
cinct. "Hoover informed me that . . . there was only one way to deal with
it. . . . He had authority to wiretap . . . Wiretapping being the ultimate
weapon."

"I told Mr. Hoover we would go forward with this program," Nixon remembered. "I called Dr. Kissinger in and indicated to him that he should
take the responsibility of checking his own staff." Kissinger, of course, complied. "Here he was in this room with J. Edgar Hoover, John Mitchell, Richard Nixon," said Kissinger's aide, Peter Rodman. "They're saying: 'Let's do
some taps.' And J. Edgar Hoover and John Mitchell say: 'Yeah, we can do
that. Bobby Kennedy did this all the time.'"

Kissinger would select suspects for surveillance. If Hoover concurred,
the taps would go in. The responsibility for finding the leakers and stopping the leaks would rest entirely on the FBI.

On the morning of May 9, Hoover picked up his telephone to hear the
unmistakable voice of Kissinger in high dudgeon. He was furious about a
front-page story in *The New York Times*. Nixon had been bombing Cambodia, a neutral nation, seeking to strike Vietcong and North Vietnamese supply depots. The bombing violated international law. But the story violated
the principles of secrecy. The president saw it as an act of treason—"a leak
which was directly responsible for the deaths of thousands of Americans."
He believed that the secret bombing could save American soldiers fighting
in South Vietnam. Kissinger conveyed his wrath to Hoover. The director's
notes of the conversation reflect it: "National security . . . extraordinarily
damaging . . . dangerous."

The Kissinger wiretaps were on. "Dr. Kissinger said he appreciated this
very much," Hoover wrote, "and he hoped I would follow it up as far as we
can take it and they will destroy whoever did this if we can find him, no
matter where he is."

Hoover gave the task of installing the taps to his intelligence chief, Bill
Sullivan. Sullivan was more than willing to follow orders from the White
House. He had had his eye on Hoover's job for years. Now he would have the
full attention of the president's men, and there was little he would not do to
serve them. He soon would have the attention of the president himself.

Sullivan secured the voluminous wiretap transcripts and logs as "Do
Not File" files. He kept them locked in an office he maintained outside of
FBI headquarters, and he provided Kissinger and his military aide, Colonel
Al Haig, with daily summaries. Nixon sent Kissinger to the FBI with in-

structions to "express your appreciation to Mr. Hoover and Mr. Sullivan for their outstanding support." His orders were to "inform Mr. Hoover that you have discussed these problems in detail with the President" and to "ask Mr. Hoover if he has any additional information or guidance which he feels would be helpful in this very difficult situation."

Some of Nixon's closest aides knew these taps fell into a twilight zone of the law. Nixon thought he had the power to spy on anyone he pleased on the grounds of national security. In 1968, Congress had passed a law saying the president could authorize wiretaps to protect the United States from foreign spies and subversives. But the targets of these taps were not KGB agents. They were thirteen American government officials and four newspaper reporters. Over the next two years, though the leaks went on, the taps never revealed a shred of incriminating evidence against anyone. But they were the first step down the road to Watergate.

On May 28, 1969, at 3:00 P.M., Nixon took a seat beside Hoover in the ceremonial East Room of the White House. Together they presided over the graduation of the eighty-third session of the FBI National Academy, a training course for American law enforcement commanders and foreign police chiefs. Minutes before, in the Oval Office, Hoover had personally delivered a set of the Kissinger wiretap summaries to the president.

In the East Room, Hoover gave Nixon a gold badge, making him an honorary member of the FBI, and Nixon spoke about the rule of law. "Our problem," the president said, "is to see to it that, all over America, our laws—the written laws—deserve respect of all Americans, and that those who carry out the law—who have that hard, difficult, grueling, sometimes dangerous task of enforcing the law—that they carry out their responsibilities in a way that deserves respect."

"Nobody knew what was right and what was wrong"

That same afternoon, in Chicago, a young FBI agent named Bill Dyson was about to be initiated into the rules of a lawless world. He remembered the day with clarity. It was the start of a new life.

Dyson was twenty-eight years old, on his first tour of duty, barely two years after joining the FBI. His boss told him he was going to be working on a wiretap. He was not exactly sure what a wiretap was, or how they worked, or what laws regulated them. But he followed his supervisor down into a windowless room in the bowels of the Bureau's office. His superiors sat him down and said: "Here's your machine."

They put him on the four-to-midnight shift listening to members of the Students for a Democratic Society. The SDS formally convened in Chicago three weeks later. One faction declared it would begin an armed struggle against the government of the United States. Over the summer, and into the fall, Dyson listened as the members of the group argued, debated, and plotted. He was witnessing the violent birth of a terrorist gang.

"I *watched* them become the Weathermen! I was *with* them when they became the Weathermen!" he said. "It was exciting. I was watching history." Almost exactly fifty years before, in Chicago, in September 1919, J. Edgar Hoover's agents had spied on the birth of the Communist Party of the United States. Dyson was following in their tradition.

The Weathermen saw themselves as revolutionaries who could overthrow America, a vision fueled in part by doses of LSD. They called themselves Communists, but their tactics were closer to those of the Italian anarchists who had bombed Washington and Wall Street in the days after World War I. "Anarchist is a very nice word for them," said John Kearney, who led the New York FBI's secret Squad 47 in many missions against the Weathermen, and later faced indictment for his warrantless break-ins. "They were terrorists."

Their leaders were white, good-looking, well-educated; some came from wealthy families. They tried to form armed alliances with the Black Panthers. They traveled to Cuba and met with representatives of the government of North Vietnam. They drilled discipline into one another with a grinding groupthink that Chairman Mao might have admired. They fought one another and slept with one another. And Dyson listened. "I knew more about these people than they knew about themselves. If you work a wiretap, a good wiretap, you will become that way," he said. "I lived with these people sometimes twenty-four hours a day, seven days a week."

But then the Weathermen became the Weather Underground. They began to shift from open rabble-rousing to clandestine bomb making in the fall of 1969. They seemed to vanish. Dyson's taps went silent. The FBI was caught flat-footed. The wiretappers traced calls to pay telephones; they placed radio transmitters in public phone booths. But the trail went cold. That sent a chill of fear through FBI intelligence chief Bill Sullivan, who had reported on September 8, 1969, that the group had "the potential to be far more damaging to the security of this Nation than the Communist Party ever was, even at the height of its strength in the 1930's."

Starting from Chicago, clandestine cells of four or more Weathermen spread across the country, from New York to San Francisco. That winter, three key members of the New York faction blew themselves up in an elegant town house on West 11th Street while trying to wire sixty sticks of dynamite in a bomb intended to kill soldiers at Fort Dix, New Jersey. After that deadly fiasco, the movement went deeper underground, but it managed to take credit for a fresh outrage every few months during the Nixon years, taunting the FBI and the White House with wild-eyed communiqués, planting bombs at will in seemingly impenetrable places. A group barely one hundred strong—with a core of a dozen decision takers and bomb makers—began to drive the government of the United States half-mad with fear as the sixties became the seventies.

Dyson, who became the FBI's lead case agent on the group, took them at their word. He judged the threat as deadly serious, and so did his superiors. The message from the underground, as he read it, was one of murderous intent: *If you don't end the war, we'll kill your Congressmen. We'll kill your Senators. We'll kill the President.*

"They were able to get into the U.S. Capitol, build a bomb into a wall, and blow it up at will," Dyson said. "They got into the Pentagon. . . . They were able to call up and say it's going to go off in exactly five minutes and it would go off in five minutes. They were as good as any terrorist group in the world in terms of their sophistication."

They carried out thirty-eight bombings. The FBI solved none.

"We didn't know how to investigate terrorism," Dyson said. "We did not have enough intelligence on these people."

That presented the FBI with a terrible problem. Its answer was to take the most drastic measures. "There were certain people in the FBI who made the decision: We've got to take a step—anything to get rid of these people. Anything!" Dyson said. "Not kill them per se, but anything went. If we suspect somebody's involved in this, put a wiretap on them. Put a microphone in. Steal his mail. Do anything!"

Dyson had questions about the rule of law: "Can I put an informant in a college classroom? Or even on the campus? Can I penetrate any college organization? What can I do? And nobody had any rules or regulations. There was nothing . . ."

"This was going to come and destroy us," he said. "We were going to end up with FBI agents arrested. Not because what they did was wrong. But because nobody knew what was right or wrong." Not knowing that difference is a legal definition of insanity. Dyson's premonitions of disaster would prove prophetic. In time, the top commanders of the FBI in Washington and New York would face the prospect of prison time for their work against the threat from the left. So would the president's closest confidants.

"Nixon ordered the FBI into this"

Nixon, Mitchell, and Ehrlichman had dinner at Hoover's home on October 1, 1969; the White House counsel recorded this rare event. They had cocktails in "a dingy, almost seedy living room," its walls covered with old glossies of Hoover with dead movie stars. They ate chili and steak in a dining room lit with lava lamps glowing purple, green, yellow, and red. After-dinner drinks were served in Hoover's basement, from a wet bar decorated with pin-up drawings of half-naked women.

The conversation was more alluring. "Hoover regaled us with stories of late-night entries and FBI bag jobs," Ehrlichman recounted. "He told us about FBI operations against domestic radicals and foreigners, and our reactions were enthusiastic and positive." Nixon and Mitchell "loved that stuff." From that night forward, Hoover had every right to believe that the president of the United States wanted him to use every power he had against the threat.

Across the country, some two million people marched against the war in Vietnam that fall. The FBI found it hard to distinguish between the kid with a Molotov cocktail and the kid with a picket sign.

Through October, November, December, and into the new year and the new decade, almost every day brought reports of threats and attacks from left-wing groups in America's biggest cities, its college campuses, and in many a small town, too. Bombs struck at Rockefeller Center in New York; the county courthouse in Franklin, Missouri; the sheriff's office in Sioux City, Nebraska. The Black Panthers shot it out with the Chicago police, and the police counterattacked with help from the FBI, killing two prominent Panther chieftains as they slept. Armed black militias, including a small gang that became known as the Black Liberation Army, allied with members of the Weather Underground. "They were trying to shoot and kill police officers," said the FBI's William M. Baker. "When they saw a white officer and a black officer working together, the Black Liberation Army, in an effort in their minds to create a revolution, would shoot both of them and then claim responsibility for it. Well, President Nixon ordered the FBI into this."

Bill Sullivan sent the word down the chain of command that winter: the ban on operations that Hoover once deemed "clearly illegal" was over. He vowed to do anything to stop the Weathermen. Sullivan's deputy, Charles D. Brennan, newly appointed as the chief of the internal security division, said the same. He felt tremendous pressure from the White House to defend the nation against "attacks against the police in general and the FBI in particular" from the left. He believed the FBI had to deal with the radicals' threat "to form commando-type units" that would carry out acts of terror, "including assassinations."

FBI agents across the country began to mount new operations aimed against peaceful marchers and violent militants alike. A deep-cover squad tried to infiltrate the far left by posing as politically radicalized Vietnam veterans well supplied with guns and drugs. Four or five of them liked their new lives so much that they never came back. "They were a bunch of renegades," said the FBI's Bernardo Perez, who drew the difficult assignment of reining them in years later.

Hoover did not know about some of the most politically charged operations. The director turned seventy-five on January 1, 1970. Sullivan and many of his top agents saw the director's powers of perception dimming, his authority slipping, his awareness of what went on from day to day at the FBI starting to fail.

"Hoover had no idea that we had agents stand there looking like they were kids in jeans and that kind of stuff at these demonstrations," said Courtland Jones, an FBI agent who had day-to-day responsibility for the Kissinger wiretaps. "Hoover's reaction was: 'Who authorized this?'"

"He was really out of touch," Jones said. "He should have bowed out, years before his death. The one thing that he never did and would never tolerate was to groom anyone to take his place."

Only one man was willing to run the risk of gunning for Hoover's job. Only one man came close to succeeding. That was Bill Sullivan, the man who knew the deepest secrets of the FBI.

34

"PULL DOWN THE TEMPLE"

A FTER HALF A CENTURY as America's counterrevolutionary in chief, Hoover no longer commanded unquestioned authority.

He had made enemies at the White House and inside the FBI, and they had started summoning the courage to denounce him. The president and the attorney general were talking about replacing him. The control of secret information had always been the primary source of Hoover's power. He had lost it.

On Monday, June 1, 1970, he made a fateful choice. He would later call it "the greatest mistake I ever made." He decided that Bill Sullivan would become his top commander, in charge of all the Bureau's criminal investigations as well as its intelligence programs. Sullivan ran the daily work of the FBI—a heady dose of power for a man known to many of his colleagues as Crazy Billy.

Hoover had thought he was loyal. He had been once. But Sullivan, COINTELPRO's creator and overlord, a master of political warfare, had been chafing under Hoover's increasingly heavy and unsteady hand, confiding in his counterparts at the CIA and his contacts at the White House that the boss had lost his nerve. He said the FBI was losing the battle against the radical left. It was time, Sullivan advised the CIA's Richard Helms, to start "moving ahead of the winds of change instead of being blown by them."

Now he had a chance to make his case directly to the president of the United States.

Nixon knew Sullivan had been handling the Kissinger wiretaps, listening in on some of the most prominent reporters and columnists in Washington as well as their suspected sources in high office. A year before, after the first taps were installed, Nixon had sent a fiercely ambitious twenty-nine-year-old White House lawyer named Tom Charles Huston over to the FBI to meet with Sullivan. Huston had been an army intelligence officer and a leader of the conservative Young Americans for Freedom; Nixon fondly called him an arrogant son of a bitch. He made Huston the point man for all White House intelligence liaisons.

Sullivan realized that the presidential aide could open the door to the Oval Office. As they conferred in secret throughout 1969 and 1970, he carefully cultivated Huston, praising his intellect and vision. Huston returned the high regard. "I do not think there was anyone in the government who I respected more," Huston said.

In Nixon's name, Huston urged Sullivan to hunt down the foreign financiers of American political ferment, to find proof that the international Communist conspiracy supported the radical left and the black militants. The demand went unsatisfied, to Nixon's displeasure. "President Nixon was insatiable in his desire for intelligence," Deke DeLoach said. "He would constantly ask the FBI for more and more intelligence to prove that the riots in our country were being caused by insurgent groups in foreign countries. And they weren't." Sullivan in turn put intense pressure on his underlings—"gave us all hell because we couldn't prove that the Soviets were behind racial and student unrest," said Jim Nolan, then a young FBI agent rising through the intelligence ranks. "We knew they were not. Nothing would have scared the Soviets more than these students."

Sullivan blamed the failure to find the proof on Hoover. He told Huston that Hoover had cut off all formal liaisons with the CIA and the military in a fit of pique; that the FBI lacked the counterintelligence skills to obtain the secrets that the White House desired; that the Bureau needed more freedom to spy on Americans, especially on students under the age of twenty-one; that the restraints on black-bag jobs, bugging, wiretapping, and surveillance were far too constricting. Huston reported all of this to Nixon. The president readily believed it. He was railing to his advisers that the top secret reports he received on his enemies, foreign and domestic, were meaningless drivel.

By the spring of 1970, Sullivan had set upon a plan to satisfy the president's thirst for secret intelligence—and to promote himself as Hoover's successor. As Sullivan's star rose at the White House, Hoover's began to fall.

"Magnified and limitless"

On Friday, June 5, 1970, Nixon called Hoover and Helms to the White House. They sat alongside Admiral Noel Gayler, director of the National Security Agency, and Lieutenant General Donald Bennett, chief of the Defense Intelligence Agency.

"The President chewed our butts," General Bennett remembered.

Nixon was on the warpath abroad and at home. Campuses across the country had exploded after Nixon invaded Cambodia and escalated the war in Vietnam. National Guardsmen had shot and killed four students at Kent State University in Ohio. More than a hundred bombings, arson attacks, and shootings had followed in May. The Weathermen and the Panthers, whose leaders had been to Cuba and Algeria for indoctrination, had shown that they could hit draft boards, police stations, and banks at will.

The president said that "revolutionary terrorism" was now the gravest threat to the United States. Thousands of Americans under the age of thirty were "determined to destroy our society"; their home-grown ideology was "as dangerous as anything they could import" from Cuba, China, or Russia. "Good intelligence," he said, was "the best way to stop terrorism."

Nixon demanded "a plan which will enable us to curtail the illegal activities of those who are determined to destroy our society." Sullivan had already drafted it. He had been working on it for two years. It would all but abolish the restraints on intelligence collection. The White House gave him the go-ahead to achieve that goal.

Sullivan convened five meetings of America's spy chiefs and their deputies. "Individually, those of us in the intelligence community are relatively small and limited," he told the first meeting, at FBI headquarters, on June 8. "Unified, our own combined potential is magnified and limitless. It is through unity of action that we can tremendously increase our intelligence-gathering potential, and, I am certain, obtain the answers the President wants." Hopes ran high among the old guard. "I saw these meetings as a perfect opportunity to get back the methods we needed," said the FBI's Bill Cregar, who ran foreign counterintelligence programs against the Soviets. "And so did Sullivan." The obstacle, both men knew, would be Hoover himself. He did not want to coordinate the FBI's work with the CIA or any other intelligence service. Quite the opposite: he had cut off communication with his counterparts so thoroughly that the link between

Huston and Sullivan was the only formal liaison left between the Bureau and the rest of the American government.

The program that emerged became known as the Huston Plan. But it was Sullivan's work from top to bottom. And it had the secret imprimatur of the president of the United States.

The plan called for America's intelligence services to work as one. The walls between them would come down. The restrictions on intelligence gathering in the United States would be lifted. The FBI's agents and their counterparts would be free to monitor the international communications of American citizens, intensify the electronic surveillance of American dissidents, read their mail, burglarize their homes and offices, step up undercover spying among freshmen and sophomores on campus—in short, to keep on doing what the Bureau had been doing for decades, but to do more of it, do it better, and do it in concert with the CIA and the Pentagon.

The plan conformed to the president's philosophy on national security: Do anything it takes. He knew that opening mail was a federal crime and that black-bag jobs were burglary. But they were the best means of gathering intelligence. And Nixon believed that if a president did it, it was not illegal.

On July 14, after Huston brought the plan to the White House, the president said he approved it. But Hoover dissented. He "went through the ceiling," Sullivan remembered, as soon as he realized that the plan would have to be carried out on his authority—not Nixon's. The president had not signed it; his approval was verbal, not written. "That leaves me alone as the man who made the decision," he said. "I'm not going to accept the responsibility myself anymore, even though I've done it for many years. . . . It is becoming more and more dangerous and we are apt to get caught."

Hoover demanded a meeting with Nixon. And he stared the president down.

Nixon believed that "in view of the crisis of terrorism," the plan was both "justified and responsible." But he realized that "it would matter little what I had decided or approved" if Hoover balked. "Even if I issued a direct order to him, while he would undoubtedly carry it out, he would soon see to it that I had cause to reverse myself. There was even the remote possibility that he would resign in protest."

Nixon withdrew the plan at Hoover's behest. His inner circle began to denounce the director as an unreliable ally in the war on revolutionary terrorism. "Hoover has to be told who is President," Huston told Haldeman on August 5. "He has become totally unreasonable and his conduct is detrimental to our domestic intelligence operations. . . . If he gets his way it is going to look like he is more powerful than the President."

The new White House counsel, a thirty-one-year-old lawyer named John W. Dean, took charge of salvaging the plan. He worked in liaison with Sullivan. Despite Hoover's dissent, electronic surveillances and surreptitious entries increased. The FBI started recruiting informants as young as eighteen. Undercover operations against the Left expanded. (The small but growing contingent of FBI agents who looked, dressed, and acted like their targets had a camaraderie and an esprit de corps all its own; the agents called themselves "Beards, Blacks, and Broads.")

These operations sometimes took place on Sullivan's say-so, sometimes at the command of Attorney General Mitchell, and sometimes on orders from the president himself.

The control of the FBI's most powerful weapons began to slip from Hoover's grasp into the hands of Nixon's political henchmen. They believed that the ideal of national security overrode the rule of law. Their mission, above all, was the re-election of the president.

"BRING ABOUT A CONFRONTATION"

The president began to think about forcing Hoover from power. "Mitchell and I had a two-hour session with the P," Haldeman wrote in his diary on February 4, 1971. "We discussed the whole question of J. Edgar Hoover and whether he should be continued."

Nixon chose a devious strategy. He told Mitchell to revive the Internal Security Division at the Justice Department under Assistant Attorney General Robert Mardian—a man Hoover personally despised, though he was an ardent anti-Communist. Nixon ordered Mardian and Sullivan to step up intelligence operations against the Left, to work "like J. Edgar used to." He was starting to speak of Hoover in the past tense. He knew that his orders could "bring about a confrontation," Haldeman wrote. "The P made it clear that Hoover has got to be replaced before the end of Nixon's first term. We need to make this point to Hoover in such a way as to get him to resign."

The attorney general began to feel out candidates to succeed Hoover. The strongest one was Sullivan—but Mitchell found him nakedly ambitious, a name-dropping wheeler-dealer. At least three other Hoover aides were jockeying for the job. The corridor chatter in the halls of Justice was vicious. "I was told five times that Hoover would be fired," Mardian said.

While a growing cohort of his enemies inside the Nixon administration plotted to supplant him, Hoover's foes on the left mounted a devastating and demoralizing attack on the secrecy and power of the Bureau itself. They pulled a black-bag job on the FBI. On the night of March 8, 1971, a band of thieves broke into the Bureau's two-man office in Media, Pennsylvania, a placid suburb outside Philadelphia, jimmying the glass-paneled door in an office across the street from the county courthouse. The job was easy; the FBI had no security system to seal the secrets inside of room 204. They stole at least eight hundred documents out of the files. The group, which called itself the Citizens' Commission to Investigate the FBI, never explained why the Media office was chosen as a target. Barry Green, whose family managed the office building, arrived at dawn to find FBI agents and police "running all over the place, trying to figure out how this could have happened and who could have done it," he remembered. "Who would invade an FBI office? It was like invading the lion's den."

Hoover reacted to the theft as if an assassin had tried to cut out his heart. He suspected the thieves were allied with the radical Catholic priests Daniel and Philip Berrigan, who had been imprisoned for destroying draft files; Hoover himself accused them, in public, on the thinnest evidence, of conspiring to kidnap Henry Kissinger. He assured the White House that arrests were imminent. But despite a nationwide investigation that lasted for at least six years, no one ever was charged in the theft. The case remained unsolved.

The Citizens' Commission to Investigate the FBI copied the stolen files and delivered them to members of Congress and the press. It took weeks, in some cases months, before the reporters began to understand the documents. They were fragmentary records of undercover FBI operations to infiltrate twenty-two college campuses with informers, and they described the wiretapping of the Philadelphia chapter of the Black Panthers. It took a year before one reporter made a concerted effort to decode a word that appeared on the files: COINTELPRO. The word was unknown outside the FBI.

In a desperate effort to keep the deepest secrets of the FBI from being exposed, Hoover ordered an end to COINTELPRO six weeks after the Media break-in. Hundreds of operations, almost all of them aimed at the

Left, were killed. Sullivan, their intellectual author, was incensed. He told his allies that Hoover had sheathed the most powerful weapon the Bureau had ever deployed to disrupt, disarm, and destroy its enemies.

Nixon revived their purpose a few weeks later.

"LET'S GET THESE BASTARDS"

The newly installed White House tapes were rolling now, and they recorded the old friendship and the new frictions between Nixon and Hoover.

Reminiscing in the Oval Office on May 26, Hoover recounted the hatred between President Johnson and Attorney General Robert F. Kennedy. He said he had warned that Kennedy would try "to steal the nomination from Lyndon" at the Democratic National Convention in 1964.

"That's what got me in bad with Bobby," Hoover said.

"In *bed* with him?" Nixon said.

"No—in *bad* with him," Hoover chortled.

Nixon then attempted a vocal impersonation of LBJ: "Ah couldn't have been President without J. Edgar Hoover. Now don't let those sons of bitches getcha." Laughter ensued.

Later that day, on the telephone, Nixon told Hoover to do anything it took to find a pair of Black Liberation Army snipers who had killed two New York City police officers. "The national security information we seek is unlimited," said Nixon. "Okay? And you'll tell the Attorney General that's what I've suggested—well, *ordered*—and you do it. Okay? Don't you agree with this?"

"I agree with it thoroughly," Hoover said.

"By God, let's get these bastards," the president said.

"I'll go all out on the intelligence on this thing," Hoover responded.

"Go in with everything you've got," Nixon said. "Surveillance, electronic and everything." The president invoked the mantra of national security; Hoover responded ritually.

Two weeks later, *The New York Times* began to publish the Pentagon Papers, a top secret history of the Vietnam War. The papers had been purloined by Daniel Ellsberg, who had worked on the study as a civilian analyst for the Defense Department. He had become a dedicated antiwar activist, and he had been trying to leak the study for many months. Hoover and Sullivan quickly identified Ellsberg as the prime suspect.

On June 17, Haldeman told the president that he thought the Brookings Institution, a think tank in Washington, might have files that could serve as evidence against Ellsberg. Nixon leaped at the idea of stealing them. "Do you remember Huston's plan? *Implement* it," said the president. "Goddamn it, get in and get those files. *Blow the safe and get it.*"

Nixon wanted political intelligence so badly that he created his own secret squad of burglars and wiretappers. He authorized the creation of a secret White House unit that had the capability to conduct those kinds of missions. The group was nicknamed the Plumbers, because in the beginning they sought to plug the leaks that plagued the president. They would carry out black-bag jobs, wiretaps, and disinformation campaigns on his behalf.

Their mastermind was a strange kind of genius named G. Gordon Liddy. He had spent five years in Hoover's FBI, from 1957 to 1962, rising to the rank of a supervisor at headquarters, where he had learned the dark arts of COINTELPRO. Liddy was installed in a cover job as general counsel for the Committee to Re-elect the President, whose chairman was John Mitchell. He drew up plans, which he presented in person in the office of the attorney general, to spend $1 million on secret agents who would kidnap antiwar leaders and spirit them off to Mexico, entrap liberal politicians with prostitutes working out of bugged houseboats, plant informants inside the campaigns of Nixon's opponents, and wiretap the Democratic Party apparatus for the 1972 presidential campaign. Mitchell disapproved of kidnapping and blackmail—in retrospect, he said, he should have thrown Liddy out the window—but the espionage elements of the plan survived.

Liddy bungled them from beginning to end. His first mission was breaking into the office of Ellsberg's psychiatrist, where he failed to find defamatory files. His last mission, nine months later, was bugging the Democratic Party headquarters at the Watergate, where he and his confreres, all former agents of the FBI and the CIA, were captured.

"Why Watergate?" said the FBI's Ed Miller, a veteran of many a black-bag job, who would soon rise to succeed Sullivan as third in command at the Bureau. "Because of Sullivan's influence on the White House . . . They became enamored with surreptitious entries as being a gangbuster investigative technique. And that's when the White House decided to create their own."

If Hoover would not do the dirty work the president wanted done, Nixon would have to do it himself.

"RAISE HOLY HELL"

The president created the Plumbers because he thought Hoover had lost the will to conduct political warfare. Many of the elements of the bill of impeachment drawn up against Nixon three years later grew out of his frustrations with the FBI, his thirst for the secrets Hoover no longer supplied, and the bugging and burglary that followed.

The Pentagon Papers case was the breaking point. Ellsberg, after going underground, surrendered on June 28, 1971. The FBI had to make a case, under the Espionage Act of 1917, that could send him to prison for the rest of his life. But "Hoover refused to investigate," Nixon said. "That's why we conducted the investigation over here. It was as simple as that."

The plot to remove J. Edgar Hoover started the next day.

The denouement began with a "bizarre story," as Nixon recounted it: "Edgar Hoover refused to investigate because Marx—Marx's daughter was married to that son-of-a-bitch Ellsberg." The father-in-law of the son-of-a-bitch was not Karl Marx, nor Groucho Marx, as Nixon pointed out, but Louis Marx, a wealthy toy manufacturer who contributed every year to a Christmas charity run by Hoover. He was officially listed at headquarters as a friend of the FBI. Sullivan and his intelligence chief, Charles Brennan, decided that Marx had to be interviewed in the Ellsberg case. He was ready to testify against his son-in-law. Hoover said no. But the interview went ahead. Hoover summarily removed Brennan as chief of the Intelligence Division.

Enraged, Sullivan tried to organize a revolt among the leaders of the FBI. The White House and the attorney general heard within hours about his fury. Mitchell told the president on June 29 that a revolution was brewing in the Bureau. "In terms of discipline, Hoover is right. In terms of his decision, he was wrong," Nixon told Mitchell. "He just cannot—and I really feel that you have to tell him this—he cannot, with my going tomorrow to address the FBI graduation, and also with the Ellsberg case being the issue—he cannot take anything which causes dissension within the FBI ranks. It's just going to raise holy hell. They'll say, 'This crotchety old man did it again,' see. That's my feeling about it."

Mitchell replied: "Well, I don't think there's any doubt about it, Mr. President. I think this might be the last straw as far as he's concerned."

Nixon said: "You tell him, 'I've talked to the President and, Edgar, he doesn't want to embarrass you in a disciplinary matter where he has overruled the director, but he feels *very* strongly. He's coming over there to the

FBI, you know, and after all, we—and he knows that discipline is important, but he feels very strongly that we must not have the Ellsberg thing be a reason for dissension in the Bureau. That could raise holy hell.' Could that be all right?"

"Yes, sir," Mitchell said. "We'll try it that way and see how it flies. I would hope that he doesn't blow his stack and leave the fold."

Nixon said: "Well, if he does now, I'll be ready."

The Supreme Court ruled on June 30 that the newspapers had the right to publish the Pentagon Papers. That ruling came down as Nixon was praising Hoover before a hundred graduates of the FBI's training academy.

"As a young Congressman I worked with him and with others in the Federal Bureau of Investigation in major investigations of various subversive elements in this country," he said. "Let me tell you something. Anybody who is strong, anybody who fights for what he believes in, anybody who stands up when it is tough is bound to be controversial. And I say that insofar as he is concerned, there may be controversy, but the great majority of the American people back Mr. Hoover."

The question was whether Nixon and Hoover still backed each other. They spoke by telephone the next day. Nixon asked Hoover what the Supreme Court decision meant for the prosecution of the Ellsberg case.

PRESIDENT NIXON: What's your public relations judgment on it, Edgar? I'd just like to know.

HOOVER: My public relations judgment, Mr. President, is that you should remain absolutely silent about it.

PRESIDENT NIXON: You would?

HOOVER: I would . . . And I think we ought to be *awful careful* what we do in this case of this man Ellsberg. Because there again, they're going to make a martyr out of him. All of the press in the country are going to, of course, come to the front that he's a martyr. And in view of what the Supreme Court has now said, I doubt whether we're going to be able to get a conviction of him.

The president was furious. "I talked to Hoover last night and Hoover is not going after this case as strong as I would like," Nixon complained to Haldeman. "There's something dragging him."

"You don't have the feeling the FBI is really pursuing this?" asked Haldeman.

"Yeah, particularly the conspiracy side," Nixon said. "I want to go after everyone. I'm not so interested in Ellsberg, but we have to go after everybody who's a member of this conspiracy."

Nixon believed to the marrow of his bones that he was up against a vast left-wing cabal—an array of forces ranging from the intelligence services of Communist dictatorships to the liberal wing of the Democratic Party—and that Western civilization hung in the balance of this struggle. On July 6, he gave a speech to newspaper and television executives at the great columned building housing the National Archives and the original copy of the Constitution of the United States. "When I see those columns," he said, "I think of what happened to Greece and Rome."

"They lost their will to live," he said. "They became subject to the decadence that destroys civilization. The United States is reaching that period."

"A HELL OF A CONFRONTATION"

Bill Sullivan had an ultimatum: Hoover had to go. He went to see Robert Mardian at the internal security division of the Justice Department, carrying a threatening weapon: two suitcases filled with transcripts and summaries of the warrantless Kissinger wiretaps on Nixon aides and newsmen. The taps were arguably unlawful; without question, they were politically explosive.

Sullivan said that Hoover could use the documents to blackmail the president of the United States—a startling if implausible idea. Deeply alarmed, Mardian called the White House. The president went on high alert.

"The P agreed to meet with J. Edgar Hoover tomorrow to seek his resignation," Haldeman wrote in his diary on Friday, September 17. But later that day, Nixon quailed at the thought. He put off the meeting, and he tried to convince the attorney general to tell the director to step down on his seventy-seventh birthday, New Year's Day 1972. Mitchell said Hoover would not accept such an order from anybody but the president.

Dreading the conversation, Nixon invited Hoover to breakfast at the White House at 8:30 on Monday, September 20. The director played it perfectly. "He was trying to demonstrate that despite his age he was still physically, mentally, and emotionally equipped to carry on," Nixon recounted in his memoirs. "I tried to point out as gently and subtly as I could that as an astute politician he must recognize that the attacks were going to mount." He was too subtle by half. Hoover replied: "More than anything else, I want to see *you* re-elected in 1972. If you feel that my staying on as head of the Bureau hurts your chances for re-election, just let me know."

The president lost his spine. "At the end of the day," Haldeman recorded, "he got around to reporting to me on his very-much-off-the-record breakfast meeting with J. Edgar Hoover. Said that it's 'no go' at this time. Hoover didn't take the bait, apparently, and is going to stay on as a political matter. He feels it's much better for the P for him to do so. He will then pull out at any point in the future when the P feels that it would be politically necessary."

Ten days later, Hoover fired Bill Sullivan and locked him out of his offices at the FBI—a decision based on his judgment that Sullivan had lost his mind. Even Sullivan's loyal subordinates were inclined to agree with that assessment. "He may have suffered a mental collapse," wrote Ray Wannall, a top FBI intelligence supervisor, who had known Sullivan since 1947, "perhaps brought on by his obsession to become FBI Director."

On the day he was forced out, Sullivan was struggling in vain to secure his files, including a copy of the poison-pen letter he had sent to Martin Luther King, among other potentially incriminating documents. In the corridor, he ran into the man Hoover had chosen to supplant him: a tall, suave thirty-year veteran of the FBI named Mark Felt, who was searching without success for the copies of the wiretap summaries that Sullivan had stolen. He was convinced that Sullivan had become a renegade, trying to claw his way to power by "playing on the paranoia and political obsessions of the Nixon administration."

Felt called Sullivan a Judas. They came close to a fistfight. In a rage, Sullivan left the Bureau for the last time.

Felt went to Hoover's inner sanctum to brief the director on the altercation. Hoover listened, shook his head sadly, and stared out the window. He had long feared a betrayal from within. "There were a few men who could tear down all that I have built up over the years," he had written. Now, for the first time, Felt saw Hoover as he was—an isolated old man, alone at the top, no longer basking in adulation, fearing for the future.

The battle over the FBI intensified. Hoover's fate was the subject of a ferocious debate in the Oval Office throughout October.

MITCHELL: We have those tapes, logs and so forth over in Mardian's safe on that background investigation, wiretapping we did on Kissinger's staff, the newspapermen and so forth . . .

EHRLICHMAN: We have all the FBI's copies.

MITCHELL: Hoover is tearing the place up over there trying to get at them . . . Should we get them out of Mardian's office before Hoover blows the safe? . . .

EHRLICHMAN: Hoover feels very insecure without having his own copy of those things because of course that gives him leverage with Mitchell and with you—and because they're illegal . . . He has agents all over this town interrogating people, trying to find out where they are . . .

PRESIDENT NIXON: He doesn't even have his own?

EHRLICHMAN: No, see, we've got 'em. Sullivan sneaked 'em out to Mardian.

MITCHELL: . . . Hoover won't come and talk to me about it. He's just got his Gestapo all over the place . . . I want to tell you that I've got to get him straightened out, which may lead to a hell of a confrontation . . . I don't know how we go about it, whether we reconsider Mr. Hoover and his exit or whether I just have to bear down on him . . .

PRESIDENT NIXON: My view is he ought to resign while he's on top, before he becomes an issue . . . The least of it is he's too old.

MITCHELL: He's getting senile, actually.

PRESIDENT NIXON: He should get the hell out of there. Now it may be, which I kind of doubt, I don't know, maybe, maybe I could just call him in and talk him into resigning.

MITCHELL: Shall I go ahead with this confrontation, then?

PRESIDENT NIXON: If he does go, he's got to go of his own volition. That's what we get down to. And that's why we're in a hell of a problem . . . I think he'll stay until he's 100 years old. I think he loves it . . . He loves it.

MITCHELL: He'll stay 'til he's buried there.

Haldeman, Ehrlichman, Mitchell, and Dean all pushed the president to force the old man out.

Nixon had come to the most perilous point of his presidency. He could ill afford to lose Hoover's loyalty. What might the director do to hold on to his power? The hint of blackmail lingered.

"We've got to avoid the situation where he could leave with a blast," Nixon said. "We may have on our hands here a man who will pull down the temple with him, including me."

The idea that Hoover could bring down the government of the United States was an extraordinary thought. It plagued the president. "I mean, he considers himself a patriot, but he now sees himself as McCarthy did," Nixon said. Would he try to topple the pillars of national security, as Senator McCarthy had done?

Then he had a brainstorm. Why not bring back Sullivan?

Ehrlichman liked the idea. "Sullivan was the man who executed all of your instructions for the secret taps," he reminded the president.

PRESIDENT NIXON: Will he rat on us?

EHRLICHMAN: It depends on how he's treated . . .

PRESIDENT NIXON: Can we do anything for him? I think we better.

EHRLICHMAN: What he wants, of course, is vindication. He's been bounced, in effect, and what he wants is the right to honorably retire and so on. I think if you did anything for Sullivan, Hoover would be offended. Right now, it would have to be a part of the arrangement . . .

PRESIDENT NIXON: He'd be a hell of an operator . . .

EHRLICHMAN: We could use him . . . He's got a fund of information and could do all kinds of intelligence and other work.

Nixon would return time and again to the thought of making Sullivan the director of the FBI. "We got to get a professional in that goddamn place," he once muttered. "Sullivan's our guy."

"It would have killed him"

An impassioned diatribe from Sullivan arrived at Hoover's home on the day that the debate over the director's future started at the White House. It read like a cross between a Dear John letter and a suicide note. "This complete break with you has been a truly agonizing one for me," he wrote. But he felt duty-bound to say that "the damage you are doing to the Bureau and its work has brought all this on."

He laid out his accusations in twenty-seven numbered paragraphs, like the counts of a criminal indictment. Some dealt with Hoover's racial prejudices; the ranks of FBI agents remained 99.4 percent white (and 100 percent male). Some dealt with Hoover's use of Bureau funds to dress up his home and decorate his life. Some dealt with the damage he had done to American intelligence by cutting off liaisons with the CIA. Some came close to a charge of treason.

"You abolished our main programs designed to identify and neutralize the enemy," he wrote, referring to COINTELPRO and the FBI's black-bag jobs on foreign embassies. "You know the high number of illegal agents operating on the east coast alone. As of this week, the week I am leaving the FBI for good, we have not identified *even one of them*. These illegal agents, as you know, are engaged, among other things, in securing the secrets of our defense in the event of a military attack so that our defense will amount to nothing. Mr. Hoover, are you thinking? Are you really capable of thinking this through? Don't you realize we are betraying our government and people?"

Sullivan struck hardest at Hoover's cult of personality: "As you know you have become a legend in your lifetime with a surrounding mythology linked to incredible power," he wrote. "We did all possible to build up your legend. We kept away from anything which would disturb you and kept flowing into your office what you wanted to hear . . . This was all part of the game but it got to be a deadly game that has accomplished no good. All we did was to help put you out of touch with the real world and this could not help but have a bearing on your decisions as the years went by." He concluded with a plea: "I gently suggest you retire for your own good, that of the Bureau, the intelligence community, and law enforcement." Sullivan leaked the gist of his letter to his friends at the White House and a handful of reporters and syndicated columnists. The rumors went out across the salons and newsrooms of Washington: the palace revolt was rising at the FBI. The scepter was slipping from Hoover's grasp.

"As political attacks on him multiplied and became increasingly shrill and unfair," Mark Felt wrote, "Hoover experienced loneliness and a fear that his life's work was being destroyed."

The president slowly pushed Hoover away from the White House. One last hurrah came at the end of 1971: an invitation to Nixon's compound at Key Biscayne, Florida, over Christmas week, and a cake to celebrate Hoover's seventy-seventh birthday aboard Air Force One during the return to Washington on New Year's Eve. But after that, over the next four months the White House logs record only three telephone calls, lasting a total of eight minutes, between Nixon and Hoover. Silence descended.

The last conversation with Hoover that anyone at the FBI recorded for posterity took place on April 6, 1972. Ray Wannall, who had spent thirty years hunting Communists for Hoover, went to the director's office to receive a promotion. Hoover began a jeremiad, a wail of pain. "That son of a bitch Sullivan pulled the wool over my eyes," he said. "He completely fooled me. I treated him like a son and he betrayed me." His lamentation went on for half an hour. Then he said good-bye.

PART IV

WAR ON TERROR

"Round up the evildoers":
President Bush at FBI headquarters after the 9/11 attacks.

35

CONSPIRATORS

O N MAY 2, 1972, in the darkness before dawn, J. Edgar Hoover died in his sleep. It rained all day as his closed casket lay on a black catafalque in the rotunda of the United States Capitol. He was buried half a mile from where he was born, alongside his parents. Forty years later, the myths and the legends are still alive.

"Oh, he died at the right time, didn't he?" Nixon said. "Goddamn, it'd have killed him to lose that office. It would have killed him."

A few minutes after Hoover's casket left the Capitol, the acting attorney general, Richard Kleindienst, telephoned his most loyal assistant at the Justice Department, L. Patrick Gray.

"Pat, I am going to appoint you acting director of the FBI," he said.

"You have to be joking," Gray replied.

Gray was fifty-five years old, and he had never held an authority greater than the command of a submarine. He still had his navy crew cut. He was a bull-headed man with a jutting jaw, a straight-arrow Nixon acolyte. He had known the president for a quarter of a century, and he revered him. He had one qualification: he would do anything Nixon asked. Now the president was entrusting Hoover's legacy to him.

In a state of awe, Gray came to the White House after Hoover's burial on May 4. Nixon gave him some sound advice. "Never, never figure that anyone's your friend," the president said. "Never, never, never . . . You've got to be a conspirator. You've got to be totally ruthless. You've got to appear to be a nice guy. But underneath you need to be steely tough. That, believe me, is the way to run the Bureau."

Gray lacked steel. He was a malleable man. He was deeply unsure of how to take control of the FBI. He dreaded being seen as "an interloper bent on pushing Hoover into the pages of history and remolding the FBI in my own likeness," he wrote in a posthumously published memoir. He knew little about the Bureau. He understood nothing of its customs and traditions. He did not comprehend the conduct of the Bureau's top commanders. He came to learn, as he wrote, that "they lied to each other and conned each other as much as they could."

Thus began the dark ages of the FBI. In a matter of months, the joint conduct of Pat Gray; his new number-two man at the Bureau, Mark Felt; and his intelligence chief, Ed Miller, would come close to destroying the house that Hoover built.

"Once Hoover died," Miller remembered mournfully, "we were absolutely deluged."

"THE DELICATE QUESTION OF THE PRESIDENT'S POWER"

Nixon called the Bureau on May 15, 1972, after George Wallace, the racist Alabama governor who had received nearly ten million votes running for president in 1968, was gravely wounded by a deluded gunman on the campaign trail.

Mark Felt answered the president's call.

"Bremer, the assailant, is in good physical shape," Felt reported. "He's got some cuts and bruises, and—"

"Good!" said Nixon. "I hope they worked him over a little more than that."

Felt laughed. "Anyway, the psychiatrist has examined him," he said, adding: "We've got a mental problem here with this guy."

Nixon wanted one thing understood. "Be sure we don't go through the thing we went through—the Kennedy assassination, where we didn't really follow up adequately. You know?" He hammered home the point. "Remember, the FBI is in charge now, and they're responsible, and I don't want any slip-ups. Okay?"

"There's no question about it," Felt answered crisply. "You're the one who's calling the shots here." Nixon liked that answer. "Right," he said. "Fine. We appreciate your help. Thank you." The conversation was over. "Yes, Mr. President," Felt said. "Bye." They never spoke again.

Felt was in charge at headquarters for far longer than he had anticipated. Gray had set out across America to visit all of the FBI's fifty-nine field offices and meet every special agent in charge. The acting director was on the road so often that agents at headquarters started calling him "Three-Day Gray." On Friday, June 17, he checked into the fashionable Newporter Inn south of Los Angeles—as did John Mitchell, now chief of CREEP, the nickname for the Committee to Re-elect the President, and Mitchell's trusted aide Robert Mardian, the former internal security chief at Justice.

All hell broke loose in Washington that weekend. The District of Columbia police arrested five men inside the offices of the Democratic National Committee at the Watergate office complex. Among them was James McCord, a former FBI agent and CIA officer now working as chief of security for CREEP. The men had burglary tools, electronic devices, and a gadget that the police thought was a bomb disguised as a smoke detector. It was a sophisticated electronic-eavesdropping device. The suspects had crisp hundred-dollar bills and Watergate Hotel keys in their pockets. Their ringleaders were the gung-ho Gordon Liddy, the former FBI agent counseling CREEP; and E. Howard Hunt, a former CIA officer who, the FBI quickly determined, worked for the president of the United States.

Supervisory special agent Daniel Bledsoe was running the major crimes desk at the FBI on the morning of Sunday, June 17, when he picked up the overnight report of the break-in. He recognized Liddy's name; he had met him at the FBI a decade before. When he heard that the burglars had been caught with eavesdropping equipment, he immediately opened a case under the federal wiretapping statutes. At about four in the afternoon, his secretary answered the phone and told him the White House was calling.

"This is Agent Supervisor Dan Bledsoe," he said. "Who am I speaking with?"

"You are speaking with John Ehrlichman. Do you know who I am?"

"Yes. You are the chief of staff there at the White House."

"That's right. I have a mandate from the President of the United States," Ehrlichman said. "The FBI is to terminate the investigation of the break-in."

Bledsoe was silent.

"Did you hear what I said?" Ehrlichman thundered. "Are you going to terminate the investigation?"

"No," Bledsoe replied. "Under the Constitution, the FBI is obligated to initiate an investigation to determine whether there has been a violation of the illegal interception of communications statute."

"Do you know that you are saying 'no' to the President of the United States?"

"Yes," the FBI agent replied.

"Bledsoe, your career is doomed," Ehrlichman said, and hung up.

Bledsoe called Mark Felt at home and recounted the conversation. "He laughed because he knew these people. In his high position, he knew what was occurring in the White House. He just laughed."

Gray learned in a telephone call from Felt on Monday morning, June 19, that the FBI's investigation of the Watergate break-in could implicate the White House. The acting director flew back to Washington and convened his first official headquarters meeting on the break-in at 4:00 P.M. on Wednesday, June 21.

Mark Felt was at the table, along with Robert G. Kunkel, special agent in charge of the Washington field office, and Charles W. Bates, chief of the FBI's Criminal Investigative Division. Bates recorded this and many other Watergate meetings in a running memorandum. He wrote: "It was agreed that this was most important, that the FBI's reputation was at stake, and that the investigation should be completely impartial, thorough and complete." Gray instructed his men that the president's counsel, John Dean, would sit in on all the FBI's interviews. Gray secretly planned to keep Dean posted about the Bureau's every move by feeding him daily summaries of the FBI's investigations and interrogations.

The next day, FBI agents questioned Charles W. Colson, special counsel to the president, with Dean sitting by his side. Colson mentioned that the Watergate burglar E. Howard Hunt had an office safe in the White House. Dean lied instinctively to the FBI. Safe? What safe? I don't know about any safe. Once they had left, he opened it, and saw two sheaves of documents inside. They were evidence of the dirty tricks the Plumbers had played for the president. He started thinking about how to hide them from the FBI.

Shortly after 10:00 A.M. on June 23, President Nixon settled on a plan to scuttle the FBI investigation. "The FBI is not under control, because Gray doesn't exactly know how to control them," Haldeman told the president. They agreed that the newly appointed deputy director of Central Intelligence, Lieutenant General Vernon Walters, a Nixon crony of long standing, would tell Gray to back off. He would raise the flag of national security and secrecy. Gray and Felt would do as they were told, Haldeman predicted confidently. "Felt wants to cooperate because he's ambitious," he said. "And that will fit rather well because the FBI agents who are working the case, at this point, feel that's what it is. This is CIA."

Nixon liked the idea. "Good deal!" he said. "Play it tough. That's the way they play it and that's the way we are going to play it."

Walters was in Gray's office by 2:30 P.M. The investigation, he told Gray, could trespass into the CIA's domain. Gray called Charles Bates the moment that Walters left his office. He made the case for standing down. Bates objected. "I again told him I felt the FBI had no choice but to continue our full investigation and obtain all the details."

Gray agonized until he answered an urgent summons from the White House at 6:30 P.M. on June 28. Inside John Ehrlichman's office, John Dean handed Gray two white manila envelopes—the documents he had taken from Hunt's safe.

"These should never see the light of day," he told Gray.

"Then why give them to me?"

"Because they are such political dynamite their existence can't even be acknowledged," Dean said. "I need to be able to say that I gave all Hunt's files to the FBI. That's what I'm doing."

Gray had a red wastebasket in his office, holding a burn bag for destroying secret documents. But he did not know what a burn bag was. Six months later, he set fire to the files in a trash bin in his backyard.

"There is little doubt," an internal FBI report later concluded, "that Mr. Gray made deplorable decisions of historic proportions."

"No holds barred"

The White House and the FBI had another crisis on their hands that summer. Nixon issued orders to escalate the war on terrorists in America. But the Bureau had lost its license to use its most powerful weapon in that battle.

The Supreme Court had banned the warrantless wiretapping of Americans in a unanimous decision on June 19, 1972—the Monday after the Watergate break-in.

A wild-eyed anarchist on the FBI's Ten Most Wanted list was at the center of the case. Pun Plamondon—minister of defense for the White Panthers, whose party platform rested largely on sex, drugs, and rock 'n' roll—stood accused of planting a bomb at the CIA's recruiting station near the University of Michigan in Ann Arbor. His lawyers correctly suspected Plamondon had been wiretapped. The federal trial judge had granted a routine defense motion for the disclosure of the government's evidence. Nixon's Justice Department refused to comply. The president's lawyers claimed that the commander in chief had an inherent and unassailable right to wiretap at will.

The government lost. A federal appeals court ruled that even the president had to obey the Fourth Amendment—the passage in the Bill of Rights protecting Americans from warrantless searches and seizures.

The Supreme Court had never upheld warrantless wiretapping within the United States. Most of the FBI's secret surveillance had been carried out in defiance of the Court—at the command of presidents and attorneys general, but sometimes on orders from Hoover and his subordinates—since 1939. The technology of electronic eavesdropping had expanded exponentially since then. Thousands of Americans were targets of government spying under Nixon.

Robert Mardian, as Nixon's internal security chief, represented the government in oral arguments before the Supreme Court. Justice Byron White had asked him bluntly: if "the President decides it's necessary to bug John Doe's phone," was there "nothing under the sun John Doe can do about it?"

Mardian had said: "The President of the United States may authorize electronic surveillance; and, in those cases, it is legal."

Justice Lewis Powell, newly appointed by President Nixon, wrote the unanimous decision rejecting that argument. "The issue before us is an important one for the people of our country and their Government," he wrote. "It involves the delicate question of the President's power, acting through the Attorney General, to authorize electronic surveillance in internal security matters without prior judicial approval. Successive Presidents for more than one-quarter of a century have authorized such surveillance in varying degrees, without guidance from the Congress or a definitive decision of this Court."

That authority was now empty.

"Although some added burden will be imposed upon the Attorney General, this inconvenience is justified in a free society to protect constitutional values," the Court ruled. "By no means of least importance will be the reassurance of the public generally that indiscriminate wiretapping and bugging of law-abiding citizens cannot occur."

The Court said the government was free to wiretap "foreign powers or their agents"—for instance, Soviet spies—but not American citizens. Not without a warrant.

The FBI had at least six warrantless taps running on the Weather Underground and the Black Panthers on the morning of the Supreme Court's ruling. They had to come out at once.

The Bureau responded by reviving black-bag jobs.

Gray called in top agents from around the country in mid-September 1972. President Nixon had ordered the FBI—along with the Pentagon, the State Department, the CIA, and the National Security Agency—to come up with a national counterterrorism plan.

The world had been transfixed ten days before by the Black September killings at the 1972 Olympic Games in Munich. Eleven Israeli athletes (and eight Palestinian attackers) had died, most of them after a bungled rescue by the West German police. President Nixon had conferred on the counter-terrorism problem with his national security adviser, Henry Kissinger, and his United Nations ambassador, George H. W. Bush. His personal secretary, Rose Mary Woods, told the president about the prophecies of a popular psychic named Jeane Dixon; the syndicated clairvoyant predicted a Pales-tinian attack against a Jewish target, such as Yitzhak Rabin, then Israel's ambassador to the United States.

"They will kidnap somebody. They may shoot somebody," Nixon told Kissinger on September 21, citing "this soothsayer, Jeane Dixon" as a source of his fears. "We have got to have a plan. Suppose they kidnap Rabin, Henry, and demand that we release all blacks who are prisoners around the United States, and we didn't and they shoot him . . . What the Christ do we do?" Nixon wondered. "We have got to have contingency plans for hijacking, for kidnapping, for all sorts of things."

On September 25, Nixon issued a secret presidential directive command-ing an all-out counterterrorism campaign. The result was the President's Cabinet Committee on Terrorism—the first full-scale effort by the Ameri-can government to address the threat. The full committee met once, and only once.

"Everybody at that meeting washed their hands like Pontius Pilate and said, 'You do it, FBI,'" Gray recounted. Nobody else wanted to take the re-sponsibility.

Gray told Mark Felt and Ed Miller, his intelligence chief, that "he had decided to reauthorize surreptitious entries," Miller said. "Well, I thought that was really good."

The first targets of the break-ins were hit in October 1972. The Bureau raided Palestinian American groups across the United States. FBI agents burglarized the files of an organization called the Arab Education League in Dallas, stole a membership list from the league's office safe, identified the group's leaders, knocked on their doors, and ran them out of the country. Gray wrote years later that the break-ins and burglaries were "clearly illegal." But he believed that he was following the president's orders.

FBI black-bag jobs against friends and families of twenty-six Weather Underground fugitives started later that month. Gray was appalled to learn that not one of the fugitives had been caught, despite a nationwide search that had gone on for nearly three years.

He ordered them "hunted to exhaustion," a submariner's command. "No holds barred," he wrote to Felt. At least seven of the burglaries were carried out by Squad 47, the secret unit based in the FBI's New York office. Under the command of John Kearney, the squad had conducted at least eight hundred black-bag jobs since the 1950s.

None of the break-ins ever produced any evidence leading to the arrest of a Weather Underground fugitive. But in time they led to federal grand jury investigations against the commanders of the FBI.

"I KNEW SOMEBODY WOULD BREAK"

The FBI veterans Liddy and McCord had been indicted on September 15, 1972, along with the five other Watergate burglars, for the bugging of the Democratic Party headquarters. But the charges ended there. The Watergate case had hit a stone wall.

Felt and his inner circle at the FBI made a decision to fight the obstruction of justice. They had personal as well as professional motives. They acted on their instincts to dismantle the roadblocks in the path of the FBI's investigation. They knew that the conspiracy and the cover-up had been orchestrated at the White House. They deeply resented the fact that the president had placed Pat Gray, a man they considered a political stooge, in charge of the FBI.

"It hurt all of us deeply," said Charles Bolz, the chief of the FBI's accounting and fraud division. Felt was Hoover's rightful heir. "Felt was the one that would have been the Director's first pick. But the Director died. And Mark Felt should have moved up right there and then. And that's what got him into the act. He was going to find out what was going on in there. And, boy, he really did."

Felt and his allies began leaking the secrets of Watergate a few weeks before the November 1972 election. Felt became famous thirty-three years later when he confessed that he was the man known as "Deep Throat," the FBI source who helped *The Washington Post* confirm the facts for its ground-breaking reports on the Watergate investigation. But he was not the only one.

The notes of Felt's first documented interview with Bob Woodward of the *Post* are now public records. "There is a way to untie the Watergate knot," he said to Woodward on October 9, 1972. "Things got out of hand." A political warfare operation against the president's enemies had gone out of control. Gray knew. The attorney general/CREEP chief, John Mitchell, knew. If Mitchell knew, the president knew. And if the facts came out, they would "ruin . . . I mean ruin" Richard Nixon.

Felt made sure that the facts were revealed by sharing information with four trusted fellow FBI men. Bob Kunkel and Charles Bates stood with Felt at the top of the FBI's chain of command in the Watergate investigation. Kunkel was in charge of the Washington field office and he briefed Felt daily. Bates kept the running chronology that served as the FBI's institutional memory of the case. Dick Long and Charles Nuzum, respectively chief and lead agent in the FBI's white-collar crime section, were masters of Watergate's paper trail. Bates and Long told a few trusted fellow agents about what they had done, and why. The word started to spread.

"They would meet at the end of the day and discuss what happened, what they knew, in the investigation," said the FBI's Paul Daly, an agent in the intelligence division. "They would make a decision, a conscious decision, to leak to the newspapers. They did that because of the White House obstructing the investigation. And they leaked it because it furnished the impetus to continue."

So street-level FBI agents turned secrets into information, and senior FBI leaders brought that information to reporters, to prosecutors, to federal grand juries, and into the public realm. That was the beginning of the end of Richard Nixon's presidency. Without the FBI, the reporters would have been lost. *The Washington Post* and *Time* magazine were the first to suggest that there were wheels within wheels in the Watergate case. *The New York Times* and the *Los Angeles Times* soon joined in. Not all of their stories were accurate. But the facts within them, taken together, sketched out a series of White House conspiracies to subvert the president's political enemies with espionage and sabotage.

Richard Nixon, his re-election imminent, took note. "I knew somebody would break," Nixon said bitterly after the first piercing stories appeared in the press. Ten days after the first big leak, he was certain about the main source.

"We know what's leaked and we know who leaked it," Haldeman told the president on October 19.

PRESIDENT NIXON: Is it somebody in the FBI?

HALDEMAN: Yes, sir . . . And it's very high up.

PRESIDENT NIXON: Somebody next to Gray?

HALDEMAN: Mark Felt.

PRESIDENT NIXON: Now why the hell would he do that?

HALDEMAN: It's hard to figure. Then again, you can't say anything about this, because we'll screw up our source . . . Mitchell is the only one that knows this. And he feels very strongly that we should—we'd better not do anything because—

PRESIDENT NIXON: Do anything? Never!

HALDEMAN: If we move on him, then he'll go out and unload everything. He knows everything that's to be known in the FBI.

PRESIDENT NIXON: Sure.

HALDEMAN: He has access to absolutely everything . . . Gray's scared to death. We've got to give him a warning . . .

PRESIDENT NIXON: What would you do with Felt? . . . Christ! You know what I'd do with him? Bastard!

The president and the FBI were now engaged in an undeclared war. Attorney General Kleindienst, following orders from the White House, told Gray five times to fire Felt. The acting director could not find the will to do it. For Felt was the more powerful man. He might not have known "everything that's to be known in the FBI," but he and his chief investigators knew more than anyone else outside the White House. Their knowledge would give them the power to go after the president himself.

"TREASONABLE PEOPLE"

Gray fell seriously ill shortly after Nixon was re-elected in a landslide on November 7, 1972. He went into the hospital near his home in Stonington, Connecticut, for abdominal surgery. His doctor released him on December 3 but ordered him to rest at home until the New Year. Mark Felt ran the FBI during Gray's two-month absence from headquarters.

Gray, still the acting director, did not know if Nixon planned to ask the Senate to confirm him, as the law required. He did not know if Nixon trusted him. He would soon have cause to wonder why he had ever trusted Nixon.

Led by John Ehrlichman, he entered the Oval Office for the second time in his life at 9:09 A.M. on February 16, 1973. Nixon got right to the point: the Senate hearings on his nomination posed a potential confrontation over the president's power to conduct secret intelligence operations.

"They would probably ask you about such things as: Do you know about any other things that the Bureau's done? Have you gotten into this domestic wiretapping?" Nixon began. "I'd say, 'Yes, we have to do it . . . What do you want us to do about this? Do you want to let people get shot?' "

Gray's mind went blank.

"Terrorism," the president said. "Hijacking is another thing. And you've got to get into that. Some of that requires wiretapping . . . We must not be denied the right to use the weapon. The idea that we're wiretapping a lot of political groups is bullshit." Gray remained speechless.

The president immediately turned to Watergate. "Would it hurt or help for you to go up there and be mashed about that?" Nixon asked.

Gray now gathered his wits. "Mr. President, I'm the man that's in the best position to handle that thing," he said confidently. "I've consistently handled it from the outset . . . I think the Administration has done a hell of a fine job in going after this thing." This was bluster, and Nixon knew it.

"You haven't been able to do anything—or have you?—up to this point, about the leaks," Nixon said. "The whole story, we've found, is coming out of the Bureau."

"Well, I'm not completely ready to buy that, Mr. President," Gray said.

What about Felt? Nixon asked pointedly.

"It would be very, very difficult to have Felt in that position without having that charge cleared up," Nixon said. "This stuff didn't leak when Hoover was there. I've never known of a leak when Hoover was there. I could talk to him in this office about everything. And the reason is that—it wasn't because they loved him, but they *feared* him. And they've got to *fear* the man at the top . . . You've got to play it exactly that way. You've got to be brutal, tough and respected . . . I understand leaking out of the CIA, those goddamned cookie-pushers. But if it leaks out of the Bureau, then the whole damn place ought to be fired."

Nixon was now sputtering and fuming. "You've got to do it like they did in the war," the president said. "In World War II, the Germans, if they went through these towns and then one of their soldiers, a sniper hit one of them, they'd line up the whole goddamned town and say until you talk you're all getting shot. I really think that's what has to be done. I mean, I don't think you can be Mr. Nice Guy over there."

"I haven't been," Gray protested. "These guys know they can't lie to me like they used to lie to Hoover."

Nixon became imperious. "Frankly, I am referring to discipline of the highest sensitivity involving what may be political matters. Partisan political matters," he said. "Let us suppose there's a leak to a certain member of the press. I've got to have a relationship here where you go out and do something and deny on a stack of Bibles."

"Right," said Gray. "I understand."

"I don't have anybody else," Nixon said. "I can't hire some asshole from the outside."

"There were times," he said, his anger boiling over, "and, and, and, Lyndon Johnson told me this same thing—when I felt that the only person in this goddamned government who was standing with me was Edgar Hoover . . . He would break his ass if he saw something that was wrong being done, if somebody was pissing on us . . . What you've got to do is to *do like Hoover.*"

By Gray's account, the president turned to Erhlichman, who nodded slightly, as if to say: go ahead. Nixon seemed to unwind, and he came back to his script.

"I think it's going to be a bloody confirmation," he said. "You've got to be prepared to take the heat and get bloodied up. But if you do go through a bloody one, let's remember that you're probably going to be in for just four years. And then they're gonna throw you out. So let's get in there and do some good for the country."

"As you know, I would never ask the Director of the Bureau to do anything that was wrong," the president said. "But I am certainly going to have to ask the Director of the Bureau at times to do things that are going to protect the security of this country."

"No problem," Gray said.

"This country," Nixon said, "this bureaucracy—Pat, you know this—it's crawling with, Pat, at best, at best, unloyal people and at worst treasonable people."

"Treasonable people," Gray repeated, dutiful and dull.

"We have got to get them, break them," Nixon said.

"Right," Gray said. "I know that."

"The way to get them is through you. See?"

"I agree. I have no problems with that."

Nixon was satisfied. He had chosen a successor. Everyone was smiling now.

"The moment you're confirmed," the president said, "we've got to have the kind of relationship we had with Hoover."

36

"THE BUREAU CANNOT SURVIVE"

O N MARCH 3, 1973, a suave-looking Iraqi in his late twenties, wearing modish sideburns and bell-bottom jeans, parked his rented Plymouth Fury and checked in at the Skyway Hotel next to John F. Kennedy International Airport in Queens, New York.

The Iraqi had arrived in New York eight weeks earlier. Shortly thereafter, the FBI had received a tip from Israeli intelligence that he might be an agent of the murderous gang called Black September, under the control of Yasser Arafat, the chief of the Palestine Liberation Organization (PLO). Black September had just murdered the American ambassador and his deputy in the Sudan.

An FBI agent interviewed the Iraqi, who explained that he had come to the United States to attend flight school and become an airline pilot.

The interview was filed away, and for a time forgotten. The agent could not be blamed for the oversight. As an institution, the FBI did not know how to investigate a terrorist. The United States had not experienced a transnational conspiracy to commit mass murder since the terrorist attacks during and after World War I.

On the morning of March 4, the Iraqi left his Fury parked next to the El Al terminal at Kennedy, where the prime minister of Israel, Golda Meir, was due to arrive in a few hours. In midtown Manhattan, his two accomplices parked their cars on Fifth Avenue, in front of two Israeli banks.

On March 5, linguists at the National Security Agency, which had just created a branch to handle the issue of international terrorism, began to translate a newly intercepted message from the Iraqi mission at the United Nations. The message had been sent to Baghdad and relayed to the PLO. It contained the outlines of a murderous plan.

As the NSA started to read the message, a tow truck operator impounded a 1973 Dodge Dart from the corner of 43rd Street and Fifth Avenue. The next morning, a 1972 Plymouth Duster at 47th Street and Fifth was towed away. Both had been ticketed for standing in a no-standing zone. An Olin rent-a-car supervisor came to the impound lot at a pier on the Hudson River to claim the Dart. He opened the trunk and stared in wonder.

A call went out to the New York Police Department's bomb squad. Its best men raced to the lot. In the back of the Dart, and then the Duster, they found plastic containers filled with gasoline, propane tanks, blocks of Semtex plastic explosive, blasting caps, batteries, and fuses. On the dashboards lay Black September and PLO propaganda, wrapped in Hebrew newspapers.

The bombs had been set to go off at noon on March 4. Had they exploded, they could have killed or maimed many hundreds of people, and terrorized many thousands more. But each had an identical flaw in the circuitry of its fuse.

The police had stumbled upon the first bomb plot in the war between Arab terrorists and the United States.

At 6:15 P.M. on March 6, the FBI joined the case. In Washington, the NSA told the Bureau about the coded message to Baghdad and warned that a third car bomb lay waiting outside the El Al terminal at JFK. Later that night, the FBI and the NYPD bomb squad found the Fury and opened the trunk.

The bomb at JFK was identical to the ones found in Manhattan, down to the faulty circuitry—but it was twice as big. Had it exploded as designed, it would have produced a fireball about fifty yards high and wide, and a destructive shock wave three times that size, ripping through the El Al terminal and into the surrounding tarmac. Airplanes at an altitude of a hundred yards or higher could have been knocked sideways.

The FBI lifted a fingerprint off the propane tank in the Fury. Eighteen years would pass before the Bureau matched the print with the bomb maker.

It only took a day for the FBI to discover that all three cars had been rented by the Iraqi whom the Bureau had interviewed weeks before. The FBI quickly traced the suspect's travels to the Skyway Motel at JFK, where they found bomb-making components. They tracked a $1,500 bank transfer he had received from Beirut. They analyzed the handwriting on his rental car agreements and his application for flight instruction at the Teterboro School of Aeronautics.

But the agents missed the phony passport he had stuffed behind an air conditioner at the Skyway; a maintenance man found it months later. And they never found his accomplices. To this day, the two men remain the most likely suspects in the assassination of Yosef Alon, the Israeli air force attaché in Washington. Alon, a leading Israeli intelligence liaison with Washington, was shot dead outside his home in Maryland four months later. The FBI's investigation of the killing was futile; the case remains officially unsolved.

On March 15, 1973, the FBI realized that the Iraqi with the Fury was responsible for all three bombs. The case against him was code-named TRIBOMB.

Six years later, the same man was stopped and questioned by the border police in Bavaria as he drove out of Germany. He was carrying a phony French passport. In the trunk of the car, police found nine more passports—along with eighty-eight pounds of explosives, eight sets of electronic timers and detonators, and $12,500 in United States currency. The wrapping on the explosives came from a pastry shop in Beirut that was a known front for terrorists. The suspect was jailed for seven months, and questioned by German and Israeli intelligence officers. He never broke. The Germans deported him to Syria. The FBI never knew.

The TRIBOMB investigation went cold. The case was fifteen years old when the FBI's Mike Finnegan revived it. In October 1990, he had been on it for two years when he received a crucial tip. The United States and its allies were on the highest intelligence alert against Iraq. Saddam Hussein had invaded Kuwait; the clock was ticking toward an American counterattack. The tip came in the form of fresh intelligence from the Israelis: the Iraqi suspect was Khalid Mohammed el-Jessem, a senior PLO lieutenant with close ties to Baghdad. The FBI put out a worldwide alert. It worked. The TRIBOMB suspect was detained on the day the first Gulf War started; he was traveling through the international airport in Rome, en route to Tunis, to attend the funeral of his close colleague, Salah Khalaf, a founder of Black September who had been assassinated after opposing Saddam Hussein.

The FBI still had the fingerprints from the bomb in the Fury. Finnegan sent them to the Italian police. They matched el-Jessem's. The Italians arrested the suspect and, after a long legal wrangle, handed him over to the FBI.

On March 5, 1993, twenty years to the day after the TRIBOMB plot was first discovered, and a week after the first terrorist attack on the World

Trade Center, the Iraqi went on trial at the federal courthouse in Brooklyn. His trial lasted three and a half days. The only issue for the jurors was the fingerprint evidence. They found him guilty in three hours. United States district judge Jack B. Weinstein gave him thirty years. "The work of the FBI was methodical and careful," the judge said as he pronounced the sentence. "Its institutional memory was faultless. Its tenacity was impressive." It had shown international terrorists that it had the power "to hunt them down anyplace in the world."

It had taken the FBI a generation to meet that standard. But its powers as a secret intelligence service first had to be destroyed and reborn.

The destruction had started the week that the TRIBOMB case began.

"A DANGEROUS GAME"

As the Bureau began to face its first confrontation with international terrorism, a struggle for power had begun that would shake the government of the United States to its foundations. On one side of the rule of law stood the president; on the other stood the FBI.

"The Bureau cannot survive, John," President Nixon said to his White House counsel, John Dean, on March 1, 1973. "It cannot survive."

To Nixon's horror, L. Patrick Gray had offered to let members of the Senate read the FBI's raw files on the Watergate investigation during his confirmation hearings. Nixon had believed that Gray wanted the job so badly he would do anything the White House commanded—including covering up the crimes of Watergate.

"For Christ's sake," the president growled, "he must be out of his mind."

The breach of secrecy was a surrender of power, like giving an enemy a sword. Nixon had a good idea what was in the FBI's files, since Gray had been backhanding copies to John Dean for nine months. They contained evidence of an elaborate conspiracy to obstruct justice.

Nixon decided that he had made a terrible mistake. He began to plot to sabotage the nomination and regain control of the FBI. His plan was cold-blooded. He would leak horror stories about the Bureau's political abuses under Presidents Kennedy and Johnson, including the bugging of Martin Luther King. He had learned the details from Dean's debriefing of Bill Sullivan—the newly installed director of the Office of National Narcotics Information at the Justice Department. The White House would feed these stories to the Senate Judiciary Committee; the senators would use them to interrogate Gray. He could not answer them in candor. He would, in John Ehrlichman's immortal phrase, twist slowly, slowly in the wind. His nomination would fail, and a more loyal man would be chosen to run the FBI.

On March 13, 1973, Dean proposed Bill Sullivan. Nixon liked the idea.

"The quid pro quo with Sullivan is that he wants someday to be back in the Bureau very badly," he said.

"That's easy," Nixon replied.

But as the president plotted, two FBI agents were sitting in the chambers of the Senate, holding the weapon that Gray had offered with an open hand.

The only member of the Judiciary Committee who had taken the time to read the raw Watergate files was Senator Roman Hruska, a law-and-order Republican from Nebraska. FBI agents delivered him twenty-six thick books, along with summaries and analyses, and he had spent six hours leafing through them, from four in the afternoon until ten at night. The senator had reached a conclusion, as FBI agent Angelo Lano reported to his superiors. "Dean had lied to us" by concealing the contents of the office safe of the Watergate burglar Howard Hunt. Lying to the FBI was a crime punishable by five years in prison.

One of the FBI's Watergate investigators slipped this information to Senator Robert Byrd, a West Virginia Democrat who had openly opposed Gray's nomination. Byrd stuck in the sword. On March 22, 1973, he asked Gray bluntly: did Dean deceive the FBI?

Gray replied: "I would have to conclude that that probably is correct, yes, sir." He did not reveal that he had destroyed the documents Dean had taken from the safe.

The president's men convened in the Oval Office, filled with false bravado, after Gray's devastating statement against Dean. Ehrlichman reported that the chairman of the Judiciary Committee, the FBI's best friend in Congress, Senator James Eastland of Mississippi, had suspended the nomination hearings. "Gray is dead on the floor," Ehrlichman told the president. "He accused your counsel of being a liar," Haldeman chimed in. "He may be dead," said Dean, " 'cause I may shoot him." Laughter all around—the last laugh captured on the White House tapes.

Late on the evening of Sunday, April 15, Ehrlichman telephoned Gray at home with bad news. Facing indictment, John Dean had determined to save himself by revealing his darkest secrets to a federal grand jury. "Dean has apparently decided to make a clean breast of things," Ehrlichman told Gray. "One of the questions that apparently they've been asking him is about the envelopes that he turned over to you."

Gray was horrified. "What the hell am I going to do about that?" he said. "The only thing I can do with this is to deny it."

Two days later, the FBI's Watergate investigators, at Mark Felt's command, knocked at the gates of the White House. "I'm worried," Ehrlichman told the president. "The FBI has just served a subpoena on our White House police." It sought the names of the people who had been cleared to enter the White House on June 18, 1972.

PRESIDENT NIXON: Jesus Christ.

EHRLICHMAN: Now what in the hell?

PRESIDENT NIXON: Where were we then?

HALDEMAN: What date?

PRESIDENT NIXON: Ah, June 18.

HALDEMAN: June 18.

EHRLICHMAN: The day of the bugging . . . Well, maybe that's the Hunt safe thing. I bet it's the Hunt safe thing . . .

PRESIDENT NIXON: I need somebody around here as counsel.

HALDEMAN: And Attorney General.

PRESIDENT NIXON: I need a Director of the FBI.

Gray confessed his role in the destruction of Watergate evidence to Attorney General Kleindienst on April 26. The attorney general called the president immediately. "This is stupidity of an unbelievable degree," Nixon said. "He'll have to resign."

Gray had served 361 days as the acting director of the FBI. His future was bleak. He faced years of criminal investigation. He contemplated killing himself. He suffered in the deepest shame for the rest of his life.

Mark Felt was certain he would be chosen to lead the FBI. He was fooling himself. He served as the acting director for three hours. Nixon instead

chose a Republican factotum named William D. Ruckelshaus, the administrator of the Environmental Protection Agency, the newly created agency in
charge of America's natural resources. His decision seemed inexplicable to
all concerned, including the nominee. But Nixon urged the job on him
with an increasing ferocity over the course of an hour.

"I had never seen the President so agitated," Ruckelshaus remembered.
"I was worried about his stability."

They finally struck a deal: he would serve a short time as the acting director until Nixon found the right man to fill Hoover's shoes. If his job
interview had been difficult, the first day of work was worse. On his
desk—Hoover's desk—was a letter to the president signed by Mark Felt
and every one of his top aides, protesting his appointment. It wasn't personal, Ruckelshaus said. "They just felt it was inappropriate to have a bird
watcher as Hoover's successor." Then Ruckelshaus went to a hastily called
staff meeting in the attorney general's office. "Dick Kleindienst emotionally
announced his resignation," Ruckelshaus said. "He was extremely bitter."

Felt's fate was sealed a few days later.

Nixon had determined beyond doubt that Felt was the source of a devastating story, printed on page 18 of *The New York Times* on the morning of
Friday, May 11, detailing the Kissinger wiretaps that Nixon had ordered
placed on presidential aides and prominent newsmen starting in 1969.

"Felt—everybody's to know that he's a goddamn traitor, and just watch
him damn carefully," Nixon said to his new chief of staff, General Al Haig,
the next day. "He has to go, of course . . . the son-of-a-bitch." Ruckelshaus,
at the president's command, ordered Felt to leave the FBI. His resignation
imminent, Felt donned the cloak of Deep Throat for a clandestine meeting
with Bob Woodward of *The Washington Post*. He said the president himself
was the key conspirator in the Watergate case.

The FBI set off on a frantic hunt to find the summaries and the transcripts of the Kissinger wiretaps, which Bill Sullivan had smuggled out of
headquarters. By the evening of May 11, FBI agents had interrogated Sullivan, Haldeman, Ehrlichman, and John Mitchell. Mitchell lied to the FBI,
saying he had never approved any of the wiretaps. But he confided that he
knew about them.

They were part of "a dangerous game we were playing," he confessed. He
told the FBI where to look for the records. The FBI's investigators were inside the White House the next day.

"The records were found two weeks into my tenure, on a Saturday, in the safe of John Ehrlichman," Ruckelshaus recalled. "An FBI agent, sent by me to the White House to guard those records and others in Ehrlichman's office, was badly shaken when the President of the United States seized his lapels and asked him what he was doing there."

The tug-of-war for control of the government was ferocious. The Watergate hearings convened by the Senate wrung damning testimony out of Nixon's foot soldiers. Pivotal stories in the press laid out the facts. But the information, almost all of it, had its source in the work of the FBI. And the information had a gathering strength, each rivulet flowing together into a mighty river, the force that lets water cut through solid rock. Backed by federal grand juries and the prosecutors who led them, the FBI's investigators preserved the rule of law against the obstruction of justice. And under law, the agents were accomplishing an act of creative destruction that the radicals of the Left could only dream of achieving.

They were bringing down the president of the United States.

"A VERY CLOSE CALL"

For the third time, and the last, Nixon chose a candidate to succeed J. Edgar Hoover.

On July 9, 1973, Clarence M. Kelley was sworn in as the second director of the FBI. He had spent a third of his life working for Hoover's Bureau, from 1940 to 1961. He had served ever since as the capable chief of police in Kansas City. Kelley was affable and sincere, a thickset meat-and-potatoes Middle American. The Senate had confirmed him quickly and unanimously.

"I don't think a cop should run the Bureau," the president once had said. "Policemen are too narrow." He had been compelled to go against his instincts. The FBI needed law and order.

Nixon flew out to Kansas City to swear Kelley into office. It was his first public appearance in a month. "I was shocked by the wounds of Watergate that were visible on the president's face," Kelley wrote later. Nixon was a haunted man. He had just proclaimed that he would not cooperate with the Senate investigation. His impeachment was the subject of serious discussion in the Congress. He was under investigation by a newly appointed special prosecutor, Archibald Cox, who was demanding that Nixon turn over his presidential documents and files. The revelation of the existence of the secret White House tapes was a week away. Cox instantly subpoenaed the tapes. Nixon defied him and fired him in October. Attorney General Elliot Richardson and his deputy Bill Ruckelshaus fell under Nixon's fusillade in the upheaval that instantly became known as the Saturday Night Massacre.

"I recall those days as being almost more than I could handle," Kelley wrote. Among the most difficult problems he confronted was a pithy two-page report that Ruckelshaus had handed him on the day he took office, listing the most pressing problems that faced the FBI. At the top of the list were the legal and moral issues raised by the FBI's secret intelligence operations, including the wiretapping, surveillance, and harassment of the American Left.

Kelley was an innocent in matters of secret intelligence. He had never handled a black-bag job, never wiretapped a suspected spy. He had never even heard of COINTELPRO. "The methodologies of these programs were unknown to me," he wrote. "It was quite an eye-opening experience." Once he started to learn about the FBI's most secret operations, he knew he had to bring them under control. "It was a delicate and sensitive matter, this pulling back," he recounted. But pull back he did.

On December 5, 1973, he sent a written warning to every one of the Bureau's 8,767 agents. He ordered them to refrain from "investigative activity that could abridge in any way the rights guaranteed citizens by the Constitution." He began to dismantle the architecture of national security that Hoover had created. By the time he was done, the FBI had eliminated 94 percent of its domestic intelligence investigations, erased more than nine thousand open cases from its books, transferred the roles and functions of national security cases to the Criminal Investigative Division, and reassigned at least 645 agents from chasing radicals to tracking common criminals.

Kelley abolished the all-pervasive powers of the Intelligence Division of the Federal Bureau of Investigation. They would not be renewed in full until the turn of the twenty-first century. For years to come, the FBI agents who hunted terrorists in America wandered in a legal wilderness, looking for signs to guide them through an uncharted land.

37

HOUSE OF CARDS

T HE COLLAPSE OF the Nixon White House set off aftershocks that cracked the walls of the FBI. Nixon had feared that the FBI might not survive the exposure of its secrets. He was prophetic.

The FBI fought in federal court to keep its COINTELPRO files sealed from the public. But when a single sheaf fell into the hands of an old enemy, and the secrets started seeping out, "the house of cards came crashing down," said Homer Boynton, who served as the FBI liaison to the White House, Congress, and the CIA.

The foe was the Socialist Workers Party, a leftist coalition with barely two thousand members. The party had worked within the American political system, albeit at its fringe. Its presidential candidates had never won more than one-tenth of one percent of the vote. The FBI's investigation of the socialists had led directly to the conviction of the party's leaders for political sedition in 1941. The FBI had penetrated the party to its core during the 1950s and 1960s. Hundreds of party members, including local and national leaders, were FBI informants. But none ever gave evidence that the party was engaged in espionage, subversion, violence, conspiracy, or any other violation of federal law. No member had ever been prosecuted—or suspected—of a terrorist act.

The first legal disclosure of the Bureau's records under the Freedom of Information Act came on December 7, 1973. The documents held a clue that the FBI had done more than infiltrate the party's ranks. The socialists soon discovered that they had been a target of a major COINTELPRO operation.

They sued the government of the United States for violating their constitutional guarantees of free speech and political assembly. The judge given charge of the case, Thomas P. Griesa, a young Republican recently appointed by President Nixon, took the suit seriously. So did the lead defendant—the new attorney general, William B. Saxbe. He had taken office on January 4, 1974, after Nixon fired the top men at Justice in his desperate attempt to keep his White House tapes under seal.

The FBI formally answered the suit a month later. It informed Judge Griesa that its COINTELPRO operations had served simply "to alert the public to the nature and activities of the Socialist Workers Party." The Bureau said its actions had been entirely lawful. It denied any part in black-bag jobs and break-ins. The files in the Bureau's New York office were filled with evidence to the contrary. The FBI was lying to a federal judge and to its superiors in the Justice Department. It wasn't the crime, as Nixon had said, it was the cover-up.

"A truthful answer," Judge Griesa later wrote, "would require disclosure of these facts. The FBI sought to avoid such disclosure."

The facts were secured in the office safe of the special agent in charge in New York, John Malone, who been burglarizing Communists since the Truman administration. Malone ran the New York office for thirteen years, from 1962 until his retirement in 1975. He was the face of the old-fashioned FBI—dead set against change. His underlings called him Cement Head.

Malone's safe held the records of 193 bag jobs against the socialists' party headquarters and offices in Manhattan during the 1950s and '60s, along with evidence gleaned by warrantless wiretaps and bugs, and copies of poison-pen letters with the aim of sparking political and racial frictions among them, destroying their reputations, their careers, and their lives.

"The FBI engaged in a prolonged series of tactics to conceal the bag jobs," Judge Griesa found. "In late 1973 or early 1974, an FBI agent in Washington dealing with the matter told the FBI case agent in New York not to advise the U.S. Attorney's office of the bag jobs. At one meeting between the FBI and the assistant U.S. attorney, the FBI representatives used the term 'confidential investigative techniques,' knowing that this reference included bag jobs. The Assistant asked for an explanation of what the term covered. The reply did not include bag jobs."

The judge concluded: "These answers were grossly deceptive."

Like the White House, the Bureau could not countenance the public revelation of its secrets. As President Nixon fell from power in the summer of 1974, demands for the disclosure of the FBI's files began building in Congress and the federal courts. Attorney General Saxbe ordered the beleaguered FBI director, Clarence Kelley, to review the Bureau's records for evidence that Hoover's agents had violated the letter and the spirit of American law.

The dirty tricks were over, the attorney general said. His proclamation was premature.

Senior FBI agents concealed crucial chapters of the Bureau's history from the Justice Department, from Congress, and from director Clarence Kelley himself. One special agent burned thousands of pages of files to prevent the secrets from leaking, said Kelley's aide, Homer Boynton. He thought it was a pity that FBI headquarters did not have a bonfire of its own.

Agents in New York and Washington made extraordinary efforts to hide the existence of five major undisclosed COINTELPRO programs from the director and the attorney general. One was aimed at a small but lethal gang of terrorists whose cause was Puerto Rican independence.

"Endless streams of sirens"

The group had just come up from underground with a new name and a terrible force. The FBI's hunt for its leaders lasted into the twenty-first century.

The roots of the FALN—Fuerzas Armadas de Liberación Nacional, or Armed Forces of National Liberation—reached back to the days when Puerto Rico was an American colony. In 1950, two days after the island became an American commonwealth, two gunmen had tried to assassinate President Truman in the name of Puerto Rican independence. Four of their fellow nationalists shot and wounded five members of Congress in the Capitol in 1954. Twenty years later, the FALN started planting bombs in New York.

The first attacks came shortly after 3:00 A.M. on October 26, 1974, when five powerful explosions ripped through Wall Street and Rockefeller Center in Manhattan, causing upwards of a million dollars' damage to banks and businesses. The second came at 11:03 P.M. on December 11, a booby-trap bomb in East Harlem that gravely wounded a rookie NYPD officer who happened to be Puerto Rican. The third came at 1:22 P.M. on January 24, 1975, in the heart of the financial district.

The FBI's Richard Hahn had been uptown on a surveillance detail, watching suspected spies among the Chinese delegation to the United Nations, when he began hearing "sirens, endless streams of sirens," from police cars heading south.

"We drove down there to see what had happened," he remembered. "Sure enough, Fraunces Tavern had been bombed."

The tavern was one of the oldest buildings in New York. In 1783 President George Washington had given his farewell address to the officers of the Continental Army from its steps. The first-floor dining room was a favorite lunchroom for the businessmen and brokers of Wall Street. A stairway to the second floor opened into the Angler's Club, a private association of wealthy fly fishermen. The blast came from a duffel bag loaded with dynamite hidden under the stairs. Four people died; sixty-three were injured, some of them grievously. The FALN communiqué taking credit for the bombing was signed in the name of Griselio Torresola, who had been shot dead trying to assassinate Harry Truman. No one was ever arrested in the killings in New York.

"It was just a continuing drumbeat of bombings and an inability to solve them," Hahn said. The FBI had no clue about the FALN. Not one of the forty agents assigned to the Fraunces Tavern case had an inkling of the identities of its members, or where the group might strike next. "We went from one suspect to another and we developed our own surveillance teams to follow these suspects around," Hahn said. "You had activists that were mouthing the same words that the FALN was mouthing in its communiqués"—marching and demonstrating, holding political rallies in public arenas—"and you really had no way of parsing out whether amongst those activists might be your suspect."

Two dozen bombings followed in rapid succession, along with bomb scares intended to terrorize New York. One hundred thousand office workers evacuated the World Trade Center and the Empire State Building after one threat. After the FALN struck banks and buildings in downtown Chicago, the FBI's Bill Dyson joined the case. He was one of the few agents in the Bureau who possessed an understanding of the thoughts and tactics of terrorists, gained from five years of experience in intelligence investigations against the Weather Underground—five futile years. He stayed on the trail of the FALN as it carried out a hundred more attacks across the nation and pulled off the most lucrative armed robbery in the history of the United States.

Dyson's work led to the creation of the FBI's first terrorist task force. It was so secret that no one at headquarters knew anything about it.

"It was done clandestinely," he said. "We used to meet at Mike's Tavern. Mike had a police bar, a true police bar. You couldn't go in there unless you buzzed and Mike recognized you as a law-enforcement officer. And he would allow us investigators, working terrorism, to go in his back room and we could meet and we could coordinate surveillances, and we could work together. But we didn't have the blessing of anybody!" Dyson was sworn in, secretly, as an inspector with the Illinois state police, whose members, along with officers of the Chicago Police Department, covertly joined the task force at Mike's Tavern. Years later, a fellow agent asked Dyson what FBI headquarters thought about this endeavor.

"We never told headquarters," he replied.

"Get to the bottom of it"

The FBI was under siege in Washington. The new Congress, elected three months after Nixon's resignation, was the most liberal in memory. In the wake of Watergate, the Senate and the House of Representatives resolved to undertake formal investigations of the nation's intelligence operations. President Gerald R. Ford realized that the revelation of those secrets would tarnish the reputations of American leaders going back to FDR. The president's top aides tried to contain the damage and limit the investigation to the CIA.

"Why not add the FBI?" the former director of central intelligence, Richard Helms, asked President Ford pointedly, face-to-face in the Oval Office. "You may as well get to the bottom of it." Deputy Attorney General Laurence Silberman agreed. "The FBI may be the sexiest part of this," he told the president's national security team on February 20, 1975. "Hoover did things which won't stand scrutiny, especially under Johnson."

Director Clarence Kelley was starting to understand that the Bureau's intelligence operations had broken the law. He feared Congress would impose strict limits on his agents. He beseeched the president to counter that threat by issuing an executive order expanding the national security powers of the FBI.

The FBI relied on laws "designed for the Civil War era, not the Twentieth

Century," he argued. The Supreme Court had "reduced to a fragile shell" the statutes against advocating revolution, he said; its ban on warrantless wiretapping of Americans had forced the Justice Department to drop its indictments against the leaders of the Weather Underground, charges built on illegal surveillance. Under the existing law, Kelley said, he doubted the Bureau's ability to gain intelligence on "terrorists and revolutionaries who seek to overthrow or destroy the Government."

If the courts or Congress questioned the legality of black-bag jobs and break-ins, Kelley and his allies in the Justice Department believed, the answer was to legalize them. On May 9, 1975, they asserted that the FBI could conduct "warrantless searches involving physical entries into private premises" if the president gave the orders.

But Watergate had washed away the old idea that the president had the powers of a king. The political climate was hardly conducive to a claim that the FBI could commit crimes on orders from the White House, even in the name of national security. After nearly seven decades of freedom from the scrutiny of outsiders, the Bureau was no longer inviolate.

"THEY GOT MY NAME!"

A confrontation was coming. Despite strong resistance at headquarters, the congressional committees investigating intelligence already were reading through the FBI's files and taking sworn statements from its commanders.

A skirmish in the corridors of the FBI was an opening battle in a long war.

The Bureau had started moving out of the Justice Department, across Pennsylvania Avenue. The new J. Edgar Hoover Building, officially dedicated on September 30, 1975, cost $126 million. It was the ugliest building in Washington: it looked like a parking garage built by the Soviet Politburo.

Members of Congress wanted tours of the old and new headquarters. The FBI's James R. Healy—a die-hard believer in the Bureau and a great admirer of Hoover—had the duty of escorting Congressman Robert Drinan, a Massachusetts Democrat, a pacifist Jesuit priest, a passionate opponent of the Vietnam War, and a proclaimed enemy of the FBI.

They passed the FBI's indoor firearms range. Healy explained that an agent only shot at a suspect in self-defense. Someone asked: What if they fire back? "Then we shoot to kill," Healy said.

"Reverend Drinan started shouting, 'They shoot to kill! They shoot to kill!'" he recounted. "I figured the guy had gone completely bonkers." Healy tried to move the congressional delegation along into a room holding index cards with the names of people in the FBI's files; the cards were the foundation of the house that Hoover had built. "Reverend Drinan said, 'Well, I'd like to see my name.' As a courtesy, I led him to a young lady who was filing the cards. I asked her to produce a few." The clerk held up the index cards with a shaking hand. The congressman snatched them away.

"They got my name!" Drinan shouted. "They got my name!"

The congressman demanded to see what else the Bureau had on him. He became one of the first Americans granted the request to see his own FBI file. It included a letter that a suspicious nun had sent to Hoover four years before, calling Father Drinan a Communist plant inside the Catholic Church.

Such was the prevailing spirit when the Senate opened its first public hearings on the FBI on November 18, 1975.

"Heads would roll"

As Director Kelley feared, congressional investigators had dug into the FBI's past and unearthed some mortifying stories—the bugging of Martin Luther King, the maintenance of a half-million pages of internal security files on Americans, the abuses of civil liberties in the COINTELPRO campaigns, and the misuses of investigative power as a weapon of political warfare.

The Senate committee concluded that the FBI had spied on Americans without just cause. It laid blame for the Bureau's violations of the law and the Constitution principally with "the long line of Attorneys General, Presidents, and Congresses who have given power and responsibility to the FBI, but have failed to give it adequate guidance, direction, and control."

But the Bureau took the rap. Public approval of the FBI plummeted. The perception of the people, shaped by the press, was plain. Respect eroded. The fear remained.

A new attorney general—Edward Levi, the fifth man to hold the office in a three-year span—saw that judgment coming. Levi put forth the first guidelines that ever governed the FBI's intelligence operations. He told Congress that they grew from the conviction that "government monitoring of individuals or groups because they hold unpopular or controversial political views is intolerable in our society." They defined domestic terrorism as a problem for law enforcement. They limited the powers at the FBI's command: the Bureau had to believe that the target of an investigation was willing to use violence before an investigation could begin. It was a high standard.

On May 8, 1976, Kelley tried to make amends to the public in a speech delivered at Westminster College in Missouri, where Winston Churchill had warned at the outset of the Cold War that an iron curtain was descending over Europe. He acknowledged that the FBI had engaged in operations that were indefensible, and he said they would never be repeated.

His performance was less than stirring. Inside the Bureau, it was instantly labeled the "I'm sorry" speech.

It was too late for apologies. Seven weeks before, on orders from the attorney general and his Civil Rights Division, Kelley had transmitted a secret order throughout the FBI. Every agent was commanded to report anything he knew about black-bag jobs that had taken place in the past decade. The responses had come back, nearly every one of them identical: no one knew anything about any break-ins or surreptitious entries. But the Civil Rights Division at the Justice Department started sorting through that thicket of lies and evasions. The FALN investigator Richard Hahn said the word had gone out among street agents in New York: "Heads would roll."

Across the United States, agents began to recoil from secret intelligence missions. I won't take that case, they said. I won't take that squad. "Nobody wants to work terrorism," remembered Bill Dyson, who had become the leader of the FBI's nationwide investigation of the FALN. "Everybody is trying to run away." Hundreds of agents thought that "nobody will support me," Dyson said. "The Bureau won't support me. The Justice Department won't support me. The citizens won't support me."

Fifty-three agents were informed they were targets of a criminal investigation, implicated in crimes committed in the name of national security. Any agent who had used bugs or black-bag jobs in counterterrorism or counterintelligence might be indicted and imprisoned.

38

"A STATE OF CONTINUAL DANGER"

T HE FBI NOW faced a case of unprecedented complexity. It had to investigate itself.

Clarence Kelley had assured the press, the public, and the president time and again that the FBI had ceased committing black-bag jobs a decade before. His top aides had told him so; they said the same to Congress and the courts in sworn testimony. On August 8, 1976, four months after he had the facts in hand, he had been forced to admit he had been fooled by experts—"knowledgeably, knowingly, intentionally deceived" by men at the top of the FBI's chain of command.

Kelley should have known this day would come. He knew from his own experience—his two decades as an FBI agent—that "very little bad news was passed along to J. Edgar Hoover." As Kelley recalled it, almost everyone at the Bureau was "afraid to tell Hoover the truth"; the boss had been "so domineering and his power over his people so intimidating" that agents concealed harsh facts from him. He attributed the deception he had suffered to "an arrogant belief at high levels in the infallibility and appropriateness of *all* FBI activities and policies"—an unquestioning belief in the public image of the Bureau.

Three days after his public confession that he had been fooled by some of the FBI's most experienced con men, Kelley announced that he had taken two dramatic steps toward reforming the Bureau.

First, he created a new force to handle internal inspections; under the watchful eyes of Justice Department prosecutors, FBI agents opened dozens of criminal investigations into their own ranks.

Second, he cut out the heart of the Intelligence Division. Apart from its work against the spies of foreign services, the FBI would henceforth handle national security cases no differently from common crimes. Secret intelligence investigations against subversive Americans would cease. It was his strongest blow against the ghosts of Hoover's past.

"A HUMILIATING AND DEGRADING EXPERIENCE"

Attorney General Edward Levi had questioned the FBI's infallibility from his first day at work.

Levi was one of the most respected lawyers in America. Balding, bespectacled, bow-tied, the son and grandson of rabbis, Levi had been president of the University of Chicago before returning to the Justice Department, where he had worked throughout World War II. Like his predecessor Harlan Fiske Stone, who had made Hoover the director half a century before, he revered the rule of law more than the power of politicians. He believed that a secret police was a menace to a free society.

Levi was just settling into his leather chair, admiring the rich wooden paneling in his new surroundings, when "an FBI agent appeared at my door without announcement," as he recalled. The agent introduced himself as Paul Daly. "He put before me a piece of paper asking my authority for the installation of a wiretap without court order and he waited for my approval."

"You're going to have to let me think about it," Levi said. "The agents might get caught going in."

"It's already in," Daly replied. "The microphone's in." That was the time-honored procedure: first the break-in to install the tap, then the approval to turn it on. The traditions of the FBI differed from the rules of criminal procedure.

Levi was astonished. "His bow tie spun around," Daly remembered.

The attorney general did not approve of warrantless searches and seizures and surveillances. In the wake of Watergate, he thought the nation would not stand for them. He was mortified to learn that the FBI's leaders had lied to Congress and the courts about the continuing practice of black-bag jobs.

He began to draft guidelines for FBI investigations, the first in the Bureau's history, governed by the principle that the government should not break the law to enforce the law. He established a clear chain of command within the Justice Department to look into criminal misconduct by agents. He gave Kelley a direct order to report on the FBI's improprieties.

"We don't ask our agents to squeal on one another," Kelley had said. But that tradition was eroding too.

The tensions at headquarters had been building ever since the FBI opened a criminal investigation of Mark Felt, the dismissed deputy director, during the denouement of the Watergate investigation. In the final days of the Nixon administration, Felt stood accused within the Bureau of smuggling documents out of the FBI and feeding them to *The New York Times.* The charge of stealing the Bureau's records was punishable by up to ten years in prison. Felt was confronted by FBI agents and advised of his constitutional rights. He had lied about his role in the leaks, skillfully, first to the agents, then in a personal letter to the director.

"Dear Clarence," he had written. "To be treated as a prime suspect in a sordid example of crass disloyalty to the FBI is a humiliating and degrading experience." He added: "Incidentally, I am not 'Deep Throat.'"

Kelley correctly surmised that there had been a concerted effort by a group of senior agents to leak the secrets of Watergate, and he had good reason to suspect that Felt had led the secret campaign. But Felt also had been his friend for two decades. Kelley's loyalties—to the FBI and to Felt—compelled him to protect Felt from prosecution. He would not embarrass the Bureau. Kelley ensured that the leak investigation was closed, and he eventually fired the man who had opened it for unspecified abuses of power. But by then, Felt's troubles had multiplied tenfold. His wife was becoming ill, physically and mentally; she later committed suicide. His daughter had disappeared into a hippie commune in California. He became the subject of a second criminal investigation by the FBI. This one could not be quashed.

On August 19, 1976, the FBI raided its own headquarters. Two teams of FBI agents, led by criminal investigators from the Civil Rights Division of the Justice Department, executed the searches in Washington. A separate FBI squad went through the New York office of the Bureau. They discovered a cache of documents no outsider had ever seen. Hoover's "Do Not File" filing system, first created before World War II, was designed to keep evidence of FBI burglaries and bugging concealed forever. It required FBI agents to destroy the original records of their secret intelligence investigations. But even Hoover occasionally erred in matters of national security. He had kept a folder in his office, labeled "Black Bag Jobs," containing a detailed description of the "Do Not File" regulations. It had somehow survived the bonfire of his personal files after his death.

It led the investigators in New York to discover twenty-five volumes of original records that had, inexplicably, been preserved. The investigation began to focus on a series of burglaries in the New York apartments of relatives and friends of the fugitive members of the Weather Underground. The break-ins had been conducted in 1972 and 1973 by the FBI's Squad 47, led by John Kearney.

Kearney, recently retired after twenty-five years at the FBI, opened his daily newspaper. He read about "a special unit being set up in the Department of Justice investigating Squad 47," he remembered. "They were interested in the unusual investigative techniques that had been used in trying to apprehend the fugitives. I had heard directly that a number of the agents had gone to testify in a grand jury, and then I had a call, an unidentified caller, who said, 'I had to give you up, John.'"

Kearney was about to be indicted for conspiracy. He was the first ranking agent in the FBI to be charged with committing crimes against the United States.

At headquarters, Clarence Kelley told a few trusted agents to run a counterinvestigation—to find out where the Justice Department was taking the case. They quickly learned that Kearney was a prime target for a criminal indictment. But he was not the only one. On August 26, a week after the initial raids, Mark Felt and Ed Miller, the FBI's retired intelligence chief, were summoned to testify in secret before a federal grand jury. The two men decided on a dangerous legal strategy. They swore that they had authorized the black-bag jobs carried out by Squad 47. They said they had had the approval of the acting director of the FBI, Pat Gray.

Their testimony made their prosecutors stop and think and argue among themselves, a debate that went to the highest levels of the Justice Department. If they indicted Felt and Miller, they would have to indict Gray as well. They would have to make a felony case against the man who had succeeded Hoover.

The charge would criminalize the FBI's traditions in the realm of intelligence. In effect, it would indict the FBI as an institution.

Felt and Miller believed that, if they went to trial, they could convince a jury that the FBI had the power to bend the law in pursuit of national security, a power that flowed directly from the president of the United States. They thought they could prove that the president's sworn duty to protect and defend the Constitution gave him to power to break and enter a citizen's door. They would assert that a president could violate the rights of an individual to preserve the interests of the nation.

They would face one more hurdle: a burden of proof. Under law, they would have to show that they carried out the break-ins to defend the United States against the agents of a foreign power. Felt and Miller both suspected that the Weather Underground fugitives received direct support from Cuba and Vietnam. The FBI in Chicago drafted an affidavit of more than one hundred single-spaced pages trying to make that argument. It was not supported by the evidence. Presidents Johnson and Nixon had demanded over and over that the FBI find the proof that the Weathermen were secret foreign agents, financed by the enemies of the United States. But the FBI had no such smoking gun.

Felt went on the Sunday morning talk show *Face the Nation* to tell the world what he had told the grand jury: he had authorized the break-ins. They were intelligence operations vital to national security. "You are either going to have an FBI that tries to stop violence before it happens or you are not," he said. "I think this is justified, and I'd do it again tomorrow."

Ed Miller put it more elegantly years later. He took his argument from the common law of centuries gone by. A man's home is his castle, he conceded. But no man can maintain a castle against the king.

The argument went back to the beginnings of the United States. "Safety from external danger is the most powerful director of national conduct," Alexander Hamilton had written in 1787. "Even the ardent love of liberty will, after a time, give way to its dictates. The violent destruction of life and property incident to war, the continual effort and alarm attendant on a state of continual danger, will compel nations the most attached to liberty to resort for repose and security to institutions which have a tendency to destroy their civil and political rights. To be more safe, they at length become willing to run the risk of being less free."

"THE SUPERHUMAN IMAGE OF THE FBI"

Until September 21, 1976, no one had ever seen a terrorist killing carried out by a foreign power in the United States.

That rainy morning, an explosion shook Sheridan Circle, about half a mile from the White House. Orlando Letelier, once Chile's ambassador to the United States, had been murdered in the streets of the capital by a powerful bomb hidden in the undercarriage of his car. His twenty-six-year-old American aide, Ronni Moffitt, died with him. Letelier and Moffitt were driving past Embassy Row when the bomb went off.

Letelier had served in the government of President Salvador Allende—first as ambassador, then as foreign minister, and finally as the minister of defense. His left-wing government was freely elected in 1970, despite the best efforts of the CIA, which had been ordered by President Nixon to keep Allende from power by any means necessary. Allende lasted three years before he died in a coup led by the far-right general Augusto Pinochet. The military junta imprisoned Letelier for a year on a freezing island. Then it expelled him.

Soon after he came to Washington to campaign against the Pinochet regime, Chile's intelligence service, DINA, made plans to assassinate him.

Pinochet and his allies—the right-wing leaders of five South American nations—had undertaken a global effort to exterminate their left-wing enemies. It was code-named Operation Condor. DINA employed murderous anti-Castro Cubans and an American soldier of fortune named Michael Townley as members of an international death squad. Before the assassination of Orlando Letelier, Henry Kissinger's State Department and George H. W. Bush's CIA were both well aware that Operation Condor contemplated political assassinations. But both expressed deep doubts that General Pinochet would risk the consequences of carrying out a terrorist act in Washington. Most American intelligence officers seemed to agree. One took exception.

"Operation Condor involves the formation of special teams from member countries to carry out sanctions up to assassination," the FBI's legal attaché in Buenos Aires, Robert Scherrer, wrote in a secret four-page report to headquarters seven days after the murders. He argued that it was possible that Pinochet and his agents had carried out the assassination.

Owing largely to the efforts of the FBI, the killing of Orlando Letelier would become a unique case: a proven act of twentieth-century state-sponsored terrorism in America.

The patient and painstaking pursuit of the case also owed something to the November 1976 election of Jimmy Carter, the first political leader to make human rights a central principle of his presidency. Carter had an unusual take on the enemies of the United States. "Peace is not the mere absence of war," Carter said when he received his nomination. "Peace is action to stamp out international terrorism."

But the new president had a hard time getting control of the instruments of American intelligence and law enforcement. The congressional inquiries of the CIA and the FBI—and the criminal investigation inside the Bureau—had led to upheavals and bitterness at both agencies. Neither was prepared to collaborate on counterterrorism. The Nixon and Ford administrations had tried to come up with a coordinated response to the threat of terrorism from abroad. Carter fared no better. Terrorism abroad was an act of war to be answered by soldiers and diplomats; terrorism at home was a crime for the FBI to solve. The United States was still years away from a strategy that would combine its law enforcement and intelligence capabilities to stop terrorists before they acted.

FBI headquarters went into a state of limbo after Carter took office in January 1977. It remained there for more than a year. The president had made it clear that he wanted a new leader for the FBI, but he could not seem to choose one. Clarence Kelley, like Pat Gray before him, twisted slowly in the wind.

"One of the things that disturbs me most about the FBI," Kelley had said at his confirmation hearings, "is the feeling that they are suffering from lack of leadership on a permanent basis, and they feel that their position of preeminence, rightfully earned, has been lowered."

He had said he hoped "to restore their feeling of confidence in themselves." But he had failed, and he knew it. "The superhuman image of the FBI, and the power and glory that accompanied it, has greatly diminished," he concluded toward the end of his career. "The FBI has descended from Mount Olympus. And, as it turns out, we are mere mortals . . . But so great and pure was the image of J. Edgar Hoover's FBI that every jot of wrongdoing—whether real, imagined, or grossly exaggerated—now commands an extraordinary amount of attention."

This had to change, he had insisted. The American people could not long endure "a crippled and beleaguered FBI."

"What was missing was good intelligence"

President Carter had spent more than a year looking for someone to lead the Bureau. His attorney general, Griffin Bell, an old friend who had been a federal appeals court judge in Georgia, considered more than fifty candidates. Finally he settled on a fellow jurist, Judge William H. Webster, a moderate Republican who had been appointed to the federal bench by Richard Nixon. Judge Webster was a Christian Scientist who projected sanctimony and probity and integrity. President Carter liked these qualities, which reflected his own image.

Webster was also haughty and harsh. "He had these steely blue eyes," said Homer Boynton, the veteran FBI agent who served as Webster's chief administrator for two years. "His voice would drop. Now, most men I worked for, when they got mad, they'd get loud. His chin would jut out, and the steely blue eyes and you'd feel about three inches tall. He could be brutal."

His first day at the Bureau, Webster made it clear that he wanted to be called "Judge." His appointment began a presidential practice of placing judges in charge of the FBI, a tradition that endured for the rest of the twentieth century.

At his swearing-in as the third director of the FBI, on February 23, 1978, Webster said the Bureau would "do the work the American people expected in the way that the Constitution demanded." Some agents found that stance unsettling. It took Webster the better part of two years to build a trusted inner circle at the FBI. It took at least that long for him to get a handle on "the Hoover hard hats," as he called them, "the old entrenched people," who, out of loyalty to Hoover, carried on his traditions without question, continually telling Webster that they were doing what Hoover would have wanted. "I had some problems with adjusting that thinking," he said later.

Webster was astonished to find that the FBI had no legal framework for its operations. The Bureau had no charter—a legal birth certificate from Congress spelling out its role. It had never had one. It still does not. Webster said from the outset that he wanted a law that defined "what people expected of us—not what we couldn't do, but what they expected us to do." He spent two years drafting it in consultation with Congress. Neither President Carter nor President Reagan acted upon it; the work was stillborn.

Webster was compelled, as he put it, "to pretend that we have a charter."

What the FBI got instead was the Foreign Intelligence Surveillance Act. The product of years of struggle among Congress, the FBI, and the CIA, it created a special court of judges, selected by the chief justice of the United States, who met in a special soundproof chamber on the top floor of the Justice Department. The court's purpose was to approve wiretapping and electronic surveillance requests by American intelligence officers—and to do it under law. For sixty years, from the start of Hoover's era, the FBI had made its own laws on taps and bugs. The court was not an obstacle to the Bureau—it approved more than seventeen thousand requests without once saying no over the next two decades. But the target had to be an agent of a foreign power. The FBI's ability to carry out secret intelligence operations was now governed by rules of law.

Judge Webster faced two tests of the FBI's ability to meet those standards shortly after he was sworn in—one secret, one painfully public.

On April 8, 1978, after an unusually forceful use of diplomatic muscle, two FBI agents took Michael Townley, the American hit man for General Pinochet's intelligence service, into their custody in Santiago, Chile. They flew him to Miami for a long interrogation. Townley had built the bomb that killed Orlando Letelier. The FBI would slowly and painstakingly build a case that would lead to the criminal convictions and imprisonment of the assassins who had worked for General Pinochet, including the general's chief of intelligence.

On April 10, the United States brought a thirty-two-count indictment against Ed Miller, once the FBI's chief of intelligence; Mark Felt, once the deputy director; and Pat Gray, once the leader of the Federal Bureau of Investigation. The charge—based on a sixty-year-old statute used principally to prosecute members of the Ku Klux Klan—was "conspiracy to injure and oppress citizens" with the weapon of warrantless searches.

The indictments infuriated hundreds of FBI agents who had worked on intelligence and terrorism cases during the 1970s. Among their ranks, sixty-nine men who had worked under Gray, Felt, and Miller during the Nixon years now had to answer to internal investigations at the Justice Department and the FBI—investigations that could cost them their jobs, their pensions, and perhaps their freedom. No one knew how many among them might face indictment.

These were some of the same agents responsible for the FBI's most sensitive cases against the enemies of the United States. They looked to Judge Webster for leadership and guidance—and absolution. Webster decided that all but six were blameless in the warrantless break-ins, and he administered discipline internally, without publicity. The Justice Department eventually decided to proceed only with the indictments against Felt and Miller. The case against Gray was dropped—to the outrage of the prosecutors—as were the charges against John Kearney, whose defense was that he had followed the orders of his superiors.

The Intelligence Division, once the strongest branch of Hoover's FBI, had been under siege by the Justice Department, and it dwindled in strength and expertise toward the end of the 1970s. Those who still served the cause wanted to revive the counterespionage effort against Soviet and Chinese spies in the United States, to hire and train FBI agents who could speak those languages, to make intelligence a career instead of a two-year tour. They wanted to hunt down the remaining fugitives of the Weather Underground and the furtive leaders of the FALN. Though the Ku Klux Klan had been defeated, a new wave of neo-Nazi groups was rising in the United States. So were armed partisans aiming to settle scores from epic battles in the Old World—the Serbs and the Croats, the Turks and the Armenians, the Irish Republican Army. Taken together, they added up to a hundred new cases a year of terrorism in America.

Webster worried about the FBI's abilities to fight these threats. "What was missing was good intelligence," he said. "We had to improve our intelligence capability."

"A FIVE-HUNDRED-YEAR FLOOD"

Robert Hanssen was a third-generation Chicago cop who joined the FBI in 1976. He spent twenty-five years in its service. He became a spy for Moscow, stealing an astonishing array of American secrets, and he went undetected by the FBI until after the turn of the century.

Hanssen had learned at a very young age that a badge could be a shield of secrecy. His father had worked on the Red squad of the Chicago police department, hunting and harassing left-wingers, abusing his authority and power, as had his father before him. Hanssen knew some of that sordid history.

"His dad and his granddad were crooked cops—and he knew that," said the FBI's Richard L. Ault, one of the founding members of the FBI Academy's Behavioral Science Unit, who debriefed Hanssen after his arrest. "He said himself, 'The bar wasn't too high for me.' It was an easy decision to make to go ahead and start his espionage." He did it for the money, more than $600,000 in all, but he also did it because he thought he could get away with it.

In March 1979, Hanssen started a two-year tour at the FBI's Soviet Counterintelligence Division in New York. Just shy of his twenty-fifth birthday, he was politically conservative, pronouncedly anti-Communist, a devout Catholic who went to mass every morning—all unexceptional attributes for an FBI agent. And like many of his fellow agents in the division, Hanssen had no training in intelligence work. The division had fallen far from its glory days. It was regarded as "a bastard godchild" at FBI headquarters, as Ault put it, a sleepy backwater where great achievements were few and far between. The Bureau's administrators saw little point in spending time teaching courses in the complexities of counterintelligence. Training came on the job if it happened at all. Mike Mason—later a top aide to FBI director Robert S. Mueller III—received a typical indoctrination in his three-hour course in counterintelligence at the FBI Academy. He remembered his trainer saying that the work was a curse to be avoided at all costs. Mason took the lesson to heart.

"I had no idea what was involved in intelligence work," he said. "All I knew was I didn't want anything to do with it."

Hanssen's supervisors had discovered his one outstanding talent a few weeks after he arrived on duty: he was one of the very few people in the FBI who understood how computers worked. They assigned him to create an automated database about the Soviet contingent of diplomats and suspected spies in New York. He had a knack for the technologies that would revolutionize the world in years to come—especially the ways in which networks were connected and information was transmitted.

The Bureau was building a new security shield for its computers. Hanssen quickly found its flaws and chinks.

His responsibilities soon included creating a monthly report on the FBI's surveillance of the Soviets. He spent many hours in the FBI's file room reading up on the history of the FBI's work against the KGB and the Soviet military intelligence service, the GRU. He learned the identities of the FBI's handful of long-standing sources within the Soviet delegations in New York.

In November 1979, Hanssen walked undetected into the midtown Manhattan offices of Amtorg, the Soviet trade mission that had served as an espionage front for six decades. The office was run by senior officers of the GRU. Hanssen knew where to go and who to see at Amtorg. That day, he volunteered his services as a spy. He turned over a sheaf of documents on the FBI's electronic surveillance of the Soviet residential compound in New York, and he set up a system for delivering new secrets every six months through encoded radio communications. Hanssen's next package contained an up-to-date list of all the Soviets in New York who the FBI suspected were spies. He delivered another revelation that shook the Soviet services to their roots: a GRU major general named Dmitri Polyakov had been working for America since 1961. He had been posted at the United Nations for most of those years. The Soviets recalled Polyakov to Moscow in May 1980. It is likely—though the question is still debated at the FBI—that Polyakov served thereafter as a channel of disinformation intended to mislead and mystify American intelligence.

Hanssen's responsibilities grew. He was given the task of preparing the budget requests for the Bureau's intelligence operations in New York. The flow of money showed the FBI's targets for the next five years—and its plans for projects in collaboration with the CIA and the National Security Agency. His third delivery to the Soviets detailed those plans. And then he decided to lie low.

If Hanssen had stopped spying then and there, the damage he wrought still would have been unequaled in the history of the FBI. William Webster himself would conduct a postmortem after the case came to light in 2001. He called it "an incredible assault," an epochal disaster, "a five-hundred-year flood" that destroyed everything in its path.

Hanssen suspended his contacts with the Soviets in New York as a major case against an American spy was about to come to light. The investigation had reached across the United States into France, Mexico, and Canada before the FBI began to focus on a retired army code clerk named Joe Helmich in the summer of 1980. He was arrested a year later and sentenced to life in prison after he was convicted of selling the Soviets the codes and operating manual to the KL-7 system, the basic tool of encrypting communications developed by the NSA. He was a lowly army warrant officer with a top secret clearance; his treason had taken place in covert meetings with Soviet intelligence officers in Paris and Mexico City from 1963 to 1966; he was paid $131,000. He had sold the Soviets the equivalent of a skeleton key that let them decode the most highly classified messages of American military and intelligence officers during the Vietnam War.

Hanssen understood one of the most important aspects of the investigation: it had lasted for seventeen years. The FBI could keep a case of counterintelligence alive for a generation. There was no statute of limitations for espionage.

"Let terrorists be aware"

America's war on communism reached a crescendo with the election of Ronald Reagan. He had been a foot soldier in the struggle ever since 1947, when he served the FBI as a confidential informer in the campaign against Hollywood leftists. He believed that the war on communism and the war on terror were the same battle.

"My fellow Americans, I'm pleased to tell you today that I've signed legislation that will outlaw Russia forever," Reagan once said with a smile during a sound check for his weekly presidential radio address. "We begin bombing in five minutes." The joke gave a glimpse into the president's mind. Reagan wanted to focus all the power he had against the Russians. He doubled the money spent at the FBI, the CIA, and the Pentagon, and quadrupled the spending on secret weapons and covert operations. He intended to build the muscle and the sinews of American intelligence for the battle with Moscow and its minions.

The president invoked the cause of counterterrorism when he closed the case against Mark Felt and Ed Miller. The FBI's veterans had been found guilty two days after Reagan won the White House in a landslide, convicted by a federal jury of conspiring to violate the constitutional rights of Americans. At their trial, they had freely admitted ordering warrantless burglaries and black-bag jobs. But they claimed they had the duty to carry them out on the president's orders. President Nixon himself had testified at the trial, as had five former attorneys general. On the stand, Nixon stood by his doctrine: a president had the power to break the law, and the FBI had the right to commit crimes at his command, in the name of national security. President Reagan agreed. His longtime chief of staff, counselor, and future attorney general, Edwin P. Meese, drafted a declaration granting Felt and Miller full and unconditional pardons.

The president signed the order shortly before he was gravely wounded by a deranged gunman on March 30, 1981. "Mark Felt and Edward Miller served the Federal Bureau of Investigation and our nation with great distinction," it said. "They had grants of authority reaching to the highest levels of government," and they had "acted on high principle to bring an end to the terrorism that was threatening our nation."

The president underscored that principle in his pardon. "America was at war in 1972," it said. "Felt and Miller followed procedures they believed essential to keep the Director of the FBI, the Attorney General, and the President of the United States advised of the activities of hostile foreign powers and their collaborators in this country." The facts did not support that phrase: the FBI's targets were not agents of foreign powers. But the pardon was a political decision. Reagan and his most powerful advisers wanted to reinstate the power of the government to spy at will within the United States, to abolish the rules instituted under Presidents Ford and Carter, and let the FBI write its own guidelines for wiretapping and bugging. Reagan vowed repeatedly to unleash American intelligence, revive its secret forces, and remove legal obstacles placed in the path of the war on terror.

Secretary of State Alexander Haig announced as soon as he was sworn in that the Soviet Union was training, financing, and arming the world's most dangerous terrorist groups. The new chief of the CIA, Reagan's wily campaign manager, William Casey, let it be known that the KGB was the world's terrorist headquarters. The charge had a few elements of truth — Soviet archives unsealed after the Cold War showed that the KGB had backed a handful of murderous Palestinian militants in the 1970s, and the East German spy service, the Stasi, had sheltered radicals who tried to assassinate Haig himself in 1979. But those facts were not known to the president and his national security team. Nor were they essential to their crusading rhetoric.

"Let terrorists be aware," President Reagan had said a week after his inauguration. If they attacked, America would deliver "swift and effective retribution."

39

THE PRICE OF SILENCE

T HE TARGETS OF the first major counterterrorism case the FBI confronted under President Reagan were America's allies in the war on communism. The FBI's Stanley Pimentel called it "one of the most gut-wrenching investigations" of his long career.

El Salvador's right-wing military regime, backed by the United States, was fighting a small armed leftist guerrilla force. The military and its death squads killed roughly 65,000 civilians, including priests, nuns, church workers, union leaders, students, and peasants. Three American nuns and a lay worker were among the dead. They were "four innocent church women who were trying to do their job of helping the poor," Pimentel said. They had been hauled out of a van, kidnapped, raped, shot at close range, and dumped on the side of a dirt road in December 1980. It was a clear case of premeditated murder, an atrocious act in a dirty war.

Pimentel, the ranking FBI legal attaché in Central America, faced formidable political obstacles. Secretary of State Haig subtly suggested that the nuns had sided with the left-wing guerrillas in El Salvador, the Farabundo Martí National Liberation Front. (The FMLN had committed political murders, but far fewer than the government.) The Reagan administration started to double and redouble American military aid to El Salvador. Salvadoran military and intelligence officials worked in tandem with CIA officers.

But Pimentel found an ally at the U.S. Embassy in El Salvador, a young political officer with a source inside the military regime. Pimentel pursued his investigation to the top of the chain of command. He strongly suspected that the orders for the killing had come from the director of the National Guard, General Carlos Eugenio Vides Casanova.

"I went to see Vides Casanova," Pimentel said. He told the general to turn over the weapons assigned to the five murder suspects, all lowly enlisted men. He planned to send the rifles to the FBI's laboratory, along with the bullets extracted from the bodies of the church women and fingerprints lifted from the scene of the crime. He soon found out that Vides Casanova had ordered the murder weapons hidden; the general planned to turn over a clean set of firearms to the FBI.

"Vides Casanova was absolutely chagrined that we had caught him in this lie," Pimentel said. "He became, of course, very irate." Nevertheless, Pimentel obtained the original weapons, placed them in a diplomatic pouch, and drove to the airport to take the evidence to the United States. Standing on the tarmac, Pimentel faced an armed confrontation. "We were surrounded by about fifty National Guard soldiers, all with automatic weapons and rifles," he said. Pimentel had a .357 Magnum loaded with six bullets. He held his ground and watched as the diplomatic pouch was loaded into the belly of the aircraft.

The FBI lab matched a rifle, bullets, and fingerprints to the soldiers at the scene of the crime. With that evidence, four National Guardsmen were convicted in the killings. But Vides Casanova was untouched. He became the minister of defense of El Salvador in 1984.

Throughout those years, FBI agents in the United States worked at cross-purposes with Pimentel. Shortly after Reagan's inauguration, the Bureau launched a nationwide terrorism investigation into CISPES, the Committee in Solidarity with the People of El Salvador. The coalition of left-wing American activists had grown significantly after the murder of the four American church workers. The Bureau's investigation was based almost entirely on intelligence supplied by Vides Casanova and his intelligence officers to an FBI informant named Frank Varelli.

The son of the former chief of the national police in El Salvador, Varelli offered his services to an FBI agent in Dallas who had no experience with international intrigue. Varelli said he had intelligence sources at the highest levels of the government of El Salvador. He confided that CISPES had forged a terrorist alliance with the leftist guerrillas of the FMLN, in concert with the Soviet Union, Cuba, Nicaragua, and Libya. He was taken at his word.

The FBI investigated some 2,375 Americans affiliated with 180 CISPES chapters across the United States. The Bureau placed these political suspects under photographic and visual surveillance, infiltrated their meetings and rallies with undercover agents and informants, investigated their church groups and campus organizations, scrutinized their financial and telephone records, searched through their garbage cans, and confronted them with aggressive face-to-face interviews.

The investigation lasted four years. It produced no evidence.

The FBI finally took a harder look at Frank Varelli. It concluded that much of what he had reported was "blatantly false," in the words of Webster's top criminal and counterterrorism aide, Oliver B. "Buck" Revell. "Some of it was concocted out of his own mind," Revell told the Senate Intelligence Committee. "And some of it was fabricated on the basis of contacts that he had initiated in El Salvador."

Those contacts were intelligence officers who worked for General Vides Casanova. The general had manipulated and misled the FBI.

Vides Casanova received a military Legion of Merit award from President Reagan, along with a green card allowing him to move to Florida. From 1988 onward he was "living fat, dumb, and happy down in the Fort Lauderdale area," Pimentel said.

"Justice has not really been done," he concluded.

"Odd man out"

While President Reagan was waging the war on communism abroad, American turncoats were stealing secrets for the Soviets from deep inside the national security establishment of the United States. Together they had undertaken the biggest attack on American military secrets since the atomic bomb spies of World War II.

In July 1981, François Mitterrand, the president of France, personally gave President Reagan a revelatory intelligence file known as the Farewell Dossier, derived from four thousand KGB documents delivered by a defector during the 1970s. It took the United States months to decipher their meaning. They described the work of Line X, a division of the Soviet intelligence directorate for science and technology. They depicted how the Soviets used the spy services of Eastern Europe—especially the Poles and the Czechs—to steal weapons technology from the United States.

"They were skillful collectors of intelligence on behalf of the Soviet Union," Webster said. "Due to some very interesting and helpful activity by the French intelligence service dealing with high-ranking KGB officials, we became aware of their program to steal our technology in the United States. The inventory list that they had supplied, or the wish list that they were given, enabled us to track their activities."

The FBI began making felony cases against members of the Polish service and the Americans who served them—chiefly crooked weapons contractors and enlisted men with money problems. A retired marine sold more than one hundred documents on American nuclear weapons systems for $250,000. A Hughes Aircraft executive received $110,000 for details about the newest American radars, aircraft combat systems, and surface-to-air missiles.

The Czech intelligence service had done even better: it penetrated the CIA. For ten years, from February 1973 to August 1983, a naturalized American named Karl F. Koecher had been working at the CIA, having convinced the Agency of his allegiance to the United States. He spent that decade smuggling highly classified data to his Communist controllers, including the names of CIA officers working at home and abroad against the Soviets.

The Hungarian intelligence service had recruited an army sergeant in West Germany, Clyde Conrad, who was in charge of the vault where the Eighth Infantry Division kept its set of NATO's operational plans for fighting World War III. Conrad sold top secret files revealing the locations of NATO's nuclear weapons and the order of battle for troops, tanks, and aircraft. He was paid more than $1 million, and he ran a ring of at least a dozen American soldiers and veterans who kept a steady flow of secrets going east across the Iron Curtain for fourteen years.

The longevity and scope of Conrad's espionage was surpassed by the work of John Walker, a navy veteran and private detective, who enlisted his brother, his son, and his best friend in a ring selling the top secret communications codes of the navy to the Soviets. The FBI only discovered Walker after his ex-wife, Barbara, made a series of telephone calls to the Bureau accusing her husband of being a spy. She was not taken seriously for five months, because she was drunk every time she called and drunk every time an agent went to interview her. But once the FBI began to investigate Walker, it took only three months before he was caught trying to deliver 129 highly classified navy documents to the KGB. He had been giving the Soviets the keys to unlock the encrypted messages of American naval forces since 1967. "There is little or no doubt he caused the death of an untold number of our troops in Vietnam," said the FBI's Robert W. Hunter, who arrested Walker.

The FBI uncovered at least sixty-eight Americans working to steal secrets for the Soviets during the 1980s. But it never found hard evidence that Moscow was behind a terrorist organization taking aim at the United States.

Though America's leaders kept raising the threat of state-sponsored terrorism, the number of attacks on the home front had plummeted. While the FBI's espionage cases multiplied threefold between 1981 and 1985, domestic terrorism cases diminished fivefold, dwindling to one a month. The FALN struck most often, killing U.S. Navy personnel, bombing FBI offices in New York, and robbing $7 million from an armored truck in Connecticut. The Weather Underground fugitives pulled off one final attack, placing a bomb beneath a bench outside the chambers of the United States Senate; the explosion, at 10:58 P.M. on November 7, 1983, injured no one, though it shattered the walls, mirrors, and chandeliers of the Republican cloakroom. But that was a last gasp. For the first time in at least twenty years, since the rise of the antiwar resistance and the renaissance of the Ku Klux Klan, no bombs were going off.

No one at the Bureau knew whether the terrorism threat was dying or evolving. William Webster wondered if it was fading away. His top aide, Buck Revell, thought it would surely rise again.

Revell, an FBI agent since 1964, was the most politically adept assistant director of his era. Like many of the best agents in the history of the FBI, he was a marine veteran; he built loyalties up and down the chain of command. He sported cowboy boots and spoke with a country-western twang; his mind was more subtle than his style.

Revell became the point man for terrorism and intelligence at the FBI. He saw himself as Judge Webster's likely successor. He was not shy about his ambitions. He had a big vision of the powers of the FBI. He wanted to create a counterterrorism division that could work around the world.

Webster had his doubts. "At first he was less than enthused," Revell said. The director had his reasons: roughly four hundred FBI agents, only 5 percent of the force, had any experience in terrorism cases, and most of them were wary of the political and legal risks of the work. Revell nonetheless persuaded Webster to declare publicly that terrorism was one of the Bureau's four top priorities, alongside counterintelligence, white-collar crime, and organized crime.

He began to meet regularly with the director of Central Intelligence, William J. Casey, and the top officials of the CIA's clandestine service. He soon became the Bureau's liaison to a secret White House counterterrorism group, led by a National Security Council staff officer, Lieutenant Colonel Oliver North, a marine running a mind-boggling number of secret missions in the Middle East and Central America. Revell became more attuned to what was happening in the White House than Webster. The director was glad to cede a measure of power, authority, and responsibility to his deputy. For months, he had been mourning the loss of his wife, who had suffered a long and painful illness and died at the age of fifty-seven.

Revell had created a small army inside the FBI in anticipation of the 1984 Olympics in Los Angeles. The Black September attacks at the Munich games twelve years before were still fresh in the memories of the organizers. No one wanted a recurrence. The FBI formed a hostage rescue team of fifty agents—many of them Vietnam veterans trained in military commando tactics. The force grew, fed by fawning publicity. Its arsenal soon included helicopters, armored personnel carriers, and tanks. The Olympics went off with barely a hitch; the biggest scare was the discovery of two hang gliders, which the FBI suspected could be used in a kamikaze operation by Palestinian terrorists. Only one thing went wrong in Los Angeles that fall.

On October 3, 1984, after a two-month investigation that began as the Olympic torch was doused, an undisciplined and untalented counterintelligence agent named Richard Miller became the first FBI man ever indicted for espionage.

The Miller case was an unsavory affair. He was a twenty-year FBI counterintelligence veteran whose life was falling apart in the months before he became a spy. The father of eight children, he had been excommunicated by the Mormon Church for adultery. He had been suspended by the FBI for two weeks without pay because he was obese. Shortly after that disciplinary action, he had willingly been recruited by a woman he knew to be a KGB agent. Svetlana Ogorodnikov enticed Miller into trading a copy of the FBI's twenty-five-page manual on foreign counterintelligence investigations in exchange for $15,000 in cash and her sexual favors. Miller was convicted and received a twenty-year sentence.

"Miller was a clown," said the FBI's Patrick J. Mullany, who worked the investigation. "He should never have been in the FBI to begin with. A pathetic case." Though the compromise of intelligence files was severe, the biggest thing the FBI lost in the case was its public reputation as a force impervious to foreign spies. The image of a desperate man trading secrets for sex with a Soviet spy was indelible to idealistic young FBI agents. "That was my first experience with espionage," said Betsey York, then at the outset of a career in FBI intelligence. "I never, ever dreamed that anybody within the FBI would ever do anything wrong. Because I always thought we were the most perfect people. And so when Richard Miller was arrested . . . I was heartbroken."

Revell was called upon to deploy his hostage rescue force shortly after that arrest. It was not a rescue effort, but a counterterrorist attack.

The FBI was on the trail of Robert Jay Mathews, a leader of a paramilitary cult called The Order. The group grew out of the Aryan Nations movement, a coalition of white racists aiming for an American Armageddon. The Order was known among its members as the Bruders Schweigen, or Silent Brotherhood, in tribute to Hitler's storm troopers. It surfaced with a crime wave that reached from Colorado to California, including two murders, the bombing of a synagogue, and armored-car robberies that reaped more than $3 million. Mathews wanted to ignite a right-wing revolution and overthrow the United States. He called America the Zionist Occupation Government.

"Mathews considered himself to be the Robin Hood of the radical right," the FBI's William H. Matens wrote, "robbing the rich Jews and giving to the Aryans, linking all these radical groups together—Klansmen, skinheads, neo-Nazis, survivalists, tax protestors, militant farmers." The FBI was astonished to learn that The Order claimed hundreds of hard-core adherents with "plans to sabotage dams and other infrastructure items such as communications and utilities in order to shut down American cities."

Mathews sowed his own destruction when he left a handgun at the last of The Order's hijackings. The FBI tracked him to a chalet on Whidbey Island, Washington, thirty miles north of Seattle in Puget Sound.

Revell sent the hostage rescue team to the island. On December 4, 1984, all hell broke loose. The team knocked heads with the FBI special agent in charge from Seattle. As they argued, Mathews opened fire. The FBI responded fiercely. Their tear gas canisters started a conflagration and the chalet burned to ashes. No rescue, much less an arrest, was possible. Mathews was incinerated. His death fed the angry fantasies of a generation of likeminded fanatics. One among them was Timothy McVeigh, the man who ignited the bomb that killed 168 Americans in Oklahoma City a decade later. The operation was considered a calamity.

But Revell and his counterterrorism cowboys won their spurs four months later by foiling a plot to kill Prime Minister Rajiv Gandhi of India during a visit to the United States. The FBI had picked up word of an assassination plot by Sikhs in New York. (Gandhi's mother, Indira, his predecessor as prime minister, had been killed by Sikh nationalists; six years later he met the same fate.) Revell sent Tom Norris, an undercover member of the hostage rescue team, to ensnare the conspirators. Norris posed as an assassin for hire. A veteran navy SEAL with a fearsome face, he had lost an eye in combat in Vietnam, and he looked like a killer. After Norris broke the case, he was invited to the Indian Embassy to accept Gandhi's gratitude.

Webster was usually wary of undercover stings; when they went wrong, they made the Bureau look like the American secret police. "I did not want to turn the FBI into a Gestapo organization," he said. "But there were times when the use of the undercover operation was the only way."

Buck Revell officially became the number-two man in the FBI in June 1985. He now had day-to-day command and control of all major cases—intelligence, investigative, criminal, counterterrorism. He was the FBI's official liaison to the White House and the CIA.

No one at the Bureau had held such a wide range of powers since the death of J. Edgar Hoover. And no one else had faced such a cavalcade of crises.

The counterterrorism capabilities of the United States were severely tested by a series of kidnappings in Lebanon. Americans were being taken hostage in the slums of Beirut. The disappearances had started fifteen months before; among the first to vanish was the CIA's station chief. The captors called themselves Islamic Jihad. But that was a cover name for a coalition of forces the United States did not comprehend.

Congress passed new laws giving the FBI the power to go after the kidnappers. For the first time, the Bureau had the legal authority to investigate terrorism against Americans abroad. It also had orders from the White House: do something, do anything, to free the hostages. Revell had to work with the CIA to form a plan. But his relationship with the Agency suffered a serious wound in the fall of 1985.

On September 22, a renegade CIA officer named Edward Lee Howard disappeared from the United States. The Agency had selected him for a deep-cover assignment in Moscow. He had undergone two years of training, which included reading some of the Agency's most sensitive files on

American operations against the Soviets. Howard was preparing to depart for his posting when the CIA determined that he was not the right man for the job: he was a drunkard and a pathological liar. Dismissed for his derelictions, Howard was bitter. The CIA was well aware of the risks of his flight; it asked the FBI to keep him under surveillance. But the Bureau lost track of him. Howard caught a flight to Helsinki and defected to the KGB. The CIA and the FBI resumed their backstabbing traditions, blaming one another for the fiasco.

The Howard affair was only one among a dozen major espionage cases that year. Two weeks later, on October 9, 1985, Robert Hanssen secretly resumed his career as a Communist spy inside the FBI. He had been made a supervisor in the Soviet counterintelligence division in New York. He promptly wrote to the most senior KGB officer in Washington that he would soon deliver documents containing "certain of the most sensitive and highly compartmented projects of the U.S. Intelligence Community."

Hanssen was true to his word. He sent the Soviets a complete compendium of double-agent operations being run by the FBI, a warning that the FBI was tunneling into the basement of the new Soviet Embassy, a rundown of the Bureau's new efforts to recruit Soviet intelligence officers, a description of the National Security Agency's decoding of Moscow's communications satellite transmissions, the details of the CIA's budget requests for the next five years, and much more. It was the biggest breach of American secrets in the history of the Cold War—with one exception.

Aldrich Ames, the chief of the Soviet counterintelligence branch of the CIA's clandestine service, had become a spy for Moscow that spring. Like Hanssen, Ames was an assiduous collector of intelligence on behalf of the Soviet Union. Along with the names of hundreds of his fellow intelligence officers, and the details of their operations, Ames sold the KGB the names of every one of the Soviets who spied for the United States.

Within weeks, Revell and the FBI's top counterintelligence officers knew something terrible had happened: two of the FBI's most valued double agents were recalled from the Soviet delegation in Washington and returned to Moscow. Soon, almost every Soviet intelligence officer who spied in secret for the United States was either behind bars or in the grave.

The KGB clearly had acquired inside knowledge of the Bureau's most valuable intelligence missions. How Moscow had done it was another question. The FBI wanted to believe the deaths and the disappearances and the blown operations could be blamed on the defection of Edward Lee Howard. But Howard knew nothing about the FBI's double agents. Nor did he know about the Bureau's efforts to recruit officers from the ranks of the Soviet delegations in Washington and New York—and nearly every one of those operations started going sour at the end of 1985.

The hunt for the source of the leaks began with great energy and intensity. In two years' time, it sputtered, stalled, and stopped. The FBI remained mystified. The CIA seemed indifferent. Their counterintelligence chiefs were furious at one another. They would not work together. They could not imagine what had gone wrong. Their investigation concluded that the problem had to be a bug, or a wiretap, or a computer. It could not conceivably be an American spy.

Traitors like Hanssen and Ames could work undetected for years on end because American counterintelligence had become a shambles. The FBI and the CIA had not been on speaking terms for most of the past forty years. The sniping and the silences between them did more harm to American national security than the Soviets.

Revell had an even bigger problem on his hands. On October 4, 1985, he had been handed the responsibility for a joint operation with the CIA to free the American hostages in Lebanon.

Nothing mattered more to Ronald Reagan. The president was aghast when he learned that the FBI and the rest of the American intelligence establishment had no idea where the captives were held or who was holding them. "Reagan was preoccupied with the fate of the hostages," remembered Bob Gates, then chief of the CIA's intelligence directorate. "No loud words or harsh indictments—none of the style of Johnson or Nixon. Just a quizzical look, a suggestion of pain, and then the request—'We just have to get those people out'—repeated nearly daily, week after week, month after month. Implicit was the accusation: *What the hell kind of intelligence service are you running if you can't find and rescue these Americans?*"

Peter Kilburn, a librarian at the American University in Beirut, had been held captive for ten months in Lebanon. Colonel North told Revell that the United States was going to pay $2 million for his freedom, with the funds provided by the politically hyperactive Texas billionaire H. Ross Perot. Middle Eastern informants would serve as go-betweens; the FBI would hand off the cash. Revell balked at ransom. He said he would not be party to a payoff. Colonel North soon came up with another concept. The FBI would remove $2 million in cash from the Federal Reserve, treat it with a chemical solution, and deliver it over to the kidnappers in Lebanon. The ransom would self-destruct in two hours.

Revell marveled at the *Mission: Impossible* concept. But he did not buy it. And Peter Kilburn was murdered on the orders of Libya's Colonel Muammar Qaddafi before the plan could be carried out.

Qaddafi's intelligence officers had placed a bomb in a West Berlin disco patronized by United States soldiers on April 5, 1986. It killed two American sergeants and a Turkish woman, and injured at least 230 others, including 79 Americans. President Reagan retaliated by bombing Tripoli and Benghazi; at least 15 people died and some 2,000 were reported wounded. Qaddafi then sent his spies into Beirut, bought Peter Kilburn from his captors, and had him executed on April 17.

The FBI organized its own counterstrike after learning that Qaddafi sought to avenge the bombing of Libya with an attack on the United States. Libyan intelligence agents tried to join forces with a group of gangsters in Chicago called El Rukn, Arabic for "the Foundation." El Rukn had started out in the 1960s as the Blackstone Rangers, a politically savvy street gang. Its leaders now posed as pious Islamists while dealing drugs and running guns; the religious motif was a cover for their criminal rackets. The FBI learned through wiretaps on El Rukn that the Libyan leader proposed to pay the Chicago gang to attack political targets in the United States. He had chosen the wrong conspirators. El Rukn knew how to sell cocaine, but it had no idea how to carry out a terrorist conspiracy. The FBI swiftly mounted a sting operation, sending an undercover agent to El Rukn's leaders. Posing as an arms dealer, the agent sold them a missile launcher. Agents quickly rounded up the group's leaders on terrorism charges.

A few weeks later, the FBI ran a similar undercover sting on a group of right-wing mercenaries who proposed to overthrow the isolated South American nation of Suriname. Three FBI undercover agents had infiltrated the group of thirteen soldiers of fortune—one posing as a crazed Vietnam veteran, another as a religious zealot, the third as an arms dealer. On July 28, 1986, the group gathered at a private airfield outside New Orleans, with weapons, ammunition, and operational plans for a revolution. The FBI arrested them all.

As these cases surfaced in screaming headlines, Revell was drawn deeper into the secret intrigues within the Reagan administration. The White House was running an international undercover operation all its own.

On July 30, 1986, North told Revell that Attorney General Ed Meese had signed off on a plan, approved by the president, to sell American missiles to the government of Iran in exchange for the release of the hostages. The Reagan administration was going to broker lethal weapons for American lives.

Revell kept a poker face. But he was thinking: is this legal? He wondered why North had shared this explosive information. He surmised it was to keep the FBI from stumbling on something even more secret. His instincts were sound. He took his doubts to Webster; the Judge consulted Meese. "The Attorney General doesn't seem to have a problem with it—which was amazing," Revell recounted. Meese had told them—falsely—that all the weapons shipments had been approved in writing by the president.

If the president did it, the FBI director concluded, that meant it was not illegal.

Revell knew that North divided his hundred-hour workweeks between the hostages in Lebanon and the counterrevolutionaries in Central America. The contras were fighting a scattershot war on communism, trying to overthrow the duly elected Marxist government of Nicaragua. North's devotion to their cause was no secret. The United States Congress had cut off American military and financial support for the contras, whose ranks included soldiers who tortured and executed civilians, including children, captured in combat. The FBI had started an investigation into soldiers of fortune suspected of smuggling weapons into Central America. The Bureau was newly alert to a gun-running operation that involved a Miami company called SAT, short for Southern Air Transport.

"On October 8, I received a call from Oliver North," Revell recounted. "He was concerned that the FBI might discover . . . that SAT was, in fact, involved in the Iran hostage situation." North had hired Southern Air Transport to ship weapons to Iran—and to the contras. Both Webster and Revell got clear signals from Attorney General Meese to back off on the investigation. They complied for a few weeks, until the facts began to leak.

The secrets spilled because the covert operations of the United States were so badly conceived, and so poorly executed, that they began to break down in public. First the crash of a cargo plane maintained by Southern Air Transport exposed the role of the White House in arming the contras in defiance of the law. Then a newspaper in Beirut revealed that the White House was smuggling weapons into Iran.

The president denied it in public. But Revell knew it was true.

On the afternoon of November 13, 1986, the White House asked Revell to review a speech that President Reagan would deliver to the American people that evening. As he pored over the draft of the speech in North's office, he pointed out five evident falsehoods.

"We did not—repeat, did not—trade weapons or anything else for hostages, nor will we," the president's draft said. The United States would never "strengthen those who support terrorism"; it had only sold "defensive armaments and spare parts" to Iran. It had not violated its stance of neutrality in the scorched-earth war between Iran and Iraq; it had never chartered arms shipments out of Miami.

Revell knew none of this was true. He warned Judge Webster, who alerted Attorney General Meese. He was ignored.

"I was sort of odd man out," Revell said.

"THE PRESIDENT HAS ASKED US TO SHUT UP"

The president delivered the speech almost precisely as drafted, word for dissembling word.

Colonel North and his superior, the president's national security adviser, Admiral John Poindexter, began shredding their records and deleting their computer files as fast as they could. But within the White House, one crucial fact emerged: they had skimmed millions of dollars in profits from the weapons sales to Iran and siphoned off the money to support the contras.

"A real bombshell," Vice President George H. W. Bush recorded in his new diary on November 22, after talking to Attorney General Meese. "It's going to be a major flap . . . The president has asked us to shut up, and that is exactly what's happening."

The silence lasted three more days. Meese made a short public statement on November 25, revealing that the missiles had been sold and the money skimmed.

Within hours, FBI agents were searching Oliver North's office. They retrieved a document from North's burn bag—an elaborately falsified statement about support for the contras, delivered in secret testimony to Congress. They dusted it and found the fingerprints of the chief of the CIA's clandestine service, Clair George. It was the beginning of a six-year investigation that reached the highest levels of the American military and intelligence establishments, the most politically perilous case the Bureau had confronted since Watergate.

FBI agents quickly questioned Vice President Bush, Attorney General Meese, the president's closest White House aides, and the chieftains of the CIA. A handful of agents, working in extreme secrecy, rapidly uncovered the most important evidence in the case: five thousand computer messages among Admiral Poindexter, Colonel North, and the National Security Council staff. In a remarkable feat of forensics, FBI agents recovered and restored the backup tapes for the internal White House e-mail system that recorded the arms sales and the diversion of funds.

The FBI's evidence also compelled a remarkable confession from the president of the United States.

"For the past three months, I've been silent on the revelations about Iran," Reagan said in a televised address to the nation on March 4, 1987. "And you must have been thinking: 'Well, why doesn't he tell us what's happening? Why doesn't he just speak to us as he has in the past when we've faced troubles or tragedies?' Others of you, I guess, were thinking: 'What's he doing hiding out in the White House?'

"Well, the reason I haven't spoken to you before now is this: You deserve the truth," the president said.

"I've paid a price for my silence," he said. "A few months ago I told the American people I did not trade arms for hostages. My heart and my best intentions still tell me that's true. But the facts and the evidence tell me it is not."

The facts and the evidence showed that the highest-ranking officers of the CIA and the National Security Council had collaborated with a remarkable gang of con men and crooks in carrying out Reagan's orders. They had committed or condoned spectacular acts of folly in the arms-for-hostages deals. The president had broken his constitutional duty to faithfully execute the laws of the United States.

Reagan concluded his speech with an announcement that he hoped would restore a measure of trust in his administration: he had nominated the FBI's William Webster to be the next director of Central Intelligence. Webster was "a man of sterling reputation," the president said. "He understands the meaning of 'rule of law.' " The choice seemed to make sense: Congress and an independent counsel were investigating the top officers of the CIA, and three dozen FBI agents armed with subpoenas were thumbing through thousands of top secret files seeking evidence of perjury and obstruction of justice. The independent counsel would conclude that President Reagan, the secretary of defense, the director of Central Intelligence, and their aides had skirted or broken the law. But President George H. W. Bush eventually granted pardons to all who faced criminal charges—including the CIA's covert operations chief, Clair George, and its counterterrorism director, Duane Clarridge.

He did as Ronald Reagan had done in absolving Mark Felt and Ed Miller. He let national security trump the rule of law.

The arrival of Judge Webster nonetheless was the end of an era at the CIA. "We probably could have overcome Webster's ego, his lack of experience with foreign affairs, his small-town America world perspective," Clarridge reflected. "What we couldn't overcome was that he was a lawyer. All of his training as a lawyer and a judge was that you didn't do illegal things. He could never accept that this is *exactly* what the CIA does when it operates abroad. We break the laws of their countries. It's how we collect information. It's why we're in business."

Clarridge and his confreres at the CIA rebelled against Webster. They felt he did not grasp the essence of secret operations. Webster's successor at the FBI faced nearly identical problems.

The selection of William Sessions, a federal judge from Texas, was a strange and surprising choice to Buck Revell and the rest of the FBI's leadership. Judge Sessions seemed willfully ignorant about the FBI's role in the national security of the United States.

The FBI began to lose its focus after Judge Sessions took office on November 2, 1987. Sessions had no experience in running an organization or overseeing investigations. At his confirmation hearings, he professed to know little about the FBI's role in national security or intelligence. Once confirmed, he seemed to regard his role as largely ceremonial, and he would lose control of the FBI long before he lost his job. He spent nearly six years as director without ever gaining command of the institution or winning the loyalty of his underlings. Buck Revell thought that the FBI's counterterrorism capabilities had been "effectively neutralized" under Sessions. By the end of the 1980s, he believed, the FBI was going "down to zero in carrying out our counter-terrorism responsibilities." Sessions went closer to zero after the turn of the decade. He reassigned more than a third of the agents working on counterterrorism to street crime assignments.

The FBI clearly believed that "terrorism was not a big deal," said Richard

Marquise, who led the Bureau's Terrorism Research and Analytical Center, a tiny box near the bottom of the hierarchy at headquarters. Marquise was the son of an FBI agent, and he joined the Bureau in 1971, three years before his father retired. He had worked under every director, including Hoover. He stayed on the counterterrorism beat long after many of his colleagues had left, working against the conventional wisdom that the threat to the United States was subsiding along with the Cold War.

"Terrorists were doing things overseas," his superiors told him. "They weren't attacking us here."

Marquise thought differently: "We were all waiting for that big one to happen."

40

MOSAIC

THE INVESTIGATION OF the bombing of Pan Am Flight 103 over Lockerbie, Scotland, depended on the FBI's ability to strike alliances with CIA analysts, Scottish constables, German intelligence officers, and Libyan double agents. Those liaisons depended on trust—a confidence hard to find between cops and spies at home and abroad. The Bureau by itself could not solve a case that reached across oceans and borders.

Pan Am 103 took off from London's Heathrow Airport, bound for New York, at 6:25 P.M. on Wednesday, December 21, 1988. Half its passengers had made a tight connection from Frankfurt. Twenty-eight minutes later, an explosion tore the 747 apart. A rain of fire started falling over Lockerbie.

One hundred eighty-nine Americans were among the two hundred fifty-nine passengers and crew. Eleven people were killed on the ground. The Scottish constabulary began to collect evidence lying scattered across 845 square miles of countryside. Within a week, with the help of British intelligence, they determined that someone had hidden a high-performance explosive, Semtex, inside a checked suitcase.

The Bureau had jurisdiction under international law; the airplane was American. But its leaders had no idea how to proceed.

"The FBI was not set up to deal with a major investigation like this," said Richard Marquise. "I blame the institution."

Marquise was given command of the FBI's task force on Lockerbie—four agents and three analysts—on January 3, 1989. He scanned the passenger list for weeks, looking for clues. The list was the stuff of conspiracy theories. It included a CIA officer, Matt Gannon, and an army intelligence major, Chuck McKee, who had been working ninety-hour weeks together in Beirut, trying to free the nine American hostages still being held in Lebanon. Gannon's father-in-law was the deputy chief of the CIA's clandestine service, and he had worked for many years in the Middle East. Six State Department officers and the chief Nazi-hunter at the Department of Justice died over Lockerbie. Another passenger, an American businessman, had the same name as a terrorist who had hijacked a Kuwaiti airliner years before.

The list of suspects encompassed almost every bitter battle between Americans and Arabs in the Middle East. The new president of the United States, George H. W. Bush, thought that the Syrians were behind Lockerbie. The FBI's Buck Revell assumed the Iranians had done it: almost six months before, in July 1988, the USS *Vincennes* had shot down Iran Air 655 over the Persian Gulf, an unprovoked attack by an errant American admiral, killing 290 passengers. The CIA suspected Ahmed Jibril, a leading Palestinian terrorist, and theorized that the Iranians had hired him to blow up the plane. Then there was always Colonel Qaddafi of Libya. He had vowed to avenge the 1986 American bombing of Tripoli, itself an act of retaliation for the Berlin disco attack that had killed two American soldiers.

The only person with hard evidence was the chief constable at Lockerbie, John Boyd, whose officers scoured the hills and valleys, searching on foot. Six weeks into the investigation, after one of Boyd's men found a fragment of a radio circuit board the size of a fingertip, the FBI knew that the Semtex explosive had been packed in a black Toshiba boom box. That was the only break in the case for many months.

"It was just painfully slow," Marquise said. "In Washington, everybody wants an answer. Right now. Who did this? How did this happen?"

The FBI convened more than one hundred American, British, Scottish, and German investigators at a hotel conference room outside Washington in May 1989. Each nation, and every agency, was chasing its own leads. There was no cooperation, no real communication.

Six months after the bombing, the FBI's Lockerbie task force was disbanded. Marquise and a small group of terrorism analysts stayed on the case.

The Scots spent the summer and the fall piecing the hundreds of thousands of shards of evidence together. They got on-the-job training from FBI veterans like Richard Hahn—a man who had been combing through the wreckage of lethal bombings for fifteen years, ever since the unsolved FALN attack on the Fraunces Tavern in New York. They learned how the damage from a blast of Semtex looked different from the scorching from the heat of flame.

The Scots soon determined that bits of clothing with tags saying "Made in Malta" had been contained in a copper Samsonite Silhouette with the radio that held the bomb. But they did not tell the FBI. Then the Germans discovered a computer printout of baggage records from the Frankfurt airport; they showed a single suitcase from an Air Malta flight had been transferred to Pan Am 103 in Frankfurt. But they did not tell the Scots. The international teams of investigators reconvened in Scotland in January 1990. Once again, it was a dialogue of the deaf. Marquise had a terrible feeling that the case would never be solved.

"We're having tons of problems with CIA. Lots of rivalry," Marquise said. "Scots are off doing their thing. You've got the Germans who are giving the records when they feel like it to the Scots. The FBI's still doing its thing. . . . Everybody's still doing their own thing."

Then, in June 1990, came small favors that paid big returns. Stuart Henderson, the new senior investigator in Scotland, shared one piece of evidence with Marquise: a photograph of a tiny piece of circuit board blasted into a ragged strip of the Maltese clothing. The Scots had been to fifty-five companies in seventeen countries without identifying the fragment. "They had no idea. No clue," Marquise said. "So they said, probably tongue-in-cheek, 'You guys try. Give it a shot.'"

The FBI crime laboratory gave the photo to the CIA. An Agency analyst had an image of a nearly identical circuit board, seized four years earlier from two Libyans in transit at the airport in Dakar, Senegal. On the back were four letters: MEBO. Nobody knew what MEBO meant.

Eighteen months had passed since the bombing of Pan Am 103.

"Cut out the chains of command"

The investigation was a mosaic of supposition and surmise. Few people at the highest levels were convinced it could be solved. Someone needed to take charge.

Robert Swan Mueller III was named chief of the Criminal Division at the Justice Department at the end of July 1990. Agents instinctively liked him, despite his aristocratic demeanor. They called him Bobby Three Sticks.

Mueller had a sharp mind, a first-rate temperament, and a high regard for well-crafted cases. The future director of the FBI was a born leader. And he was a marine.

Mueller had gone from Main Line Philadelphia and Princeton to lead a rifle platoon in combat in Vietnam. An official report from a December 11, 1968, battle in Quang Tri province praised his courage during a search-and-destroy mission. Confronting a force of two hundred North Vietnam Army troops, Second Lieutenant Mueller "fearlessly moved from one position to another, directing the accurate counter-fire of his men and shouting words of encouragement to them. With complete disregard for his own safety, he . . . personally led a team across the fire-swept terrain to recover a mortally wounded Marine who had fallen in a position forward of the friendly lines." He was awarded, among other citations, the Bronze Star for valor.

His appointment at the Justice Department came at a critical moment for the FBI. Saddam Hussein had invaded Kuwait; the United States prepared to go to war in the Persian Gulf. The FBI recorded the nervous twitching of terrorism alerts, perceived as threats from Iraq to attack targets in the United States. But money and manpower allotted to counterterrorism were low and sinking. So was morale, owing in no small part to the leadership of director William Sessions. "Getting Director Sessions' full attention was challenging," said Bill Baker, the newly appointed FBI criminal division chief, who forged a close and critical alliance with Mueller.

Mueller put Marquise in full charge of the Lockerbie case. No FBI intelligence analyst ever had run a major investigation before. Marquise reported directly to Baker, and Baker to Mueller. His orders were to turn intelligence into evidence.

"We literally cut out the chains of command at headquarters," Marquise said. "We brought in the CIA. We brought the Scots. We brought MI5 to Washington. And we sat down and we said, 'We need to change the way we're doing business. We need to start doing this right . . . We need to start sharing information.' "

Marquise had never had the authority to pick up the telephone and call his counterparts in Scotland. He made that first call in November 1990. Things started to change quickly.

Marquise learned that a Scottish magistrate's court had uncovered the mystery of MEBO—Mebo was a Swiss electronics company that had been doing business with Libya for almost twenty years. Armed with that fact, he found out that an owner of the firm, Edwin Bollier, had hand-delivered a detailed letter to the U.S. Embassy in Vienna days after the Lockerbie bombing.

The FBI never would have looked for it without the tip from the Scots. It said, in essence: Pan Am 103 was a Libyan operation. Bollier knew what he was talking about: Mebo had built twenty sophisticated timers for the Libyans.

Bollier's letter—vital evidence in an international terrorism investigation—had been sitting unread for almost two years.

Marquise knew from bitter experience how often the FBI had no idea what was in its own files. The Bureau was a pyramid of paper, and it stayed that way well into the twenty-first century. While Marquise was running the FBI's Terrorism Research and Analytical Center from 1986 to 1988, the Bureau had come up with a database called the Terrorist Information System. The system was "totally useless," he said. "You'd spend all kinds of time putting things in and you couldn't get things out . . . It would have said 'No Record' for probably ninety-five percent of the major cases in the Bureau. We tried to sell it to people for years but it was so user-unfriendly. It was a great concept that didn't work."

"WE WERE GOING TO GO FORWARD"

By the start of 1991, Marquise had the rough outlines of a circumstantial case against Qaddafi and Libya. He felt a momentum building.

"We've got FBI agents teamed with Scottish cops, teamed with Maltese cops, covering leads in Malta, doing things on one sheet of music," he said. "We're sharing information incredibly. We're starting to come up with the names of Libyan intelligence officers. And one of them is a guy by the name of Abdel Baset Ali al Megrahi."

A shopkeeper in Malta picked out a picture of Megrahi as a man who had bought some of the clothing found at the crime scene in Lockerbie. Immigration records showed that Megrahi had been in Malta the same day the clothes were purchased. In February 1991, as the Gulf War raged, the FBI invited Edwin Bollier for a weeklong interview. He tentatively identified a picture of Megrahi as a Libyan who ran a front company that did business with Mebo in Zurich.

"I'm pretty excited," Marquise said. "Everybody's pretty excited." He briefed Robert Mueller, who coolly reminded him that he had a long way to go.

Marquise needed to turn intelligence into evidence. He needed a witness who could link Megrahi to the Samsonite suitcase with the Semtex. He needed to find someone who knew that the suitcase carried the bomb from Air Malta 180 to Pan Am 103. He went back to the CIA. The Agency told him, belatedly, that it had once had a Libyan informant named Abdul Majid Giaka at the international airport in Malta. He had gone on the CIA's payroll four months before Lockerbie. He was on it the night Pan Am 103 was bombed. But the Agency had dropped him a few months later, deeming him a fabricator milking his interrogators for money.

Marquise was dying to talk to Majid, no matter how dubious he seemed to the CIA. In June 1991, the Agency flew him from a navy ship off the coast of Malta to give the FBI the chance to interview him in Virginia. Justly wary of its informant, the CIA imposed one condition: Don't tell anybody.

Marquise weighed the odds and broke the rules. He picked up the telephone and called his Scottish counterpart. "If you ever tell anybody about this, I'll get fired," he said to Stuart Henderson. "The guy's in the U.S. We think he may have some information but we don't know. We're going to start to interview him tomorrow."

Majid was debriefed for at least two weeks during September 1991. He insisted that he knew three facts. He identified Megrahi as an intelligence officer serving as Libya's airline security chief. He said that Megrahi's subordinate in Malta had a cache of Semtex. And he said he had seen Megrahi with a large brown suitcase at the airport in Malta during the weeks before the Lockerbie bombing. Majid was without doubt an unreliable witness. But the FBI had faith that he was telling the truth on those three points. Marquise thought he had the foundation of a case that would stand up in court.

It came down to a question of law or war. The decision was up to the president.

The United States could try to kidnap Megrahi; it had nabbed terrorists overseas before. But snatching him in Libya was beyond the capabilities of the CIA or the military. It could try to kill him. That was beyond conscience at the time: shortly before the Lockerbie bombing, when Israel had sent a hit team to Tunis to kill Abu Jihad, the second in command of the Palestine Liberation Organization, the United States had openly condemned the act as a political assassination.

The president could attack Libya with bombs and missiles. Reagan had targeted Qaddafi after Libya's spies blew up the La Belle disco in Berlin five years before, citing the right to use force in self-defense under Article 51 of the UN Charter. But the evidence then was airtight; the Lockerbie case now demanded an equivalent proof.

President George H. W. Bush believed that terrorists were criminals, not enemy combatants. He chose to go to court. Mueller strongly concurred. They would follow the law where it led. Marquise said: "We were going to go forward with our prosecution and announce the results to the world."

Megrahi was indicted in the United States and Scotland on November 15, 1991. It took almost a decade to convict him. Another decade passed before it was clear beyond doubt that Colonel Qaddafi himself had ordered the attack on Pan Am 103 in a pitiless act of revenge against the United States and the United Kingdom. The circle of retribution was completed when an American Predator spy plane helped the colonel's enemies hunt him down before they killed him in Libya, twenty-three years after the Lockerbie attack.

41

THE BLIND SHEIKH

THE WEEK THE Pan Am 103 indictment came down, a murder trial opened in Manhattan Criminal Court. The defendant was El-Sayyid Nosair, an Egyptian immigrant wearing a white skullcap and robes, and a follower of Omar Abdel Rahman, a holy warrior known as the Blind Sheikh. Nosair was charged with the murder of Meir Kahane, the leader of the Jewish Defense League, a group later labeled a terrorist organization by the state of Israel.

Among the spectators was a $500-a-week FBI informant named Emad Salem, a balding, bearded veteran of the Egyptian army. Salem sat with the defendant's associates, chatting with them in the corridor during breaks, working his way into their lives.

Salem was an ingratiating man who had been working as a house detective at the Woodward Hotel in midtown Manhattan when Nancy Floyd, an FBI foreign counterintelligence agent, approached him in April 1991. Floyd told Salem that the hotel was frequented by suspected Russian spies. Would he help her keep watch over them?

Salem said, in so many words, Who cares about the Cold War and the Russians? I can tell you about the holy war and the Blind Sheikh.

Agent Floyd had never heard of the Blind Sheikh. Few had. But she liked Salem, which was easy to do, and she trusted him, which was a leap of faith. She recruited Salem as an informant and introduced him to a fellow FBI agent, John Anticev, who had joined the Bureau four years before and served on the Joint Terrorism Task Force in New York.

Anticev was very interested in El-Sayyid Nosair. The FBI had photographed some of his associates taking target practice with semiautomatic weapons and playing at paramilitary exercises. But the FBI never saw a terrorism connection in the Kahane murder case, or the role the Blind Sheikh had played in it. The task force had taken forty-seven boxes of evidence from Nosair's apartment after his arrest. The FBI had warehoused them. Within them was Nosair's diary, written in Arabic. It recorded the sheikh's calls for a holy war. It explicitly described plans for an attack on New York aimed at "destroying the structure of their civilized pillars . . . and their high world buildings of which they are proud."

The diary went unread for three years. At the time, the FBI had only one translator capable of reading and understanding Arabic. "If it had been properly translated, processed, authenticated and analyzed," Buck Revell later testified, the FBI would have seen "a direct association between the assassin of Meir Kahane and the group that conspired and eventually did bomb the World Trade Center."

Who could imagine that the spirit of the anarchists who bombed Wall Street and Washington at the end of World War I had been revived? Who could think that the Islamists who drove the Soviet army from Afghanistan were turning their anger on America? Who could believe the Bureau was about to confront another battle in the crusades between Christians and Muslims? It was all close to inconceivable in the spring of 1991. The investigations that the FBI's counterterrorism section opened up during those months were almost all focused on small right-wing groups—the Los Angeles Area Skinheads, the Aryan Women's League, the Texas Reserve Militia—whose members were more likely to harm themselves than to threaten the peace and security of the United States.

"We were feeling pretty good" in those days, Buck Revell said. "The Cold War had ended, we believed our side had won, Communism in the U.S. and its affiliated organizations were largely defunct. Communism as a global movement was essentially discredited. Terrorism was held in check in the U.S. and was descending on an international scale . . . All in all we had done a good job in dealing with the threat of terrorism in spite of a lot of problems along the way."

Emad Salem was offering the FBI a look into the future. The Bureau did not see it coming.

"SHAKE THE EARTH UNDER THEIR FEET"

Salem started attending Nosair's murder trial on November 4, 1991, and he quickly befriended the defendant's supporters. They were elated when the jurors brought in a split verdict. There was no question that Nosair had killed Kahane. Yet he was convicted only of gun possession and assault. The judge said at the sentencing that the jury must have been out of its collective mind. Then he gave Nosair a maximum of twenty-two years, saying: "I believe the defendant conducted a rape of this country, of our Constitution and of our laws, and of people seeking to exist peacefully together."

Salem visited Nosair at the notorious Attica state prison, making the long drive upstate and back with members of the sheikh's circle. Soon he was listening in as they plotted to bomb the symbols of American power. Salem met the sheikh, the intellectual author of the plot, and he heard first-hand about the plans to bring the jihad to America. "Salem's penetration had been so thoroughly successful that he'd had intimate access to Abdel Rahman himself, almost from the start," marveled Andrew McCarthy, a gung-ho federal prosecutor in Manhattan.

Salem gave the FBI the names and identities of almost every one of the men who were plotting to blow up the World Trade Center. He did not know their target. But his new friends told him it would be something big, something the world had never seen before. This was something new in the annals of the FBI: firsthand intelligence on a terrorist plot as it took shape.

The cell could have—and should have—been uncovered long before the attack. But the FBI's investigation stopped dead at the end of June 1992, when the Bureau dropped Emad Salem as an informant.

The decision was made by Carson Dunbar, the thirty-nine-year-old chief of the FBI's foreign counterintelligence squad in New York. He suspected that Salem was a double agent for Egyptian intelligence. Significantly, the fear that Salem might be a foreign spy outweighed his warning of a terrorist attack. But Dunbar and his agents had a deeper dread.

"We couldn't let you make a bomb," FBI agent Anticev told Salem. "If that bomb, let's say, goes off at a synagogue and kills two, three people, and that it comes out that an agent of the FBI participated in making the bomb—forget it, they would go berserk, the press would say we knew, we'd be sued, people would be fired." The Bureau would have had to bear an unspeakable shame.

FBI agent Floyd was shocked by Dunbar's decision. "This thing was handled completely wrong from the very beginning," she told Salem. She thought that "the people on the squad didn't have a clue of how to operate . . . That the supervisors didn't know what was going on. That they hadn't taken the time to learn the history."

Salem knew the history better than most. The Blind Sheikh had been one of the leaders of the Egyptian Islamic Jihad organization for many years. He preached that political violence was sanctioned by God. His imprisonment in Cairo had followed his ideological support for the 1981 assassination of President Anwar Sadat.

The sheikh had been on the State Department's terrorist watch list, with good reason, yet he had won a visa to the United States in 1990. A CIA officer working undercover as a State Department consular official had issued it—an inexplicable snafu, since the CIA's own files described him as "Egypt's most militant Sunni cleric and a close associate of the Egyptian Jihad movement."

The sheikh made no great secret of his aspirations. "We must be terrorists," he said in a January 16, 1993, sermon at his Brooklyn mosque. "We must terrorize the enemies of Islam and frighten them and disturb them and shake the earth under their feet."

"This will drive the whole world crazy"

A palace coup struck the FBI on January 19, 1993, in the final hours of the presidency of George H. W. Bush. William Sessions was accused of official misconduct in his capacity as director of the Federal Bureau of Investigation.

Isolated at headquarters, detached from his daily responsibilities, entranced by the ceremonial perquisites of his power, Sessions had frittered away his authority. An internal revolt at the Bureau had been rising in the eighteen months since Sessions sent his most powerful rival, the well-connected Buck Revell—everyone's favorite FBI agent in the Reagan and Bush administrations—to serve out the end of his career in Dallas.

Now the Justice Department had completed a 194-page report accusing Judge Sessions of petty corruption—trying to shave his income taxes, using government funds to build a $9,890 security fence at his house, blocking an investigation into an alleged sweetheart deal on his home mortgage, arrogating his powers of office for his pleasure and comfort. None of these were criminal charges. Nonetheless, the report was read as a political and personal indictment of the director's integrity and character. "I must ask you to do the right thing for your Bureau and your country," Revell wrote to Sessions. "Resign while you still have some semblance of dignity and before you do further harm to an agency that you have professed to honor and respect."

Every director of the FBI since Hoover had been confirmed by the Senate to serve a ten-year term, at the pleasure of the president. Bush could act upon the recommendation of his attorney general and remove Sessions from office before the next president was inaugurated on January 20. Or he could do nothing, and let Bill Clinton solve the problem. He decided to leave the problem to the new president, a malevolent parting gift.

Proudly defiant, Sessions refused to acknowledge the accusations. He pretended that he could not hear the calls to step down, though they came from within the Bureau itself. Six months passed—six crucial months—with a punch-drunk and powerless man sequestered in his chambers at the FBI.

The ability to command and control the FBI did not prove to be one of President Clinton's talents. Sessions sat in silent defiance. Clinton's first two nominees for attorney general quickly failed; both had hired illegal immigrants as nannies, in violation of the law. Without an attorney general, he could hardly fire the head of the FBI. Three weeks into his administration, on February 11, 1993, Clinton made his final choice: Janet Reno, the chief state prosecutor in Miami. She became the first woman attorney general and the longest-serving holder of the office in the twentieth century. As was the case with her president, she would find the FBI a source of constant sorrow.

"Quickly, when I came into office, I learned that the FBI didn't know what it had," Reno later testified. "The right hand didn't know what the left hand was doing." Agents at the dawn of the Internet age lived in a sixty-four-kilobyte world. By the time the FBI installed new information technology, it was already obsolete. Reno was shocked to discover that the FBI could not do basic database searches. The Bureau could not put its case files into a computerized system to store and retrieve information. Field offices worked in isolation from one another and from headquarters. Agents had no way to connect with one another. Even at the elite terrorist task forces, paper files stacked up on floors, potentially devastating wiretaps went unread for lack of translators, patterns went unseen.

"Sometimes I thought we had made progress, but then we'd find something else that we didn't know we didn't have," Reno said. "It was very difficult for the FBI to get that problem solved."

She began to learn the best and the worst about the FBI a few days after she took office.

On Friday, February 26, 1993, a 1,500-pound bomb loaded into a rented truck detonated in the six-story basement parking garage underneath

Tower One of the World Trade Center. It was the biggest terrorist explosion in the United States since the Black Tom blast shattered Manhattan and scarred the Statue of Liberty from across New York Harbor in 1916.

Six people died in the World Trade Center explosion, and more than a thousand were injured by the shock waves, the smoke, and the shrapnel. The concrete tiers of the basement garage collapsed down to the bedrock. The bomb crater was roughly 110 feet wide. A crucial fragment came out of the wreckage three days after the explosion: a shattered truck frame, bearing a vehicle identification number. It came from a Ryder van rented the week before in New Jersey. It was the great good fortune of the FBI that one of the conspirators was foolish enough to return to the Ryder rent-a-truck company, report the van stolen, and demand the return of his $400 deposit.

"The speed at which this occurs and the luck involved here is just phenomenal!" marveled Richard Hahn, on the scene at the World Trade Center, two decades into his FBI career as a terrorism investigator. Four of the conspirators were arrested. But the round-up was not rapid enough.

The bomb maker had fled the country. Abdul Basit Mahmoud Abdul Karim—better known as Ramzi Yousef—was a twenty-five-year-old Pakistani who had arrived in the United States from Afghanistan in December. Poised and articulate, Yousef spoke seven languages, and he had studied chemistry and engineering at British universities. He was part of a global network that reached from the canyons of Wall Street to the mountains of the Hindu Kush.

The conspiracy was still alive. Its outlines were barely visible to the FBI. Many of its members were underground in New York.

Hat in hand, the FBI's John Anticev went back to Emad Salem and asked him to go undercover again. Their conversation was bitter. Salem was furious that he had been forced out of the investigation.

"I told you they will blow bombs in New York City and you didn't do nothing about it," he railed. "You drop me out of the case."

Anticev said he had been "blocked at every turn" by the "bureaucratic bullshit" of his cautious superiors.

"I want to talk to the head of the FBI," Salem said. "The information I supplied, it was expensive and valuable enough to save the country's ass from this bomb . . . How many disasters would be created if the World Trade Centers collapse out of some stupid assholes trying to play Muslims?"

Salem did not talk to the head of the FBI, who was in any case all but incommunicado. But after an agonized debate, he went back on the FBI payroll as an informant. Salem received more than $1 million for his work. He was brave to the point of danger. At crucial turns he came close to playing the role of agent provocateur. But he made the case that put the Blind Sheikh in prison.

On May 7, 1993, Salem had a long conversation with one of the Blind Sheikh's most trusted aides, a Sudanese native named Siddig Ali. He learned that the sheikh wanted his men to blow up the United Nations—"the big house," he called it. Salem then consulted with the cleric himself. On May 23, the informant arrived at the sheikh's apartment in Jersey City, carrying a briefcase wired for sound.

"I wish to know in regards to the United Nations, do we consider it the house of the devil?" Salem said. "Because my strike is a devastating one, not a screw-up like the one that took place at the Trade Center . . ."

The sheikh responded: "Find a plan, find a plan . . . to inflict damage, inflict damage on the American army itself. But the United Nations . . . will be a disadvantage for the Muslims. It will harm them deeply."

"So forget about the United Nations?"

"No."

"We keep it in the army."

"Yes."

On May 27, Siddig told Salem that the United Nations plot was back on. And he had two new targets: the Lincoln and Holland tunnels, the lifelines connecting Manhattan to mainland America. The plan was to hit all three landmarks at once.

"The big house, I will take care of it," Siddig said. "There will be five minutes between each of them. Boom! God, the whole world! Boom! This will drive the whole world crazy."

The key conspirators met at a safe house in Queens on the evening of June 23, 1993. The building was wired for video and sound by the FBI. They started filling fifty-five-gallon oil drums with fuel oil and ammonium nitrate fertilizer, a basic recipe for homemade terrorist bombs since the 1970s. Or so they thought: Salem had sabotaged the saboteurs by supplying them with $150 worth of Scotts Super Turf Builder, a fertilizer with no explosive force.

The arrests were swift—with one exception.

The Blind Sheikh took refuge at a Brooklyn mosque. The argument over how to handle him caused great consternation at the FBI. No one in command authority wanted to make the case against him. From Sessions on down, to a man they demurred. They thought it best to ask President Hosni Mubarak of Egypt to extradite him. It would be so much easier to deport the sheikh—to make him disappear back into the Egyptian prison where he once belonged. The assistant director in charge of the FBI in New York, James Fox, was most adamantly against prosecuting the case in court.

The FBI's leaders knew an indictment would raise some harsh questions. Street agents and their superiors in New York had known about the World Trade Center bombers for many months. The terrorist task force had held the Nosair diary in its hands—and never read it. The FBI had placed Salem as an informer among the jihadis fourteen months before the bombing—and let him go.

Attorney General Reno had to stiffen their collective spine. At the end of an hour of debate with the leaders of the FBI and her top prosecutors, she tapped her knuckles on a conference table, knocking on wood, and decided to indict the sheikh on a charge of seditious conspiracy, a statute invoked very rarely since the Red raids of 1920.

The attorney general also advised the president to dismiss William Sessions as the director of the FBI for his "serious deficiencies in judgment." The Sessions years had ended with a disastrous confrontation between hundreds of FBI agents, including the hostage rescue force, and a millennial Christian sect, the Branch Davidians, in Waco, Texas. The FBI had used tear gas against the barricaded and heavily armed group, giving its leader the apocalypse he desired. Eighty of the Davidians, including twenty-five children, had died in the fire that followed. Judge Sessions let Janet Reno take the blame.

To his enduring sorrow, Bill Clinton chose yet another pious judge to run the Bureau. Louis J. Freeh had been a good FBI agent for six years and a first-rate prosecutor for a decade before he donned his black robes and ascended to the bench in 1991, at the precocious age of forty-one. He was arguably the best-qualified FBI director since J. Edgar Hoover; he thought Clinton was the most talented politician since Richard Nixon.

That made their mutual contempt all the more tragic. It undermined the FBI and ultimately damaged the United States.

42

FLAWS IN THE ARMOR

S HORTLY AFTER Louis Freeh was sworn in as the fifth director of the FBI on September 1, 1993, he turned in his White House pass. He refused to enter the Oval Office. His reasons were pure and simple. Freeh regarded President Clinton not as commander in chief but as the subject of a criminal case.

The FBI had opened the first of a never-ending series of investigations into Clinton's personal and political conduct. As a consequence, Freeh found it extraordinarily difficult to talk to Clinton on any matter. Over the course of Clinton's eight years in office, the two men spoke no more than five or six times, face-to-face or on the phone.

"He came to believe that I was trying to undo his presidency," Freeh wrote in a memoir. The director soon regretted accepting his appointment at the FBI. But he would not leave for fear that the president would replace him with a political hack.

Freeh knew the estrangement undermined the FBI. "The lost resources and lost time alone were monumental," he wrote. "So much that should have been straightforward became problematic in the extreme." But he felt compelled to keep a distance from the president. It deepened as the years went by. It became a danger to the United States.

"One of the greatest flaws that our government now faces," warned James Steinberg, the deputy national security adviser, was an FBI that stood in silence and isolation, "totally disconnected from the president or the White House."

The chief counterterrorism aides at the National Security Council, Steven Simon and Daniel Benjamin, found Freeh "extraordinarily unresponsive" to their growing fears of a terrorist attack. "His mistrust of the White House grew so strong that it seems to have blinded him," they wrote. But they knew that Clinton could do nothing about it: "The one remedy available to the President by law, dismissing Freeh, was a political impossibility. A chief executive who was being investigated by the FBI could not fire the FBI director: it would be another Saturday Night Massacre, the second coming of Richard Nixon."

Freeh, who had finished law school in the final months of the Watergate scandal, came to conclude that Clinton was worse than Nixon. The director's sense of virtue, highly developed since his days as an altar boy, served as a cleansing force after the reign of Judge Sessions, and his reverence for the Bureau, rooted in his six years as a street agent, ran deep. But they did not sanctify the FBI. His cultivation of Congress brought the Bureau a billion-dollar budget increase and thousands of new agents. But it did not make the FBI a more powerful institution of government. Freeh was personally incorruptible. But the FBI was not.

Freeh infuriated the White House almost every day for more than seven years. One case among many was the FBI's immense investigation into allegations that China's intelligence services had bought political influence at the White House through illegal campaign contributions. When President Clinton expressed disbelief at the allegations, Freeh responded that the White House was lying.

The Bureau spent far more time and energy on the case than it did on any terrorism investigation during the Clinton years. It brought several criminal charges against Chinese contributors, some of whom were influence peddlers without particular ideologies or politics. But Freeh's FBI managed to bury the fact that its most highly valued source on Chinese espionage in the United States, a politically wired California woman named Katrina Leung, had been spying for China throughout the 1980s and 1990s. All the while, she was having sex with the special agent in charge of her case, a top supervisor of the FBI's China Squad, James J. Smith—and occasionally with a leading FBI counterintelligence expert on China, William Cleveland. The Bureau paid Leung more than $1.7 million for her work as an intelligence asset.

The FBI suspected for the better part of a decade that Leung was a double agent. But no one wanted to embarrass the Bureau. The case festered for years. Not until after Freeh's departure was it clear that the Chinese, Russian, and Cuban intelligence services all had penetrated the FBI in the 1990s.

So had a member of the world's most dangerous and least-known terrorist organization. His name was Ali Mohamed. Al-Qaeda had a double agent posing as an informer for the FBI.

"MAKE THE AMERICAN PEOPLE SUFFER"

The United States did not suffer a single terrorist attack, foreign or domestic, in 1994. But the threat of a catastrophic blow against the nation became part of the everyday life of the FBI at the start of 1995.

"Merely solving this type of crime is not enough," Freeh told Congress in a written statement at the time. "It is equally important that the FBI thwart terrorism before such acts can be perpetrated." But without intelligence, the Bureau would have to depend on blind luck and shoe leather.

On the night of January 6, 1995, Ramzi Yousef, the architect of the World Trade Center bomb, was in a sixth-floor apartment in Manila, the capital of the Philippines, cooking chemicals with his colleague Abdul Hakim Murad. At about 10:45 P.M., a security guard saw the two men running downstairs, carrying their shoes. Smoke poured from their apartment window. Murad was arrested, but Yousef escaped and caught a flight out of Manila.

The police searched the apartment and found a smoldering bomb factory—chemicals, timers, batteries, fuses—along with documents and a laptop computer. The data, locked in encrypted files, took many days to decode and decipher. But they confirmed Murad's confession to the most ambitious plot in the annals of international terrorism.

The Manila plan was code-named Bojinka. Yousef and five of his allies intended to place sophisticated time bombs aboard a dozen 747s—United, Delta, and Northwest flights bound for the United States from Manila, Tokyo, Seoul, Singapore, Bangkok, and Taipei. Each man would board a flight, leave on its first stopover, and catch another connection. A few hours later, the bombs would bring down the 747s over the Pacific. If the flights were full and the plot went off as planned, roughly 3,500 people would die over the course of a day, as the bombs exploded one by one.

The United States announced a $2 million reward for information leading to the arrest of Yousef. Three weeks later, one of his cohorts cashed in.

On February 7, the Pakistani military intelligence service, in the company of a handful of armed State Department security officers, arrested Yousef at a bed-and-breakfast not far from the U.S. Embassy in Islamabad. The next day, three FBI agents flew him back to the United States. On the plane, Yousef proudly claimed credit for the World Trade Center bombing. Lew Schiliro, the FBI's top agent in New York, met the flight and escorted a blindfolded Yousef onto a helicopter. They were headed for the Metropolitan Correctional Center in lower Manhattan.

The night was clear and cold. The helicopter banked over New York Harbor. "We allowed him to remove the blindfold," Schiliro remembered. "He focused his eyes as the helicopter was adjacent to the World Trade Center. One of the agents that was onboard the helicopter said to Mr. Yousef that the World Trade Center was still standing. And in no uncertain terms, Yousef's response was 'It would not have been, had we had more money.'"

On March 20, a millennial Japanese cult called Aum Shinrikyo, led by a blind guru claiming to be Jesus Christ incarnate, released vials of home-made nerve gas inside five subway cars in Toyko. Fifteen people were killed, dozens blinded, and thousands injured. Aum Shinrikyo had thousands of members, controlled tens of millions of dollars, and already had conducted attempts at mass murder using anthrax and botulism. But not a single American intelligence officer knew anything about the cult.

On April 12, the police in Manila turned Abdul Hakim Murad over to FBI special agents Frank Pellegrino and Tom Donlon. Their captive spoke freely to the agents as they flew to Alaska, refueled, and took off for New York. He was a Kuwaiti who had attended two flight schools in the United States; he had dreamed of hijacking a plane in Washington and crashing it into the headquarters of the CIA. Murad told the FBI agents that he had been working on the Bojinka plot with Ramzi Yousef for six months. He said the goal was "to make the American people and the American government suffer" for the foreign policy of the United States in the Middle East.

On April 19, a rented Ryder truck loaded with 4,800 pounds of fuel oil and ammonium nitrate blew up the nine-story federal government headquarters in Oklahoma City, Oklahoma. Terrorism experts on television immediately blamed the attack on Islamic fundamentalists. But the perpetrator was a patriotic American. A right-wing militant named Timothy McVeigh had chosen the second anniversary of the Branch Davidian disaster in Texas to attack an outpost of the government of the United States. A highway patrolman arrested McVeigh ninety minutes after the explosion. He was speeding down the interstate with a gun in his glove box and no license plates on his car. The FBI found the axle of his rented truck, with its telltale vehicle identification number, two blocks from the blast. The evidence was ironclad within two days, though the FBI relentlessly conducted twenty-five thousand interviews over the next two years. The Oklahoma City bombing was by far the deadliest terrorist attack in the history of the United States. The explosion killed 168 people and wounded 850.

On April 24, the president of the California Forestry Association, the timber industry lobbying group, was killed by a bomb inside a package mailed to his office. It was the latest of sixteen deadly attacks attributed by the FBI to an unknown suspect. The investigation—called UNABOM because the first targets were universities and airlines—had been going on for seventeen years.

This eleven-week barrage of bombs and plots seemed disconnected—a madman in the Midwest, a millennial cult in Japan, a jihad cell in Manila. But there were patterns in it. Bomb throwers once wanted to create political theater. Now they wanted to burn the theater down. Terrorism once had been a game of nations. Now it was starting to look like a global gang war.

Terrorism was in a state of transformation. Counterterrorism was not.

After the Manila bomb plot was discovered, President Clinton sought a dramatic expansion of the FBI's wiretapping and surveillance powers. The most conservative Congress in twenty years stopped him. Congress stripped the bill of its major statutes—and revived them all six years later in the Patriot Act.

Months of haggling left only three meaningful measures. The new legislation controlled the sale of explosives. It created secret trial procedures for terrorism suspects. And it gave the president a green light to "disrupt, dismantle and destroy international infrastructures used by international terrorists." *International infrastructures* was political language. The intent of the law was clear: destroy the terrorists. But first the United States had to find them.

On June 21, 1995, Clinton signed a secret order intended to create a new regime of American counterterrorism. He placed the FBI at its pinnacle. How this could work when the president and the FBI director would not speak was left, like so much else, unsaid.

"We will not allow terrorism to succeed," Presidential Decision Directive 39 (PDD 39) began. "Through our law-enforcement efforts, we shall make clear that there is no higher priority than the pursuit, arrest, and prosecution of terrorists."

PDD 39 placed the FBI in charge of detecting hidden arsenals of nuclear, biological, and chemical weapons with "robust and rapidly deployable counterterrorism teams." Hoover had started worrying about that threat nearly fifty years before. The FBI had fewer than five agents dedicated to weapons of mass destruction in 1995. Attorney General Reno immediately asked Congress for 175 more. She got them.

The directive made the rendition of terrorist suspects—kidnapping them abroad and bringing them to trial—"a matter of the highest priority" for the FBI. Rendition had been used rarely, and with fanfare, under Presidents Reagan and Bush in the past decade. It would become a commonplace under Clinton, but carried out in secret.

The president told the Bureau to "collect, analyze and disseminate intelligence on terrorist groups and on activities of international terrorists in the United States." That order had no real precedent. The FBI could gather intelligence well enough. But it had no capacity to analyze it. It lacked three essential elements: it did not have the people, it did not have the computers, and it did not have the time.

The directive contained one hurdle still higher: "The Directors of Central Intelligence and FBI together shall personally ensure that their Agencies achieve maximum cooperation regarding terrorism," it said. "The CIA and FBI shall ensure timely exchanges of terrorist information." They had to share intelligence. They had to talk to one another. They had to work together.

The task of enforcing this shotgun wedding fell to one of the authors of the presidential directive, the intelligence director of the National Security Council, a cigar-chomping, tightly wound, forty-two-year-old staff man named George J. Tenet. On July 3, 1995, twelve days after the president signed the order, Tenet took office as the deputy director of Central Intelligence. He ran the CIA from day to day, and he continued to run it for the next nine years. He soon became the acting director, then the director, and Louis Freeh swore him in at his ascension.

Forging links with the FBI was one of the many seemingly impossible missions Tenet faced. He thought he could make it happen. He started by making friends with Freeh. Tenet's parents ran a Greek diner in Queens. Freeh's father had been a trucking company dispatcher in Brooklyn. The two men got along; they trusted each other. Maybe the FBI and the CIA could get along as well.

They decided to trade counterterrorism chiefs. Four senior FBI agents were seconded to the Agency; four CIA officers were deputized at the Bureau. The swap became known as the hostage exchange program. Almost no one volunteered.

Dale Watson, the FBI assistant special agent in charge in Kansas City, was selected as the first hostage. He was informed that he would become the number-two man at the CIA's new counterterrorism center. He was as qualified as anyone: he had worked the Oklahoma City bombing as well as the Bureau's counterintelligence operations against Iranian spies. Watson weighed the chances of success and decided to stay in Kansas City. He said no twice. The third time was an order. He would rise in two years' time to become the FBI's counterterrorist in chief.

Watson learned quickly on his new assignment that the Bureau and the Agency could perform remarkable feats of detection together. What to do with the intelligence they gathered was another question.

The FBI had obtained Ramzi Yousef's address book from the police in the Philippines. Tracing the names and telephone numbers in the book, the Bureau discovered that a man in the emirate of Qatar using the name Khalid Sheikh had sent a $660 wire transfer to one of the World Trade Center bombers only days before the attack. The CIA learned five facts about the man in Qatar. He worked as a government engineer. He was Ramzi Yousef's uncle. He was deeply involved in the plot to blow up 747s. He had been associated with al-Qaeda and its affiliates for seven years. His full name was Khalid Sheikh Mohammed.

A sealed and secret indictment against him was handed up by a federal grand jury in New York at the start of 1996. The CIA and the FBI located him in Doha, the capital of Qatar, a nation newly allied with the American military. They conferred in secret with the American ambassador, Patrick Theros, who had been the State Department's counterterrorism deputy. Together they decided to ask the emir of Qatar for his help in hunting down Khalid Sheikh Mohammed. The emir stalled. One of his ministers sent word to the suspect that the Americans were after him. Fleeing to a remote province of Pakistan, beyond the reach of American intelligence and law enforcement, and then across the border to Afghanistan, Khalid Sheikh Mohammed began working with al-Qaeda on a plan to finish what the World Trade Center bombers had started.

Watson came to understand that terrorists in the most remote nations on earth could strike the United States at will, attacking embassies, military bases, and other symbols of American power. The FBI as constituted could not dismantle or destroy them. It would have to be remade for that mission.

The Bureau had received hundreds of millions of dollars in extra funds from Congress to hire hundreds of new agents and intelligence analysts for the war on terror. Freeh doubled the number of his overseas legal attachés, creating an FBI presence in nations like Saudi Arabia and Pakistan. He met with dozens of kings, princes, emirs, and other heads of state in his effort to create a worldwide intelligence service. The FBI now had unquestioned authority to take the lead when terrorists killed Americans abroad. Freeh himself took command of the investigation of the bombing of Khobar Towers in Dhahran, on the edge of the Persian Gulf in Saudi Arabia, on June 25, 1996.

Nineteen American military personnel had been killed, and 372 injured, when a tanker truck packed with explosives destroyed the eight-story Khobar Towers housing complex. The bomb was slightly bigger than the one in Oklahoma City. The dead were members of the 4404th Fighter Wing, which patrolled the skies over Iraq, enforcing a no-fly zone from the King Abdul Aziz Airbase.

Freeh dispatched hundreds of agents and forensics experts to Dhahran, and he personally went with them. He remembered them sifting through tons of debris in the blazing heat, "exhausted, many sick and dehydrated, working until they literally dropped, in some cases, down on their knees, digging with their fingers," sorting bits of human flesh and bone.

Freeh became obsessed with the case. Thirteen Saudis were implicated, but Freeh surmised, through circumstantial evidence, that the government of Iran was behind the bombing. He thought the case against Iran could be made in court. He also thought that he could flatter and cajole Saudi princes into sharing criminal evidence and, ultimately, handing over the suspects. When his charm offensive failed, he lashed out—first at the royal family, then at the president. Freeh became convinced that Clinton lacked the political will and the moral force to avenge the Americans killed at Khobar. He thought the United States should retaliate against Iran for an act of war. He pushed the case with a passionate and personal devotion for five years. But he was almost alone in his judgments. He did not persuade the White House, the State Department, the Pentagon, or the Justice Department to punish Iran's mullahs or the Iranian military. Freeh was forced to conclude that "Khobar represented a national security threat far beyond the capability or authority of the FBI."

While Freeh haggled with Saudi princes, the FBI opened a criminal case against the Saudi pariah Osama bin Laden in September 1996. He had been described in the CIA's files up until then as a wealthy financier who bankrolled terrorism. But days before, bin Laden had issued his first declaration of war against the United States. In a message from Afghanistan, published by an Arabic-language newspaper in London, he had praised the Khobar bombing and warned America to withdraw its troops from Saudi Arabia.

"Nothing between us needs to be explained," bin Laden wrote. "There is only killing."

"WHAT KIND OF WAR?"

The FBI's investigation into bin Laden was not a paper case. The Bureau had a witness.

An al-Qaeda defector, Jamal al-Fadl, a Sudanese who had stolen $110,000 from bin Laden's coffers in Khartoum, had turned up at the U.S. Embassy in the neighboring nation of Eritrea, on the Horn of Africa, at the start of the summer. "I have information about people, they want to do something against your government," he told a State Department officer. "I told her I was in Afghanistan and I work with group and I know in fact those people, they try to make war against your country and they train very hard, they do their best to make war against your country."

"What kind of war?" she asked al-Fadl.

"Maybe they try to do something inside United States and they try to fight the United States Army outside, and also they try make bomb against some embassy outside," he replied. "I work with them more than nine years."

Three CIA officers debriefed al-Fadl for three weeks. Then, in the newfound spirit of counterterrorism cooperation, the Agency turned him over to the FBI.

Daniel Coleman, a grizzled twenty-three-year FBI veteran attached to the Joint Terrorism Task Force in New York and the CIA's counterterrorism center, flew to Germany with Patrick Fitzgerald, a young prosecutor in charge of national security cases at the federal courthouse in Manhattan. They talked to al-Fadl every day for two weeks. They brought him back to New York, and he remained in the Bureau's around-the-clock custody for the next two years. Coleman and his fellow agents came to like him. They nicknamed him Junior.

By January 1997, Junior had given the FBI a deep look at al-Qaeda's origins, its structure, its ambitions, and its leaders. He told the FBI that bin Laden had been vowing to attack the United States for at least three years. America was a snake, bin Laden had said to his followers. Al-Qaeda had to cut off its head.

That same month, Dale Watson returned to FBI headquarters as chief, International Terrorism Section, National Security Division. On orders from the director, Watson spent an inordinate amount of time chasing shadows in the Khobar Towers case. But he was now more interested in the future than the past. He had learned a lot at the CIA. The Agency had thousands of people sitting and thinking. One of his core missions was to find a way for the FBI to think.

Clinton's Presidential Decision Directive 39 had ordered the Bureau to analyze secret intelligence on terrorist threats, and to create strategies to disrupt and destroy them before they struck again. Freeh had promised to deploy a squadron of strategic analysts for that mission. Strategic analysis was the big picture, the power to know what your enemy is thinking. It was not about what happened five minutes ago, but what might happen five months from now; not a smart guess, but sifted and refined intelligence. Without it, taking action usually was a shot in the dark.

Watson looked around headquarters wondering: Where were all the analysts? They had been hired in 1995 and 1996, fifty or more of them, many with advanced degrees. But they had been shocked at the state of intelligence at the FBI. Where were the computers? Where were the data? Most of the new hires left within a year. They felt they had been treated like furniture, not federal investigators. By the turn of the century, the FBI had one analyst working on al-Qaeda.

Watson presided over the FBI's Radical Fundamentalist Unit and a new Osama bin Laden Unit. He had seven agents, including Dan Coleman, working on the bin Laden case, under the assistant special agent in charge of counterterrorism in New York, John O'Neill. But at headquarters, "no one was thinking about the counterterrorism program—what the threat was and what we were trying to do about it," Watson said. "And when that light came on, I realized that, hey, we are a reactive bunch of people, and reactive will never get us to a prevention." No one was thinking about where al-Qaeda's next target might be—and "no one was really looking."

But one FBI agent was talking about it in public, and that was O'Neill. He was a showboat and a self-promoter, but he studied al-Qaeda with a steely gaze. O'Neill believed, and he would tell anyone who listened, that the group had the capability to strike the United States at a time and place of its choice. "The balance of power has shifted," he warned in a speech in Chicago that spring. "No intelligent state will attack the United States in the foreseeable future because of our military superiority. So the only way these individuals can attack us and have some effect is through acts of terrorism."

Freeh had promised to come up with a plan to meet the threat. He assured Congress that he would "double the 'shoe-leather' for counterterrorism investigations." But that promise came after Congress had already tripled his counterterrorism budget to $301 million a year and increased the FBI's spending from $2.4 billion to $3.4 billion under Clinton. On paper, Freeh had 1,300 agents and an equal number of analysts and support staff assigned to counterterrorism. In reality, the force was not nearly as strong as the numbers made it seem.

The FBI's fifty-six field offices were supposed to draw up counterterrorism strategies and report to headquarters. Section chiefs at headquarters would incorporate the field office reports into elements of a five-year strategy. Division chiefs would absorb that work and report to the director. The director would come up with a Strategic Plan, capital S, capital P. The FBI had been working on the Strategic Plan since the attack on the World Trade Center. It was never done.

Watson came to confide in Richard Clarke, the counterterrorism chief at the White House. Clarke worked around the clock. His hair had gone gray in his forties, and his skin was as pale as skim milk. He looked like he had been living in a bomb shelter for a decade, waiting for the bombs to fall. In a way, that was true. Clarke had Oliver North's old office at the National Security Council suite next to the White House. A sign on the mantel of the nineteenth-century fireplace read: THINK GLOBALLY/ACT LOCALLY. Clinton gave him a title to go with his responsibilities: national counterterrorism coordinator.

Clarke was trying to coordinate everything from the Pentagon down to the police. He wanted to raise the fear of terrorism in the United States to the right level. He wanted to protect Americans from attack—a goal he saw as "almost the primary responsibility of the Government"—but he had little faith in Freeh's ability to assist in that mission. He thought the FBI had no concept of the terrorist threat to America. "They never provided analysis to us, even when we asked for it," he said. "I don't think that throughout that ten-year period we really had an analytical capability of what was going on in this country."

Clarke believed that "Freeh should have been spending his time fixing the mess the FBI had become, an organization of fifty-six princedoms without any modern information technology to support them. He might have spent more time hunting for terrorists in the United States, where Al Qaeda and its affiliates had put down roots." Instead, he was playing the role of chief investigator in the Khobar Towers and Chinese espionage investigations. But Clarke thought that "his personal involvement appeared to contribute to the cases going down dark alleys, empty wells."

Watson came to a graver conclusion. He told Clarke: "We have to smash the FBI into bits and rebuild it."

"I WANTED TO HURT THE BUREAU"

The director was trying to keep that from happening.

Freeh faced a cascading series of calamities as President Clinton was sworn in for his second term, on January 20, 1997. His falling-out with the White House was now complete. Freeh did not speak to the president at all for almost four years.

Attorney General Reno made it clear in public and in private that her trust in Freeh was broken. The break came the week before Clinton's re-election, when the chief of the FBI's violent crime section pleaded guilty to obstruction of justice—the highest-ranking headquarters man ever imprisoned for a felony. He had destroyed documents about the Hostage Rescue Team's killing of the wife of a right-wing militant during a confrontation in the remote Idaho town of Ruby Ridge; an FBI sharpshooter had taken the woman's life as she cradled her eleven-month-old daughter in her arms. There were no warrants for her arrest. She was not wanted for a crime. Freeh was forced to acknowledge that the FBI had violated the Constitution by allowing its agents to shoot on sight. In a fit of virtue, Freeh then destroyed the career of his deputy director, once his good friend, for sending the team to the scene of the standoff.

Freeh came close to the breaking point himself. He had accused the president of lying, and the president returned his fire, during the four-year-long investigations of campaign contributors and crooked politicos who had tried to influence Clinton. The independent prosecutor who worked these cases in tandem with the FBI was near the end of his rope, after spending $30 million, until he heard that a twenty-four-year-old former White House intern named Monica Lewinsky had granted Clinton sexual favors. The FBI watched over the White House physician as he executed an order to extract Clinton's DNA, by taking a blood sample from the president's arm. With that evidence came proof that the president had lied under oath about the affair. Many months of entertaining torment ensued, ending with a formal impeachment in the House, a trial in the Senate, and a hung jury verdict.

Freeh saw the investigation as a matter of principle: Clinton had forfeited his political life and his immortal soul for a few minutes of private pleasure. The president saw it as "a Stalinist show trial," a political search-and-destroy mission, "an unconscionable waste of the FBI's assets"—hundreds of agents "who could have been working on crime, drugs, terror, things that actually make a difference"—and thus a danger to the security of the United States. The director of the Secret Service, Lew Merletti, whose job was to protect the president's life, understandably agreed. While the FBI was "investigating the foibles of the President and Monica," he said, "a number of senior al Qaeda operatives were traveling the United States."

Freeh had his own scandals to investigate. A decade earlier, FBI espionage operations in New York had started to go wrong. Now the Bureau thought it knew why. A member of the foreign counterintelligence squad had begun stealing secret documents and selling them to the Russians in the summer of 1987. He had continued to spy for Moscow after the end of the Cold War.

Earl Pitts had seemed like an archetype of an agent: he was good-looking, square-jawed, buttoned-down, once an army captain and a law clerk for a conservative federal judge. But three months after he arrived in his new post, he was spying for Moscow. It took the FBI a decade to detect him.

"I wanted to hurt the Bureau," he said in a jailhouse confession after he received a twenty-seven-year sentence on June 27, 1997. He insisted that he was a patriot who loved his country, and yet he hated the FBI, in which he had served for fourteen years, with a passion. "The Bureau prides itself on keeping secrets," he said. "And I was going to hurt that." His baffled interrogators could only conclude that he was a well-mannered madman. "Nothing was sacred to Pitts," said the federal prosecutor in the case.

The true cost of the treason committed by the traitors in American counterintelligence during the 1980s and 1990s can be measured in blood and treasure. A dozen or more foreign agents who worked for the Bureau and the CIA were executed. American perceptions of major political and military developments abroad were manipulated by disinformation fed to the United States by Moscow. Many hundreds of millions of dollars spent on the secret development of American weapons went to waste. The Russians, the Chinese, and the Cubans misled and mystified the FBI, sending hundreds of agents down blind alleys for years on end.

Counterintelligence was a crucial ingredient of counterterrorism. It was the one field where the CIA and the FBI had to cooperate at all costs. If they failed, the United States was in danger. Terrorists and spies alike struck at flaws in America's armor, looking for its heart.

43

AN EASY TARGET

O N AUGUST 21, 1997, the FBI's Dan Coleman walked out of the United States Embassy in Nairobi, Kenya, hunting for al-Qaeda.

Marine sentries guarded the doorway of the ugly brown building, three steps from a sidewalk teeming with street preachers and homeless children. Guided by Kenyan police through the gray streets, Coleman and two CIA colleagues drove through the heart of the biggest city in East Africa.

They arrived at the squalid home of Wahid el-Hage, a naturalized American citizen, born a Catholic in Lebanon, who had lived for years in Texas. He was not home that day. He was in Afghanistan with Osama bin Laden.

Coleman was following a solid lead: Junior al-Fadl had identified el-Hage as al-Qaeda's African quartermaster. Inside his house, while the Kenyan police double-talked el-Hage's American wife, Coleman seized diaries, business records, and a PowerBook. A CIA technician copied the computer's hard drive. It held messages to and from key members of al-Qaeda in Nairobi. "The cell members in East Africa are in great danger," one message said. "They should know that now they have become America's primary target."

The Kenyan police told el-Hage upon his return to Nairobi that his life was in danger. He and his family flew back to the United States. Within days, he was under interrogation by the FBI and the federal grand jury in New York. On September 23, 1997, he was asked about the last time he had seen bin Laden and what he knew about al-Qaeda's plans to strike American military and diplomatic outposts. He was questioned about al-Qaeda's operational status in the United States and seventeen other nations, including Kenya, Saudi Arabia, Egypt, and Afghanistan. He was grilled about the people whose names appeared in his notebooks.

One was a man who had been known to the FBI for almost five years: Ali Mohamed.

"I was introduced to al Qaeda"

Ali Mohamed had volunteered his services to the FBI shortly after the first World Trade Center bombing in 1993. At first glance, he must have seemed like a godsend.

Mohamed was a fit, fair-skinned, clean-cut man of forty, a seventeen-year veteran of the Egyptian military, who had offered himself to both the CIA and the United States Army. The army said yes. He had taken a four-month training course for foreign officers at Fort Bragg, California, and he joined the army in 1986. He was only a supply sergeant. But he had given lectures on Islamic terrorism to Green Berets at the Special Operations Command in Fort Bragg, and his superiors had commended him for his work.

He applied for a job at the FBI in 1990 and again in 1991, seeking work as an Arabic-language specialist who could conduct interviews, listen to wiretaps, and translate documents. At the time, the Bureau was not accepting Arabic-speakers, but the San Francisco office bit when Mohamed offered up well-concocted stories suggesting a criminal connection between Mexican smugglers and Palestinian terrorists. Though his application to become a full-time translator was still pending, he was on the books as an FBI informant by 1992.

In April 1993, Mohamed had driven to Vancouver to pick up a friend at the airport. But his colleague—a fellow Egyptian army veteran who had joined the jihad—had been detained after he was found to be in possession of two forged Saudi passports. The Royal Canadian Mounted Police had questioned Mohamed as well. He explained that he was working for the FBI and he offered the telephone number of his Bureau contact in San Francisco. The Canadians released Mohamed after the agent vouched for him.

When Mohamed returned to California, he told the FBI an astonishing story. The Bureau's agents did not comprehend him.

Mohamed had revealed that he had secretly joined the Egyptian Islamic Jihad organization after his first training course at Fort Bragg. "I was introduced to al Qaeda—al Qaeda is the organization headed by Osama bin Laden—through my involvement with the Egyptian Islamic Jihad," Mohamed later told a federal judge, recounting what he had told the FBI. He had "conducted military and basic explosives training for al Qaeda in Afghanistan," as well as "intelligence training . . . how to create cell structures that could be used for operations."

It was the first time that anyone at the FBI had ever heard of al-Qaeda or bin Laden.

The Bureau's agents in San Francisco had not reported his revelations to Washington or New York. In the meantime, he had returned to work for al-Qaeda, helping to build the Nairobi cell. At bin Laden's command, he had gone to Nairobi to stake out potential targets for a bombing. He took photographs of the U.S. Embassy and brought them to bin Laden in Khartoum, the capital of Sudan. Bin Laden looked at the pictures and pointed to the ramp leading to an underground garage. He said that would be the best place to drive a truck laden with explosives.

The next time the FBI contacted Ali Mohamed, they had an ominous conversation. A defense lawyer preparing for the sedition trial of the Blind Sheikh notified the federal prosecutor, Andrew McCarthy, that he wanted Mohamed to testify at the trial. On McCarthy's orders, the FBI's Harlan Bell, one of the very few Arabic-speaking special agents in the Bureau, tracked down Mohamed by telephone in Nairobi and told him that they needed to talk. Mohamed flew back to California for a tense confrontation with Bell and McCarthy, in a conference room in Santa Barbara on December 9, 1994.

"He had been pitched to me as an engaging friendly by his handlers—FBI agents in Northern California with whom he was purportedly cooperating," McCarthy recalled. "It quickly became clear who was picking whose pocket." McCarthy came away from the conversation with a gut feeling that the Bureau was being conned by a terrorist; he thought "the FBI should be investigating him rather than allowing him to infiltrate." But McCarthy did not have the information he needed to confirm his instinct, because the Bureau had withheld what it knew about its informant: "It was not until much later that I learned Mohamed had told FBI agents in California that bin Laden ran an organization called al Qaeda."

The members of the FBI's new Radical Fundamentalist Unit knew nothing about Ali Mohamed and al-Qaeda at the time. They usually had no idea what investigations their colleagues were pursuing. Nor did their supervisors really know what was going on in the field. The FBI had individual experts but no institutional knowledge. The FBI's fifty-six field offices worked in isolation. Agents rarely talked to analysts. The terrorism task forces across the country rarely talked to headquarters. And the director still was not talking to the White House.

"Kill the Americans"

In early September 1997, two weeks after he left Nairobi, Dan Coleman confronted Ali Mohamed over a meal at a Sacramento restaurant. The Egyptian was working as a security guard for a California military contractor. While the two men talked, FBI agents searched Mohamed's home and mirror-imaged his computer.

Their conversation was one-sided. Coleman's interview notes record a barrage of taunts: "MOHAMED stated . . . that he loved bin Laden and believed in him. MOHAMED admitted that he had trained people in 'war zones' and added that war zones can be anywhere. MOHAMED indicated that he knew lots of people and was well trusted and could put people together with people that they need."

A stronger warning came on February 23, 1998. Bin Laden and his new ally, Ayman al-Zawahiri, the leader of the Egyptian Islamic Jihad group, sent a proclamation from Afghanistan. The two men had joined forces, creating the first global terrorist group, and their words were published across the world.

"We issue the following fatwa to all Muslims," they said. "To kill the Americans and their allies—civilians and military—is an individual duty for every Muslim who can do it in any country in which it is possible to do it."

Using the fruits of Dan Coleman's investigation in Nairobi, the federal prosecutor in charge of the New York grand jury, Patrick Fitzgerald, was preparing an indictment against bin Laden. Attorney General Janet Reno authorized the monitoring of al-Qaeda's cell phones and satellite phones inside and outside the United States. But as the surveillance started picking up signs and signals of a gathering attack, the investigation began to sputter and stall.

The FBI kept hunting for al-Qaeda in Africa. The CIA was preparing to capture or kill bin Laden in Afghanistan. They had between them evidence of his next attack in hand: the el-Hage files and the wiretaps on four telephones in Nairobi revealed the identities of at least four men in an al-Qaeda bomb plot. But America's leading counterterrorists were too busy making war on one another to perfect their plans.

The chief of the FBI's national security division, John O'Neill, refused to share the el-Hage files with the Agency. After the CIA seized al-Qaeda records in a raid in Azerbaijan, the head of the CIA's Bin Laden Unit, Michael Scheuer, refused to share them with the FBI. The two men built walls mortared by mutual hatred. When O'Neill died in the second World Trade Center attack, Scheuer said his death was "the only good thing" that happened that day. "O'Neill poisoned relations between the FBI and the CIA," Scheuer said. "He withheld information from the FBI's partners in the intelligence community; he misled the congressional intelligence committees; and he disrupted anti-al-Qaeda operations overseas."

"Steeled toward waiting for the fall"

The United States ambassador to Kenya, Prudence Bushnell, remembered everything that happened when the bomb exploded in Nairobi on August 7, 1998.

"I thought to myself that the building was going to collapse, that I was going to tumble down all those stories, and that I was going to die, and every cell in my body was just steeled toward waiting for the fall," she said.

She was covered with blood, but whether it was her own or the blood of others, she could not tell. "I saw the charred remains of what was once a human being," she recalled. "I saw the back of the building completely ripped off, and utter destruction, and I knew that no one was going to take care of me."

Two men in a pickup truck loaded with a ton of explosives had driven to the entrance of the embassy's underground parking lot, just as bin Laden had instructed Ali Mohamed four years before. The explosion shattered the embassy from its façade to its back wall, and brought down a commercial office building next door. Twelve Americans and 212 Kenyans died. Nearly five thousand people were injured, many blinded and mutilated by flying glass.

The ambassador knew there was an al-Qaeda cell in Nairobi, and she strongly suspected bin Laden wanted to attack her embassy. "I had been told in Washington that we wanted to disrupt his activities, which seemed pretty sensible," she said. Then an Egyptian had walked into the embassy and informed a CIA officer that the building would be bombed. "I was assured that the guy had done the same thing a number of times to other embassies in Africa," the ambassador said. "He was considered a flake." He was not. He was one of the bombers that struck the U.S. Embassy in Dar es Salaam, Tanzania, a few minutes after the Nairobi attack, killing eleven people and wounding eighty-five.

The first wave of FBI agents—more than 250 of them—started arriving in Nairobi overnight. The Bureau eventually deployed close to 900 people on the East Africa embassy bombings, the biggest overseas investigation in its history.

Ambassador Bushnell did not want them to appear as an occupying army. She had "tough negotiations about whether they would come with guns," and she convinced the special agent in charge of the arriving force, Sheila W. Horan, one of the first women ever to hold power at the FBI, to make the agents wear street clothes, carry their weapons discreetly, and work with the Kenyan police. "It was the Kenyans who were knocking on doors, but nobody was particularly fooled," the ambassador said. "The last thing I needed was to deal with lies about how people were being treated by the police and FBI."

The first man to confess was Mohamed Odeh, a Palestinian born in Saudi Arabia, raised in Jordan, and educated in the Philippines. He had been arrested by the immigration police in the international airport in Karachi, Pakistan, carrying a crudely forged passport and bearing chemical traces of explosives on his body. It took a week before he was returned to Kenya and interviewed by the FBI. By then, the police had searched his residence in Nairobi, where they found sketches of the area surrounding the American embassy, along with budget ledgers for weapons and training.

Odeh sat down with the FBI's John Anticev—the same agent who had handled the undercover investigation of the first World Trade Center bombing—at police headquarters in Nairobi on August 15. The suspect told the story of his life. He had pledged loyalty to bin Laden and al-Qaeda five years before, in Peshawar, Pakistan. He had been working on the Nairobi bomb plot for months.

"He stated that the reason he was talking to us now was because the people that he was with were pushing him and pushing him and pushing him and they're all gone and he's left here facing big problems," Anticev recounted. Odeh thought the bombing was "a blunder. He didn't like the fact that so many civilians and Kenyans were killed. He said that the bombing of Khobar Towers was a hundred times better and that the individual who drove the truck with the explosives should have got it into the building or died trying."

It soon became clear that Odeh was denouncing his confederate—the second man to confess.

Mohamed al-Owhali had been riding shotgun in the truck that destroyed the embassy. He had panicked at the last moment. When a Kenyan security guard refused to raise the wooden bar at the entrance to the parking garage, al-Owhali jumped from the truck, tossed a stun grenade, and fled on foot. Badly wounded by the explosion, he had stopped at his hotel and then checked himself into a hospital. The hotel clerk alerted the Kenyan police, who found him at the hospital, searched him, pulled a detailed copy of the plans for the bombing from his pants pocket, and arrested him.

"He wanted to tell his entire story from the beginning to the end," said the FBI's Steve Gaudin, who began to take the suspect's confession in a crowded Nairobi police station over the course of the next week. Gaudin had been on vacation at the New Jersey shore when called to duty in Nairobi. He had never worked an international terrorism case. He would work on nothing else for the next five years.

Al-Owhali was a wealthy twenty-one-year-old Saudi, born in Liverpool, England, educated not only in the Koran and the sharia religious laws, but in history and political science. He had left his family to join the jihad in Afghanistan two years before. "He had met with Mr. bin Laden several times and had expressed to him interest in missions that he would like to do," the FBI agent said. "Mr. bin Laden told him: 'Take your time. Your mission will come in time.'"

The interrogation went deep into the plans and the goals of al-Qaeda. "Al-Owhali explained to me that Osama bin Laden is at the very top of al-Qaeda but that he has several senior military leaders directly under him, and that bin Laden provides the political objectives to these military leaders," Gaudin said. "These people would then provide the instructions down to the lower chains of command." That summer, al-Owhali had learned that his mission was to serve as a suicide bomber.

"There were several reasons why the embassy in Nairobi was picked," al-Owhali told Gaudin. "First, there was a large American presence at the U.S. Embassy in Nairobi; the ambassador of the U.S. Embassy was a female, and if the bomb resulted in her being killed, it would further the publicity for the bombing. There were also a number of Christian missionaries at the embassy. And lastly . . . it was an easy target."

Al-Owhali completed his confession by revealing bin Laden's grandest ambitions: "There are targets in the U.S. that we could hit, but things aren't ready yet, we don't have everything prepared to do that yet," he told Gaudin. "We have to have many attacks outside the United States and this will weaken the U.S. and make way for our ability to strike within the United States."

The FBI relayed the confessions from Nairobi to Washington. For the first time, the United States had ironclad evidence that it was under attack by al-Qaeda.

On August 20, 1998, President Clinton retaliated with a barrage of cruise missiles. The targets were training camps outside Khost, Afghanistan, and a pharmaceutical factory outside Khartoum, Sudan. The CIA thought bin Laden was at the training camp; the intelligence was already stale. The Agency also had reported that the pharmaceutical plant was a chemical-weapons factory; the evidence proved unusually frail. The counterattack was perceived around the world as a fiasco, compounded by the president's public confession that the FBI had caught him lying about his sex life. His humiliation was all but complete, his impeachment all but assured.

Louis Freeh arrived in Nairobi a few hours before the cruise missiles started spinning in their launching tubes. "He and I were to meet the following morning," Ambassador Bushnell remembered. "That night, however, I received an urgent telephone call advising me the Director was coming over to see me immediately." She got out of bed and threw on some clothes. "When Freeh arrived he was beside himself," the ambassador said. "He had just learned that the U.S. was going to launch missile attacks and no one had given him prior warning. He wanted to know what I knew—which was less than he, at that point—and what my plan was."

Freeh evidently feared that the missile attacks would spark an Islamic uprising in Kenya, where fewer than one in ten people were Muslims. He told the ambassador: "I assume that you're going to evacuate. I'm removing all FBI personnel. I have five seats left on the plane coming in that I'll give to you. You can decide whom you want to send out." Then he dashed off.

Bushnell was astonished. She called her security officers to her home. "We looked at one another with both shock and bemusement," she recounted. "Given the anger Kenyans were feeling toward al Qaeda, and the small number of Muslims in Nairobi, about the worst we would experience was the ire of people coming back from Friday prayers at a mosque some distance away. We decided to close the embassy at noon, advise people to stay home, and see what happened," she said. "Nothing. Meanwhile, the FBI with all of their long guns, short guns and soft suits had high-tailed it."

Freeh did not bring all his agents out of Africa. On August 27 and 28, a week after the cruise missile attacks, the FBI's John Anticev and Steve Gaudin separately brought Odeh and al-Owhali to New York, under the formal procedures of criminal rendition. Without a suggestion of coercion or the hint of a threat, the FBI had obtained their full confessions along with crucial information about the global reach of al-Qaeda. Among other things, al-Owhali had provided a telephone number in Yemen that served as an international switchboard for bin Laden.

On November 4, 1998, an indictment unsealed in the United States Court House in the Southern District of New York charged bin Laden and twenty other members of al-Qaeda with carrying out the embassy bombings. Ten of the defendants wound up serving life sentences. El-Hage, Odeh, and al-Owhali were convicted on the evidence delivered by the FBI.

Federal prosecutor Patrick Fitzgerald had tried to strengthen the indictments by compelling the duplicitous Ali Mohamed, the leading al-Qaeda operative in America, to talk. As Mohamed later confessed: "After the bombing in 1998, I made plans to go to Egypt and later to Afghanistan to meet bin Laden. Before I could leave, I was subpoenaed to testify before the grand jury in the Southern District of New York. I testified, told some lies." He denied, under oath, that he had trained bin Laden and his men in the techniques of terrorism, intelligence, and counterintelligence.

Fitzgerald and the FBI agents who worked with him in New York all knew that Ali Mohamed was working for al-Qaeda. They decided to arrest him then and there. Two years later, he pleaded guilty in open court to serving as bin Laden's first deep-penetration agent in America and a key conspirator in the embassy bombings. Then the United States made him vanish; no record of his imprisonment exists. He was an embarrassment to the FBI.

"ARREST THE EMPEROR"

After all the trials in *U.S. v. Bin Laden*, eleven of the attackers were still at large—including the lead defendant.

Eleanor Hill, an experienced federal prosecutor serving as staff director for two congressional intelligence committees, asked an FBI agent in New York about the strategy against al-Qaeda. "It's like telling the FBI after Pearl Harbor, 'Go to Tokyo and arrest the emperor,' " he said. "The Southern District doesn't have any cruise missiles."

Fitzgerald did not want missiles. He wanted a bulldozer to tear down "the Wall."

The Justice Department had erected the Wall to comply with the Foreign Intelligence Surveillance Act (FISA) of 1978. For sixty years before that law, the FBI had wiretapped on orders from the attorney general, or at J. Edgar Hoover's say-so. For the twenty years since, federal judges who met in secret—the FISA court—oversaw the FBI's surveillance of suspected spies and terrorists. They legalized the warrantless bugs and taps Hoover once had used at will.

The FBI had been left to decide when to share intelligence with federal prosecutors. But it had mishandled that power more than once. In 1995, new guidelines ordered agents to get advance approval from the Justice Department. The rules were badly written and widely misread. The FBI's leaders compounded and reinforced their misinterpretation. In the field, and at headquarters, FBI agents working intelligence cases thought they could not talk to outsiders—including other agents working criminal cases.

"Here were the ground rules," Fitzgerald said. "We could talk to the FBI agents working the criminal case; we could talk to the New York City Police Department; we could talk to other Federal agencies in the Government, including the intelligence community; we could talk to citizens, foreign police, and foreign intelligence, including spies. We did that. We went overseas to talk to people. We could even talk to Al Qaeda. . . . But we had a group of people we were not allowed to talk to. And those were the FBI agents across the street in Manhattan working the parallel intelligence investigation. We could not talk to them."

The Wall was a maze of misunderstandings, created in large measure by the breakdown in communications at Freeh's FBI. Agents perceived walls where none existed. Their misconceptions had disastrous consequences for the struggle against suspected terrorists.

Louis Freeh reported to Congress that he had reorganized the FBI at the start of 1999. Counterterrorism and counterintelligence were the new top priorities. But his testimony was little more than empty words and wishful thinking.

"Did we have a war plan?" the FBI counterterrorism chief, Dale Watson, asked rhetorically. "Absolutely, we did not." He tried to push the Bureau forward. It was like leaning on the great monolith of the Hoover Building and trying to move it off its foundations. He called it "the hardest thing we ever tried to do."

Watson thought the Bureau's work in Nairobi had been a breakthrough. The intelligence the agents had gathered had opened up two hundred leads against al-Qaeda. He wanted to focus the FBI on the mission.

On December 4, 1998, the headline on the President's Daily Brief, the most secret intelligence document in the government of the United States, read: "Bin Ladin Preparing to Hijack US Aircraft and Other Attacks." It was a secondhand report picked up by the CIA from the Egyptian intelligence service, but no one ever had seen anything like it. "Bin Ladin might implement plans to hijack US aircraft before the beginning of Ramadan on 20 December," the warning read. "Two members of the operational team had evaded security checks during a recent trial run at an unidentified New York airport." The imputed motive was freeing the imprisoned bombers of the World Trade Center and the American embassies in Africa.

Clinton's terrorism czar, Richard Clarke, saw Watson as his best ally at the FBI. In his role as chief of the National Security Council's counterterrorism group, he told Watson to alert the New York City police and the Federal Aviation Administration about the threat report. New York's airports went to maximum security.

From that day forward, Watson tried to underscore the urgency of Clarke's counterterrorism campaign throughout the FBI. He ordered every one of the Bureau's fifty-six field offices to develop an understanding of the threat. But many if not most remained unaware. He summoned agents from across the country to meet with Clarke. They got the full treatment: Clarke's portfolio was filled with portents of attacks; his standard briefing covered bacteria, viruses, and cyber warfare on top of more traditional acts of terrorism.

The meeting went down in the annals of the FBI as the "Terrorism for Dummies" seminar.

"There is a problem convincing people that there is a threat," Clarke said. "There is disbelief and resistance. Most people don't understand. C.E.O.'s of big corporations don't even know what I'm talking about. They think I'm talking about a fourteen-year-old hacking into their Web sites.

I'm talking about people shutting down a city's electricity, shutting down 911 systems, shutting down telephone networks and transportation systems. You black out a city, people die. Black out lots of cities, lots of people die." He now envisioned the deaths of hundreds or thousands of Americans at the hands of Islamic terrorists.

Clarke despaired of the FBI's ability to defend the nation. He nonetheless trusted Dale Watson, the only constant connection between the FBI and the president's closest aides. They shared reports on every conceivably credible terrorist threat.

The warnings became an alarm that rang throughout the days and nights of 1999. One said al-Qaeda had clandestine cells inside the United States. A second said terrorists were going to assassinate the secretary of state, the secretary of defense, and the director of Central Intelligence. A third said bin Laden was trying to obtain nuclear weapons. They came in a scalding and unceasing stream. No one knew which might be true.

Freeh decided in April 1999 that the best thing to do was to put Osama bin Laden on the FBI's Ten Most Wanted list. The Bureau offered a $5 million reward for information leading to his arrest.

Throughout the year, America's counterterrorism chiefs worked with their allies among intelligence services across the world on the extraordinary rendition of suspected members of al-Qaeda and the Egyptian Islamic Jihad. Elaborate plans to kidnap bin Laden in Afghanistan were disrupted by a military coup in Pakistan. Eighty-seven accused terrorists were secretly detained in places like Albania, Bulgaria, Azerbaijan, and the United Arab Emirates. All were sent to prison in Cairo. At the end of November, the Jordanian intelligence service arrested sixteen men and accused them of being al-Qaeda members plotting to attack Americans. They found two American citizens among the suspects, a fact that riveted the FBI and the CIA. Both men had roots in California. One was a computer engineer in Los Angeles who had worked at a charity organization that was starting to look like an al-Qaeda front.

Then, on December 14, 1999, an alert United States Customs agent in Port Angeles, Washington, stopped a nervous twenty-three-year-old Algerian named Ahmed Ressam who was crossing over from Canada on the last ferry of the evening. He had explosives in his trunk and plans to blow them up at the Los Angeles International Airport. The case galvanized the government into an all-out millennium alert. Watson and the White House counterterrorism group met around the clock. They sought an extraordinary number of FISA wiretaps; Janet Reno authorized at least one warrantless search on her own authority.

Clarke convened two emergency cabinet meetings. At the second one, on December 22, Louis Freeh made a rare appearance at the White House. Among the group gathered in the subterranean Situation Room were the secretary of defense, the secretary of state, and the chairman of the Joint Chiefs of Staff. The record reflects that Freeh talked about an array of wiretaps and investigations. The FBI was looking at people in Brooklyn who might have known Ahmed Ressam. It was working with the Royal Canadian Mounted Police to check out suspects in Montreal. It was running down an uncorroborated report from a foreign intelligence service about threatened attacks in seven American cities. His rambling presentation was the high point of his cooperation with the White House in the 1990s.

On New Year's Eve, the leaders of American counterterrorism filled the FBI's new Strategic Information and Operations Center, a $20 million, forty-thousand-square-foot, thirty-five-room command post at headquarters that served as the bureau's own situation room. Freeh and Watson stood watch through the night. Three A.M. came on the East Coast as midnight struck in California on New Year's Day. The counterterrorism chiefs exhaled and had a drink.

But for the rest of Freeh's days in office, the FBI suffered a series of wounds, many self-inflicted, that would scar the United States and American intelligence for years. "We had neither the will nor the resources to keep up the alert," Freeh wrote. "That's what really worried me: not December 31, 1999, but January 1, 2000, and beyond."

"ACTION REQUIRED: NONE"

On January 15, a twenty-four-year-old Saudi, Khalid al-Mihdhar, caught a United Airlines flight from Bangkok to Los Angeles. The CIA had tracked al-Mihdhar for ten days before the flight. The Agency had identified him as an al-Qaeda member, by tracing the telephone number in Yemen that the FBI had obtained from Nairobi, the phone that served as a global switchboard for jihad.

He had left Yemen and checked into a hotel in Dubai, where an intelligence officer copied his Saudi passport and its multiple-entry visa to the

United States. He had flown to Malaysia and met a chemist known to the CIA. Remarkably, the Agency had photos of the meeting, a conclave of terrorists who had worked from the Mediterranean to the Pacific.

But the CIA did not tell the FBI that al-Mihdhar had a ticket to Los Angeles. Nor did the CIA report that his traveling companion was a known terrorist named Nawaf al-Hazmi. The internal CIA cable on them was stamped ACTION REQUIRED: NONE.

Their trail was lost before they cleared the airport immigration desk. The two men settled in San Diego. They used their true names on a rental agreement, their driver's licenses, and their telephone numbers, listed in public directories. They spent many hours in the company of a gregarious fellow Saudi who was a longtime FBI counterterrorism informant. They soon started taking flying lessons. The informant never notified the FBI.

Throughout January and February, Richard Clarke worked with Dale Watson and his counterparts on twenty-nine proposals to expand the counterterrorism capabilities of the United States. The White House approved every one and asked Congress for $9 billion to support them. The big ideas for the FBI included setting up joint terrorism task forces at every one of the fifty-six field offices, increasing the number of Arabic-speakers, and reporting on wiretaps in real time instead of leaving thousands of hours of tapes unheard.

Watson took these ambitions and expanded them into an enormous initiative he called MAXCAP 2005. The FBI was going to become an intelligence service. Every field office would be staffed, trained, and equipped "to prevent and effectively respond to acts of terrorism." The Bureau would collect, analyze, and report strategic, operational, and tactical intelligence. It would finally get online and create a computer system to connect its agents to the world and one another. Thus armed, the FBI would establish sound relationships with the American intelligence community, foreign spy services, state and local law enforcers, military and technology contractors, the Justice Department, and the White House in the war on terror.

Watson asked Congress for $381 million in new funds to hire and train roughly 1,900 new counterterrorism agents, analysts, and linguists. He got enough money for 76 people. He presented his strategy to all the FBI's special agents in charge in the field. Almost all of them thought it was a pipe dream. He went to the Training Division, where three days of the sixteen-week course for new agents were devoted to national security, counterterrorism, and counterintelligence. It would take time to change the traditional curriculum, the trainers told him.

In March and April, as the last year of the Clinton administration began to run out, Attorney General Reno ordered Freeh to fulfill his promises on counterterrorism and counterintelligence in a matter of months. "Implement a system to ensure the linkage and sharing of intelligence," she commanded. "Share it internally and then share it securely with other agencies." She implored him to "utilize intelligence information currently collected and contained in FBI files," and to use that knowledge "to identify and protect against emerging national security threats." Reno said she insisted upon these goals because "I kept finding evidence that we didn't know we had. And I would talk to somebody, and they'd say, 'Well, just wait till we get automated.'" At a minimum, she wanted some assurance that the FBI knew what it had in its own files.

The director swallowed his pride and hired IBM's network operations chief, Bob Dies, to fix the FBI's computers. The expert took a long look at the state of the Bureau's technologies. The average American teenager had more computer power than most FBI agents. The field offices worked with the digital infrastructures of the 1970s. They could not perform a Google search or send e-mails outside their offices. "You guys aren't on life support," Dies told Freeh. "You're dead."

The Bureau's information technology systems had to be overhauled. Freeh and Dies convinced Congress to let the FBI spend $380 million over the next three years to create Trilogy: new computers, servers, and software to let agents read documents, analyze evidence, and communicate with one another and the outside world. Five years, ten project directors, and fifteen IT managers later, the Trilogy program had to be reworked, redesigned, and rebuilt, and the software had to be scrapped. Roughly half the money had been wasted.

As Trilogy was conceived during the spring and summer of 2000, an entire sector of the Bureau began collapsing. Freeh had created a new Investigative Services Division, once known as the Office of Intelligence, to work alongside the Counterterrorism Division at the FBI. It was supposed to be devoted to strategic analysis. An internal audit soon showed that two-thirds of its personnel were unqualified. The new division was rejected and shunned; it worked in isolation and silence. It would last two years before it was disbanded at the nearly unanimous demand of the FBI's assistant directors.

The director's power and authority were fading in Washington and around the world. He was proud of the fact that he had traveled to sixty-eight countries and met, by his account, with more than two thousand foreign leaders in the name of the FBI. But he saw that he was losing face among the world's security ministers, princes, and secret-police chiefs, a fact that he figured was a consequence of the international ridicule over the president's sexual peccadilloes.

On the evening of April 6, 2000, Freeh flew to Pakistan to meet its military dictator, General Pervez Musharraf. That morning, a man had walked into the FBI's Newark office with a warning of an al-Qaeda plot to hijack a 747. He said he was supposed to meet half a dozen men who were part of the plan, launched in Pakistan, and that a trained pilot was on the hijacking team. Though he took a lie detector test, the FBI was never sure if he was telling the truth. The next day, in a Lahore military cantonment built by the British officers of the Raj, Freeh presented General Musharraf with an ultimatum. He had a warrant for the arrest of Osama bin Laden, and he wanted the general to execute it immediately.

"Musharraf laughed," Freeh reported. He refused to help.

That same week, about five hundred miles to the west in Afghanistan, al-Qaeda's leaders were videotaping a highly threatening verbal assault on the United States. Bin Laden swore once again to take vengeance for the imprisonment of the Blind Sheikh and the embassy bombers. He wore a Yemeni dagger on his belt. That clue went unseen until the tape was broadcast five months later, when his plans were ripe.

In those months of silence from the world's most wanted terrorist, some of the Bureau's leaders thought the danger was subsiding. "FBI investigation and analysis indicates that the threat of terrorism in the United States is low," the deputy assistant director for counterterrorism, Terry Turchie, testified to a House national security panel on July 26. He talked about the arrests of fringe groups who had sabotaged veal-processing plants in the name of animal rights, right-wing militiamen who were stockpiling explosives, and a cigarette-smuggling gang that sent money to Hezbollah in Lebanon. Bin Laden went unmentioned.

The Bureau had opened close to two hundred terrorism cases since the East Africa attacks two years before, the majority aimed at suspected members of al-Qaeda and their allies. Dozens went awry after Justice Department attorneys saw a pattern of mistakes and misrepresentations in the cases. At least one hundred applications for national security wiretaps filed by the FBI with the FISA court were legally defective. The cause, as the FBI's inspector general later determined, was the Bureau's continuing inability to grasp the rules of law that governed American intelligence. The judges issued new edicts intended to keep criminal cases against terrorists from being dismissed due to government misconduct.

Mary Jo White was doing everything in her power to keep those cases alive. She was the United States attorney in Manhattan, and she had worked on secret intelligence investigations with the FBI for two decades. White had overseen all of the nation's major terrorism prosecutions for seven years, from the Blind Sheikh to the embassy bombings trial. She saw Nairobi as a harbinger.

She began her remarks in a public speech on September 27, 2000, by noting the previous night's black-tie gala marking the twentieth anniversary of the FBI's Joint Terrorism Task Force, at the Windows on the World restaurant: "The celebration was held, very appropriately, at the World Trade Center."

She said it was imperative for the FBI and the Justice Department to preserve the rule of law in the investigations, indictments, and trials of terrorists. "Even the least of these defendants—in terms of role and evidence—is capable of walking out of a courtroom and committing new terrorist acts," she said. "They would likely do so with enhanced zeal and ruthlessness, and they would enjoy greater status in the terrorist world for having beaten the American system of justice."

The United States would have to depend on the work of the FBI, she said. But she feared that nothing might stop the next assault on America. She warned that "we must and we do expect similar attacks in the future."

44

ALL OUR WEAPONS

A STEADY ROAR OF rage at the FBI reverberated after the shock of the September 11, 2001, attacks. The anger culminated in a debate at the highest levels of the government over dismantling the Bureau and building a new intelligence service in its place.

"We can't continue in this country with an intelligence agency with the record the FBI has," said Thomas Kean, the Republican chairman of the National Commission on Terrorist Attacks upon the United States, known as the 9/11 Commission. "You have a record of an agency that's failed, and it's failed again and again and again."

The collapse of the counterterrorism and counterintelligence divisions of the FBI had been a long time coming. The anguish and frustration of the Bureau's best agents had grown unbearable during Louis Freeh's last months in office. Computers and information systems failed. Leadership in Washington failed. Communications between Freeh, two attorneys general, and two presidents failed almost completely. FBI agents who served the cause of national security had fought against their superiors and the system they served. They almost won.

"Some connected the dots," said the FBI's Gabrielle Burger, who worked counterterrorism and counterintelligence for a decade. "Their voices were a whisper."

One of those voices belonged to Catherine Kiser, a secret intelligence stalwart who had devoted a quarter of a century of her life to the FBI. She was one of its great successes, and she witnessed two of its greatest disasters. Born in 1950, raised in the Bronx, the daughter of a New York City police officer, she went to work teaching second-graders at a public school, only to be laid off when the city almost went bankrupt in 1975. Wondering what to do with her life, she met a second cousin at a family funeral. He was a federal narcotics agent, and he told her that the FBI was hiring women. It took two years, but in 1978, she became the seventy-eighth female special agent in the history of the Bureau.

Six years into her career, in 1984, after struggles with skeptical and sexist superiors, she started working spy cases. The FBI had been a man's world—usually men of Irish or Italian heritage schooled by Jesuits and raised in a closed culture of police and priests. Kiser had the background but more foresight; her mind was open. She would become one of the more influential women at the FBI.

She was among the first FBI agents stationed at the new National Counterintelligence Center at the CIA in 1996. Over the next four years, she led scores of seminars about spying; she was in high demand at the FBI's Training Academy, where she schooled new agents on the laws governing counterintelligence and counterterrorism.

Kiser was the sole FBI liaison agent stationed at the National Security Agency from 1999 to 2002. The NSA's headquarters in Fort Meade, Maryland, was the center of America's electronic-eavesdropping and data-mining powers, tapping into the world's telephones and computers, circling the earth with spy satellites, and monitoring secret portals at telecommunications companies. Kiser knew the rules when agents wanted national security warrants from the FISA court to spy on foreign enemies. She served as a human switchboard, one of the only people in America who could connect FBI agents with Fort Meade. On her desk sat an array of computers, including her kludge of an FBI laptop, a frail connection to headquarters, and telephones that never seemed to stop ringing.

After working counterintelligence for sixteen years, she had developed a finely honed sixth sense: suspicion. It served her well one morning in January 2001 when she received a call from FBI headquarters. The man on the phone was a stranger to her.

He said: "Hello, Cathy. This is Bob Hanssen. How are you?"

She replied: "Fine. And who are you?"

Hanssen curtly introduced himself as a newly appointed member of the FBI's senior executive service. He was brusque, bordering on rude; Hanssen did not like women in authority. He instructed Kiser to set up some meetings with "high-profile people at NSA who can tell me about NSA's computer infrastructure." Kiser turned him down on instinct, first on the telephone, then face-to-face at headquarters a few days later.

After twenty-two years of spying for Moscow, Hanssen had finally become the target of an espionage investigation that dated back to the Cold War. The FBI had suspected the wrong man: a CIA officer who had bitterly protested his innocence. The confrontation had become a running battle between the Bureau and the Agency. In a last-ditch effort to resolve the investigation, the FBI had paid a retired Russian spy a multimillion-dollar finder's fee for stealing a file on the case from the KGB's intelligence archives. It came wrapped in the same garbage bag that Hanssen had used to seal the FBI documents he smuggled to the Russians. It held not only his fingerprints but a fourteen-year-old tape of him talking with his KGB contact.

The voice, with its Chicago accent, was unmistakable: it was Hanssen.

Two days before the incriminating tape arrived, he had delivered to the Russians close to one thousand pages of documents. They included the names of FBI counterintelligence sources throughout the United States, Canada, and England; they held data the Bureau had delivered to the White House, the Pentagon, the State Department, and the National Security Agency. He had downloaded all of it from the Bureau's Automated Case Support system; it was child's play for him. "Any clerk in the Bureau could come up with stuff on that system," Hanssen said during the debriefings after his arrest on February 18, 2001. "What I did is criminal, but it's criminal negligence . . . what they've done on that system."

Kiser had to help assess the damage Hanssen had done to the NSA; it was a harrowing task. "People lined up outside my office with frightened, shocked looks on their faces," she said. "NSA employees had been in meetings with this man during the normal course of business. They had known him for years. The FBI and the intelligence community were in a state of shock and disbelief . . . It was out of control."

The Hanssen case broke four weeks into the presidency of George W. Bush. It was, at the time, the worst embarrassment in the recent history of the FBI. The case sapped what was left of Louis Freeh's spirit. He decided to resign, effective June 1, 2001, with more than two years left in his decade-long appointment. He gave no advance notice to the new attorney general, John Ashcroft, who had been mortified by the news of the Hanssen affair on his first day in office.

Freeh left while the FBI was fighting to resolve the facts behind the latest attack by al-Qaeda. Two suicide bombers had piloted a small boat filled with five hundred pounds of high explosive alongside the USS *Cole*, which was refueling in Yemen en route to the Persian Gulf. The blast blew a forty-five-foot hole in the $800 million navy destroyer, killing seventeen navy personnel and wounding more than forty. The best among the FBI agents on the case had been schooled and steeled in Nairobi. But the investigation in Yemen was far harder: the government, the army, and the police were closer in their sympathies to al-Qaeda than America. Six suspects were in custody in Yemen, but the FBI could not confirm their links to al-Qaeda. The FBI needed the CIA to make the case. But their confrontation over Hanssen had escalated the tensions between them to the highest levels since the end of the Cold War.

Kiser was still trying to sort through her damage report in the Hanssen case when she took another urgent call on August 17, 2001. FBI special agent Harry Samit was on the line from Minneapolis. She recognized his name; she had taught him in a counterterrorism training course. Samit, a former navy aviator based at the FBI's Minneapolis field office, was in a high state of tension. The day before, he had confronted an Algerian with a French passport and an expired visa named Zacarias Moussaoui. Samit had been acting on a tip from a fellow navy pilot who ran a flight school: Moussaoui was studying how to handle a 747, but he did not care about takeoffs or landings. The Algerian had $3,000 in his money belt, a three-inch folding dagger in his pocket, and an aggressive attitude when Samit and an immigration agent arrested him on a visa charge. He angrily insisted that he had to get back to flight school.

"He's a bad dude," Samit said to Kiser. "I have a very bad feeling about him."

He wanted a FISA warrant from the Foreign Intelligence Surveillance Court to search Moussaoui's laptop computer. But he could not get the request past the lawyers at headquarters without hard evidence that the suspect was a terrorist.

"We need a link to al-Qaeda," he said.

She went running down the hall looking for help and finding little; it was 4:30 P.M. on a Friday in August. Over the next three weeks, she contacted everyone she knew at the FBI, the CIA, and the NSA, relaying Samit's warnings. "I was trying and trying and trying to get something," she said. "They weren't making the link. There was a breakdown in communication." It was one among many. Five weeks before, an FBI special agent in Phoenix, Ken Williams, had sent a report to the FBI's Radical Fundamentalist Unit and the Osama bin Laden Unit at the Counterterrorism Division. Williams and a fellow agent, a newly hired Arabic-speaking ex-cop named George Piro, had gathered evidence that al-Qaeda had a network of adherents at American flight schools. Williams urged a nationwide investigation. He was unsurprised when headquarters took no action; thirteen years of experience had taught him that counterintelligence and counterterrorism were "bastard stepchildren" at the FBI. He said: "I knew that this was going to be at the bottom of the pile."

Samit never heard about the Phoenix memo. Almost no one did. It was one among some sixty-eight thousand counterterrorism leads awaiting action at headquarters. The Bin Laden Unit alone had taken in more than three thousand leads in the past few months; counterterrorism director Dale Watson had two analysts looking at them. The fact that terrorists were taking flying lessons went unnoticed.

Samit pleaded with the headquarters supervisors at ITOS, the International Terrorism Operations Section, which oversaw the Radical Fundamentalist and bin Laden squads. He reported over the next week that Moussaoui was "preparing for a terrorist attack." He got nowhere. Samit's immediate superior in Minneapolis, FBI special agent Greg Jones, begged headquarters to listen. He said he wanted to keep the suspect from "flying an airplane into the World Trade Center."

Samit later called the conduct of FBI headquarters in the summer of 2001 "criminal negligence." Kiser said she would be haunted all her life by the thought that "those idiots at ITOS didn't let anybody know."

She received a despondent e-mail from Samit on the afternoon of Monday, September 10, 2001. He reported that ITOS had rejected his request for a search warrant. He was instructed that "FBI does not have a dog in this fight," and he was told to let the immigration service handle the case. "At this point I am so desperate to get into his computer, I'll take anything," he wrote to Kiser. "I am not optimistic. Thanks for your help and assistance. Take care, Harry."

Kiser responded almost immediately, at 3:45 P.M. "You fought the good fight. God help us all if the next terrorist incident involves the same type of plane. Take care, Cathy."

"ROUND UP THE EVILDOERS"

The Bureau had gone through the summer of 2001 without a leader. Five weeks passed after Freeh's formal resignation before President Bush announced Robert Mueller's nomination in the Rose Garden of the White House on July 5. "The next ten years will bring more forms of crime, new threats of terror from beyond our borders and within them," the president had said. "The Bureau must secure its rightful place as the premier counter-espionage and counterterrorist organization in the United States."

The Senate took two months to confirm Mueller. On August 2, the day he won a unanimous vote of approval, he underwent prostate cancer surgery. Another month passed before he took office on Tuesday, September 4. That same day, the National Security Council's Richard Clarke warned his superior, Condoleezza Rice, that an attack by al-Qaeda could come without warning in the not-too-distant future. He went unheeded. He did not alert Mueller. He said: "I didn't think the FBI would know whether or not there was anything going on in the United States by al Qaeda."

The new director's first week at the FBI was a blur of briefings on everything from the wreckage left by Robert Hanssen to the procedures for evacuating Washington in the event of a nuclear attack. On the morning of September 11, Mueller was being brought up to date on the *Cole* investigation. Like almost everyone else in America, he saw the disasters on television. Al-Qaeda had turned airplanes into guided missiles.

Within three hours, the FBI's counterterrorism director had telephoned Clarke in the White House Situation Room. "We got the passenger manifests from the airlines," Dale Watson said. "We recognize some names, Dick. They're al-Qaeda." Clarke replied: "How the fuck did they get on board?" The question would take two years to answer.

For the next three years, Mueller would rise before dawn, read through the overnight reports of threats and portents, arrive at headquarters for a 7:00 A.M. counterterrorism briefing, confer with the attorney general at 7:30, travel in an armored limousine to the White House, and talk to the president at 8:30. The subject was almost always the same. As Bush recounted in his memoir, "I told Bob that I wanted the Bureau to adopt a wartime mentality . . . Bob affirmed: 'That's our new mission, preventing attacks.'"

Mueller was now in charge of the biggest investigation in the history of civilization. Within forty-eight hours, he had four thousand special agents running down leads in the United States, twenty legal attachés working with foreign law enforcement agencies overseas, thrice-daily conference calls with all fifty-six field offices, hundreds of legal subpoenas, and at least thirty emergency search warrants approved by the Foreign Intelligence

Surveillance Court. All the FBI could do was reconstruct a global crime scene and regroup for the next attack.

Mueller clearly did not yet command and control what the FBI knew about the threat. On September 14, he said publicly: "The fact that there were a number of individuals that happened to have received training at flight schools here is news, quite obviously. If we had understood that to be the case, we would have—perhaps one could have averted this."

That day, Congress authorized the president to use "all necessary and appropriate force" against the terrorists. The FBI was about to become one of those forces.

Waves of fear lashed at the foundations of the United States. Every ringing telephone in Washington sounded like an air raid alert. The specter of terrorist assaults with nuclear, biological, and chemical weapons surged every day and broke and rose again each night. The CIA was convinced they were coming, at the command of al-Qaeda's leaders, safe in their Afghan redoubts. The president wanted a shield to hold back the tide and a sword to beat back the invaders. He sent a paramilitary team to Afghanistan; American missile strikes and bombing raids were imminent.

Bush went to FBI headquarters to unveil a Most Wanted Terrorist list with twenty-two names. "Round up the evildoers," he told the agents assembled at the Hoover Building. "Our war is against evil."

His vice president, Dick Cheney, knew where the weaponry was kept. He had served four years as secretary of defense under Bush's father and as White House chief of staff under Ford. The attacks transformed him into the imperial commander of American national security.

Under Cheney's direction, the United States moved to restore the powers of secret intelligence that had flourished for fifty-five years under J. Edgar Hoover. In public speeches, the president, the vice president, and the attorney general renewed the spirit of the Red raids. In top secret orders, they revived the techniques of surveillance that the FBI had used in the war on communism.

The FBI arrested more than 1,200 people within eight weeks of the attacks. Most were foreigners and Muslims. None, so far as could be determined, was a member of al-Qaeda. Some were beaten and abused during "their continued detention in harsh conditions of confinement," as the Justice Department's inspector general later reported. Hundreds were imprisoned for months under a "hold until cleared" policy imposed on the FBI by

Attorney General Ashcroft. The policy was neither written nor debated. No one told Mueller about it. One of Ashcroft's terrorism lawyers, aware that innocent people were imprisoned, wrote that the FBI director would "want to know that the field isn't getting the job done . . . we are all getting screwed up because the Bureau's SACs [special agents in charge] haven't been told explicitly they must clear, or produce evidence to hold, these people and given a deadline to do it." Mueller learned about the policy and the problems it created six months later.

Ashcroft also ordered the indefinite detention of at least seventy people, including about twenty American citizens, under the Material Witness statute, a federal law generally used in immigration proceedings. Thirty were never brought before a tribunal. Four were eventually convicted of supporting terrorism. Two were designated enemy combatants.

Ashcroft defended the nationwide dragnet in a speech to American mayors. The FBI, he said, had been called on to combat "a multinational network of evil." He was explicit about the detention of suspected terrorists. "Robert Kennedy's Justice Department, it is said, would arrest mobsters for spitting on the sidewalk," he said. The FBI would use "the same aggressive arrest and detention tactics in the war on terror. Let the terrorists among us be warned: If you overstay your visa—even by one day—we will arrest you. If you violate a local law, you will be put in jail and kept in custody as long as possible. We will use every available statute. We will seek every prosecutorial advantage. We will use all our weapons."

The attorney general also spelled out some of the authorities the FBI would use under the Patriot Act, which passed the Senate that same day: capturing e-mail addresses, tapping cell phones, opening voice-mails, culling credit card and bank account numbers from the Internet. All of this would be done under law, he said, with subpoenas and search warrants.

But the Patriot Act was not enough for the White House. On October 4, Bush commanded the National Security Agency to work with the FBI in a secret program code-named Stellar Wind.

The program was ingenious. In time, Mueller would decide that it also was illegal.

The director of the National Security Agency, General Michael V. Hayden, had told tens of thousands of his officers in a video message: "We are going to keep America free by making Americans feel safe again." Immediately after the September 11 attacks, Hayden said, he had "turned on the spigot of NSA reporting to FBI in, frankly, an unprecedented way." He and his chief of signals intelligence, Maureen Baginski, had been sending the FBI a torrent of raw data—names, telephone numbers, and e-mail addresses mined from millions of communications entering and leaving America. The intent was a hot pursuit of anyone in the United States who might be linked to al-Qaeda, under the auspices of the Foreign Intelligence Surveillance Court. The action was legal but illogical, Hayden said. "We found that we were giving them too much data in too raw form"; as a result, hundreds of FBI agents spent much of the fall of 2001 chasing thousands of false leads. "It's the nature of intelligence that many tips lead nowhere," he said, "but you have to go down some blind alleys to find the tips that pay off."

The president and the vice president wanted the FBI to execute searches in secret, avoiding the strictures of the legal and constitutional standards set by the Foreign Intelligence Surveillance Court. The answer was Stellar Wind. The NSA would eavesdrop freely against Americans and aliens in the United States without probable cause or search warrants. It would mine and assay the electronic records of millions of telephone conversations— both callers and receivers—and the subject lines of e-mails, including names and Internet addresses. Then it would send the refined intelligence to the Bureau for action.

Stellar Wind resurrected Cold War tactics with twenty-first-century technology. It let the FBI work with the NSA outside of the limits of the law. As Cheney knew from his days at the White House in the wake of Watergate, the NSA and the FBI had worked that way up until 1972, when the Supreme Court unanimously outlawed warrantless wiretaps.

Stellar Wind blew past the Supreme Court on the authority of a dubious opinion sent to the White House the week that the Patriot Act became law. It came from John Yoo, a thirty-four-year-old lawyer in the Justice Department's Office of Legal Counsel who had clerked for Justice Clarence Thomas. Yoo wrote that the Constitution's protections against warrantless searches and seizures did not apply to military operations in the United States. The NSA was a military agency; Congress had authorized Bush to use military force; therefore he had the power to use the NSA against anyone anywhere in America.

The president was "free from the constraints of the Fourth Amendment," Yoo wrote. So the FBI would be free as well.

Mueller was caught between the president's command and the law of the land. He knew it was foolhardy to flout the chief judge of the Foreign Intelligence Surveillance Court, an irascible Texan named Royce Lamberth who had presided over secret surveillance warrants for seven years. The judge had once destroyed the career of a senior FBI counterintelligence agent who he believed had deliberately deceived him. ("We sent a message to the FBI: You've got to tell the truth," the judge said later. "What we found in the history of our country is you can't trust these people.")

Mueller already had won Lamberth's trust; the judge had approved hundreds of national security surveillances, without formal hearings, at the director's personal request. Now the president had ordered the FBI to abuse that trust, ignore the court, and abjure its authority. Very gingerly, without disclosing the underlying existence of Stellar Wind, Mueller worked out a way to signal that some of the warrants he sought were based on intelligence gleaned from the NSA. The chief judge said he and his successor made arrangements with Mueller whereby surveillances were approved "based on the oral briefing with the director of the FBI." The arrangement, unprecedented and precarious, held for almost two years.

But the frictions at the FBI grew with the fear of a new al-Qaeda attack. Mueller tried to smooth over the tension among the counterterrorism commanders in Washington. He maintained that he worked in harmony with the CIA and Tenet. "The thought of regularly sharing Bureau information is something that J. Edgar Hoover would likely have resisted," Mueller said, "and he may well be turning around in his grave to understand the extent to which, since September 11th, there has been the interchange of information between ourselves and the CIA."

The Bureau's working relationships with the rest of the government remained a constant struggle. The attorney general was appalled when the FBI failed to find a mad scientist sending letters filled with anthrax spores to television newsrooms, newspapers, and United States senators. The FBI focused for four years on the wrong man. The Bureau was drowning in false leads; its networks were crashing; its desktop computers still required twelve clicks to save a document.

The FBI had no connectivity with the rest of American intelligence. Headquarters could not receive reports from the NSA or the CIA classified at the top secret level—and almost everything was classified top secret. Fresh intelligence could not be integrated into the FBI's databases.

The pressures on the Bureau's top people were inhuman. Counterterrorism directors held on for a year at best before burning out. Mueller's chiefs of staff lasted a little longer; his information technology executives even less.

As the war on terror went worldwide, the most dangerous personnel crisis Mueller faced was in the field. The fight between the FBI and their counterterrorism counterparts burned through America's chain of command, a slow fuse that ran from the CIA's secret prisons all the way to the White House.

Mueller began to assign the first of more than one thousand FBI agents to the theaters of war in November and December 2001. Their assignments were to collect intelligence and interrogate prisoners. The FBI's interrogation policies were set in stone: no brutality, no violence, and no intimidation.

Some FBI agents went to military posts in Afghanistan, some to the United States Navy base at Guantánamo Bay. A handful of FBI agents joined secret capture-or-kill missions with the CIA against al-Qaeda suspects. On March 28, 2002, they took their first prize captive: a Palestinian working for al-Qaeda in Faisalabad, Pakistan. He was gravely wounded in a firefight; the raid had struck a safe house where a group of militants had gathered. Strapped to a gurney, he was flown to the CIA's newly created secret prison—a "black site" in a warehouse at the Udon Thani air force base in the far northeast of Thailand, near the border of Laos.

"The other day we hauled in a guy named Abu Zubaydah," President Bush said at a Republican fund-raiser in Greenwich, Connecticut, on April 9. "He's one of the top operatives plotting and planning death and destruction on the United States. He's not plotting and planning anymore. He's where he belongs." Relying on the CIA's subsequent reports, the president later called the prisoner al-Qaeda's number-three man and bin Laden's chief of operations.

"A NATIONAL TREASURE"

The first Americans to question Abu Zubaydah were two of the FBI's eight Arabic-speaking agents: Steve Gaudin, a veteran of the Nairobi bombing, and Ali Soufan, who had led the *Cole* investigation in Yemen. Soufan was thirty years old, a native of Lebanon with a master's degree in international relations from Villanova University, and he had joined the FBI on something of a whim in 1997. He had won fame within the closed world of American counterterrorism for his knowledge as an investigator and his finesse as an interrogator. Major General Michael Dunleavy, the military commander at Guantánamo, where Soufan conducted interrogations and won confessions, called him "a national treasure."

Soufan approached the wounded prisoner at the black site with a soft voice and a storehouse of foreknowledge. "I asked him his name," Soufan later testified. "He replied with his alias. I then asked him: 'How about if I call you Hani?' That was the name his mother nicknamed him as a child. He looked at me in shock, said okay, and we started talking."

Within the course of two days, the prisoner identified a photograph of Khalid Sheikh Mohammed, the planner of the al-Qaeda attacks. It was the FBI's biggest breakthrough to date. "Before this," Soufan testified, "we had no idea of KSM's role in 9/11 or his importance in the al Qaeda leadership structure."

The CIA officer at the black site relayed the report to his headquarters. The CIA's director, George Tenet, was unhappy to learn that the FBI was leading the questioning. He ordered a CIA counterterrorism team to take over in Thailand. "We were removed," Soufan said. "Harsh techniques were introduced"—at first, stripping the prisoner of his clothes and depriving him of sleep for forty-eight hours at a time—and "Abu Zubaydah shut down and stopped talking." Then the FBI took over again. The prisoner revealed that he had run logistics and travel for al-Qaeda and gave up information that led to the May 8 arrest of Jose Padilla, a Chicago street-gang hoodlum who had converted to Islam in prison, consorted with al-Qaeda in Pakistan and Afghanistan, and had dreams of setting off a radioactive dirty bomb in Washington.

The CIA falsely claimed credit for the arrest and wrested back control of the interrogation. Its officers blasted the prisoner with noise, froze him with cold, and buried him in a mock coffin. Soufan and Gaudin protested. The CIA officers told them the techniques had been approved at the highest levels of the American government.

Soufan said he contacted FBI headquarters to report that he was witnessing "borderline torture." He refused to take part. The Bureau's counterterrorism chief, Pasquale D'Amuro, pulled both agents from Thailand around the end of May. But he did not raise the issue with Mueller for at least two months. The director learned about it after the line had been crossed.

On August 1, the Justice Department's Office of Legal Counsel granted the CIA's request to begin water-boarding Abu Zubaydah. The technique, tantamount to torture, was designed to elicit confessions through the threat of imminent death by drowning. That same day John Yoo, now a deputy to Attorney General Ashcroft, advised the White House that the laws against torture did not apply to American interrogators. The president, the vice president, the secretary of defense, and the director of Central Intelligence approved.

The FBI did not. "We don't do that," D'Amuro said to Mueller some weeks later. D'Amuro had overseen the investigation and prosecution of the East Africa embassy bombings. He knew that terrorists would talk to the FBI. He also believed that prisoners would say anything to stop the torture, and that their inventions would send the FBI chasing phantoms. And he was convinced that the secret torture would come out one way or another: FBI agents would have to testify about it in court. Their credibility, and criminal cases against terrorists, would be destroyed if they took part in torture, or condoned it. He wanted to be able to say the FBI's hands were clean.

Both men understood that they might someday face their own interrogation, under television lights in a chamber of Congress, or in a courtroom under oath.

Mueller was caught again between the rule of law and the requisites of secrecy. He agreed with D'Amuro in principle. But he also kept his silence. He put nothing in writing. The argument about whether the FBI could countenance torture went on.

The CIA water-boarded Abu Zubaydah eighty-three times in August and kept him awake for a week or more on end. It did not work. A great deal of what the CIA reported from the black site turned out to be false. The prisoner was not bin Laden's chief of operations. He was not a terrorist mastermind. He had told the FBI everything he knew. He told the CIA things he did not know.

"You said things to make them stop, and those things were actually untrue, is that correct?" he was asked five years later in a tribunal at Guantánamo.

"Yes," he replied. "They told me, 'Sorry, we discover that you are not Number Three, not a partner, not even a fighter.'"

The techniques of torture continued in Afghanistan and Cuba, and FBI agents again bore witness.

In mid-September Soufan talked to an al-Qaeda prisoner named Ramzi Binalshibh, who was chained naked to the floor in a CIA black prison at the Bagram air base outside Kabul. He said he was starting to obtain "valuable actionable intelligence" before CIA officers ordered him to stop talking forty-five minutes later. On September 17, they flew their prisoner to a second black site in Morocco, then on to Poland; under extreme duress he described plots to crash airplanes into Heathrow Airport and Canary Wharf in London. He was also diagnosed as a schizophrenic.

Soufan went on to Guantánamo, one among more than four hundred FBI agents who served at the navy base over the course of the next two years. Half of them would report abuses by interrogators.

Among the prisoners Soufan questioned was an al-Qaeda operative named Mohammed al-Qahtani, captured by Pakistani forces as he fled Afghanistan. The FBI had identified him with fingerprints as the twentieth hijacker, the one who never made his flight: arriving in the United States at the Orlando Airport, speaking no English, without a return ticket, he had been detained by customs and immigration agents, fingerprinted, photographed, and deported back to Dubai shortly before the attacks.

Soufan tried to get al-Qahtani to talk over the course of a month at Guantánamo, where the prisoner was placed in the navy brig, in a freezing cell where the lights burned through the night. But Soufan could not break him with words.

Army officers demanded "a piece of al-Qahtani" and "told the FBI to step aside" in October. They questioned him for twenty-hour stretches, leashed him and made him perform dog tricks, stripped him naked and paraded him, froze him to the point of hypothermia, wrapped him from the neck up in duct tape, confronted him with snarling dogs, and ordered him to pray to an idol shrine.

By October 22, 2002, FBI agents at Guantánamo had started a running file that they later labeled "War Crimes."

An e-mail from Cuba, which circulated at the top of the Counterterrorism Division in November, alerted top officials to what the agents were seeing and hearing. "Those who employ these techniques may be indicted, prosecuted, and possibly convicted," Spike Bowman, the chief of the FBI's national security law unit, advised his colleagues at headquarters. "We can't control what the military is doing," he wrote. "But we need to stand well clear of it, and we need to get as much information as possible to . . . Mueller as soon as possible."

No one got the information to Mueller.

The FBI agents at Guantánamo continued to report what their counterparts were doing. The gist of their reports went from the lawyers at the FBI to the highest levels of the Justice Department. But Mueller's closest aides shielded him from an increasingly fierce battle—"ongoing, longstanding, trench warfare," in the words of Ashcroft's chief of staff—at Justice, the CIA, the Pentagon, and the White House. The argument over interrogation, intelligence, torture, and the law went on for more than a year.

Ali Soufan resolved it in his own way. He left the FBI in 2005—a rare event in American government, a resignation of conscience over a matter of honor.

"No one was more shocked"

Mueller was embroiled in another ferocious argument over the rule of law and the role of the FBI as the interrogation fight festered. Vice President Cheney had wanted to send the American military to a Muslim enclave in Lackawanna, a dead-end upstate New York town by the Canadian border. The troops were going to seize six suspected al-Qaeda supporters—all of them Americans—charge them as enemy combatants, and send them to Guantánamo forever.

The fear was that the suspects in Lackawanna were ticking time bombs, a sleeper cell of secret al-Qaeda agents in America. All had family roots in Yemen. All had traveled to Afghanistan. But Mueller convinced the White House to let the FBI round them up rather than sending in the army.

The investigation had fused the powers of the FBI, the CIA, and the National Security Agency. They came together in a flash on a remote road in Yemen on November 3, 2002, when a Predator drone aircraft armed with a Hellfire missile destroyed a pickup truck carrying two wanted terrorists among its passengers. One was a member of al-Qaeda implicated in the bombing of the *Cole*; he had been traced by a combination of Soufan's investigation, NSA data mining, and CIA surveillance. Another was Kamal Derwish, who had lived in Lackawanna, consorted with the arrested suspects, and counseled them to go to Afghanistan. He was the subject of a sealed indictment in the case. His sentence was final: the first American targeted and killed by Americans in the war on terror.

As President Bush made the case for a wider war against Iraq in his State of the Union address on January 28, 2003, he called the six men in Lacka-wanna an al-Qaeda cell. The FBI would conclude that this was not true. No evidence ever surfaced that they had planned an attack. They were not sleeper agents. They were malleable young men who meekly cooperated with the government. They drew relatively light sentences of seven years. Three of them entered the federal witness protection program and testified on behalf of the United States at Guantánamo tribunals.

The case set off an intense debate at headquarters that went on after the suspects pleaded guilty. If the FBI had been thinking like an intelligence service, it could have worked with one or more of the Lackawanna suspects to penetrate al-Qaeda in Afghanistan. Should the Bureau have recruited them as spies instead of arresting them?

Mueller had no way to resolve such questions. The Bureau still had no capacity to use intelligence as a weapon of national security. It was con-sumed by reacting to the events of the day, the hour, and the minute. It could not see over the horizon. It was hard for Mueller and his deputies to see beyond the edges of their own desks. Mueller was trying to double the number of counterterrorism agents and intelligence analysts at the FBI, but the machinery ground with unbearable inertia.

By the time the United States started the war against Iraq on March 19, 2003, Mueller and his new counterterrorism director, Larry Medford, the third man to hold the post in fourteen months, were being battered with hundreds of daily threat reports flowing out of the Middle East. They were blindsided by breakdowns in Mueller's carefully cultivated arrangements with the Foreign Intelligence Surveillance Court over the FBI's role in the secret Stellar Wind program. The White House had just ordered the Bureau to investigate the threat posed by tens of thousands of Iraqis living in the United States. The congressional 9/11 Commission was about to hold its first public hearings, and it seemed certain that the director would be called to account for the FBI's failures, past and present. The pressures of the end-lessly ringing telephones and the demands to stop the next attack and the wartime mentality commanded by the president were shattering for some agents. On April 29, after being awakened by a call at 4:30 A.M., the chief of the Counterterrorism Division's Iran unit took his life with his own gun.

On May 1, President Bush declared that major combat operations in Iraq were over and America's mission had been accomplished. Mueller thought he might have a moment to breathe and think. He made a decision intended, in his words, at "transforming the Bureau into an intelligence agency."

Mueller created an Office of Intelligence at the FBI out of thin air and hired the chief of signals intelligence at the National Security Agency as its director. She was the most powerful woman in the American intelligence community. Almost no one at the FBI had ever heard of her.

Maureen Baginski was a career NSA officer who had started out as a Russian analyst and risen to command authority. At the turn of the century, when the NSA found itself unable to keep pace with the explosion of encrypted information on the Internet, and the agency's supercomputers sputtered and crashed, General Hayden had put Baginski in charge of fixing things. Her SIGINT directorate was the biggest single component of the United States espionage establishment; she commanded a budget that rivaled the FBI's $4 billion and a workforce bigger than the FBI's nearly eleven thousand agents. She also had run Stellar Wind since its inception.

Mueller made her his right hand. She would be by his side at every crucial meeting. He gave her an office down the hall from his and told her to go to work. But at the start she had no staff and no money; it took her a year to assemble a staff of fifty, the size of a large marine platoon. And in that time she won little support from the field. She pushed her message out to the special agents in charge across America: they were now part of a twenty-first-century intelligence service. Every field office was to create and run its own intelligence group and report to headquarters on the threats they faced. They were dubious.

Baginski almost instantly became known to the men of the FBI as the Vision Lady. She reported back to Mueller that it would take years to realize the transformation. They were in a marathon, she said, not a race for the swift or the short-winded.

Mueller also moved to create a full-scale FBI field office in Baghdad. Before the war began, he had signed an order establishing the FBI's role in Iraq as an intelligence mission intended to capture enemy leaders, exploit secret documents, and to uncover potential threats to the United States. The original plan was to send seventy agents at a time. More than 1,500 FBI agents, analysts, and evidence technicians would wind up working in Iraq.

At first, life was good. The city was secure in May and June. Thousands of Iraqi intelligence files were stacked in American command posts. The FBI's special agent in charge, serving on a three-month rotation, held rank equivalent to that of a three-star general. He had a desk in the bath house by the swimming pool at Saddam Hussein's presidential palace, in the Green Zone held by American forces.

Within weeks, the mission took a bad turn. The FBI was ordered to work with the interim interior minister of Iraq to rebuild law enforcement in the nation. The minister was Bernard Kerik, the New York police commissioner at the time of the 9/11 attacks and a long-standing friend to the Bureau. Money was no object for him. Bricks of shrink-wrapped hundred-dollar bills were available for everything from informant networks to computer systems.

But Kerik left Baghdad after ninety days, on September 2, 2003, mission unaccomplished. The only things he left behind were 50,000 Glock pistols in a warehouse. Bush named him the new leader of the Department of Homeland Security; an FBI investigation derailed the nomination and led to Kerik's indictment and imprisonment for fraud.

The FBI's training of the Iraqi police was interrupted by a series of immediate emergencies. Car bombs were going off everywhere. The FBI combed through the wreckage of the Jordanian embassy and the United Nations headquarters and the Red Cross in Baghdad. The American military had to call on the Bureau to collect evidence from a growing number of crime scenes—suicide attacks, roadside bombs, and sniper assaults on military checkpoints and police stations—as its control of the occupied city began to slip.

Days after Kerik departed, the FBI's agents were assigned to interrogate prisoners at Abu Ghraib, the biggest prison in Baghdad. They took thousands of fingerprints and conducted hundreds of interviews in the last three months of 2003. Agents were eager to find detainees who had served as Iraqi intelligence officers or had traveled to the United States. But they were loath to work inside the chaotic main building at Abu Ghraib, preferring to talk to detainees in tents or trailers. Nor did they work at night, when the compound was mortared by insurgents. So they started to hear the rumors of the torture and the deaths inside the prison only in November and December 2003. Not until January 21, 2004, did they learn firsthand from an army captain that there were videotapes of beatings and rapes. A senior FBI agent in Baghdad, Edward Lueckenhoff, relayed the news to headquarters. It was the first time anyone in Washington had heard about the evidence that would surface more than three months later, tarnishing the honor of the United States around the world.

Three of Mueller's senior counterterrorism aides weighed the report and decided to do nothing. It was out of their jurisdiction and above their pay grades. They did not want to wreck the FBI's relationships with the military and the CIA in Iraq. Something more important was about to happen. The FBI was about to get the first crack at High Value Detainee Number One.

Saddam Hussein and George Piro sat down for the first of their twenty-five conversations inside the razor-wired walls of Camp Cropper, the American military's brightly lit prison at the edge of Baghdad International Airport, shortly after 7:00 A.M. on February 7, 2004.

Piro had started his career at the FBI looking for al-Qaeda in Phoenix, Arizona, five years before. He was now one among a dozen native Arabic-speakers at the Bureau, and on his second tour in Baghdad. He had been born and raised in Beirut, and his voice had a distinctive Lebanese lilt that Saddam liked. They were soon on a first-name basis.

Piro was born around the time that Saddam first took power in Iraq. He was thirty-four years old, a tall, thin man with a bright-eyed intensity. He had been a police officer in Turlock, California, a town one hundred miles east of San Francisco, a home for decades to a community of Assyrian Christians from the Middle East. His parents had moved there in 1982, when he was twelve, to escape the war tearing through Beirut.

Piro had been preparing for six weeks to question Saddam. His interview reports show that the rapport he established and the rigor of his inquiries produced revelations that riveted the White House. Saddam said he had used the telephone only twice and rarely slept in the same bed two nights running since the first American war against Iraq began in 1991. He despised Osama bin Laden as a Sunni Muslim zealot. He was now prepared to die at the hands of his captors.

Six days into the debriefing, Piro questioned Saddam intensely and repeatedly about the elusive Iraqi chemical and biological arsenal that was President Bush's justification for the American invasion.

Where were the weapons of mass destruction? he asked. Did they exist at all? They did not, Saddam said. It had been a long-running bluff, a deception intended to keep the Iranians, the Israelis, and the Americans at bay.

"We destroyed them. We told you," he told Piro on February 13, 2004. "By God, if I had such weapons, I would have used them in the fight against the United States." He was telling the truth.

The FBI—not for the first time—had produced evidence that undermined a presidency. "No one was more shocked and angry than I," Bush wrote in his memoirs. "I had a sickening feeling every time I thought about it. I still do."

45

"IF WE DON'T DO *THIS*, PEOPLE WILL DIE"

O N THE DAY after Pearl Harbor, President Roosevelt gave J. Edgar Hoover the power to monitor all telecommunications traffic in and out of the United States. Three weeks after 9/11, President Bush handed Robert Mueller an authority almost as strong.

For twenty-nine months following Bush's order, the FBI had tracked thousands of telephones and Internet addresses in the United States under the aegis of the National Security Agency. "Every day," as Mueller said, the Bureau investigated "e-mail threats from all around the world saying that this particular terrorist activity is going to occur in the United States."

The task of "neutralizing al Qaeda operatives that have already entered the U.S. and have established themselves in American society is one of our most serious intelligence and law enforcement challenges," Mueller told a closed-door meeting of the Senate Select Committee on Intelligence on February 24, 2004. Now the director faced a task as daunting. He had to defy the president and the vice president of the United States, confront them in a showdown over secrecy and democracy, and challenge them in the name of the law.

At least three separate global eavesdropping programs had been mining and assaying the electronic ether under the rubric of Stellar Wind. At least two of them violated the Constitution's protections against warrantless searches and seizures. Mueller saw no evidence that the surveillances had saved a life, stopped an imminent attack, or discovered an al-Qaeda member in the United States.

Stellar Wind had to be reauthorized by the signatures of President Bush and Attorney General Ashcroft every forty-five days. They acted on the basis of reports from the CIA—intelligence officers called them "the scary memos"—justifying the continuing surveillance. The number of people who knew the facts was exceedingly small, but it was growing. A handful of Justice Department lawyers and intelligence court judges thought the programs were unconstitutional and their power had to be controlled. They convinced James Comey, the newly appointed number-two man at the Justice Department. And Comey soon won a convert in Robert Mueller.

On March 4, Mueller and Comey agreed that the FBI could not continue to go along with the surveillance programs. The scope of the searches had to be altered to protect the rights of Americans. They thought Attorney General Ashcroft could not re-endorse Stellar Wind as it stood. Comey made his case to his boss in an hour-long argument at the Justice Department that day, and Ashcroft concurred. Comey was a persuasive advocate. One of the FBI's favorite prosecutors, the grandson of an Irish police commissioner, he had worked with skill and intensity on terrorism cases as the United States attorney in Manhattan for two years after the al-Qaeda attacks. The trust vested in him that day showed that the awe-inspiring force of American national security rested on personal relationships as well as statutory powers.

That night, hours after Comey won him over, Ashcroft suffered a wave of excruciating nausea and pain. Doctors diagnosed a potentially fatal case of gallstone pancreatitis. He was sedated and scheduled for surgery. With Ashcroft incapacitated, Comey was the acting attorney general and chief law enforcement officer of the United States.

Stellar Wind had to be reauthorized on March 11. Seven days of struggle lay ahead, a tug-of-war between security and liberty. Mueller was "a great help to me over that week," Comey said.

The FBI director met Vice President Cheney at the White House at noon on March 9. They stared at one another across the table in the corner office of the president's chief of staff, Andrew Card. Cheney was adamant: no one had the right to challenge the president's power. The spying would continue at his command. It would go on with or without the Justice Department's approval.

"I could have a problem with that," Mueller replied. His notes of the meeting say that he told the vice president that the FBI had to "review legality of continued participation in the program."

On March 10, President Bush ordered Card and the White House counsel Alberto Gonzales to go to the intensive care unit at George Washington University Hospital, one mile northwest of the White House, and to get Ashcroft's signature. An FBI security detail guarded Ashcroft's room. He had come out of surgery the day before. He was in no condition to receive guests, much less sign secret presidential orders. The president called the hospital at 6:45 P.M. and insisted on talking to Ashcroft. His wife took the call.

The president told her that it was a matter of national security. She would not hand over the phone. The FBI agents had the presence of mind to alert Ashcroft's chief of staff that the president's men were on their way. He called Comey. The acting attorney general called Mueller, asking him to meet him at the hospital and bear witness to the confrontation.

They raced to the intensive care unit. Comey got there first. He walked into the darkened room and saw that Ashcroft was fading: "I immediately began speaking to him . . . and tried to see if he could focus on what was happening. And it wasn't clear to me that he could. He seemed pretty bad off." Comey stepped out into the hallway and called Mueller again. The director said he would be there in a few minutes. He wanted to speak with his agents. He ordered them to make sure that the president's men did not throw the acting attorney general out of the hospital room.

The FBI agents recorded that Card and Gonzales entered at 7:35 P.M. Gonzales stood at the head of the bed holding a manila envelope with the presidential authorization inside. He told Ashcroft he wanted his signature.

Ashcroft lifted his head off his pillow. He refused. "In very strong terms," he said the program was illegal; his argument was "rich in both substance and fact—which stunned me," Comey said. Then Ashcroft laid down his head and said: "But that doesn't matter, because I'm not the attorney general. There is the attorney general." And then he pointed at Comey.

Mueller crossed paths with the president's empty-handed emissaries as they stalked out. They were about to cross swords.

The president signed the authorization alone in the White House on the morning of March 11. It explicitly asserted that his powers as commander in chief overrode all other laws of the land. Mueller met with White House chief of staff Card at noon. His notes say that he told Card that "the WH was trying to do an end run" around the law.

Mueller drafted a letter of resignation by hand at 1:30 A.M. on March 12, 2004. "In the absence of clarification of the legality of the program from the Attorney General," he wrote, "I am forced to withdraw the FBI from participation in the program. Further, should the President order the continuation of the FBI's participation in the program, and in the absence of further legal advice from the AG, I would be constrained to resign as Director of the FBI."

Seven hours later, Mueller went to the morning briefing with the president at the White House. It had been a busy night in the world of counterterrorism. In Madrid, Islamic jihadists claiming inspiration from al-Qaeda had set off ten bombs in four commuter trains. They killed 191 people and wounded 1,800, the worst terrorist attack in Europe since the bombing of Pan Am 103 over Lockerbie in 1988. The FBI was looking for links to the United States.

After the meeting, the president stood alone with Mueller in the Oval Office. Bush now realized that the FBI director, the attorney general, and his deputy were in rebellion. Mueller told Bush face-to-face that he would resign if the FBI was ordered to continue warrantless searches on Americans without an order from the Department of Justice. Mueller said he had an "independent obligation to the FBI and to DOJ to assure the legality of actions we undertook," according to his recently declassified notes of the meeting. "A presidential order alone could not do that."

Both men had sworn upon taking office to faithfully execute the laws of the United States. Only one still held to his oath.

The president pleaded ignorance of the law and the facts. He said he hadn't known there had been legal problems with Stellar Wind. He said he hadn't known Ashcroft had been in the hospital. He said he hadn't known Mueller and Comey had been blowing the whistle. He was almost surely deceiving the director, and deliberately.

Without doubt he saw a political disaster at hand. "I had to make a big decision, and fast," Bush wrote in his memoirs. "I thought about the Saturday Night Massacre in October 1973"—when Nixon defied the Justice Department over his secret tapes, forced the attorney general and his deputy to resign, and destroyed his presidential aura of power. "That was not a historical crisis I was eager to replicate. It wouldn't give me much satisfaction to know I was right on the legal principles while my administration imploded and our key programs in the war on terror were exposed in the media."

Bush promised to put the programs on a legal footing. This did not happen overnight. It took years. But based on the president's promise, Mueller and his allies backed down from their threats to resign. Bush kept the secret for twenty more months. The man who first blew the whistle on the warrantless surveillance was a Justice Department lawyer named Thomas Tamm; his father and his uncle had been two of J. Edgar Hoover's closest aides at headquarters. By the time the first facts were revealed in *The New York Times*, both Ashcroft and Comey had resigned from the Bush administration.

Mueller's stand against the president stayed secret far longer. But Comey told a select audience at the National Security Agency what Mueller had heard from Bush and Cheney at the White House:

> "If we don't do *this*, people will die." You can all supply your
> own *this*: "If we don't collect this type of information," or "If we
> don't use this technique," or "If we don't extend this authority." It is
> extraordinarily difficult to be the attorney standing in front of the
> freight train that is the need for *this* . . . It takes far more than a sharp
> legal mind to say "no" when it matters most. It takes moral character. It
> takes an ability to see the future. It takes an appreciation of the damage
> that will flow from an unjustified "yes." It takes an understanding that,
> in the long run, intelligence under law is the only sustainable
> intelligence in this country.

Mueller testified in public before the 9/11 Commission one month later, on April 14, 2004, and he never breathed a word of what had happened at the White House. He never has.

"The beginnings of an intelligence service"

The commission and Congress accepted the director's assurance that the FBI could safeguard both liberty and security. But they asked more from Mueller. They wanted to know that the FBI was using the full powers Congress had granted it under the Patriot Act of 2001.

It was, but not always well. On May 6, 2004, the FBI arrested an Oregon attorney, Brandon Mayfield, on a material witness warrant in connection with the Madrid bombings. He was an American citizen who had converted to Islam. The FBI had used every wiretapping and surveillance tool it had against Mayfield for seven weeks. The case rested on the FBI's misreading of a fingerprint lifted from a plastic bag in Madrid. Spanish police had told the FBI legal attaché in Madrid that Mayfield was the wrong man. He was nonetheless arrested after that warning. The arrest led to two weeks of harsh imprisonment in solitary confinement before he was freed; he later won a formal apology and a $2 million settlement from the government.

The Patriot Act, written swiftly, in a state of fear, had greatly expanded the force of national security letters, a tactic rarely used before 9/11. The letters commanded banks, credit bureaus, telephone companies, and Internet service providers to turn over records about their customers to the FBI. They also compelled the recipients to remain silent—they could tell no one, not even a lawyer. They had the combined power of a subpoena and a gag order. The FBI was sending out close to one thousand of these letters a week; more than half the targets were American citizens. FBI agents said they were indispensable investigative tools, the bread and butter of counterterrorism in the United States. But the letters, like warrantless wiretaps, were also a form of breaking and entering. An FBI supervisor could write them without a judge's order or a prosecutor's request.

By September 2004, federal judges were starting to find them unconstitutional. The courts struck down the provisions of the Patriot Act that gave the FBI those powers; Congress rewrote the law to preserve them. The Bureau now had to justify the gag order to a judge, but the letters continued.

The FBI's counterterrorism agents also were abusing their power by creating "exigent letters"—emergency subpoenas for thousands of telephone records—without telling anyone at headquarters. An endless succession of assistant directors, deputies, and special agents in charge did not learn the rules or their roles. Mueller said: "We did not have a management system in place to assure that we were following the law." He conceded that the Bureau had misused the Patriot Act to obtain intelligence.

The testimony that the 9/11 Commission heard left many of the commissioners thinking that the Bureau should be rebuilt. They seriously considered creating a new domestic intelligence service to supplant the FBI. Mueller fought a three-front battle with the commission, the Congress, and the White House to keep the Bureau from becoming a house divided, with law enforcement on one side and intelligence on the other. The struggle went on every day through the summer and fall of 2004, and into the next year.

The only part of the commission's report on the FBI that was written into law was an order commanding the creation of "an institutional culture with substantial expertise in, and commitment to, the intelligence mission." Mueller had been trying to do that for years. His progress was slow and uneven, but he soon achieved his goal of doubling the number of intelligence analysts at the FBI. There were now two thousand of them, and they were no longer assigned to answer phones and empty the trash.

Mueller had confidently reported to the commission that he was making great strides, "turning to the next stage of transforming the Bureau into an intelligence agency." But the FBI was at least five years away from that goal.

The president had been compelled to create his own intelligence commission after conceding that the weapons of mass destruction in Iraq were a mirage. Federal appeals court judge Laurence Silberman led it. He was Cheney's choice; the two were of one mind about the Bureau. They had been for thirty years, ever since Silberman was deputy attorney general and Cheney President Ford's chief of staff. Back then, after Nixon fell, the White House had sent Silberman to search the secret files of J. Edgar Hoover. The judge had had a barb out for the Bureau ever since.

"It was the single worst experience of my long governmental service," Judge Silberman told his fellow judges. "Hoover had indeed tasked his agents with reporting privately to him any bits of dirt on figures such as Martin Luther King, or their families. Hoover sometimes used that information for subtle blackmail to ensure his and the Bureau's power . . . I think it would be appropriate to introduce all new recruits to the nature of the secret and confidential files of J. Edgar Hoover. And in that connection this country—and the Bureau—would be well served if his name were removed from the Bureau's building."

Silberman's report on the FBI, in the works throughout the winter of 2004 and sent to the White House on March 31, 2005, was a steel-wire scrubbing. "It has now been three and a half years since the September 11 attacks," the report's chapter on the Bureau began. "Three and a half years after December 7, 1941, the United States had built and equipped an army and a navy that had crossed two oceans, the English Channel, and the Rhine; it had already won Germany's surrender and was two months from vanquishing Japan. The FBI has spent the past three and a half years building the beginnings of an intelligence service." The report warned that it would take until 2010 to accomplish that task.

The report bore down hard on the FBI's intelligence directorate, created by Mueller two years before. It concluded that the directorate had great responsibility but no authority. It did not run intelligence investigations or operations. It performed no analysis. It had little sway over the fifty-six field groups it had created. No one but the director himself had power over any of these fiefs.

"We asked whether the Directorate of Intelligence can ensure that intelligence collection priorities are met," the report said. "It cannot. We asked whether the directorate directly supervises most of the Bureau's analysts. It does not." It did not control the money or the people over whom it appeared to preside. "Can the FBI's latest effort to build an intelligence capability overcome the resistance that has scuppered past reforms?" the report asked. "The outcome is still in doubt." These were harsh judgments, all the more stinging because they were true.

If the FBI could not command and control its agents and its authorities, the report concluded, the United States should break up the Bureau and start anew, building a new domestic intelligence agency from the ground up.

With gritted teeth, Mueller began to institute the biggest changes in the command structure of the Bureau since Hoover's death. A single National Security Service within the FBI would now rule over intelligence, counterintelligence, and counterterrorism. The change was imposed effective in September 2005. As the judge had predicted, it would take the better part of five years before it showed results.

"Who is calling shots?"

The war in Iraq was throwing sand into the FBI's gears. Hundreds of agents had rotated through Iraq, and hundreds more labored at the FBI's crime lab in Quantico, Virginia, taking part in a battle that seemed to have no end. They analyzed tens of thousands of fingerprints and biometric data from prisoners, looking for leads on al-Qaeda. They worked to capture, analyze, and reverse-engineer tens of thousands of fragments of the improvised explosive devices that were killing American soldiers.

Members of the FBI's vaunted hostage rescue team, trained in commando tactics, were in high demand in both Iraq and Afghanistan. Some had been through four tours of duty in battle, more than any soldier in the war, by the summer of 2005.

The team was now preparing a military assault on a terrorist who had been on the FBI's Most Wanted list for more than twenty years.

The Bureau had been after Filiberto Ojeda Ríos ever since the January 1975 bombing of the Fraunces Tavern in New York, one of the first murderous terrorist attacks of the modern age. The Puerto Rican independence movement's armed forces, the FALN, had taken the credit. The FBI had run COINTELPRO operations against the independence movement throughout the sixties and early seventies; Hoover himself had cited "the increasing boldness" of their political programs and "the courage given to their cause by Castro's Cuba."

Ojeda was the FALN's commander. He had been trained by the Cuban intelligence service from 1961 to 1967, and he had returned to Puerto Rico as a revolutionary. Arrested by an FBI agent in San Juan, he jumped bail and fled to New York, where he worked under the protection of Castro's intelligence officers at the Cuban mission to the United Nations. By the start of 1974, Ojeda had organized the FALN in New York and Chicago.

The FBI blamed the group for more than 120 terrorist bombings over the next decade; the attacks had killed a total of six people and done millions of dollars of damage. The Bureau got a lucky break on November 1, 1976, when a heroin addict broke into the FALN's secret hideout in the Westown section of Chicago, looking for something to steal. He found a cache of dynamite and he tried to sell it on the street. Two days later, on November 3, 1976, the Chicago police and the FBI heard about his offer and got a warrant to search the apartment he had burglarized. They found the first working bomb factory ever discovered in a terrorist investigation in the United States. The safe house held explosives, batteries, propane tanks, watches, and a treasure trove of documents. The investigation led to a series of indictments. The FBI had wounded the FALN, but it did not kill the group.

Ojeda fled again to Puerto Rico, from which he oversaw the assassination of a United States Navy sailor in San Juan in 1982 and directed a $7.1 million Wells Fargo bank robbery in Connecticut in 1983. The FBI believed that half the money went to Cuban intelligence.

A new FBI special agent in charge in San Juan, Luis Fraticelli, had created a fifteen-member terrorism squad. Tracking down Ojeda was its top priority. Thirty years had passed since the Fraunces Tavern bombing.

During the summer of 2005, the squad determined that the seventy-two-year-old fugitive was living in a small house up a dirt road outside an isolated hamlet on the western edge of Puerto Rico. Fraticelli asked for the hostage rescue team to hunt him down.

FBI headquarters approved the deployment. Ten snipers and a support team landed in Puerto Rico ten days later, on September 23, 2005. There was going to be no negotiation. No member of the team spoke Spanish.

But the plan went awry. A helicopter dropped the hostage rescue force in the wrong location. Their cover was blown quickly. By the time they found Ojeda's house, a crowd had gathered down the road, chanting "FBI assassins." Shots were fired—by the FBI and its target—at 4:28 P.M. A standoff ensued. The assault team hunkered down. Rain started falling as night drew near. The FBI's leaders, monitoring events from headquarters, grew worried.

Willie Hulon—the FBI's sixth counterterrorism director in four years under Mueller—called his superior, Gary Bald, the FBI's new national security chief.

"Bald believed that there was confusion regarding who was in command," an understated after-action report recounted. He wrote in his notes: "Who is calling shots?" The answer was three different FBI chieftains.

In San Juan, the highly stressed special agent in charge wanted an immediate attack. In Quantico, the commander of the hostage rescue team wanted to send in fresh troops. In Washington, Hulon wanted to see a written plan of attack. As midnight approached, Bald told the team to stand down. Its members strongly disagreed. Their commander dispatched a new team from Dulles International Airport at 1:00 A.M. on September 24. They entered the small white house, pierced with 111 bullet holes, shortly after noon. They found Ojeda's body on the floor with a loaded and cocked Browning 9mm handgun by his side. He had been dead since the first exchange of gunfire. No one at headquarters faulted the team that took him down. Ojeda was a terrorist and an assassin, and he had fired on the FBI, wounding one agent, before he died.

But "Who is calling shots?" was a resounding question. Given the continuing inability of the commanders of the FBI and their agents in the field to communicate, it was hard to see who could put them on the same wavelength. The ever-changing leadership of the FBI's counterterrorism and intelligence chiefs made it harder. Most had cashed out for more rewarding jobs as security directors at credit-card companies, casinos, and cruise lines.

Every morning, Mueller read through the daily threat reports that came out of the new National Counterterrorism Center, up to twenty pages a day of captured e-mails, tips from foreign intelligence services, interviews with informants, and reports about suspicious characters from state and local police. On an average day, the FBI's in-house threat-tracking system, called

Guardian, recorded as many as one hundred alerts. The great majority turned out to be false alarms.

The FBI had to find a way to analyze it all, choose targets for investigations, and turn those investigations into arrests and indictments that would stand up in court and be counted as victories against the enemy. Mueller still needed to make intelligence into a tool for law enforcement.

There was a way. Mueller needed a new general and a new strategy.

"THIS IS ON OUR WATCH"

He found the commander he had been looking for in Philip Mudd, the prematurely gray and deceptively mild-mannered deputy director of the CIA's Counterterrorist Center. They had testified together for years in classified briefings; Mueller liked the way his new recruit thought and spoke. Mudd was a professional intelligence analyst, a twenty-year veteran of the CIA who had served as the National Security Council's director for Persian Gulf and Middle East issues and worked in Kabul with the American ambassador in Afghanistan.

Mudd became the chief of the FBI's National Security Division on April 27, 2006. Though he had been unraveling secrets all his life, he confessed that the FBI mystified him.

"It took me maybe six to twelve months to understand," he said. "We're not about *collecting* intelligence. We're about looking at a problem and using our combined intelligence and law-enforcement skills to *do something* about that problem in a way that provides security for Los Angeles or Chicago or Tuscaloosa. This is a profound difference, in my judgment, between the other intelligence challenges I've seen over time.

"This is bigger, harder, and it has, in some ways, greater implications for the security of this country," he said. "This is on our watch. If we don't get it right, it's our bad."

Mueller and Mudd took a hard look at the correlation of forces in the war on terror in the spring and summer of 2006. The Bush administration was flagging. The attempts by the administration to use spies and soldiers to capture and interrogate suspected terrorists were starting to collapse. Torture tainted testimony against the suspects, making their conviction by American juries next to impossible. And the Supreme Court ruled that the president did not have the authority to create war crimes tribunals at Guantánamo.

Bush had fired his CIA director, and he was about to jettison his defense secretary. His attorney general, Alberto Gonzales, the former White House counsel, was widely regarded as a weak reed. Vice President Cheney's top national security aide, I. Lewis "Scooter" Libby, had been convicted of perjury and obstruction of justice for lying about a CIA leak investigation; he was the highest-ranking White House official convicted of a felony since the Iran-contra imbroglio. The war in Iraq was going badly. Al-Qaeda was still rampant; its methods were metastasizing; the images from Abu Ghraib became a recruiting poster across the world. After the embarrassing exposure of the extralegal aspects of the Stellar Wind eavesdropping program, Congress worked to expand the warrantless wiretapping powers of the government. It eventually legalized parts of the president's secret surveillance; it made eavesdropping inside America easier. Since much of the world's telecommunications traffic is routed through the United States, regardless of its origins, the NSA and the FBI could trap an international e-mail stored on a Microsoft server or trace a call switched through an AT&T office without a warrant. Nonetheless, five years of hot pursuit had failed to find a single al-Qaeda suspect in America. Yet the FBI had an ominous sense that they were out there somewhere.

There was another way to smoke them out. What had worked for Hoover against the Ku Klux Klan and the Communist Party of the United States could work for Mueller against the threat of Islamic terrorism. The FBI would seek and arrest potential terrorists with undercover stings. It was a time-honored strategy that criminal investigators understood and intelligence agents savored. It combined secret investigations with the satisfaction of big arrests and blazing headlines. It required two essential elements: a convincing con man as the informant and a credulous suspect as the target. No jury in Los Angeles, Chicago, or Tuscaloosa would accept an argument of entrapment by an accused terrorist handcuffed and shackled by the FBI.

Over the next three years—until the FBI found its first actual al-Qaeda operative in America—the undercover sting became a central strategy of counterterrorism in America. Mueller made it official in a speech on June 23, 2006, announcing the arrests of seven men in a Miami slum who were accused of plotting to blow up the Sears Tower in Chicago, the tallest building in America. Mueller called the men members of a "homegrown terrorist cell . . . self-recruited, self-trained, and self-executing. They may not have any connection to al-Qaeda or to other terrorist groups. They share ideas and information in the shadows of the Internet. They gain inspiration from radical websites that call for violence. They raise money by committing low-level crimes that do not generate much attention. They answer not to a particular leader, but to an ideology. In short, they operate under the radar."

The Liberty City Seven, as they were called, were half-bright thugs without the apparent means or the skills to carry out an attack on anything bigger than a liquor store. Their plotting was more aspirational than operational, as the FBI's deputy director, John Pistole, put it—a phrase that would often be repeated. It took three trials to convict five of the men. But case after case against the homegrown threat followed across the country. An undercover FBI agent in Illinois trailed a twenty-two-year-old thug who traded his stereo speakers for four fake hand grenades; he said he intended to kill shoppers in a mall outside Chicago during Christmas week of 2006. In another investigation, Mueller singled out the work of a former Green Beret in Ohio who had tracked two naturalized Americans from Jordan as they lifted weights, slugged down steroids, and talked about murdering American soldiers in Iraq.

More than half the major cases the FBI brought against accused terrorists from 2007 to 2009 were stings. The Bureau unveiled a spectacular-sounding indictment on May 8, 2007, charging a plot to attack the military base at Fort Dix, New Jersey, with heavy weapons. The ringleaders were three pot-smoking petty criminals in their twenties, all illegal immigrants from Albania, and their brother-in-law, a Palestinian cabdriver. They had taped themselves at a shooting range, shouting "God is great," and they brought the tape to a video clerk to convert it to a DVD. He called the FBI, which infiltrated the group with an informant, who offered to provide assault rifles and grenades. An even more frightening case emerged on June 3, 2007, when the FBI arrested a sixty-three-year-old suspect, who had once worked at Kennedy Airport in New York, and charged him with leading a plot to blow up aviation fuel tanks and pipelines surrounding the passenger terminals. The informant, a convicted cocaine dealer, recorded his target on tape: "To hit John F. Kennedy, wow," he said. "They love JFK—like the man. If you hit that, the whole country will be in mourning. It's like you can kill the man twice."

A thirty-one-year-old former navy signalman was convicted on March 5, 2008, in a case based in large part upon an e-mail he had sent seven years before. The defendant, born Paul Hall, had changed his name to Hassan Abu-Jihad, a choice that had raised no eyebrows when he joined the navy. While aboard the USS *Benfold* in the Persian Gulf in April 2001, five months after the bombing of the *Cole*, he had sent messages to an online jihad forum in London embracing al-Qaeda and disclosing the deployment of ten navy ships to the Gulf. He received a twenty-five-year sentence.

These cases made good stories. The FBI represented them as real-time threats from real-life radicals in the United States. As long as the nation did not suffer an actual attack, most Americans cared little that some of the cases were concoctions, that the FBI sometimes supplied the guns and missiles, that not every e-mail was a fuse for an explosive, or that the plotters might not be homegrown terrorists but garden-variety lunatics.

The FBI had more than seven hundred million terrorism-related records in its files. The list of suspected terrorists it oversaw held more than 1.1 million names. Finding real threats in the deluge of secret intelligence remained a nightmarish task. The Bureau's third attempt to create a computer network for its agents was floundering, costing far more and taking far longer than anyone had feared. It remained a work in progress for years to come; only one-third of the FBI's agents and analysts were connected to the Internet. Mueller had the authority to hire two dozen senior intelligence officers at headquarters. By 2008, he had found only two. Congress continued to flog the FBI's counterterrorism managers for their failures of foresight and stamina; Mueller had now seen eight of them come and go.

And the FBI's relentless focus on fighting terrorism had an unforeseen consequence. The investigation and prosecution of white-collar crime plummeted, a boon to the Wall Street plunderings that helped create the greatest economic crisis in America since the 1930s.

Mueller remained in high repute as the Bush administration came to a close. So did Mudd, who stayed on as the director's senior intelligence aide. With guidance from the secretary of defense, the former director of central intelligence Robert Gates, they began to develop a global counterterrorism strategy that won favor with both parties in Congress and both candidates running for the White House in the fall of 2008. All three would stay on under the next president. All three would shape his strategies.

"THE PURPOSE THAT HAS ALWAYS GUIDED OUR POWER"

On April 28, 2009, President Barack Obama came to the Hoover Building for a public celebration of the FBI's hundredth anniversary. A crowd of clerks and secretaries began to assemble in the central courtyard of the

Bureau's concrete fortress. The FBI's elite, bearing their gold badges, walked out to the courtyard with Obama. The centennial banner, drooping slightly, hung at the back wall.

"Back in 1908, there were just thirty-four special agents reporting to Theodore Roosevelt's attorney general. Today, there are over 30,000 men and women who work for the FBI," the president began. "So much has changed in the last one hundred years," he said, turning on the charm. "Thank God for change." The crowd went wild.

"I also know that some things have remained constant," he said, his voice leveling. "The rule of law—that is the foundation on which America was built. That is the purpose that has always guided our power. And that is why we must always reject as false the choice between our security and our ideals."

Obama had come of age as a champion of civil liberties and constitutional law. In the Oval Office, he took a harder line than he had proclaimed in public. His choices on counterterrorism sometimes shocked his supporters. He decided to hunt and kill al-Qaeda in Afghanistan and Pakistan. The United States carried the fight to thousands who adhered to the credo of jihad. Guided by the imperative of preventing the next attack, he went beyond what his predecessors had done to solve the conundrums of counterterrorism. He was the first president since the end of the Cold War to coordinate America's military and intelligence powers into lethal forces under clear-cut rules.

Under Obama, the CIA and the Pentagon obliterated hundreds of terrorist suspects, and sometimes civilians as well, with a ceaseless barrage of rockets fired by drones over Afghanistan and Pakistan. While American commandos killed Osama bin Laden and other al-Qaeda leaders, the State Department used muscular diplomacy to win cooperation from many of the nations of Islam, aided by the uprisings of the Arab Spring, led by rebellions against dictators in the name of democracy. To maintain law and order in the war on terror, Obama gave the FBI control over the toughest al-Qaeda captives, the high-value detainees. He entrusted Robert Mueller and his agents with the task of arresting and interrogating terrorists without mangling American laws and liberties.

The FBI was now a part of a growing global network of interwoven national security systems, patched into a web of secret information shared among police and spies throughout America and the world. The Bureau trapped more suspects with more stings, and more sophisticated ones. It sometimes worked at the edge of the law, and arguably beyond, in the surveillance of thousands of Americans who opposed the government with words and thoughts, not deeds or plots. But it also used superior intelligence work to arrest Najibullah Zazi, an Afghan immigrant allied with al-Qaeda, and to bring him to a federal court in New York, where he pleaded guilty to plotting to plant a bomb in a subway as the tenth anniversary of 9/11 approached. In October 2011, another al-Qaeda-inspired terrorist, Umar Farouk Abdulmutallab, pleaded guilty to trying to destroy a Delta airliner with 278 passengers over Detroit on the previous Christmas Day. He had explosives planted in his underwear.

The federal judge asked him if he knew he had broken the law. "Yes, U.S. law," he said. The cases were proof that terrorist suspects could be tried and convicted in American courts under law, without military tribunals or confessions extracted by torture in secret prisons.

On the home front, Americans had become inured to the gaze of closed-circuit cameras, the gloved hands of airport guards, and the phalanx of cops and guardsmen in combat gear. Many willingly surrendered liberties for a promise of security. They might not love Big Brother, but they knew he was part of the family now.

Yet there was still a sign that the rule of constitutional law might govern counterterrorism in the years to come. A new set of guidelines for the FBI's intelligence investigations emerged on November 7, 2011. It followed from a decade of struggle over how to use the immense powers thrust upon the Bureau in the war on terror, and three years of trying to repair the damage done in the name of national security under the Bush administration.

The FBI's new rules set specific legal limits on intelligence searches and seizures, wiretaps and bugs, data mining and electronic eavesdropping, the trapping and tracing of e-mails and cell phones. The 460-page manual, made public with significant deletions, looked like something new in the twenty-first century. It looked as if the American government was trying, in good faith, to balance liberty and security.

The FBI, which still has no legal charter from Congress, had been fighting for a century over what it could do in the name of national security. Attorney General Edward Levi had been the first to try to govern the Bureau thirty-five years earlier, in the wake of Watergate. He had acted in the tradition of Justice Harlan Fiske Stone, the pillar of the law who first appointed J. Edgar Hoover, and who had warned that a secret police was a menace to a free society.

The FBI might now have created the first realistic operating manual for running a secret intelligence service in an open democracy. The new rules said at the outset that "rigorous obedience to constitutional principles and guarantees is more important than the outcome of any single interview, search for evidence, or investigation." They made it clear that the FBI could not investigate people for "opposing war or foreign policy, protesting government actions, or promoting certain religious beliefs," or because they were aliens or anarchists or Arab Americans. The unleashing of the unlimited powers of the FBI's ability to conduct unwarranted searches and seizures and surveillances now required a declaration of war by Congress rather than a secret presidential decree. These principles once might have seemed self-evident, but the FBI had violated them time and again in the past.

The continuity of Robert Mueller contributed to this change. No other FBI director ever had the stability to serve the ten-year term that Congress had imposed on the office after Hoover's death. Some had left in disgrace or disrepute. Mueller had persevered. He passed the milestone a decade after the 9/11 attacks. Obama asked him to stay on for two more years. He would serve until September 2013, if he could withstand the pressure of each passing day. He would be approaching seventy by then, and he had aged in office, his hair white, his face gray, his eyes weary, as every morning brought a barrage of fresh threats and false alarms. But ever since he had confronted a president over the limits of his powers to spy on American citizens, he had stood for a principle. He had said back then that he wanted no historian to write: "You won the war on terrorism, but you sacrificed your civil liberties."

The chance remained that the principle might prevail, the possibility that in a time of continual danger Americans could be both safe and free.

AFTERWORD

This work owes its life to Robert D. Loomis, who has been making books at Random House for fifty-five years, a career as long as J. Edgar Hoover's. He knew Hoover and they shared a Jack Daniel's or two back in the day. Working side by side with Bob, my manuscript on his desk and his pencil in his hand, has been one of the great pleasures of my life, an experience only the luckiest authors have had.

At Random House, a remarkable team turned our manuscript into a book. My deepest thanks to Gina Centrello, Tom Perry, Susan Kamil, Benjamin Dreyer, Theresa Zoro, Ben Steinberg, Andy Ward, Amelia Zalcman, Avideh Bashirrad, Erika Greber, Susanna Sturgis, Lisa Feuer, Richard Elman, Steve Messina, Carole Lowenstein, Susan Turner, Beck Stvan, Barbara Fillon, and Lisa Barnes. I owe enormous gratitude to the world's best literary agent, Kathy Robbins, and her staff, including David Halpern, Louise Quayle, and Mike Gillespie. My thanks also go to counselor F. Richard Pappas, Esq., and to Matthew Snyder at CAA.

Enemies has been blessed by great fortune in the timing of the release of documents kept secret since World War II. In recent months, the FBI has declassified thousands of records that provided depth and scope for this book. The Bureau's official historian, John H. Fox, Jr., and his staff have performed a public service by publishing these documents online, a labor for which they deserve acclaim.

Many of the oral histories in this book have been compiled and copyrighted by the Society of Former Special Agents of the Federal Bureau of Investigation, and are cited here with the written and oral permission of the society. The intelligence files of J. Edgar Hoover were provided to me after a twenty-six-year effort initiated under the Freedom of Information Act and brought to fruition by David Sobel of the Electronic Frontier Foundation. I thank him and the FBI personnel who worked to complete the declassification.

The FBI has a squad of public relations officers whose skill and experience is exceeded only by the Pentagon's. I have chosen not to work directly with them to preserve the integrity of the book and to spare readers the wooden prose of press releases. The FBI nonetheless provides a significant amount of public information online within the limits of a bureaucracy bound by secrecy.

I have worked with secret documents and investigated secret agencies for twenty-five years. I know that no outsiders—and few insiders—comprehend the full scope of the secret operations of the government. This book is incomplete. It nonetheless represents an effort to write a chapter of the history of the United States over the past century. Readers may argue, but I believe the records cited in this book speak for themselves. They are the annals of Americans' fight to be safe and to be free.

We will forgo our freedom in the future if we fail to read our history. "A popular Government without popular information or the means of acquiring it, is but a Prologue to a Farce or a Tragedy or perhaps both," James Madison wrote at the beginning of our nation's continuing struggle to create a free republic. "Knowledge will forever govern ignorance, and a people who mean to be their own Governors, must arm themselves with the power knowledge gives."

NOTES

PRIMARY SOURCES

- Federal Bureau of Investigation records declassified under the Freedom of Information Act (FBI/FOIA)

- Federal Bureau of Investigation oral histories complied by the Society of Former Special Agents of the Federal Bureau of Investigation (FBI/FBIOH)

- Federal Bureau of Investigation records and correspondence in the Foreign Relations of the United States volumes *Emergence of the Intelligence Establishment: 1945–1950* and *The Intelligence Community: 1950–1955* (FRUS Intelligence)

- Foreign Affairs Oral History (FAOH): more than fifteen hundred oral histories of American diplomats (and diplomats who served as intelligence officers) have been compiled by the Association for Diplomatic Studies and Training and many are available online at http://www.adst.org/Oral_History.htm

- Franklin D. Roosevelt Presidential Library (FDRL)

- Harry S. Truman Presidential Library (HSTL)

- Dwight D. Eisenhower Presidential Library (DDEL)

- John F. Kennedy Presidential Library (JFKL)

- Richard M. Nixon Presidential Library (RMNL)

- Gerald R. Ford Presidential Library (GRFL)

- Jimmy Carter Presidential Library (JCL)

- George H. W. Bush Library (GHWBL)

- Records of the Senate Select Committee to Study Governmental Operations with Respect to Intelligence Activities (hereinafter "Church Committee" or CC)

- Federal Bureau of Investigation records and documents published on the FBI's history website, http://vault.fbi.gov/ (FBI), were an invaluable source for this book. Interested readers may peruse the Bureau's original files on the ACLU, the American Nazi Party, COINTELPRO, Fidel Castro, the Freedom Riders, Martin Luther King, Jr., Saddam Hussein, and other subjects ranging from Jimmy Hoffa to Jimi Hendrix. A unique collection of records on the origins of the Communist Party of the United States of America dating to 1919 is at http://www.marxists.org/history/usa/eam/index.html.

Part I · Spies and Saboteurs

1. Anarchy

3 **"He worked Sundays and nights"**: O'Brian interview, CBS News, May 2, 1972 (the day that Hoover died).

4 **"I sometimes have thought"**: Fennell interview, in Ovid Demaris, *The Director: An Oral Biography of J. Edgar Hoover* (New York: Harper's Magazine Press, 1975).

4 **"cool relentless logic"**: Hester O'Neill, "J. Edgar Hoover's Schooldays," *American Boy and Open Road*, Sept. 1954.

5 **"filled our unsuspecting communities"**: President Wilson's war message to Congress, April 2, 1917.

5 **"When we declared war"**: O'Brian quoted in *The New York Times*, Oct. 9, 1918.

5 **"Immense pressure"**: John Lord O'Brian, "New Encroachments on Individual Freedom," *Harvard Law Review* 66, no. 1 (Nov. 1952), p. 14.

6 **Von Papen began to build a propaganda machine**: On the scope of the German effort, see testimony of A. Bruce Bielaski (Director, Bureau of Investigation, Department of Justice), Senate Judiciary Committee, 65th Congress, 2nd Session, Dec. 6, 1918 (Washington, D.C.: Government Printing Office, 1919).

6 **"We might as well admit openly"**: Bernstorff cited in Arthur S. Link, *Wilson: The Struggle for Neutrality, 1914–1915* (Princeton, N.J.: Princeton University Press, 1960), p. 378.

6 **"the gravest threats"**: Woodrow Wilson, Third Annual Message to Congress, Dec. 7, 1915.

2. Revolution

7 **"I believe in power"**: Theodore Roosevelt letter to George Otto Trevelyan, June 19, 1908, in Joseph Bucklin Bishop, *Theodore Roosevelt and His Time Shown in His Own Letters* (New York: C. Scribner's Sons, 1920), pp. 92–94.

8 **"The time of the great social revolutions has arrived"**: Theodore Roosevelt, *American Ideals, and Other Essays, Social and Political* (New York: G. P. Putnam's Sons, 1897), p. 304.

8 **"anarchy is a crime"**: Theodore Roosevelt, First Annual Message to Congress, Dec. 3, 1901, online at the American Presidency Project, http://www.presidency.ucsb.edu.

9 **"I have always been averse"**: Attorney General Brewster cited in Homer Cummings and Carl McFarland, *Federal Justice: Chapters in the History of Justice and the Federal Executive* (New York: Macmillan, 1937), p. 373.

9 **"These people should all be marked"**: Robert A. Pinkerton, "Detective Surveillance of Anarchists," *North American Review* 173, no. 540 (1901), p. 39.

10 "the methods of Russian spies and detectives": Unsigned editorial in the *Salem* (Oregon) *Capitol Journal,* reprinted in the *Portland Oregonian,* July 8, 1905, cited in Jerry A. O'Callaghan, "Senator Mitchell and the Oregon Land Frauds, 1905," *Pacific Historical Review* 21, no. 3 (Aug. 1952), p. 261; "outrageous conduct": Attorney General Wickersham to President Taft, May 10, 1912, NARA RG 60, Jones Pardon file case.

10 "ROOSEVELT, in his characteristic dynamic fashion": Findlay to Hoover, "Memorandum for the Director: Re: Early History of the Bureau of Investigation, United States Department of Justice," Nov. 19, 1943.

11 "The Department of Justice": Annual Report of the Attorney General of the United States, 1907, online at www.fbi.gov/libref/historic/history/origins.

11 "American ideas of government": *Hearings of House Appropriations Committee on Deficiency Appropriations,* 59th Congress, 2nd Session (1907). On Jan. 17, 1908, the chairman of the House Appropriations Committee, Representative James A. Tawney, a Minnesota Republican, laid a trap for Attorney General Bonaparte. The Appropriations Committee controlled the course of federal spending. Bonaparte was asked, in an open hearing, how many Secret Service agents and private eyes the Justice Department had hired over the past year. "It would be difficult to say," he replied, trying his best to avoid the question. He was reminded that there was a specific amount of money authorized for the Secret Service and a legal requirement that the appropriation be limited to that service alone. Had he ever employed private detectives as well? "We have to employ certain special agents from time to time," Bonaparte replied. "We have to have some detective service. . . . But you do not need a great many, and you must remember that the class of men . . . is one you have to employ with a good deal of caution."

"They are not always a high type of man?" Bonaparte was asked. "No, sir," Bonaparte replied.

Congressman Tawney not only blocked Bonaparte's request for federal money to create the new Bureau of Investigation, but he went one step further: he wrote a provision into the federal budget barring the Justice Department from using Secret Service agents as investigators.

11 "ready to kick the Constitution": Twain to Rev. J. H. Twichell, Feb. 16, 1905, *Mark Twain's Letters* (New York: Harper & Brothers, 1919), p. 766.

11 On July 26, 1908: The FBI's records note June 29, 1908, as the date when Bonaparte dipped into his miscellaneous funds to hire Secret Service agents (sources differ as to whether it was eight, nine, or ten agents). But the Bureau calls the date of the formal signed order, July 26, 1908, its official founding day.

The order Bonaparte signed creating a permanent "force of special agents" reads as follows:

> All matters relating to investigations under the Department, except those to be made by bank examiners, and in connection with the naturalization service, will be referred to the Chief Examiner for a memorandum as to whether any member of the force of special agents under his direction is available for the work to be performed. No authorization of expenditure for special examinations shall be made by any officer of the Department, without first ascertaining whether one of the regular force is available for the service desired, and, in case the service cannot

be performed by the regular force of special agents of the Department, the matter will be specially called to the attention of the Attorney General, or Acting Attorney General, together with a statement from the Chief Examiner as to the reasons why a regular employee cannot be assigned to the work, before authorization shall be made for any expenditure of any money for this purpose. CHARLES J. BONAPARTE, Attorney General.

The glorified accountant who held his job by patronage and bore the title of "chief examiner" was, in effect, the director of the Bureau of Investigation in its first years.

12 **"The difficulties encountered"**: Bonaparte to Roosevelt, Jan. 14, 1909, online at www.fbi.gov/libref/historic/history/origins.htm.

12 **"The Attorney General knows"**: Bonaparte, Annual Report of the Attorney General of the United States, December 1908, online at www.fbi.gov/libref/historic/history/origins.htm.

3. TRAITORS

13 **"vicious spies and conspirators"**: Woodrow Wilson, "Address on Flag Day at Washington," June 14, 1917.

14 **"I believe in the right of free speech"**: Ernest Freeberg, *Democracy's Prisoner: Eugene V. Debs, the Great War, and the Right to Dissent* (Cambridge, Mass.: Harvard University Press, 2008), pp. 98–104.

14 **"traitors, scoundrels, and spies"**: Statement of Senator Lee Overman, *Congressional Record*, 65th Congress, 2nd Session, April 4, 1918 (Washington, D.C.: Government Printing Office, 1919).

Senator Overman convened Judiciary Committee hearings on the Red threat only two months after the end of World War I. The hearings in many ways anticipated the work of Senator Joseph McCarthy more than thirty years later. They influenced the course of the great Red scare of 1919.

In January 1919, Overman took testimonies on Germany's wartime espionage against the United States. The hearings were a bust, since not a single act of German sabotage had troubled the nation since Black Tom.

Senator Overman and his Judiciary Committee colleagues quickly turned their attention to the international Communist conspiracy. "I do not know whether we can go into this question right now, under our resolution, and investigate Bolshevism," the senator said. But they did, and immediately.

Archibald E. Stevenson, a thirty-five-year-old Wall Street lawyer and a self-proclaimed expert on the Red threat, riveted the committee. Stevenson said that thousands upon thousands of Americans—ministers, professors, politicians, publishers—were in thrall to the Russian Revolution. He named hundreds of names, including nationally respected figures like Jane Addams, the Chicago social reformer, and Charles Beard, one of America's foremost historians. Some were active Bolshevik agents, he said; others were deluded intellectuals.

The ideas of Marx, Lenin, and Trotsky were being spread like poison by outwardly respectable Americans, Stevenson told the senators. The Russians were pouring money, people, and propaganda into the United States, and their American agents were carrying the Russian Revolution to every city and industrial center in the country through secret committees called soviets.

14 **"There is quite a deal of hysteria":** Attorney General Gregory to T. U. Taylor, April 1918, cited in Charles McCormick, *Seeing Reds: Federal Surveillance of Radicals in the Pittsburgh Mill District, 1917–1921* (Pittsburgh: University of Pittsburgh Press, 2002), p. 64.

14 **"an enormous overlapping":** Memorandum of F. X. O'Donnell, Oct. 24, 1938, cited in "An Analysis of FBI Domestic Security Intelligence Investigations: Authority, Official Attitudes, and Activities in Historical Perspective," FBI, Oct. 28, 1975.

15 **At its height the league claimed:** Bruce Bielaski of the Bureau of Investigation told Congress in December 1918 that the American Protective League peaked at between 300,000 and 350,000 strong, though other government officials put its membership at 250,000.

15 **"the gravest danger"** and **"very dangerous":** McAdoo to Wilson, June 2, 1917, and Wilson to Gregory, June 4, 1917, in *The Public Papers of Woodrow Wilson*, 42, pp. 410–411 and 416, online at http://www.presidency.ucsb.edu/woodrow_wilson.php; **"derelict in not having sought a remedy":** Wilson quoted in John F. Fox Jr., "Bureaucratic Wrangling over Counterintelligence, 1917–18," online at www.cia.gov/library/center-for-the-study-of-intelligence/csi-publications/csi-studies/studies.

15 **"in effect, and perhaps in fact":** *The New York Times*, Aug. 4, 1917, p. 6; **put the IWW out of business:** cited in Melvyn Dubofsky, *"We Shall Be All": A History of the Industrial Workers of the World* (Chicago: University of Illinois Press, 2000), p. 233.

16 **"No one can make a goat of me":** De Woody quoted in *The New York Times*, Sept. 6, 1918, p. 1.

17 **"the greatest scoop in history":** David A. Langbart, "Five Months in Petrograd in 1918: Robert W. Imbrie and the US Search for Information in Russia," *Studies in Intelligence* 52, no. 1 (March 2008), CIA, Center for the Study of Intelligence.

The documents in question were delivered by the American government propaganda council, the Committee on Public Information, created by President Wilson to boost popular support for the war. The committee produced powerful posters, newsreels, and speeches—along with some strange characters, among them Edgar Sisson, a prominent magazine editor dispatched to Russia as the chief of American propaganda. Sisson was posted at the American consulate in Petrograd, present-day St. Petersburg, as the Bolshevik revolution overthrew the czar's government. He talked the United States ambassador into paying 20,000 rubles for the documents, offered for sale by the publisher of a local scandal sheet. Sisson thought he had "the greatest scoop in history," in the words of the State Department's top lawyer. He delivered his smoking guns to President Wilson, who ordered their release to every big newspaper in America. Wilson, against the counsel of his War Department, sent American troops to fight the Bolsheviks. The Americans were still fighting after World War I officially ended on Nov. 11, 1918.

21 **the newly opened Soviet diplomatic offices:** Moscow's official representative was a German citizen named Ludwig Martens; he sought diplomatic recognition from the

United States in vain. Like most foreign embassies, Martens's office was designed to serve as a trade mission, a propaganda outlet, and an espionage station, not just a diplomatic post.

To J. Edgar Hoover, the very existence of Martens seemed to prove a sinister alliance between wartime Germany and revolutionary Russia. A German citizen born and raised in Russia, interned in England as a German alien during the war, he declared himself a German upon arriving in New York, then announced himself as the Soviet ambassador. He found American industrialists happy to trade with Moscow—if they were paid in hard cash. Above all, the Soviets wanted American troops out of Russia—and American technology in.

21 **"a mass formation of the criminals of the world":** A. Mitchell Palmer, "The Case Against the Reds," *Forum* 63 (February 1920), pp. 173–185.

22 **"the poison of disorder, the poison of revolt":** *Addresses of President Wilson,* U.S. 66th Congress, 1st Session, Senate, doc. 120, vol. 435 (Washington, D.C.: Government Printing Office, 1920).

23 **sixty-one . . . agents and thirty-five undercover informers:** Hoover, "Memorandum Upon the Work of the Radical Division, Aug. 1, 1919, to March 15, 1920," Bureau of Investigation, RG65, NARA.

23 **Teams of lock pickers:** In 1919, "a shock-team of FBI, ONI, and New York police representatives succeeded in 'picking-the-lock' of the safe of the Japanese Consul General in New York, where they discovered a Japanese Naval Code," a Navy officer of the era recorded. "This code was photographed, page-by-page, and rephotographed a year or two later to pick up extensive printed changes. The cipher used with this code was not too difficult and we were literally surfeited with blessings." Capt. Laurance F. Safford, "A Brief History of Communications Intelligence in the United States," National Security Agency (declassified March 1982).

24 **"the mad march of Red fascism":** Hoover testimony before House Committee on Un-American Activities, March 26, 1947.

24 **"a vigorous and comprehensive investigation":** Flynn memo, Aug. 12, 1919, reprinted in "Investigation into Activities of the Department of Justice, Letter from the Attorney General," 66th Congress, 1st Session, Nov. 15, 1919.

24 **Palmer had scoured the statutes:** Letter from the attorney general in response to a Senate resolution of Oct. 17, 1919, *Report on the Activities of the Bureau of Investigation of the Department of Justice Against Persons Advising Anarchy, Sedition, and the Forcible Overthrow of the Government* (Washington, D.C.: Government Printing Office, Nov. 17, 1919), pp. 5–13. Attorney General Palmer had just lost a test case against three members of a tiny gang of Spanish-speaking anarchists in Buffalo, New York, who had published a pamphlet of blood-curdling rhetoric. A federal judge had tossed out the indictment on July 24, 1919, saying it had no basis in law.

25 **"terrorists . . . ready for any sort of work":** Edgar B. Speer, "The Russian Workingmen's Association, sometimes called the Union of Russian Workers," April 8, 1919, Bureau of Investigation, NARA M-1085, reel 931, doc. 313846. On Aug. 15, 1919, the New York City police, spurred by the Lusk Committee and Archibald Stevenson, conducted a second raid on the Russian house on East 15th Street. On the ground floor, they found a classroom full of immigrants learning to read and write—and studying revolution, the raiders supposed. On the top floor three men were editing

a Russian-language newspaper called *Bread and Freedom*. The three were swiftly indicted on state charges of criminal anarchy on Aug. 20. The charges were not front-page news.

4. COMMUNISTS

26 **"secret sessions of the heads"**: August H. Loula, "Communist Party Convention: Day 1–Sept. 1, 1919," Department of Justice/Bureau of Investigation Files, NARA M-1085, doc. 313848. Loula was keenly aware of "the importance of preserving the cover of our confidential informants," keeping their identities secret and their work out of the public record, as the Bureau's chief, Bill Flynn, recorded. The Socialists left Chicago divided and downhearted; one of their leaders would call the Communist movement that emerged from the divide "a ludicrous fiasco" run by a rabble of Russians and "a handful of American intellectuals with a generous sprinkling of Department of Justice agents."

26 **"the whole game has been played"**: Confidential Informant No. 121, "In Re: Communist Party Convention, Sept. 1–7, 1919," Department of Justice/Bureau of Investigation Files, NARA M-1085, doc. 313846.

27 **"The name of this organization"**: Constitution of the Communist Party of America. Report to the Communist International (Chicago: Communist Party of America, n.d. [1919]).

27 **"cutthroats and pimps"**: Jacob Spolansky et al., "In Re: Communist Meeting at West Side Auditorium, Chicago," Sept. 21, 1919, DoJ/BoI Investigative Files, NARA M-1085, docs. 313846 and 313848.

27 **"to overthrow the Government"**: J. Edgar Hoover, "Brief on the Communist Party," submitted to the Committee on Rules, House of Representatives, 66th Congress, 2nd Session (Washington, D.C.: Government Printing Office, 1920).

27 **Soviet archives exhumed after the Cold War ended**: The question of whether the Comintern underwrote American Communists is settled by Comintern archives. It did. But how much it sent is still open to question. The archives show approval for four secret subsidies in precious metals and diamonds totaling more than two million Russian rubles in 1919 and 1920. That sum that cannot be precisely converted to U.S. dollars but could be hundreds of thousands of dollars, or even millions depending on how the valuables were exchanged. However, an emissary of the Communist Party of America asked the Comintern for more modest sums in 1920, suggesting a lesser level of largesse on Moscow's part. This $60,000 budget request for the Communist Party of America, made to the Comintern by Louis C. Fraina in August 1920, included $20,000 for "Prisoners—defense, support of dependents," $15,000 for "Agitation among the Negro," $10,000 for "Agitation among the soldiers and sailors," and $15,000 to start up three newspapers.

29 **"and if not, why not"**: "Letter from the Attorney General Transmitting in Response to a Senate Resolution of Oct. 17, 1919" (Washington, D.C.: Government Printing Office, Nov. 17, 1919).

29 **Communist Party chiefs in Chicago**: Special Agent August Loula went back to the Russian hall, now the headquarters of the Communist Party of America, to seize

some seditious pamphlets in October. He confronted the party's leaders face-to-face. As he reported, they asked him "how they came to be honored by a visit from the Agent of the Department of Justice." He answered that when he came back, he would have "an invitation for them to select rooms in the County Jail." But when he read the pamphlet, he glumly concluded that "it does not contain matter upon which prosecution could be based." August H. Loula, "A Visit to Communist Party Head-quarters, Chicago–Oct. 14, 1919," DoJ/BoI Investigative Files, NARA M-1085, doc. 202600-14.

29 **On October 27, Hoover was in New York:** Hoover's report on his New York trip is recounted in Kenneth Ackerman, *Young J. Edgar: Hoover, the Red Scare, and the Assault on Civil Liberties* (New York: Carroll & Graf, 2007), pp. 102–105.

29 **"It is the desire of the Bureau of Investigation":** Hoover to Caminetti, Nov. 3, 1919, NARA RG85, file 85-54235/36. The celebrations marking the second anniversary of the Russian Revolution began in New York at nightfall, with speeches by Santeri Nuorteva, the number-two man at the Soviet diplomatic offices in Manhattan, and Benjamin Gitlow, the Socialist state assemblyman turned Communist Labor Party leader. Bureau of Investigation agents in the audience took word-for-word notes in shorthand.

30 **1,182 suspects had been arrested:** List, Union of Russian Workers (Raid of Nov. 7, 1919), Memorandum for Mr. Burke, DoJ/BoI Investigative Files NARA M-1085, doc. 202600-14; Annual Report of the Commissioner General of Immigration to the Secretary of Labor: Fiscal Year Ended June 30, 1920 (Washington, D.C.: Government Printing Office, 1920).

30 **"They would destroy":** Briefs quoted in J. Edgar Hoover, *Masters of Deceit* (New York: Henry Holt & Co., 1958), p. vi.

31 **"To gather a correct, up-to-date list":** M. J. Davis, "In re: Communist Party," Dec. 4, 1919, NARA M-1085, reel 931, doc. 313846.

31 **"a considerable number of affidavits":** Hoover to Caminetti, Dec. 16, 1919, NARA M-1085, doc. 313846.

31 **"The crowd was very cocky":** Hoover quoted in *New York Tribune*, Dec. 22, 1919; **"Haven't I given you":** The source of the quotation is Congressman William Vaile of Colorado, *Congressional Record*, Jan. 5, 1920.

31 **"It was 4:20 A.M.":** Emma Goldman, *Living My Life* (New York: Dover Publications, 1970), pp. 716–717.

5. "Who is Mr. Hoover?"

33 **"The Communist Party is practically busted":** The agent's identity remains uncertain. He evidently penetrated the executive committee of the Communist Party. He may have been Clarence Hathaway, a founding member of the CPUSA, and an FBI informant from 1920 onward. His undercover surveillance report went from Brigadier General Marlborough Churchill, the chief of Military Intelligence, to Hoover's desk on Jan. 12, 1920, NARA M-1085, doc. 313846. Although the American Communists had many factions in their first decade, Ruthenberg was "the founder of the

Communist Party in the United States," in the words of Jay Lovestone, an early member and later one of the nation's leading anti-Communists.

34 **"Arrange with your undercover informants"**: Burke to Kelleher, Dec. 27, 1919, published in "Charges of Illegal Practices of the Department of Justice," United States Senate, 66th Congress, 3rd Session (Washington, D.C.: Government Printing Office, 1921), pp. 12–14.

34 **"All instructions previously issued"**: Telegram to Agents in Charge, initialed JEH, Jan. 2, 1920, NARA M-1085, doc. 313846.

34 **"About 25 aliens were apprehended"**: Myron J. Blackmon, Special Agent in Charge, "Report of the Red Raid in Buffalo, NY, Night of Jan. 2/3, 1920," filed Jan. 14, 1920, NARA M-1085, doc. 202600–1613.

35 **"The attack upon our organization"**: Charles E. Ruthenberg, "Report of the Executive Secretary to the Central Executive Committee of the Communist Party of America," Jan. 18, 1920.

35 **"The Department of Justice of the United States"**: A. Mitchell Palmer, "The Case Against the 'Reds,'" *Forum* 63 (1920), pp. 173–185.

36 **"The revolutionary conspiracy is international"**: Hoover, "Report on Radical Division," reprinted in *Attorney A. Mitchell General Palmer on Charges Made Against Department of Justice,* 65th Congress, 2nd Session, June 1, 1920.

37 **"I am strongly opposed"**: Francis Fisher Kane's letter was printed in *Survey* 43, Jan. 31, 1920, pp. 501–503.

37 **"As an aftermath"**: Judge Anderson's speech was reported in the weekly *Harvard Alumni Bulletin* and reprinted in *LaFollette's Magazine* 12, no. 2 (February 1920), p. 3. On Anderson's record as United States Attorney and his handling of the Deer Island habeas corpus case, see his entry in *The Yale Biographical Dictionary of American Law.*

38 **"I'll take great pleasure"**: Skeffington quoted in *Boston Globe,* Jan. 13, 1920.

40 **"Q: Who is Mr. Hoover?"**: The proceedings before Judge Anderson are cited in the National Popular Government League's "Report upon the Illegal Practices of the U.S. Department of Justice," May 1920.

40 **"This case seems"**: Ibid.

41 **"The plot is nationwide"**: *The New York Times,* April 30 and May 1, 1920.

42 **"creatures of the imagination of the Attorney General"**: Hoover, Report on Radical Division, in *Palmer on Charges,* p. 186.

42 **"the real story of the red menace"**: Hoover to Palmer, May 5, 1920, Department of Justice file 209264.

43 **"an assault upon the most sacred"**: *Report to the American People upon the Illegal Practices of the Department of Justice,* National Popular Government League, Washington, D.C., 1920.

45 **Hoover said: "No, sir"**: *Report upon the Illegal Practices,* op. cit.

45 **"the wrecking of the communist parties"**: Hoover report to Congress on the General Intelligence Division, Oct. 5, 1920. He was half-right. Comintern files made public at the end of the century show that dues-paying membership of the Communist Party in the United States plummeted after the raids, from 23,744 in December 1919 to 2,296 in February 1920, then rose to 8,223 in April 1920; fewer than one thousand of those who remained on the rolls spoke English.

45 **"the radical situation":** Hoover report to Congress on the General Intelligence Division, Oct. 5, 1920.

46 **"We'll get them":** *The New York Times,* Sept. 19, 1920.

6. UNDERWORLDS

47 **"I am not fit for this office":** Harding quoted by a close adviser, Nicholas Murray Butler, the president of Columbia University, in Butler, *Across the Busy Years: Recollections and Reflections* (New York: Charles Scribner's Sons, 1939), vol. 1, p. 411.

47 **"Daugherty has been my best friend":** Francis Russell, *The Shadow of Blooming Grove: Warren G. Harding and His Times* (New York: McGraw-Hill, 1968), p. 427.

48 **"We made an effort":** Hoover to Burns, Sept. 20, 1921, NARA M-1085, doc. 202600-1617-53.

48 **"holding us responsible":** "Circular Letter to the Membership of the United Communist Party," NARA M-1085, doc. 202600-14.

49 **"Soviet Russia is the enemy of mankind":** Harry M. Daugherty, *The Inside Story of the Harding Tragedy* (1932; Boston: Western Islands, 1975), p. 119.

49 **In the spring and summer of 1921:** C. J. Scully, "In re: Communist Activities—Special Report," May 1, 1921, NARA M-1085, doc. 202600-1775-8.

49 **"Rules for Underground Party Work":** Communist Party of America leaflet, undated, Comintern Archive, Russian State Archive of Socio-Political History (hereinafter RGASPI).

50 **secret four-day meeting:** H. J. Lenon, "Unity Convention of Communist Parties," NARA M-1085, doc. 202600-2265.

50 **Clarence Hathaway:** Hathaway was identified as an FBI informant from 1920 onward in a March 23, 1960, memo to Hoover on a meeting between Morris Childs, the FBI's highest-ranking infiltrator of the CPUSA, and top CP leaders Eugene Dennis and Gus Hall. The memo was declassified by the FBI in a thirty-five-volume file on the Childs operation, code-named SOLO, and published on Aug. 2, 2011, on the FBI's website: vault.fbi.gov/solo. The document identifying Hathaway is at volume 19, page 29 of the file.

50 **"The Communist Party is definitely an outlaw organization":** C. E. Ruthenberg (writing under his pseudonym "David Damon"), *The Communist* 1, no. 2 (August 1921). Communist membership figures are taken from Comintern records and C. E. Ruthenberg's own estimates published in *The Communist* 1, no. 9 (July 1922).

52 **"The word went out through the underworld":** The snappy prose is from Hoover's 1938 memoir, *Persons in Hiding* (New York: Little, Brown), ghostwritten by his favorite journalist, Courtney Riley Cooper.

52 **"trays with bottles carrying":** Alice Roosevelt Longworth, *Crowded Hours* (New York: Charles Scribner's Sons, 1933), pp. 320–325.

52 **"Communists and most subversive activities":** Hoover to Attorney General Robert Jackson, April 1, 1941.

53 **The deciding ballot was cast by Agent K-97:** Reflecting on the referendum, Max Bedacht, one of the delegates at Bridgman, wrote of the undercover Bureau man: "I became personally acquainted with the most contemptible creature in human form,

the *agent provocateur* . . . police agents who help instigate the committing of deeds which can be construed as crimes." Bedacht himself went undercover. He became a leading liaison between American Communists and Soviet intelligence; in 1932 he recruited the young editor of a Marxist journal by the name of Whittaker Chambers to serve Moscow as a spy. Max Bedacht, "Underground and Above: A Memoir of American Communism in the 1920s," unpublished memoir, Tamiment Library, New York University.

53 **"The radical chieftains":** *St. Joseph* [Mich.] *Herald-Press,* Aug. 24, 1922.

54 **"advocated crime, sabotage, violence, and terrorism":** C. E. Ruthenberg, "Foster Verdict a Triumph for Communism in the United States," *The Worker,* April 21, 1923.

54 **two workers on his payroll:** William Z. Foster, "Report on the Labor Union Situation in the United States and Canada," Dec. 16, 1922, by William Z. Foster, Comintern Archive, f. 515, op. 1, d. 99, l. 1–2.

54 **"virtually nonexistent":** J. Edgar Hoover, *On Communism* (New York: Random House, 1969), p. 5.

54 **civil war:** Daugherty, *Inside Story of the Harding Tragedy,* pp. 119–125; **But Daugherty and Hoover escalated:** "Lawless Disorders and Their Suppression," Appendix to the Annual Report of the Attorney General for 1922; Washington, pp. 1–25.

55 **"played into the hands of the radicals":** Daugherty, *Inside Story,* p. 166. Bureau memos on Senator Borah's speech calling for the release of fifty-three men still imprisoned under the Espionage Act were filed on March 12, 1923.

56 **"My image as a Bolshevik":** Burton K. Wheeler with Paul F. Healy, *Yankee from the West* (Garden City, N.Y.: Doubleday, 1962), pp. 200–204. While United States senators such as Borah and Wheeler backed recognition of Russia, American socialists were denouncing the Soviets for killing real and imagined enemies of the state. Eugene Debs had fired off a telegram to the Kremlin in November 1922, saying: "I protest with all civilized people in the name of our common humanity" against political murder committed by the Communists. Debs telegram to Lenin quoted in *The New York Call,* November 1922.

56 **"the Communist leader in the Senate":** Daugherty, *Inside Story,* p. 214.

56 **"the most colossal conspiracy":** Richard A. Whitney, *Reds in America* (New York: Beckwith Press, 1924), pp. 17–19, 48–54.

57 **"If you knew of a great scandal":** Russell, *Shadow of Blooming Grove,* p. 582.

58 **"Get rid of this Bureau of Investigation":** Crim testimony, *Investigation of the Hon. Harry M. Daugherty,* United States Senate, 68th Congress, 1st Session, Vol. 3, p. 2570ff.

58 **"exceedingly bad odor":** Alpheus Thomas Mason, *Harlan Fiske Stone: Pillar of the Law* (New York: Viking, 1956), pp. 147–149.

7. "They never stopped watching us"

60 **"ultra-radical":** Hoover to Stone, July 31, 1924, FBI files, ACLU.

61 **"I think we were wrong," "to leave my desk each day,"** and **"We never knew":** in "They Never Stopped Watching Us: A Conversation Between Roger Baldwin and Alan F. Westin," *Civil Liberties Review* 4 (November/December 1977), p. 25.

62 **"The activities of the Communists"**: Hoover to Donovan, Oct. 18, 1924, FBI. Hoover gave this answer to his immediate superior, the newly appointed chief of the Criminal Division of the Justice Department, William J. Donovan, destined to become the leader of American espionage during World War II and the godfather of the CIA.

63 **"official matters"**: The statute enacted in 1916 says "the Attorney General may appoint officials . . . to detect and prosecute crimes against the United States [and] to conduct such other investigations regarding official matters under the control of the Department of Justice and the Department of State as may be directed by the Attorney General." Nearly sixty years later, President Ford's attorney general, Edward H. Levi, testified that this statute could not stand scrutiny: "the statutory basis for the operations of the Bureau cannot be said to be fully satisfactory."

63 **"This Bureau cannot afford"**: Whitehead, *The FBI Story: A Report to the People* (New York: Random House, 1956), p. 71.

64 **"see that every secrecy is maintained"**: Hoover to Special Agents in Charge, Aug. 6, 1927, FBI/FOIA.

64 **"the entire membership of all New York unions"**: David Williams, " 'They Never Stopped Watching Us': FBI Political Surveillance, 1924–1936," *UCLA Historical Journal* 2 (1981).

8. RED FLAGS

65 **"The workers of this country"**: House Committee to Investigate Communist Activities, Investigation of Communist Propaganda, 71st Congress, 2nd Session (1930), p. 348.

66 **"no department of the government"**: Hamilton Fish, Jr., "The Menace of Communism," *The Annals* 156 (Philadelphia: American Academy of Political and Social Science, 1931), pp. 54–61.

66 **"never been established by legislation"**: Memorandum of a telephone call between J. Edgar Hoover and Congressman Fish, Jan. 19, 1931, cited in "Counterintelligence Between the Wars," *CI Reader*, National Counterintelligence Executive.

66 **"to secure a foothold"**: Hoover to Attorney General Mitchell, Jan. 2, 1932, cited in "Counterintelligence Between the Wars," *CI Reader*, National Counterintelligence Executive.

67 **"active Communist unit"**: Hoover to Kelley, Jan. 20, 1931, cited in "They Never Stopped Watching Us."

69 **"We are now engaged in a war"**: Cummings quoted in Kenneth O'Reilly, "A New Deal for the FBI: The Roosevelt Administration, Crime Control, and National Security," *Journal of American History* 69, no. 3 (1982).

70 **"the criminal standing army"**: Hoover's warning about 4.3 million criminals at large in America were debunked, albeit quietly, in a report to the Senate by the Brookings Institution, included in *Investigation of Executive Agencies of the Government*, 75th Congress, 1st Session (1937).

Part II · World War

9. The Business of Spying

73 **"a very careful and searching investigation"**: Hoover memorandum of conversation, May 10, 1934.
74 **"subversive activities in the United States"**: Hoover memos, Aug. 24 and 25, 1936.
76 **"men of zeal, well-meaning"**: *Olmstead v. U.S.*, 227 U.S. 438 (1928).
79 **"probably have laughed"**: Vetterli to FBI HQ, July 25, 1938, cited in Raymond J. Batvinis, *The Origins of FBI Counterintelligence* (Lawrence: University Press of Kansas, 2007), p. 23. My retelling of the Rumrich case relies on research by Batvinis, a former FBI counterintelligence agent, whose account is the first complete and straightforward narrative of the tale.
80 **On October 14, 1938, Hoover:** Hoover's plans for intelligence and counterintelligence are in two crucial documents: "The Work, Function, Organization of the Federal Bureau of Investigation in Time of War," Oct. 14, 1938; and Hoover's memorandum, enclosed with letter from Cummings to Roosevelt, Oct. 20, 1938. The documents are cited, respectively, in Batvinis, *Origins,* and "Counterintelligence Between the Wars," and together represent a basis for regarding Hoover as the true founding father of central intelligence in the United States.
80 **"He stated that he had approved"**: Hoover memorandum, Nov. 7, 1938.

10. The Juggler

81 **"You know I am a juggler"**: FDR quoting himself at a special study group on Latin America, May 15, 1942, Presidential Diary, p. 1093, Henry Morgenthau Papers, FDRL. The quotation forms the thesis of Warren F. Kimball's classic study, *The Juggler: Franklin Roosevelt as Wartime Statesman* (Princeton, N.J.: Princeton University Press, 1991).
81 **"On June 26, 1939, FDR"**: It read: "It is my desire that the investigation of all espionage, counter-espionage, and sabotage matters be controlled and handled by the Federal Bureau of Investigation of the Department of Justice, the Military Intelligence Division [MID] of the War Department, and the Office of Naval Intelligence [ONI] of the Navy Department. The Directors of these three agencies are to function as a committee to coordinate their activities."
82 **"take charge of investigative work"**: Public statement of the president, Sept. 6, 1939. Attorney General Murphy said at a news conference held the same day: "Foreign agents and those engaged in espionage will no longer find this country a happy hunting ground for their activities. There will be no repetition of the confusion and laxity and indifference of twenty years ago. We have opened many new FBI offices throughout the land. Our men are well prepared and well trained. At the same time, if you want this work done in a reasonable and responsible way it must not turn into a witch-hunt. We must do no wrong to any man. Your government asks you to co-

operate with it. You can turn in any information to the nearest local representative of the Federal Bureau of Investigation."

83 **"Twenty years ago inhuman and cruel things"**: Murphy quoted in J. Woodford Howard Jr., *Mr. Justice Murphy: A Political Biography* (Princeton, N.J.: Princeton University Press, 1968), pp. 205–210.

84 **"Same rule prevails"**: Hoover notation, Tamm to Hoover, Dec. 22, 1937, FBO/FOIA.

84 **"inconsistent with ethical standards"**: *Nardone II,* 308 U.S. 338.

85 **"greatly concerned"**: Hoover to Jackson, April 13, 1940, Library of Congress, Robert H. Jackson Papers, Box 94, Folder 8.

85 **"the very definite possibility"**: Hoover to L. M. C. Smith, Chief, Neutrality Laws Unit, Nov. 28, 1940, FBI, *CI Reader,* "The Custodial Detention Program."

86 **"the various so-called radical"**: Tolson to Hoover, Oct. 30, 1939, FBI, *CI Reader,* "Scope of FBI Domestic Intelligence."

86 **"liberty in this country"**: Memo to E. A. Tamm, Nov. 9, 1939, FBI, *CI Reader,* "Scope of FBI Domestic Intelligence."

86 **"watched carefully"**: Memo to E. A. Tamm, Dec. 2, 1939, FBI, *CI Reader,* "Scope of FBI Domestic Intelligence."

86 **"entirely confidential"**: Hoover to Field Offices, Dec. 6, 1939, FBI, *CI Reader,* "Scope of FBI Domestic Intelligence."

87 **August T. Gausebeck:** The *Rueckwanderer* plot is detailed in Norman J. W. Goda, "Banking on Hitler: Chase National Bank and the Rückwanderer Mark Scheme, 1936–1941," in *U.S. Intelligence and the Nazis,* published by the National Archives Trust Fund Board, Washington, D.C., 2005. The work is based on documents released and analyzed by the National Archives interagency working group on Nazi records.

88 **"undoubtedly sound"**: Franklin D. Roosevelt, Confidential Memorandum for the Attorney General, May 21, 1940, FDRL. Roosevelt's next attorney general, Francis D. Biddle, later wrote: "The memorandum was evidently prepared in a hurry by the President personally, without consultation, probably after he had talked to Bob [Attorney General Jackson]. It opened the door pretty wide to wiretapping of anyone suspected of subversive activities. Bob didn't like it, and, not liking it, turned it over to Edgar Hoover without himself passing on each case." Francis Biddle, *In Brief Authority* (Garden City, N.Y.: Doubleday, 1967), p. 167.

88 **at least 6,769 warrantless wiretaps:** Attorney General Edward H. Levi testimony, Nov. 6, 1975, Senate Select Committee to Study Governmental Operations with Respect to Intelligence Activities (hereinafter "Church Committee").

88 **"The Federal Bureau of Investigation"**: Attorney General Jackson to Justice Department heads, undated.

88 **"the difference between 'investigative' activity and 'intelligence' activity"**: Hoover to Jackson, April 1, 1941; reprinted in *From the Secret Files of J. Edgar Hoover,* edited with commentary by Athan Theoharis (Chicago: Ivan R. Dee, 1993), pp. 184–193.

89 **"The President thought"**: Early to Hoover, May 21, 1940, FDR Library. FDR's thirst for political intelligence on his domestic enemies, and his correspondence with Hoover about that intelligence, is detailed in Douglas M. Charles, *J. Edgar Hoover and the Anti-Interventionists: FBI Political Surveillance and the Rise of the Domestic Security States, 1939–1945* (Columbus: Ohio State University Press, 2007).

90 **"all telephone conversations"**: Hoover to Watson, Sept. 28, 1940, FDR Library.

11. SECRET INTELLIGENCE

92 **The question for the FBI:** The Bureau's handling of the Sebold case was detailed for the first time by Raymond J. Batvinis in his 2007 monograph, "The Origins of FBI Counterintelligence." Batvinis was to my knowledge the first author to review the Sebold case file; my account follows his. American intelligence files say that "the FBI previously had been advised of Sebold's expected arrival, his mission, and his intentions to assist them in identifying German agents in the United States." During one of his four attempts to flee Germany during his forced conscription and training by the Abwehr, Sebold gave a detailed statement to the American vice consul in Cologne.

94 **"a long meeting on coordinated intelligence":** Beatrice B. Berle and Travis B. Jacobs, eds., *Navigating the Rapids, 1918–1971: From the Papers of Adolf Berle* (New York: Harcourt, 1973), p. 321.

12. "TO STRANGLE THE UNITED STATES"

96 **Very little was written about it:** The *History of the SIS* is dated May 22, 1947, unsigned, in five volumes, declassified and released under the Freedom of Information Act in 2007. Volume 1, running 42 pages, is a remarkable document, despite some key deletions in the name of national security. It contains a frank discussion of the FBI's failures, and it evidently was not intended for an outsider's eyes. The administrative files of the SIS are also eye-opening; they are available at the National Archives, in Record Group 65. Quotes from the SIS history are cited herein as *History of the SIS*.

97 **"We certainly picked some fine lemons":** Hoover's notation on FBI radiogram, undated, attached to *History of the SIS*.

98 **"the names of agents that he knew of":** Dallas Johnson interview, FBI Oral History Project (FBI/FBIOH).

99 **"to be in a position":** Hoover to Watson, March 5 and 6, 1941, FDRL.

100 **"the Bureau is marking time":** Hoover to Jackson, April 4, 1941.

101 **"It appears almost certain":** This message and the following Japanese cables intercepted by Magic are reprinted in *CI Reader*, op. cit.

104 **"central enemy intelligence organization":** Thomas F. Troy, *Donovan and the CIA: A History of the Establishment of the Central Intelligence Agency* (Frederick, Md.: University Publications of America, 1984), p. 59.

105 **"the resultant super-Intelligence Agency":** Hoover, General Miles, and Admiral Kirk signed this "Report on Coordination of the Three Intelligence Services," dated May 29, 1941, but transmitted to the War Department on June 5, 1941.

105 **He taped the call:** Transcript of telephone call, July 5, 1941, FBI, Nichols file, reprinted in *From the Secret Files of J. Edgar Hoover*, edited with commentary by Athan Theoharis (Chicago: Ivan R. Dee, 1993), pp. 332–334. The call came after the president asked Astor to handle a very sensitive personal matter: FDR's dissolute cousin Kermit, who was Astor's close friend and President Teddy Roosevelt's son, was on an alcoholic bender and had disappeared with a masseuse named Herta Peters; there

was an off chance that the woman was a German spy. Astor handed this hot potato to the FBI.

106 **"a movement to remove me"**: Do Not File memo, Hoover to Tolson and Tamm, Sept. 23, 1941, *From the Secret Files of J. Edgar Hoover*, p. 339.

107 **"He abhorred homosexuality"**: DeLoach oral history, FBI/FBIOH.

107 **"authority to collect and analyze"**: Troy, *Donovan and the CIA*, pp. 419–423.

107 **"You can imagine how relieved"**: H. Montgomery Hyde, *Room 3603: The Story of the British Intelligence Center in New York During World War II* (New York: Farrar Straus, 1963), pp. 169ff.

108 **"The President was greatly impressed"**: Ibid.

13. Law of War

109 **"It was illegal. It was burglary"**: Chiles oral history, FBI/FBIOH.

111 **"Nothing was said"**: Francis Biddle, *In Brief Authority* (Garden City, N.Y.: Doubleday, 1962), pp. 328ff.

114 **In the fall of 1942**: Details of the investigation were declassified by the National Archives and analyzed by Norman J. W. Goda of the Archives interagency working group on Nazi records. See Goda's "Banking on Hitler: Chase National Bank and the Rückwanderer Mark Scheme," in *U.S. Intelligence and the Nazis*, published by the National Archives Trust Fund Board.

115 **"I do strongly recommend"** and **"I am most anxious and willing"**: Hoover to Strong, Sept. 10, 1942; Administrative Files of the SIS.

116 **"You must remember"**: John Walsh oral history, FBI/FBIOH.

116 **The civilians of the Radio Intelligence Division**: George E. Sterling, "The U.S. Hunt for Axis Agent Radios." Sterling's work was printed in *Studies in Intelligence*, the Central Intelligence Agency's in-house publication, vol. 4 (spring 1960); declassified circa 2007.

The heart of the FCC's Radio Intelligence Division (RID) was made up of hundreds of civilians who ran a network built around twelve main monitoring stations, sixty smaller outposts, and ninety mobile units in the United States. Their job was to police the airwaves. The routine beat for the patrolman of the ether was to cruise the radio spectrum, checking the regular landmarks of transmissions, searching for strange signals, and alerting headquarters in Washington to hunt down enemy stations.

The RID had been picking up and tracking down the radio signals of the clandestine networks of German espionage in Latin America and the Caribbean since the spring of 1941. Over the next eight months, the division listened as the network spread to six nations, with three major stations in Brazil and a fourth in Chile, all in direct communication with the Abwehr in Hamburg. The targets of the German espionage were British and American troops, military aircraft and ships, and the establishment of agent networks throughout the United States. German U-boats were sinking British and American ships all over the Atlantic. British intelligence formed a close liaison with the RID and started schooling the Americans in German codes and ciphers.

On Jan. 15, 1942, five weeks after Pearl Harbor, the RID sent its best people to Brazil, Chile, Mexico, Paraguay, Cuba, and Martinique. They carried suitcase-sized mobile detection units for hunting down clandestine transmitters, whose locations had been fixed to within a few hundred yards by the radio police in the United States. The RID also sent squads to Colombia, Venezuela, Ecuador, Peru, Uruguay, and Haiti to work with the governments of those nations to establish monitoring networks.

On Feb. 11, 1942, RID monitoring stations in Miami, Pittsburgh, and Albuquerque picked up signals from Portugal: SAID THERE IS TO BE DISEMBARKMENT ENGLISH AMERICAN TROOPS DAKAR NEXT FIFTEEN DAYS. WHY NO REPORTS MOST URGENT. The Americans fixed the location of the transmitter outside Lisbon. British commandos took out the Portuguese station and its operators. In Chile, five months of hot pursuit by the radio detectives cleaned out the German spy ring and its transmitters. With the exception of Argentina, whose pro-German government stiff-armed the Americans, so it went throughout most of Latin America.

The Brazilian investigation was the crowning achievement.

When the RID detected a Nazi radio network in Brazil, "they had their monitoring equipment and they would find these clandestine radio signals," the FBI's John Walsh remembered. "Through triangulation they would locate where they were and they could keep moving in until they came close to it. At that point then the Bureau would make arrangements with the local authorities to have these people arrested."

A case in point: an RID monitor in Laredo, Texas, picked up a coded message from Rio de Janeiro, Brazil. It was a simple cipher and quickly broken: QUEEN MARY REPORTED OFF RECIFE BY STEAMSHIP CAMPEIRO AT 18:00 MIDDLE EUROPEAN TIME. The *Queen Mary* was carrying 10,000 American and Canadian troops to war. The Germans in Brazil were tracking her movement for their masters in Hamburg, who would relay her position to U-boats trying to sink her in the Atlantic.

In pursuit of the ship, the German Navy began unrestricted warfare within Brazil's coastal waters. The RID's chief in Brazil, felicitously named Robert Linx, already had mapped the Nazi network. He had fixed the locations of six Nazi radios in Rio, tracking them down with his portable directional finder, monitoring their broadcasts. Linx reported to the U.S. ambassador in Brazil. Hours before German U-boats started hunting the *Queen Mary* as she left the dock in Rio and headed for her home port on a newly altered route, the Brazilian police wrapped up the Axis spy ring, arresting 200 suspects and crushing the German intelligence effort.

116 **"An Agent could not be expected":** *History of the SIS,* vol. 1, pp. 14ff.

14. THE MACHINE OF DETECTION

119 **"a very likely source of information":** Hoover to Attorney General, Feb. 14, 1943, FBI, cited in Katherine A. S. Sibley, *Red Spies in America: Stolen Secrets and the Dawn of the Cold War* (Lawrence: University Press of Kansas, 2004). Sibley's book is the single best source, bar none, on the origins of Soviet espionage in America.

120 **"It was obvious":** The transcript of the wiretap and the FBI's summary of the conversation are reproduced and reliably reconstructed from fragments of declassified

FBI documents cited in *Red Spies in America* and John Earl Haynes, Harvey Klehr, and Alexander Vassilev, *Spies: The Rise and Fall of the KGB in America* (New Haven, Conn.: Yale University Press, 2009).

121 **"like children lost in the woods"**: Duggan's quote comes from a 1940 KGB file cited in Haynes, Klehr, and Vassilev, *Spies*, p. 239.

121 **"a human side of Edgar Hoover"**: Biddle, *In Brief Authority*, pp. 258–259.

122 **"a 'custodial detention' list of citizens"**: Biddle to Assistant Attorney General Hugh Cox and Hoover, July 6, 1943, DOJ, cited in "The Scope of FBI Counterintelligence," *CI Reader*, National Counterintelligence Executive, Director of National Intelligence, pp. 178–181.

123 **"where revolutionary preachings are given"**: Memo for the Director, Aug. 19, 1940, FBI, *CI Reader*, "Scope of FBI Domestic Intelligence."

123 **"opposed to the American way of life"**: Hoover to M. F. McGuire, Assistant to the Attorney General, Aug. 21, 1940, FBI, *CI Reader*, "Scope of FBI Domestic Intelligence."

123 **"who may be dangerous"**: Hoover to FBI Field Offices, "Dangerousness Classification," Aug. 14, 1943, FBI/FOIA.

123 **"key figures"**: Security Index cards were supposed to be prepared "only on those individuals of the greatest importance to the Communist movement"; as of early 1946, after the list was cut back, there were 10,763 Security Index cards on "communists and members of the Nationalist Party of Puerto Rico." D. M. Ladd to Hoover, Feb. 27, 1946, FBI, *CI Reader*, "The Custodial Detention Program."

15. ORGANIZING THE WORLD

127 **"the system that has worked so successfully"**: Donovan to Clark, Aug. 29, 1945, FBI, collected in FRUS Intelligence, pp. 24–26.

127 **"He was in possession"**: Donald Shannon, oral history interview, Sept. 4, 2003, FBI/FBIOH.

128 **"to be in a position"**: Hoover to Watson, March 5, 1941, FDRL.

PART III · Cold War

16. NO GESTAPO

131 **"the right to guide"**: Churchill quoted in Raymond A. Callahan, *Churchill: Retreat from Empire* (Wilmington, Del.: SR Books, 1984), p. 185.

131 **"The joint chiefs of staff"**: The military was widely opposed to Donovan. The United States had three different and opposing teams of spies and secret agents out in the world as the Allies fought to deliver a death blow to Nazi Germany. One was Hoover's. One was Donovan's. And one belonged to the army intelligence chief, General George Veazey Strong.

The general's service was code-named The Pond. Strong had created it shortly after taking his post as chief of army intelligence in the fall of 1942. Its orders were to uncover spying and subversion against the United States by its wartime allies, the British and the Soviets. "Its existence was not known," Brigadier General Hayes Kroner said in secret postwar testimony at a closed congressional hearing; only a very few men, including "the President himself, who had to know by virtue of his approving certain operations, knew it existed." The generals had put a highly unusual army officer, John "Frenchy" Grombach, in charge of The Pond. His orders were impressive: "He would not only institute a secret intelligence service, looking to the current war effort, but he would lay the foundation for a perpetual, a far-seeing, a far-distant, continuing secret intelligence service," General Kroner testified. "That was the birth of high-level intelligence, secret intelligence operations in our government."

The FBI knew Frenchy Grombach well. "As you know," read a report circulated among Hoover's top national security aides, "Colonel Grombach for the past five years has been handling ultra secret intelligence work for the Army and the White House." The colonel long served as an FBI source on Communist influence inside American intelligence.

132 **"their use as a secret intelligence agency"**: Park Report, Rose A. Conway files, OSS/ Donovan folder, HSTL; **"drastic action"**: Colonel Richard Park, Jr., Memorandum for the President, April 13, 1945, FBI/FOIA.

133 **"I said, 'What the hell is this?'"**: Vaughan interview, in Ovid Demaris, *The Director: An Oral Biography of J. Edgar Hoover* (New York: Harper's Magazine Press, 1975), p. 109.

134 **"future communications along that line"**: Vaughan to Hoover, April 23, 1945, HSTL.

134 **"building up a Gestapo"**: FRUS Intelligence, p. 4 (HST conversation with White House budget director Harold D. Smith, May 4, 1945).

135 **"a dumb son of a bitch"**: HST oral history quoted in Merle Miller, *Plain Speaking: An Oral Biography of Harry S. Truman* (New York: Berkley, 1974), p. 226.

135 **Hoover had renewed his power**: See Athan Theoharis, *The FBI and American Democracy: A Brief Critical History* (Lawrence: University Press of Kansas, 2004). We know much of what we know about FBI wiretapping thanks to tireless work over three decades by Theoharis.

A Truman Library oral history given by Attorney General Tom Clark's executive assistant H. Graham Morison—fascinating but unfortunately unverifiable—suggests that at least some wiretap authorizations were rejected during 1946 and 1947:

MORISON: . . . One of my most difficult tasks was those little slips—about just like this, not much larger than that—which would come in from J. Edgar Hoover for authority to wiretap.

Q: Requests from J. Edgar Hoover for wiretapping?

MORISON: Yes. I accumulated those damn things in my desk drawer until I had about fifty and then Edgar called the Attorney General and said, "I want to know why some fifty requests for wiretaps were not acted upon."

He said, "Well, I guess Graham Morison has them. It is his job to first review them."

So, he called and asked about them. I said, "Tom, you revere our Constitution; I know you do, I've talked to you about it. There is no authority in law and it is in contradiction of the civil rights of a free people to permit this invasion of their privacy...." And he said, "Well, Edgar's coming up. You have to carry the ball."

I said, "I'll be delighted to."

So he came up and the Attorney General asked me to state my position to Hoover. ... I said, "Mr. Hoover, about the requested wiretaps. You studied law, as I did. I have a great reverence for our Constitution, and as a lawyer, I am persuaded that you know and I know that we have absolutely no authority—however you may feel about it and despite your desire to know about the actions of citizens—to invade their privacy in peacetime. It makes a mockery out of our Constitution and as far as I'm concerned, I will not let you do it."

And he said, "Well, Mr. Attorney General, what about you?"

Tom Clark replied, "Well, whatever he says, Edgar, I will follow." ... It's a strange thing, but after this incident Tom said, "My God, I thought I would never see the day when somebody would 'buck' Edgar! He has walked over every Attorney General since Attorney General Stone...."

And I said, "Well, blame it on me."

He said, "That's what I intend to do." We never had any repercussions, but it ended the matter while I was there.

Q: Did you block those wiretaps?

MORISON: Every one of them.

Q: Were there no wiretaps by the FBI during the Truman administration?

MORISON: None that required the approval of the Attorney General were authorized while I was Executive Assistant in '46 or '47. There may have been some after I left that post.

135 "to confine the FBI": FRUS Intelligence, p. 4 (HST conversations with White House budget director Smith, July 6 and Sept. 5, 1945).

137 "The future welfare of the United States": Hoover to Clark, Aug. 29, 1945, FRUS Intelligence, pp. 24–26.

137 "Donovan's plans": Hoover to Clark, Sept. 6, 1945, FRUS Intelligence, pp. 31–32.

137 "FBI Plan for United States Secret World-Wide Intelligence Coverage": undated but prepared on Sept. 21, 1945, FBI/FOIA. "The FBI plan provides for the joint operation in every country of the world of the Office of Military Intelligence, the Office of Naval Intelligence, and the Federal Bureau of Investigation," Hoover's presentation read. "Foreign and domestic intelligence are inseparable and constitute one field of operation," he argued. "The Communist movement originated in Russia but operates in the United States. To follow these organizations access must be had to their origin and headquarters in foreign countries as well as to their activities in the United States." Hoover's intelligence reports for the White House in the summer of

1945 covered the subversive activities of Soviets, Germans, Japanese, Chinese, Filipinos, French, Italian, Koreans, Poles, Spaniards, Yugoslavs, and Puerto Ricans in the United States.

137 **"I visited President Truman"**: Chiles to Hoover, Oct. 2, 1945, FBI, FRUS Intelligence, pp. 55–56. In 1990, forty-five years after Hoover sent him to see Truman at the White House, Morton Chiles recorded a home video recounting the conversation: "Mr. Hoover sent me over to see President Truman . . . because it was very urgent that someone get to Mr. Truman before he signed an executive order [which would] put Wild Bill Donovan in charge of world-wide intelligence . . . [Truman] was very grateful that I had come over to brief him on this because he knew nothing of it. He said that Roosevelt never told him anything." Chiles memoir, FBI/FBIOH.

138 **"the President had stated flatly"**: Minutes of the 168th Meeting of the Secretary of State's Staff Committee, Nov. 20, 1945, FRUS Intelligence, pp. 118–120.

138 **"The Americans are currently investigating"**: "Bob" to Moscow Center, Nov. 20, 1945, KGB file obtained by Alexander Vassilev and reproduced in Haynes, Klehr, and Vassilev, *Spies: The Rise and Fall of the KGB in America,* p. 519.

139 **"President Truman was not a man"**: DeLoach oral history, FBI/FBIOH.

17. SHOWDOWN

140 **"Completely unworkable"**: Hoover to Attorney General, Jan. 15, 1946, FBI/FOIA; The attorney general objected to his blunt language: Ladd to Hoover, Subject: "Worldwide Intelligence," Jan. 18, 1946, FBI/FOIA. President Truman's aides deplored FDR's decision to divide the world among the FBI, the army, and the navy. At the White House on Jan. 9, they warned him that the nation was "approaching the subject of intelligence in a most unintelligent fashion." They proposed a new triad of power—the secretaries of war, state, and navy would be served by a new director of Central Intelligence. He would unify military intelligence and have dominion over the FBI. The Bureau would be demoted in the pantheon of American power. Harold D. Smith, "White House conference on intelligence activities," Jan. 9, 1946, FRUS Intelligence, pp. 170–171.

141 **the first director of Central Intelligence**: Three directors of Central Intelligence served Truman from January 1946 to July 1947. They led a small and disorganized service called the Central Intelligence Group. The Central Intelligence Agency was created when Truman signed the National Security Act on July 26, 1947. The powers of the Agency were expanded in 1949.

141 **"He wanted it understood"**: Hoover to Tolson, Tamm, Ladd, and Carson, Jan. 25, 1946, FBI/FOIA.

141 **"General Eisenhower inquired"**: Hoover to Tolson, Tamm, Ladd, and Carson, Jan. 25, 1946, FBI/FOIA.

141 **"What do you want me to do?"**: William W. Quinn, *Buffalo Bill Remembers: Truth and Courage* (Fowlerville, Mich.: Wilderness Adventure Books, 1991), pp. 234–267.

142 **"It is of the utmost urgency"**: Souers to Truman, April 17, 1946, FRUS Intelligence, p. 276.

143 **"She was a flake"**: Jack Danahy, FBI Oral History Project interview, FBI/FBIOH. The

Soviet spy network Bentley served was managed by her lover, Jacob Golos, who had died in 1943. The FBI already had a file on Golos. The Bureau had seen him meet the long-vanished Soviet spy Gaik Ovakimian back in 1941. Ovakimian, in turn, had come to the United States in 1933, when the Roosevelt administration first recognized the Soviets and allowed Moscow to establish diplomatic posts in Washington and New York.

144 **"There is an enormous Soviet espionage ring"**: Hoover memorandum, May 29, 1946, FBI/FOIA.

144 **"It *was* a time of some hysteria"**: Oral history interview with Tom C. Clark, Oct. 17, 1972, HSTL.

144 **"in the event of an emergency"**: Ladd to Hoover, Feb. 27, 1946, FBI, reprinted in *CI Reader*, "The Postwar Expansion of FBI Domestic Intelligence."

144 **"intensify its investigation"**: Hoover to Attorney General, Personal and Confidential, March 8, 1946, FBI, *CI Reader*.

145 **"Move rapidly"**: Hoover notation on memo from Tamm to Hoover, July 18, 1946, FBI/FOIA.

145 **"All investigative files"**: C. H. Carson, "Closing of [Deleted] Office" and "Closing of SIS Offices," Aug. 22 and Sept. 9, 1946, FBI/FOIA.

145 **"to avoid offending Mr. Hoover"**: Tamm to Hoover, Aug. 10, 1946, FRUS Intelligence. Hoover's rage was not quelled. When Attorney General Clark protested Hoover's unilateral withdrawal from the Western Hemisphere, FBI assistant director Ed Tamm gave him a piece of Hoover's mind: "[Director of Central Intelligence] Vandenberg had the effrontery" to hire "men who had deserted from the service of the FBI" as his "alleged intelligence representatives," he told Clark. These men were "definitely persona non grata" with Hoover.

145 **"Watch with meticulous care"**: Hoover notation on memo to Ladd, April 10, 1947, FBI/FOIA. Emphasis in original. Hoover took delight in every snafu that the Central Intelligence Group suffered. Its new station chief in Paraguay, whose Spanish was faulty, registered himself at his hotel as an American ambassador. By coincidence, the actual American ambassador to Paraguay, Willard L. Beaulac, left the country for a conference in Washington that day. The nation's newspapers and radio stations had a field day reporting that Beaulac had been replaced by a mysterious stranger. An FBI radiogram reported the embarrassing incident. "Well, CIG is starting off true to form," Hoover wrote on his copy of the report.

145 **"The 'empire builders' "**: Hoover notation on memo from Ladd, June 2, 1947, FBI/FOIA.

145 **"a major blow"**: Acheson to National Intelligence Authority, Aug. 5, 1946, FRUS Intelligence, pp. 286–287.

146 **"I think we ought to have a showdown"**: Hoover notation on memo to Ladd, Oct. 29, 1946, FBI/FOIA.

146 **"the threat of infiltrating"**: "FBI Plan for United States Secret World-Wide Intelligence Coverage," no date (but updated circa Sept. 1946), FBI/FOIA. The plan was continually updated; this version was included in a package of documentation in preparation for Hoover's congressional testimony on the legislation that became the National Security Act of 1947.

18. "Red fascism"

147 **On September 26, 1946:** Clark Clifford, "Report to the President," Sept. 26, 1946, HSTL; **"Reds, phonies, and 'parlor pinks' ":** Truman diary entry cited in David McCullough, *Truman* (New York: Simon & Schuster, 1992), p. 517.

149 **"Communism, in reality":** Hoover testimony, House Committee on Un-American Activities, March 26, 1947.

150 **"Who's that young man?":** Bradshaw Mintener interview, Ovid Demaris, *The Director: An Oral Biography of J. Edgar Hoover* (New York: Harper's Magazine Press, 1975), pp. 120–121.

19. Surprise Attack

151 **"Very strongly anti-FBI":** Clifford notes of conversation with Truman, May 2, 1947, HSTL.

151 **"a Frankenstein":** Snyder oral history, HSTL.

151 **He artfully twisted the arms:** Hoover's off-the-record briefing was printed at the FBI on July 3, 1947. Its delivery to selected congressmen working on the National Security Act came on Hoover's terms—off the record. It appears here for the first time.

152 **"very frank in his statement":** [Deleted] to Ladd, April 17, 1947, FBI/FOIA.

153 **"the raw material for building":** Testimony of Allen W. Dulles, Hearing of the Committee on Expenditures in the Executive Departments, June 27, 1947. The hearing was closed; a sole surviving copy of the transcript of the testimony of key witnesses was kept in a locked safe at CIA headquarters. Staff members of the House Intelligence and Government Operations committees unearthed it in 1982.

153 **"It is a tragedy":** Hoover notation on memo from Victor Keay to H. B. Fletcher re: Criticism of CIA, FBI/FOIA, Oct. 28, 1948; **"If the people of this nation":** Memorandum for Mr. Ladd re: Central Intelligence Agency, Aug. 11, 1948, FBI/FOIA.

153 **"It strikes me as a waste":** Hoover notation on memo to Ladd, Aug. 19, 1947, FBI/FOIA; **"*Please* cut out all":** Hoover notation on memo, Ladd to Hoover, Oct. 23, 1947, FBI/FOIA, emphasis in original; **"Waste no time on it":** Hoover notation on memo for Ladd, Dec. 11, 1947, FBI/FOIA.

153 **"the present widespread belief":** "Subject: Intelligence Matters," Top Secret memorandum of conversation by John H. Ohly, special assistant to secretary of defense, Oct. 24, 1947, HSTL.

154 **"the smuggling into the United States":** Forrestal to Hoover, Dec. 20, 1948, Top Secret letter quoting Hoover memo to Forrestal dated Nov. 1, 1947, HSTL. Hoover's Nov. 1, 1947, warning to Forrestal on the threat of Soviet atomic terrorism served as a political catalyst. Stratagems to subvert Stalin consumed the secretary of defense, who became a driving force behind the creation of the new clandestine service of the CIA and its overseas operations. The goal was nothing less than undermining the Soviet state, freeing the captive nations of Eastern Europe, and rolling Russia's borders back to where they had been before World War II. The chief of the new covert

operations outfit, Frank Wisner, sought the FBI's help in vetting Russian and Eastern European exiles in the United States whom he sought to train and equip as political shock troops to attack Stalin and his allies. Hoover's men were happy to oblige, as the task enabled them to add to Hoover's dossiers on the CIA. Their boss cast an extremely skeptical gaze on Wisner and his men, whose plans went down in the FBI files as "Project 'X.'"

155 **The United States Army's Signal Intelligence Service:** The navy had its own project aimed at Soviet communications in the Pacific. The army and navy combined their attack before the end of World War II. The American code-making and code-breaking effort became the National Security Agency in 1952.

156 **At that point, General Carter W. Clarke:** On or before Sept. 1, 1947, Clarke briefed the FBI's liaison to army code breakers, Special Agent S. Wesley Reynolds, on the gist of the Soviet diplomatic messages. The FBI's official historian, John F. Fox, Jr., has recorded that "Clarke asked Reynolds if the Bureau knew of any Soviet cover names that might help his team's effort. Reynolds soon turned over a list of 200 known cover names that the FBI had acquired. Most of them had not been found in the traffic to that point." The army gave the FBI received fragments of their decryptions. Reynolds filed them; but "the message fragments were placed in a safe and forgotten" for nine months. John J. Fox, Jr., "In the Enemy's House: Venona and the Maturation of American Counterintelligence," presented at the Oct. 27, 2005, Symposium on Cryptologic History, National Security Agency.

157 **"In view of loose methods":** Hoover worried about the disclosure of secrets throughout the American intelligence community. For example, the question of who knew about the army's payment of $150,000 a year to American communications companies in exchange for copies of foreign diplomatic cables in the Venona program vexed Hoover as well as army general A. R. Bolling, who told the FBI that "only a few people, including the President and the Secretary of Defense" knew about the deal, and advised the Bureau to hold the fact very tightly. Keay memo to Ladd, May 6, 1949, FBI/FOIA. On the opening of the FBI investigation that led to the execution of the Rosenbergs, the documentation includes Ladd to Hoover, Jan. 8, 1953, "re: Julius Rosenberg, Ethel Rosenberg, Espionage-R"; Hoover to New York field office, Aug. 18, 1949; and New York field office to headquarters, Aug. 18, 1949, all first cited in FBI historian Fox's 2005 conference report at the NSA, "In the Enemy's House: Venona and the Maturation of American Counterintelligence." Hoover first wrote in May 1952 that the army and the FBI might consider reading the CIA into Venona despite its "loose methods" and "questionable personnel." Hoover note on a memo from Belmont to Ladd, May 23, 1952, FBI/FOIA.

157 **"We now had dozens":** Robert J. Lamphere and Tom Shachtman, *The FBI-KGB War: A Special Agent's Story* (Macon, Ga.: Mercer University Press, 1995), pp. 96–97.

157 **"I am going through":** Truman to Churchill, July 10, 1948, cited in David McCullough, *Truman* (New York: Simon & Schuster, 1992), pp. 648–649.

158 **"like an animated shuttlecock":** Pearson wrote in his Sept. 26, 1948, syndicated newspaper column, Washington Merry-Go-Round, that the "handsome FBI-man Lou Nichols" met every few days with the chairmen of HUAC and the Senate investigations subcommittee. How did Pearson know this? He correctly suspected that Hoover's men had him under surveillance. So he put Hoover's man under surveil-

lance. He wrote in that same column: "This town's name is not Moscow, but it's gotten to be a place where sleuths tail other sleuths almost as much as the NKVD secret police do."

158 **"an acquittal under very embarrassing circumstances"**: Jones memo to Ladd, Jan. 16, 1947, FBI, cited by the official FBI historian John J. Fox, Jr., "In the Enemy's House: Venona and the Maturation of American Counterintelligence," presented at the Oct. 27, 2005, Symposium on Cryptologic History.

159 **One was Laurence Duggan**: Duggan was grilled by the FBI in December 1948 after Chambers went public; and the next week by his old Soviet intelligence contacts. He died five days later by jumping or falling out of a sixteenth-story window. Hiss was indicted for perjury by a federal grand jury in December 1948 after denying under oath that he had given State Department documents to Chambers. He was convicted and sentenced to five years. Chambers had lied to the grand jury too, but without penalty. Soviet intelligence files published in 2009 proved Hiss had been a spy.

159 **"No, I was not"**: The executive-session testimony Chambers gave was never officially released. Excerpts from the transcript were first published in Sam Tanenhaus, *Whittaker Chambers: A Biography* (New York: Modern Library, 1998), pp. 216–219. The open testimony is at p. 221.

The question of why the FBI deliberately ignored what Chambers had confessed to A. A. Berle in September 1939 and in his first interview with the Bureau in May 1942 has a pointed answer. The journalist Isaac Don Levine had been the go-between for Berle; Hoover had blackballed him in the summer of 1939; when Hoover blackballed you, you and your associates stayed blackballed. Levine had embarrassed the Bureau. He had written a series of stories for the *Saturday Evening Post*—a magazine with five million subscribers—which told the story of Soviet espionage in America for the first time. It was the story of Walter Krivitsky, a senior Soviet intelligence officer who had broken with Stalin, defected in Paris, met with the American ambassador, William Bullitt, and won his help to come to the United States. His information had helped convince Bullitt, once an ardent supporter of Soviet recognition, that Stalin's government was a gigantic conspiracy to commit murder. Ambassador Bullitt, a journalist himself in his youth, knew and trusted Levine as a talented foreign correspondent. He vouchsafed for the Soviet defector.

The *Saturday Evening Post* stories were riveting. They described how Stalin liquidated his real and imagined rivals. They detailed how the Soviet secret police had stolen the passports of the American volunteers who had fought in the Spanish Civil War and used the documents for the international travels of Soviet espionage agents. They laid out in some detail the workings of the Soviet foreign intelligence apparatus in the United States—and they suggested that the Soviets had been running rings around the FBI for years.

The FBI had interviewed Krivitsky twice in New York, the first time shortly after the first article appeared in print. He was the first Soviet spy to speak with anyone at the Bureau. A retired senior FBI counterintelligence officer, Raymond J. Batvinis, reviewed the Krivitsky case file more than sixty years after it was closed. He concluded that Hoover himself decided that Krivitsky could not be trusted and should not be believed. Hoover based his judgment on an editor's note accompanying the first article that described Krivitsky as "still a believer in the true Communism of

Lenin." That was too much for Hoover. He then wrote off Levine because he had written Krivitsky's story. His ban tainted Berle's report. "How can we make sense of the FBI's failure to recognize a unique and extraordinarily valuable source of information that could have broken open Soviet intelligence activities in the Western Hemisphere like an egg?" Batvinis wrote in 2007, with the perspective of a man who had spent his career hunting spies. He concluded that Hoover and his men simply lacked "the professional skills" they needed to interview and understand a defecting Soviet intelligence officer. The result was a lost decade.

160 **"Hoover did his thing"**: Spingarn oral history, March 29, 1967, HSTL, and Spingarn interview in Ovid Demaris, *The Director: An Oral Biography of J. Edgar Hoover* (New York: Harper's Magazine Press, 1975).

160 **"That was contrary to our whole tradition"**: Spingarn oral history, March 29, 1967, HSTL.

160 **"We began to fall out"**: Tom C. Clark oral history, Oct. 17, 1972, HSTL.

160 **"the program for the detention of Communists"**: [Deleted] to Ladd, "CIA Requests for Information Concerning Aliens," Nov. 19, 1948, FBI/FOIA.

161 **"For some months representatives"**: Hoover to Souers, July 7, 1950, FRUS Intelligence.

161 **Congress secretly financed**: In 1971, in a signing statement repealing the Emergency Detention Act of 1950, President Nixon said: "No President has ever attempted to use the provisions of this act. And while six detention camps were established and funded by the Congress, none of them was ever used for the purposes of this legislation. In fact, all six camps have been abandoned or used for other purposes since 1957."

161 **Dewey defeats Truman**: One of the fifty reporters who unanimously predicted Truman's defeat was Bert Andrews, the Washington bureau chief of the reputable Republican daily the *New York Herald Tribune,* who had just won the Pulitzer Prize for a series on the loyalty and security programs. He was a secret confidant for Nixon and Chambers and he plied both men ruthlessly for scoops; riding the arc of the Red hunt, he vowed that he could make Nixon president. When Truman saw the fifty-to-nothing prediction of the press, he said: "I know every one of those fifty fellows. There isn't one of them has enough sense to pound sand in a rat hole."

20. PARANOIA

163 **"She bestrides the world like a Colossus"**: Robert Payne, *Report on America* (New York: John Day, 1949), p. 3.

163 **"She gives the impression"**: Jan. 4, 1945, KGB file cited by Haynes, Klehr, and Vassilev in *Spies,* pp. 288–289. The report on Judith Coplon, aka Sima, was not a decoded Venona message but a file transcribed by Vassilev from KGB archives. The Soviet central intelligence agency changed its name thirteen times between 1917 and 1991. KGB, short for Committee on State Security, was adopted in March 1954 and lasted until Oct. 1991. The Soviet military intelligence service, which also changed its name, is hereinafter GRU, short for Chief Intelligence Directorate.

165 **"O.K.—H."**: Memo to Ladd, Nov. 11, 1949, FBI, cited in Alan F. Westin, "The

Wire-Tapping Problem: An Analysis and a Legislative Proposal," *Columbia Law Review* 52, no. 2 (November 1952), pp. 165–208. Westin's analysis contains extensive excerpts from the Coplon trial and appeals record, including the fact that 50 FBI agents monitored the Coplon taps, that an FBI agent gave false testimony at the first trial, and that the FBI destroyed the wiretap records before the second trial.

165 **"the entire Coplon affair":** Lamphere and Shachtman, *The FBI-KGB War,* pp. 115–122.

166 **By September 7, 1949, informed:** MI5 records cited in Michael S. Goodman, "Who Is Trying to Keep What Secret from Whom and Why? MI5-FBI Relations and the Klaus Fuchs Case," *Journal of Cold War Studies* 7, no. 3 (2005), pp. 124–146.

166 **"Fuchs knew as much":** Keay to Fletcher, "Klaus Fuchs: Espionage," Feb. 21, 1950, FBI/FOIA.

167 **"But after that connection with Gold":** Donald Shannon, FBI Oral History Project interview, Sept. 4, 2003, FBI/FBIOH.

167 **"Take note":** Hoover notation, Ladd to Hoover, "Subject: Foocase," Feb. 16, 1950, FBI/FOIA.

167 **"What the competitors have on them":** Moscow Center to KGB New York, April 10, 1950, Vassilev transcription cited in Haynes, Klehr, and Vassilev, *Spies.*

168 **"At the Hall he had a reputation":** National Security Agency, "L'Affaire Weisband," in *Breaches in the Dike—the Security Cases,* NSA DOCID 3188691.

168 **"implemented a set of defensive measures":** Vassilev transcription of March 1949 and July 1949 KGB files; "The FBI began piecing together": National Security Agency, "L'Affaire Weisband."

168 **"Mr. Hoover was not one who trusted anyone":** Furgerson oral history, FBI/FBIOH.

169 **"It is outrageous":** Hoover note on memo, Keay to Ladd, April 7, 1949, FBI/FOIA.

Trying to battle Allen Dulles for the title of American intelligence czar, Hoover wrote to Dulles staking out his claims. The FBI's authority covered all the foreigners in the United States whom the CIA was trying to recruit and run as agents overseas—not only aliens and defectors but foreign students and businessmen. In short, the CIA should not fish in the FBI's waters. This was a very sore point.

Dulles had convinced members of Congress to draft new and sweeping legislation. The CIA Act of 1949 strengthened and expanded the power of the director of Central Intelligence, the office Dulles sought. Among those proposed powers was the CIA's right to bring foreigners into the United States for training as spies and saboteurs against Stalin. Hoover saw this legislative language as a threat to America. What if the aliens turned out to be double agents? What if a Russian defector learned about American intelligence and then returned to Moscow? Hoover wrote in his royal-blue hand that he would fight "this astounding provision," endorsed by Dulles and his allies at the CIA.

Upon further review, Hoover decided the whole bill was a disaster. "Make certain," he instructed, "that we in no way at any time approve the overall proposition. We oppose its enactment & it is viciously bad."

Hoover wrote to the attorney general that Dulles and his allies threatened "hopeless confusion" on the home front. His warning went unheeded. The CIA Act was rammed through Congress in great secrecy, with next to no debate. It granted the Agency, among other powers, a secret budget hidden in the Pentagon's ledgers, the right to spend that money without accounting for it, the license to bring one hundred aliens a year into the United States and grant them permanent residence status without regard to their past war crimes or terrorist conduct, and a degree of freedom in conducting domestic operations, short of serving as a secret police.

The battle that Hoover and Dulles had begun to wage would shape American intelligence for decades. The fight between the FBI and the CIA started in Washington but it soon spread across the country and overseas. Their theater of war was, on occasion, a theater of the absurd.

Admiral Roscoe Hillenkoetter, Truman's director of Central Intelligence, knew he was unqualified; he had said so himself. But the admiral deeply resented being undermined by Wild Bill Donovan, Allen Dulles, and their favorite CIA officer, Frank Wisner, who ran the Agency's rapidly expanding worldwide campaign of commando operations and psychological warfare against Stalin. All three were leaking derogatory information as part of the Dulles campaign to become director. The admiral took the issue to President Truman and to Hoover; he advised the FBI that "the President had bitterly criticized General Donovan for trying to meddle in CIA affairs and had also termed him 'a prying SOB.' "

Hoover happily placed Harry Truman's pungent observations in his CIA dossier. On April 5, 1950, Hoover's file grew thicker. Hoover had picked up word that Wisner's officers were working in Hollywood, "trying to recruit undercover Intelligence persons in the movie colony out here," as a letter from a reliable informant read. "One of the 'lines' used is that the FBI is all washed up . . . There is quite a whispering campaign going on which is untrue and unfair." Enraged, Hoover demanded a full-scale field investigation of Wisner, his Hollywood recruiters, and their "slanderous statements against the Bureau."

The FBI's liaison at the CIA, Cartha "Deke" DeLoach—a young agent who emulated Hoover in appearance, word, and deed—told the director of Central Intelligence that Wisner's men were "infringing on the jurisdiction of the FBI" and "slanderously trying to undermine the Bureau." The admiral began a long lament against Wisner. He was a lord of misrule; " 'bad elements' and incompetent personnel" were rife among his officers. But his star was ascending. The admiral said Wisner would soon take over every branch of the CIA's worldwide clandestine service; his patron Allen Dulles would be close behind him. The admiral told the FBI agent that he would resign from the CIA as soon as he could find a ship that the president would let him command.

Wisner ran the only branch of the American government on which Hoover did not have a handle. "What do we know of him?" Hoover had written on the first FBI memo to mention Wisner, which misidentified him as a "prominent newspaperman," rather than a well-bred lawyer who had run operations in Romania for Wild Bill Donovan in World War II.

Hoover was appalled to learn, as he soon did, that Wisner's outfit had more money and more power than the FBI.

170 **"This is the most shocking picture":** Hoover note on memo, Mohr to Tolson, "CIA Appropriations," Aug. 18, 1951, FBI/FOIA.

21. "It looks like World War III is here"

171 **"espionage, sabotage, subversive activities"**: Truman statement, July 24, 1950, HSTL. Some of Truman's aides were shocked at the scope of this statement. "How in Hell did this get out?" the national security aide Stephen Spingarn wrote to his White House colleague, George Elsey. "Don't know—thought you were handling," replied Elsey, who suspected Hoover was attempting a power grab.

171 **"ten substantial and highly reliable"**: FBI report to White House, "Present International Situation and the Role of American Communists in the Event of War," Aug. 24, 1950, HSTL.

175 **sexual entrapment and blackmail by foreign intelligence services:** The Soviets ran operations called honey traps. An attractive young woman (or an attractive young man) would flirt with an American abroad. Their coupling took place in a hotel room wired by the KGB. The American would be confronted with pictures of the tryst and a proposition: work with Moscow or face the music. The CIA grappled with cases of this kind in the Truman years. The longtime CIA station chief in Switzerland, a homosexual, had fallen into a honey trap; he was under suspicion of succumbing and serving the Soviets. He was recalled to Washington and he shot himself. The CIA hushed up the case, but the FBI knew a thing or two about it. A few years later, the most powerful foreign policy columnist in Washington, Joe Alsop, fell into a honey trap with a young man in Moscow. The FBI knew all about that one. The FBI also knew, as few did, that throughout the years Whittaker Chambers had been an underground Soviet agent, he had constantly picked up men for furtive one-night stands in New York and Washington. He had broken with communism and homosexuality at exactly the same time. The secrets and the sex—the fake names, the encoded language, the thrills and dangers—had been two sides of one coin to Chambers.

175 **"The Soviets knew"**: Conway oral history, FBI/FBIOH.

175 **Sex Deviates Program:** The origins and scope of the Sex Deviates Program and the Responsibilities Program are laid out in a report to Hoover from the FBI Executives' Conference, chaired by Tolson, "Dissemination of Information by the Bureau Outside the Executive Departments," Oct. 14, 1953, FBI/FOIA.

176 **"General Smith seemed to be"**: Hoover memorandum for Tolson and Ladd, Oct. 18, 1950, FBI/FOIA. Hoover was particularly concerned about a CIA officer named Carmel Offie, who worked under the CIA's clandestine services chief, Frank Wisner. He suspected that Offie was an espionage agent for Israel. He knew for a fact that Offie had well-connected friends in high places all over Washington, that he was a social butterfly with an ear for hot gossip and an eye out for loose lips, and that he was a flamboyant and promiscuous homosexual with a police record for having had oral sex in a public rest room in Lafayette Park, across the street from the White House.

Hoover had the record. An FBI memo to Hoover preparing him for his meeting with General Smith read: "We have on several occasions found it necessary to advise CIA of arrest records received at the Identification Division which reflected the homosexual activity of CIA employees. The case of Carmel Offie represents a typical example. Offie, as you know, remained on the CIA payroll for a long period of time after CIA became acquainted with the fact that he was a homosexual.

"You will recall that Offie is currently being investigated by the FBI due to his alleged participation in Israeli espionage activities," the memo concluded.

177 **"He has been very cooperative"**: Roach to Belmont, transmitting Papich memo, Sept. 27, 1954, FBI/FOIA.

177 **"widely exposed to penetration"**: Keay to Belmont, with Hoover note, transmitting Papich memo, "Central Intelligence Agency/Security of its Operations," July 2, 1952, FBI/FOIA.

178 **"Pursuant to your request"**: Ladd to Hoover, June 24, 1952, FBI/FOIA.

22. No Sense of Decency

179 **Nixon called twice a day**: Ed Tamm, a top aide to Hoover who became a federal judge, recalled that during the Eisenhower administration, "right before the director left for the office, Nixon called him, every morning," and called again "every night, and told him what was going to happen tomorrow and who he was going to see." Tamm interview cited in Curt Gentry, *J. Edgar Hoover: The Man and the Secrets* (New York: W. W. Norton, 1991), p. 404.

179 **"day-to-day and person-to-person"**: "FBI Liaison Activities," Jan. 26, 1953, FBI/FOIA.

180 **"Our bible was Executive Order 10450"**: Walsh interview, Foreign Affairs Oral History (FAOH).

180 **"It was not a good time"**: Grand interview, FAOH.

180 **"The FBI reported to me"**: Attorney General Herbert Brownell, "The Fight Against Communism," national radio and television address, April 9, 1954.

182 **"robbing the whole of the war industry"**: The anonymous letter to Hoover, dated Aug. 7, 1943, was reproduced in the National Security Agency's 1995 release of historical documents from the Venona files.

182 **"How many other like situations"**: Hoover notation on memo from Ladd, June 23, 1947, FBI, cited in John F. Fox, Jr., "What the Spiders Did: U.S. and Soviet Counterintelligence Before the Cold War," *Journal of Cold War Studies* 11, no. 3 (Summer 2009), p. 222. My reconstruction of the career of Boris Morros comes from the decoded Venona documents and the work of John Earl Haynes, Harvey Klehr, and Alexander Vassilev in *Spies: The Rise and Fall of the KGB in America*, pp. 445–453. The key Soviet agent ensnared in the Mocase was a longtime illegal known as Jack Soble, whose cover was a shaving-brush company with importing and exporting offices in Paris. Soble's agents in America included Martha Dodd Stern, the daughter of an American ambassador to Germany; her husband, Alfred Stern, a millionaire New York investment broker; Jane Foster Zlatovski, an 11th-generation American and a veteran of Wild Bill Donovan's Office of Strategic Services, and her husband, George Zlatovski, an army intelligence officer during and after World War II.

183 **"No one need erect"**: McCarthy to Hoover, July 30, 1952, FBI/FOIA.

184 **"McCarthy is a former Marine"**: *San Diego Evening Tribune* interview with Hoover, Aug. 22, 1953, cited in Gentry, *J. Edgar Hoover: The Man and the Secrets*, p. 431.

184 **"neither sacrosanct nor immune":** Transcript of telephone conversation between Allen and Foster Dulles cited in David M. Barrett, *The CIA and Congress: The Untold Story from Truman to Kennedy* (Lawrence: University Press of Kansas, 2005), p. 184.

184 **"Senator McCarthy had found":** Papich to Hoover, Aug. 5, 1953, FBI files, DDEL.

184 **"thirty-one potentially friendly witnesses":** The reports to Hoover and the quotations from conversations between the FBI and McCarthy's staff during the summer and fall of 1953 are recorded in three separate documents: an untitled 12-page report attached to a memo from Roach to Belmont, July 14, 1953, FBI/FOIA; Belmont to Boardman, "Senate Permanent Subcommittee on Investigations (Army-McCarthy Hearings)/Communist Penetration of Central Intelligence Agency," July 28, 1953, FBI/FOIA; and an appended "Analysis of Alleged Communist Penetration into the Central Intelligence Agency Involving Past and Present Employees," July 28, 1953, FBI/FOIA.

186 **"My boys, I am convinced":** Hagerty diaries, June 8, 1954, DDEL.

23. GAME WITHOUT RULES

188 **"The President stated":** Roach to Belmont, "Doolittle Study of Covert Operations/Central Intelligence Agency," Aug. 18, 1954, FBI/FOIA.

188 **"I have a completely defeatist attitude":** Hoover note, Keay to Belmont, "Central Intelligence Agency," Aug. 18, 1954, FBI/FOIA. Hoover's attitude brightened when he saw a detailed FBI report on Doolittle's interview with the CIA's Jim Angleton, who was about to take charge of the Agency's counterintelligence operations. Angleton's work spilled over into domestic politics; like Hoover, he saw American leftists as Moscow's puppets. He also ran a section called Special Projects, salvaging the wreckage of blown covert operations. The report came via Angleton himself, Hoover's best spy inside the CIA. Hoover could not have had a more useful source, short of a wiretap on Allen Dulles.

Hoover and Angleton appeared to have little in common on the surface, save anticommunism. Hoover was one of the most recognized people in America, the tough cop who looked like a well-fed bulldog. Angleton was one of the most shadowy men in Washington, a tubercular chain-smoker who resembled a wraith. But they thought alike. They grasped the intricacies of counterintelligence operations, where one spy service tries to penetrate another unseen. They were skilled at the political intrigues of Washington, where backstabbing is an art form, and alliances struck at noon are betrayed at midnight.

On Aug. 19, 1954, "Angleton advised that he 'opened up' " to the Doolittle group, telling them "exactly how he felt about his agency." The CIA's covert operations were racked by "confusion, duplication, and waste of manpower and money," Angleton said. Many had "failed miserably."

Angleton went on to report that "CIA's counterespionage coverage was disgracefully weak." The men he had to work with included "inexperienced personnel . . . many who became connected with the Agency simply for the ride."

Angleton said the CIA was "incapable of doing an efficient job if political and psychological warfare operations were to be handled jointly with divisions responsible for espionage and counterespionage activities." Running coups, broadcasting propaganda, fixing elections, and bribing politicians was not intelligence work. The real work was the collection of information through espionage—stealing secrets. Hoover could not have agreed more.

Doolittle asked how the FBI and the CIA were getting along. Angleton said that "as far as he was concerned, the relations were excellent." At his level, perhaps they were. But at the top, they were terrible.

189 **"How in the world"**: Keay to Belmont, incorporating Papich memo, "Relations with Central Intelligence Agency; Interview with Allen Dulles, May 22, 1954," FBI/FOIA.

189 **"Doolittle viewed the Bureau"**: Belmont to Boardman, "Doolittle Study of Covert Operations/Central Intelligence Agency," Aug. 30, 1954, FBI/FOIA.

189 **"some of its weaknesses and defects"**: Hoover to Tolson, Nov. 19, 1954, FBI/FOIA.

189 **"We are facing"**: Doolittle "Report on the Covert Activities of the Central Intelligence Agency," Sept. 30, 1954, declassified Aug. 20, 2001, CIA.

190 **"The ideal solution"**: Hoover to Tolson, Nov. 19, 1954, FBI/FOIA.

190 **"His February 28, 1955, report"**: Belmont was a key member of the NSC planning board subcommittee; the report, "Study of Possible Hostile Soviet Actions," was adopted by the president and the NSC on March 31, 1955.

190 **"Plans for the detention"**: Hoover report, "The Internal Security Program," NSC 5509, part 8, April 8, 1955.

190 **"most important goal"**: Hoover report to General Mark Clark, Jan. 25, 1955, FBI/FOIA.

24. THE LONG SHADOW

191 **Using cobalt-60:** Belmont to Roach, "Director's Briefing: National Security Council, March 8, 1956," dated March 22, 1956, FBI/FOIA. This is the only known record that shows the discussion of a "dirty bomb" using cobalt-60 at the NSC briefing.

191 **"Sometimes it is necessary"**: Minutes of the 279th meeting of the National Security Council, March 8, 1956, partly declassified with deletions, DDEL.

192 **Hoover had asked:** On March 8, 1955, Hoover wrote to Attorney General Brownell trying to renew the approvals for warrantless wiretaps he had won in his May 21, 1940, letter from President Roosevelt. Hoover pointedly asked Brownell if that letter still gave the FBI legal authority for wiretapping. If not, Hoover asked the attorney general "to present this matter to President Eisenhower to determine whether he holds the same view." Brownell wrote back eight days later: "I personally explained to the President, the Cabinet, the National Security Council and the Senate and House Judiciary Committees during 1954 the present policy and procedure on wiretaps. . . . I do not think it necessary to reopen the matter at this time."

192 **"Surveillances weren't the answer"**: Jack Danahy, FBI/FBIOH.

193 **"We had a group sort of like the Dirty Dozen"**: James R. Healy, May 3, 2007, FBI/FBIOH.

193 **"we were using every means"**: Graham J. Desvernine, FBI/FBIOH, Oct. 4, 2006. Desvernine soon joined a small group "whose responsibility was solely the surveil-

lance and recording of conversations from within the car of William Z. Foster"—the head of the Communist Party of the United States. Hoover had been after him since the Bridgman raids of 1922. Foster had run for president three times, in 1924, 1928, and 1932—and been imprisoned only once, and briefly, for his work. His car was the setting for one-on-one meetings among the CPUSA's dwindling brain trust. William Z. Foster, the grandfather of the CPUSA, would die in 1961 in Moscow, where he was buried in the Kremlin wall.

193 **"a program of intelligence collection"**: Edward S. Miller, FBI/FBIOH, May 23, 2008. The CIA's brilliant but doomed Berlin Tunnel project, conceived and executed by the cashiered FBI agent Bill Harvey, was the crown jewel of Program C.

194 **"We broke into the house"**: John F. McCormack, Oct. 31, 2006, FBI/FBIOH.

196 **"the terrific propaganda"**: Sullivan oral history interview, in Demaris, *The Director*, pp. 76–77. Emphasis in original.

196 **"He was a brilliant chameleon"**: Sullivan oral history interview, in Demaris, *The Director*, pp. 76–77.

196 **"Brash, brilliant"**: Cartha D. "Deke" DeLoach, *Hoover's FBI: The Inside Story by Hoover's Trusted Lieutenant* (Washington, D.C.: Regnery, 1995), pp. 270–271.

197 **"This is a rough, tough, dirty business"**: Sullivan deposition, Church Committee, Nov. 1, 1975.

198 **"connections with the Communist party"**: Summaries of FBI field office reports in "Scope of FBI Domestic Intelligence," *CI Reader*.

198 **"The Negro situation"**: Hoover to New York Special Agent in Charge, Oct. 2, 1956, FBI/FOIA.

199 **"exploit the enforcement"**: Hoover statement, "Racial Tension and Civil Rights," presented March 9, 1956, DDEL.

199 **"The Klan was dead"**: McCormack oral history, FBI/FBIOH.

199 **"Headquarters came out with instructions"**: Fletcher D. Thompson oral history, FBI/FBIOH. As Thompson recounted, a handful of FBI agents worked the Klan beat in the 1950s: "We had one agent up in Summerton, South Carolina, by the name of E. Fleming Mason, who was one of the Bureau characters—he had a number of high-level informants," Thompson remembered. "Never did he ask them, nor did he arrange the interview, but it just so happened that he ran into them at one place or another and they 'volunteered' this information. I remember one report in particular. Fleming said he was driving down the road one morning and he noticed his socks didn't match and he stopped at this country store to buy a pair of socks. And he saw his friend, the Exalted Cyclops, and 'he volunteered the following information . . .' "

199 a black **"messiah"**: The instructions to the field for the 1968 iteration of the "Black Nationalist" COINTELPRO read: "Prevent the rise of a 'messiah' who could unify and electrify the militant black nationalist movement. Malcolm X might have been such a 'messiah'; he is the martyr of the movement today. Martin Luther King . . . King could be a real contender."

199 **"He was very consistent"**: Sullivan oral history, Demaris, *The Director*, p. 226.

200 **"a CP member with no official title"**: Redacted FBI document dated June 25, 1957, and first cited in David J. Garrow, "The FBI and Martin Luther King," *Atlantic Monthly*, July-August 2002.

25. "Don't trust anybody"

202 **At a formal state luncheon:** United States Ambassador Donald Norland, then a young State Department officer attending the luncheon, overheard Hoover and Nixon as they "talked very animatedly . . . very concerned about the President's health." Norland oral history, FAOH.

202 **"You may be President":** Richard Nixon, *RN: The Memoirs of Richard Nixon* (New York: Simon & Schuster, 1990), p. 184.

203 **"They lived in sheer opulence":** DeLoach, *Hoover's FBI*, p. 103.

204 **"Communism," to quote the director:** Hoover speech, "Communist Illusion and Democratic Reality."

204 **"The word was that this guy's crazy":** Mogen oral history, FBI/FBIOH.

205 **a forged American passport:** Hayhanen had gone before an American diplomat in Helsinki, Finland, bearing the birth certificate of a long-dead boy named Eugene Maki, who had been born to Finnish immigrants in Idaho. The document had been obtained by Soviet agents in America sometime late in the 1940s. He had sailed from England aboard the *Queen Mary* and arrived at New York City on Oct. 21, 1952, carrying a freshly issued American passport awarded on the basis of the birth certificate. Passport fraud was an issue that drove Hoover to distraction. In 1955, he had helped install a personal and political ally, Frances Knight, as the head of the passport office at the State Department, where she worked with a dozen FBI agents. She served Hoover and the FBI with unswerving devotion for twenty-two years. "She was extremely right-wing," recalled Ronald Somerville, a longtime director of the State Department's Bureau of Consular Affairs. "She provided to the FBI and received from the FBI comprehensive reporting on the movements of Americans abroad. She was very active in denying passports to people whose loyalty might be questioned" (Ronald Somerville oral history, FAOH).

205 **the FBI identified sixteen:** 444th Meeting of the National Security Council, May 13, 1960, FRUS 1958–1960, Volume 10, Part 1.

205 **"The FBI kept a keen eye":** William D. Morgan oral history, FAOH.

205 **"One thing about Reino":** Edmund J. Birch oral history, FBI/FBIOH, Aug. 28, 2005.

206 **"a wetback camp":** Gamber oral history, FBI/FBIOH.

207 **"If we discovered a Soviet spy":** Eisenhower at 444th Meeting of the National Security Council, May 13, 1960, FRUS 1958–1960, Volume 10, Part 1.

208 **"We have been trying":** Belmont to Boardman, "Subject: Courier system between Communist Party USA and Communist Party, Soviet Union," Aug. 30, 1957, FBI/FOIA.

208 **The FBI's first debriefings:** The thirty-volume, 4,252-page set of files, an initial release of a far larger dossier, is available online at an FBI website, http://vault.fbi.gov/solo.

210 **"When I introduced him to Hoover":** Nixon oral history interview with Frank Gannon, May 12, 1983, University of Georgia, http://www.libs.uga.edu/media/collections/nixon/nixonday3.html. Emphasis in original.

26. IMMORAL CONDUCT

211 **"This is what happens"**: Hoover note, Rosen to Hoover, March 7, 1959, FBI/FOIA.

212 **"The ensuing problems and publicity"**: Graham Desvernine, FBI/FBIOH, op. cit.

212 **"hoodlum connections"**: Jones to DeLoach, "Senator John F. Kennedy of Massachusetts," July 7, 1960, FBI/FOIA.

214 **"Mitchell had been found"**: Hoover memorandum for Tolson et al., Oct. 14, 1960, FBI/FOIA.

214 **"The President expressed amazement"**: Ibid.

27. "MURDER WAS IN STYLE"

216 **"Castro was to be done away with"**: McAndrews to Rosen, Oct. 19, 1960; "You are advised": Hoover to SAC, Chicago, Airtel/June Mail, June 19, 1961, captioned "Subject: Samuel M. Giancana," FBI/FOIA.

217 **"Senator Homer E. Capehart"**: Papich to Frohbose, "Subject: Fulgencio Batista/Internal Security—Cuba," July 20, 1959, FBI/FOIA.

218 **"If it was highly politically explosive"**: Katzenbach oral history, RFKL.

218 **Eisenhower himself had named**: Memorandum of Conversation between Eisenhower and Secretary of State Christian Herter, Aug. 30, 1960, DDEL. Congressman Cooley, chairman of the House Agriculture Committee, became the target of an unprecedented FBI investigation into political corruption inside Congress four weeks after the start of the Kennedy administration. The congressman, on the take from Dominican Republic dictator Trujillo, was lobbying the new secretary of state, Dean Rusk, for changes in the administration of the law affecting sugar quotas; Trujillo and his families stood to gain or lose millions of dollars. On Feb. 16, 1961, twenty-six days after the new administration took power, Attorney General Robert Francis Kennedy approved FBI wiretaps on Cooley's secretary's telephone in the Capitol, on a lobbyist for the Dominican Republic, and on three Department of Agriculture employees; the FBI later bugged a hotel room where Cooley met with representatives of the Dominican Republic. The question of a dictator having a powerful congressman in his pocket was not simply a question of political corruption. It took on national security implications as presidents tried to cope with the question of dictatorships—Cuba's among others—in the Caribbean. Excerpts from the records of a Feb. 14, 1961, meeting between Rusk and Cooley, which took place two days before RFK approved the wiretaps, give a flavor of the case:

> Secretary Rusk opened the conversation by stating that the Administration accepted a 21-month extension of the sugar bill, wanted it enacted as soon as possible, but felt it of great importance that the bill, as submitted by Congressman Cooley, be amended to give the President discretionary power with respect to that portion of the Cuban quota which might otherwise have to be allocated to the Dominican Republic.

The Secretary based this letter request primarily on the serious potential threat to United States and hemisphere security which is presented by the present situation in Cuba. He indicated that it was essential to take vigorous action to prevent the Castro regime from continuing its efforts to upset peaceful and friendly regimes in Latin America and from becoming a more serious military threat to the United States. . . . To many of these Latin American countries, led by Venezuela, the Dominican Republic presents an equally serious threat to their stability. Failure of the United States to see the problem of Trujillo as a threat equally as serious as Castro will deprive us of the support and sympathy which we need. . . .

To these people it is incomprehensible that the United States should be willing to punish Castro by not buying sugar in Cuba and then turn to the Dominican Republic to replace much of it. It is a windfall and a reward when they think only punishment is justified.

From a United States standpoint, we are also concerned about the current political activities of Trujillo. His propaganda machine, which is well financed, is extremely active and a cause of concern to our intelligence agencies. His publicity has become violently anti-American and sympathetic to many Soviet interests. There is evidence that his regime is in contact with Soviet bloc and Castro representatives.

Congressman Cooley [and House Speaker John McCormack] pressed a number of questions with respect to what we expected to happen in the Dominican Republic if Trujillo was upset. Their great fear was that this prevented an opportunity for a Castro-sponsored regime to take over. . . . Congressman Cooley indicated that he had been discussing the problem of Dominican Republic sugar with a number of people in recent days. . . . Everyone he had talked to had agreed with the Secretary that our Latin American policy would be seriously prejudiced by continued United States purchases of former Cuban quota sugar from the Dominican Republic. He was, therefore, sympathetic to the idea of giving the President discretionary authority. However, he thought it would be desirable in order to secure an orderly transition and prevent a Castro-type take-over if Trujillo could be persuaded that now was a good time for him to retire to some quiet part of the world. He was known to have a substantial fortune abroad. . . . Congressman Cooley suggested that he knew some people who were close friends of Trujillo and could carry such a message to him. They would be persuasive and he thought he might listen to them. He thought this should be done before any action was taken on sugar legislation.

The Secretary protested strongly that there was not time to undertake such a step, even if it were a wise thing to do, before enacting sugar legislation. In addition he felt that the persuasiveness of any such approach would be greatly increased if the President had already been given discretionary authority to cut off the Dominican Republic allotment before Trujillo was talked to. Otherwise, he could still hope that his friends in Washington could save the day for him as they had in the past.

219 **"Get into the underground":** Farland oral history interview, FAOH. A West Virginia native who married the daughter of a coal-company owner, Farland had become a wealthy man, and retired from the FBI after the war, but he had kept his hand in

Washington, becoming a major campaign contributor to the Republican Party, and joining the State Department as a troubleshooter in 1955.

His career path was highly unusual. Farland went on to serve as Kennedy's ambassador to Panama (one of only two Republicans ever to serve as an ambassador under JFK). He became Nixon's ambassador to Iran and Pakistan—where, in the crowning covert mission of his career, he secretly smuggled Henry Kissinger over the Himalayas for secret talks with the Communist leaders of China.

When Farland arrived in the Dominican Republic, the FBI had been embroiled for three years in the case of the kidnapping and killing of an American. A twenty-three-year-old American pilot named Gerald Murphy, who flew for a Dominican airline, had disappeared. His parents in Oregon had mobilized their congressman, Charles Porter, who had demanded an FBI investigation. A federal grand jury had convened in Washington. The case led to the prosecution of a rogue ex-FBI man named John J. Frank. Frank had become one of the people he pursued—an international criminal. After joining the CIA for a short tour, he had parlayed his position into a more lucrative post: a secret agent for Trujillo.

Frank had played a central role in the murder of Jesús de Galíndez, a Columbia University professor who had tutored Trujillo's children, fled the dictator's regime, and moved to New York, where he wrote a book about Trujillo's crimes. Galíndez had reported threats against his life to the New York office of the FBI, to no avail. Frank arranged for Galíndez to be kidnapped at the subway stop outside the gates of Columbia University, stuffed in a car, driven out to a small airfield on Long Island, and thrown into the back of a private aircraft. The plane had been chartered by Joe Zicarelli, a prominent member of the Mafia in New Jersey and a henchman for Trujillo. The pilot was Gerald Murphy. Murphy flew Galíndez down to the Dominican Republic. Trujillo killed Galíndez. Then he murdered Murphy and his Dominican co-pilot in order to keep the conspiracy a secret.

Frank had been arrested and indicted on four counts of serving Trujillo as an unregistered foreign agent, the Justice Department's strategy for charging spies under diplomatically delicate circumstances. The logical next step, from the prosecutor's standpoint, was to indict the Dominican consul general in New York in the conspiracy to kidnap Galíndez. The FBI reports that guided the grand jury proceedings came from wiretaps placed on the Dominican embassy in Washington. The case was monitored by the attorney general, the chief of the Justice Department's criminal division, and Hoover himself.

Trujillo had overseen the plot. How would Washington deal with him? The United States never had charged a foreign leader with capital crimes committed on American soil. President Eisenhower had been questioned on that very issue at a news conference: Did the FBI have jurisdiction to investigate whether "agents of a dictatorship which enjoys diplomatic immunity here are assassinating persons under the protection of the United States flag?" Ike had replied: "I don't know anything about this."

Hoover assured the president that the FBI was on top of the case. But he balked. He informed the Justice and State departments that the case against Trujillo and his henchmen was not "sufficiently watertight."

Ultimately the president would have to decide to kill the investigation or cut the knot that bound American interests to a tyrant.

The former FBI agent, John J. Frank, was ultimately convicted as an unregistered foreign agent of Trujillo's dictatorship, but he never revealed any details of the larger conspiracy.

220 **"Senator Eastland was one"**: Dearborn oral history, FAOH. If the Trujillo case had been pursued as a criminal matter, even as formidable a senator as Eastland could have been charged with acting as an agent of a foreign power.

The political intelligence Farland and Dearborn developed—almost all of which made its way through back channels to the FBI—included the sordid details of visits of other American luminaries on Trujillo's payroll.

The former American ambassador to the Court of Saint James's—the immensely wealthy and ambitious Joseph Kennedy, father of Jack and Bobby—sent a family retainer, a society gossip columnist named Igor Cassini. Then the business magnate Bill Pawley brought a bipartisan team—Bebe Rebozo, who was Nixon's close friend, and Senator George Smathers of Florida, Jack Kennedy's best buddy on Capitol Hill. "Smathers, Bill Pawley and Bebe Rebozo and I all went to see Trujillo," Dearborn recounted. "Smathers gave him this talk. He said, 'Generalissimo, you have the opportunity to be a great hero in this hemisphere. You have the opportunity to be one of the few dictators, one of the only dictators, who was ever able to turn his country into a democracy during his lifetime. If you would do that you would really be a hero to your people and to the hemisphere.'"

Dearborn said: "I sat there thinking, 'Oh Lord, you don't know who you are talking to.'"

220 **"Castro has among his chief lieutenants"**: Four reports from Farland as well as information clearly derived from him are in FRUS 1958–1960, Volume 6, *American Republics*, "United States policy regarding certain political developments in the Caribbean and Central American area," pp. 357–459.

220 **"a considerable amount of information"**: Hoover cited in "Memorandum of a Meeting, Department of State, Jan. 29, 1959," pp. 357–360.

220 **"offered his services"**: M. A. Jones to DeLoach, Subject: Frank Fiorini, aka Frank Anthony Sturgis, IS [Internal Security]/Cuba, April 1, 1959, FBI/FOIA. Summaries of the Sturgis memo went to the CIA, leading to the recruitment of Sturgis. They also went, in a sanitized form, to the State Department. In the summer and fall of 1959, Farland's reporting from the DR and stepped-up FBI surveillance of Cuban intrigues in the United States began to reach a critical mass.

The reporting from the Dominican Republic and Cuba proved a pivotal factor in Hoover's decision to open up a new front for the FBI in 1959: the systemic bugging and wiretapping of the Mob. Farland's reporting on the connection among American politicians, organized crime, and Caribbean strongmen eroded Hoover's long-held resistance.

Hoover got into the act in the summer of 1959 as a Senate subcommittee stepped up its public interrogation of Mafia dons. The driving force of the Senate subcommittee, known as the Rackets Committee, was its counsel, Robert F. Kennedy. RFK, drawing on his experience as minority counsel for the McCarthy committee, hired three talented ex-FBI agents as rackets investigators. One of them, Walter Sheridan, also had worked for the National Security Agency and had gained experience in the uses of electronic surveillance.

An illegal bug planted in Las Vegas serendipitously led the FBI into the CIA's plots against Castro. On Oct. 31, 1960, the Bureau picked up an arrest report from the Las Vegas police department. A hotel maid had stumbled on a bug being installed on orders from a detective named Arthur Balletti. The detective had been hired by a private eye named Robert Maheu—an ex-FBI agent who worked for the billionaire Howard Hughes, moonlighting as a CIA informant and a servant of the Vegas mob. The target of the bug was Giancana's two-timing girlfriend, the nightclub singer Phyllis McGuire. Hoover's handwritten orders pushed the FBI full speed ahead: "Yes & press vigorously on Giancana, Maheu & Balletti. H."

The Las Vegas bugging arrest allowed the FBI to lean heavily on Maheu, who eventually laid out the details of the 1960 CIA-Mafia contract on Castro.

221 **"I went all by myself"**: Farland oral history, FAOH.

222 **"ex-FBI agents"**: Testimony of Richard Bissell, former CIA clandestine division director, Church Committee, July 22, 1975.

222 **"to remove Trujillo"**: Herter to Eisenhower, "Possible Action to Prevent Castroist Takeover of Dominican Republic," April 14, 1960, DDEL.

Trujillo's enemies were emboldened by Ambassador Farland and his number-two man, Henry Dearborn, who succeeded him as the acting ambassador. Both Americans had assured the conspirators that the United States would smile upon their work. "Ambassador Farland had had contacts with the opposition and had brought me in on them," Dearborn said. The opposition did not trust the CIA, but "they had gotten to trust Farland and me. So I carried on the contacts with the opposition, reporting to CIA. We were using all these weird means of communication because we didn't want to be seen with each other. Things like notes in the bottom of a grocery bag, rolled up in cigars. They were asking us for advice at times. They were asking us for help at times.

"They developed an assassination plot," Dearborn said. "I knew they were planning to do it. I knew how they were planning to do it. I knew, more or less, who was involved. Although I was always able to say that I personally did not know any of the assassins, I knew those who were pulling the strings.

"What they wanted from the U.S.," Dearborn said, "was moral support and, later, material and token weapon support." They were not disappointed. The CIA sent them three .38 caliber pistols and four machine guns, delivered to the Dominican Republic in a State Department diplomatic pouch. By the time the weapons arrived, Farland, the FBI agent turned ambassador extraordinary, had returned to Washington.

222 **"he was being bombarded"**: Memorandum of Conference with the President, May 13, 1960, Office of Staff Secretary, Eisenhower Papers, DDEL. General Andrew Goodpaster, Ike's military aide, wrote the memorandum on May 16. The president was in the foulest mood on May 13—weathering, in his words, in "a great storm" over the CIA's U-2 spy plane that had crashed during a secret flight over the Soviet Union. The pilot, Francis Gary Powers, was a prisoner in Moscow (he was eventually exchanged for the Soviet spy known as Colonel Rudolph Abel). The Soviet leader Nikita Khrushchev had humiliated the United States. Ike's anger can be inferred from the record created by General Goodpaster.

28. Dangerous Man

223 **"rather frightening":** Robert F. Kennedy oral history, JFKL.

223 **"Bobby was trying to take over the FBI":** DeLoach oral history, LBJL.

223 **Hoover had told his old friend:** The eyewitnesses to the demands from Joe Kennedy that JFK take RFK as attorney general—and Hoover's personal approval of that choice—were JFK's friend Senator George Smathers of Florida; RFK's aide John Seigenthaler; and Hoover's assistant, Cartha "Deke" DeLoach. "Some of Bobby and the President's personality may have come from old man Joe Kennedy, who didn't mind bowling people over," DeLoach said, perceptively. "He loved the usage of power, and so did the President and Bobby—Bobby, I think, more than the President."

224 **"We did it for the reason":** Robert F. Kennedy oral history, JFKL.

224 **"He offended the FBI":** Katzenbach oral history, JFKL.

224 **"most unpleasant":** RFK oral history, JFKL.

225 **"The great problem now":** RFK handwritten notes cited in Church Committee report.

226 **"I kept the Kennedys from firing Hoover":** Evans oral history, in Deborah Hart Strober and Gerald S. Strober, *The Kennedy Presidency: An Oral History of the Era* (Washington, D.C.: Brassey's, 2003), p. 269.

226 **"For years CIA has not played":** Hoover notations on memos, [Deleted] to Sullivan, April 2, 1962, and Evans to Belmont, April 20, 1963; FBI/FOIA.

226 **"analyze the weaknesses of US intelligence":** Director, FBI, to the Attorney General, "The Central Intelligence Agency," blind memorandum hand-delivered April 21, 1961; Belmont to Parsons, "Central Intelligence Agency/Report for the Attorney General," April 21, 1961.

227 **"The driver of the bus":** Joseph G. Kelly oral history, FBI/FBIOH, Aug. 29, 2004.

228 **"We had a leak":** Crockett oral history, FAOH.

228 **"Sheridan was the principal":** LBJ White House tapes, Nov. 17, 1964, LBJL.

229 **"The leaker was one Otto Otepka":** Crockett oral history, FAOH.

29. Rule by Fear

230 **"When I heard":** RFK oral history, JFKL. Kennedy set the date of this revelation in 1961; some historians believe the meeting was in 1962, but the circumstantial evidence suggests the earlier date is correct. Hoover went on high alert after King and Levison met the attorney general and his top civil rights aides in a private dining room at the Mayflower Hotel—an odd choice of venue, since Hoover usually took his lunch at the Mayflower. Hoover quickly learned about the meeting. It represented, to him, a Communist penetration—a secret agent's access to the highest levels of the American government. No one took any notes that survived, but the conversation remained in the memory of those who were there. Kennedy advised King that the Justice Department had little jurisdiction to protect civil rights leaders from the Klan or southern lawmen. Sit-ins and civil disobedience were not the way, Kennedy advised; an orderly campaign for blacks to register and vote was the right

path. After the lunch, Kennedy's assistant John Seigenthaler took King aside and warned him about Levison: the man was a known Communist, and King would best be rid of him. King replied, in so many words, that it would be hard to break that tie.

230 **The substance of their conversation:** Hoover memo to Tolson, Belmont, Sullivan, DeLoach, Jan. 9, 1962; Evans to Belmont, Feb. 2, 1962; Bland to Sullivan, Feb. 3, 1962, FBI/FOIA.

231 **Lesiovsky's meeting with Levison:** The FBI's surveillance of the meeting was the result of a very lucky break: a member of the Soviet delegation who worked for the Soviet military intelligence service had offered to serve the FBI as an agent in place. On March 13, 1962, the FBI reported that Dmitri Polyakov, code-named Top Hat, had identified every member of the Soviet diplomatic delegation in New York and Washington who served as a spy for Moscow. Top Hat helped the FBI track diplomatic developments at a high level. SA Edward F. Gamber to SAC New York, "Subject: United Nations Personnel—USSR," March 13, 1962, FBI/FOIA. On the Levison connection to the KGB's Lesiovsky, Birch oral history, FBI/FBIOH.

232 **"Under no circumstances":** Hoover notation, Bland to Sullivan, Feb. 3, 1962, FBI/FOIA.

232 **"that bastard":** The March 22, 1962, meeting between Hoover and JFK has been reconstructed through existing White House records by Robert Kennedy's and Martin Luther King's best biographers, Evan Thomas and Taylor Branch, respectively, but they both rely on hearsay evidence for the "bastard" quotation reproduced here.

232 **"I expressed astonishment":** Hoover's May 9, 1962, memo for the record was published by the Church Committee in 1975.

232 **"Courtney I hope":** Hoover, May 22, 1961, memo to RFK and RFK's notation, quoted in Church Committee, *Assassination Plots, Interim Report: Alleged Assassination Plots Involving Foreign Leaders*, pp. 127–128. Hoover's memo reported that the FBI had interviewed the CIA's security chief, Sheffield Edwards: "Colonel Edwards advised that in connection with CIA's operation against Castro he personally contacted Robert Maheu," an ex–FBI agent who worked, simultaneously, for the CIA, the Mafia, and the Las Vegas billionaire Howard Hughes. The memo noted that Maheu had served the CIA "as a 'cut-out' in contacts with Sam Giancana, a known hoodlum in the Chicago area."

233 **"Levison influenced him":** RFK oral history, JFKL. RFK's close aide and successor, Nick Katzenbach, agreed. "Given the Bureau's statement about Levison as being true, and given the way they stated it which was flatly and positively and—from really making it spooky as far as the source is concerned—I'd no reason to doubt that," Katzenbach said in his own oral history for the JFK Library.

Levison told King they should break off their relationship, he told the historian Arthur Schlesinger, Jr., in 1976: "The movement needed the Kennedys too much. I said it would not be in the interests of the movement to hold on to me if the Kennedys had doubts."

But as the historian David J. Garrow has written, after reviewing FBI records released a decade ago:

> King remained reluctant to lose Levison's assistance and counsel, and thus he detailed a mutual friend, the young African-American attorney Clarence B. Jones,

of New York, to serve as a telephonic intermediary between himself and Levison. Marshall and Robert Kennedy picked up on the ruse almost immediately, and within days Kennedy had authorized the wiretapping of Jones's home and office. Kennedy considered adding a tap on King as well, but decided to hold off.

In early August of 1963 King happened to stay at Jones's home for several days, at which point both the FBI and, by extension, the Kennedys were introduced to a new aspect of King's life—namely, his sexual endeavors, which in subsequent months would all but replace Levison as the focus of the FBI's surveillance of King. But at that time Marshall and Robert Kennedy were far more worried by the extensive evidence of King and Levison's communication by way of Jones. The wiretap in Jones's office recorded King saying, "I'm trying to wait until things cool off—until this civil rights debate is over—as long as they may be tapping these phones, you know. . . ."

David J. Garrow, "The FBI and Martin Luther King," *Atlantic Monthly*, July–August 2002.

233 **Hoover commanded the FBI:** Director to SAC Atlanta, "Communist Infiltration of the Southern Christian Leadership Conference: Internal Security," July 20, 1962, FBI/FOIA.

233 **"The Klan got involved":** Woodcock oral history, FBI/FBIOH.

234 **"I go in to see Hoover":** Davis oral history, FBI/FBIOH.

235 **"The 19 million Negroes":** William C. Sullivan, "Communist Party USA/Negro Question/Internal Security—Communist," Aug. 23, 1963, with Hoover notations and Sullivan's response, FBI/FOIA.

235 **"a really politically explosive document":** Katzenbach oral history, RFK Oral History Project, JFKL.

236 **eight wiretaps and sixteen bugs:** Brennan to Sullivan, "Subject: Martin Luther King Jr./Security Matter—Communist," April 18, 1968, FBI/FOIA. The taps on King's home telephones remained in place until April 1965; the SCLC taps until June 1966.

236 **"It's a moral issue":** McGorray oral history, FBI/FBIOH.

236 **"Hoover was telling me":** Jack Danahy oral history, FBI/FBIOH.

236 **"King is a 'tom cat' ":** Sullivan to Belmont, with Hoover notation, Jan. 27, 1964, FBI/FOIA.

236 **4,453 members:** William C. Sullivan, "Communist Party USA/Negro Question/Internal Security—Communist," Aug. 23, 1963, FBI/FOIA.

236 **"I have some news for you":** William Manchester, *The Death of a President* (New York: Harper & Row, 1967), pp. 195–196. The source for this account was Robert F. Kennedy but, as always, it was his word against Hoover's. "Manchester is a liar but it was obvious he was fed this by R.F.K.," Hoover scribbled in a note to his aides on Feb. 15, 1967. FBI/FOIA.

237 **"Oswald was a confidential informant":** DeLoach to Mohn, "Assassination of the President/Allegation That Oswald Was an FBI Informant," Feb. 7, 1964, FBI/FOIA.

237 **"their training, violent tendencies":** Sullivan to Belmont, Nov. 26, 1963, FBI/FOIA.

237 **"gross incompetency," "We failed," and "a direct admission":** Hoover and DeLoach memos, Dec. 10, 1963, and Oct. 14, 1964; cited in "The Investigation of the Assassina-

tion of John F. Kennedy," a staff report of the Church Committee conducted in 1975 but classified and unpublished until 2000.

30. "YOU GOT THIS PHONE TAPPED?"

239 **"Edgar, I don't hear you well"**: LBJ/Hoover, LBJ telephone tapes, Feb. 27, 1964, LBJL.

239 **"You're my brother"**: LBJ/Hoover, LBJ telephone tapes, Nov. 29, 1963, LBJL.

240 **"J. Edgar Hoover is a household word"**: Lyndon B. Johnson, Remarks Honoring J. Edgar Hoover, May 8, 1964.

240 **"One of the troubles"**: McGeorge Bundy oral history, LBJL.

240 **"Mr. Hoover's going down"**: RFK to LBJ, LBJ telephone tapes, July 10, 1964, LBJL.

241 **"I have no dealings with the FBI"**: RFK to LBJ, LBJ telephone tapes, July 21, 1964, LBJL.

241 **"Mr. Johnson at all times"**: DeLoach oral history, LBJL.

241 **"three sovereignties"**: The quotation of LBJ comes from Burke Marshall, RFK's civil rights deputy at Justice. Marshall oral history, LBJL. It was Marshall's idea to use the FBI against the Klan. In a written proposal that RFK sent to the White House on June 5, 1964, Marshall presented the Klan's work as "terrorism" and a threat to the internal security of the United States. Marshall strongly recommended that the FBI identify Klansmen and work undercover to expose the Klan's infiltration of state and local law enforcement in the Deep South: "The techniques followed in the use of specially trained, special-assignment agents in the infiltration of Communist groups should be of value," Marshall wrote. "I recommend taking up with the Bureau the possibility of developing a similar effort to meet this new problem."

242 **"We have found the car"**: Hoover to LBJ, LBJ telephone tapes, June 21, 1964, LBJL.

242 **"I haven't got a better friend"**: LBJ to Hoover, LBJ telephone tapes, June 24, 1964, LBJL.

242 **"You ought to review"**: Dulles to Hoover and LBJ, LBJ telephone tapes, June 26, 1964, LBJL.

244 **"Mr. Hoover never would have changed"**: Marshall oral history, Strober and Strober, *The Kennedy Presidency*, p. 317.

244 **"I want you to gather intelligence"**: Billy Bob Williams oral history, FBI/FBIOH.

244 **"Martin Luther King yelled"**: Donald Cesare oral history, FBI/FBIOH.

246 **"I paid him close"**: Cesare oral history, FBI/FBIOH. No informant in FBI history ever had been paid that much, as far as is known. Some funds for paying FBI informants were raised by Jewish business community leaders in Mississippi, according to several agents, including James O. Ingram, one of the more accomplished counter-Klansmen at the FBI. Jews in Jackson, Miss., "had long supported the FBI, by money and their efforts to help us. They made available money to the FBI for informants," Ingram said. It is unclear whether Delmar Dennis, whose recruitment dated to the summer of 1964, received funds that originated from outside the FBI. Important FBI informants among Mississippi Klansmen defected before Dennis, including Sgt. Wallace Miller of the Meridian Police Department.

247 **"There would be a Klan meeting"**: Joseph J. Rucci, Jr., oral history, FBI/FBIOH.

248 **"The Bureau was doing"**: Billy Bob Williams oral history, FBI/FBIOH.

248 **"the race riots"**: Hoover to LBJ, LBJ telephone tapes, Sept. 9, 1964, LBJL.

248 **"I'm very grateful to you"**: LBJ to Hoover, LBJ telephone tapes, Oct. 23, 1964, LBJL.

249 **"He told me he had spent"**: RFK oral history, JFKL.

250 **"He *knows* Martin Luther King"**: LBJ to DeLoach, LBJ telephone tapes, Nov. 20, 1964, LBJL.

250 **"He flatly denied"**: Nicholas deB. Katzenbach, *Some of It Was Fun: Working with RFK and LBJ* (New York: Norton, 2008), p. 154.

250 **"I'll tell you"**: LBJ to Katzenbach, LBJ telephone tapes, March 4, 1965, LBJL.

251 **"We had this case wrapped up"**: Shanahan oral history, FBI/FBIOH.

251 **"We will not be intimidated"**: LBJ televised remarks, March 26, 1965, LBJL.

31. "The man I'm depending on"

253 **"We're really going"**: LBJ to Mann, LBJ telephone tapes, April 24, 1965, LBJL.

254 **"We have no evidence"**: Undersecretary Thomas Mann to United States Ambassador Tap Bennett, Feb. 25, 1965, Foreign Relations of the United States, 1964–1968, Volume 32, Dominican Republic.

254 **"With Bureau approval"**: Estill oral history, FBI/FBIOH.

255 **"In my opinion"**: Director of Central Intelligence Raborn to President Johnson, April 29, 1965, LBJ telephone tapes, LBJL.

257 **"They fly us down in this C-130"**: Paul Brana oral history, FBI/FBIOH.

258 **"I arrived at the Regency Hotel"**: Kennedy M. Crockett, Memorandum for the Record, Johnson Library, National Security File, May 18, 1965, with copies to Mann, Vance, Helms, Vaughn, and Bromley Smith for Bundy. Balaguer was identified as a recruited FBI source by Wallace Estill and Paul Brana. The record is in Foreign Relations of the United States, 1964–1968, Volume 32, Dominican Republic. Balaguer's FBI handler, Heinrich Von Eckardt, was, implausibly, the son and namesake of the German ambassador to Mexico during World War I; the ambassador had been an addressee of the Zimmerman Telegram, the intercepted cable that drew America into the Great War.

259 **"Have we done that"**: This tape is shot through with deletions made in the name of national security. Though edited here for length, it conveys a president at the edge of his endurance. The Dominican crisis drove LBJ half-mad, in the eyes of some of his top aides. "Highly dubious reports from J. Edgar Hoover" agitated the president's mind, said Undersecretary of State George Ball. "The President became the desk officer on the thing. He ran everything himself . . . This became a thing of such passion, almost an obsession." But Johnson was starting to lose faith in his own judgment. "I don't always know what's right," LBJ said to Fortas on May 23. "Sometimes I take other people's judgments, and I get misled. Like sending troops in there to Santo Domingo. But the man that misled me was *Lyndon Johnson*. Nobody else! I did that!"

261 **"What would my instruction"**: David Atlee Phillips, *The Night Watch: 25 Years of Peculiar Service* (New York: Atheneum, 1977), p. 155.

261 **"provide excellent fodder"**: Memorandum of Conversation, Washington, Sept. 1,

1965, Foreign Relations of the United States, 1964–1968, Volume 32, Dominican Republic.

262 **"That whole operation was really weird"**: Crimmins oral history, FAOH.

262 **"It is an awful mess"**: Hoover to President Johnson, Sept. 10, 1965, LBJ telephone tapes, LBJL.

263 **"The President expected"**: "Subject: Presidential Election in the Dominican Republic," Dec. 29, 1965, in Foreign Relations of the United States, 1964–1968, Volume 32, Dominican Republic. The memorandum from acting director of Central Intelligence Helms to the CIA's deputy director for plans Desmond FitzGerald deserves a fuller quotation:

> I want to reiterate, for the record, that the President told the Director and me on more than one occasion between May and mid-July, he expected the Agency to devote the necessary personnel and material resources in the Dominican Republic required to win the presidential election for the candidate favored by the United States Government. The President's statements were unequivocal. He wants to win the election, and he expects the Agency to arrange for this to happen.
>
> If you are finding road blocks in the way of getting on with this operation, I would appreciate being advised, so that the difficulties can be identified to the President with the aim of securing his influence on the side of financial allocations in support of the appropriate candidate. RH

263 **"Hoover has furnished"**: Rostow to Johnson, "Balaguer's First Appointments," June 11, 1966, Foreign Relations of the United States, 1964–1968, Volume 32, Dominican Republic.

32. Clearly Illegal

264 **"The Chinese and North Vietnamese"**: Hoover memo for the record, April 28, 1965, cited in Church Committee, "COMINFIL Investigations—The Antiwar Movement and Student Groups."

264 **"We were engaged almost every weekend"**: Gamber oral history, FBI/FBIOH.

264 **"The demonstrations have been marked"**: Hoover to FBI Special Agents in Charge, May 3, 1966, cited in Church Committee, "Civil Disturbance Intelligence."

265 **"I was, frankly, astounded"**: Katzenbach, *Some of It Was Fun,* p. 182. Katzenbach realized that the surveillance of Martin Luther King was potential political dynamite. The FBI planted its last bug on King in November 1965. But wiretaps on King's close adviser, the suspected Communist Stanley Levison, remained in place.

265 **Hoover had installed 738 bugs**: FBI assistant director James Gale to FBI assistant director Cartha DeLoach, May 27, 1966, FBI/FOIA.

266 **"Students for a Democratic Society, which"**: Hoover memo for the record, April 28, 1965, FBI/FOIA.

266 **"Wire taps and microphones"**: Hoover to Katzenbach, Sept. 14, 1965, FBI/FOIA.

267 **"He cannot be trusted"**: M. A. Jones to DeLoach, Aug. 2, 1965, FBI/FOIA, cited in Church Committee, "Warrantless FBI Electronic Surveillance."

267 **"Just how gullible can he be!":** Hoover notation on memo to Tolson, "Subject: letter to Sen. Edward Long," Jan. 21, 1966, FBI/FOIA.

267 **"He was always willing":** Cartha D. "Deke" DeLoach, *Hoover's FBI: The Inside Story by Hoover's Trusted Lieutenant* (Washington, D.C.: Regnery, 1995), p. 58. Fortas had to step down from the Supreme Court in 1969 because of his ethical transgressions; his conduct in *Black v. U.S.* stayed secret for two decades. Fred Black was a business associate of Bobby Baker's; Baker was the secretary of the United States Senate when Lyndon Johnson was the majority leader, and he had been accused, but not yet convicted, of political corruption. Hoover had it on good authority (including bugs and wiretaps) that Baker had been a procurer of prostitutes for senators of both parties.

268 **"No more such techniques":** Hoover notation, Sullivan to DeLoach, July 19, 1966. FBI/FOIA.

Breaking and entering clearly violated the Fourth Amendment's ban on unwarranted searches and seizures. So did mail opening, as the Supreme Court had ruled in an 1878 case, *Ex Parte Jackson*:

> The constitutional guaranty of the right of the people to be secure in their papers against unreasonable searches and seizures extends to their papers, thus closed against inspection, wherever they may be. . . . No law of Congress can place in the hands of officials connected with the postal service any authority to invade the secrecy of letters and such sealed packages in the mail; and all regulations adopted as to mail matter of this kind must be in subordination to the great principle embodied in the fourth amendment of the Constitution.

268 **"clearly illegal":** "Such a technique involves trespass . . . ," Sullivan memo with Hoover's notation, July 19, 1966, all reprinted in Church Committee files and in Theoharis, *From the Secret Files of J. Edgar Hoover,* pp. 129–130; 147–152. LBJ and RFK may not have fully grasped the legal and technical differences between a wiretap on a telephone line, which could be legally authorized, and a bug, a hidden microphone whose installation usually required breaking and entering without a warrant.

268 **"In our time in the Bureau":** Miller oral history, FBI/FBIOH.

269 **"Someone got to the old man":** Church Committee staff summary of Louis Tordella interview, June 16, 1975. The CIA's James Angleton accurately assessed the effect that the changing political climate had on Hoover. "The Congress was delving into matters pertaining to FBI activities," he said. "Mr. Hoover looked to the President to give him support in terms of conducting those operations. And when that support was lacking, Mr. Hoover had no recourse." Angleton testimony, Church Committee hearings, Sept. 24, 1975.

269 **"Hoover put us out of business":** Cregar classified testimony, Aug. 20, 1975, Church Committee staff files.

Hoover had threatened to pull the plug on the FBI's surveillances once before: "I want consideration given to terminating *all* technicals—H." That note came thundering down from the director on July 21, 1958. "Terminating all technicals" would have meant an end to electronic surveillance—the use of bugs and the break-ins required to install them—and the destruction of hundreds of American intelligence operations. The root of Hoover's wrath was a CIA leak to Congress about a Soviet defector. Hoover's anger faded, but his threat to pull the FBI's bugs from every secret hiding place in America remained.

270 **For the next decade, from 1966 to 1976:** A grand total of eleven espionage cases were brought against Americans in that decade, and nine of them were investigated by military intelligence and tried by military courts. The primary cause of this decline in FBI counterespionage and counterintelligence was the ceaseless demand by presidents Johnson and Nixon to focus on the political warfare against the American Left. LBJ told Deke DeLoach "that much of the protest concerning his Vietnam policy, particularly the hearings in the Senate," could be traced to the Soviets and their allies. The statistics and the underlying causes are analyzed in *Espionage Against the United States by American Citizens, 1947–2001*, Defense Personnel Security Research Center, July 2002.

270 **"That guy traveled":** Edmund Birch oral history, FBI/FBIOH.

271 **"King was told by Levison":** Hoover to LBJ, July 25, 1967, LBJ telephone tapes, LBJL.

271 **"disrupt, misdirect, discredit":** FBI headquarters to field offices, Aug. 25, 1967, FBI/FOIA.

272 **liberal-minded men:** The intelligence coordination among Attorney General Clark, Deputy Attorney General Christopher, the military, the CIA, and the FBI was detailed first in hearings before the Senate Judiciary Subcommittee on Constitutional Rights on April 9 and 10, 1974, and later in the Church Committee's reports. The major programs undertaken by the FBI, the CIA, and the military were code-named Shamrock and Minaret.

272 **"I don't want anybody to know":** LBJ to Hoover, Feb. 14, 1968, LBJ telephone tapes, LBJL. The full context of these heated discussions is in Foreign Relations of the United States, 1964–1968, Volume 7, November 1–12, 1968: South Vietnamese Abstention from the Expanded Peace Conference; the Anna Chennault Affair.

274 **"The Negro youth and moderates":** FBI headquarters to field offices, April 3, 1968, FBI/FOIA. Hoover's "dead revolutionaries" warning came the day before the assassination of Martin Luther King.

275 **"I have been appalled":** FBI headquarters to field offices, July 23, 1968, FBI/FOIA.

275 **"He became a kind of Messiah":** Hoover memorandum for the record to Tolson, DeLoach, Sullivan, and Bishop, June 19, 1969, FBI/FOIA.

275 **"We've lost Thieu":** LBJ telephone tapes, Nov. 1, Nov. 4, Nov. 8, Nov. 12, and Nov. 13, 1968. LBJ determined—after the election—that he could not prove the charge. The FBI, at LBJ's command, eventually traced five telephone calls placed from the campaign plane of Republican vice presidential candidate Spiro Agnew in Albuquerque, New Mexico. One was a telltale: a conversation between Nixon's clandestine emissary, Anna Chennault, at a Nixon command center in Washington, and an Agnew aide named Kent Crane, a former CIA officer. The tapes and conversations on the Chennault intrigue are recorded in Foreign Relations of the United States, 1964–1968, Volume 7, November 1–12, 1968: South Vietnamese Abstention from the Expanded Peace Conference; the Anna Chennault Affair.

276 **"If it hadn't been for Edgar Hoover":** Nixon, *RN: The Memoirs of Richard Nixon*, pp. 357–358. The telephone call to Hoover during the Nixon meeting is recorded in LBJ's daily diary.

33. The Ultimate Weapon

277 "The risk of war": Nixon's sworn deposition in *Halperin v. Kissinger*, Jan. 15, 1976.

277 "I will warn you now": Nixon, *RN: The Memoirs of Richard Nixon*, pp. 357–358.

277 "my closest personal friend": Nixon White House tapes, May 3, 1972.

278 "he'd come in alone": Nixon White House tapes, Feb. 16, 1973.

278 "Almost unbelievable conversation": H. R. Haldeman, *The Haldeman Diaries: Inside the Nixon White House* (New York: G. P. Putnam's Sons, 1994), p. 192.

278 "florid and fat-faced": John Ehrlichman, *Witness to Power: The Nixon Years* (New York: Simon & Schuster, 1982), pp. 156–157.

278 "conducted, without a search warrant": Nixon response to interrogatories, Church Committee, March 9, 1976.

278 "That was Mr. Hoover's common practice": Grand jury testimony of Richard Nixon, June 24, 1975, Watergate Special Prosecution Force Records, online at http://www.archives.gov/research/investigations/watergate/nixon-grand-jury/.

279 "This is the way civilizations": Nixon statement on campus disorders, March 22, 1969.

280 "Attorneys General seldom directed": Nixon testimony, *U.S. v. Felt*, Oct. 29, 1980.

280 "his friend and White House confidant": Ehrlichman, *Witness to Power*, pp. 156–159.

281 "What is this": The outrage of Nixon and Kissinger at the leaks, and their handling of the wiretaps, is best summarized in Walter Isaacson, *Kissinger: A Biography* (New York: Simon & Schuster, 1992, 2005), pp. 212–227.

281 "Within days": Nixon, *RN: Memoirs*, p. 387.

282 "Hoover informed me": Nixon deposition, *Halperin v. Kissinger*.

282 "Here he was in this room": Rodman oral history, FAOH.

282 "a leak which was directly responsible": Nixon deposition, *Halperin v. Kissinger*.

282 "Dr. Kissinger said": Hoover memorandum of conversation with Kissinger, May 9, 1969, FBI, July 9, 1969, 5:05 P.M.

283 "express your appreciation": "Talking Points for Meeting with J. Edgar Hoover, Wednesday, June 4, 1969," Library of Congress, Kissinger Papers, Box TS 88.

284 "Here's your machine": Dyson oral history, FBI/FBIOH.

284 "the potential to be far more damaging": Sullivan to DeLoach, Sept. 8, 1969, FBI/FOIA.

287 "attacks against the police": Brennan to Sullivan, Feb. 3, 1969, FBI/FOIA.

287 "to form commando-type units": Brennan to Sullivan, Jan. 26, 1970, FBI/FOIA.

287 "They were a bunch of renegades": Perez oral history, FBI/FBIOH.

287 "Hoover had no idea": Jones oral history, FBI/FBIOH.

34. "Pull down the temple"

288 "the greatest mistake I ever made": Mark Felt and John O'Connor, *A G-Man's Life: The FBI, Being "Deep Throat," and the Struggle for Honor in Washington* (New York: Public Affairs, 2006), p. 121.

288 **"moving ahead of the winds"**: Sullivan to Helms, Oct. 24, 1968, FRUS 1964–1968, Volume 33.

289 **"I do not think"**: Huston testimony, Church Committee, Sept. 23, 1975.

289 **"President Nixon was insatiable"**: DeLoach oral history, FBI/FBIOH.

289 **"gave us all hell"**: Nolan oral history, FBI/FBIOH.

290 **"The President chewed our butts"**: Staff summary of Bennett testimony, Church Committee, June 5, 1975.

290 **"revolutionary terrorism"**: "Presidential Talking Paper: Meeting with J. Edgar Hoover, Richard Helms, Lt. Gen. Bennett and Adm. Gayler, June 5, 1970," Haldeman White House Files.

290 **"Individually, those of us"**: Sullivan memorandum, June 6, 1970, Church Committee files.

290 **"I saw these meetings"**: Cregar testimony, Church Committee staff summary, Aug. 20, 1975.

291 **"went through the ceiling"**: Sullivan deposition, Nov. 1, 1975, Church Committee.

291 **"in view of the crisis of terrorism"**: Nixon, *RN: Memoirs,* pp. 474–475.

292 **"Hoover has to be told"**: Huston to Haldeman, Aug. 5, 1970.

292 **"Mitchell and I"**: Haldeman, *Haldeman Diaries,* p. 243.

293 **"I was told five times"**: Mardian oral history, Strober and Strober, *The Nixon Presidency,* p. 225.

293 **"running all over the place"**: Mark Wagenveld, "Delco Raid Forced Changes in FBI," *Philadelphia Inquirer,* March 8, 1996.

294 **"to steal the nomination"**: Nixon White House tapes, May 26, 1971.

294 **"The national security information"**: Ibid.

295 **"Do you remember Huston's plan?"**: Nixon White House tapes, June 17, 1971.

295 **"Why Watergate?"**: Miller oral history, FBI/FBIOH.

296 **"Hoover refused to investigate"**: Nixon White House tapes, May 9, 1973.

296 **"In terms of discipline"**: Nixon White House tapes, June 29, 1971.

297 **"As a young Congressman"**: Nixon at graduation exercises of the FBI National Academy, June 30, 1971.

299 **"He was trying to demonstrate"**: Nixon, *RN: Memoirs,* pp. 598–599; "At the end of the day": Haldeman, *Haldeman Diaries,* p. 357.

299 **"He may have suffered"**: Ray Wannall, *The Real J. Edgar Hoover: For the Record* (Paducah, Ky.: Turner Publishing, 2000), p. 146.

299 **"playing on the paranoia"**: Felt and O'Connor, *A G-Man's Life,* pp. 116–121.

299 **"There were a few men"**: Hoover memorandum of conversation with Rep. H. Allen Smith, May 23, 1966, FBI/FOIA.

300 **"We have those tapes"**: Nixon White House tapes, Oct. 8, 1971.

301 **"We've got to avoid the situation"**: Nixon White House tapes, Oct. 25, 1971.

301 **"Sullivan was the man"**: Ibid.

301 **"We got to get a professional"**: Nixon White House tapes, March 13, 1973.

303 **"As political attacks on him multiplied"**: Felt and O'Connor, *A G-Man's Life,* p. 160.

303 **"That son of a bitch Sullivan"**: Wannall, *The Real J. Edgar Hoover,* p. 147.

PART IV · **War on Terror**

35. CONSPIRATORS

307 "Oh, he died": Nixon White House tapes, June 2, 1972.

307 "Pat, I am going to appoint you": L. Patrick Gray III with Ed Gray, *In Nixon's Web: A Year in the Crosshairs of Watergate* (New York: Times Books, 2008), pp. 17–18.

307 "Never, never figure": Nixon White House tapes, May 4, 1972.

307 "an interloper bent on pushing"; "they lied to each other": Gray, *In Nixon's Web*, pp. 23–27.

308 "Once Hoover died": Miller oral history, FBI/FBIOH.

310 "He laughed because": Bledsoe oral history, FBI/FBIOH.

310 "It was agreed": C. W. Bates, "Subject: James W. McCord Jr. and Others," June 22, 1972, FBI/FOIA.

310 "The FBI is not under control": Nixon White House tapes, June 23, 1972.

311 "I again told him": C. W. Bates, "Subject: James W. McCord Jr. and Others," June 22, 1972, FBI/FOIA.

311 "These should never see the light of day": Gray, *In Nixon's Web*, pp. 81–82. Dean corroborated Gray's account in his Watergate testimony.

311 "There is little doubt": "FBI Watergate Investigation/OPE Analysis," July 5, 1974, FBI/FOIA.

312 if "the President decides": The oral arguments and the ruling are from the Supreme Court records of *U.S. v. U.S. District Court*, decided June 19, 1972, and more commonly known as the *Keith* case, after the federal trial court judge whom the Justice Department sued to prevent the disclosure of the warrantless wiretaps. It soon became clear why the Justice Department had fought so long and so hard against the disclosures. The FBI had placed a warrantless tap on the White Panther headquarters in Ann Arbor. The Bureau also had overheard the defendant Plamondon on a warrantless tap aimed at discovering ties between Black Panthers and Palestinian radicals; that surveillance had been part of a highly classified program called MINARET, in which the FBI and the National Security Agency had collaborated to spy on members of the radical antiwar and black power movements since 1967.

313 "They will kidnap somebody": Nixon White House tapes, Sept. 21, 1972.

313 "Everybody at that meeting": Gray, *In Nixon's Web*, p. 117.

313 "he had decided to reauthorize": Miller oral history, FBI/FBIOH.

314 "hunted to exhaustion" and "No holds barred": Miller oral history, FBI/FBIOH; Felt and O'Connor, *A G-Man's Life*, pp. 259–260. See also Gray, *In Nixon's Web*, pp. 117ff. The FBI's Paul Daly led the subsequent internal investigation of John Kearney, leader of the FBI's Squad 47: "I believe I counted up over eight hundred break-ins, for which he was commended." The Justice Department eventually dropped the case against Kearney, once its investigators understood that he had been following orders from the top of the chain of command.

314 "It hurt all of us deeply": Bolz oral history, FBI/FBIOH.

315 "There is a way to untie the Watergate knot": Woodward notes, October 9, 1972,

Harry Ransom Center, www.hrc.utexas.edu/exhibitions/web/woodstein/deepthroat/
felt.

315 **"They would meet at the end of the day":** Daly oral history, FBI/FBIOH.

316 **"We know what's leaked":** Nixon White House tapes, Oct. 19, 1972.

316 **"we'll screw up our source":** The White House knew thanks to Roswell Gilpatric—
a lawyer for *Time* and once JFK's deputy secretary of defense. The magazine's top
editors had ordered their reporter, Sandy Smith, to identify Felt as his own source.
Then they betrayed his confidence by telling Gilpatric, who told his friend John
Mitchell that Felt was leaking the FBI's secrets.

317 **"They would probably ask you":** Nixon White House tapes, Feb. 16, 1973; Gray, *In
Nixon's Web*, pp. 152–77.

36. "THE BUREAU CANNOT SURVIVE"

320 **An FBI agent interviewed the Iraqi:** Finnegan testimony, *United States v. Khalid
Mohammed el-Jessem*, United States District Court for the Eastern District of New
York, 73 CR 500, March 6, 1993.

The case against el-Jessem, aka Kahlid Jawary, is reconstructed here from the federal court records of his 1993 trial; a partially declassified National Security Agency
history, "The First Round: NSA's Efforts Against International Terrorism in the
1970's"; an FBI situation report sent out under Director L. Patrick Gray's name,
"Black September Organization Activities," dated March 25, 1973; and Santo F. Russo,
"In re Extradition of Khaled Mohammed El Jassem: The Demise of the Political Offense Provision in U.S.-Italian Relations," *Fordham International Law Journal* 16, no.
4 (1992). After serving sixteen years of his sentence, the Iraqi was deported to the
Sudan in February 2009.

323 **"The Bureau cannot survive":** Nixon White House tapes, March 1, 1973.

323 **"For Christ's sake":** Nixon White House tapes, March 1, 1973.

324 **"The quid pro quo":** Nixon White House tapes, March 13, 1973.

324 **"Dean had lied to us":** Gebhardt to Baker, "Subject: Confirmation," March 7, 1973,
FBI Watergate Special Prosecutor Files.

324 **"I would have to conclude":** Hearings on the Nomination of L. Patrick Gray, Senate
Judiciary Committee, March 22, 1973.

324 **"Gray is dead":** Nixon White House tapes, March 22, 1973.

325 **"Dean has apparently decided":** Gray, *In Nixon's Web*, p. 238.

325 **"I'm worried":** Nixon White House tapes, April 17, 1973.

325 **"This is stupidity":** Nixon White House tapes, April 26, 1973.

326 **"I had never seen":** Ruckelshaus speech to National Association of Former U.S. Attorneys, Oct. 3, 2009.

326 **"Felt—everybody's to know":** Nixon White House tapes, May 12, 1973.

326 **"a dangerous game we were playing":** FBI Special Agent Nick Stames interview with
John H. Mitchell, May 11, 1973, FBI/FOIA.

327 **"I don't think a cop should run the Bureau":** Nixon White House tapes, Oct. 25, 1971.
There were strong rumors at the FBI that Nixon's choice had come down to either

Clarence Kelley or Bill Sullivan. The FBI's Paul Daly said: "Kelley told me that when he went in to interview with the President . . . he sat beside Sullivan, and Sullivan went in first and came out, then he went in. And it was a very close call." Nixon's available presidential records do not confirm that Sullivan was signed in at the White House that day.

327 **"I was shocked by the wounds"**: Clarence M. Kelley and James Kirkpatrick Davis, *Kelley: The Story of an FBI Director* (Kansas City, Mo.: Andrews, McMeel & Parker, 1987), p. 116.

37. HOUSE OF CARDS

330 **"The FBI engaged in a prolonged series"**: *Socialist Workers Party v. Attorney General*; 73 Civ. 3150; 642 F. Supp. 1357 (Southern District of New York).

332 **"sirens, endless streams of sirens"**: Hahn oral history, FBI/FBIOH.

333 **"It was done clandestinely"**: Dyson oral history, FBI/FBIOH.

333 **"Why not add the FBI?"**: Memorandum of Conversation, Oval Office, Jan. 4, 1975, Gerald R. Ford Presidential Library.

333 **"The FBI may be the sexiest part of this"**: Memorandum of Conversation, White House, Feb. 20, 1975, GRFL.

333 **"designed for the Civil War era"**: Kelley to Attorney General, Aug. 7, 1974, FBI/FOIA.

334 **"warrantless searches"**: John C. Kenney, Acting Assistant Attorney General, filing in *U.S. v. Ehrlichman,* United States Court of Appeals for the District of Columbia, May 9, 1975.

334 **a die-hard believer in the Bureau**: Healy oral history, FBI/FBIOH.

335 **"the long line of Attorneys General"**: Church Committee, *Federal Bureau of Investigation,* at 1–2 (statement of Chairman Frank Church).

335 **"government monitoring"**: Testimony of Attorney General Edward H. Levi, FBI Oversight: Hearings before the Subcommittee on Civil and Constitutional Rights of the House Committee on the Judiciary, April 6, 1976.

336 **"Nobody wants to work terrorism"**: Dyson oral history, FBI/FBIOH.

38. "A STATE OF CONTINUAL DANGER"

337 **"knowledgeably, knowingly, intentionally deceived"**: Kelley transcript, *Meet the Press,* Aug. 8, 1976.

337 **"very little bad news"**: Kelley and Davis, *Kelley: The Story of an FBI Director,* pp. 39–40.

338 **"an FBI agent appeared at my door"**: Edward H. Levi, address to Los Angeles County Bar Association, Nov. 18, 1976.

338 **"You're going to have to let me think"**: Daly oral history, FBI/FBIOH.

339 **"We don't ask our agents to squeal"**: Kelley news conference, July 14, 1975, FBI/FOIA/Black Bag Jobs file, Vol. 13, p. 82.

339 **"Dear Clarence"**: Felt to Kelley, personal communication, June 20, 1974, FBI/FOIA/Felt file, Vol. 10, p. 169.

341 A man's home is his castle: Miller oral history, FBI/FBIOH.

341 "Safety from external danger": Alexander Hamilton, *The Federalist* no. 8.

343 "One of the things that disturbs me": Kelley confirmation hearings, Senate Judiciary Committee, June 19, 1973.

343 "The superhuman image": Kelley public statement, FBI headquarters, Aug. 11, 1976.

343 "a crippled and beleaguered FBI": Kelley public statement, FBI headquarters, Aug. 11, 1976.

344 "He had these steely blue eyes": Boynton oral history, FBI/FBIOH.

344 "do the work": Webster oral history, Miller Center of Public Affairs, presidential oral history program, Aug. 21, 2002.

344 "to pretend that we have a charter": Webster oral history, Miller Center.

346 "What was missing": Webster oral history, FBI/FBIOH.

347 "a bastard godchild": Ault interview, FBI/FBIOH.

347 "I had no idea": Mason oral history, FBI/FBIOH.

347 he was one of the very few: During the 1980s and 1990s, the Bureau wasted well over $1 billion on computer systems that never worked. Among the first of these failed technologies was a 1980s database called the Terrorist Information System. It was supposed to provide instant readouts on 200,000 people and 3,000 organizations. "Great concept," said Richard A. Marquise, later one of the FBI's leading terrorism investigators. "Totally useless."

348 "an incredible assault": Webster et al., "A Review of FBI Security Programs," Commission for Review of FBI Security Programs, Justice Department, March 2002.

39. The Price of Silence

351 "one of the most gut-wrenching investigations": Pimentel oral history, FBI/FBIOH.

353 "blatantly false": Revell testimony, Senate Intelligence Committee, Feb. 23, 1988.

353 From 1988 onward: In Oct. 2009, the United States Department of Homeland Security began judicial proceedings to deport Vides Casanova on the grounds that he had tortured political prisoners in El Salvador. A final judgment was scheduled as this book went to press in January 2012.

353 "They were skillful collectors": Webster oral history, FBI/FBIOH.

354 "There is little or no doubt": Hunter oral history, FBI/FBIOH.

355 "At first he was less than enthused": Oliver "Buck" Revell and Dwight Williams, *A G-Man's Journal* (New York: Pocket Books, 1998), p. 217.

357 "That was my first experience with espionage": York oral history, FBI/FBIOH.

357 "Mathews considered himself": Matens memoir reprinted in FBI/FBIOH.

358 "I did not want to turn the FBI": Webster oral history, FBI/FBIOH.

360 "Reagan was preoccupied": Robert M. Gates, *From the Shadows: The Ultimate Insider's Story of Five Presidents and How They Won the Cold War* (New York: Simon & Schuster, 1996), p. 397.

362 "The Attorney General doesn't": Revell deposition, *Report of the Congressional Committees Investigating the Iran/Contra Affair*, June 11, 1987, pp. 909ff.

363 "I was sort of odd man out": Ibid.

363 "A real bombshell": Vice President Bush's diary entry for Nov. 22 and his FBI inter-

view on Dec. 12, 1986, are described in the *Final Report of the Independent Counsel for Iran/Contra Matters*, United States Court of Appeals for the District of Columbia, Aug. 4, 1993.

365 **"We probably could have overcome"**: Duane R. Clarridge with Digby Diehl, *A Spy for All Seasons: My Life in the CIA* (New York: Scribner, 1997), p. 371.

365 **"effectively neutralized"**: Revell, *A G-Man's Journal*, p. 296.

365 **"down to zero"**: Revell testimony, House Committee on International Relations, Oct. 3, 2001.

365 **"terrorism was not a big deal"**: Marquise oral history, FBI/FBIOH.

40. Mosaic

367 **"The FBI was not set up"**: Marquise oral history. The FBI's work on Pan Am 103 is minutely described in Marquise's book on the case: *SCOTBOM: Evidence and the Lockerbie Investigation* (New York: Algora Publishing, 2006).

370 **"fearlessly moved"**: Robert S. Mueller III combat citation (2nd Platoon, H Company, 2nd Battalion, 4th Regiment, 3rd Marine Division), Dec. 11, 1968.

370 **"Getting Director Sessions' full attention"**: Baker oral history, FBI/FBIOH.

373 **Megrahi was indicted:** Qaddafi turned Megrahi over to the long arm of international law in 1999. He was found guilty by a Scottish court sitting in the Netherlands in 2001, but released in 2009 after a diagnosis of cancer and threats against the British government by Qaddafi. In February 2011, Qaddafi's justice minister, after defecting during the NATO attack on Libya, said unequivocally that Qaddafi had commanded the bombing of Pan Am 103.

41. The Blind Sheikh

375 **"destroying the structure of their civilized pillars"**: *United States v. Abdel Rahman*, 93 Cr. 181, United States District Court, Southern District of New York, Government exhibit 76T.

375 **"If it had been properly"**: Revell testimony, House Committee on International Relations, Oct. 3, 2001.

375 **"We were feeling pretty good"**: Revell testimony, House Committee on International Relations, Oct. 3, 2001.

376 **"I believe the defendant"**: *State of New York v. El Sayyid Nosair*, sentencing hearing, Jan. 29, 1992, Manhattan Criminal Court.

376 **"Salem's penetration had"**: Andrew C. McCarthy, *Willful Blindness: A Memoir of the Jihad* (New York: Encounter Books, 2009), p. 10.

376 **"We couldn't let you make a bomb"**: Salem recorded his conversations with both the FBI and the targets of the investigation on his own; transcripts of the tapes quoted here were introduced as trial evidence in *United States v. Abdel Rahman*. As Assistant United States Attorney Andrew McCarthy wrote: "Salem had installed a home recording system that would have made the Nixon White House blush. He would sometimes wear amateur body wires to meetings with FBI agents and cops. He was

not systematic about it. When he was out of tape and wanted to make new recordings, he would haphazardly grab an old tape and record over it. But what tapes he had, he maintained—here, there and everywhere in the clutter of his home. All sixty-seven of them, capturing well over two thousand conversations which I was just thrilled beyond words to have to share with over a dozen salivating defense lawyers. Salem wanted to help the FBI and, in his supreme self-confidence, believed he could infiltrate the jihad group. He would not try it, however, unless he was given iron-clad assurance that he was involved only in intelligence-gathering, just as it had been with the Russians, and not in an investigation regarding which his public testimony might one day be required . . . The [FBI] agents misled Salem, Salem lied to the agents, and it ended in a disastrous parting of the ways."

377 **"Egypt's most militant Sunni cleric"**: Unsigned CIA analysis, "Hizballah Ties to Egyptian Fundamentalists," in CIA *Near East and South Asia Review*, April 24, 1987, CIA/FOIA.

378 **"Quickly, when I came into office"**: Reno testimony, National Commission on Terrorist Attacks upon the United States (9/11 Commission), April 14, 2004.

379 **"The speed at which this occurs"**: Hahn oral history, FBI/FBIOH.

379 **"I told you they will blow bombs"**: *United States v. Abdel Rahman*.

380 **"The big house, I will take care of it"**: *United States v. Abdel Rahman*.

42. FLAWS IN THE ARMOR

382 **"He came to believe"**: Louis J. Freeh with Howard Means, *My FBI: Bringing Down the Mafia, Investigating Bill Clinton, and Fighting the War on Terror* (New York: St. Martin's, 2005), pp. 177ff. Freeh's book is a classic Washington memoir, though often dubious and disingenuous. I cite it only to reflect Freeh's direct experience. Freeh distorts many aspects of his dealings with the White House. A small case in point: The FBI created a pointless controversy after it mistakenly sent the Clinton White House the files on four hundred people who had held security clearances under Presidents Reagan and Bush. When these files turned up, Freeh's aides asserted that Clinton had solicited them. That was false. But Freeh publicly protested that the White House was smearing the good name of the FBI. This was a symptom of a far more serious problem.

382 **"One of the greatest flaws"**: Steinberg oral history, Sept. 27, 2000, National Security Council Project, Brookings Institution/Center for International and Security Studies, University of Maryland; **"His mistrust of the White House"**: Clinton's national security aides Steven Simon and Daniel Benjamin reported in *The Age of Sacred Terror* (New York: Random House, 2002), p. 301. More pithily, Clinton's political aide John Podesta told the reporter John Harris, then at *The Washington Post*, that Freeh's first name never passed Clinton's lips: it was always *Fucking Freeh*, as in *Fucking Freeh has screwed us again*.

383 **When President Clinton expressed:** Freeh, *My FBI*, p. 263. The FBI's expenditure of working hours on the Chinese campaign contributions case exceeded all terrorism investigations from 1995 to 2002: "Federal Bureau of Investigation Casework and Human Resource Allocation," Office of the Inspector General, Justice Department,

September 2003. On the Katrina Leung case and its suppression during Freeh's tenure at the FBI, see "A Review of the FBI's Handling and Oversight of FBI Asset Katrina Leung," Office of the Inspector General, Justice Department, May 2006. FBI Agent Smith was sentenced to three years' probation and a $10,000 fine. FBI Agent Cleveland—"a very religious man who was universally well regarded, dedicated to the FBI, and considered a mainstay in the FBI's China Program in the 1980s and early 1990s," according to the inspector general's report—was not charged with a crime. As the investigation surfaced, Cleveland was the chief of security at a leading American nuclear weapons research laboratory.

384 **"Merely solving this type":** Freeh's statement comes from the FBI's fiscal 1995 budget request to Congress.

385 **"We allowed him":** Schiliro interview by Lowell Bergman and Tim Weiner, Sept. 18, 2001. PBS broadcast, "Looking for Answers," Oct. 9, 2001. The facts of Yousef's arrest are taken from the records of his criminal trial, *United States v. Yousef,* and the appeals court's summary in the case. The FBI did not arrest Yousef in a safe house owned by Osama bin Laden, as was widely reported at the time.

385 **"to make the American people":** Pellegrino testimony, *United States v. Yousef* (appeals court record dated April 4, 2003).

386 **"disrupt, dismantle and destroy":** The Antiterrorism and Effective Death Penalty Act of 1996, 22 USC 2237.

386 **"We will not allow terrorism to succeed":** Presidential Decision Directive 39, "U.S. Policy on Counterterrorism," June 21, 1995, declassified Jan. 27, 2009.

389 **"exhausted, many sick":** Freeh testimony, Senate and House Joint Intelligence Committee, hereinafter Joint Inquiry, Oct. 8, 2002.

390 **"Khobar represented":** Ibid.

390 **"I have information about people":** Al-Fadl testimony, *U.S. v. Osama bin Laden,* 98 Cr. 1023, Feb. 7, 2001.

391 **"no one was thinking":** Watson interview, Joint Inquiry staff report, "Strategic Analysis," p. 338.

392 **"The balance of power has shifted":** O'Neill speech, National Strategy Forum, Chicago, Illinois, June 11, 1997.

392 **"double the 'shoe-leather' ":** Freeh testimony, Senate Intelligence Committee, Jan. 28, 1998.

392 **"almost the primary responsibility":** Clarke interview and Clarke testimony, 9/11 Commission.

393 **"Freeh should have been spending"** and **"We have to smash":** Richard C. Clarke, *Against All Enemies: Inside America's War on Terror* (New York: Free Press, 2004), pp. 116, 219.

394 **"a Stalinist show trial":** Clinton interview, Ken Gormley, *The Death of American Virtue* (New York: Random House, 2010), p. 249.

394 **"I wanted to hurt the Bureau":** Ault oral history, FBI/FBIOH. Ault debriefed Pitts at length after his conviction.

43. AN EASY TARGET

396 **"The cell members in East Africa"**: The message was first published by *Frontline* in a PBS/*New York Times* documentary series, "Hunting Bin Laden," and later entered into evidence in *U.S. v. Bin Laden*.

397 **"I was introduced to al Qaeda"**: Plea hearing, *United States of America v. Ali Mohamed*, 98 Cr. 1023, United States District Court, Southern District of New York, Oct. 20, 2000.

398 **"He had been pitched to me"**: McCarthy, *Willful Blindness*, pp. 301–303.

399 **"MOHAMED stated"**: Coleman affidavit, *U.S. v. Ali Abdelseoud Mohamed*, sealed complaint prepared September 1998 but undated.

400 **"the only good thing"**: Scheuer testimony, House Foreign Affairs Committee, April 17, 2007.

400 **"O'Neill poisoned relations"**: Michael Scheuer, *Marching Toward Hell: America and Islam After Iraq* (New York: Simon & Schuster, 2008), p. 279.

400 **"I thought to myself"**: Bushnell testimony, *U.S. v. Bin Laden*, March 1, 2001. The author covered the 1998 embassy attack in Nairobi. A full factual summary of the case, which adds to (and significantly subtracts from) previous published accounts of the investigations, is found in the consolidated decision *In re Terrorist Bombings of U.S. Embassies in East Africa*, United States Court of Appeals for the Second Circuit, Nov. 24, 2008.

400 **"I had been told"**: Bushnell oral history, Foreign Affairs Oral History Project, July 21, 2005.

401 **"He stated that the reason"**: Anticev testimony, *U.S. v. Bin Laden*, Feb. 28, 2001.

402 **"He wanted to tell"**: Gaudin testimony, *U.S. v. Bin Laden*, Jan. 8, 2001.

403 **"He and I were to meet"**: Bushnell oral history, FAOH, July 21, 2005. Freeh's memoir gives an entirely different account, placing him in command in Dar es Salaam at the time of the cruise missile attacks. News articles of the day place him in Nairobi, suddenly cutting his visit short, squaring with Ambassador Bushnell's story.

404 **"After the bombing in 1998"**: Mohamed guilty plea, *U.S. v. Ali Abdelseoud Mohamed*, Oct. 13, 2000.

404 **After all the trials**: Fitzgerald's grand jury originally handed up a secret indictment in *U.S. v. Bin Laden* on June 8, 1998, charging bin Laden with "conspiracy to attack defense utilities of the United States." It was a misfire. Fitzgerald had used a copy of el-Hage's computer files to link al-Qaeda to the killing of American troops in Somalia during the "Black Hawk Down" battle of Mogadishu five years before. The charge was unsupported by the evidence, and it would have to be redrawn. Though the sealed indictment gave the United States the theoretical power to disrupt or destroy al-Qaeda anywhere in the world, it had little effect in the world outside the court house.

405 **"It's like telling the FBI"**: Hill testimony, Joint Inquiry, Oct. 8, 2002.

405 **"Here were the ground rules"**: Fitzgerald testimony, Senate Judiciary Committee, Oct. 20, 2003. FISA actually imposes few restrictions upon intelligence and law enforcement coordination. But the FBI nonetheless developed a Byzantine system in

which "dirty" teams of intelligence investigators and "clean" teams of criminal investigators worked the same terrorist cases. "This became so complex and convoluted," said one top FBI official, Michael Rolince, "that in some FBI field offices, agents perceived 'walls' where none actually existed."

406 **"Did we have a war plan?"** and **"the hardest thing"**: Watson testimony, Joint Inquiry, Sept. 26, 2002. Watson was perhaps the only senior official at the FBI who heeded a call to arms issued on Dec. 8, 1998, a month after the indictment of bin Laden. George Tenet, the director of Central Intelligence, had issued a directive that he intended to resound throughout the government of the United States. "We must now enter a new phase in our effort against bin Laden," it said. "Each day we all acknowledge that retaliation is inevitable and that its scope may be far larger than we have previously experienced. We are at war. I want no resources or people spared in this effort." An aide faxed the memo to the leaders of the American intelligence community, but it had little palpable effect. Those same leaders had convened with Tenet and resolved that unless they made "sweeping changes," the United States was likely to suffer "a catastrophic systemic intelligence failure." The date of that report was Sept. 11, 1998.

406 **"There is a problem"**: The author interviewed Clarke and reported highlights of his briefing in a profile in *The New York Times* on Feb. 1, 1999, at about the time Clarke delivered his seminar to the FBI.

408 **"We had neither the will"**: Freeh, *My FBI*, p. 296.

409 **a chemist known to the CIA**: The chemist in Malaysia also signed letters of introduction for an Algerian with a French passport named Zacarias Moussaoui, who entered the United States as his patron's business representative and promptly enrolled at the Airman Flight School in Norman, Oklahoma.

409 **"to prevent and effectively respond"**: Freeh testimony, "Threat of Terrorism to the United States," written submissions to Senate Appropriations, Armed Services, and Intelligence committees, May 10, 2001.

410 **"Implement a system"**: Reno testimony, 9/11 Commission, April 13, 2004.

410 **"You guys aren't on life support"**: Freeh, *My FBI*, p. 280.

411 **"Musharraf laughed"**: Freeh, *My FBI*, p. 287. The account of the informant's approach to the FBI's Newark office in April 2000 is in a 9/11 Commission report dated April 13, 2004.

411 **"FBI investigation and analysis"**: Turchie testimony, House Subcommittee on National Security, July 26, 2000.

412 **"The celebration was held"**: Mary Jo White, "Prosecuting Terrorism in New York," address to the Middle East Forum, New York, Sept. 27, 2000.

44. ALL OUR WEAPONS

413 **"We can't continue in this country"**: Kean public statement to reporters and witnesses, 9/11 Commission hearings, April 13, 2004.

413 **"Some connected the dots"**: Burger oral history, FBI/FBIOH.

414 **"Hello, Cathy. This is Bob Hanssen"**: Kiser oral history, FBI/FBIOH.

415　**it was Hanssen:** *U.S. v. Hanssen,* affidavit in support of arrest, United States District Court, Eastern District of Virginia, Crim. 1-118-A.

415　**"Any clerk in the Bureau":** Hanssen debriefing cited in William Webster et al., "A Review of FBI Security Programs," Department of Justice, March 2002.

417　**"bastard stepchildren":** Williams cited in Eleanor Hill, "The FBI's Handling of the Phoenix Electronic Communication and Investigation of Zacarias Moussaoui Prior to Sept. 11, 2001," Joint Inquiry, Senate and House intelligence committees staff report, Sept. 24, 2002.

417　**sixty-eight thousand counterterrorism leads:** Hill, "The FBI's Handling of the Phoenix Electronic Communication." FBI headquarters also fumbled when a leading agent in the *Cole* investigation, Steve Bongardt, learned through a misdirected e-mail that one of the original members of the al-Qaeda cell in Yemen, Khalid al-Mihdhar, had received a renewed visa to re-enter the United States. On Aug. 29, 2001, his superiors told him to stand down: it was not his case. "Someday somebody will die," he wrote in a message to his overseers, "—and Wall or not—the public will not understand." Al-Mihdhar was one of the 9/11 hijackers.

417　**"flying an airplane":** Samit testimony, *U.S. v. Moussaoui,* March 20, 2006.

417　**"criminal negligence":** Samit testimony, *U.S. v. Moussaoui,* March 20, 2006. Moussaoui had been recruited by al-Qaeda. He was being held in reserve for a second wave of attacks.

417　**She received a despondent e-mail:** Kiser's e-mails to Samit and his responses were reported by the Joint Inquiry and the 9/11 Commission, although neither agent was identified by name. Kiser recorded an oral history for the Society of Former Special Agents of the FBI in October 2009, in which she detailed the correspondence. "It was awful," she said. "We all knew ... And we didn't even know about the Phoenix memo. Because those idiots in ITOS [the FBI's international terrorism section] didn't let anybody know. Dale Watson didn't even know about the Phoenix memo. We would've done a scrub on these flight schools! And that would've scared these guys! And would they have done something else? Probably. But it wouldn't have been the magnitude of what we experienced."

　　"You had kind of connected the dots," her interviewer said.

　　"I did," she said. "A small cadre of agents connected those dots."

418　**"I didn't think the FBI":** Clarke testimony, 9/11 Commission, April 8, 2004. White House terrorism chieftain Clarke had no faith that the FBI would ever provide any reporting on al-Qaeda. "The Phoenix memo, the Minnesota case, whatever," he said. "Not just a few hints were missed." The failures went back for many years.

　　"I know the abuses the FBI engaged in—in the 1950s and 1960s—" he said, but "by the 1980s or 1990s we should have recognized the need for domestic intelligence collection. . . . It doesn't mean you become a totalitarian state if you do a good job of oversight and control. We needed to have a domestic intelligence collection and analysis capability, and we did not have it."

418　**"We got the passenger manifests":** Clarke, *Against All Enemies,* pp. 13–14.

418　**"I told Bob":** George W. Bush, *Decision Points* (New York: Crown, 2010), p. 8.

419　**"Round up the evildoers":** Bush address at FBI headquarters, Oct. 10, 2001.

419　**"hold until cleared":** The policy, its consequences, and the delays in informing

Mueller are documented in "The September 11 Detainees," Office of Inspector General, Department of Justice, April 2003.

420 **"Robert Kennedy's Justice Department"**: John Ashcroft, "Remarks for the U.S. Mayors Conference," Oct. 25, 2001.

420 **"We are going to keep America free"**: General Michael V. Hayden, "What American Intelligence and Especially the NSA Have Been Doing to Defend the Nation," address at National Press Club, Jan. 23, 2006.

420 **"turned on the spigot of NSA reporting"**: Hayden, address at National Press Club, Jan. 23, 2006.

421 **"free from the constraints"**: John Yoo, "Authority for Use of Military Force to Combat Terrorist Activities Within the United States," Office of Legal Counsel, Department of Justice, Oct. 23, 2001; declassified March 2, 2009.

422 **"We sent a message to the FBI"**: Lamberth address, American Library Association, June 23, 2007.

422 **"The thought of regularly sharing"**: Mueller speech, Stanford Law School, Oct. 18, 2002.

423 **"The other day we hauled"**: Remarks by President Bush, Republican luncheon, Hyatt Regency Hotel, Greenwich, Conn., April 9, 2002.

424 **"a national treasure"**: General Dunleavy quoted in "A Review of the FBI's Involvement in and Observations of Detainee Interrogations in Guantanamo Bay, Afghanistan, and Iraq," Office of Inspector General, Department of Justice, Oct. 2009.

424 **"I asked him his name"**: Soufan testimony, Senate Judiciary Committee, May 13, 2009.

425 **"We don't do that"**: D'Amuro's discussions with Mueller are cited in "A Review of the FBI's Involvement in and Observations of Detainee Interrogations in Guantanamo Bay, Afghanistan, and Iraq," Office of Inspector General, Department of Justice, Oct. 2009.

425 **"They told me, 'Sorry' "**: Transcript, Combatant Status Tribunal Review, Guantánamo Bay, March 27, 2007.

426 From **"a piece of al-Qahtani"** to **"as soon as possible"**: "A Review of the FBI's Involvement in and Observations of Detainee Interrogations in Guantanamo Bay, Afghanistan, and Iraq," Office of Inspector General, Department of Justice, Oct. 2009.

427 **"ongoing, longstanding, trench warfare"**: Ibid.

45. "IF WE DON'T DO *THIS*, PEOPLE WILL DIE"

432 **"Every day"**: Mueller testimony, Senate Judiciary Committee, Sept. 17, 2008.

432 **"neutralizing al Qaeda operatives"**: Mueller classified testimony to Senate Intelligence Committee, Feb. 24, 2004, cited in Jack Goldsmith, "Memorandum for the Attorney General Re: Review of Legality of the [Deleted] Program," Office of Legal Counsel, Department of Justice, May 6, 2004 (declassified in part March 9, 2011).

433 **"I could have a problem with that"**: Mueller's conversation with Cheney, his resignation letter, and his contemporaneous notes of his confrontation with the president are all cited in "Unclassified Report on the President's Surveillance Program," an extraordinary joint effort by the inspectors general of the Pentagon, the Justice

Department, the CIA, the NSA, and the Director of National Intelligence, July 10, 2009.

436 **"If we don't do *this*"**: James Comey, address to National Security Agency, May 20, 2005, reprinted in *The Green Bag* 10, no. 4 (Summer 2007), George Mason University School of Law.

437 **"We did not have a management system"**: Mueller testimony, Senate Homeland Security and Governmental Affairs Committee, Sept. 30, 2009.

437 **"an institutional culture"**: Intelligence Reform and Terrorism Prevention Act of 2004, P.L. 108-458.

438 **"turning to the next stage"**: *The FBI's Counterterrorism Program Since September 2001, Report to the National Commission on Terrorist Attacks upon the United States,* April 14, 2004.

438 **"It was the single worst experience"**: Silberman speech, First Circuit Judicial Conference, Newport, R.I., June 2005.

438 **"It has now been three and a half years"**: Commission on the Intelligence Capabilities of the United States Regarding Weapons of Mass Destruction, Report to the President of the United States, March 31, 2005.

440 **"the increasing boldness"**: Hoover to SAC, San Juan, Aug. 4, 1960, FBI/FOIA.

441 **"Bald believed that there was confusion"** and **"Who is calling shots?"**: Cited in "A Review of the September 2005 Shooting Incident Involving the Federal Bureau of Investigation and Filiberto Ojeda Ríos," Office of the Inspector General, Department of Justice, August 2006.

442 **"It took me maybe six to twelve months"**: Mudd testimony, Senate Intelligence Committee, Oct. 23, 2007.

443 **"homegrown terrorist cell"**: Mueller speech, City Club of Cleveland, June 23, 2006.

444 **"To hit John F. Kennedy, wow"**: Indictment, *U.S. v. Russell Defreitas et al.,* June 3, 2007.

446 **"Back in 1908"**: Obama speech, FBI headquarters, April 28, 2009.

448 **"rigorous obedience to constitutional principles"**: *Domestic Investigations and Operations Guide,* Federal Bureau of Investigation, October 15, 2001, declassified in part and published online at http://vault.fbi.gov on November 7, 2011.

448 **"You won the war"**: Mueller testimony, April 14, 2004, 9/11 Commission.

INDEX

ABOUT THE AUTHOR

TIM WEINER won the Pulitzer Prize for his reporting and writing on secret intelligence and national security. As a correspondent for *The New York Times* he covered the Central Intelligence Agency in Washington and terrorism in Afghanistan, Pakistan, the Sudan, and other nations. *Enemies* is his fourth book. His *Legacy of Ashes: The History of the CIA* won the National Book Award and was acclaimed as one of the year's best books by *The New York Times, The Economist, The Washington Post, Time,* and many other publications. *The Wall Street Journal* called *Betrayal* "the best book ever written on a case of espionage." He is now working on a history of the American military.

About the Type

This book was set in Minion, a 1990 Adobe Originals typeface by Robert Slimbach. Minion is inspired by classical, old-style typefaces of the late Renaissance, a period of elegant, beautiful, and highly readable type designs. Created primarily for text setting, Minion combines the aesthetic and functional qualities that make text type highly readable with the versatility of digital technology.